The American Pageant

The American Pageant

A History of the Republic
Volume I

9th Edition

Thomas A. Bailey
David M. Kennedy
Stanford University

D. C. Heath and Company
Lexington, Massachusetts   Toronto

Acquisitions Editor: James Miller
Developmental Editor: Sylvia Mallory
Production Editor: Karen Wise
Designer: Cia Boynton/Alwyn Velásquez
Production Coordinator: Michael O'Dea
Photo Researcher: Mark Corsey
Text Permissions Editor: Margaret Roll
Cover Design: Alwyn Velásquez
Cover Photo Credits (from back to front): Library of Congress; Massilon Museum; Library of Congress; Schlesinger Library, Radcliffe College; Bettmann Archive; Smithsonian Institution; Library of Congress. Background map, "The United States and the Relative Position of the Oregon and Texas," published by James Wyld, London, 1854. Reprinted courtesy of the Museum of Our National Heritage, Lexington, Massachusetts.

THOMAS A. BAILEY, a native Californian, taught American history for nearly forty years at Stanford University, his alma mater. Always a popular teacher, he also served as a visiting professor at Harvard, Cornell, Johns Hopkins, and other institutions. Long regarded as among the nation's leading diplomatic historians, he was honored by his colleagues in 1968 by election to the presidency of the Organization of American Historians. Though he was the author, co-author, or editor of some twenty books in the field of American history, he was most proud of *The American Pageant*, through which, he liked to say, he had taught American history to some two million students.

DAVID M. KENNEDY is William Robertson Coe Professor of History and American Studies at Stanford University, where he has taught since 1967. A native of Seattle, he received his undergraduate education at Stanford and earned his Ph.D. at Yale University in American Studies, combining the fields of history, literature, and economics. His first book, *Birth Control in America: The Career of Margaret Sanger* (1970) was honored with both the Bancroft Prize and the John Gilmary Shea Prize. His study of World War I, *Over Here: The First World War and American Society* (1980), was a Pulitzer Prize nominee. He is currently working on a volume in *The Oxford History of the United States* covering the period from 1929 to 1945. Kennedy has twice been recognized by Stanford's graduating class for the effectiveness of his teaching and in 1988 was presented with the Dean's Award for Distinguished Teaching. He has chaired Stanford's program in international relations, served as Associate Dean of the School of Humanities and Sciences, and is currently the chair of the Stanford History Department. He has lectured at many schools and universities in the United States, as well as in Italy, Turkey, Denmark, Finland, Ireland, England, and Germany. Married and the father of three children, in his leisure time he enjoys hiking, river-running, and fly-fishing and still foolishly attempts an occasional game of soccer.

Preface

An old story about Kaiser Wilhelm of Germany recounts that he once visited the state astronomical observatory at Bonn, clattered noisily with his retinue up to the astronomer who was gazing through his telescope at the heavens, and asked, "Well, my dear Professor Argelanger, what's new in the starry sky?" The venerable scientist paused a moment, looked up, and replied, "And does Your Majesty already know the old?" Wilhelm reportedly laughed good-naturedly at the old astronomer's exposure of his ignorance.

Our own fast-paced, high-technology age is often obsessed with all the things that are allegedly new in the world. But like Kaiser Wilhelm, if we do not know the old, we will have pitifully little ability to evaluate the new—or even to recognize what is truly new and what is not. The study of history gives us that ability to understand the new in addition, of course, to giving us an appreciation of the triumphs and follies of the past itself. As the Philadelphia author Agnes Repplier wrote nearly a century ago: "I used to think that ignorance of history meant only a lack of cultivation and a loss of pleasure. Now I am sure that such ignorance impairs our judgement by impairing our understanding, by depriving us of standards, of the power to contrast, and the right to estimate."

Those are the intellectual skills that *The American Pageant* tries to cultivate. It seeks to develop in readers the capacity for balanced judgment and informed understanding about American society by holding up to the present the mirror and measuring rod that is the past. It deals with the past on its own terms, to be sure, but in ways that will help readers to think critically about where America is today by examining where it has been.

In its journey across the centuries, American history has taken twists and turns embracing the full range of human experiences, from the highest idealism to the most shameful injustice, from soaring accomplishments to bitter defeats, from foul crimes to fabulous inventions. *The American Pageant* tries to portray vividly all these dramas from the American past without sacrificing a sense of the often sobering seriousness and complexity of history.

The American Pageant has long enjoyed a reputation as one of the most readable, popular, and effective textbooks in the field of American history. Readers have often commented that it is one of the few textbooks with a personality, and it owes much of that distinctive character to its original author, Thomas A. Bailey. In nearly four decades of teaching at Stanford University, he cultivated a classroom style that he transposed to the pages of his textbook. That style emphasized, above all, clarity and concreteness. It also included mastery of the narrative form, and occasional leavening with a dollop of wit. I have done my best to preserve all those personality traits in this revision.

Like earlier revisions, this one has been guided by two principles: first, the obligation to incorporate into the historical record the histories of many people who until recently were only dimly visible to historians—including women, the working class, native Americans, African-Americans, Hispanics, Asians, and certain religious communities; second, the belief that the main drama and the urgent interest of American history reside in the public arena where these and other groups have both cooperated and contended with one another. In that sometimes noisy forum, Americans have shaped the civic culture in which they all necessarily live. Thus this ninth edition of *The American Pageant,* like its predecessors, lays special emphasis on the great public issues that have dominated national life: the Revolution and the making of the Constitution, slavery and the Civil War, the struggles of minorities for full access to the American dream, the transformation of the economy from an agricultural to an industrial to a post-industrial basis, relations with other nations (including wars), the never-ending debates about social justice and the proper role of government, and the evolution of major public institutions like political parties. Political history, in short, forms the spine of the *Pageant*'s account, but that spine is firmly connected to the full body of social, economic, and intellectual history that makes up the organic whole of the American past.

Throughout the book, I have tried to help the reader see those connections by drawing out the ways in which political developments have been shaped by ideas, religious beliefs, social conditions, and economic and technological change, as well as by events in areas of the world outside the United States. Readers will thus find substantially new treatment of the Federalist era of the 1790s, emphasizing the complex interaction of different political philosophies, colorful personalities, and the upheavals of the French Revolution in molding the first American political party system. I have also extensively revised the discussion of religion, immigration, and the economy in the early nineteenth century in order to clarify the several streams of history that fed the antislavery movement and led eventually to the Civil War. The account of the Civil War itself is entirely new, reflecting the light that recent scholarship has shed on the interrelationships between military developments and politics in wartime, culminating in the great triumph of emancipation and the great frustration and ultimate failure of Reconstruction to give African-Americans their full measure of freedom.

Similarly, the discussion of the post-1945 period has been completely revised to make clear the connections between America's unique geopolitical position in the world at the end of World War II and social developments like suburbanization, the baby boom, the revolution in the status of women, and the eventual decline in this country's international economic position that set in after 1970. The discussion of the civil-rights movement in particular has been substantially enlarged and enriched to reflect the brilliant surge in recent scholarship on the subject. I have also added a complete discussion of the Ronald Reagan presidency, putting it in historical perspective as perhaps the most consequential presidency since Franklin D. Roosevelt's.

Also new in this ninth edition of the *Pageant* are eighteen special essays, all richly illustrated, entitled "Makers of America." These essays focus on the diverse ethnic and racial groups that compose our strikingly pluralistic society. They provide fascinating portraits of the lives of immigrant peoples before they arrived on American soil, or, in the case of native Americans, before contact with European and African civilizations. They also discuss the fates of those peoples over time as members of American society.

To assist students in reviewing the material, I have also added chronologies to the end of each chapter. In addition, most of the end-of-chapter "Varying Viewpoints" essays on historiography have been revised and lengthened, in response to changes in recent scholarship and at the request of many instructors and students that this useful feature be expanded. All bibliographies have been thoroughly updated; many new boxed quotations have been added; the statistical profile of the American people in the Appendix has been brought completely up to date; and new, improved maps and illustrations have been inserted into virtually every chapter.

A revised teaching supplement, the *Instructor's Resource Guide,* is also available with this edition. It features summaries of chapter themes, chapter outlines, suggestions and resources for lectures, character sketches of key historical figures, ideas for classroom debates, and discussion questions. To enrich class presentations further, the instructor can draw from the enlarged package of full-color Map Transparencies, offering a wealth of important map topics explored in the *Pageant.* In addition, the student *Guidebook;* instructor's *Quizbook,* and *HeathTest Plus Computerized Testing Program* have been expanded and rewritten to be fully compatible with this edition. And *The American Spirit,* a companion collection of primary-source documents, has been revised and in many places supplemented with new documents to reflect the changes in the *Pageant.*

While undertaking these improvements, I have tried to preserve all those elements that have made *The American Pageant* distinctive and useful to countless students over the years: clarity, a strong chronological narrative, and a lively writing style that aims to grab and hold the reader's interest. I hope that readers of this book will take from it a renewed appreciation of what has gone before and a seasoned perspective on what is to come. And I hope that they will both learn and enjoy from the reading of it, as I have gained both understanding and pleasure from the writing of it.

Acknowledgments

Many people contributed to this revision. Foremost among them are the countless students and teachers who have written unsolicited letters of comment or inquiry. I have learned from each of them. Several colleagues also gave me the benefit of their assistance, including:

> John E. Baur, California State University, Northridge
> Ronald Goldberg, Thomas Nelson Community College
> Wendy F. Hamand, Eastern Illinois University
> William F. Holmes, University of Georgia
> Gary Huey, Ferris State University
> John McGreevey, Stanford University
> Bruce Schulman, University of California, Los Angeles
> Shung-Tse Sha, University of the District of Columbia
> Victor D. Starlard, University of Arkansas, Pine Bluff
> Robert Sterling, Joliet Community College
> Mark W. Summers, University of Kentucky
> Wendy Wall, Stanford University
> Stephen G. Weisner, Springfield Technical Community College

My warm thanks to each of them.

David M. Kennedy

Contents

Maps

Charts and Tables

Sail, sail thy best, ship of Democracy,
Of value is thy freight, 'tis not the Present only,
The Past is also stored in thee,
Thou holdest not the venture of thyself alone, not of
the Western continent alone,
Earth's résumé entire floats on thy keel, O ship, is
steadied by thy spars,
With thee Time voyages in trust, the antecedent
nations sink or swim with thee,
With all their ancient struggles, martyrs, heroes, epics,
wars, thou bear'st the other continents,
Theirs, theirs as much as thine, the destination-port
triumphant. . . .

Walt Whitman
Thou Mother with Thy Equal Brood, 1872

The American Pageant

1

New World Beginnings, 1492–1670

. . . For I shall yet live to see it [Virginia] an Inglishe nation.

Sir Walter Raleigh, 1602

Planetary Perspectives

Several billion years ago that whirling speck of dust known as the earth, fifth in size among the planets, came into being.

About six thousand years ago—only the day before yesterday geologically—recorded history of the Western world began. Certain peoples of the Middle East, developing a primitive culture, gradually emerged from the haze of the past.

Nearly five hundred years ago—only yesterday—European explorers stumbled on the American continents. This epochal achievement, one of the most dramatic in the chronicles of humankind, opened breathtaking new vistas and forever altered the future of both the Old World and the New.

The two new American continents eventually brought forth a score of sovereign republics. By far the most influential of this brood—the United States—was born a pygmy and grew to be a giant. It was destined to leave a deep imprint upon the rest of the world as a result of its refreshingly liberal ideals, its revolutionary democratic experiment, and its boundless opportunities for the common folk of foreign lands. The enormous output of its robust economy ultimately made it a decisive weight in the world balance of power. Its achievements in science, technology, and the arts shaped people's lives in every corner of the planet.

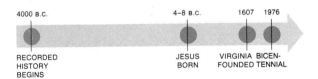

The American Republic, which is still relatively young when compared with the Old World, was from the outset uniquely favored. It started from scratch on a vast and virgin continent, which was so sparsely peopled by Indians that they were to be eliminated or shouldered aside. This rare opportunity for a great social and political experiment may never come again, for no other huge, fertile, and relatively unin-habited areas are left in the temperate zones of this increasingly crowded planet.

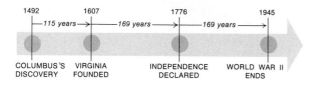

Despite its marvelous development, the United States will one day reach its peak, like Greece and Rome. Its glory will eventually fade, as did theirs. But whatever uncertainties the future may hold, the past at least is secure and will richly repay examination.

Indirect Discoverers of the New World

The American continents were slow to yield their virginity. The all-conquering Romans, a half century after the birth of Christ, expanded their empire northwestward as far as Britain. But for nearly fifteen hundred years thereafter, the New World lay unknown and unsuspected to Europeans, awaiting its discoverers. Blond-bearded Norse seafarers from Scandinavia chanced upon the northeastern shoulder of North America about A.D. 1000. They landed at a place abounding in wild grapes, which they named Vinland. But their settlements were soon abandoned, and the discovery was forgotten, except in Scandinavian saga and song.

America was to be mainly a child of Europe, not of a specific country, such as England. One must seek in the Old World that momentous chain of events that led to a drive toward the Far East—and a completely accidental discovery of the New World.

Christian Crusaders must take high rank among the indirect discoverers of America. Tens of thousands of these European warriors, clad in shining armor, invaded Palestine from the eleventh to the fourteenth century. They were avowedly attempting to wrest the Holy Land from the polluting hand of the Moslem "infidel." Foiled in their repeated assaults, these Christian soldiers did manage to come into closer contact with the exotic delights of Asia— delights already introduced to Europe on a limited scale. European "barbarians" learned more fully the value of spices for spoiled and monotonous food; of silk for rough skins; of drugs for aching flesh; of perfumes for unbathed bodies; and of colorful draperies for gloomy castles.

But the luxuries of the Far East were prohibitively expensive in Europe. They had to be transported enormous distances from the Spice Islands (Indonesia), China, and India, in creaking ships and on swaying camel back, to the ports of the eastern Mediterranean. Moslem middlemen exacted a heavy toll en route. By the time the strange-smelling goods reached the Italian merchants at Venice and Genoa, they

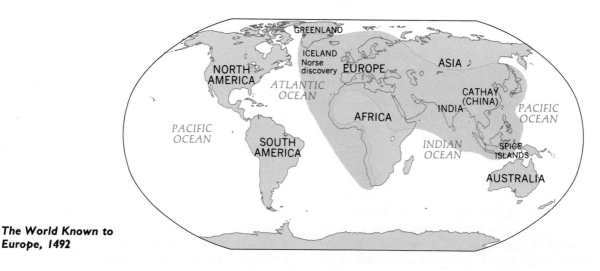

The World Known to Europe, 1492

were so costly that purchasers and profits alike were narrowly limited. Consumers and distributors of Western Europe were naturally eager to find a less costly route to the riches of Eastern Asia—one that would also break the monopoly of the Italian cities.

European appetites were further whetted when footloose Marco Polo, an Italian adventurer, returned to Europe in 1295, after a stay of nearly twenty years in China. Several years later, while a war prisoner, he dictated a classic account of his travels. He, too, must be regarded as an indirect discoverer of the New World, for his book, with its descriptions of rose-tinted pearls and golden pagodas, stimulated European desires for a cheaper route to the treasures of the Orient.

An urge to find a shortcut waterway to Eastern Asia was strong, but success awaited new horizons and new technology. Fortunately the Renaissance, which dawned in the fourteenth century, shot hopeful rays of light through the mists of the Middle Ages. An atmosphere of rebirth nurtured a healthy spirit of optimism, self-reliance, and venturesomeness. Better maps reduced superstitious fears of the unknown. The mariner's compass, possibly borrowed from the Arabs, eliminated some of the uncertainties of navigation. Printing presses, introduced about 1450, facilitated the spread of scientific knowledge.

Columbus Comes upon a New World

The spirit of the Renaissance also stimulated the ambition of several European monarchs. As these kings gradually subordinated the nobles, the modern national state emerged in Western Europe from the feudalism of the Middle Ages. This new type of government alone had the unity, power, and resources to shoulder the formidable tasks of discovery, conquest, and colonization.

The first nations to unite were the first to flourish as colonial empire builders—Portugal, Spain, England, France, and the Netherlands. Those countries that did not achieve unity until the nineteenth century, notably Germany and Italy, were left with crumbs dropped by the early feasters.

Little Portugal took the lead in discovering what came to be the coveted water route to the Far East. A courageous band of Portuguese navigators, edging cautiously down the pistol-handle coast of Africa, pushed southeasterly in the general direction of Asia. In 1488, four

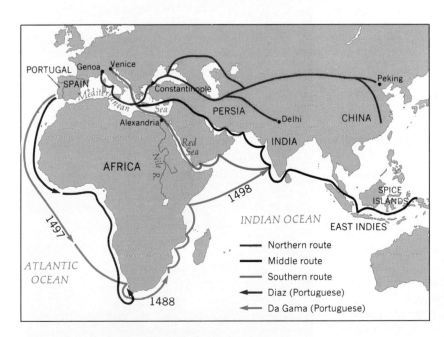

Trade Routes with the East
Goods on the early routes were passed through so many hands along the way that their ultimate source remained mysterious to Europeans.

years before Columbus chanced upon America, Bartholomeu Diaz rounded the southernmost tip of the Dark Continent. Complete success crowned Portuguese efforts in 1498 when Vasco da Gama finally reached India (hence the name "Indies," given to all the mysterious lands of the Orient). He coaxed few jewels and spices from the natives, but later voyagers reaped lush profits from this treasure trove.

Portuguese empire builders ultimately established flourishing trading stations in India, Africa, China, and the East Indies. Immense wealth flowed to European coffers from these ventures. In turn, the ballooning prices of Asian products collapsed, and the monopolistic grip of the Italian commercial cities was broken.

The kingdom of Spain became united—an event pregnant with destiny—late in the fifteenth century. This new unity resulted primarily from the marriage of two sovereigns, Ferdinand and Isabella, and from the brutal expulsion of the "infidel" Moslem Moors. Glorying in their new strength, the Spaniards were eager to outstrip their Portuguese rivals in the race for the fabled Indies.

Christopher Columbus, a skilled Italian seaman, now stepped upon the stage of history. A man of vision, energy, resourcefulness, and courage, he finally managed, after heartbreaking delays, to gain the ear of the Spanish rulers. Like all of his informed contemporaries, he was convinced that the world was round. Then why not find the way to East Asia by sailing directly westward into the darkness of the Atlantic, instead of eastward for unnecessary miles around Africa?

The Spanish monarchs at last decided to gamble on the persistent mariner. They helped outfit him with three tiny but seaworthy ships, manned by a motley crew. Daringly, he spread the sails of his cockleshell craft. Winds were friendly and progress was rapid, but the superstitious sailors, fearful of sailing over the edge of the world, grew increasingly mutinous. Nearly six long weeks passed and failure loomed ahead when, on October 12, 1492, land was sighted— an island in the Bahamas. A new world thus swam within the vision of Europeans.

Columbus's sensational achievement has obscured the fact that he was one of the most successful failures in history. Seeking a new water route to the fabled Indies of the East, he had in fact bumped into an enormous land barrier blocking the ocean pathway. For decades thereafter explorers strove to get through it—or around it. The truth gradually dawned that sprawling new continents had been discovered. Yet Columbus stubbornly maintained until his death in 1506 that he had skirted the rim of the "Indies." So certain was he that he called the near-naked natives "Indians," a gross geographical misnomer that somehow stuck.

The Earliest Americans

Ironically, the remote ancestors of these native Americans were the true discoverers of America. Some twenty thousand years earlier, they had begun to venture from Asia across the land bridge that then connected Siberia and Alaska.

Mosaic Mask of Aztec God Quetzalcoatl   *According to some Aztec legends, Quetzalcoatl, the god of civilization, goodness, and light, sailed from Mexico's east coast in ancient times to some distant mythic land, promising one day to return. Fatefully, many Indians in 1519 at first welcomed the Spanish invader Hernando Cortes as the returning god. (The Granger Collection.)*

North American Indian Tribes at the Time of European Colonization *This map illustrates the great diversity of the Indian population—and suggests the inappropriateness of identifying all the Native American peoples with the single label* Indian. *The more than two hundred tribes were deeply divided by geography, language, and life-style.*

Roaming slowly southward through the silent vastness of the untracked wilderness, they eventually reached the far tip of South America. They continued to trek across the Asian-American isthmus for thousands of years, until rising seas submerged it and left this far-flung part of the family of man marooned for millennia on the now-isolated American continents.

Time did not stand still for these aboriginal Americans. Over the centuries they split into

Incan Art *This golden figurine, wrapped in Peruvian cloth, illustrates both the wealth and the refinement of Incan society. (Lee Boltin, private collection.)*

hundreds of tribes, with different languages, religions, and cultures. Some of them evolved stunning civilizations. Incas in Peru, Aztecs in Mexico, and Mayans in Central America developed advanced agricultural techniques, based primarily on the cultivation of maize, which is Indian corn. Numbering their population in the millions, these sophisticated societies erected bustling, elaborately carved stone cities, rivaling in size those of Columbus's Europe. They carried on commerce, studied mathematics, and made strikingly accurate astronomical observations.

Indian life in North America was less advanced, though some groups reached high levels of development. The Mound Builders of the lower Mississippi Valley built large permanent settlements around rectangular plazas. They used iron tools, wore woven fabrics, and buried their dead in collective graves covered by mounds. Their influence radiated as far as the Great Lakes area until—around the time of Columbus's discovery—powerful enemies virtually destroyed their culture. The Pueblos in the Rio

Taos Indian Pueblo *This sprawling adobe apartment house in present-day New Mexico looks today much as it did when Spanish explorers penetrated the upper Rio Grande Valley in the sixteenth century. Among the Spanish contributions to Pueblo Indian culture were the dome-shaped baking ovens, whose design, in turn, had entered Spain from Africa. (Shostal Associates, New York.)*

Grande Valley constructed elaborate irrigation systems and were dwelling in villages of multi-storied, terraced buildings when the Spanish made contact with them in the late sixteenth century. (*Pueblo* means "village" in Spanish.) The Creeks in the Southeast practiced a democratic style of government that led Europeans later to include them among the "civilized tribes." The Iroquois in the Northeast, inspired by their legendary leader Hiawatha, developed the political skills to sustain a robust military confederacy, which menaced Indian and European neighbors alike for more than a century (see "Makers of America," pp. 8–9).

These exceptions aside, most native peoples lived in small, scattered, and impermanent settlements. Tribes would gather into dense encampments along a riverbank at spawning time and then disperse in small bands of two or three families for the winter's hunting. In more settled agricultural tribes, women tended the crops while men hunted, fished, gathered fuel, and cleared fields for planting—often by setting massive forest fires. Deliberate torching of thousands of acres of woods also created better hunting habitats, especially for deer. This Indian burning accounted for the open, parklike character of the eastern woodlands that so amazed early European explorers.

But for the most part the land did not heavily feel the hand of the Indians upon it—partly because the Indians were so few in number. Perhaps ten million Native Americans dwelled in all of the present-day United States at the time of Columbus's arrival. They were so thinly spread across the land that vast areas were virtually uninhabited, with whispering, primeval forests and sparkling, virgin waters.

When Worlds Collide

Two ecosystems—the fragile, naturally evolved networks of relations among organisms in a stable environment—commingled and clashed when Columbus waded ashore. The flora and fauna of the Old and New Worlds had been separated from one another for thousands of years. European explorers marveled at the strange sights that greeted them—buffalo, iguanas, and "snakes with castanets" (rattlesnakes). Native

Benjamin Franklin later commented on the attractiveness of Indian life to Europeans: "When an Indian child has been brought up among us, taught our language and habituated to our customs, yet if he goes to see his relations and make one Indian ramble with them, there is no persuading him ever to return. [But] when white persons of either sex have been taken prisoners by the Indians, and lived awhile among them, though ransomed by their friends, and treated with all imaginable tenderness to prevail with them to stay among the English, yet in a short time they become disgusted with our manner of life, and the care and pains that are necessary to support it, and take the first good opportunity of escaping again into the woods, from whence there is no reclaiming them." (Letter to Peter Collinson, May 9, 1753.)

New World plants like tobacco, corn (maize), beans, tomatoes, and especially the lowly potato revolutionized the international economy and fed the rapid population growth of Europe. These were among the most important Indian gifts to the Europeans.

In exchange, the Europeans introduced cattle, swine, and horses to the New World. Indian tribes like the Blackfoot, the Sioux, and the Apaches swiftly adopted the horse, transforming their culture. They became less sedentary and more nomadic, roaming on horseback over the grassy Great Plains in pursuit of the buffalo.

Unwittingly, the Europeans also brought other organisms in the dirt on their boots and the dust on their clothes, as well as in their bodies—such as the seeds of Kentucky bluegrass, dandelions, and daisies and the germs that caused smallpox, yellow fever, and malaria. Old World diseases devastated the Native Americans. During their millennia of isolation in the Americas, the Indians had rooted out most of the Old World's killer maladies. But generations of freedom from those illnesses had also wiped out necessary antibodies. Devoid of any natural resistance to European sicknesses, Indians died in droves. In the century after Columbus's landfall, nearly 90 percent of the Native American

The Iroquois

Long before the crowned heads of Europe turned their eyes and their dreams of empire toward the New World, a great military power had emerged in the Mohawk Valley of what is now New York State. The Iroquois Confederacy, dubbed by whites the "League of the Iroquois," bound together five Indian nations—the Mohawks, the Oneidas, the Onondagas, the Cayugas, and the Senecas. According to Iroquois legend, it was founded in the late 1500s by two leaders, Deganawidah and Hiawatha. This proud and potent league vied initially with neighboring Indians for territorial supremacy, then with the French, British, and Dutch for control of the fur trade. Ultimately, infected by the white man's diseases, intoxicated by his whiskey, and menaced by his muskets, the Iroquois struggled for their very survival as a people.

The building block of Iroquois society was the longhouse. This wooden structure deserved its descriptive name. Only twenty-five feet in breadth, the longhouse stretched from eighty to two hundred feet in length. Each building contained three to five fireplaces around which gathered two nuclear families, consisting of parents and children. All families residing in the longhouse were related, their connections of blood running exclusively through the maternal line. A single longhouse might shelter a woman's family and those of her mother, sisters, and daughters—with the oldest woman being the honored matriarch. When a man married, he left his childhood hearth in the home of his mother to join the longhouse of his wife. Men dominated in Iroquois society, but they owed their positions of prominence to their mothers' families.

As if sharing one great longhouse, the five nations joined in the Iroquois Confederacy but kept their own separate fires. Although they celebrated together and shared a common policy

Elm Bark Longhouse, c. 1600

The Hiawatha Belt *This woven belt symbolized the formation of the Iroquois Confederacy. The pine tree in the center was an emblem of the Confederacy, and the joined rectangles represented the individual member nations. (New York State Museum.)*

"Old Broken-Nose" *An Onondaga mask. (Museum of the American Indian, Heye Foundation.)*

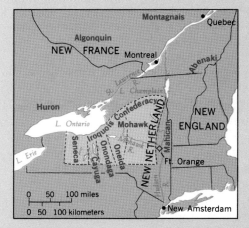

Iroquois Lands and European Trade Centers, c. 1590–1650

toward outsiders, they remained essentially independent of one another. On the eastern flank of the League, the Mohawks, known as the Keepers of the Eastern Fire, specialized as middlemen with European traders, while the outlying Senecas, the Keepers of the Western Fire, became fur suppliers.

After banding together to end generations of warfare among themselves, the Five Nations vanquished their rivals, the neighboring Hurons, Eries, and Petuns. But the arrival of gun-toting Europeans threatened this supremacy and enmeshed the Iroquois in a web of diplomatic maneuverings. Throughout the seventeenth and eighteenth centuries, they allied alternately with the British against the French and vice versa, for a time successfully working

this perpetual rivalry to their own advantage. But when the American Revolution broke out, the Confederacy could reach no consensus on which side to support. Each tribe was left to decide independently; most, though not all, sided with the British. The ultimate British defeat left the Confederacy in tatters. Many Iroquois, especially the Mohawk, moved to new lands in British Canada; others ended up on reservations in western New York.

Reservation life proved unbearable for a proud people accustomed to dominion over a vast territory. Morale sank; brawling, feuding, and alcoholism became rampant. Out of this morass arose a prophet, an Iroquois called Handsome Lake. In 1799 angelic figures clothed in traditional Iroquois garb appeared to Handsome Lake in a vision and warned him that the moral decline of his people must end if they were to endure. He awoke from his vision to warn his tribespeople to mend their ways. His socially oriented gospel inspired many Iroquois to forsake alcohol, to affirm family values, and to revive old Iroquois customs. Handsome Lake died in 1815, but his teachings, in the form of the Longhouse religion, survive to this day.

A Carolina Indian Woman and Child *A painting by John White, who was a member of the Raleigh expedition of 1585. Notice that the Indian girl carries a European doll, illustrating the mingling of cultures that had already begun. (The Granger Collection.)*

population perished. By 1592, a combination of disease, enslavement, and armed Spanish aggression had reduced the civilization of the Arawaks in Hispaniola from about 5 million people to 250. Enraged and vengeful, Indians kneaded infected blood into their masters' bread, to little effect. Perhaps it was poetic justice that the Indians took a kind of revenge by infecting the early explorers with syphilis, injecting that noxious disease for the first time into Europe.

The Spanish Conquistadores

Gradually Europeans realized that the American continents held rich prizes of their own—especially the glittering gold of the advanced Indian civilizations in the southern continent.

Spain secured its claim to Columbus's discoveries in the Treaty of Tordesillas (1494), dividing with Portugal the "heathen lands" of the New World. The lion's share went to Spain, but Portugal received compensating territory in Africa and Asia, and also title to lands that would one day be Brazil.

Spain now became the dominant exploring and colonizing power in the 1500s. Love of God joined with the lure of gold in spurring the Spaniards on, as zealous priests sought to convert the pagan natives to Catholic Christianity. On Spain's long roster of heroic deeds two spectacular exploits must be headlined. Vasco Nuñez Balboa, hailed as the discoverer of the Pacific Ocean, waded into the foaming waves off Panama in 1513 and claimed for his king all the lands washed by that sea! Ferdinand Magellan started from Spain in 1519 with five tiny ships. After discovering the storm-lashed strait off South America that bears his name, he was slain by the natives in the Philippines, but his one remaining vessel creakily completed the first circumnavigation of the globe in 1522.

Other ambitious Spaniards ventured into North America. In 1513 Juan Ponce de León discovered Florida, which he thought an island. Debauched by high living, he was seeking the mythical fountain of youth. He found instead death—from an Indian arrow. Francisco Coronado, in quest of golden cities that turned out to be adobe pueblos, wandered in 1540–1542 with a clanking cavalcade through Arizona and New Mexico as far east as Kansas. His expedition discovered en route two impressive natural wonders: the Grand Canyon of the Colorado and enormous herds of buffalo (bison). A half-century later, Spanish settlers began to trickle into the Rio Grande Valley. They treated the Indians cruelly—severing one foot of each survivor of a battle in 1599—and were temporarily driven out of the region by an Indian uprising in 1680.

Hernando de Soto, with six hundred armor-plated men, undertook a fantastic gold-seeking expedition during 1539–1542. Floundering through marshes and pine barrens, from Florida westward, he discovered and crossed the majestic Mississippi north of the Arkansas River. After brutally misusing the Indians with iron collars and fierce dogs, he at length died of

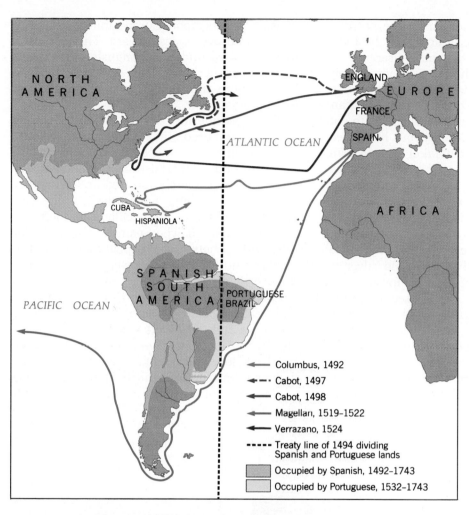

Principal Voyages of Discovery *Spain, Portugal, France, and England reaped the greatest advantages from the New World, but much of the earliest exploration was done by Italians, notably Christopher Columbus of Genoa. John Cabot, another native of Genoa (his original name was Giovanni Caboto), sailed for England's King Henry VII. Giovanni da Verrazano was a Florentine employed by France.*

Columbus, 1492
Cabot, 1497
Cabot, 1498
Magellan, 1519–1522
Verrazano, 1524
Treaty line of 1494 dividing Spanish and Portuguese lands
Occupied by Spanish, 1492–1743
Occupied by Portuguese, 1532–1743

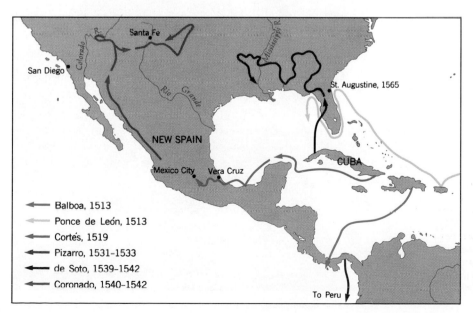

Principal Spanish Explorations and Conquests *Note that Coronado traversed northern Texas and Oklahoma. In present-day eastern Kansas he found, instead of the great golden city he sought, a drab encampment, probably of Wichita Indians.*

Balboa, 1513
Ponce de León, 1513
Cortés, 1519
Pizarro, 1531–1533
de Soto, 1539–1542
Coronado, 1540–1542

fever and wounds. His remains were secretly buried at night in the Mississippi, lest the Indians abuse the dead body of their abuser.

Hernando Cortés, with seven hundred men and eighteen horses (which awed the horseless natives), tore open the coffers of the Mexican Aztecs in 1519–1521. Burning his ships to cut off any hope of retreat, Cortés drove his armed force inland to the Aztec capital of Tenochtitlán (Mexico City). There he swiftly overwhelmed the emperor Montezuma and, with the dauntingly superior technology of armor and gunpowder, extinguished all resistance to his conquest. Francisco Pizarro, an ironfisted conqueror, crushed the Peruvian Incas in 1532 and added another incredible hoard of gold and silver to the loot from Mexico. The Spanish invaders not only robbed the Indians but subsequently enslaved them and put them to work digging up precious metals. By 1600, Spain was swimming in New World silver, mostly from the fabulously rich mines at Potosi in present-day Bolivia.

The Spanish conquerors (*conquistadores*), curiously enough, were indirect founders of the United States. Their phenomenal success excited the envy of the English and helped spur some of the early attempts at colonization. Moreover, the dumping of the enormous Indian treasure chests upon Europe inflated the currency and drove prices upward. The pinch further distressed underpaid English toilers, many of whom in turn were later driven to the New World. There, ironically, they challenged Spanish supremacy.

These plunderings by the Spaniards unfortunately obscured their substantial colonial achievements and helped give birth to the "black legend." This false concept meant that the conquerors merely tortured and butchered the Indians ("killing for Christ"), stole their gold, infected them with smallpox, and left little but misery behind. The Spanish invader did kill thousands of natives and exploit the rest, but he intermarried with them as well, creating a distinctive South American culture of *mestizos*— people of mixed Indian and European heritage. He erected a colossal empire, sprawling from California and the Floridas to Tierra del Fuego. He transplanted and engrafted his culture, laws, religion, and language and laid the foundations for a score of Spanish-speaking nations.

The bare statistics of Spain's colonial empire are alone impressive. By 1574, thirty-three years before the first primitive English shelters in Virginia, there were about two hundred Spanish cities and towns in North and South

Indians Working in the Silver Mines at Potosi, New Spain (now Bolivia), 1590   *Out of silver and the sweat of these New World native peoples, the Spanish wrung an enormous fortune that made Spain among the wealthiest nations of Europe in the sixteenth century. (The Granger Collection.)*

America. A total of 160,000 Spanish inhabitants, mostly men, had subjugated some 5 million Indians—all in the name of the gentle Jesus. Majestic cathedrals dotted the land, printing presses were turning out books, and literary prizes were being awarded. Two distinguished universities were chartered in 1551, one at Mexico City and the other at Lima, Peru. Both of them antedated Harvard, the first college established in the English colonies, by eighty-five years.

It is clear that the Spaniards, who had more than a century's head start over the English, were genuine empire builders in the New World. As compared with their Anglo-Saxon rivals, their colonial establishment was larger and richer, and it lasted more than a quarter of a century longer.

England's Imperial Stirrings

Feeble indeed were the efforts of England in the 1500s to compete with the sprawling Spanish Empire. As Spain's ally in the first half of the century, England took little interest in establishing its own overseas colonies. But after the Protestant Queen Elizabeth mounted the English throne in 1558, rivalry with Catholic Spain intensified.

Hardy English freebooters swarmed out upon the shipping lanes. They sought to promote the twin goals of Protestantism and plunder by seizing Spanish treasure ships and raiding Spanish settlements, even though England and Spain were technically at peace. The most famous of these semipiratical "sea dogs" was the courtly Francis Drake. He plundered his way around the planet, returning in 1580 with his ship heavily ballasted with Spanish booty. The venture netted profits of about 4,600 percent to his financial backers, among whom, in secret, was Queen Elizabeth. Defying Spanish protest, she brazenly knighted Drake on the deck of his barnacled ship.

The bleak coast of Newfoundland was the scene of the first English attempt at colonization, which collapsed when its promoter, Sir Humphrey Gilbert, lost his life at sea in 1583. Gilbert's ill-starred dream inspired his gallant half brother Sir Walter Raleigh to try again in

Main Sources of the Puritan "Great Migration" to New England, 1620–1650

Sir Walter Raleigh (c. 1552–1618) Here he is shown "drinking tobacco," as smoking was first called. He is credited with introducing both tobacco and the potato into England. A dashing courtier, he launched important colonizing failures in the New World. After seducing (and marrying) one of Queen Elizabeth's maids of honor, he fell out of favor and was ultimately beheaded for treason.

Elizabeth I (1533–1603)   Although accused of being vain, fickle, prejudiced, and miserly, she proved to be an unusually successful ruler. She never married (the "Virgin Queen"), although various royal matches were projected. (National Portrait Gallery, London.)

down came in 1588, when the lumbering Spanish flotilla, 130 strong, hove into the English Channel. The English sea dogs fought back. Using craft that were swifter, more maneuverable, and more ably manned, they inflicted heavy damage on the cumbersome, overladen Spanish ships. Then a devastating storm arose (the "Protestant wind"), scattering the crippled Spanish fleet.

The defeat of the Spanish Armada was a red-letter day in American history. It dampened the fighting spirit of Spain and helped ensure England's naval dominance in the North Atlantic. It started England well on the way to becoming master of the seas—a fact of enormous importance to the American people.

A wondrous flowering of the English national spirit also bloomed in the wake of the Spanish Armada's defeat. A golden age of literature dawned in this exhilarating atmosphere, with Shakespeare, at its forefront, making occasional poetical references to England's American colonies. The English were seized with restlessness, with thirst for adventure, and with curiosity about the unknown. Everywhere there blossomed a new spirit of self-confidence, of vibrant patriotism, and of boundless faith in the future of the English nation. When England and Spain finally signed a treaty of peace in 1604, the English people were poised to plunge headlong into the planting of their own colonial empire in the New World.

England on the Eve of Empire

England's scepter'd isle, as Shakespeare called it, throbbed with social and economic change as the seventeenth century opened. Its population was mushrooming, from some 3 million people in 1550 to about 4 million in 1600. In the evergreen English countryside, landlords were "enclosing" croplands for sheep grazing, forcing many small farmers ("yeomen") into precarious tenancy or off the land altogether. It was no accident that the woolen districts of eastern and western England—where Puritanism had taken strong root—supplied many of the earliest immigrants to America. When economic depression hit the woolen trade in the late 1500s, thousands of footloose yeomen took to the

warmer climes. Raleigh organized a group of settlers who landed in 1585 on North Carolina's Roanoke Island, off the coast of Virginia—a vaguely defined region named by the "Virgin Queen" Elizabeth in honor of herself. With Raleigh busy at home, the hapless Roanoke colony mysteriously vanished, swallowed up by the wilderness.

These pathetic English failures at colonization contrasted embarrassingly with the glories of the Spanish Empire, whose profits were enriching Spain beyond its most ambitious dreams of avarice. Philip II of Spain, self-anointed foe of the Protestant Reformation, used part of his imperial gains to amass an "Invincible Armada" of ships for an invasion of England. The show-

roads. They drifted about England, chronically unemployed, often ending up as beggars and paupers in cities like Bristol and London.

This remarkably mobile population alarmed many contemporaries. They concluded that England was burdened with a "surplus population," though twentieth-century London holds twice as many people as did all of England in 1600.

At the same time, laws of primogeniture decreed that only eldest sons were eligible to inherit landed estates. The landholders' ambitious younger sons—like Gilbert, Raleigh, and Drake —were forced to seek their fortunes elsewhere. Bad luck plagued their early, lone-wolf enterprises. But by the early 1600s the joint-stock company—forerunner of the modern corporation—was perfected. It enabled a considerable number of investors, called "adventurers," to pool their capital.

Peace with a chastened Spain provided the opportunity for English colonization. Population growth provided the workers. Unemployment, as well as a thirst for adventure, for markets, and for religious freedom, provided the motives. Joint-stock companies provided the financial means. The stage was now set for a historic effort to establish an English beachhead in the still uncharted American wilderness.

England Plants the Jamestown Seedling

In 1606, two years after peace with Spain, the hand of destiny beckoned toward Virginia. A joint-stock company, known as the Virginia Company of London, received a charter from King James I of England for a settlement in the

> *King James I had scant enthusiasm for the Virginia experiment, partly because of his hatred of tobacco smoking, which had been introduced into the Old World by the Spanish discoverers. In 1604 he published the pamphlet* A Counterblast to Tobacco: *"A custom loathsome to the eye, hateful to the nose, harmful to the brain, dangerous to the lungs, and in the black stinking fume thereof, nearest resembling the horrible Stygian smoke of the pit [Hades] that is bottomless."*

New World. The main attraction was the promise of gold, combined with a strong desire to convert the Indians to Christianity and to find a passage through America to the Indies. Like most joint-stock companies of the day, the Virginia Company was intended to endure for only a few years, after which its stockholders hoped to liquidate it for a profit. This arrangement put severe pressure on the luckless colonists, who were threatened with abandonment in the wilderness if they did not quickly strike it rich on the company's behalf. Few of the investors thought in terms of long-term colonization. Apparently no one even faintly suspected that the seeds of a mighty nation were being planted.

The charter of the Virginia Company is a significant document in American history. It guaranteed to the overseas settlers the same rights of Englishmen that they would have enjoyed if they had stayed at home. This precious boon was gradually extended to the other English colonies and became a foundation stone of American liberties.

*The Tudor Rulers of England**

NAME, REIGN	RELATION TO AMERICA
Henry VII, 1485–1509	Cabot voyages, 1497, 1498
Henry VIII, 1509–1547	English Reformation begun
Edward VI, 1547–1553	Strong Protestant tendencies
"Bloody" Mary, 1553–1558	Catholic reaction
Elizabeth I, 1558–1603	Break with Rome final; Drake; Spanish Armada defeated

* See p. 34 for continuation of table.

Unluckily, the site selected in 1607 for the tiny colony was Jamestown, on the wooded and malarial banks of the James River, named in honor of King James I. Although the spot was easy to defend, it was mosquito-infested and devastatingly unhealthful.

The early years at Jamestown proved to be a nightmare for all concerned—except the buzzards. Forty would-be colonists perished during the initial voyage in 1606–1607. Another expedition in 1609 lost its leaders and many of its precious supplies in a shipwreck in Bermuda. Of the 400 settlers who managed to make it to Virginia, only 60 survived the "starving time" winter of 1609–1610. Ironically, the woods rustled with game and the rivers flopped with fish, but the greenhorn settlers wasted valuable time grubbing for nonexistent gold when they should have been gathering provisions. Diseased and despairing, the colonists dragged themselves aboard homeward-bound ships in the spring of 1610—only to be met at the mouth of the James River by a relief party, which ordered them back to Jamestown.

Disease continued to reap a gruesome harvest among the Virginians, and Indian raids added to the death toll. One Indian uprising in 1622 left 347 settlers dead. By 1625, Virginia contained only some 1200 hard-bitten survivors of the nearly 8000 adventurers who had tried to start life anew in the ill-fated colony.

Virginia was saved from collapse at the start largely by the leadership and resourcefulness of an intrepid young adventurer, Captain John Smith. Taking over in 1608, he whipped the gold-hungry colonists into line with the rule, "He who will not work shall not eat." The brown-skinned Indian maiden Pocahontas may not have saved his life, as he dramatically related, by suddenly interposing her head between his and the war clubs of his Indian captors, but there can be little doubt that she contributed to the salvation of the colony by helping to preserve peace and provide foodstuffs. At times of scarcity the settlers were forced to eat "dogges, Catts, Ratts, and Myce." One hungry man killed, salted, and ate his wife, for which misbehavior he was executed.

Virginia: Child of Tobacco

John Rolfe, who married Pocahontas in 1614 and became father of the tobacco industry, was also an economic savior of the Virginia colony. By 1616 he perfected methods of raising and curing the pungent weed, eliminating much of the bitter tang. Tobacco-rush days began, as crops were planted even in the streets of Jamestown and between the numerous graves. So heavy was the concentration on the yellow leaf that some foodstuffs had to be imported.

Virginia's prosperity was finally built on tobacco smoke. This "bewitching weed" played a vital role in putting the colony on firm foundations and in setting an example for other successful colonizing experiments. But tobacco—King Nicotine—was something of a tyrant. It was ruinous to the soil when greedily planted in successive years, and it enchained the prosperity of Virginia to the fluctuating price of a single crop. Tobacco also promoted the broad-acred plantation system and with it a brisk demand for fresh labor.

In 1619, the year before the Plymouth Pilgrims landed in New England, what was described as a Dutch warship appeared off Jamestown and sold some twenty black Africans. (The

Pocahontas (c. 1595–1617) Taken to England by her husband, she was received as a princess. She died when preparing to return, and her infant son ultimately reached Virginia, where hundreds of his descendants have lived, including the second Mrs. Woodrow Wilson. (National Portrait Gallery, Smithsonian Institution, Washington, D.C.)

scanty record does not reveal whether they were purchased as lifelong slaves or as servants committed to limited years of servitude.) Yet black slaves were too costly for most of the hard-pinched white colonists to acquire, and for decades they were imported only in driblets. Virginia counted but three hundred blacks in 1650, although by the end of the century blacks made up approximately 14 percent of the colony's population.

Representative self-government was also born in primitive Virginia, in the same cradle with slavery and in the same year—1619. The London Company authorized the settlers to summon an assembly, known as the House of Burgesses. A momentous precedent was thus feebly established, for this assemblage was the first of many miniature parliaments to mushroom from the soil of America.

As time passed, James I grew increasingly hostile to Virginia. He detested tobacco and he distrusted the representative House of Burgesses, which he branded a "seminary of sedition." In 1624 he revoked the charter of the bankrupt and beleaguered Virginia Company, thus making Virginia a royal colony directly under his control.

Maryland: Catholic Haven

Maryland—the second plantation colony but the fourth English colony to be planted—was founded in 1634 by Lord Baltimore, of a prominent English Catholic family. He embarked upon the venture partly to reap financial profits and partly to create a refuge for his co-religionists. Protestant England was still persecuting Roman Catholics; among numerous discriminations, a couple seeking wedlock could not be legally married by a Catholic priest.

Absentee proprietor Lord Baltimore hoped that the 200 settlers who founded Maryland at St. Marys, on Chesapeake Bay, would be the vanguard of a vast new feudal domain. Huge estates were to be awarded to his largely Catholic relatives, and gracious manor houses, modeled on those of England's aristocracy, were intended to sprout from the fertile forests. As in Virginia, colonists proved willing to come only if offered the opportunity to acquire land of their

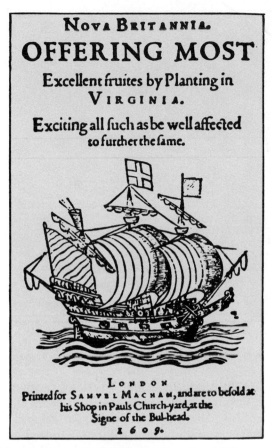

Advertisement of a Voyage to America, 1609

own. Soon they were dispersed around the Chesapeake region on modest farms, and the haughty land barons, mostly Catholic, were surrounded by resentful backcountry planters, mostly Protestant. Resentment flared into open rebellion near the end of the century, and the Baltimore family for a time lost its proprietary rights.

The wife of a Virginia governor wrote to her sister in England in 1623 of her voyage: "For our Shippe was so pestered with people and goods that we were so full of infection that after a while we saw little but throwing folkes over board. It pleased god to send me my helth till I came to shoare and 3 dayes after I fell sick but I thank god I am well recovered. Few else are left alive that came in that Shippe. . . ."

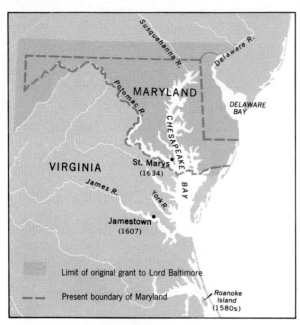

Early Maryland and Virginia

Despite these tensions, Maryland prospered. Like Virginia, it blossomed forth in acres of tobacco. Like Virginia, it depended for labor in its early years mainly on white indentured servants—penniless persons who bound themselves to work for a number of years to pay their passage. In both colonies it was only in the later years of the seventeenth century that black slaves began to be imported in large numbers.

Lord Baltimore, a canny soul, permitted unusual freedom of worship at the outset. He hoped that he would thus purchase toleration for his own fellow worshipers. But the heavy tide of Protestants threatened to submerge the Catholics and place severe restrictions on them, as in England. Faced with disaster, the Catholics of Maryland threw their support behind the famed Act of Toleration, which was passed in 1649 by the local representative assembly.

Maryland's new religious statute guaranteed toleration to all Christians. But it decreed the death penalty for those, like Jews and atheists, who denied the divinity of Jesus. The law thus sanctioned less toleration than had previously existed in the settlement, but it did extend a temporary cloak of protection to the uneasy Catholic minority. One result was that when the colonial era ended, Maryland probably shel-

tered more Roman Catholics than any other English-speaking colony in the New World.

Colonizing the Carolinas

Civil wars convulsed England in the 1640s. King Charles I had dismissed Parliament in 1629, and when he eventually recalled it in 1640, the members were mutinous. Finding their great champion in the Puritan-soldier Oliver Cromwell, they ultimately beheaded Charles in 1649, and Cromwell ruled England for nearly a decade. Finally, Charles II, son of the decapitated king, was restored to the throne in 1660.

Colonization had been interrupted during this period of bloody unrest. Now, in the so-called Restoration period, empire building resumed with even greater intensity—and royal involvement. The Carolinas, named in honor of the restored king, were formally created in 1670, after Charles II granted to eight of his court favorites—Lords Proprietors—an expanse of wilderness ribboning across the continent to the Pacific. These aristocratic founders hoped to grow foodstuffs to provision the sugar plantations in Barbados and to export non-English products like wine, silk, and olive oil.

South Carolina prospered by developing close economic ties with the flourishing British West Indies. In a broad sense, the mainland colony was but the most northwesterly of those islands. Indian slaves were among the colony's earliest exports. Manacled captives from the colony's interior were sent to work in the West Indian cane fields and sugar mills. Others were dis-

Early Carolina Coins   *These copper halfpennies bore the image of an elephant, an unofficial symbol of the colony, and a prayer for the Lords Proprietors. (Larry Stevens/Nawrocki Stock Photo.)*

patched to New England. One Rhode Island town in 1730 counted over two hundred Indian slaves from Carolina in its midst.

After much experimentation, rice emerged as the principal export crop in South Carolina. Rice was then an exotic food in England; no rice seeds were sent out from London in the first supply ships to South Carolina. But rice was grown in Africa, and the Carolinians were soon paying premium prices for west African slaves experienced in rice cultivation. The Africans' agricultural skill and their relative immunity to malaria (thanks to a genetic trait that also made them and their descendants susceptible to sickle-cell anemia) made them ideal laborers on the hot and swampy rice plantations. By 1710 they constituted a majority of Carolinians.

Moss-festooned Charles Town—also named for the king—rapidly became the busiest seaport in the South. Many high-spirited sons of English landed families, deprived of an inheritance, came to the Charleston area and gave it a rich aristocratic flavor. The village became a colorfully diverse community, to which French Protestant refugees and others were attracted by religious toleration.

Nearby, in Florida, the Catholic Spaniards bitterly resented the intrusion of these Protestant English heretics. South Carolina's frontier was often aflame. Spanish-incited Indians brandished their tomahawks, and armor-clad warriors of Spain frequently unsheathed their swords during the successive Anglo-Spanish wars. But by 1700 South Carolina was too strong to be wiped out.

The Thirteen Original Colonies

NAME	FOUNDED BY	YEAR	CHARTER	MADE ROYAL	1775 STATUS
1. Virginia	London Co.	1607	{1606, 1609, 1612}	1624	Royal (under the Crown)
Plymouth	Separatists	1620	None		(Merged with Mass., 1691)
Maine	F. Gorges	1623	1639		(Bought by Mass., 1677)
2. New Hampshire	John Mason and others	1623	1679	1679	Royal (absorbed by Mass., 1641–1679)
3. Massachusetts	Puritans	c. 1628	1629	1691	Royal
4. Maryland	Lord Baltimore	1634	1632	——	Proprietary (controlled by proprietor)
5. Connecticut	Mass. emigrants	1635	1662	——	Self-governing (under local control)
6. Rhode Island	R. Williams	1636	{1644, 1663}	——	Self-governing
New Haven	Mass. emigrants	1638	None		(Merged with Conn., 1662)
7. N. Carolina	Virginians	1653	1663	1729	Royal (separated informally from S.C., 1691)
8. New York	Dutch	c. 1613			
	Duke of York	1664	1664	1685	Royal
9. New Jersey	Berkeley and Carteret	1664	None	1702	Royal
10. S. Carolina	Eight nobles	1670	1663	1729	Royal (separated formally from N.C., 1712)
11. Pennsylvania	William Penn	1681	1681	——	Proprietary
12. Delaware	Swedes	1638	None	——	Proprietary (merged with Penn., 1682; same governor, but separate assembly, granted 1703)
13. Georgia	Oglethorpe and others	1733	1732	1752	Royal

The wild northern expanse of the huge Carolina grant bordered on Virginia. From the older colony there drifted down a motley group of poverty-stricken outcasts and religious dissenters. Many of them had been repelled by the rarefied atmosphere of Virginia, dominated as it was by big-plantation aristocrats belonging to the Church of England. North Carolinians, as a result, have been called "the quintessence of Virginia's discontent." The newcomers, who frequently were "squatters" without legal right to the soil, raised their tobacco and other crops on small farms, with little need for slaves.

Distinctive traits developed rapidly in North Carolina. The poor but sturdy inhabitants, regarded as riffraff by their snobbish neighbors, earned a reputation for being irreligious and hospitable to pirates. Isolated from neighbors by raw wilderness and stormy Cape Hatteras, "graveyard of the Atlantic," the North Carolinians developed a strong spirit of resistance to authority. Their location between aristocratic Virginia and aristocratic South Carolina caused the area to be dubbed "a vale of humility between two mountains of conceit." Following much friction with governors, North Carolina was officially separated from South Carolina in 1712, and subsequently each segment became a royal colony.

North Carolina shares with tiny Rhode Island several distinctions. These two outposts were the most democratic, the most independent-minded, and the least aristocratic of the original thirteen English colonies.

Late-Coming Georgia: The Buffer Colony

Pine-forested Georgia, with the harbor of Savannah nourishing its chief settlement, was formally founded in 1733. It proved to be the last of the thirteen colonies to be planted—fifty-two years after Pennsylvania. Chronologically it belongs elsewhere, but geographically it may be grouped with its southern neighbors.

Georgia was valued by the English crown chiefly as a buffer. It would serve to protect the more valuable Carolinas from inroads by vengeful Spaniards from Florida and by the hostile French from Louisiana. Georgia in truth suffered much buffeting, especially when wars broke out between Spain and England in the European cockpit. As a vital link in imperial defense, the exposed colony received monetary subsidies from the British government at the outset—the only one of the "original thirteen" to enjoy this boon in its founding stage.

Named in honor of George II of England, Georgia was launched by a high-minded group of philanthropists. Aside from producing silk and wine, and strengthening the empire, they were determined to create a haven for wretched souls imprisoned for debt. The ablest of the founders was the dynamic soldier-statesman James Oglethorpe, who became keenly interested in prison reform after one of his friends had died in a debtor's jail. As an able military leader, Oglethorpe repelled savage Spanish attacks. As an imperialist and a philanthropist, he saved "the Charity Colony" by his energetic leadership and by mortgaging heavily his own personal fortunes.

The hamlet of Savannah, like Charleston, was a melting-pot community. German Lutherans and kilted Scots Highlanders, among others, added color to the pattern. All Christian worshipers except Catholics enjoyed religious toleration. Many Bible-toting missionaries arrived to work among debtors and Indians. Prominent among them was young John Wesley, who later returned to England and founded the Methodist church.

Early Carolina and Georgia Settlements

Georgia grew with painful slowness and at the end of the colonial era was perhaps the least populous of the colonies. Prosperity through a large-plantation economy was thwarted by an unhealthful climate, by early restrictions on black slavery, and by demoralizing Spanish attacks.

The Plantation Colonies

Certain distinctive features were shared by England's southern mainland colonies: Maryland, Virginia, North Carolina, South Carolina, and Georgia.

Broad-acred, these outposts of empire were all in some degree dominated by a plantation economy. Profitable staple crops were the rule, notably tobacco and rice, though to a lesser extent in small-farm North Carolina. Slavery was found in all the plantation colonies, though only after 1750 in reform-minded Georgia. Immense acreage in the hands of a favored few fostered a strong aristocratic atmosphere, except in North Carolina and to some extent in debtor-tinged Georgia. The wide scattering of plantations and farms, often along stately rivers, made the establishment of churches and schools both difficult and expensive. In 1671 the governor of Virginia thanked God that no free schools or printing presses existed in his colony.

All the plantation colonies permitted some religious toleration. The tax-supported Church of England became the dominant faith, though weakest of all in nonconformist North Carolina.

All the plantation colonies were in some degree expansionary. "Soil butchery" by excessive growing of tobacco drove settlers westward, and the long, lazy rivers invited penetration of the continent.

CHRONOLOGY

c. 18,000 B.C.	First humans cross into Americas from Asia
c. 4000 B.C.	First civilized societies develop in the Middle East
c. A.D. 1000	Norse voyagers discover and briefly settle in North America
c. A.D. 1100–1300	Christian Crusades arouse European interest in the East
1488	Diaz rounds southern tip of Africa
1492	Columbus lands in the Bahamas
1519–1521	Cortés conquers Mexico for Spain
1585	Raleigh founds Roanoke colony
1588	England defeats Spanish Armada
1607	Virginia colony founded at Jamestown
1619	First black Africans arrive in Jamestown
	Virginia House of Burgesses established
1634	Maryland colony founded
1649	Charles I beheaded; Cromwell rules England
1660	Charles II restored to English throne
1670	Carolina colony created
1712	North Carolina separated from South Carolina
1733	Georgia colony established

Varying Viewpoints

The history of discovery and the earliest colonization raises perhaps the single most fundamental question about all American history. Should it be understood as the extension of European civilization into the New World or as the gradual development of a uniquely "American" culture? An older school of thought tended to emphasize the Europeanization of America. Historians of that persuasion thus paid close attention to the situation in Europe, particularly in England and Spain, in the fifteenth and sixteenth centuries. They also focused on the various means by which the values and institutions of the mother continent were exported to the new lands in the western sea. Some European writers have varied this general question by asking what transforming effect the discovery of America had on Europe itself. But both these approaches are Eurocentric. More recently, historians have concentrated on the distinctive aspects of America, especially the interactions among the various races in the Western Hemisphere. This approach stresses the adaptations of native, African, and European cultures to the challenges of life in a strange new environment and emphasizes the creation of a uniquely *American* society and culture.

Select Readings

Primary Source Documents

Richard Hakluyt, *Divers Voyages Touching the Discovery of America and the Islands Adjacent,** edited by J. W. Jones (1850), supplied the rationale for the establishment of English colonies in North America. John Smith, "Generall Historie of Virginia," in *Travels and Works of Captain John Smith,** edited by Edward Arber (1910), is the account of the amazing, vain man who steered Jamestown through its first few years.

Secondary Sources

The international economic background to colonization is sketched in Ralph Davis, *The Rise of the Atlantic Economies* (1973). More theoretical is Immanuel Wallerstein, *The Modern World-System: Capitalist Agriculture and the Origins of the European World in the Sixteenth Century* (1974). The immediate English backdrop is colorfully presented in Peter Laslett, *The World We Have Lost* (1965), and in Carl Bridenbaugh, *Vexed and Troubled Englishmen, 1590–1642* (1968). Samuel E. Morison has written several masterful accounts of the discoveries; among the best are *Admiral of the Ocean Sea* (2 vols., 1942; condensed as *Christopher Columbus, Mariner,* 1956), *The European Discovery of America: The Northern Voyages,* A.D. *500–1600* (1971), and *The European Discovery of America: The Southern Voyages,* A.D. *1492–1616* (1974). A modern classic is Wallace Notestein, *The English People on the Eve of Colonization, 1603–1630* (1954). The ablest summation of the Spanish experience is Charles Gibson, *Spain in America* (1966); James Lang, *Conquest and Commerce: Spain and England in the Americas* (1975), is a comparative chronicle of colonial rivalries. A fascinating brief synthesis of early European contact with the Americas is J. H. Elliott, *The Old World and the New, 1492–1650* (1970). D. W. Meinig presents a geographical overview of immigration in *The Shaping of America: A Geographical Perspective on 500 Years of History. Atlantic America, 1492–1800* (1986). Bernard Bailyn offers a detailed statistical portrait of a single group of immigrants in *Voyagers to the West: A Passage in the Peopling of America on the Eve of*

---

*An asterisk indicates that the document, or an excerpt from it, can be found in Thomas A. Bailey and David M. Kennedy, eds., *The American Spirit: United States History as Seen by Contemporaries, 7th ed.* (Lexington, Mass: D. C. Heath and Company, 1991).

the Revolution (1986). A concise summary of his broad argument on patterns of immigration can also be found in *The Peopling of British North America: An Introduction* (1986). A marvelously illustrated volume, portraying the impact of America on the European imagination, is Hugh Honour, *The New Golden Land* (1975). Contact between Indian and European cultures is handled in Wilcomb E. Washburn, *The Indian in America* (1975), in Francis Jennings, *The Invasion of America* (1975), and in James Axtell, *The Invasion Within: The Contest of Cultures in Colonial America* (1985). Brian M. Fagan reviews the sketchy evidence concerning the earliest humans to arrive in the Americas in *The Great Journey: The Peopling of Ancient America* (1987). Nathan Wachtel presents the Indians' view of the Spanish conquest in *The Vision of the Vanquished* (1977). See also Karen Ordahl Kupperman, *Settling with the Indians: The Meeting of English and Indian Cultures in America, 1580–1640* (1980). The impact of Indian-white relations on the environment is the subject of William Cronon's intriguing *Changes in the Land* (1983) and Calvin Martin's provocative *Keepers of the Game* (1978). Alfred Crosby discusses *The Columbian Exchange: The Biological Consequences of 1492* (1972). The Chesapeake region has recently received much fresh attention, especially in Aubrey C. Land et al., *Law, Society, and Politics in Early Maryland* (1977); Thad W. Tate and David L. Ammerman, eds., *The Chesapeake in the Seventeenth Century* (1979); and Paul G. E. Clemens, *The Atlantic Economy and Colonial Maryland's Eastern Shore* (1980). The most comprehensive account of the various colonial economies is contained in John J. McCusker and Russell R. Menard, *The Economy of British North America, 1607–1789* (1985). The role of slavery in early colonial society gets perceptive treatment in Edmund S. Morgan, *American Slavery, American Freedom* (1975). See also Winthrop Jordan's monumental *White over Black* (1968) and Peter Wood's account of South Carolina, *Black Majority* (1974). Gary Nash analyzes relations among all three races in *Red, White, and Black: The Peoples of Early America* (1974).

2

Completing the Thirteen Colonies, 1619–1700

*God hath sifted a Nation that he might send
Choice Grain into this Wilderness.*

*William Stoughton
[of Massachusetts Bay], 1699*

The Protestant Reformation Produces Puritanism

Little did the German monk Martin Luther know, when he nailed his protests against Catholic doctrines to the door of Wittenberg's cathedral in 1517, that he was shaping the destiny of a yet unheralded nation. Denouncing the authority of priests and popes, Luther declared that the Bible alone was the source of God's word. He ignited a fire of religious reform (the "Protestant Reformation") that licked its way across Europe for more than a century, dividing peoples, toppling sovereigns, and kindling the spiritual fervor of millions of men and women—some of whom helped to found America.

The reforming flame burned especially brightly in the bosom of John Calvin of Geneva. This somber and severe religious radical elaborated Luther's ideas in ways that profoundly af-

fected the thought and character of generations of Americans yet unborn. Calvinism became the dominant theological credo not only of the New England Puritans but of other American settlers as well, including Scotch Presbyterians, French Huguenots, and communicants of the Dutch Reformed church.

Calvin spelled out his basic doctrine in a learned Latin tome of 1536, *Institutes of the Christian Religion*. God, he argued, was all-powerful and all-good. Humans, because of the corrupting effect of original sin, were weak and wicked. God was also all-knowing—and he knew who was going to heaven and who to hell. Since the first moment of creation, some souls —the *elect*—had been destined for eternal bliss and others for eternal torment. Good works could not save those whom *predestination* had marked for the infernal fires.

But neither could the elect count on their predetermined salvation and lead lives of wild, immoral abandon. For one thing, no one could be certain of his or her status in the heavenly ledger. Gnawing doubts about their eternal fate plagued Calvinists. They constantly sought, in themselves and others, signs of *conversion,* or the receipt of God's free gift of saving grace. Conversion was thought to be an intense, identifiable personal experience in which God revealed to the elect their heavenly destiny. Thereafter they were expected to lead "sanctified" lives, demonstrating by their holy behavior that they were among the "visible saints."

These doctrines swept into England just as King Henry VIII was breaking his ties with the Roman Catholic church in the 1530s, making himself the head of the Church of England. Henry would have been content to retain Roman rituals and creeds, but his action powerfully stimulated some English religious reformers to undertake a total purification of English Christianity. Many of these *Puritans,* as it happened, came from the commercially depressed woolen districts. Calvinism, with its message of stark but reassuring order in the divine plan, fed on this social unrest and provided spiritual comfort to the economically afflicted. As time went on, Puritans grew increasingly unhappy over the snail-like progress of the Protestant Reformation in England. They burned with pious zeal to see the Church of England wholly de-Catholicized.

All Puritans agreed that only "visible saints" should be admitted to church membership. But the Church of England was open to all comers, which meant that the "saints" had to share pew and communion rail with the damned. Gagging on this unholy fraternizing, a group of extreme Puritans, known as Separatists, vowed to break away entirely from the Church of England.

King James I, a shrewd Scotsman, was head of both the state and the church in England. He quickly perceived that if his subjects could defy him as their spiritual leader, they might one day defy him as their political leader, as in fact they later defied his son, Charles I. He therefore threatened to harass the more bothersome Separatists out of the land.

The Pilgrims End Their Pilgrimage at Plymouth

The most famous congregation of Separatists, fleeing royal wrath, departed for Holland in 1608. During the ensuing twelve years of toil and poverty, they were increasingly distressed by the "Dutchification" of their children. They longed to find a haven where they could live and die as English men and women—and as purified Protestants. America was the logical refuge, despite the early ordeals of Jamestown, and despite tales of cannibals roasting steaks from their white victims before open fires.

A group of the Separatists in Holland, after negotiating with the Virginia Company, at length secured rights to settle under its jurisdiction. But their crowded *Mayflower,* sixty-five days at sea, missed its destination and arrived off the rocky coast of New England in 1620, with a total of 102 persons. One had died en route—an unusually short casualty list—and one had been born and appropriately named Oceanus. Fewer than half of the entire party were Separatists. Prominent among the nonbelongers was a peppery and stocky soldier of fortune, Captain Myles Standish, dubbed by one of

Seventeenth-Century New England Settlements

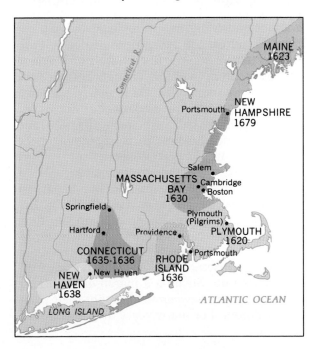

his critics "Captain Shrimp." He later rendered indispensable service as an Indian fighter and negotiator.

The Pilgrims did not make their initial landing at Plymouth Rock, as commonly supposed, but undertook a number of preliminary surveys. They finally chose for their site the shore of inhospitable Plymouth Bay. This area was outside the domain of the Virginia Company, and consequently the settlers became squatters. They were without legal right to the land and without specific authority to establish a government.

Before disembarking, the Pilgrim leaders drew up and signed the brief Mayflower Compact. Though setting an invaluable precedent for later written constitutions, this document was not a constitution at all. It was a simple agreement to form a body politic and to submit to the will of the majority under the regulations agreed upon. The compact was signed by forty-one adult males, eleven of them with the exalted rank of "mister," though not by the servants and two seamen. The pact was a promising step toward genuine self-government, for soon the adult male settlers were assembling to make their own laws in open-discussion town meetings—a great laboratory of liberty.

The Pilgrims' first winter of 1620–1621 took a grisly toll. Only 44 out of the 102 survived. At one time only 7 were well enough to lay the dead in their frosty graves. Yet when the *Mayflower* sailed back to England in the spring, not a single one of the courageous band of Separatists left. As one of them wrote, "It is not with us as with other men, whom small things can discourage."

God made his children prosperous, so the Pilgrims believed. The next autumn, that of 1621, brought bountiful harvests and with them the first Thanksgiving Day in New England. In time the frail colony found sound economic legs in fur, fish, and lumber. The beaver and the Bible were the early mainstays: the one for the sustenance of the body, the other for the sustenance of the soul. Plymouth proved that the English could maintain themselves in this uninviting region.

The Pilgrims were extremely fortunate in their leaders. Prominent among them was the cultured William Bradford, a self-taught scholar

> William Bradford wrote in Of Plymouth Plantation, "Thus out of small beginnings greater things have been produced by His hand that made all things of nothing, and gives being to all things that are; and, as one small candle may light a thousand, so the light here kindled hath shone unto many, yea in some sort to our whole nation."

who read Hebrew, Greek, Latin, French, and Dutch. He was chosen governor thirty times in the annual elections. Among his major worries was his fear that independent, non-Puritan settlers "on their particular" might corrupt his godly experiment in the wilderness. Bustling fishing villages and other settlements did sprout to the north of Plymouth, on the storm-lashed shores of Massachusetts Bay, where many people were as much interested in cod as God.

Quiet and quaint, the little colony of Plymouth was never important economically or numerically. It claimed only seven thousand souls by 1691, when, still charterless, it merged with its giant neighbor, the Massachusetts Bay Colony. But the tiny settlement of Pilgrims was big both morally and spiritually.

The Bay Colony Bible Commonwealth

The Separatist Pilgrims were dedicated extremists—the purest Puritans. More moderate Puritans sought to reform the Church of England by boring from within. Though resented by bishops and monarchs, they slowly gathered support, especially in Parliament. But when Charles I dismissed Parliament in 1629 and sanctioned the anti-Puritan persecutions of the reactionary Archbishop William Laud, many Puritans saw catastrophe in the making.

In 1629, an energetic group of non-Separatist Puritans, fearing for their faith and for England's future, secured a royal charter to form the Massachusetts Bay Company. They proposed to plant a sizable settlement in the infertile Massachusetts area, with Boston soon becoming its hub. Stealing a march on both king and church, the newcomers brought their charter with them. For many years they used it as a

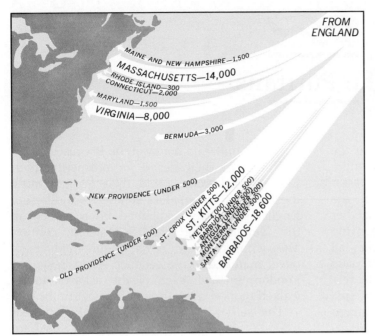

FROM ENGLAND

MAINE AND NEW HAMPSHIRE—1,500
MASSACHUSETTS—14,000
RHODE ISLAND—300
CONNECTICUT—2,000
MARYLAND—1,500
VIRGINIA—8,000
BERMUDA—3,000
NEW PROVIDENCE (UNDER 500)
OLD PROVIDENCE (UNDER 500)
ST. CROIX (UNDER 500)
ST. KITTS—12,000
NEVIS—4,000
BARBUDA (UNDER 500)
ANTIGUA (UNDER 500)
MONTSERRAT (UNDER 200)
SANTA LUCIA (UNDER 500)
BARBADOS—18,600

The Great Puritan Migration, c. 1630–1642
Much of the early history of the United States was written by New Englanders, who were not disposed to emphasize the larger exodus of Puritans to the southerly islands. When the mainland colonials declared independence in 1776, they hoped that these island outposts would join them, but the existence of the British navy had a chilling effect.

kind of constitution, out of easy reach of royal authority. They steadfastly denied that they wanted to separate from the Church of England, only from its impurities. But back in England the highly orthodox Archbishop Laud snorted that the Bay Colony Puritans were "swine which rooted in God's vineyard."

The Massachusetts Bay enterprise was singularly blessed. The well-equipped expedition of 1630, with eleven vessels carrying nearly a thousand immigrants, started the colony off on a larger scale than any of the other English settlements. Continuing turmoil in England tossed up additional enriching waves of Puritans on the shores of Massachusetts in the following decade (see "Makers of America," pp. 28–29). During the "Great Migration of the 1630s, about seventy-five thousand refugees left England. But not all of them were Puritans, and only about fourteen thousand came to Massachusetts. Many were attracted to the warm and fertile West Indies, especially the sugar-rich island of Barbados. More Puritans came to this Caribbean islet, rather surprisingly, than to all of Massachusetts.

Many fairly prosperous, educated persons immigrated to the Bay Colony, including Governor John Winthrop, a well-to-do pillar of English so-

ciety. A successful attorney and manor lord in England, Winthrop eagerly accepted the offer to become governor of the Massachusetts Bay Colony, believing that he had a *calling* from God to lead the new religious experiment. He served as governor or deputy governor for nineteen years. The resources and skills of talented settlers like Winthrop helped Massachusetts to prosper, as fur trading, fishing, and shipbuilding blossomed into important industries, especially fish and ships. Massachusetts Bay Colony rapidly shot to the fore as both the biggest and the most influential of the New England outposts.

Massachusetts also benefited from a shared sense of purpose among most of the first settlers. "We shall be as a city upon a hill," a beacon to humanity, declared Governor Winthrop. The Puritan bay colonists believed that they had a *covenant* with God, an agreement to build a holy society that would be a model for humankind.

Building the Bay Colony

These common convictions deeply shaped the infant colony's life. Soon after arrival, the franchise was extended to all "freemen"—adult males who belonged to the Puritan congrega-

The Puritans

Almost alone among English voyagers to the New World, the Puritans transplanted entire communities from the Old Country to Massachusetts. Women as well as men braved the seas, old as well as young, parents together with children, humble servants accompanying haughty masters and mistresses. And they all came at once, or nearly so. In the twelve years between 1629 and 1642—a decade of cruel religious repression by King Charles I and of sustained economic depression—some fourteen thousand swarmed to New England. The Puritans came to escape poverty as well as persecution, to establish a godly commonwealth, and to enjoy the milk and honey of the Promised Land.

United in their desire for prosperity, their English background, and their Puritan faith, the Puritans nonetheless sprang from different English stocks and so planted different seeds in the New England soil. Seventeenth-century Massachusetts Bay never regimented itself, never marched to the cadence set in Boston or London; instead, each of the colony's towns walked to its own slightly different drumbeat.

The settlers of Rowley, Massachusetts, for example, hailed from Yorkshire in northern England, a region of small, old-fashioned farms little touched by the fever of commercialization that had swept through other areas of English society. Rowley's founders brought their traditions with them; as in England, they granted families very small farming plots and maintained vast common fields, worked by and for the benefit of the whole community. They even tried to continue the old Yorkshire regional specialty of hemp making, despite its unsuitability to the soil and climate of their new environment.

Land Use in Rowley, Massachusetts, c. 1650 *Note the small private plots and large common fields. (Adapted from map drawn by Richard J. Stinely in* In English Ways, *by David G. Allen. © 1981, University of North Carolina Press.)*

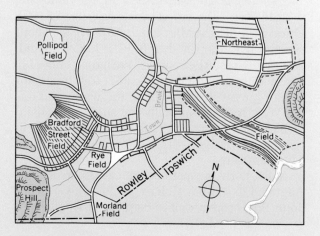

Town Meetinghouse, Hingham, Massachusetts
Erected in 1681, it is still in use today. (Margo Taussig Pinkerton/New England Stock Photo.)

Mistress Anne Pollard. *(Massachusetts Historical Society, Boston.)*

English Spindled Chair Brought from the Old World to the New *(Museum of Fine Arts, Boston. Photo by Richard Cheek.)*

The settlers of Watertown, Massachusetts, on the other hand, transferred the very different practices of their home region of East Anglia. That area had been the hub of the British cloth-making industry. A fervid commercial spirit animated East Anglia, where farms were run like businesses. Farmers there engaged in a brisk land trade and tilled no common fields. This entrepreneurial streak accompanied the East Anglian Puritans to Watertown—a town without common fields, where local regulations were designed to spur on economic development.

Political practices, too, revealed the English antecedents of the various Puritan towns. In Ipswich, Massachusetts, a town settled by Puritans from East Anglia, the governors ruled with an iron hand. Like the officials of their native region in England, the political leaders of Ipswich summarily escorted unwelcome strangers beyond the town's boundaries, reproved the lazy, and comforted the old and sick. The ruling selectmen were drawn almost exclusively from the town's wealthiest families and served long terms in office.

The chaos of nearby Newbury marked a strong contrast to the staid politics of Ipswich. Newbury was planted by migrants from western England, a region with little tradition of local government. Newbury's local politics was bitter and contentious, and officeholders were hard pressed to win reelection to a second term.

So the saintly Puritans tried to raise their "New Canaan" in the wilderness by rebuilding their old homes from the counties and boroughs of the British Isles, importing a diversity of English models into Massachusetts. By the end of the seventeenth century, however, the Puritans' imperial masters in London tightened the reins on their wayward colonies and circumscribed the towns' precious autonomy. But the diverse heritage of fiercely independent New England towns endured, reasserting itself during the American Revolution and persisting even to this day.

tions, which in time came to be called collectively the Congregational church. Unchurched men remained voteless in provincial elections, as did women. On this basis, about two-fifths of adult males enjoyed the franchise in provincial affairs, a far larger proportion than in contemporary England. Town governments, which conducted much important business, were even more inclusive. There all male property holders, and in some cases other residents as well, enjoyed the priceless boon of publicly discussing local issues, often with much heat, and of voting on them by a majority-rule show of hands.

Yet the provincial government, liberal by the standards of the time, was not a democracy. The able Governor Winthrop feared and distrusted the "commons" as the "meaner sort" and thought that democracy was the "meanest and worst" of all forms of government. "If the people be governors," asked one Puritan clergyman, "who shall be governed?" True, the freemen annually elected the governor and his assistants, as well as a representative assembly called the General Court. But only Puritans—the "visible saints" who alone were eligible for church membership—could be freemen. And according to the doctrine of the covenant, the whole purpose of government was to enforce God's laws—which applied to believers and unbelievers alike. Moreover, unbelievers as well as believers paid taxes for the government-supported church.

Religious leaders thus wielded enormous influence in the Massachusetts "Bible Commonwealth." They powerfully influenced admission to church membership, by conducting public interrogations of persons claiming to have experienced conversion. Prominent among the early clergy was fiery John Cotton. Educated at England's Cambridge University, a Puritan citadel, he emigrated to Massachusetts to avoid persecution for his criticism of the Church of England. In the Bay Colony he devoted his considerable learning to defending the government's duty to enforce religious rules. Profoundly pious, he sometimes preached and prayed up to six hours in a single day.

But the power of the preachers was not absolute. A congregation had the right to hire and fire its minister and to set his salary. Clergymen were also barred from holding formal political office. Puritans in England had suffered too much at the hands of a "political" Anglican clergy to permit in the New World another unholy union of religious and governmental power. In a limited way, the bay colonists thus endorsed the idea of the separation of church and state.

The Puritans were a worldly lot, despite—or even because of—their spiritual intensity. Like John Winthrop, they believed in the doctrine of a "calling" to do God's work on this earth. They shared in what was later called the "Protestant ethic," involving serious commitment to work and to engagement in the world of affairs. Legend to the contrary, they also enjoyed simple pleasures: they ate plentifully, drank heartily, sang songs occasionally, and made love discreetly. Like other peoples of their time, in both America and Europe, they passed laws aimed at making sure these pleasures stayed simple by repressing certain human instincts. In New Haven, for example, a young married couple was fined twenty shillings for the crime of kissing in public, and in later years Connecticut came to be dubbed "the Blue Law State." (It was so named for the blue paper on which the repressive laws—also known as "sumptuary laws"—were printed.)

Yet life was serious business, and hellfire was real—a hell where sinners shriveled and shrieked for divine mercy. An immensely popular poem in New England, selling one copy for every twenty persons, was clergyman Michael Wigglesworth's "Day of Doom" (1662). Especially horrifying were his descriptions of the fate of the damned:

> They cry, they roar for anguish sore,
>   and gnaw their tongues for horrour.
> But get away without delay,
>   Christ pitties not your cry:
> Depart to Hell, there may you yell,
>   and roar Eternally.

Trouble in the Bible Commonwealth

The Bay Colony enjoyed a high degree of social harmony, stemming from common beliefs, in its early years. But even in this tightly knit community, dissension soon appeared. Quakers, who flouted the authority of the Puritan clergy, were persecuted with fines, floggings, and ban-

Anne Hutchinson, Dissenter *Mistress Hutchinson (1591–1643) held unorthodox views that challenged the authority of the clergy and the very integrity of the Puritan experiment in Massachusetts Bay Colony. (Mike Mazzaschi/ Stock, Boston.)*

ishment. In one extreme case, four Quakers who defied expulsion, one of them a woman, were hanged on the Boston Common.

A sharp challenge to Puritan orthodoxy came from Mistress Anne Hutchinson. She was an unusually intelligent, strong-willed, and talkative woman, ultimately the mother of fourteen children. Swift and sharp in theological argument, she carried to logical extremes the Puritan doctrine of predestination. She claimed that a holy life was no sure sign of salvation and that the truly saved need not bother to obey the law of either God or man. This assertion, known as *antinomianism* (from the Greek, "against the law"), was high heresy.

Brought to trial in 1638, the quick-witted Hutchinson bamboozled her clerical inquisitors for days, until she eventually boasted that she had come by her beliefs through a direct revelation from God. This was even higher heresy. The Puritan magistrates had little choice but to banish her, lest she pollute the entire Puritan experiment. She set out on foot for Rhode Island, though pregnant. She finally moved to New York, where she and all but one of her household were killed by Indians. Back in the Bay Colony, the pious John Winthrop sadly saw "God's hand" in her fate.

More threatening to the Puritan leaders was a personable and popular Salem minister, Roger Williams. Williams was a young man with radical ideas and an unrestrained tongue. An extreme Separatist, he hounded his fellow clergymen to make a clean break with the corrupt Church of England. He also challenged the legality of the Bay Colony's charter, which he condemned for expropriating the land from the Indians without fair compensation. As if all this were not enough, he went on to deny the authority of civil government to regulate religious behavior—a seditious blow at the Puritan idea of government's very purpose.

Their patience exhausted by 1635, the Bay Colony authorities found Williams guilty of disseminating "newe & dangerous opinions" and ordered him banished. He was permitted to remain several months longer because of illness, but he kept up his criticisms. The outraged magistrates, fearing that he might organize a rival colony of malcontents, made plans to exile him to England. But Williams foiled them.

The Rhode Island "Sewer"

Aided by friendly Indians, Roger Williams fled to the Rhode Island area in 1636, in the midst of a bitter winter. At Providence, the courageous and far-visioned Williams built a Baptist church, probably the first in America. He established complete freedom of religion, even for Jews and Catholics. In this respect he was not only far ahead of his age but ahead of any of the other English settlements in the New World. He demanded no oaths regarding one's religious beliefs, no compulsory attendance at worship, no taxes to support a state church. He even sheltered the abused Quakers, although disagreeing sharply with their views.

Those outcasts who clustered about Roger Williams enjoyed additional blessings. They exercised simple manhood suffrage from the start, though this boon was later modified by a property qualification. Opposed to special privilege of any sort, the doughty Rhode Islanders managed to achieve remarkable freedom of opportunity.

Other scattered settlements soon dotted Rhode Island. They consisted largely of malcontents and exiles, some of whom could not bear the stifling theological atmosphere of the Bay Colony. Many of these restless souls in "Rogues' Island," including Anne Hutchinson, had little in common with Roger Williams—except banishment. The Puritan clergy back in Boston sneered at Rhode Island as "that sewer" in which the "Lord's debris" had collected and rotted.

Planted by dissenters and exiles, Rhode Island became strongly individualistic and stubbornly independent. With good reason "Little Rhody" was later known as "the traditional home of the otherwise minded." Begun as a squatter colony in 1636 without legal standing, it finally established rights to the soil when it secured a charter from Parliament in 1644. A huge bronze statue of the "Independent Man" appropriately stands today on the dome of the statehouse in Providence.

New England Spreads Out

The smiling valley of the Connecticut River, one of the few highly fertile expanses of any size in all New England, had meanwhile attracted a sprinkling of Dutch and English settlers. Hartford was founded in 1635. The next year witnessed a spectacular beginning of the centuries-long westward movement across the continent. An energetic group of Boston Puritans, led by the Reverend Thomas Hooker, swarmed as a body into the Hartford area, with Mrs. Hooker riding a horse litter.

Three years later, in 1639, the settlers of the new Connecticut River colony drafted in open meeting a trailblazing document known as the Fundamental Orders. It was in effect a modern constitution, which established a regime democratically controlled by the "substantial" citi-

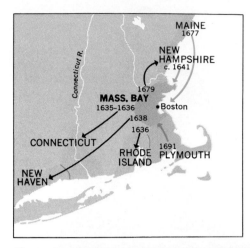

Massachusetts Bay, the Hub of New England *All earlier colonies grew into it; all later colonies grew out of it.*

zens. Essential features of the Fundamental Orders were later borrowed by Connecticut for its colonial charter and ultimately for its state constitution.

Another flourishing Connecticut settlement began to spring up at New Haven in 1638. It was a prosperous community, founded by Puritans who contrived to set up an even closer church-government alliance than in Massachusetts. Although only squatters without a charter, the colonists dreamed of making New Haven a flourishing seaport. But they fell into disfavor with Charles II, as a result of having sheltered two of the judges who had condemned his father, Charles I, to death. In 1662, to the acute distress of the New Havenites, the crown granted a charter to Connecticut that merged New Haven with the more democratic settlements in the Connecticut Valley.

Far to the north, enterprising fishermen and fur traders had been active on the coast of Maine for a dozen or so years before the founding of Plymouth. After disheartening attempts at colonization in 1623 by Sir Ferdinando Gorges, this land of lakes and forests was absorbed by Massachusetts Bay after a formal purchase in 1677 from the Gorges heirs. It remained a part of Massachusetts for nearly a century and a half and then became a separate state.

Granite-ribbed New Hampshire also sprang from the fishing and trading activities along its narrow coast. It was absorbed in 1641 by the grasping Bay Colony, under a strained interpretation of the Massachusetts charter. The king, annoyed by this display of greed, arbitrarily separated New Hampshire from Massachusetts in 1679 and made it a royal colony.

Seeds of Colonial Unity and Independence

A path-breaking experiment in union was launched in 1643, when four colonies banded together to form the New England Confederation. Old England was then deeply involved in civil wars, and hence the colonials were thrown upon their own resources. The primary purpose of the confederation was defense against foes or potential foes, notably the Indians, the French, and the Dutch. Purely intercolonial problems,

Philip, King of Mount Hope *Philip was not only shot and killed but, as a "traitor" to the king, beheaded, drawn, and quartered. His head was exhibited at Plymouth for many years. (The Granger Collection.)*

such as runaway servants and criminals who had fled from one colony to another, also came within the jurisdiction of the confederation. Each member, regardless of size, wielded two votes—an arrangement highly displeasing to the most populous colony, Massachusetts Bay.

The confederation was essentially an exclusive Puritan club. It consisted of the two Massachusetts colonies (the Bay Colony and bantam-sized Plymouth) and the two Connecticut colonies (New Haven and the scattered valley settlements). The Puritan leaders blackballed Rhode Island, as well as the Maine outposts. These places, it was charged, harbored too many heretical or otherwise undesirable characters. Shockingly, one of the Maine towns had made a tailor its mayor and had even sheltered an excommunicated minister of the gospel.

Weak though it was, the confederation was the first notable milestone on the long and rocky road toward colonial unity. The delegates took tottering but urgently needed steps toward acting together on matters of intercolonial importance. Rank-and-file colonists, for their part, received valuable experience in delegating their votes to properly chosen representatives.

The New England Confederation functioned usefully during the bloody war in 1675–1676 with the Indian chieftain King Philip, whose followers struck back at encroachments by whites on their lands. Several hundred settlers were killed and dozens of towns were burned, but the whites finally emerged victorious. If the confederation had been continued and strengthened, it almost certainly would have spared the colonials much grief in their subsequent conflicts with the French and Indians.

Back home in England, the king had paid little attention to the American colonies during the early years of their planting. They were allowed, in effect, to become semiautonomous commonwealths. This era of benign neglect was prolonged when the crown, struggling to retain its power, became enmeshed during the 1640s in civil wars with the parliamentarians.

But when Charles II was restored to the English throne in 1660, the royalists and their Church of England allies were once more firmly in the saddle. Puritan hopes of eventually purifying the old English church withered. Worse, Charles II was determined to take an active, ag-

The Stuart Dynasty in England*

NAME, REIGN	RELATION TO AMERICA
James I, 1603–1625	Va., Plymouth founded; Separatists persecuted
Charles I, 1625–1649	Civil wars, 1642–1649; Cavalier tradition; Mass., Md. founded
(Interregnum, 1649–1660)	Commonwealth; Protectorate (the Cromwells)
Charles II, 1660–1685	The Restoration; Carolinas, Penn., N.Y. founded; Conn. chartered
James II, 1685–1688	Catholic trend; Glorious Revolution, 1688
William & Mary, 1689–1702	King William's War, 1689–1697
(Mary died 1694)	

*See p. 15 for predecessors; p. 89 for successors.

gressive hand in the management of the colonies. His plans ran headlong against the habits that decades of relative independence had bred in the colonists.

Deepening colonial defiance was nowhere more glaringly revealed than in Massachusetts. One of the king's agents in Boston was mortified to find that royal orders had no more effect than old issues of the London *Gazette*. Punishment was soon forthcoming. As a slap at Massachusetts, Charles II gave rival Connecticut in 1662 a sea-to-sea charter grant, which legalized the squatter settlements. The very next year the outcasts in Rhode Island received a new charter, which gave kingly sanction to the most religiously tolerant government yet devised in America. A final and crushing blow fell on the stiff-necked Bay Colony in 1684, when its precious charter was revoked by the London authorities.

Andros Promotes the First American Revolution

Massachusetts suffered further humiliation in 1686, when the Dominion of New England was created by royal authority. Unlike the homegrown New England Confederation, it was imposed from London. Embracing at first all New England, it was expanded two years later to include New York and East and West Jersey. The Dominion also aimed at bolstering colonial defense in the event of war with the Indians, and hence from the imperial viewpoint of London was a statesmanlike move.

More importantly, the Dominion of New England was designed to promote urgently needed efficiency in the administration of the English Navigation Laws. Those laws reflected the intensifying colonial rivalries of the seventeenth century. They sought to stitch England's overseas possessions more tightly to the motherland, by throttling American trade with countries not ruled by the English crown. Like colonial peoples everywhere, the Americans chafed at such confinements, and smuggling became an increasingly common and honorable occupation.

At the head of the new dominion stood autocratic Sir Edmund Andros, an able English military man, conscientious but tactless. Establishing headquarters in Puritanical Boston, he

Andros's Dominion of New England

generated much hostility by his open affiliation with the despised Church of England. The colonials were also outraged by his noisy and Sabbath-profaning soldiers, who were accused of teaching the people "to drink, blaspheme, curse, and damn."

Andros was prompt to use the mailed fist. He ruthlessly curbed the cherished town meetings; laid heavy restrictions on the courts, the press, and the schools; and revoked all land titles. Dispensing with the popular assemblies, he taxed the people without the consent of their duly elected representatives. He also strove to enforce the unpopular Navigation Laws and suppress smuggling. Liberty-loving colonials, accustomed to unusual privileges during long decades of neglect, were goaded to the verge of revolt.

The people of old England, likewise resisting oppression, stole a march on the people of New England. In 1688–1689 they engineered the memorable Glorious (or Bloodless) Revolution. Dethroning the despotic and unpopular Catholic James II, they enthroned the Protestant rulers of the Netherlands, the Dutch-born William III and his English wife, Mary, daughter of James II.

When the news of the Glorious Revolution reached America, the ramshackle Dominion of New England collapsed like a house of cards. A Boston mob, catching the fever, rose against the existing regime. Sir Edmund Andros attempted to flee in woman's clothing but was betrayed by boots protruding beneath his dress. He was then shipped off to England.

Massachusetts, though rid of the despotic Andros, did not gain as much from the upheaval as it had hoped. In 1691 it was arbitrarily made a royal colony, with a new charter and a new royal governor. The permanent loss of the ancient charter was a staggering blow to the proud Puritans, who never fully recovered. Worst of all, the privilege of voting, once a monopoly of church members, was now to be enjoyed by all qualified male property holders.

England's Glorious Revolution had a far-flung impact, for unrest erupted from New England to the Carolinas. The upheaval resulted in a permanent abandonment of many of the objectionable features of the Andros system, as well as a temporary breakdown of the new imperial policy of enforcing the Navigation Laws.

Yet residues remained of Charles II's effort to assert tighter administrative control over his empire. More British officials—judges, clerks, customs officials—were now staffing the courts and strolling the wharves of British America. Many were incompetent, corrupt hacks who knew little and cared less about American affairs. Appointed by influential patrons in far-off England, they blocked by their presence the rise of local leaders to positions of political power. Aggrieved Americans viewed them with mounting contempt and resentment as the eighteenth century wore on.

Old Netherlanders at New Netherland

Late in the sixteenth century, the oppressed people of the Netherlands unfurled the standard of rebellion against Catholic Spain. After bloody and protracted fighting, they finally succeeded, with the aid of Protestant England, in winning their independence.

The seventeenth century—the era of Rembrandt and other famous artists—was a golden age in Dutch history. This vigorous little lowland nation finally emerged as a major commercial and naval power and then ungratefully challenged the supremacy of her former benefactor, England. Three great Anglo-Dutch naval wars were fought in the seventeenth century, with as many as a hundred ships on each side. The sturdy Dutch dealt blows about as heavy as they received.

Holland also became a leading colonial power, with by far its greatest activity in the East Indies. There it maintained an enormous and profitable empire for over three hundred years. The Dutch East India Company was virtually a state within a state and at one time supported an army of 10,000 men and a fleet of 190 ships, 40 of them men-of-war.

Seeking greater riches, this enterprising company employed an English explorer, Henry Hudson. Disregarding orders to sail northeast, he ventured into Delaware Bay and New York

**The Seal of New Netherland,
1630**   *The central figure of the beaver
is a reminder of the importance of fur-
trading in the life of the raw colony.
(The Museum of the City of New York.)*

Bay in 1609 and then ascended the Hudson
River, hoping that at last he had chanced upon
the coveted shortcut through the continent.
But, as the event proved, he merely filed a
Dutch claim to a magnificently wooded and wa-
tered area.

Much less powerful than the mighty Dutch
East India Company was the Dutch West India
Company, which maintained profitable enterprises in the Caribbean. At times it was less interested in trading than in raiding and at one
fell swoop in 1628 captured a fleet of Spanish
treasure ships laden with loot worth $15 mil-
lion. The company also established outposts in
Africa and a flourishing sugar industry in
Brazil, which for several decades was its principal center of activity in the New World.

New Netherland, in the beautiful Hudson
River area, was planted in 1623–1624 on a permanent basis. Established by the Dutch West
India Company for its quick-profit fur trade, it
was never more than a secondary interest of the
founders. The company's most brilliant stroke

**Early Settlements in the Middle Colonies,
with Founding Dates**

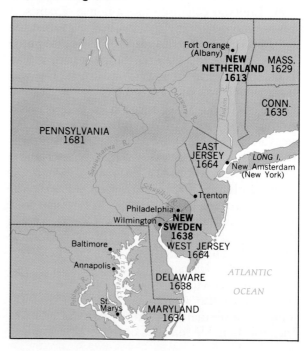

New Amsterdam, c. 1653 *The site of latter-day New York, this colonial village was still in Dutch hands in 1653, as illustrated by the Dutch-style windmill. (Museum of the City of New York.)*

was to buy Manhattan Island from the Indians (who did not actually "own" it) for trinkets worth about $24—22,000 acres of what is now perhaps the most valuable real estate in the world for one-tenth of a cent an acre.

New Amsterdam—later New York City—was a company town. It was run by and for the Dutch company, in the interests of the stockholders. The investors had no enthusiasm for religious toleration, free speech, or democratic practices; and the governors appointed by the company as directors-general were usually harsh and despotic. In response to repeated protests by the colonists, a semirepresentative body was at length reluctantly granted. Religious dissenters who opposed the official Dutch Reformed church were looked upon with suspicion, and for a while Quakers were savagely abused.

This picturesque Dutch colony took on a strongly aristocratic tinge and retained it for generations. Vast feudal estates fronting the Hudson River, known as patroonships, were granted to promoters who would settle fifty persons on them. One of the largest in the Albany area was slightly larger than the later state of Rhode Island.

Colorful little New Amsterdam attracted a cosmopolitan population, as is common in seaport towns. A French Jesuit missionary, visiting in the 1640s, noted that eighteen different languages were being spoken in the streets.

The later babel of immigrant tongues was thus foreshadowed.

Friction with English and Swedish Neighbors

Vexation of various sorts beset the Dutch company-colony from the beginning. The directors-general were largely incompetent, though Washington Irving's later characterization of one of them as "a beer barrel on skids" is unfair. Company shareholders demanded their dividends, even at the expense of the colony's welfare. The Indians, infuriated by Dutch cruelties, retaliated with horrible massacres. As a defense measure, the hard-pressed settlers on Manhattan Island erected a stout wall, from which Wall Street derived its name.

New England was hostile to the growth of its Dutch neighbor, and the people of Connecticut finally ejected intruding Hollanders from their verdant valley. Three of the four member colonies of the New England Confederation were eager to wipe out New Netherland with military force. But Massachusetts, which would have had to provide most of the troops, vetoed the proposed foray.

The Swedes in turn trespassed on Dutch preserves, from 1638 to 1655, by planting the anemic colony of New Sweden on the Delaware River. This was the golden age of Sweden, during and following the Thirty Years' War of 1618–1648, in which its brilliant King Gustavus Adolphus had carried the torch for Protestantism. This outburst of energy in Sweden caused it to enter the costly colonial game in America, though on something of a shoestring.

Resenting the Swedish intrusion on the Delaware, the Dutch dispatched a small military expedition in 1655. It was led by the ablest of the directors-general, the energetic and hotheaded Peter Stuyvesant, who was dubbed "Father Wooden Leg" by the Indians. The main fort fell after a bloodless siege, whereupon Swedish rule came to an abrupt end. The colonists were absorbed by New Netherland.

New Sweden was never important. It faded away, leaving behind in later Delaware a sprinkling of Swedish place names and Swedish log cabins (the first in America), as well as an admixture of Swedish blood.

Dutch Residues in New York

The days of the Dutch on the Hudson were numbered, for the English regarded them as intruders. In 1664, after the imperially ambitious Charles II had granted the area to his brother, the Duke of York, a strong English squadron appeared off the decrepit defenses of New Amsterdam. A fuming Peter Stuyvesant, short of all munitions except courage, was forced to surrender without firing a shot. New Amsterdam was thereupon renamed New York, in honor of the Duke of York. England won a splendid harbor, strategically located in the middle of the mainland colonies, and a stately Hudson River penetrating the interior. The English banner now waved triumphantly, with the removal of this foreign wedge, over a solid stretch of territory from Maine to the Carolinas.

As the neglected stepchild of a trading company, New Netherland was destined from the beginning to be English. Lacking vitality, and representing only a secondary commercial interest of the Dutch, it lay under the shadow of the vigorous English colonies to the north. In addition, it was honeycombed with New England immigrants. Numbering about one-half of New Netherland's ten thousand souls in 1664, they might in time have seized control from within.

Peter Stuyvesant (1602–1682) *Despotic in government and intolerant in religion, he lived in a constant state of friction with the prominent residents of New Netherland. When protests arose, he replied that he derived his power from God and the company, not the people. He opposed popular suffrage on the grounds that "the thief" would vote "for the thief" and "the rogue for the rogue." (Culver Pictures.)*

The conquered Dutch province tenaciously retained many of the illiberal features of earlier days. An autocratic spirit survived, and the aristocratic element gained strength when certain corrupt English governors granted immense acreage to their favorites. Influential landowning families—such as the Livingstons and the De Lanceys—wielded disproportionate power in the affairs of colonial New York. These monopolistic land policies, combined with the lordly atmosphere, discouraged many European immigrants from coming. The physical growth of New York was correspondingly retarded.

The short-lived Dutch colony contributed little of major significance, whether to democracy, government, education, toleration, or literature. A possible exception would be the Knickerbocker themes that Washington Irving developed in the nineteenth century with such charm. The Dutch peppered place names over the land, including Harlem (Haarlem), Brooklyn (Breuckelen), and Hell Gate (Hellegat). They likewise left their imprint on the gambrel-roofed architecture. As for social customs and folkways, no other foreign group of comparable size has made so colorful a contribution. Noteworthy were Easter eggs, Santa Claus, waffles, sauerkraut, bowling, sleighing, skating, and kolf (golf)—a dangerous game played with heavy clubs and forbidden in settled areas.

Penn's Holy Experiment in Pennsylvania

A remarkable group of dissenters, commonly known as Quakers, arose in England during the mid-1600s. Their name derived from the report that they "quaked" when under deep religious emotion. Officially they were known as the Religious Society of Friends.

Yearly Meeting of the Quakers, London, 1696
William Penn, a prominent Quaker in both America and England, sits to the right of the presiding officer. (Friends Historical Library at Swarthmore College.)

Quakers were especially offensive to the authorities, both religious and civil. They refused to support the established Church of England with taxes. They built simple meetinghouses, without a paid clergy, and "spoke up" themselves in meetings when moved. Believing that they were all children in the sight of God, they kept their broad-brimmed hats on in the presence of their "betters" and addressed others with simple "thees" and "thous," rather than with conventional titles. They would take no oaths, because Jesus had said, "Swear not at all." This peculiarity often embroiled them with government officials, for "test oaths" were still required to establish the fact that a person was not a Roman Catholic.

The Quakers, beyond a doubt, were a people of deep conviction. They abhorred strife and warfare and refused military service. As advocates of passive resistance, they would turn the other cheek and rebuild their meetinghouse on the site where their enemies had torn it down. Their courage and devotion to principle finally triumphed. Though at times they seemed stubborn and unreasonable, they were a simple, devoted, democratic people, contending in their own high-minded way for religious and civic freedom.

William Penn, a well-born and athletic young Englishman, was attracted to the Quaker faith in 1660, when only sixteen years old. His father, disapproving, administered a sound flogging. After various adventures in the army (the best portrait of the peaceful Quaker has him in armor), the youth firmly embraced the despised faith and suffered much persecution. The courts branded him a "saucy" and "impertinent" fellow. Several hundred of his less fortunate coreligionists died of cruel treatment, and thousands more were fined, flogged, or cast into "nasty stinking prisons."

Penn's thoughts naturally turned to the New World, where a sprinkling of Quakers had already fled, notably to Rhode Island, North Carolina, and New Jersey. Eager to establish an asylum for his people, he also hoped to experiment with liberal ideas in government and at the same time make a profit. Finally, in 1681, he managed to secure from the king an immense grant of fertile land, in consideration of a monetary debt owed to his deceased father by the

William Penn Signs a Treaty with the Indians   *The peace-loving Quaker founder of Pennsylvania made a serious effort to live in harmony with the Indians, but the westward thrust of white settlement eventually caused friction, as in other colonies. (The Thomas Gilcrease Institute of American History and Art, Tulsa, Oklahoma.)*

crown. The king called the area Pennsylvania ("Penn's Woodland") in honor of the sire. But the modest son, fearing that critics would accuse him of naming it after himself, sought unsuccessfully to change the name.

Pennsylvania was by far the best advertised of all the colonies. Its founder—the "first American advertising man"—sent out paid agents and distributed countless pamphlets printed in English, Dutch, French, and German. Unlike the lures of many another American real estate promoter, then and later, Penn's inducements were generally truthful. He especially welcomed forward-looking spirits and substantial citizens, including industrious carpenters, masons, shoemakers, and other manual workers. His liberal land policy, which encouraged substantial holdings of land, was instrumental in attracting a heavy inflow of immigrants.

Quaker Pennsylvania and Its Neighbors

Penn formally launched his colony in 1681. His task was simplified by the presence of several thousand "squatters"—Dutch, Swedes, English,

Welsh—who were already scattered along the banks of the Delaware River. Philadelphia, meaning "brotherly love" in Greek, was more carefully planned than most colonial cities and consequently enjoyed wide and attractive streets. Penn farsightedly bought land from the Indians, including Chief Tammany, later patron saint of New York's political Tammany Hall. His treatment of the native peoples was so fair that the Quaker "broad brims" went among them unarmed and even employed them as baby tenders.

Penn's new proprietary regime was unusually liberal and included a representative assembly elected by the landowners. There was no tax-supported state church. Freedom of worship was guaranteed to all residents, although Penn, under pressure from London, was forced to deny Catholics and Jews the privilege of voting or holding office. The death penalty was imposed only for treason and murder, as compared with some two hundred capital crimes in England.

Among other noteworthy features, no provision was made by the peaceloving Quakers of Pennsylvania for a military defense. No restrictions were placed on immigration, and naturalization was made easy. The humane Quakers early developed a strong dislike of black slavery, and in the genial glow of Pennsylvania some progress was made toward social reform.

With its many liberal features, Pennsylvania attracted a rich mix of ethnic groups. They included numerous religious misfits who were repelled by the harsh practices of neighboring colonies. This Quaker haven boasted a surprisingly modern atmosphere in an unmodern age and to an unusual degree afforded economic opportunity, civil liberty, and religious freedom. Even so, there were some "blue laws" aimed at "ungodly revelers," stage plays, playing cards, dice, May games, and excessive hilarity.

Under such generally happy auspices, Penn's brainchild grew lustily. The Quakers were shrewd businesspeople, and in a short time the settlers were exporting grain and other foodstuffs. Within two years Philadelphia claimed three hundred houses and twenty-five hundred people. Within nineteen years—by 1700—the colony was surpassed in population and wealth only by long-established Virginia and Massachusetts.

William Penn, who altogether spent about four years in Pennsylvania, was never fully appreciated by his colonists. His governors, some of them incompetent and tactless, quarreled bitterly with the people, who were constantly demanding greater political control. Penn himself became too friendly with James II, the deposed Catholic king. Thrice arrested for treason, thrust for a time into a debtors' prison, and racked by apoplectic seizures, he died full of sorrows. His enduring monument was not only a noble experiment in government but also a new commonwealth. Based on civil and religious liberty, and dedicated to freedom of conscience and worship, it held aloft a hopeful torch in a world of semidarkness.

Small Quaker settlements flourished next

In a Boston lecture (1869), Ralph Waldo Emerson declared, "the sect of the Quakers in their best representatives appear to me to have come nearer to the sublime history and genius of Christ than any other of the sects."

door to Pennsylvania. New Jersey was started in 1664, when two noble proprietors received the area from the Duke of York. A substantial number of New Englanders, including many whose weary soil had petered out, flocked to the new colony. One of the proprietors sold West New Jersey in 1674 to a group of Quakers, who here set up a sanctuary even before Pennsylvania was launched. East New Jersey was also acquired in later years by the Quakers, whose wings were clipped in 1702 when the crown combined the two Jerseys in a royal colony.

Swedish-tinged Delaware consisted of only three counties—two at high tide, the witticism goes—and was named after Lord de la Warr. Harboring some Quakers, and closely associated with Penn's flourishing colony, Delaware was granted its own assembly in 1703. But until the American Revolution it remained under the governor of Pennsylvania.

The Middle Way in the Middle Colonies

The middle colonies—New York, New Jersey, Delaware, and Pennsylvania—enjoyed certain features in common.

In general, the soil was fertile and the expanse of land was broad, unlike rock-bestrewn New England. Pennsylvania, New York, and New Jersey came to be known as the "bread colonies," by virtue of their heavy exports of grain.

Rivers also played a vital role. Broad, languid streams—notably the Susquehanna, the Delaware, and the Hudson—tapped the fur trade of the interior and beckoned adventuresome spirits into the backcountry. The rivers had few cascading waterfalls, unlike New England's, and hence presented little inducement to manufacturing with water-wheel power.

A surprising amount of industry nonetheless flourished in the middle colonies. Virginal forests abounded for lumbering and shipbuilding. The presence of deep river estuaries and landlocked harbors stimulated both commerce and the growth of seaports, such as New York and Philadelphia. Even Albany, more than a hundred miles up the Hudson, was a port of some consequence in colonial days.

The middle colonies were in many respects midway between New England and the southern plantation group. Except in aristocratic New York, the landholdings were generally intermediate in size—smaller than in the big-acreage South but larger than in small-farm New England. Local government lay somewhere between the personalized town meeting of New England and the diffused county government of the South. There were fewer industries in the middle colonies than in New England, more than in the South.

Yet the middle colonies, which in some ways were the most American part of America, could claim certain distinctions in their own right. Generally speaking, the population was more ethnically mixed than that of other settlements. The people were blessed with an unusual degree of religious toleration and democratic control. Earnest and devout Quakers, in particular, made a contribution to human freedom out of all proportion to their numbers. Desirable land was more easily acquired in the middle colonies than in New England or in the tidewater South. One result was that a considerable amount of economic and social democracy prevailed, though less so in aristocratic New York.

Modern-minded Benjamin Franklin, entering Philadelphia as a seventeen-year-old youth with a roll of bread under each arm, found a congenial home in the urbane atmosphere of the city. It is true that he was born a Yankee in Puritanical Boston, but, as one Pennsylvanian later boasted, "He came to life at seventeen, in Philadelphia."

By the mid–eighteenth century, the thirteen colonies as a group revealed striking similarities, even though they had developed wide differences. They were all basically English. They all exercised certain priceless Anglo-Saxon freedoms. They all possessed some measure of self-government, though by no means complete democracy. They all enjoyed some degree of religious toleration and educational opportunity. They all afforded unusual advantages for economic and social self-development. Finally—and perhaps most significantly—they were all separated from home authority by a billowing ocean moat three thousand miles (4,800 kilometers) wide.

CHRONOLOGY

1517	Martin Luther begins Protestant Reformation
1536	John Calvin of Geneva publishes *Institutes of the Christian Religion*
1620	Pilgrims sail on the *Mayflower* to Plymouth Bay
1624	Dutch found New Netherland
1629	Charles I dismisses Parliament and persecutes Puritans
1630	Puritans found Massachusetts Bay Colony
1635–1636	Roger Williams convicted of heresy and founds Rhode Island colony
1635–1638	Connecticut and New Haven colonies founded
1643	New England Confederation formed
1655	New Netherland conquers New Sweden
1664	England seizes New Netherland from Dutch East and West Jersey colonies founded
1675–1676	King Philip's War
1681	William Penn founds Pennsylvania colony
1688–1689	Glorious Revolution overthrows Stuarts and Dominion of New England

Varying Viewpoints

For many years, historians of the first century of colonial life in British North America focused on the efforts of the colonists to stake out a social order free of the constraints of the mother country. The struggle of the Massachusetts Bay Puritans to escape the regimentation of English society and to seize the religious freedom and economic equality proffered by the American wilderness formed the centerpiece of this interpretation, which was conspicuous in the work of Perry Miller, among others. Similarly, the founding of Quaker settlements in New Jersey and Pennsylvania, and the attempt of Dutch New Yorkers to maintain their cultural heritage, revealed the discord between the colonies and the mother country.

Recent studies, including those by Gary Nash and Patricia Bonomi, have shifted the drama of early American history from the transatlantic to the domestic stage. This perspective emphasizes the contests for economic and political supremacy within the colonies, such as the efforts of the Massachusetts Bay elite to ward off the challenges of religious "heretics" and an increasingly restless lower class. Nowhere was such internal conflict so prevalent as in the ethnically diverse middle colonies, where factional conflict became the distinguishing feature of public life. Some historians even find, in the turbulent middle colonies, the seeds of the later competitive American political system.

Select Readings

Primary Source Documents

John Winthrop, "A Modell of Christian Charity" (1630), in *The American Primer,* edited by Daniel Boorstin, outlines the goals of the Puritan errand into the wilderness. Winthrop's "Speech on Liberty"* (1645), in his *History of New England* (1853), established the colony's fundamental political principles. William Bradford, *Of Plymouth Plantation,** edited by Samuel E. Morison (1952), is a rich contemporary account.

Secondary Sources

New England has received more scholarly attention than any other colonial region. An incisive short account is Edmund S. Morgan's *The Puritan Dilemma: The Story of John Winthrop* (1958). A brilliant and complex intellectual history is Perry Miller's *The New England Mind* (2 vols., 1939, 1953), a work that has long been a landmark for other scholars. Sacvan Bercovitch traces the heritage of the New England temperament in *The Puritan Origins of the American Self* (1975). See also his *The American Jeremiad* (1978). Edmund S. Morgan describes the crisis that beset the original Puritans when their children displayed a lesser degree of religiosity in *Visible Saints* (1963). Economic questions receive critical attention from Bernard Bailyn in *The New England Merchants in the Seventeenth Century* (1955). Sidney Ahlstrom's *Religious History of the American People* (1972) is comprehensive. John T. Ellis pays special attention to religious issues in *Catholics in Colonial America* (1965), as does Edmund S. Morgan in *Roger Williams: The Church and State* (1967). David S. Lovejoy discusses the impact of England's Glorious Revolution on the colonies in *The Glorious Revolution in America* (1975). Areas outside New England are dealt with in Gary Nash, *Quakers and Politics: Pennsylvania, 1681–1726* (1971); Patricia Bonomi, *A Factious People: Politics and Society in Colonial New York* (1971); and Frederick Tolles, *Meetinghouse and Countinghouse* (1948). Timothy H. Breen, *Puritans and Adventurers* (1980), draws contrasts between Virginia and New England.

3

American Life in the Seventeenth Century, 1607–1692

Being thus passed the vast ocean, and a sea of troubles before in their preparation . . . , they had now no friends to wellcome them, nor inns to entertaine or refresh their weatherbeaten bodys, no houses or much less towns to repaire too, to seeke for succore.

William Bradford, Of Plymouth Plantation

The Unhealthy Chesapeake

Life in the American wilderness was nasty, brutish, and short for the earliest Chesapeake settlers. Malaria, dysentery, and typhoid took a cruel toll, cutting ten years off the life expectancy of newcomers from England. Half the people born in early Virginia and Maryland did not survive to celebrate their twentieth birthdays. Few of the remaining half lived to see their fiftieth—or even their fortieth, if they were women.

The disease-ravaged settlements of the Chesapeake grew only slowly in the seventeenth century, mostly through fresh immigration from England. The great majority of immigrants were single men in their late teens and early twenties, and most perished soon after arrival. Surviving males competed for the affec-

tions of the extremely scarce women, whom they outnumbered nearly six to one in 1650 and still outnumbered by three to two at the end of the century. Eligible women did not remain single for long.

Families were both few and fragile in this ferocious environment. Most men could not find mates. Most marriages were destroyed by the death of a partner within seven years. Scarcely any children reached adulthood under the care of two loving parents, and almost no one knew a grandparent. Weak family ties were reflected in the many pregnancies among unmarried young girls. In one Maryland county, more than a third of all brides were already pregnant when they spoke their marriage vows.

Yet despite these hardships, the Chesapeake colonies struggled on. The native-born inhabitants eventually acquired immunity to the killer diseases that had ravaged the original immigrants. The presence of more women allowed more families to form, and by the end of the seventeenth century the white population of the Chesapeake was growing on the basis of its own birthrate. As the eighteenth century opened, Virginia, with some fifty-nine thousand souls, was the most populous colony. Maryland, with about thirty thousand, was the third largest (after Massachusetts).

The Tobacco Economy

Though unhealthy for human life, the Chesapeake was immensely hospitable to tobacco cultivation. Profit-hungry settlers often planted tobacco before they planted corn. (Cornfields were also feared as staging areas for Indian ambushes.) Seeking fresh fields to plant to tobacco, these new immigrants plunged ever farther up the river valleys, provoking Indian attacks.

Leaf-laden ships annually hauled some 1.5 million pounds (680,000 kilograms) of tobacco out of Chesapeake Bay by the 1630s and almost 40 million pounds (18 million kilograms) a year by the end of the century. This enormous production depressed prices, but colonial Chesapeake tobacco growers responded to falling prices in the familiar way of farmers: by planting still more acres to tobacco and bringing still more product to market.

More tobacco meant more labor, but where was it to come from? Families formed too slowly to provide it by natural population increase. Indians died too quickly on contact with whites to be a reliable labor force. African slaves cost too much money. But England still had a "surplus" of displaced yeoman farmers, desperate for employment. Many of them, as "indentured servants," voluntarily mortgaged the sweat of their bodies for several years to Chesapeake masters. In exchange they received transatlantic passage and eventual "freedom dues," including a few barrels of corn, a suit of clothes—and perhaps a small parcel of land.

Both Virginia and Maryland employed the "headright" system to encourage the importation of servant workers. Under its terms, whoever paid the passage of a laborer received the right to acquire fifty acres of land. Masters—not the servants themselves—thus reaped the benefits of landownership from the headright system. Some masters, men who already had at least some modest financial means, soon parlayed their investments in servants into huge fortunes in real estate. They became the great

A Tobacco Plantation   As the white managers look on, slave workers load tobacco in barrels for shipment on the waiting vessels in the background. (The Granger Collection.)

merchant-planters, lords of vast riverfront estates that came to dominate the agriculture and commerce of the southern colonies. Hungry for both labor and land, Chesapeake planters brought some 100,000 indentured servants to the region by 1700. These "white slaves" represented more than three-quarters of all European immigrants to Virginia and Maryland in the seventeenth century.

Indentured servants led a hard but hopeful life in the early days of the Chesapeake settlements. They looked forward to becoming free and acquiring land of their own after completing their term of servitude. But as prime land became scarcer, masters became increasingly resistant to including land grants in "freedom dues." The servants' lot grew harsher as the seventeenth century wore on. Misbehaving servants, such as a housemaid who became pregnant or a laborer who killed a hog, might be punished with an extended term of service. Even after formal freedom was granted, penniless freed workers often had little choice but to hire themselves out for pitifully low wages to their former masters.

Frustrated Freedmen and Bacon's Rebellion

An accumulating mass of footloose, impoverished freemen was drifting discontentedly about the Chesapeake region by the late seventeenth century. Mostly single young men, they were frustrated by their broken hopes of acquiring land, as well as by their gnawing failure to find single women.

The swelling numbers of these wretched bachelors rattled the established planters. The Virginia assembly in 1670 disenfranchised most of the landless knockabouts, accusing them of "having little interest in the country" and causing "tumults at the election to the disturbance of his majesty's peace." Virginia's Governor Berkeley lamented his lot as ruler of this rabble: "How miserable that man is that governs a people where six parts of seven at least are poor, endebted, discontented, and armed."

Berkeley's misery soon increased. About a thousand Virginians broke out of control in

Early Tobacco Advertising *Crude woodcut labels like this were used to identify various "brands" of tobacco. (The Granger Collection.)*

1676, under the leadership of a twenty-nine-year-old planter, Nathaniel Bacon. Many of the rebels were frontiersmen who had been forced into the untamed backcountry in search of virgin land. They fiercely resented Berkeley's friendly policies toward the Indians, whose thriving fur trade the governor monopolized. When Berkeley refused to retaliate for a series of savage Indian attacks on frontier settlements, Bacon and his followers took matters into their own hands. They fell murderously upon the Indians, friendly and hostile alike, chased Berkeley from Jamestown, and put the torch to the capital. Chaos swept the raw colony, as frustrated freemen and resentful servants—described as "a rabble of the basest sort of people"—went on a rampage of plundering and pilfering.

As this civil war in Virginia ground on, Bacon suddenly died of disease, like so many of his fellow colonials. Berkeley thereupon crushed the uprising with brutal cruelty, hanging more than

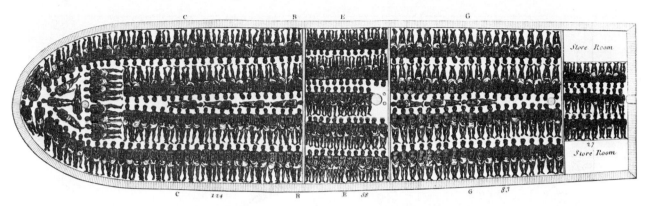

The "Middle Passage" *Human cargo in the hold of a slave ship. (The Mariners Museum.)*

twenty rebels. Back in England Charles II complained, "That old fool has put to death more people in that naked country than I did here for the murder of my father."

The distant English king could scarcely imagine the depths of passion and fear that Bacon's Rebellion excited in Virginia. Bacon had ignited the smoldering unhappiness of landless former servants, and he had pitted the hard-scrabble backcountry frontiersmen against the haughty gentry of the tidewater plantations. The rebellion was now suppressed, but these tensions remained. Lordly planters, surrounded by a still-seething sea of malcontents, anxiously looked about for less-troublesome laborers to toil in the restless tobacco kingdom. Their eyes soon lit on Africa.

Colonial Slavery

Perhaps 10 million Africans were carried in chains to the New World in the three centuries or so following Columbus's discovery. Only about 400,000 of them ended up in North America, the great majority arriving after 1700. Most of the early human cargoes were hauled to Spanish and Portuguese South America or to the sugar-rich West Indies.

Africans had been brought to Jamestown as early as 1619, but as late as 1670 they numbered only about 2,000 in Virginia (out of a total population of some 35,000 persons) and about 7 percent of the 50,000 people in the southern plantation colonies as a whole. Hard-pinched white colonists, struggling to stay alive and to hack crude clearings out of the forests, could not afford to pay high prices for slaves who might die soon after arrival. White servants might die, too, but they were far less costly.

Drastic change came in the 1680s. Rising wages in England shrank the pool of penniless folk willing to gamble on a new life or an early death as indentured servants in America. At the same time, the large planters were growing increasingly fearful of the multitudes of potentially mutinous former servants in their midst. By the mid-1680s, for the first time, black slaves outnumbered white servants among the plantation colonies' new arrivals. In 1698 the Royal African Company lost its crown-granted monopoly on carrying slaves to the colonies. Enterprising Americans, especially Rhode Islanders, rushed to cash in on the lucrative slave trade, and the supply of slaves increased steeply. More than ten thousand Africans were pushed ashore in America in the decade after 1700, and tens of thousands more in the next half-century. Blacks accounted for nearly half the population of Virginia by 1750. In South Carolina they outnumbered whites two to one.

Most of the slaves who reached North America came from the west coast of Africa, including the area stretching from present-day Senegal to Angola. They were originally captured by African coastal tribes, who traded them in crude markets on the shimmering tropical beaches to itinerant European—and American—flesh merchants. Usually branded and bound, the captives were herded aboard sweltering ships for

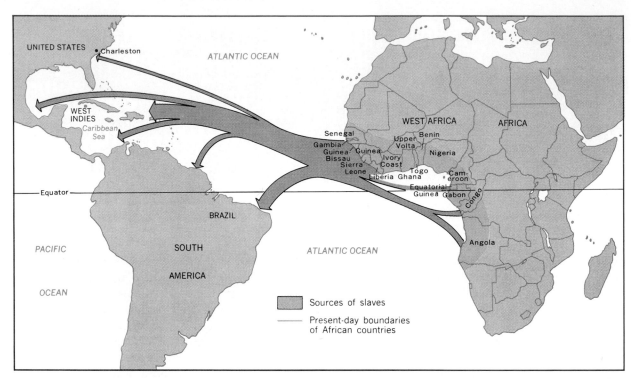

Main Sources of African Slaves, c. 1500 to c. 1800 *The three centuries of the "African Diaspora" scattered blacks all over the New World, with about 400,000 coming to the English colonies.*

the gruesome "middle passage," on which death rates ran as high as 20 percent. Terrified survivors were eventually shoved onto auction blocks in New World ports like Newport, Rhode Island, or Charleston, South Carolina, where a giant slave market flourished for more than a century.

A few of the earliest African immigrants gained their freedom, and some even became slaveowners themselves. But as the number of Africans in their midst increased dramatically toward the end of the seventeenth century, white colonists reacted remorselessly to this supposed racial threat.

Charleston, South Carolina, c. 1735 *Scarcely half a century old when this painting was done, Charleston was the largest city in the mostly rural southern colonies. This watercolor by Bishop Roberts is believed to be the earliest painting of Charleston. (Colonial Williamsburg Foundation.)*

Earlier in the century the legal difference between a slave and a servant was unclear. But now the law began to make sharp distinctions between the two—largely on the basis of race. Statutes appeared that formally decreed the iron conditions of slavery for blacks. These earliest "slave codes" made blacks *and their children* the property (or "chattels") for life of their white masters. Some colonies made it a crime to teach a slave to read or write. Not even conversion to Christianity could qualify a slave for freedom. Thus did the God-fearing whites put the fear of God into their hapless black laborers. Slavery might have begun in America for economic reasons, but by the end of the seventeenth century, it was clear that racial discrimination also powerfully molded the American slave system.

Africans in America

In the deepest South, slave life was especially harsh. The climate was hostile to health, and the labor was life-draining. The widely scattered South Carolina rice and indigo plantations were lonely hells on earth where gangs of mostly male Africans toiled and perished. Only fresh imports could sustain the slave population under these cruel conditions.

Blacks in the tobacco-growing Chesapeake region had a somewhat easier lot. Tobacco was a less physically demanding crop than those of the deeper South. Tobacco plantations were larger and closer to one another than rice plantations. The size and proximity of these plantations permitted the slaves more frequent contact with friends and relatives. By about 1720 the proportion of females in the Chesapeake slave population had begun to rise, making family life possible. The captive black population of the Chesapeake area soon began to grow not only through new imports but also through its own fertility—making it one of the few slave societies in history to perpetuate itself by its own natural reproduction.

Native-born African-Americans contributed to the growth of a stable and distinctive slave culture, a mixture of African and American elements of speech, religion, and folkways (see "Makers of America," pp. 50–51). On the sea islands off South Carolina's coast, blacks evolved a unique language, *Gullah* (probably a corruption of *Angola*, the African region from which many of them had come). It blended English with several African languages, including Yoruba, Ibo, and Hausa. Through it many African words have passed into American speech—such as *goober* (peanut), *gumbo*

An Indigo Plantation
Indigo, used to make blue dye for textiles, was a major product of the southernmost colonies. As shown here, black slaves furnished most of the labor on indigo plantations. (The New York Public Library.)

From African to African-American

Dragged in chains from the shores of West Africa, the first African-Americans struggled to preserve their diverse African heritages from the ravages of slavery. Their sons and daughters, the first generation of American-born slaves, melded these various African traditions—Guinean, Ibo, Yoruba, Angolan—into a distinctive African-American culture. Their achievement sustained them during the cruelties of enslavement and has endured to enrich American life to this day.

With the arrival of the first Africans in the seventeenth century, a cornucopia of African traditions poured into the New World: handicrafts and skills in numerous trades; a plethora of languages, musics, and cuisines; even rice-planting techniques that conquered the inhospitable soil of South Carolina. It was North America's rice paddies, tilled by experienced West Africans, that introduced rice into the English diet and furnished so many English tables with the sticky staple.

These first American slaves were mostly males. Upon arrival they were packed off to small isolated farms, where social contact with other Africans, especially with women, was an unheard-of luxury. Yet their legal status was at first uncertain. A few African-Americans were able to buy their own freedom in the seventeenth century. One, Anthony Johnson of Northampton County, Virginia, actually became a slaveholder himself.

But by the beginning of the eighteenth century, a settled slave society was emerging in the southern colonies. Laws tightened; slave traders stepped up their deliveries of hu-

Gourd Fiddle; Africans Destined for Slavery   Made in early-nineteenth-century Maryland, this instrument was directly adapted from African designs and is a fine example of the importation of native traditions into the New World. The drawing depicts the brutality that Africans bound for foreign servitude experienced in the slave markets of coastal Africa. (left, Smithsonian Neg. 81-11790; right, Library of Congress.)

An Account of the Number of Negroes delivered in to the Iſlands of Barbados, Jamaica, and Antego, from the Year 1698 to 1708, ſince the Trade was Opened, taken from the Accounts ſent from the reſpective Governours of thoſe Iſlands to the Lords Commiſſioners of Trade, whereby it appears the African Trade is encreas'd to four times more ſince its being laid Open, than it was under an Excluſive Company.

Between what Years deliver'd.	No. of Negroes delivered into Barbados.	Number delivered into Jamaica.	Number delivered into Antego.
Between the 8 April, 1698 To April 1699	} 3436		
To April 1700	3080		
To 5 ditto 1701	4311		
To 10 ditto 1702	9213		
To 31 Mar. 1703	4561		
To 5 April 1704	1876		
To 2d. ditto 1705	3319		
To 5 ditto 1706	1879		
To 12 May 1707	2720		
To 29 April 1708	1018		
Between 29 Sept. 1698 and 29 Decemb. 1698		} 1273	
Between 7 April 1699 and 28 March 1700		} 5766	
From 28 Mar. to 3 Apr. 1701		6668	
3 Apr. 1701. to 20 dit. 1702		8505	
20 dit. 1702 to 12 dit. 1703		2238	
12 dit. 1703 to 18 dit. 1704		2711	
18 dit. 1704 to 24 dit. 1705		3421	
24 dit. 1705 to 27 dit. 1706		5462	
27 dit. 1706 to 22 dit. 1707		2122	
22 dit. 1707 to 26 dit. 1708		6633	
To June 1708		187	
1698			18
June 1699			212
Between June 1700 and 24 April 1701			} 364
Between 24 April 1701 and 30 March 1702			} 2395
To April 1703			1670
To Nov. 1704			1551
To 1705			269
To 1706			530
To 1707			114
	35409	44376	7123

Beſides which there are 7 Separate Ships named in the foregoing Liſt for Antego, but not the Number of Negroes, ſo we may well compute them at 1200 more, which arriv'd between 1699 and 1700.

A Royal African Company Account Log of Slaves Imported to the West Indies, 1698–1708 Note the rapid expansion of the slave trade as the eighteenth century opened. (Historical Society of Pennsylvania.)

man cargo; large plantations formed. Most significantly, a new generation of American-born slaves joined their forebears at labor in the fields. By 1740 large groups of slaves lived together on sprawling plantations, the American-born outnumbered the African-born, and the importation of African slaves slowed.

Forging a common culture and finding a psychological weapon with which to resist their masters and preserve their dignity were daunting challenges for American born slaves. Plantation life was beastly, an endless cycle of miserable toil in the field or foundry from sunup to sundown. Female slaves were forced to perform double duty. At the end of a day's backbreaking work, women were expected to sit up for hours spinning, weaving, or sewing to clothe themselves and their families.

Yet even with so little time for society and so little commonality of language and custom, a vibrant culture flowered. Women used the knitting and weaving time to discuss child-rearing and to develop close female bonds. In this they carried on a West African tradition of separate female social networks. Cut off from African religions, most slaves became Christians, but at their Sunday and nighttime prayer meetings African-Americans adapted Christianity to their own purposes, adding African-influenced music and rituals to the services. Methodism, one of the most popular denominations in the slave quarters, banned dancing as sinful. But unlike their staid, white fellow-communicants, African-Americans ingeniously circumvented this stricture: three or four people would stand still in a ring, clapping hands and beating time with their feet (but never crossing their legs, so therefore not officially "dancing"); others would walk around the ring, singing in unison. This "ring shouting" derived from African religions. Modern American dances, among them the 1920s craze the Charleston, in turn descended from this "not dancing" dancing.

Black Christianity differed from white Christianity in theology as well as fervor. Blacks rejected predestination and emphasized the lowly earthly place of Jesus and the earthly deliverance of Joshua, Daniel, and Moses. And they retained an African idea of a heaven where they would be united with their ancestors.

Thus were diverse African traditions alloyed with New World innovations, and thus was American culture endowed in its turn. Much of American music and literature, as well as religion, was born in the slave quarters, but only at the bitter cost of generations of human agony.

Yarrow Mamout When Charles Willson Peale painted this portrait in 1819, Mamout was over 100 years old. A devout Muslim brought to Maryland as a slave, he eventually bought his freedom and settled in Georgetown. (Historical Society of Pennsylvania.)

A Merchant Planter's Home and Its Dining Room *Simple by later standards, this house was home to the family of a substantial planter in the seventeenth century. It stands on land in the Virginia Tidewater region first acquired by Adam Thoroughgood, who arrived in Virginia Colony as an indentured servant in 1621. By 1635, as a freeman, he had recruited 105 settlers to the colony and was rewarded, according to the practice of the "headright system," with the title to some 5350 acres along the Lynnhaven River. There his grandson erected this house in about 1680. It was continuously occupied by the Thoroughgood family for more than two centuries, until the 1920s. (The Chrysler Museum.)*

(okra), and *voodoo* (witchcraft). The ringshout, a West African religious dance performed by shuffling in a circle while answering a preacher's shouts, was brought to colonial America by slaves and eventually contributed to the development of jazz. The banjo and the bongo drum were other African contributions to American culture.

Slaves also helped powerfully to build the country with their labor. A few became skilled artisans—carpenters, bricklayers, and tanners. But chiefly they performed the sweaty toil of clearing swamps, grubbing out trees, and other menial tasks. Condemned to life under the lash, slaves naturally pined for freedom. A slave revolt erupted in New York City in 1712 that cost the lives of a dozen whites and caused the execution of twenty-one blacks, some of them burned at the stake over a slow fire. More than fifty resentful South Carolina blacks exploded in revolt in 1739 and tried to march to Spanish Florida, only to be stopped by the local militia. But in the end the slaves in the South proved to be a more reliable labor force than the white indentured servants they gradually replaced. No

slave rebellion in American history matched the scale of Bacon's Rebellion.

Southern Society

As slavery spread, the gaps in the South's social structure widened. The rough equality of poverty and disease of the early days was giving way to a defined hierarchy of wealth and status in the early eighteenth century. At the top of the social ladder perched a small but powerful covey of great planters. Owning gangs of slaves and vast domains of land, they ruled the region's economy and virtually monopolized political power. A clutch of extended clans—such as the Fitzhughs, the Lees, and the Washingtons—possessed among them horizonless tracts of Virginia real estate, and together they dominated the House of Burgesses. Just before the Revolutionary War, 70 percent of the leaders of the Virginia legislature came from families established in Virginia before 1690—the famed "first families of Virginia," or "FFVs."

Yet, legend to the contrary, these great seventeenth-century merchant planters were not silk-swathed cavaliers gallantly imitating the ways of English country gentlemen. They did eventually build stately riverfront manors, occasionally rode to the hounds, and some of them even cultivated the arts and accumulated distinguished libraries. But for the most part they were a hardworking, businesslike lot, laboring long hours over the problems of plantation management. Few problems were more vexatious than the unruly, often surly servants. One Virginia governor had such difficulty keeping his servants sober that he struck a deal allowing them to get drunk the next day if they would only lay off the liquor long enough to look after his guests at a celebration of the queen's birthday in 1711.

Beneath the planters—far beneath them in wealth, prestige, and political power—were the small farmers, the largest social group. They tilled their modest plots and might own one or two slaves, but they lived a ragged, hand-to-mouth existence. Still lower on the social scale were the landless whites, most of them luckless

former indentured servants. Beneath them were those persons still serving out the term of their indenture. Their numbers gradually diminished as black slaves increasingly replaced white indentured servants toward the end of the seventeenth century. The oppressed black slaves, of course, remained enchained in society's basement.

Few cities sprouted in the colonial South, and consequently an urban professional class, including lawyers and financiers, was slow to emerge. Southern life revolved around the great plantations, distantly isolated from one another. Waterways provided the principal means of transportation. Roads were so wretched that in bad weather funeral parties could not reach church burial grounds—an obstacle that accounts for the development of family burial plots in the South, a practice unlike anything in old England or New England.

The New England Family

Nature smiled more benignly on pioneer New Englanders than on their disease-plagued fellow colonists to the south. Clean water and cool temperatures retarded the spread of killer microbes. In stark contrast to the fate of Chesapeake immigrants, settlers in seventeenth-century New England *added* ten years to their life spans by migrating from the Old World. One settler claimed that "a sip of New England's air is better than a whole draft of old England's ale." The first generations of Puritan colonists enjoyed, on the average, about seventy years on this earth—not very different from the life expectancy of present-day Americans.

In further contrast with the Chesapeake, New Englanders tended to migrate not as single individuals but as families, and the family remained at the center of New England life. Almost from the outset, New England's population grew from natural reproductive increase. The people were remarkably fertile, even if the soil was not.

Early marriage encouraged the booming birthrate. Women typically wed by their early twenties and produced babies about every two years thereafter until menopause. Ceaseless childbearing drained the vitality of many pio-

Mrs. Elizabeth Freake and Baby Mary *This portrait of a Boston mother and child in about 1674 suggests the strong family ties that characterized early New England society. (Worcester Art Museum.)*

Early Advertising *Appeal in England for American colonists.*

neer women, as the weather-eroded colonial tombstones eloquently reveal. A number of the largest families were borne by several mothers, though claims about the frequency of death in childbirth have probably been exaggerated. But the dread of death in the birthing bed haunted many women, and it was small wonder that they came to fear pregnancy. A married woman could expect to experience up to ten pregnancies and rear as many as eight surviving children. Massachusetts governor William Phips was one of twenty-seven children, all by the same mother. A New England woman might well have dependent children in her household from the earliest days of her marriage until the day of her death, and child raising became virtually her full-time occupation.

The longevity of the New Englanders contributed to family stability. Children grew up in nurturing environments where they received love and guidance not only from their parents but from their grandparents as well. This novel intergenerational continuity has inspired the observation that New England "invented" grandparents. Family stability was reflected in low premarital pregnancy rates (again in contrast with the Chesapeake) and in the generally strong, tranquil social structure characteristic of colonial New England.

Life in the New England Towns

Sturdy New Englanders evolved a tightly knit society, the basis of which was small villages and farms. This development was natural in a people anchored by geography and hemmed in by the Indians, the French, and the Dutch. Puritanism likewise made for unity of purpose—

Graveyard Art *These New England colonists evidently died in the prime of life. Carving likenesses on grave markers was a common way of commemorating the dead. (American Antiquarian Society.)*

A Colonial Kitchen *Simple but well-provisioned, this restored kitchen from a Massachusetts house of 1684 illustrates the tidy, unpretentious prosperity of colonial New England. (Essex Institute.)*

and for concern about the moral health of the whole community. It was no accident that the nineteenth-century crusade for abolishing black slavery—with Massachusetts agitators at the forefront—sprang in some degree from the New England conscience, with its Puritan roots.

In the Chesapeake region the expansion of settlement was somewhat random and was usually undertaken by lone-wolf planters on their own initiative, but New England society grew in a more orderly fashion. New towns were legally chartered by the colonial authorities, and the distribution of land was entrusted to the steady hands of sober-minded town fathers, or "proprietors." After receiving a grant of land

Puritan Textbooks *A page from the* New England Primer; *and the hornbook for children, so called because the printing was protected by transparent horn.*

from the colonial legislature, the proprietors moved themselves and their families to the designated place and laid out their town. It usually consisted of a meetinghouse, which served as both the place of worship and the town hall, surrounded by houses. Also marked out was a village green, where the militia could drill. Each family received several parcels of land, including a woodlot for fuel, a tract suitable for growing crops, and another for pasturing animals.

Towns of more than fifty families were required to provide elementary education, and a majority of the adults knew how to read and write. As early as 1636, just eight years after the colony's founding, the Massachusetts Puritans established Harvard College, today the oldest corporation in America, to train local boys for the ministry. Only in 1693, eighty-six years after the founding of Jamestown, did the Virginians establish their first college, William and Mary.

Puritans ran their own churches, and democracy in Congregational church government led logically to democracy in political government. The town meeting, in which the freemen met together and each man voted, exhibited democracy in its purest form. New England villagers from the outset gathered regularly in their meetinghouses to elect their officials, appoint schoolmasters, and discuss such mundane matters as road repairs. The town meeting, observed Thomas Jefferson, was "the best school of political liberty the world ever saw."

The Half-Way Covenant and the Salem Witch Trials

Yet worries plagued the God-fearing pioneers of these tidy New England settlements. The pressure of a growing population was gradually dispersing the Puritans onto outlying farms, far from the control of church and neighbors. And while the core of Puritan belief still burned brightly, the passage of time was dampening the first generation's flaming religious zeal. About the middle of the seventeenth century a new form of sermon began to be heard from Puritan pulpits—the "jeremiad." Taking their cue from the doom-saying Old Testament prophet Jeremiah, earnest preachers scolded parishioners for their waning piety. Especially alarming was the apparent decline in conversions—testimonials by individuals that they had received God's grace and therefore deserved to be admitted to the church as members of the elect. Troubled ministers in 1662 announced a new formula for church membership, the "Half-Way Covenant." It offered partial membership rights to persons not yet converted.

The Half-Way Covenant dramatized the difficulty of maintaining at fever pitch the religious devotion of the founding generation. Jeremiads continued to thunder from the pulpits, but as time went on, the doors of the Puritan churches swung fully open to all comers, whether converted or not. This widening of church membership gradually erased the distinction between the "elect" and other members of society. In effect, strict religious purity was somewhat sacrificed to the cause of wider religious participation. Interestingly, from about this time onward women made up a larger proportion of Puritan congregations.

Women also played a prominent role in one of New England's most frightening religious episodes. A group of adolescent girls in Salem, Massachusetts, claimed to have been bewitched by certain older women. A hysterical "witch-hunt" ensued, leading to the legal lynching in 1692 of twenty persons, nineteen of whom were hanged and one of whom was pressed to death. Two dogs were also hanged. Larger-scale witchcraft persecutions were then common in Europe, and several outbreaks had already flared forth in the colonies. But the reign of hor-

Salem Witchcraft Hysteria   *In this notorious tract of 1693, the Puritan minister Cotton Mather defended the death-sentence verdicts of several trials for witchcraft. (The Granger Collection.)*

ror in Salem grew not only from the superstitions of the age but also from the unsettled social and religious conditions of the rapidly evolving Massachusetts village. The Salem witchcraft delusion marked an all-time high in American experience of popular passions run wild and seriously weakened the prestige of the Puritan clergy, some of whom had supported it.

The New England Way of Life

Oddly enough, the story of New England was largely written by rocks. The heavily glaciated soil was strewn with countless stones, many of which were forced to the surface after a winter freeze. In a sense the Puritans did not possess the soil; it possessed them by shaping their

The Saugus Iron Works   *Built in 1646, this primitive Massachusetts iron works flourished for only a few years. Now restored, it stands as mute testimony to New England's painful struggle, beginning even in the seventeenth century, for economic self-sufficiency. (Saugus Iron Works NHS.)*

character. Scratching a living from the protesting earth was an early American success story. Back-bending toil put a premium on industry and penny-pinching frugality, for which New Englanders became famous. Traditionally sharp Yankee traders, some of them palming off wooden nutmegs, made their mark. Connecticut came in time to be called good-humoredly "the Nutmeg State." Cynics exaggerated when they said that the three stages of progress in New England were "to get on, to get honor, to get honest."

The grudging land also left colonial New England less ethnically mixed than its southern neighbors. European immigrants were not attracted in great numbers to a site where the soil was so stony—and the religion so sulfurous.

Climate likewise molded New England, where the summers were often uncomfortably hot and the winters cruelly cold. Many early immigrants complained of the region's extremes of weather. Yet the soil and climate of New England eventually encouraged a diversified agriculture and industry. Staple products like tobacco did not flourish, as in the South. Black slavery, although attempted, could not exist profitably on small farms, especially where the surest crop was stones. No broad, fertile hinterland, comparable to that of the South, beckoned

people inland. The mountains ran fairly close to the shore, and the rivers were generally short and rapid.

Repelled by the rocks, the hardy New Englanders turned instinctively to their fine natural harbors. Hacking timber from their dense forests, they became experts in shipbuilding and commerce. They also ceaselessly exploited the self-perpetuating codfish lode off the coast of Newfoundland—the fishy "gold mines of New England," which have yielded more wealth than all the treasure chests of the Aztecs. During colonial days the wayfarer seldom got far from the sound of the ax and hammer, or the swift rush of the ship down the ways to the sea, or the smell of rotting fish. As a reminder of the importance of fishing, a handsome replica of the "sacred cod" is proudly displayed to this day in the Massachusetts State House in Boston.

The Sacred Cod   *As displayed in the Boston State House. (George M. Cushing.)*

The combination of Calvinism, soil, and climate in New England made for energy, purposefulness, sternness, stubbornness, self-reliance, and resourcefulness. Righteous New Englanders prided themselves on being God's chosen people. They long boasted that Boston was "the hub of the universe"—at least spiritually. A famous jingle of later days ran:

> I come from the city of Boston
> The home of the bean and the cod
> Where the Cabots speak only to Lowells
> And the Lowells speak only to God.

New England's impact on the rest of the nation has been incalculable. Countless thousands of New Englanders, ousted by their sterile soil, were destined to pull up stakes and re-create New England towns from Ohio to Oregon and all the way to Hawaii. A people courageous, conscientious, and willing to sacrifice for their beliefs, they made the idealism represented by Plymouth Rock a national symbol. As flinty as their stones, as stiff as their cuffs and collars, they cross-fertilized innumerable other communities with their ideals and democratic practices. The New England conscience inspired many later reformers and added something indispensable to the fiber and backbone of the American people.

The Early Settlers' Days and Ways

The cycles of the seasons and the sun set the schedules of all the earliest American colonists, men as well as women, blacks as well as whites. The overwhelming majority of colonists were farmers. They planted in the spring, tended their crops in the summer, harvested in the fall, and prepared in the winter to begin the cycle anew. They usually rose at dawn and went to bed at dusk. Chores might be performed after nightfall only if they were "worth the candle," a phrase that has persisted in American speech.

Women, slave or free, on southern plantations or northern farms, wove, cooked, cleaned, and cared for children. Men cleared land; fenced, planted, and cropped it; cut firewood; and butchered livestock as needed. Children helped with all these tasks, while picking up such schooling as they could.

Life and Death in Colonial America *This embroidery suggests the stoic resolve of a colonial mother, with one child in a coffin and another in its cradle. (The Connecticut Historical Society.)*

Life was humble but comfortable by contemporary standards. Compared to most seventeenth-century Europeans, Americans lived in affluent abundance. Land was relatively cheap, though somewhat less available in the planter-dominated South than elsewhere. In the northern and middle colonies, an acre of virgin soil cost about what American carpenters could earn in one day as wages, which were roughly three times those of their European counterparts.

"Dukes don't emigrate," the saying goes, for if people enjoy wealth and security, they are not likely to risk exposing their lives in the wilderness. Similarly, the very poorest members of a society may not possess even the modest means needed to pull up stakes and seek a fresh start in life. Accordingly, most white migrants to early colonial America came neither from the aristocracy nor from the dregs of European society—with the partial exception of the impoverished indentured servants.

Crude frontier life did not in any case permit the flagrant display of class distinctions, and seventeenth-century society in all the colonies had a certain simple sameness to it, especially in the more egalitarian New England and middle colonies. Yet many settlers, who considered themselves to be of the "better sort," tried to re-create on a modified scale the social structure they had known in the Old World. To some extent, they succeeded, though yeasty democratic forces frustrated their full triumph. Resentment against upper-class pretensions helped to spark outbursts like Bacon's Rebellion of 1676 in Virginia and the uprising of Maryland's Protestants toward the end of the seventeenth century. In New York, animosity between lordly landholders and aspiring merchants fueled Leisler's Rebellion, an ill-starred and bloody little insurgency that rocked New York City from 1689 to 1691.

For their part, would-be American blue bloods resented the pretensions of the "meaner sort" and passed laws to try to keep them in their place. Massachusetts in 1651 prohibited poorer folk from "wearing gold or silver lace," and in eighteenth-century Virginia a tailor was fined and jailed for arranging to race his horse—"a sport only for gentlemen." But these efforts to reproduce the finely stratified societies of Europe proved feeble in the early American wilderness, where equality and democracy found fertile soil—at least for white people.

CHRONOLOGY

1619	First Africans arrive in Virginia
1636	Harvard College founded
1662	Half-Way Covenant for Congregational church membership established
1670	Virginia Assembly disenfranchises landless freemen
1676	Bacon's Rebellion
1680s	Mass expansion of slavery in colonies
1689–1691	Leisler's Rebellion
1692	Salem witch trials
1693	College of William and Mary founded
1698	Royal African Company slave trade monopoly ended
1712	New York City slave revolt
1739	South Carolina slave revolt

Varying Viewpoints

The simultaneous evolution of a rigid racial caste system and democratic political traditions in the British colonies has long perplexed students of early America. For many generations historians, most of them of Yankee stock, resolved the apparent paradox by locating the seeds of democracy in New England. The aggressive independence of the people, best expressed by the boisterous town meetings, spawned the American obsession with freedom. On the other hand, this view holds, the slave societies of the South were hierarchical, aristocratic communities under the sway of a few powerful planters.

Recent studies have questioned this interpretation. First, they point out the many undemocratic features of colonial New England. Second, they note that Washington, Jefferson, and Madison—the architects of American government and its commitment to liberty—all hailed from slaveholding Virginia. In fact, nowhere were republican principles stronger than in Virginia. This realization has sparked new speculation about the relationship between American slavery and American freedom. Some scholars, notably Edmund S. Morgan, see the willingness of wealthy planters to concede the equality and freedom of all white males as a device to ensure racial solidarity and mute class conflict. In this view, the concurrent emergence of slavery and democracy poses no paradox. Racism muffled animosity between rich and poor and fostered the devotion to equality (for whites) that became the hallmark of American democracy.

Select Readings

Primary Source Documents

Adolph B. Benson, ed., *The America of 1750*; *Petar Kalm's Travels in North America* (1937) records the observations of a visiting Swedish naturalist with a keen eye for the behavior of human fauna. The first slave laws of Virginia are collected in Warren M. Billings, ed., *The Old Dominion in the Seventeenth Century** (1975), as are firsthand accounts of Bacon's Rebellion. See also George L. Burr, ed., *Narratives of the Witchcraft Cases, 1648–1706** (1914).

Secondary Sources

A general survey is Clarence Ver Steeg, *The Formative Years* (1964). On life and labor in the Chesapeake, consult Thad W. Tate and David L. Ammerman, eds., *The Chesapeake in the Seventeenth Century* (1979); Wesley F. Craven, *The Southern Colonies in the Seventeenth Century* (1949); and Edmund S. Morgan, *American Slavery, American Freedom* (1975), which concentrates on race and class relations. Further probing economic conflicts and their role in the introduction of slavery is Timothy H.

Breen and Stephen Innes, *Myne Owne Ground: Race and Freedom on Virginia's Eastern Shore, 1640–1676* (1980). Gloria Main chronicles *The Tobacco Colony: Life in Early Maryland, 1650–1719* (1982), while Darrett B. Rutman and Anita H. Rutman examine Virginia in *A Place in Time: Middlesex County, Virginia, 1650–1750* (1984). Daniel Blake Smith looks *Inside the Great House: Planter Family Life in Eighteenth-Century Chesapeake Society* (1980). Kenneth A. Lockridge analyzes the life of one of Virginia's most celebrated residents in *The Diary and Life of William Byrd II of Virginia, 1674–1744* (1987). Winthrop Jordan's magnificent *White over Black: American Attitudes toward the Negro, 1550–1812* (1968) discusses the evolution of racial attitudes. Life in New England's towns and homes is scrutinized in Edmund S. Morgan, *Puritan Family* (1944); Bernard Bailyn, *Education in the Forming of American Society* (1960); Sumner C. Powell, *Puritan Village* (1963); Darrett Rutman, *Winthrop's Boston* (1965); John Demos, *A Little Commonwealth: Family Life in Plymouth Colony* (1970); Philip Greven,

Four Generations: Population, Land, and Family in Colonial Andover, Massachusetts (1970); Kenneth Lockridge, *New England Town: Dedham* (1970); Roger Thompson, *Women in Stuart England and America* (1974); Lyle Koehler, *A Search for Power: The "Weaker Sex" in Seventeenth-Century New England* (1980); Laurel T. Ulrich, *Good Wives: Image and Reality in the Lives of Women in Northern New England, 1650–1750* (1982); Stephen Innes, *Labor in a New Land: Economy and Society in Seventeenth Century Springfield* (1983); and Philip Greven, *The Protestant Temperament* (1977), which analyzes child-rearing practices. Robert Pope examines *The*

Half-Way Covenant: Church Membership in Puritan New England (1969). David Grayson Allen emphasizes the persistence of English customs in *In English Ways: The Movement of Societies and the Transferral of English Local Law and Custom to Massachusetts Bay in the Seventeenth Century* (1981). Witchcraft is the subject of Paul Boyer and Stephen Nissenbaum's *Salem Possessed* (1974) and John Demos's massive *Entertaining Satan* (1982). A sweeping survey that emphasizes the diversity of cultures already present in seventeenth-century America is E. Brooks Holifield, *Era of Persuasion: American Thought and Culture, 1521–1680* (1989).

Colonial Society on the Eve of Revolution, 1700–1775

Driven from every other corner of the earth, freedom of thought and the right of private judgment in matters of conscience direct their course to this happy country as their last asylum.

Samuel Adams, 1776

Conquest by the Cradle

The common term *thirteen original colonies* is misleading. There were thirty-two colonies under British rule in North America by 1775, including Canada, the Floridas, and the various islands of the Caribbean. But only thirteen of them unfurled the standard of revolt. A few of the nonrebels, such as Canada and Jamaica, were larger, wealthier, or more populous than some of the thirteen. And even among the revolting thirteen, dramatic differences in economic organization, social structure, and ways of life were evident.

All the eventually rebellious colonies did have one outstanding feature in common: their population was growing by leaps and bounds. In 1700 they contained fewer than 300,000 souls, about 20,000 of whom were black. By 1775, 2.5 million persons inhabited the thirteen colonies,

of whom about half a million were black. White immigrants made up nearly 400,000 of the increased number, and black "forced immigrants" accounted for almost as many again. But most of the spurt stemmed from the remarkable natural fertility of all Americans, white and black. To the amazement and dismay of Europeans, the colonists were doubling their numbers every twenty-five years. Unfriendly Dr. Samuel Johnson, back in England, growled that the Americans were multiplying like their own rattlesnakes. They were also a youthful people, whose average age in 1775 was about sixteen.

This population boom had political consequences. In 1700 there were twenty English subjects for each American colonist. By 1775 the English advantage in numbers had fallen to three to one—setting the stage for a momentous shift in the balance of power between the colonies and England.

The bulk of the population was cooped up east of the Alleghenies, although by 1775 a vanguard of pioneers had trickled into the stump-studded clearings of Tennessee and Kentucky. The most populous colonies in 1775 were Virginia, Massachusetts, Pennsylvania, North Carolina, and Maryland—in that order. There were only four communities that might properly be called cities: Philadelphia, including suburbs, was first with about 34,000, while New York, Boston, and Charleston were strung out behind. About 90 percent of the people lived in rural areas.

A Mingling of the Races

Colonial America was a melting pot and had been from the outset. The population, although basically English in stock and language, was picturesquely mottled with numerous foreign groups.

Heavy-accented Germans constituted about 6 percent of the total population, or 150,000, by 1775. Fleeing religious persecution, economic oppression, and the ravages of war, they had flocked to America in the early 1700s and had settled chiefly in Pennsylvania. They belonged to several different Protestant sects—primarily Lutheran—and thus further enhanced the religious diversity of the colony. Known popularly but erroneously as the Pennsylvania Dutch (a corruption of the German word *Deutsch*), they totaled about one-third of the colony's population. In Philadelphia the street signs were painted in both German and English.

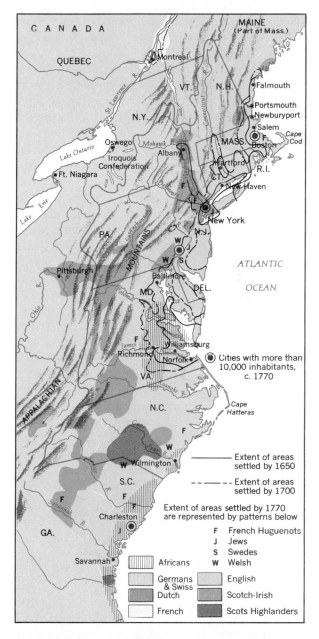

Immigrant Groups in 1775 *America was already a nation of diverse nationalities in the colonial period. This map shows the great variety of immigrant groups, especially in Pennsylvania and New York. It also illustrates the tendency of later arrivals, particularly the Scotch-Irish, to push into the backcountry.*

A young Frenchman named Crèvecoeur wrote about 1770 of the diverse population: "They are a mixture of English, Scotch, Irish, French, Dutch, Germans, and Swedes. From this promiscuous breed, that race now called Americans have arisen. . . . I could point out to you a family whose grandfather was an Englishman, whose wife was Dutch, whose son married a French woman, and whose present four sons have now four wives of different nations."

These German newcomers moved into the backcountry of Pennsylvania, where their splendid stone barns gave—and still give—mute evidence of industry and prosperity. Not having been brought up English, they had no deep-rooted loyalty to the British crown, and they clung tenaciously to their German language and customs.

The Scotch-Irish (see "Makers of America," pp. 66–67), who in 1775 numbered about 175,000, or 7 percent of the population, were an important non-English group, although English-speaking. They were not Irish at all, but turbulent Scots Lowlanders. Over a period of many decades, they had first been transplanted to Northern Ireland, where they had not prospered. The Irish Catholics already there, hating Scotch Presbyterianism, resented the intruders and still do. The economic life of the Scotch-Irish was severely hampered, especially when the English government placed burdensome restrictions on their production of linens and woolens.

Early in the 1700s tens of thousands of embittered Scotch-Irish finally pulled up stakes and came to America, chiefly to tolerant and deep-soiled Pennsylvania. Finding the best acres already taken by Germans and Quakers, they pushed out onto the frontier. There many of them illegally but defiantly squatted on the unoccupied lands and quarreled with both Indian and white owners. When the westward-flowing Scotch-Irish tide lapped up against the Allegheny barrier, it was deflected southward into the backcountry of Maryland, down Vir-

ginia's Shenandoah Valley, and into the western Carolinas. Already experienced colonizers and agitators in Ireland, the Scotch-Irish proved to be superb frontiersmen, though their readiness to visit violence on the Indians repeatedly inflamed the western districts. By the mid–eighteenth century, a chain of Scotch-Irish settlements lay scattered along the "great wagon road," which hugged the eastern Appalachian foothills from Pennsylvania to Georgia.

It was said, somewhat unfairly, that the Scotch-Irish kept the Sabbath—and all else they could lay their hands on. Pugnacious, lawless, and individualistic, they brought with them the Scottish secrets of whiskey distilling and dotted the Appalachian hills and hollows with their stills. They cherished no love for the British government that had uprooted them—or for any other government, it seemed. They led the armed march of the Paxton Boys on Philadelphia in 1764, protesting the Quaker oligarchy's lenient policy toward the Indians, and a few years later spearheaded the Regulator movement in North Carolina, a small but nasty insurrection against eastern domination of the colony's affairs. Many of them—including the youthful Andrew Jackson—eventually joined the embattled American revolutionists. All told, about a dozen future presidents were of Scotch-Irish descent.

Approximately 5 percent of the multicolored colonial population consisted of other European groups. These embraced French Huguenots, Welsh, Dutch, Swedes, Jews, Irish, Swiss, and Scots Highlanders—as distinguished from the Scotch-Irish. Except for the Scots Highlanders, such hodgepodge elements felt little loyalty to the British crown. By far the largest single non-English group was African, accounting for nearly 20 percent of the colonial population in 1775 and heavily concentrated in the South.

The population of the thirteen colonies, though mainly Anglo-Saxon, was perhaps the most mixed to be found anywhere in the world. The South, holding about 90 percent of the slaves, already displayed its historic black-and-white racial composition. New England, mostly staked out by the original Puritan migrants, showed the least ethnic diversity. The middle colonies, especially Pennsylvania, received the

*Estimated Population Elements, 1790** *
(Based on Family Names)

ETHNIC GROUPS	NUMBER	PERCENTAGE
English and Welsh	2,605,699	66.3%
Scotch (including Scotch-Irish)	221,562	5.6
German	176,407	4.5
Dutch	78,959	2.0
Irish	61,534	1.6
French	17,619	0.4
All other whites	10,664	0.3
African	757,181	19.3
GRAND TOTAL	3,929,625	

*Rossiter, *A Century of Population Growth* (1909). Later estimates by Barker and Hansen (1931) are not used here because they are confused by the inclusion of Spanish and French elements *later* a part of the United States.

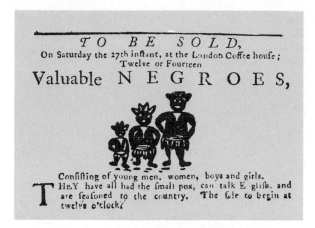

A Pennsylvania Advertisement for Slaves in the 1760s Note that the slaves are said to have had smallpox and to be able to speak English. (Rare Book Division, The New York Public Library, Astor, Lenox and Tilden Foundations.)

bulk of later white immigrants and boasted an astonishing variety of peoples. Outside of New England, about one-half the population was non-English in 1775. Of the fifty-six signers of the Declaration of Independence in 1776, eighteen were non-English, and eight had not been born in the colonies.

The Structure of Colonial Society

In contrast with contemporary Europe, eighteenth-century America was a shining land of equality and opportunity—with the notorious exception of slavery. No titled nobility dominated society from on high, and no pauperized underclass threatened it from below. Most white Americans, and even some free blacks, were small farmers. Clad in buckskin breeches, they owned modest holdings and tilled them with their own hands and horses. The cities contained a small class of skilled artisans, with their well-greased leather aprons, as well as a few shopkeepers and tradespeople, and a handful of unskilled casual laborers. The most remarkable feature of the social ladder was the rags-to-riches ease with which an ambitious colonial, even a former indentured servant, might rise from a lower rung to a higher one, quite unlike in old England.

Yet in contrast with seventeenth-century America, colonial society on the eve of the Revolution was beginning to show signs of stratification and barriers to mobility that raised worries about the "Europeanization" of America. The gods of war contributed to these developments. The armed conflicts of the 1690s and early 1700s had enriched a number of merchant princes in the New England and middle colonies. They laid the foundations of their fortunes with profits made as military suppliers. Roosting regally atop the social ladder, these elites now feathered their nests more finely. They sported imported clothing and dined at tables laid with English china and gleaming silverware. Prominent persons came to be seated in churches and schools according to their social rank. (Future President John Adams was placed fourteenth in a class of twenty-four at Harvard, where ability also affected one's standing.)

The plague of war also created a class of widows and orphans, who became dependent for their survival on charity. Both Philadelphia and New York built almshouses in the 1730s to care for the destitute. Yet the numbers of poor people remained tiny compared to the numbers in England, where about a third of the population lived in impoverished squalor.

In the New England countryside the descendants of the original settlers faced more limited prospects than had their pioneering forebears. As the supply of unclaimed soil dwindled and families grew, existing landholdings were subdivided and the average size of farms shrank

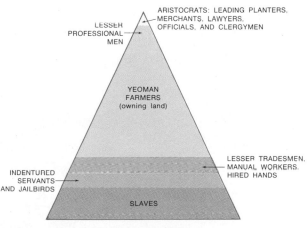

The Colonial Social Pyramid, 1775 (an approximation)

The Scotch-Irish

As the British Empire spread its dominion across the seas in the seventeenth and eighteenth centuries, great masses of people poured into its ever-widening realms. Their migration unfolded in stages. They journeyed from farms to towns, from towns to great cities like London and Bristol, and eventually from the seaports to Ireland, the Caribbean, and the North American colonies. Among these intrepid wanderers, few were more restless than the Scotch-Irish, the settlers of the first American West. Never feeling at home in the British Empire, these perennial outsiders always headed for its most distant outposts. They migrated first from their native Scottish lowlands to Northern Ireland and then on to the New World. And even in North America, the Scotch-Irish remained on the periphery, ever distancing themselves from the reach of the English crown and the Anglican church.

Poverty weighed heavily on the Scottish lowlands in the 1600s; one observer winced at the sight of the Scots, with "their hovels most miserable, made of poles, wattled and covered with thin sods," their bodies shrunken yet swollen with hunger. But Scotland had long been an unyielding land, and it was not simply nature's niggardliness that drove the lowlanders to the ports. The spread of commercial farming forced many Scots from the land and subjected others to merciless rent increases at the hands of the land-owning *lairds* (lords)—a practice called rack-renting. Adding insult to injury, the British authorities repeatedly persecuted the Presbyterian Scots, squeezing taxes from their barren purses to support the hated Anglican church.

Not surprisingly, then, some 200,000 Scots immigrated to neighboring Ireland in the 1600s. So great was the exodus that Protestant Scots eventually outnumbered Catholic natives

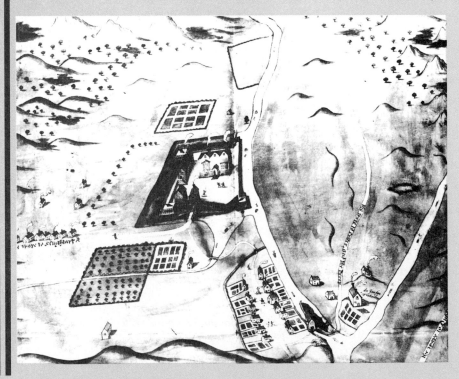

A Scotch "Plantation" in Seventeenth-Century County Tyrone, Northern Ireland (Green Studio, Dublin.)

This British advertisement of 1738 urged Scotch-Irish Protestants to settle in colonial New York. (New-York Historical Society.)

This Scotch Presbyterian church, built in 1794, still stands in Alexandria, Virginia. (Presbyterian Church, Department of History.)

in the several northern Irish counties that compose the province of Ulster. Still, Ireland offered only slender and temporary relief to many Scots. Although the north was prosperous in comparison with the rest of that unhappy nation, making a living was still devilishly hard in Ireland. Soon the Scots discovered that their migration had not freed them from their ancient woes. Their Irish landlords, with British connivance, racked rents just as ferociously as their Scottish *lairds* had done. Under such punishing pressures, waves of these already once-transplanted Scots, now called Scotch-Irish, fled yet again across the sea throughout the 1700s. This time their destination was America.

Most debarked in Pennsylvania, seeking the religious tolerance and abundant land of William Penn's commonwealth. But these unquiet people did not stay put for long. They fanned out from Philadelphia into the farmlands of western Pennsylvania. Blocked temporarily by the Allegheny Mountains, these early pio-

neers then migrated south along the backbone of the Appalachian range, slowly filling the backcountry of Virginia, the Carolinas, and Georgia. There they built farms and towns, and these rickety settlements bore the marks of Scotch-Irish restlessness. While their German neighbors typically erected sturdy homes and cleared their fields meticulously, the Scotch-Irish satisfied themselves with floorless, flimsy log cabins; they chopped down trees, planted crops between the stumps, exhausted the soil fast, and . . . moved on.

Almost every Scotch-Irish community, however isolated or impermanent, maintained a Presbyterian church. Religion was the bond that yoked these otherwise fiercely independent folk. In backcountry towns, churches were erected before law courts, and clerics were pounding their pulpits before civil authorities had the chance to raise their gavels. In many such cases the local religious court, known as the Session, passed judgment on crimes like burglary and trespassing as well as on moral and theological questions. But the Scotch-Irish, despite their intense faith, were no theocrats, no advocates of religious rule. Their bitter struggles with the Anglican church made them stubborn opponents of established churches in the United States, just as their seething resentment against the king of England ensured that the Scotch-Irish would be well represented among the Patriots in the American Revolution.

Slave-Catcher Advertisement *Runaway slaves were so numerous in colonial days that newspapers kept on hand stock woodcuts like those reproduced here. One Virginia owner offered five pounds reward for the return of Toby, a fourteen-year-old mulatto boy "with a scar on the right side of his throat" and with "an old brown jacket, tow shirt and check trousers, which are supposed to be worn out by this time."*

drastically. Younger sons were increasingly forced to hire out as wage laborers—or eventually, to seek virgin tracts of land beyond the Appalachians.

In the South the power of the great planters continued to be bolstered by their disproportionate ownership of slaves. The riches created by the growing slave population in the eighteenth century were not distributed evenly among the whites. Wealth was concentrated in the hands of the largest slaveowners, widening the gap between the prosperous gentry and the "poor whites," who were increasingly forced to become tenant farmers.

In all the colonies the ranks of the lower classes were further swelled by the continuing stream of indentured servants, many of whom ultimately achieved prosperity and prestige. Two became signers of the Declaration of Independence.

Far less fortunate than the voluntary indentured servants were the paupers and convicts involuntarily shipped to America. Altogether, about fifty thousand "jayle birds" were dumped on the colonies by the London authorities. This riffraff crowd—including robbers, rapists, and murderers—was generally sullen and undesirable, and not bubbling over with goodwill for the king's government. But many convicts were the unfortunate victims of circumstances and of

a viciously unfair English penal code that included about two hundred capital crimes. Some of the deportees, in fact, came to be highly respectable citizens.

Least fortunate of all, of course, were the black slaves. They enjoyed no equality with whites and dared not even dream of ascending the ladder of opportunity. Oppressed and degraded, the slaves were America's closest approximation to Europe's volatile lower classes, and fears of black rebellion plagued the white colonists. Some colonial legislatures, notably South Carolina's in 1760, sensed the dangers present in a heavy concentration of resentful slaves and attempted to restrict or halt their importation. But the British authorities vetoed all such efforts. Many colonials looked upon this veto as a callous disregard of their welfare, although it was done primarily in the interests of imperial policy and of the British and New England slave trade. Thomas Jefferson, himself a slaveholder, assailed such vetoes in an early draft of the Declaration of Independence, but his proposed clause was finally dropped, largely out of regard for southern sensibilities.

Clerics, Physicians, and Jurists

Most honored of the professions was the Christian ministry. In 1775 the clergy wielded less influence than in the early days of Massachusetts, when piety had burned more warmly. But they still occupied a position of high prestige.

Most physicians, on the other hand, were poorly trained and not highly esteemed. Not until 1765 was the first medical school established, although European centers attracted some students. Aspiring young doctors served

On doctors and medicine Benjamin Franklin's **Poor Richard's Almanack** *offered some homely advice:*

"God heals and the doctor takes the fee."

"He's the best physician that knows the worthlessness of most medicines."

"Don't go to the doctor with every distemper, nor to the lawyer with every quarrel, nor to the pot for every thirst."

for a while as apprentices to older practitioners and were then turned loose on their "victims." Bleeding was a favorite and frequently fatal remedy; when the physician was not available, a barber was often summoned.

Plagues were a constant nightmare. Especially dreaded was smallpox, which afflicted one out of five persons, including the heavily pock-marked George Washington. A crude form of inoculation was introduced in 1721, despite the objections of many physicians and some of the clergy, who opposed tampering with the will of God. Powdered dried toad was a favorite prescription for smallpox. Diphtheria was also a deadly killer, especially of young people. One epidemic in the 1730s took the lives of thousands. This grim reminder of their mortality may have helped to prepare many colonists in their hearts and minds for the religious revival that was soon to sweep them up.

At first the law profession was not favorably regarded. In this pioneering society, which required much honest manual labor, the parties to a dispute often presented their own cases in court. Lawyers were commonly regarded as noisy windbags or troublemaking rogues; an early Connecticut law classed them with drunkards and brothel keepers. When future President John Adams was a young law student, the father of the woman whom he eventually married frowned upon him as a suitor.

By about 1750, seaboard society had passed the pioneering stage, and trained attorneys were generally recognized as useful. Able to defend colonial rights against the crown on legal grounds, lawyers like the eloquent James Otis and the flaming Patrick Henry took the lead in the agitation that led to revolt. Other lawyer-orators played hardly less important roles in forging new constitutions and in serving in representative bodies.

Workaday America

Agriculture was the leading industry, involving about 90 percent of the people. Tobacco continued to be the staple crop in Maryland and Virginia. The fertile middle ("bread") colonies produced large quantities of grain, and by 1759 New York alone was exporting eighty thousand

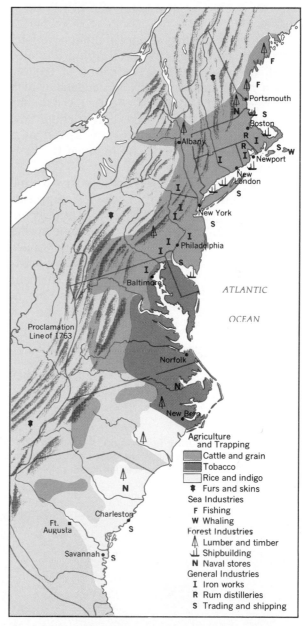

The Colonial Economy *By the eighteenth century, the various colonial regions had distinct economic identities. The northern colonies grew grain and raised cattle, harvested timber and fish, and built ships. The Chesapeake colonies and North Carolina were still heavily dependent on tobacco, while the southernmost colonies grew mostly rice and indigo. Cotton, so important to the southern economy in the nineteenth century, had not yet emerged as a major crop.*

barrels of flour a year. Seemingly the farmer had only to tickle the soil with a hoe and it would laugh with a harvest. Overall, Americans probably enjoyed a higher standard of living than the masses of any country in history up to that time.

Fishing (including whaling), though ranking far below agriculture, was rewarding. Pursued in all the colonies, this harvesting of the sea was a major industry in New England, which exported smelly shiploads of dried cod to the Catholic countries of Europe. The fishing fleet also stimulated shipbuilding and served as a nursery for the seamen who manned the navy and merchant marine.

A bustling commerce, both coastwise and overseas, enriched all the colonies, especially the New England group, New York, and Pennsylvania. Commercial ventures and land speculation, in the absence of later get-rich-quick schemes, were the surest avenues to speedy wealth. Yankee seamen were famous in many climes not only as skilled mariners but as tightfisted traders. They provisioned the Caribbean sugar islands with food and forest products. They hauled Spanish and Portuguese gold, wine, and oranges to London, to be exchanged for industrial goods, which were then sold for a juicy profit in America.

The so-called triangular trade was infamously profitable, though small in relation to total colonial commerce. A skipper, for example, would leave a New England port with a cargo of rum and sail to the Gold Coast of Africa. Bartering the fiery liquor with African chiefs for captured African slaves, he would proceed to the West Indies with his screaming and suffocating cargo sardined below deck. There he would exchange the survivors for molasses, which he would then carry to New England, where it would be distilled into rum. He would then repeat the trip, making a handsome profit on each leg of the triangle.

Manufacturing in the colonies was of only secondary importance, although there was a surprising variety of small enterprises. As a rule, workers could get ahead faster in soil-rich America by tilling the land. Huge quantities of "kill devil" rum were distilled in Rhode Island and Massachusetts; and even some of the "elect of the Lord" developed an overfondness for it. Handsome beaver hats were manufactured in quantity, despite British restrictions. Smoking iron forges, including Pennsylvania's Valley

Sea Captains Carousing in Surinam, 1757–1758 This playful portrayal of Yankee sea captains in Dutch Guiana is a reminder of the distant trade connections established by American shippers in the colonial era. The lively ale-house merriment also confirms that not all seamen were sober-sided Puritans. (The Saint Louis Art Museum.)

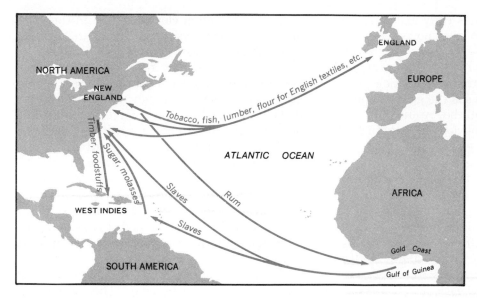

Colonial Trade Patterns, c. 1770 *Future President John Adams noted about this time that "the commerce of the West Indies is a part of the American system of commerce. They can neither do without us, nor we without them. The Creator has placed us upon the globe in such a situation that we have occasion for each other."*

Forge, likewise dotted the land and in fact were more numerous in 1775, though generally smaller, than those of England. In addition, household manufacturing, including spinning and weaving by women, added up to an impressive output. As in all pioneering countries, strong-backed laborers and skilled craftspeople were scarce and highly prized. In early Virginia a carpenter who had committed a murder was freed because his woodworking skills were needed.

Lumbering was perhaps the most important single manufacturing activity. Countless cartloads of virgin timber were consumed by shipbuilders, at first chiefly in New England and then elsewhere in the colonies. By 1770 about four hundred vessels of assorted sizes were splashing down the ways each year, and about one-third of the British merchant marine was American-built.

Colonial naval stores—such as tar, pitch, rosin, and turpentine—were highly valued, for Britannia was anxious to gain and retain a mastery of the seas. London offered generous bounties to stimulate production of these items; otherwise Britain would have had to turn to the uncertain and possibly hostile Baltic areas. Towering trees, ideal as masts for His Majesty's navy, were marked with the king's broad arrow for future use. The luckless colonial who was caught cutting down this reserved timber was subject to a fine. Even though there were countless unreserved trees and the ones marked were being saved for the common defense, this shackle on free enterprise engendered considerable bitterness.

Americans held an important flank of a thriving, many-sided Atlantic economy by the dawn of the eighteenth century. Yet strains appeared

Early Lumbering *An eighteenth-century sawmill in colonial New York. (The William L. Clements Library.)*

in this complex network as early as the 1730s. Fast-breeding Americans demanded more and more English products—yet the slow-growing English population early reached the saturation point for absorbing imports from America. How, then, could the colonists sell the goods to make the money to buy what they wanted in England? The answer was obvious: by seeking foreign (non-English) markets.

By the eve of the Revolution the bulk of Chesapeake tobacco was filling pipes in France and other Continental countries, though it passed through the hands of British re-exporters, who took a slice of the profits. More important was the trade with the West Indies, especially the French islands. West Indian purchases of North American timber and foodstuffs provided the crucial cash for the colonists to continue to make their own purchases in England. In 1733, bowing to pressure from influential British West Indian planters, Parliament passed the Molasses Act, aimed at squelching North American trade with the French West Indies. If successful, this scheme would have struck a crippling blow to American international trade and to the colonists' standard of living. American merchants responded by bribing and smuggling their way around the law. Thus was foreshadowed the impending imperial crisis, when headstrong Americans would revolt rather than submit to the dictates of a far-off Parliament, apparently bent on destroying their very livelihood.

Horsepower and Sailpower

All sprawling and sparsely populated pioneer communities are cursed with oppressive problems of transportation. America, with a scarcity of both money and workers, was no exception.

Not until the 1700s were there roads connecting even the major cities, and these dirt thoroughfares were treacherously poor. A wayfarer could have rumbled along more rapidly over the Roman highways in the days of Julius Caesar, nearly two thousand years earlier. It actually took twenty-nine days for the news of the Declaration of Independence—the story of the year—to reach Charleston from Philadelphia.

Roads were often clouds of dust in the summer and quagmires of mud in the winter. Stagecoach travelers braved such additional dangers as tree-strewn roads, rickety bridges, carriage overturns, and runaway horses. A wayfarer venturesome enough to journey from Philadelphia to New York, for example, would not think it amiss to make a will and assemble the family for prayers before departing.

Where man-made roads were wretched, heavy reliance was placed on God-grooved waterways. Population tended to cluster along the banks of navigable rivers. There was also much coastwise traffic, and although it was slow and undependable, it was relatively cheap and pleasant.

Taverns sprang up along the main routes of travel, as well as in the cities. Their attractions customarily included such items as bowling alleys, pool tables, bars, and gambling equipment. Before a cheerful, roaring log fire all social classes would mingle, including the village loafers and drunks. The tavern was yet another cradle of democracy.

Gossips also gathered at the taverns, which were clearinghouses of information, misinformation, and rumor—frequently stimulated by alcoholic refreshment and impassioned political talk. A successful politician, like the wire-pulling Samuel Adams, was often a man who had a large alehouse acquaintance in places like Boston's Green Dragon Tavern. Taverns were important in crystallizing public opinion and proved to be hotbeds of agitation as the Revolutionary movement gathered momentum.

An intercolonial postal system was established by the mid-1700s, although private couriers remained. Some mail was handled on credit. Service was slow and infrequent, and secrecy was problematical. Mail carriers, serving long routes, would sometimes pass the time by reading the letters entrusted to their care.

Dominant Denominations

Two "established," or tax-supported, churches were conspicuous in 1775: the Anglican and the Congregational. A considerable segment of the population, surprisingly enough, did not

could be heard, sedition flowed freely from pulpits. Presbyterianism, Congregationalism, and rebellion were triplets. Many of the leading Anglican clergymen, aware of what side their tax-provided bread was buttered on, naturally supported their king.

Anglicans in the New World were seriously handicapped by not having a resident bishop, whose presence would be convenient for the ordination of young ministers. American students of Anglican theology had to travel to England to be ordained. On the eve of the Revolution there was serious talk of creating an American bishopric, but the scheme was violently opposed by many non-Anglicans, who feared a tightening of the royal reins. This controversy poured holy oil on the smoldering fires of rebellion.

Religious toleration had indeed made enormous strides in America, at least when compared with halting steps abroad. Roman Catholics were still generally discriminated against, as in England, even in office holding. But there were fewer Catholics in America, and hence the antipapist laws were less severe and

Established (Tax-Supported) Churches in the Colonies, 1775 *

COLONIES	CHURCHES	YEAR DISESTABLISHED
Mass. (incl. Me.)	Congregational	1833
Connecticut		1818
New Hampshire		1819
New York	Anglican (in N.Y. City and three neighboring counties)	1777
Maryland	Anglican	1777
Virginia		1786
North Carolina		1776
South Carolina		1778
Georgia		1777
Rhode Island	None	
New Jersey		
Delaware		
Pennsylvania		

*Note the persistence of the Congregational establishment in New England.

Franklin's *Poor Richard's Almanack* contained such thoughts on religion as:

"A good example is the best sermon."

"Many have quarreled about religion that never practiced it."

"Serving God is doing good to man, but praying is thought an easier service, and therefore more generally chosen."

"How many observe Christ's birthday; how few his precepts! O! 'tis easier to keep holidays than commandments."

less strictly enforced. In general, people could worship—or not worship—as they pleased.

The Great Awakening

In all the colonial churches, religion was less fervid in the early eighteenth century than it had been a century earlier, when the colonies were first planted. The Puritan churches in particular sagged under the weight of two burdens: their elaborate theological doctrines and their compromising efforts to liberalize membership requirements. Churchgoers increasingly complained about the "dead dogs" who droned out tedious, overerudite sermons from Puritan pulpits. Some ministers, on the other hand, worried that many of their parishioners had gone soft and that their souls were no longer kindled by the hellfire of orthodox Calvinism. Liberal ideas began to challenge the old-time religion, and some worshipers now proclaimed that human beings were not necessarily predestined to damnation but might save themselves by good works. A few churches grudgingly conceded that spiritual conversion was not necessary for church membership. Together, these twin trends toward clerical intellectualism and lay liberalism were sapping the spiritual vitality from many denominations.

The stage was thus set for a rousing religious revival. Known as the Great Awakening, it exploded in the 1730s and 1740s and swept through the colonies like a fire through prairie grass. The Awakening was first ignited in

The Wetherburn Tavern
*A meticulously restored eigh-
teenth-century tavern in Colonial Williamsburg, Virginia.
Alehouses like this not only
provided food, drink, and shelter to American colonials, but
were also raucous arenas for
the exchange of political ideas.
(Colonial Williamsburg
Foundation.)*

worship in any church. And in those colonies where there was an "established" religion, only a minority of the people belonged to it.

The Church of England, whose members were commonly called Anglicans, became the official faith in Georgia, North and South Carolina, Virginia, Maryland, and a part of New York. Established also in England, it served in America as a major prop of kingly authority. British officials naturally made vigorous efforts to impose it on additional colonies, but they ran into a stone wall of opposition.

In America the Anglican church fell distressingly short of its promise. Secure and self-satisfied, like the parent establishment in England, it clung to a faith that was less fierce and more worldly than the religion of Puritanical New England. Sermons were shorter; hell was less scorching; and amusements, like Virginia fox hunting, were less frowned upon. So dismal was the reputation of the Anglican clergy in seventeenth-century Virginia that the College of William and Mary was founded in 1693 to train a better class of clerics.

The influential Congregational church, which had grown out of the Puritan church, was formally established in all the New England colonies, except independent-minded Rhode Island. At first Massachusetts taxed all residents to support Congregationalism but later relented and exempted members of other

well-known denominations. Presbyterianism, though closely associated with Congregationalism, was never made official in any colonies.

Ministers of the gospel, turning from the Bible to this sinful world, increasingly grappled with burning political issues. As the early rumblings of revolution against the British crown

Estimated Religious Census, 1775

NAME	NUMBER	CHIEF LOCALE
Congregationalists	575,000	New England
Anglicans	500,000	N.Y., South
Presbyterians	410,000	Frontier
German churches (incl. Lutheran)	200,000	Pa.
Dutch Reformed	75,000	N.Y., N.J.
Quakers	40,000	Pa., N.J., Del.
Baptists	25,000	R.I., Pa., N.J., Del.
Roman Catholics	25,000	Md., Pa.
Methodists	5,000	Scattered
Jews	2,000	N.Y., R.I.
EST. TOTAL MEMBERSHIP	1,857,000	
EST. TOTAL POPULATION	2,493,000	
PERCENTAGE CHURCH MEMBERS	74%	

Northampton, Massachusetts, by a tall, delicate, and intellectual pastor, Jonathan Edwards. Perhaps the deepest theological mind ever nurtured in America, Edwards proclaimed with burning righteousness the folly of believing in salvation through good works and affirmed the need for complete dependence on God's grace. Warming to his subject, he painted in lurid detail the landscape of hell and the eternal torments of the damned. "Sinners in the Hands of an Angry God" was the title of one of his most famous sermons. He believed that hell was "paved with the skulls of unbaptized children."

Edwards's preaching style was learned and closely reasoned, but his stark doctrines sparked a warmly sympathetic reaction among his parishioners in 1734. Four years later, the itinerant English parson George Whitefield loosed a different style of evangelical preaching on America and touched off a conflagration of religious ardor that revolutionized the spiritual life of the colonies. A former alehouse attendant, Whitefield was an orator of rare gifts. His magnificent voice boomed sonorously over thousands of enthralled listeners in an open field. One of England's greatest actors of the day commented enviously that Whitefield could make audiences weep merely by pronouncing the word *Mesopotamia* and that he would "give a hundred guineas if I could only say 'O!' like Mr. Whitefield."

Triumphally touring the colonies, Whitefield trumpeted his message of human helplessness and divine omnipotence. His eloquence reduced Jonathan Edwards to tears and even caused the skeptical and thrifty Benjamin Franklin to empty his pockets into the collection plate. During these roaring revival meetings, countless

George Whitefield Preaching *Americans of both sexes and all races and sections were spellbound by Whitefield's emotive oratory. (National Portrait Gallery, London.)*

sinners professed conversion, while hundreds of the "saved" groaned, shrieked, or rolled in the snow from religious excitement. Whitefield soon inspired American imitators. Taking up his electrifying new style of preaching, they heaped abuse on sinners and shook enormous audiences with emotional appeals. One preacher cackled hideously in the face of hapless wrongdoers. Another, naked to the waist, leaped frantically about in the light of flickering torches.

Orthodox clergymen, known as "old lights," were deeply skeptical of the emotionalism and the theatrical antics of the revivalists. "New light" ministers, on the other hand, defended the Awakening for its role in revitalizing American religion. Congregationalists and Presbyterians split over this issue, and many of the believers in religious conversion went over to the Baptists and other sects more prepared to make room for emotion in religion. The Awakening left many lasting effects. Its emphasis on direct,

> Jonathan Edwards preached hellfire, notably in one famous sermon: "The God that holds you over the pit of hell, much as one holds a spider or some loathsome insect over the fire, abhors you, and is dreadfully provoked. His wrath toward you burns like fire; he looks upon you as worthy of nothing else but to be cast into the fire."

emotive spirituality seriously undermined the older clergy whose authority had derived from their education and erudition. The schisms it set off in many denominations greatly increased the numbers and the competitiveness of American churches. It encouraged a fresh wave of missionary work among the Indians and even among black slaves, many of whom also attended the mass open-air revivals. It led to the founding of such "new light" centers of higher learning, as Dartmouth, Brown, Rutgers, and Princeton. Perhaps most significant, the Great Awakening was the first spontaneous mass movement of the American people. It tended to break down sectional boundaries as well as denominational lines and contributed to the growing sense that Americans had of themselves as a single people, united by a common history and shared experiences.

Schools and Colleges

A time-honored English ideal regarded education as a boon reserved for the aristocratic few, not for the unwashed many. Education should be for leadership, not citizenship, and primarily for the male sex. Only slowly and painfully did the colonials break the chains of these ancient restrictions.

Puritan New England, largely for religious reasons, was more zealously interested in education than any other section. Dominated by the Congregational church, it stressed the need for Bible reading by the individual worshiper. The primary goal of the clergy was to make good Christians rather than good citizens. A more

John Adams, the future second president, once wrote to his wife: "The education of our children is never out of my mind. Train them to virtue. Habituate them to industry, activity, and spirit. . . . For God's sake make your children hardy, active, and industrious; for strength, activity, and industry will be their only resource and dependence."

secular approach was evident late in the eighteenth century, when some children were warned:

> He who ne'er learns his A.B.C.
> Forever will a blockhead be.
> But he who learns his letters fair
> Shall have a coach to take the air.

Education, principally for boys, flourished almost from the outset in New England. This densely populated region boasted an impressive number of graduates from the English universities, especially Cambridge, the intellectual center of England's Puritanism. New Englanders, at a relatively early date, established primary and secondary schools, which varied widely in the quality of instruction and in the length of time that their doors remained open each year. Back-straining farm labor drained much of the youth's time and energy.

Fairly adequate primary and secondary schools were also hammering knowledge into the heads of reluctant "scholars" in the middle colonies and in the South. Some of these institutions were tax-supported; others were privately operated. The South, with its white and black population diffused over wide areas, was severely handicapped in attempting to establish an effective school system. Wealthy families leaned heavily on private tutors.

The general atmosphere in the colonial schools and colleges continued grim and gloomy. Most of the emphasis was placed on religion and on the classical languages, Latin and Greek. The stress was not on experiment and reason, but on doctrine and dogma. The age was one of orthodoxy, and independence of thinking was discouraged. Discipline was quite severe, with many a mettlesome lad being sadistically "birched" with a switch cut from a birch tree. Sometimes punishment was inflicted by indentured-servant teachers, who could themselves be whipped for their failures as workers and who therefore were not inclined to spare the rod.

College education was regarded—at least at first in New England—as more important than instruction in the ABCs. Churches would wither if a new crop of ministers was not trained to lead the spiritual flocks. Many well-to-do families, especially in the South, sent their boys abroad to English institutions.

For purposes of convenience and economy, nine local colleges were planted during the colonial era. Student bodies were small, numbering about 200 boys at the most; and at one time a few lads as young as eleven were admitted to Harvard. Instruction was poor by present-day standards. The curriculum was still heavily loaded with theology and the "dead" languages, although by 1750 there was a distinct trend toward "live" languages and other modern subjects. A significant contribution was made by Benjamin Franklin, who had a large hand in launching what became the University of Pennsylvania, the first American college free from denominational control.

Culture in the Backwoods

The dawn-to-dusk toil of pioneer life left little vitality or aptitude for artistic effort. Americans were too busy chopping down trees to sit around painting landscapes, especially when a hostile Indian might burst from a nearby bush. There was no strong esthetic tradition; many of the clergy, in fact, regarded art as an invention of the Devil.

As the colonists gradually acquired some wealth and leisure, their surplus energy went

Harvard College *An eighteenth-century needlepoint.* *(Massachusetts Historical Society.)*

into religious and political leadership, not art. The materialistic atmosphere was not favorable to artistic endeavor. One famous painter, John Trumbull of Connecticut (1756–1843), was discouraged in his youth by his father with the chilling remark, "Connecticut is not Athens." Charles W. Peale (1741–1827), best known for his portraits of George Washington, ran a museum, stuffed birds, and practiced dentistry.

Colonial Colleges

NAME	ORIGINAL NAME (IF DIFFERENT)	LOCATION	OPENED OR FOUNDED	DENOMINATION
1. Harvard		Cambridge, Mass.	1636	Congregational
2. William and Mary		Williamsburg, Va.	1693	Anglican
3. Yale		New Haven, Conn.	1701	Congregational
4. Princeton	College of New Jersey	Princeton, N.J.	1746	Presbyterian
5. Pennsylvania	The Academy	Philadelphia, Pa.	1751	Nonsectarian
6. Columbia	King's College	New York, N.Y.	1754	Anglican
7. Brown	Rhode Island College	Providence, R.I.	1764	Baptist
8. Rutgers	Queen's College	New Brunswick, N.J.	1766	Dutch Reformed
9. Dartmouth (begun as an Indian missionary school)		Hanover, N.H.	1769	Congregational

Tea Set, by Paul Revere   *The famed horseman of the Revolution was a silversmith by trade. These finely wrought pieces illustrate not only the high degree of his skill but also the growing prosperity and refined tastes of his clients in late eighteenth-century Boston. (The Metropolitan Museum of Art, Bequest of A. T. Clearwater, 1933.)*

Gifted Benjamin West (1738–1820) and precocious John S. Copley (1738–1815) succeeded in their ambition to become famous painters, but they had to go to England to complete their training. Only there could they find subjects who had the leisure to sit for their portraits and the money to pay handsomely for them. Copley was regarded as a Loyalist during the Revolutionary War, while West, a close friend of George III and official court painter, was buried in London's St. Paul's Cathedral.

Architecture was largely imported from the Old World and modified to meet the peculiar climatic and religious conditions of the New World. Even the lowly log cabin was apparently borrowed from Sweden. The red-bricked Georgian style, so common in the pre-Revolutionary decades, was introduced about 1720 and is best exemplified by the beauty of· now-restored Williamsburg, Virginia.

Colonial literature, like art, was generally undistinguished, and for much the same reasons. One noteworthy exception was the precocious poet Phillis Wheatley (c. 1753–1784), a slave girl brought to Boston at age eight and never formally educated. Taken to England when twenty years of age, she published a book of verse and subsequently wrote other polished poems that revealed the influence of Alexander Pope. Her verse compares favorably with the best of the poetry-poor colonial period, but the remarkable fact is that she could overcome her severely disadvantaged background and write any poetry at all.

Many-sided Benjamin Franklin, often called "the first civilized American," also shone as a literary light. Although his autobiography is now a classic, he was best known to his contemporaries for *Poor Richard's Almanack,* which he edited from 1732 to 1758. This famous publication, containing many pithy sayings culled from the thinkers of the ages, emphasized such homespun virtues as thrift, industry, morality, and common sense. Examples are: "What maintains one vice would bring up two children"; "Plough deep while sluggards sleep"; "Honesty is the best policy"; and "Fish and visitors stink in three days." *Poor Richard's* was well known in Europe and was more widely read in America than anything else except the Bible. As a teacher of both old and young, Franklin had an incalculable influence in shaping the American character.

Science, rising above the shackles of superstition, was making some progress, though lagging behind the Old World. A few botanists, mathematicians, and astronomers had won some repute, but Benjamin Franklin was perhaps the only first-rank scientist produced in the American colonies. His spectacular but dangerous experiments, including the kite-flying episode proving that lightning was a form of electricity, won him numerous honors in Europe. But his mind had a practical turn, and among his numerous inventions were bifocal spectacles and the highly efficient Franklin stove. His lightning rod, not surprisingly, was condemned by the less-liberal clergy as "presuming on God" by attempting to control the "artillery of the heavens."

portunity, freedom of speech, freedom of the press, freedom of assembly, and representative government. And these democratic seeds, planted in rich soil, were to bring forth a lush harvest in later years.

Colonial Folkways

Everyday life in the colonies may now seem glamorous, especially as reflected in antique shops. But judged by modern standards, it was drab and tedious. For the mass of the people, the labor was heavy and constant—from daybreak to backbreak.

Food was plentiful, though the diet could be coarse and monotonous. Americans probably ate more bountifully, especially of meat, than any people in the Old World. Lazy or sickly was the person whose stomach was empty.

Basic comforts now taken for granted were lacking. Churches were not heated at all, except for charcoal foot-warmers that the women carried. During the frigid New England winters, the preaching of hellfire may not have seemed altogether unattractive. Drafty homes were poorly heated, chiefly by inefficient fireplaces. There was no running water in the houses, no plumbing, and probably not a single bathtub in all colonial America. Flickering lights were inadequate, for illumination was provided by candles and whale-oil lamps. Garbage disposal was primitive. Long-snouted hogs customarily ranged the streets to consume refuse, while buzzards, protected by law, flapped greedily over tidbits of waste.

Amusement was eagerly pursued where time and custom permitted. The militia assembled periodically for "musters," which consisted of several days of drilling, liberally interspersed with merrymaking and eyeing the girls. On the frontier, pleasure was often combined with work at house-raisings, quilting bees, husking bees, and apple parings. Funerals and weddings everywhere afforded opportunities for social gatherings, which customarily involved the swilling of much strong liquor.

Winter sports were common in the North, while in the South card playing, horse racing, cockfighting, and fox hunting were favorite pas-

Heated Public Gathering *The spirit of the New England town meeting. (Library of Congress.)*

times. George Washington, not surprisingly, was a superb rider. In the non-Puritanical South, dancing was the rage—jigs, square dances, the Virginia reel—and the agile Washington could swing his fair partner with the best of them.

Other diversions beckoned. Lotteries were universally approved, even by the clergy, and were used to raise money for churches and colleges, including Harvard. Stage plays became popular in the South but were disapproved in the Quaker and Puritan colonies and in some places were even forbidden by law. Many of the New England clergy regarded playacting as time-consuming and immoral; they preferred religious lectures, from which their flocks derived much spiritual satisfaction.

Holidays were everywhere celebrated, but Christmas was frowned upon in New England as an offensive reminder of "Popery." "Yuletide is fooltide" was a common Puritan sneer. Thanksgiving Day came to be a truly American festival, for it combined thanks to God with an opportunity for jollification, gorging, and guzzling.

England's American colonists in 1775 were a remarkable people: restless, energetic, ambitious, resourceful, ingenious, and independent-minded. With every passing year they were less willing to bow their necks to the yoke of overseas authority. They were like a fast-growing and vigorous youngster who is coming of age and who expects to be treated as an adult and not as a lackey. With a boundless continent before them, with impressive pioneer achievements behind them, and with an astonishing fertility within them, they had caught a vision of their destiny and were preparing to grasp it. Woe unto him who should try to thwart them!

CHRONOLOGY

1693	College of William and Mary founded
1721	Smallpox inoculation introduced
1732	First edition of *Poor Richard's Almanack*
1734	Jonathan Edwards begins Great Awakening
1734–1735	Zenger free-press trial in New York
1738	George Whitefield spreads Great Awakening
1746	Princeton College founded
1760	Britain vetoes South Carolina anti–slave trade measures
1764–1769	Brown, Rutgers, Dartmouth colleges founded
1764	Paxton Boys
1768–1771	Regulator protests

Varying Viewpoints

Many historians, notably Richard Bushman, see pre-Revolutionary America as an expanding, opening society. In this view, colonial society was losing the religious discipline and social hierarchy of the founding generations, as Americans poured out onto the frontier or sailed the commercial seaways in search of fortune and adventure. These scholars portray the Great Awakening as further evidence of the erosion of social constraints. They argue that unbridled religious enthusiasm, directed by itinerant preachers, displayed the kind of questing for personal autonomy that eventually led to demands for national independence.

The opposing view, shown by Gary Nash and Kenneth Lockridge, emphasizes declining opportunities in colonial society. Pressure on land and the continued dominance of church and parental authority gave rise to a landless class, forced to till tenant plots in the countryside or find manual labor in the cities. The simmering discontent of this growing lower class, according to this interpretation, exploded first in the Great Awakening and later in the American Revolution.

Select Readings

Primary Source Documents

Noting the ethnic diversity of colonial American society, Michel Guillaume Jean de Crèvecoeur's *Letters from an American Farmer* (1904)* and Benjamin Franklin's "Observations on the Increase of Mankind,"* in Jared Sparks, ed., *The Works of Benjamin Franklin* (1840), respectively celebrate and express unease at that diversity. Franklin's entertaining *Autobiography** (1868) is an indispensable guide to the values and preoccupations of his time. It includes an account of George Whitefield's visit to Philadelphia during the Great Awakening.

Secondary Sources

Social history is painted with broad strokes in James Henretta, *The Evolution of American Society, 1700–1815* (1973), and Daniel Boorstin, *The Americans: The Colonial Experience* (1958). Richard Hofstadter takes a suggestive snapshot view in *America at 1750* (1971). Population trends are detailed in Evarts B. Greene and Virginia D. Harrington, *American Population before the Federal Census of 1790* (1932), and in Robert V. Wells, *The Population of the British Colonies in America before 1776* (1975). Black "immigrants" are studied in Philip D. Curtin, *The African Slave Trade: A Census* (1969); indentured servants, in Abbot E. Smith, *Colonists in Bondage* (1947); and colonial immigration in general, in the early portions of Maldwyn Jones, *American Immigration* (1960). Jackson T. Main astutely analyzes *The Social Structure of Revolutionary America, 1763–1788* (1965). Access to the ballot is scrutinized in Chilton Williamson, *American Suffrage: From Property to Democracy, 1760–1860* (1961). Large-scale economic patterns are traced in Edwin J. Perkins, *The Economy of Colonial America* (1980), and in Alice II. Jones, *The Wealth of a Nation to Be: The American Colonies on the Eve of the Revolution* (1980). The toiling classes are probed in Gerald W. Mullin, *Flight and Rebellion: Slave Resistance in Eighteenth-Century Virginia* (1972); Gary B. Nash, *The Urban Crucible: Social Change, Political Consciousness and the Origins of the American Revolution* (1979); Allen Kulikoff, *Tobacco and Slaves: The Development of Southern Cultures in the Chesapeake, 1680–1800* (1986); and Rhys Isaac, *The Transformation of Virginia, 1740–1790* (1982). Nash and Isaac link social conflict to the Great Awakening, as does Richard L. Bushman, *From Puritan to Yankee: Character and Social Order in Connecticut, 1690–1765* (1967). Patricia Bonomi also emphasizes religious conflict as a promoter of Revolutionary ideology in *Under the Cope of Heaven: Religion, Society, and Politics in Colonial America* (1986). Religious revivalism is chronicled in Edwin S. Gaustad, *The Great Awakening in New England* (1957). Cultural history is imaginatively presented in Howard M. Jones, *O Strange New World: American Culture in the Formative Years* (1964). Comprehensive is Henry May, *The Enlightenment in America* (1976). The sometimes heroic dedication to education is portrayed by Lawrence Cremin, *American Education: The Colonial Experience, 1607–1783* (1970); and the general social implications of the early educational system are studied in James Axtell, *School upon a Hill* (1974). Colonial politics are interpreted in a most suggestive way in Bernard Bailyn, *The Origins of American Politics* (1965). More fine-grained local studies are Charles S. Sydnor, *Gentlemen Freeholders* (1952); Richard L. Bushman, *King and People in Provincial Massachusetts* (1985); Jackson Turner Main, *Society and Economy in Colonial Connecticut* (1985); Patricia Bonomi, *A Factious People: Politics and Society in Colonial New York* (1971); James T. Lemon, *The Best Poor Man's Country* (1972), which deals with Pennsylvania; and Daniel Blake Smith, *Inside the Great House: Planter Family Life in Eighteenth-Century Chesapeake Society* (1980). Timothy Breen examines the ways in which the increasing indebtedness of the Virginia planters changed their behavior in *Tobacco Culture: The Mentality of the Great Tidewater Planters on the Eve of Revolution* (1985).

5

The Duel for
North America, 1608–1763

A torch lighted in the forests of America set all Europe in conflagration.

Voltaire, c. 1756

France Finds a Foothold in Canada

France was another latecomer in the scramble for New World real estate, like England and Holland, and for basically the same reasons. It was convulsed during the 1500s by foreign wars and domestic strife, including the frightful clashes between the Roman Catholics and the Protestant Huguenots. On St. Bartholomew's Day, 1572, over ten thousand Huguenots—men, women, and children—were butchered in cold blood.

A new era dawned in 1598 when the Edict of Nantes, issued by the crown, granted limited toleration to the French Protestants. Religious wars ceased, and in the 1600s France blossomed into the mightiest and most feared nation in Europe. Leadership of a high order was provided by a series of brilliant ministers and by the vainglorious King Louis XIV. *Le Grand*

Monarque reigned majestically, beginning as a five-year-old boy, for an incredible seventy-two years (1643–1715). Though involved with a glittering court and numerous mistresses, he was deeply interested in overseas colonies and bestirred himself to promote their welfare.

Success finally crowned the exertions of France in the New World. In 1608, the year after Jamestown, the permanent beginnings of a vast empire were established at Quebec, a rocky sentinel commanding the St. Lawrence River. The leading figure was Samuel de Champlain, an intrepid soldier and explorer whose energy and leadership fairly earned for him the title "Father of New France."

Champlain entered into friendly relations—a fateful friendship—with the nearby Huron Indian tribes. Yielding to their entreaties, he joined them in battle against their feathered foes, the federated Iroquois tribes of the upper

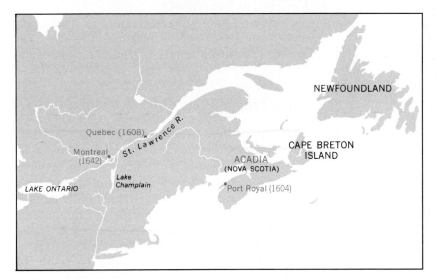

Early French Settlements *By the 1990s French-speakers made up nearly 25 percent of the total Canadian population of about 26 million, and a strong separatist movement had developed among them in Quebec—just one legacy of the colonial-era duel for North America.*

New York area. Two shots from the "lightning sticks" of the whites routed the terrified Indians, who left behind three dead and one wounded. France, to its sorrow, thus earned the lasting enmity of the Iroquois tribes. They thereafter hampered French penetration of the Ohio Valley, ravaged French settlements, and served as allies of the British in the prolonged struggle for supremacy on the continent.

The government of New France (Canada) finally fell under the direct control of the king, after various commercial companies had faltered or failed. This royal regime was almost completely autocratic. There were no popularly elected assemblies, as in the English colonies; there was no trial by jury—merely the decision of the magistrate.

Population in Catholic New France grew with painful slowness: as late as 1750 there were only sixty thousand or so whites. Landowning French peasants, unlike the dispossessed English tenant farmers who embarked for the British colonies, had little economic motive to move. Protestant Huguenots, who might have had a religious motive to migrate, were denied a refuge in this raw colony. The French

Champlain Fights the Iroquois, 1609 *This illustration commemorates the battle on Lake Champlain. Champlain's explorations extended French claims as far inland as Wisconsin. He was fittingly buried in Quebec. (The Granger Collection.)*

France's American Empire at Greatest Extent, 1700

government, in any case, favored its Caribbean island colonies, rich in sugar and rum, over the snow-cloaked wilderness of Canada.

New France Fans Out

New France did contain one valuable resource: the beaver. European fashion-setters valued beaver-pelt hats for their warmth and opulent appearance. To adorn the heads of Europeans, French fur-trappers ranged over the woods and waterways of North America in pursuit of beaver. These colorful *coureurs de bois* (runners of the woods) were also runners of risks—two-fisted drinkers, free spenders, free livers and lovers. They littered the land with scores of place names, including Baton Rouge (red stick), Terre Haute (high land), Des Moines (some monks), and Grand Teton (big breast).

Singing, paddle-swinging French *voyageurs* also recruited Indians into the fur business. The Indian fur flotilla arriving in Montreal in 1693 numbered four hundred canoes. But the fur trade had some disastrous drawbacks. Indians were decimated by the white man's diseases

Chief of the Taensa Indians Receiving La Salle, March, 1682 *Driven by the dream of a vast North American empire for France, La Salle spent years exploring the Great Lakes region and the valleys of the Illinois and Mississippi Rivers. This scene of his encounter with an Indian chieftain is imaginatively recreated by the nineteenth-century artist George Catlin. (A Detail. The National Gallery of Art, Washington, D.C., The Paul Mellon Collection.)*

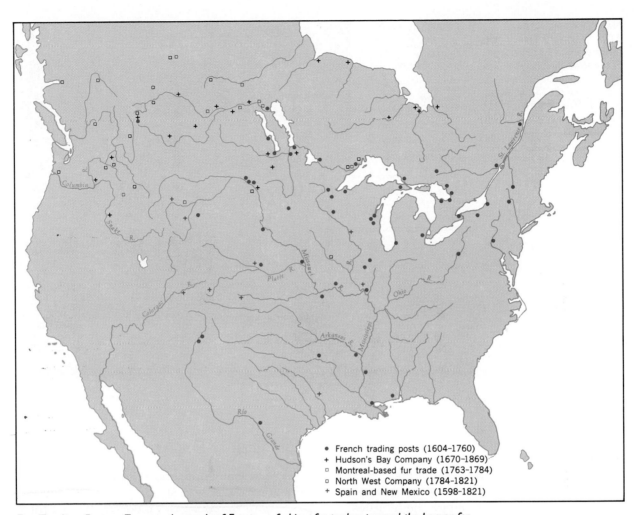

Fur-Trading Posts *To serve the needs of European fashion, fur-traders pursued the beaver for more than two centuries over the entire continent of North America. They brought many Indians for the first time into contact with white culture.*

and debauched by his alcohol—"firewater"—often adulterated with pepper. Slaughtering beaver by the boatload violated many Indians' religious beliefs and sadly demonstrated the shattering effect that contact with Europeans wreaked on traditional Indian ways of life.

Pursuing the sharp-toothed beaver ever deeper into the heart of the continent, the French trappers and their Indian partners hiked, rode, snowshoed, sailed, and paddled amazing distances. They trekked in a huge arc across the Great Lakes, into present-day Saskatchewan and Manitoba, along the valleys of the Platte, the Arkansas, and the Missouri, west to the Rockies, and south to the border of Texas. In the process, they extinguished the beaver population in many areas, inflicting incalculable ecological damage.

French Catholic missionaries, notably the Jesuits, labored zealously to save the Indians for Christ and from the fur-trappers. Some of the Jesuit missionaries, their efforts scorned, suffered unspeakable tortures at the hands of the Indians. But though they made few permanent converts, the Jesuits played a vital role as explorers and geographers.

Other explorers sought neither souls nor beaver, but empire. To thwart English settlers pushing into the Ohio Valley, Antoine Cadillac founded Detroit, "the City of Straits," in 1701. To check Spanish penetration into the region of the Gulf of Mexico, haughty and ambitious

New Orleans, About 1720 This early French map shows the modest beginnings of the strategic river-port, gateway to the Mississippi (here called the "St. Louis River"). (The Granger Collection.)

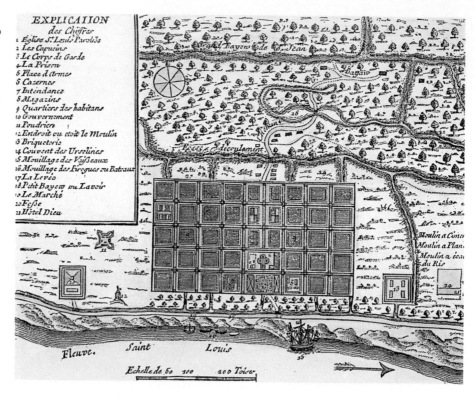

Robert de La Salle floated down the mighty Mississippi in 1682 to the point where it mingles with the gulf. He named the great interior basin "Louisiana," in honor of his sovereign, Louis XIV. Dreaming of empire, he returned to the gulf three years later with a colonizing expedition of four ships. But he failed to find the Mississippi delta, landed in Spanish Texas, and in 1687 was murdered by his mutinous men.

Undismayed, French officials persisted in their efforts to block Spain on the Gulf of Mexico. They planted several fortified posts in what is now Mississippi and Louisiana, the most important of which was New Orleans (1718). Commanding the mouth of the Mississippi River, this strategic semitropical outpost also tapped the fur trade of the huge interior valley. The fertile Illinois country—where the French established forts and trading posts at Kaskaskia, Cahokia, and Vincennes—became the garden of France's North American empire. Surprising amounts of grain were floated down the Mississippi for transshipment to the West Indies and to Europe.

The Clash of Empires

As the seventeenth century neared its sunset, a titanic struggle was shaping up for mastery of the North American continent. It involved three civilizations: English, French, and Spanish. From 1688 to 1763, four bitter wars convulsed Europe. All four of these conflicts were world wars. They amounted to a death struggle for domination in Europe as well as in the New World and were fought on the waters and on the soil of two hemispheres. Counting these first four clashes, there have been nine world wars since 1688. The American people, whether as British subjects or as American citizens, were unable to stay out of a single one of them. Isolation from the broils of Europe was all too often a hope rather than a reality.

The first two wars, known in America as King William's War and Queen Anne's War, pitted British colonials against the French coureurs de bois and their Indian allies. Both France and England at this stage did not consider America worth the commitment of regular

Later English Monarchs*

NAME, REIGN	RELATION TO AMERICA
William III, 1689–1702	War of Spanish Succession begun
Anne, 1702–1714	Queen Anne's War, 1702–1713
George I, 1714–1727	Navigation Laws laxly enforced ("salutary neglect")
George II, 1727–1760	Ga. founded; King George's War; French and Indian War
George III, 1760–1820	American Revolution, 1775–1783

*See pp. 15, 34 for earlier ones.

troops, so a kind of primitive guerrilla warfare prevailed. French-inspired Indians ravaged with torch and tomahawk the British colonial frontiers, visiting especially horrible violence on the villages of Schenectady, New York, and Deerfield, Massachusetts. Spain, eventually allied with France, probed from its Florida base at outlying South Carolina settlements. For their part, the English colonials failed miserably in attempts to capture Quebec and Montreal but did temporarily seize the stronghold of Port Royal in Acadia.

Peace terms, signed at Utrecht in 1713, revealed how badly France and its Spanish ally had been beaten. England was rewarded with French-populated Acadia (renamed Nova Scotia, or New Scotland) and the wintry wastes of Newfoundland and Hudson Bay. These immense tracts applied the pincers to the St. Lawrence settlements of France, foreshadowing their ultimate doom. A generation of peace ensued, during which Britain provided its American colonies with decades of "salutary neglect"—fertile soil for the roots of independence.

By the treaty of 1713 the British had won limited trading rights in Spanish America, but these later involved much friction over smuggling. Ill feeling flared up when the English Captain Jenkins, encountering Spanish revenue authorities, had one ear sliced off by a sword. The Spanish commander reportedly sneered, "Carry this home to the King, your master, whom, if he were present, I would serve in like fashion." The victim, with a tale of woe on his tongue and a shriveled ear in his hand, aroused furious resentment when he returned home to England.

The War of Jenkins's Ear, curiously but aptly named, broke out in 1739 between the English and the Spaniards. It was confined to the Caribbean Sea and to the much-buffeted buffer colony of Georgia, where philanthropist-soldier James Oglethorpe fought his Spanish foe to a standstill.

The Nine World Wars

DATES	IN EUROPE	IN AMERICA
1688–1697	War of the League of Augsburg	King William's War, 1689–1697
1701–1713	War of Spanish Succession	Queen Anne's War, 1702–1713
1740–1748	War of Austrian Succession	King George's War, 1744–1748
1756–1763	Seven Years' War	French and Indian War, 1754–1763
1778–1783	War of the American Revolution	American Revolution, 1775–1783
1793–1802	Wars of the French Revolution	Undeclared French War, 1798–1800
1803–1815	Napoleonic Wars	War of 1812, 1812–1814
1914–1918	World War I	World War I, 1917–1918
1939–1945	World War II	World War II, 1941–1945

British Territory after Two Wars, 1713

English
French
Spanish
Unexplored

This small-scale scuffle with Spain in America soon merged with the large-scale War of Austrian Succession in Europe. Once again, France allied itself with Spain. Once again, a rustic force of New Englanders invaded New France. With help from a British fleet and with much good luck, the raw and sometimes drunken recruits captured a reputedly impregnable French fortress, Louisbourg, on Cape Breton Island, commanding the approaches to the St. Lawrence River.

When the peace treaty of 1748 handed Louisbourg back to their French foe, the victorious New Englanders were outraged. The glory of their arms—never terribly lustrous in any event—seemed tarnished by the wiles of Old World diplomats. Worse, Louisbourg was still a cocked pistol pointed at the heart of the American continent. France, powerful and unappeased, still clung to its vast holdings in North America.

New Englanders Capture Louisbourg, 1745 When the final peace settlement returned this fortress to France, the American colonials felt betrayed by their British masters. (Yale University Art Gallery, The Mabel Brady Garvan Collection.)

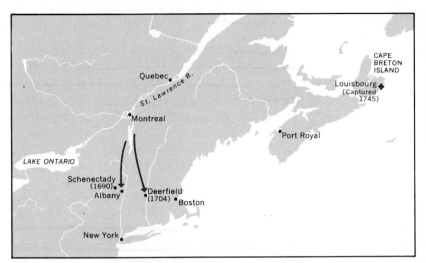

Scenes of the French Wars *The arrows indicate French-Indian attacks. The primitive settlement of Schenectady was burned to the ground in the raid of 1690. At Deerfield the attackers killed fifty inhabitants, took over one hundred prisoners, and sent the rest of the village's three hundred residents fleeing for their lives into the wintry February wilderness.*

George Washington Inaugurates War with France

As the drama unfolded in the New World, the Ohio Valley became the chief bone of contention between the French and British. The Ohio country was the critical area into which the westward-pushing English would inevitably penetrate. It was the key to the continent that the French had to retain, particularly if they were going to link their Canadian holdings with those of the lower Mississippi Valley. By the mid-1700s the English colonials, painfully aware of these basic truths, were no longer so reluctant to bear the burdens of empire. Alarmed by French land-grabbing and cutthroat fur-trade competition in the Ohio Valley, they were determined to fight for their economic security and for the supremacy of their way of life in North America.

Rivalry for the lush lands of the upper Ohio Valley brought tensions to the snapping point. In 1749 a group of English colonial speculators, chiefly influential Virginians, including the Washington family, had secured rights to some 500,000 acres in this region. In the same disputed wilderness the French were in the process of erecting a chain of forts commanding the strategic Ohio River. Especially formidable was Fort Duquesne at the strategic point where the Monongahela and Allegheny rivers join to form the Ohio—the later site of Pittsburgh.

In 1754 the governor of Virginia ushered George Washington, a twenty-one-year-old surveyor and fellow Virginian, onto the stage of history. Washington was sent to the Ohio country as a lieutenant colonel in command of about 150 Virginia militiamen. Encountering a small detachment of French troops in the forest about forty miles from Fort Duquesne, the Virginians opened fire—the first shots of the globe-girdling new war. The French leader was killed, and his men retreated. An exultant Washington wrote: "I heard the bullets whistle, and believe me, there is something charming in the sound." It soon lost its charm.

The French promptly returned with reinforcements, which surrounded Washington in

The Ohio Country, 1753-1754

back of his hastily constructed breastworks, Fort Necessity. After a ten-hour siege he was forced to surrender his entire command in July 1754—ironically the Fourth of July. But he was permitted to march his men away with the full honors of war.

With the shooting already started and in danger of spreading, the British authorities in Nova Scotia took vigorous action. Understandably fearing a stab in the back from the French Acadians, whom England had acquired in 1713, the British brutally uprooted some four thousand of them in 1755. These unhappy French deportees were scattered as far south as Louisiana, where the descendants of the French-speaking Acadians are now called "Cajuns" and number nearly a million.

Global War and Colonial Disunity

The first three Anglo-French colonial wars had all started in Europe, but the tables were now reversed. A fourth struggle, known as the French and Indian War, began in America. Touched off by George Washington in the wilds of the Ohio Valley in 1754, it rocked along on an undeclared basis for two years and then widened into the most far-flung conflict the world had yet seen—the Seven Years' War. It was fought not only in America but in Europe, in the West Indies, in the Philippines, in Africa,

and on the ocean. The Seven Years' War was a seven-seas war.

In Europe the principal adversaries were England and Prussia on one side, arrayed against France, Spain, Austria, and Russia on the other. The bloodiest theater was in Germany, where Frederick the Great deservedly won the title of "Great" by repelling French, Austrian, and Russian armies, often with the opposing forces outnumbering him three to one. The London government, unable to send him effective troop reinforcements, liberally subsidized him with gold. Luckily for the English colonials, the French wasted so much strength in this European bloodbath that they were unable to throw an adequate force into the New World. "America was conquered in Germany," declared Britain's great statesman William Pitt.

In previous colonial clashes, the Americans had revealed an astonishing lack of unity. Colonists who were nearest the shooting had responded much more generously with volunteers and money than those enjoying the safety of remoteness. Even the Indians had laughed at the inability of the colonials to pull together. Now, with musketballs already whining in the Ohio country, the crisis demanded concerted action.

In 1754 the British government summoned an intercolonial congress to Albany, New York, near the Iroquois Indian country. Travel-weary delegates from only seven of the thirteen colonies showed up. The immediate purpose was to keep the scalping knives of the Iroquois tribes loyal to the British in the spreading war. The chiefs were harangued at length and then presented with thirty wagonloads of gifts, including guns.

The longer-range purpose at Albany was to achieve greater colonial unity and thus bolster the common defense against France. A month before the congress assembled, ingenious Benjamin Franklin published in his *Pennsylvania Gazette* the most famous cartoon of the colonial era. Showing the separate colonies as parts of a disjointed snake, it broadcast the slogan, "Join, or Die."

Franklin himself, a wise and witty counselor, was the leading spirit of the Albany Congress.

Famous Cartoon by Benjamin Franklin *Delaware and Georgia were omitted.*

His outstanding contribution was a well-devised scheme for colonial home rule. It was unanimously adopted by the Albany delegates but was spurned by the individual colonies and by the London regime. To the colonials, it did not seem to give enough independence; to the British officials, it seemed to give too much. The disappointing result confirmed one of Franklin's sage observations: all people agreed on the need for union, but their "weak noddles" were "perfectly distracted" when they attempted to agree on details.

Braddock's Blundering and Its Aftermath

The opening clashes of the French and Indian War went badly for the English colonials. Haughty and bullheaded General Braddock, a sixty-year-old officer experienced in European warfare, was sent to Virginia with a strong detachment of British regulars. After gathering scanty supplies from the reluctant colonists, he set out in 1755 with some two thousand men to capture Fort Duquesne. A considerable part of his force consisted of ill-disciplined colonial militiamen ("buckskins"), whose behind-the-tree methods of fighting Indians won "Bulldog" Braddock's professional contempt.

Braddock's expedition, dragging heavy artillery, moved slowly. Axmen laboriously hacked a path through the dense forest, thus opening a road that was later to be an important artery to the West. A few miles from Fort Duquesne, Braddock encountered a much smaller French and Indian army. At first the enemy force was repulsed, but it quickly melted into the thickets and poured a murderous fire into the ranks of the redcoats. George Washington, an energetic and fearless aide to Braddock, had two horses shot from under him and four bullet holes in his coat, and Braddock himself was mortally wounded. The entire force was routed after appalling losses.

Inflamed by this easy victory, the Indians took to a wider warpath. The whole frontier from Pennsylvania to North Carolina, left virtually naked by Braddock's bloody defeat, felt their fury. Scalping forays occurred within eighty miles of Philadelphia, and in desperation the local authorities offered bounties for Indian scalps: $50 for a woman's and $130 for a brave's. George Washington, with only three hundred men, did heroic work in helping to defend the scorched frontier.

The British launched a full-scale invasion of Canada in 1756, now that the undeclared war in America had at last merged into a world conflict. But they unwisely tried to attack a number of exposed wilderness posts simultaneously, instead of throwing all their strength at Quebec and Montreal. If these strongholds had fallen, all the outposts to the west would have withered on the vine for lack of riverborne supplies. But the British ignored such sound strategy, and defeat after defeat tarnished their arms, both in America and in Europe.

Pitt's Palms of Victory

In the hour of crisis Britain brought forth, as it repeatedly has, a superlative leader—William Pitt. A tall and imposing figure, whose

William Pitt (1708–1778) *He opposed the king's stubborn policies against the colonies but never favored complete independence. Fort Duquesne, falling to Britain in the French and Indian War, was renamed Pittsburgh in his honor. (The Granger Collection.)*

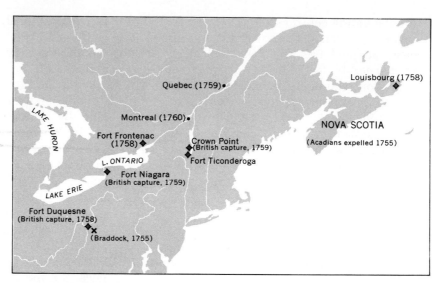

Events of 1755–1760

flashing eyes were set in a hawklike face, he was popularly known as the "Great Commoner." Pitt drew much of his strength from the common people, who admired him so greatly that on occasion they kissed his horses. A splendid orator endowed with a majestic voice, he believed passionately in his cause, in his country, and in himself.

In 1757 Pitt became a foremost leader in the London government. Throwing himself headlong into his task, he soon earned the title "Organizer of Victory." He wisely decided to soft-pedal assaults on the French West Indies, which had been bleeding away much British strength, and to concentrate on the vitals of Canada—the Quebec-Montreal area. He also picked young and energetic leaders, thus bypassing incompetent and cautious old generals.

Pitt first dispatched a powerful expedition in 1758 against Louisbourg. The frowning fortress, though it had been greatly strengthened, fell after a blistering siege. Wild rejoicing swept England, for this was the first significant British victory of the entire war.

Quebec was next on Pitt's list. For this crucial expedition he chose the thirty-two-year-old James Wolfe, who had been an officer since the age of fourteen. Though slight and sickly, Wolfe combined a mixture of dash with painstaking attention to detail. The British attackers were making scant progress when Wolfe, in a daring move, sent a detachment up a poorly guarded part of the rocky eminence protecting Quebec. This vanguard scaled the cliff, pulling itself upward by the bushes and showing the way for the others. In the morning the two armies faced each other on the Plains of Abraham on the outskirts of Quebec; the British under Wolfe and the French under the Marquis de Montcalm. Both commanders fell fatally wounded, but the French were defeated and the city surrendered (see "Makers of America", pp. 96–97)

The battle of Quebec ranks as one of the most significant engagements in British and American history. When Montreal fell in 1760, the French flag waved in Canada for the last time. By the peace settlement at Paris (1763), French power was thrown completely off the continent of North America, leaving behind a fertile French population that is to this day a strong minority in Canada. This bitter pill was sweetened somewhat when the French were allowed to retain several small but valuable sugar islands in the West Indies, and two never-to-be-fortified islets in the Gulf of St. Lawrence for fishing stations. A final blow came when the

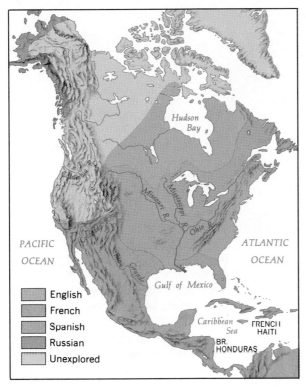

North America before 1754

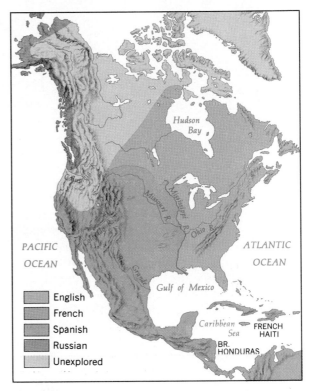

North America after 1763 (after French losses)

French, to compensate their luckless Spanish ally for its losses, ceded to Spain all trans-Mississippi Louisiana, plus the outlet of New Orleans. Spain, for its part, turned Florida over to England in return for Cuba, where Havana had fallen to British arms.

Great Britain thus emerged as the dominant power in North America, while taking its place as the leading naval power of the world.

Restless Colonials

England's colonials, baptized by fire, emerged with increased confidence in their military strength. They had borne the brunt of battle at first; they had fought bravely beside the crack British regulars; and they had gained valuable experience, officers and men alike. In the closing days of the conflict some twenty thousand American recruits were under arms.

The French and Indian War, while bolstering colonial self-esteem, simultaneously shattered the myth of British invincibility. On Braddock's bloody field the "buckskin" militia had seen the demoralized regulars huddling helplessly together or fleeing their unseen enemy.

Ominously, friction had developed during the war between arrogant English officers and the raw colonial "boors." Displaying the contempt of the professional soldier for amateurs, the British refused to recognize any American militia commission above the rank of captain—a demotion humiliating to "Colonel" George Washington. They also showed the usual condescension of snobs from the civilized Old Country toward the "scum" who had confessed failure by fleeing to the "outhouses of civilization." General Wolfe referred to the colonial militia, with exaggeration, as "in general the dirtiest, most contemptible, cowardly dogs that you can conceive." Energetic and hardworking American settlers, on the other hand, sensed that they were the cutting edge of British civilization. They believed that they deserved credit rather

The French

At the height of his reign in the late seventeenth century, Louis XIV, France's "Sun King," turned his smoldering desires westward to the New World. He envisioned there a bountiful New France, settled by civilizing French pioneers, in the maritime provinces of Acadia and the icy expanses of Quebec. But his dreams flickered out like candles before the British juggernaut in the eighteenth century, and his former New World subjects had to suffer foreign governance in the aftermath of the French defeats in 1713 and 1763. Over the course of two centuries, many chafed under the British yoke and eventually found their way to the United States.

The first French to leave Canada were the Acadians, the settlers of the seaboard region that now comprises Nova Scotia, New Brunswick, Prince Edward Island, and part of Maine.

In 1713 the French crown ceded this territory to the British, who demanded that the Acadians either swear allegiance to Britain or withdraw to French territory. At first doing neither, they managed to escape reprisals until *Le Grand Derangement* ("the Great Displacement") in 1755, when the British expelled them at bayonet point. The Acadians fled far south to the French colony of Louisiana, where they settled among the sleepy bayous, planted sugar cane and sweet potatoes, practiced Roman Catholicism, and spoke the French dialect that came to be called Cajun (a corruption of the English word *Acadian*.) Their settlements were tiny and secluded, many of them accessible only by small boat.

For generations these insular people were scarcely influenced by developments outside their tight-knit communities. Louisiana passed

Modern-Day Quebec *A bit of the old world in the new. (Joseph Nettis/ Stock, Boston.)*

Acadian Architecture *This architectural style was transplanted to the "Cajun" bayous of Louisiana. (Cameramann International Ltd.)*

Franco-American Mill Workers in New England, c. 1910 *(Museum of American Textile History.)*

through Spanish, French, and American hands, but the Cajuns kept to themselves. Cajun women sometimes married German, English, or Spanish men—today one finds such names as Schneider and Lopez in the bayous—but the outsiders were always absorbed completely into the large Cajun families. Not until the twentieth century did Cajun parents surrender their children to public schools and submit to a state law restricting French speech. Only in the 1930s, with a bridge-building spree engineered by Governor Huey Long, was the isolation of these bayou communities broken.

In 1763, as the French settlers of Quebec fell under British rule, a second group of French people began to leave Canada. By 1840 what had been an irregular southward trickle of Quebecois swelled to a steady stream, depositing most of the migrating French-Canadians in New England. These nineteenth-century emigrants were not goaded by bayonets but driven away by the lean harvests yielded by Quebec's short growing season and scarcity of arable land. They frequently recrossed the border to visit their old homes, availing themselves of the train routes opened in the 1840s between Que-

bec and Boston. Most hoped someday to return to Canada for good.

They emigrated mostly to work in New England's lumberyards and textile mills, gradually establishing permanent settlements in the northern woods. Like the Acadians, these later migrants from Quebec stubbornly preserved their Roman Catholicism. And both groups shared a passionate love of their French language, believing it to be the cement that bound them, their religion, and their culture together. As one French-Canadian explained: "Let us worship in peace and in our own tongue. All else may disappear but this must remain our badge." Yet today, almost all Cajuns and New England French-Canadians speak English.

North of the border, in the land that these immigrants left behind, Louis XIV's dream lingers on in the Canadian province of Quebec. Centuries have passed since the British won the great eighteenth-century duel for North America, but the French language still adorns the road signs of Quebec and rings out in its classrooms, courts, and markets, eloquently testifying to the continued vitality of French culture in North America.

than contempt for risking their lives to erect a New World empire.

British officials were further distressed by the reluctance of the colonials to support the common cause wholeheartedly. American shippers, using fraudulent papers, developed a golden traffic with the enemy ports of the Spanish and French West Indies. This treasonable trade in foodstuffs actually kept some of the hostile islands from starving at the very time when the British navy was trying to subdue them. In the last year of the war the British authorities, forced to resort to drastic measures, forbade the export of all supplies from New England and the middle colonies.

Other colonials, self-centered and regarding the war as remote, refused to provide troops and money for the conflict. They demanded the rights and privileges of Englishmen, without the duties and responsibilities of Englishmen. Not until Pitt had offered to reimburse the colonies for a substantial part of their expenditures—some £900,000—did they move with some enthusiasm. If the Americans had to be bribed to defend themselves against a relentless and savage foe, would they ever unite to strike the mother country?

The curse of intercolonial disunity, present from early days, had continued throughout the recent hostilities. It had been caused mainly by enormous distances; by geographical barriers like rivers; by conflicting religions, from Catholic to Quaker; by varied nationalities, from German to Irish; by differing types of colonial governments; by many boundary disputes; and by the resentment of the crude backcountry settlers against the aristocratic bigwigs.

Yet unity received some encouragement during the French and Indian War. When soldiers and statesmen from widely separated colonies met around common campfires and council tables, they were often agreeably surprised by what they found. Despite deep-seated jealousy and suspicion, they discovered that they were all fellow Americans who generally spoke the same language and shared common ideals. Barriers of disunity began to melt, although a long and rugged road lay ahead before a nation could emerge.

Americans: A People of Destiny

The removal of the French menace in Canada profoundly affected American attitudes. While the French hawk had been hovering in the North and West, the colonial chicks had been forced to cling close to the wings of the mother hen. Now that the hawk was killed, they could range far afield with a new spirit of independence.

The French, humiliated by the British and saddened by the fate of Canada, consoled themselves with one wishful thought. Perhaps the loss of their American empire would one day result in Britain's loss of its American empire. In a sense the history of the United States began with the fall of Quebec and Montreal; the infant republic was cradled on the Plains of Abraham.

The Spanish and Indian menaces, in like manner, were removed by the recent war. Spain was eliminated from Florida, although now entrenched in Louisiana and New Orleans. And the Indian allies of France were left in the lurch. A violent postwar flare-up against the whites occurred in the Ohio Valley and Great Lakes region in 1763, with the vengeful chieftain Pontiac as the principal leader. Catching the British napping, the Indians wiped out a number of their posts. But the whites swiftly and cruelly retaliated. The British commander ordered blankets infected with smallpox to be distributed among the Indians. Such tactics

The Reverend Andrew Burnaby, an observant Church of England clergyman who visited the colonies in the closing months of the French and Indian War, scoffed at any possibility of unification (1760): ". . . for fire and water are not more heterogeneous than the different colonies in North America. Nothing can exceed the jealousy and emulation which they possess in regard to each other. . . . In short . . . were they left to themselves there would soon be a civil war from one end of the continent to the other, while the Indians and Negroes would . . . impatiently watch the opportunity of exterminating them all together."

Settled Areas at End of French and Indian War, 1763 *This map, showing the colonies thirteen years before the Declaration of Independence, helps to explain why the British would be unable to conquer their offspring. The colonials were spreading rapidly into the backcountry, where the powerful British navy could not flush them out. During the Revolutionary War, the British at one time or another captured the leading colonial cities—Boston, New York, Philadelphia, and Charleston; but the more remote interior remained a sanctuary for rebels.*

crushed the uprising and pacified the frontier, temporarily.

Land-hungry American colonials were now free to burst over the dam of the Appalachian Mountains and flood out over the grassy western lands. A tiny rivulet of pioneers like Daniel Boone had already trickled into Tennessee and Kentucky; other courageous settlers were preparing for the long, dangerous trek over the mountains.

Then, out of a clear sky, the London government issued its Proclamation of 1763. It flatly prohibited settlement in the area beyond the Appalachian Mountains, pending further adjustments. The truth is that this hastily drawn document was not designed to oppress the colonials at all, but to work out the Indian problem fairly and prevent another bloody eruption like Pontiac's uprising.

But countless Americans, especially land speculators, were dismayed and angered. Was not the land beyond the mountains their birthright? Had they not, in addition, bought it with their blood in the recent war? In complete defiance of the paper proclamation, they clogged the westward trails. In 1765 an estimated one thousand wagons rolled through the town of Salisbury, North Carolina, on their way "up west." This wholesale flouting of royal authority boded ill for the longevity of British rule in America.

The French and Indian War also caused the colonials to develop a new vision of their ultimate destiny. With the path cleared for the conquest of a continent, with their birthrate high and their energy boundless, they sensed that they were a potent people on the march. And they were in no mood to be restrained.

Lordly Britons, whose suddenly swollen empire had tended to produce swollen heads, were in no mood for back talk. Puffed up over their recent victories, they were already annoyed with their unruly colonials. The stage was set for a violent family quarrel.

CHRONOLOGY

1598	Edict of Nantes
1608	Champlain colonizes Quebec
1643	Louis XIV becomes King of France
1682	La Salle explores Mississippi River to the Gulf of Mexico
1689–1697	King William's War (War of the League of Augsburg)
1702–1713	Queen Anne's War (War of Spanish Succession)
1718	French found New Orleans
1739	War of Jenkins's Ear
1740–1748	King George's War (War of Austrian Succession)
1754	Washington battles French on frontier
	Albany Congress
1756–1763	French and Indian War (Seven Years' War)
1757	Pitt emerges as leader of British government
1759	Battle of Quebec
1763	Peace of Paris
	Pontiac's uprising
	Proclamation of 1763

Varying Viewpoints

The duel for North America was but one episode in the epochal story of the worldwide expansion of European commerce and culture after 1500. Dominated by the "imperial school," a group of historians who see transatlantic economic stresses as leading to revolution, scholarly inquiry has revolved around four principal questions: How did New World developments fit into the overall pattern of rivalries among the great European powers? What were the relative strengths and weaknesses of the British and French imperial systems that spelled the final triumph of the British and the defeat of the French? How well or poorly did the British Empire function? Finally, were the Americans well or badly treated in the British imperial system? In short, how economically justifiable was the eventual American Revolution?

Social historians have recently looked at the colonial rivalries in a different light. They view the social and economic dislocations wrought by war as a stimulus to class conflict and revolutionary ferment. Some scholars have also asked whether the Revolution would have occurred at all without the British victory over the French in North America. If a powerful, Catholic, hostile France had retained its foothold in Canada, the British colonials might have thought twice about challenging their mother country.

Select Readings

Primary Source Documents

"The Albany Plan of the Union" was the first great statement of colonial unity; "The Proclamation of 1763" forbade settlement west of the Appalachians. Both are collected in Henry Steele Commager, *Documents of American History.*

Secondary Sources

The workings of the British mercantile system are detailed in Charles M. Andrews's vast *Colonial Period of American History* (4 vols., 1935–1938) and in Lawrence H. Gipson's still more ambitious *British Empire before the American Revolution* (15 vols., 1936–1970). Further efforts to analyze the colonial empire are James Henretta, *"Salutary Neglect": Colonial Administration under the Duke of Newcastle* (1972), and Michael Kammen's especially interesting *Empire and Interest* (1970). The French colonial effort is described in George M. Wrong, *The Rise and Fall of New France* (2 vols., 1928). Calvin Martin, *Keepers of the Game* (1978), offers a provocative interpretation of the fur trade and its impact on Indian societies. See also Shepard Krech III, ed., *Indians, Animals and the Fur Trade: A Critique of Keepers of the Game* (1981). The Anglo-French struggle is recounted in Howard H. Peckham, *The Colonial Wars, 1689–1762* (1964). Alan Rogers, *Empire and Liberty: American Resistance to the British Authority, 1755–1763* (1974), investigates American participation in the Seven Years' War. Fred Anderson focuses on colonial soldiers in *A People's Army: Massachusetts Soldiers and Society in the Seven Years' War* (1984). Classic accounts are Francis Parkman's several volumes, including *Count Frontenac and New France under Louis XIV* (1877), *Montcalm and Wolfe* (2 vols., 1884), and *A Half-Century of Conflict* (1892). Parkman's tomes are condensed, without serious loss of flavor, in *The Battle for North America,* edited by John Tebbel (1948), and *The Parkman Reader,* edited by Samuel E. Morison (1955). An impressive biography is Douglas S. Freeman, *Young Washington* (2 vols., 1948), a subject treated in less detail in James T. Flexner, *George Washington: The Forge of Experience* (1965). See also Bernhard Knollenberg's revealing *George Washington: The Virginia Period* (1965).

6

The Road
to Revolution, 1763–1775

The Revolution was effected before the war commenced. The Revolution was in the minds and hearts of the people.

John Adams, 1818

The Deep Roots of Revolution

In a broad sense, the American Revolution was not the same thing as the American War of Independence. The war itself lasted only eight years. But the Revolution lasted over a century and a half and began when the first permanent English settlers set foot on the new continent. Insurrection of thought usually precedes insurrection of deed. Over the years such a ferment had occurred in the thinking of the colonists that the Revolution was partially completed in their minds before the musketballs began to fly. America was a revolutionary force from the day of its discovery.

England's colonies were settled largely by emigrants who were discontented or rebellious in spirit—by people who had failed to adjust themselves to their harsh lot in the Old World. Most of them had not been able to get along, whether socially, politically, economically, or religiously. Some of them were tired of taking off their hats and standing bareheaded in the presence of their "betters." Others wanted a larger share in government, or a richer portion of this world's goods, or an opportunity to worship God in their own peculiar way.

The nightmare of crossing the Atlantic normally lasted about six to eight weeks, often much longer. Ships were frequently turned into "floating coffins" by food shortages or epidemics of disease; in one extreme case 350 of 400 passengers and crew perished. Cannibalism was not unknown, and starving voyagers fought over the bodies of vermin. As a sailor's song ran:

> We ate the mice, we ate the rats,
> And through the hold we ran like cats.

Such a perilous crossing left many emotional scars. Survivors who staggered ashore on the promised land were, as a rule, isolated spiritually from the faraway Old World. They were more than ever aware that the long arm of the London government, enfeebled by 3,000 miles

(4,800 kilometers) of ocean, could not reach them nearly so effectively as at home. Distance weakens authority; great distance weakens authority greatly.

America's lonely wilderness likewise stimulated ideas of independence. Back in England some villagers had lived near graveyards that contained the bones of their ancestors for a thousand years past. Born into such conservative surroundings, the poor peasants did not question the social rut in which they found themselves. But in the New World they were not held down by the scowl of their overlords.

In America all was strange, crude, different. Dense forests and the rugged pioneering conditions changed patterns of living and consequently habits of thought. Those wretched settlers perished who could not adapt themselves to their raw surroundings, and hundreds of the early Virginia colonists paid the supreme penalty. Before long, Americans were eating Indian corn, wearing Indian moccasins and buckskin, and in extreme instances on the frontier uttering the war whoop as they scalped their fallen Indian foe. Hacking a home out of the wildwood with an ax developed strength, self-confidence, individualism, and a spirit of independence.

As the Americans matured, they acquired privileges of self-government enjoyed by no other colonial peoples. They set up thirteen parliaments of their own and aped the parliamentary methods of England. Ultimately they came to regard their own legislative bodies as more or less on a footing with the great mother of parliaments in London. One governor of Rhode Island would wear no wig unless it had been made in England and was exactly like that worn by the speaker of the British House of Commons.

Adam Smith, the Scottish "Father of Modern Economics," frontally attacked mercantilism in 1776: "To prohibit a great people, however, from making all that they can of every part of their own produce, or from employing their stock and industry in the way that they judge most advantageous to themselves, is a manifest violation of the most sacred rights of mankind."

The Mercantile Theory

Britain's empire was acquired in a "fit of absent-mindedness," as the old saying goes, and there is much truth in it. ~~Not one of the original thirteen colonie~~s, except Georgia, ~~was formally planted by the British government. The actual founding was done haphazardly by trading companies, religious groups, land speculators, and others.~~ Ignoring the high-minded and far-visioned aspirations of pioneering Puritans, Quakers, and other colonizers, authorities in London scarcely dreamed that a new nation was being born.

~~Machinery in Britain for controlling the colonies was relatively simple.~~ As it had evolved by 1696, the ~~principal agency was the Board~~ of ~~Trade,~~ joined in an advisory capacity by certain other prominent officials. With the passage of time, interest in the board flagged, an~~d membership on it became something of a joke.~~ Yet the ~~recommendations of the board~~ regarding the colonies ~~were often made into law, either~~ by ~~act of Parliament or in regulations adopted~~ by ~~the Privy Council (the king's advisers).~~

The theory that shaped and justified English exploitation of the American colonies was called mercantilism. Mercantilist ideas lay behind the policies of all the major trading nations of Europe from the sixteenth to the eighteenth centuries. The leading powers relied on strong central governments to direct their economies. They all sought to achieve economic (and military) self-sufficiency by exporting more than they imported and thereby amassing huge reserves of precious metals. ~~According to mercantile doctrine, colonies existed only to help the mother country meet those goals. Colonist~~s ~~were regarded more or less as tenant~~s. They were expected to produce tobacco and other products needed in England and not to bother their heads with dangerous dreams of economic independence or self-government.

Specifically, how were the American colonies to benefit England? First of all, they were to ensure Britain's naval supremacy by furnishing ships, ships' stores, sailors, and trade. In addition, they were to provide a profitable consumers' market for the English manufacturers at home and were discouraged from buying the products of other countries. Finally, they were to keep gold and silver money within the empire by growing products, such as sugar, that otherwise would have to be bought from foreigners. The ideal of "buy British" would thus be promoted in a manner that foreshadowed later protective tariffs.

Mercantilist Trammels on Trade

Parliament passed numerous measures to enforce the mercantile system. Most famous were the Navigation Laws. The first of these, enacted in 1650, was aimed at rival Dutch shippers who were elbowing their way into the American carrying trade. The Navigation Laws worked to restrict commerce to and from the colonies to English vessels. Such regulation not only kept money within the empire but bolstered the British and colonial merchant marine, which in turn was an indispensable auxiliary to the Royal Navy.

An alert Parliament from time to time enacted additional laws that were favorable to England. European goods consigned to America had to be landed first in England, where customs duties could be collected and where the British middleman would get his cut of the profit. Still other curbs required certain "enumerated" products, notably tobacco, to be shipped to England and not to a foreign market, though prices in Europe might be higher.

In the interests of the empire, settlers were even restricted in what they might produce at home. They were forbidden to manufacture for export certain products, such as woolen cloth and beaver hats, because the colonies were supposed to complement and not compete with English industry.

Americans also felt the pinch in the area of currency. No banks existed in the colonies, and the money problem on the eve of the Revolution was acute. Industrious colonials were now busily buying more goods from England than they were selling to her, so the difference had to be made up in hard cash. Every year gold and silver money, much of it in quaint Spanish coins from the West Indies, was drained out of the colonies. The colonials simply did not have enough left for the convenience of everyday

purchases. Barter became necessary, and even butter, nails, pitch, and feathers were used for purposes of exchange.

Currency problems came to a boil when dire need finally forced many of the colonies to issue paper money, which unfortunately depreciated. British merchants and creditors, understandably worried, squawked so loudly that Parliament was compelled to act. It restrained the colonial legislatures from printing paper currency and from passing lax bankruptcy laws—practices that might result in defrauding British

> As the Boston Gazette *declared in 1765, "A colonist cannot make a button, a horseshoe, nor a hobnail, but some snooty ironmonger or respectable buttonmaker of Britain shall bawl and squall that his honor's worship is most egregiously maltreated, injured, cheated, and robbed by the rascally American republicans."*

The Female Combatants *Britain is symbolized as a lady of fashion, and her rebellious daughter as an Indian princess. (Courtesy of The Print Collection, Lewis Walpole Library, Yale University.)*

merchants. The Americans, who felt that their welfare was again being sacrificed, reacted angrily. Another burning grievance was thus heaped upon the pile of combustibles already smoldering.

London officialdom naturally kept a watchful eye on the legislation passed by the colonial assemblies. If such laws conflicted with British regulations or policy, they might be summarily declared null and void by the Privy Council.

This "royal veto" was in fact used rather sparingly—469 times in connection with 8,563 laws. But the colonists nevertheless fiercely resented it. They felt aggrieved when, in the interests of England, they were forbidden to make reforms that they deemed desirable, such as curbing the degrading trade in African slaves.

Paul Revere, c. 1768 *This painting by John Singleton Copley of the famed silversmith-horseman challenged convention—but reflected the new democratic spirit of the age—by portraying an artisan in working clothes. Note how Copley has depicted the serene confidence of the master craftsman and Revere's quiet pride in his work. (Museum of Fine Arts, Boston. Gift of Joseph W., William B., and Edward H. R. Revere.)*

The Merits of Mercantilism

Red-blooded Americans have long regarded the British mercantile system as thoroughly selfish and deliberately oppressive, if not downright malicious. The truth is that until 1763 the Navigation Laws imposed no intolerable burden, partly because they were laxly enforced. Ingenious colonial merchants early learned to disregard or evade restrictions that they found vexatious. In fact, some of the early American fortunes were amassed by wholesale smuggling. Wealthy and vain John Hancock of Massachusetts came to be known as the "King of Smugglers," though his illicit activity was greatly exaggerated.

Americans, in addition, were fortunate enough to reap direct benefits from the mercantile system. London paid liberal bounties or price supports to those colonials who produced ships' parts and ships' stores, even though English competitors complained heatedly. When independence came, the bounties dried up and many of these American producers were forced to the wall.

Virginia tobacco planters, in particular, enjoyed valuable privileges. While forbidden to ship their pungent yellow leaf to any place other than England, the planters were guaranteed a monopoly of the British market. Tobacco growing was also outlawed in England and Ireland, although the plant had already been raised in England with some success.

American colonials additionally fared well in other fields. They enjoyed the undiluted rights of Englishmen, as well as unusual opportunities for self-government. They were not compelled to tax themselves to support a professional army and navy for protection against the French, Dutch, Spaniards, Indians, and pirates. Although the colonists went to some little expense in "training" militias, they enjoyed the shield of a strong army of British redcoats and the mightiest navy in the world—without a penny of cost. After independence, the American people would themselves be required to pay the costs of maintaining a tiny army and navy, both of which afforded inadequate protection.

In manufacturing and trade the New World settlers did not fare badly. They were denied the privilege of fabricating specified articles for export, notably fur hats, but this regulation worked no serious hardships, because it was laxly enforced and because other pursuits were usually more profitable. Americans were forced to deal with the British middleman, but they would have done so anyhow, owing to a common language, standard pounds and shillings, liberal credit arrangements, and familiar business methods.

"Prosperity trickles down" is a common saying; and it is true that the Americans enjoyed a generous share of Britain's profits under the time-honored mercantile system. The average American was probably better off economically than the average English person at home. If the colonies existed for the benefit of England, it was hardly less true that England existed for the benefit of the colonies. The well-meaning officials in London were working for the welfare of the empire as a whole, and they gave overall unity to its policies. A wise owner does not disembowel or starve the goose that lays the golden eggs. Mistakes were made by the British authorities, but they were not, until revolt had erupted, the mistakes of malice.

Mercantilism had sufficient merit to be widely adopted and long perpetuated. All other colonial nations of that age, including Spain and France, embraced mercantilistic principles completely and enforced them ironhandedly. Elements of mercantilism have endured to the present day, even in the United States. Manufacturers, workers, and farmers seek to ensure their prosperity through protective tariffs, and the government tries to enhance national security by prohibiting the export of high-technology products with possible military applications.

The Menace of Mercantilism

Even when painted in its rosiest colors, the mercantile system burdened the colonials with annoying liabilities. Economic initiative was stifled because Americans were not at complete liberty to buy, sell, ship, or manufacture under conditions that they found most profitable. The southern colonies, as "pets," were generally favored over the northern ones, chiefly because

> *English statesman Edmund Burke warned in 1775: "Young man, there is America—which at this day serves for little more than to amuse you with stories of savage men and uncouth manners; yet shall, before you taste of death, show itself equal to the whole of that commerce which now attracts the envy of the world."*

they grew non-English products like tobacco, sugar, and rice. Revolution was one seed that sprouted vigorously from the stony soil of New England, for the proud descendants of the Puritans greatly resented being treated like unwanted relatives.

One-crop Virginians, despite London's preference for the southern colonies, also nursed rankling grievances. Forced to sell their tobacco in England, they were at the mercy of British merchants, who often gouged them. Many of the fashionable Virginia planters were plunged into debt by the falling price of tobacco and were forced to buy their necessities in England by mortgaging future crops. Some debts, becoming hereditary, were bequeathed from one generation to the next.

Impoverished Virginia thus joined restless Massachusetts in agitating for revolt against England. Unfriendly critics sneered that the Virginians' cry, "Liberty or Death," might better have been "Liberty or Debt." While this charge was unfair in many cases, countless Virginians welcomed the opportunity to end their economic bondage to the mother country.

Finally—and of supreme importance—mercantilism was debasing to the Americans. The colonies, many of them felt, were being used or milked, as cows are milked. They were to be kept in a state of perpetual economic adolescence and never allowed to come of age. As Benjamin Franklin wrote in 1775:

> We have an old mother that peevish is
>   grown;
> She snubs us like children that scarce walk
>   alone;
> She forgets we're grown up and have sense
>   of our own.

Revolution broke out, as Theodore Roosevelt later remarked, because England failed to recognize an emerging nation when it saw one.

The Stamp Tax Uproar

The costly Seven Years' War, which ended in 1763, marked a new relationship between Britain and her transatlantic colonies. A revolution in British colonial policy precipitated the American Revolution.

Victory-flushed Britain emerged from the conflict possessing one of the biggest empires in the world—and also, less happily, the biggest debt. It amounted to £140 million, about half of which had been incurred in defending the American colonies. British officials wisely had no intention of asking the colonials to help pay off this crushing burden. But London felt that the Americans should be asked to defray one-third the cost of maintaining a garrison of some ten thousand redcoats, presumably for the colonies' own protection.

Prime Minister George Grenville, an honest and able financier not noted for tact, moved vigorously. Dedicated to efficiency, he aroused the resentment of the colonials in 1763 by ordering the British navy to enforce the Navigation Laws. He also secured from Parliament the so-called Sugar Act of 1764, the first law ever passed by that body for raising revenue in the colonies for the crown. Among various provisions, it increased the duty on foreign sugar imported from the West Indies. After bitter protests from the colonials, the duties were lowered substantially, and the agitation died down. But resentment was kept burning by the Quar-

A Royal Stamp *The motto in French is translated "Shame to him who evil thinks." (The Granger Collection.)*

tering Act of 1765. It required certain colonies to provide food and quarters for British troops.

Then in the same year, 1765, Grenville imposed the most ominous measure of all: a stamp tax, to raise revenues to support the new military force. The Stamp Act required the use of stamped paper or the affixing of stamps, certifying payment of tax. Involved were about fifty trade items and certain types of commercial and legal documents, including playing cards, pamphlets, newspapers, diplomas, bills of lading, and marriage licenses.

Grenville regarded all these measures as reasonable and just. He was simply asking the Americans to pay their fair share for colonial defense, through taxes that were already familiar in England. In fact, Englishmen for two generations had endured a stamp tax far heavier than that passed for the colonies.

Yet the Americans were angrily aroused at what they regarded as Grenville's fiscal aggression. The new laws pinched their pocketbooks and, even more ominously, menaced the local liberties they had come to assume as a matter of right. Thus, some colonial assemblies defiantly refused to comply with the Quartering Act or voted only a fraction of the supplies that it called for.

Worse still, Grenville's noxious legislation seemed to jeopardize the basic rights of the colonists as Englishmen. Both the Sugar Act and the Stamp Act provided for trying offenders in the hated admiralty courts, where juries were not allowed. The burden of proof was on the defendants, who were assumed to be guilty unless they could prove themselves innocent. Trial by jury and the doctrine of "innocent until proved guilty" were ancient privileges that the English people everywhere, including the American colonials, held most dear.

And why was a British army needed at all in the colonies, now that the French were expelled from the continent and Pontiac's warriors crushed? Could its real purpose be to whip rebellious colonials themselves into line? Many Americans began to sniff the strong scent of a conspiracy to strip them of their historic liberties. They lashed back violently, and the Stamp Act became a target that drew their most ferocious fire.

A Parody of the "Fatal Stamp"

Angry throats raised the cry, "No taxation without representation." There was some irony in the slogan, because the seaports and tidewater towns that were most wrathful against the Stamp Act had long denied full representation to their own backcountry pioneers. But now the agitated colonials took the high ground of principle. They vividly recollected the theories of popular government developed during England's own Puritan revolution a century earlier. American firebrands hurled these doctrines back at their English masters, who were stunned at the keenness of the colonials' historical memory.

The Americans made a distinction between "legislation" and "taxation." They conceded the right of Parliament to legislate about matters that affected the entire empire, including the regulation of trade. But they steadfastly denied the right of Parliament, in which no Americans were seated, to impose taxes on Americans. Only their own elected colonial legislatures, the Americans insisted, could legally tax them. Taxes levied by the distant English Parliament amounted to robbery, a piratical assault on the sacred rights of property.

Grenville dismissed these American protests as hairsplitting absurdities. The power of Parliament was supreme and undivided, he asserted, and in any case the Americans *were* represented in Parliament. Elaborating the theory of "virtual representation," Grenville claimed that every member of Parliament represented all British subjects, even those Americans in Boston or Charleston who had never voted for a member of the London Parliament.

The Americans scoffed at the notion of virtual representation. And at bottom, they did not really want direct representation in Parliament, which might have seemed like a sensible compromise. If they had obtained it, any gouty member of the House of Commons could have proposed an oppressive tax bill for the colonies, and the American representatives, few in numbers, would have stood bereft of a principle with which to resist.

Thus the principle of no taxation without representation was supremely important, and the colonials clung to it with tenacious consistency. When the English replied that the sovereign power of government could not be divided between "legislative" authority in London and "taxing" authority in the colonies, they forced the Americans to deny the authority of Parliament altogether and to begin to consider their own political independence. This chain of logic eventually led to revolutionary consequences.

Protesting the Stamp Act, 1765 *Angry colonists burn the hated tax stamps in a bonfire. (The Granger Collection.)*

Parliament Forced to Repeal the Stamp Act

Colonial outcries against the hated stamp tax took various forms. The most conspicuous assemblage was the Stamp Act Congress of 1765, which brought together in New York City twenty-seven distinguished delegates from nine colonies. After dignified debate, the members drew up a statement of their rights and grievances and besought the king and Parliament to repeal the odious legislation.

The Stamp Act Congress, which was largely ignored in England, made little splash at the time in America. But it did do something to break down sectional suspicions, for it brought together around the same table leaders from the different and rival colonies. It was one more

halting but significant step toward intercolonial unity.

More effective than the congress was the widespread adoption of nonimportation agreements against British goods. Woolen garments of homespun became fashionable, and the eating of lamb chops was discouraged so that the wool-bearing sheep would be allowed to mature. Nonimportation agreements were in fact a promising stride toward union; they spontaneously united the American people for the first time in common action.

Violence also attended colonial protests. Groups of ardent spirits, known as Sons of Liberty and Daughters of Liberty, took the law into their own hands. Crying "Liberty, Property, and No Stamps," they enforced the nonimportation agreements against violators, often with a generous coat of tar and feathers. Houses of unpopular officials were ransacked, their money was stolen, and stamp agents were hanged on liberty poles, albeit in effigy.

Shaken by violence, the machinery for collecting the tax broke down. On that dismal day in 1765 when the new act was to go into effect, the stamp agents had all been forced to resign, and there was no one to sell the stamps. While flags flapped at half-mast, the law was openly and flagrantly defied—or rather, nullified.

England was hard hit. America then bought about one-quarter of all British exports, and about one-half of British shipping was devoted to the American trade. Merchants, manufacturers, and shippers suffered from the colonial nonimportation agreements, and hundreds of laborers were thrown out of work. Loud demands converged on Parliament for repeal of the Stamp Act. But many of the members could not understand why 7.5 million Britons had to pay heavy taxes to protect the colonies, while some 2 million colonials refused to pay for only one-third of the cost of their own defense.

After a stormy debate, and as a matter of expediency and not of right, Parliament in 1766 reluctantly repealed the Stamp Act. At the same time, and by an overwhelming vote, it saved face by passing the Declaratory Act. This futile measure proclaimed that Parliament had the right "to bind" the colonies "in all cases whatso-

Hanging John Huske in Effigy   *A Paul Revere engraving showing the fate in America of an alleged supporter of the Stamp Act. (American Antiquarian Society.)*

white lead, paper, and tea. Townshend, seizing on a dubious distinction between internal and external taxes, made this tax, unlike the Stamp Act, an indirect customs duty payable at American ports. But to the colonials, this was a distinction without a difference. For them, the real difficulty remained taxes—in any form—without representation.

Flushed with their recent victory over the stamp tax, the colonists were in a rebellious mood. The impost on tea was especially irksome, for an estimated 1 million persons drank the refreshing brew twice a day, and even tipplers used it when alcohol was not available.

The new Townshend revenues, worse yet, would be used to pay the salaries of the royal governors and judges in America. From the standpoint of efficient administration by London, this was a reform long overdue. But the ultrasuspicious Americans, who had beaten the royal governors into line by controlling the purse, regarded Townshend's tax as another attempt to enchain them. Their worst fears took on greater reality when the London govern-

ever." A bare assertion of this right was but a feeble victory for parental authority, for the unruly colonials had proved that the London government could be forced to yield to boycotts and mob action.

America forthwith burst into an uproar of rejoicing. Grateful residents of New York erected a leaden statue to King George III—a tribute that was later melted into thousands of bullets to be fired at his own troops.

The Townshend Tea Tax and the Boston "Massacre"

Control of the British ministry was now seized by the gifted but erratic "Champagne Charley" Townshend, a man who could deliver brilliant speeches in Parliament while drunk. Rashly promising to pluck feathers from the colonial goose with a minimum of squawking, he persuaded Parliament in 1767 to pass the Townshend Acts. The most important of these new regulations was a light import duty on glass,

Redcoats Landing in Boston   *(The Granger Collection.)*

The Boston Massacre, 1770 *This widely reprinted engraving by Paul Revere was both art and propaganda. (Library of Congress.)*

ment, after passing the Townshend taxes, suspended the legislature of New York in 1767 for failure to comply with the Quartering Act.

Nonimportation agreements, previously potent, were quickly revived against the Townshend Acts. But they proved less effective than those devised against the Stamp Act. The colonials, again enjoying prosperity, took the new tax less seriously than might have been expected, largely because it was light and indirect. They found, moreover, that they could secure smuggled tea at a cheap price, and consequently smugglers increased their activities, especially in Massachusetts.

British officials, faced with a breakdown of law and order, landed two regiments of troops in Boston in 1768. Many of the soldiers, as might be expected, were drunken and profane characters. Liberty-loving colonials, resenting the presence of the red-coated "ruffians," taunted the "bloody backs" unmercifully.

A clash was inevitable. On the evening of March 5, 1770, a crowd of some sixty townspeople set upon a squad of about ten "bloody backs," one of whom was hit by a club and another of whom was knocked down. Acting apparently without orders but under extreme provocation, the troops opened fire and killed or wounded eleven "innocent" citizens. One of the first to die was Crispus Attucks, described by contemporaries as a powerfully built runaway "mulatto" and as a leader of the mob. Both sides were in some degree to blame, and in the subsequent trial (in which future president John Adams served as defense attorney for the soldiers) only two of the redcoats were found guilty of manslaughter. They were released after being branded on the hand.

The so-called Boston Massacre further inflamed the colonials against the British, especially after the conviction spread that the Americans had been wholly unoffending. Paul Revere, the artist-horseman, wrote:

Unhappy Boston! see thy sons deplore
Thy hallowed walks besmear'd with guiltless
  gore.

Massacre Day was observed in Boston as a patriotic holiday until 1776, when the more glorious Fourth of July eclipsed it.

The Seditious Committees of Correspondence

By 1770 King George III, then only thirty-two years old, was strenuously attempting to restore the declining power of the British monarchy. He was a good man in his private morals, but he proved to be a bad ruler. Earnest, industrious, stubborn, lustful for power, and later plagued with periodic fits of supposed madness, he surrounded himself with cooperative "yes men," notably his corpulent prime minister, Lord North.

The ill-timed Townshend Acts had failed to produce revenue, though producing near-rebellion. Net proceeds from the tax in one year were £295, and during that time the annual military costs to Britain in the colonies had mounted to £170,000. Nonimportation agreements, though feebly enforced, were pinching British manufacturers. The government of Lord North, bowing to various pressures, finally persuaded Parliament to repeal the Townshend revenue duties. But the three-pence tax on tea was retained to keep alive the principle of parliamentary taxation.

Flames of discontent in America continued to be fanned by numerous incidents, including the redoubled efforts of the British officials to enforce the Navigation Laws. Resistance was further whipped up by a master propagandist and engineer of rebellion, Samuel Adams of Boston, a cousin of John Adams. Unimpressive in appearance (his hands trembled), he lived and breathed only for politics. His friends had to buy him a presentable suit of clothes when he left Massachusetts on intercolonial business. Zealous, tenacious, and courageous, he was ultrasensitive to infractions of colonial rights. Cherishing a deep faith in the common people, he appealed effectively to what was called his "trained mob." Skillful also as a pamphleteer, he soon became known as the "Penman of the Revolution."

Samuel Adams's signal contribution was to organize in Massachusetts the local committees of correspondence. After he had formed the first

one in Boston during 1772, some eighty towns in the colony speedily set up similar organizations. Their chief function was to spread propaganda and information by interchanging letters and thus keep alive opposition to British policy. One critic referred to the committees as "the foulest, subtlest, and most venomous serpent ever issued from the egg of sedition." No more effective device for stimulating resistance could have been contrived.

Intercolonial committees of correspondence were the next logical step. Virginia led the way in 1773 by creating such a body as a standing committee of the House of Burgesses. Within a short period of time every colony had established a central committee through which it could exchange ideas and information with other colonies. These intercolonial groups, which were supremely significant in stimulating and disseminating sentiment in favor of united action, evolved directly into the first American congresses.

Tea Parties at Boston and Elsewhere

Thus far—that is, by 1773—nothing had happened to make rebellion inevitable. Nonimportation was weakening. Increasing numbers of colonials were reluctantly paying the tea tax, because the legal tea was now cheaper than the smuggled tea and cheaper than tea in England. Even John Adams on one occasion hoped that the tea he was drinking was smuggled Dutch tea, but he could not be sure and did not want to know.

A new ogre entered the picture in 1773. The powerful British East India Company, overburdened with 17 million pounds of unsold tea, was facing bankruptcy. If it collapsed, the London government would lose heavily in tax revenue. The ministry therefore decided to assist the company by awarding it a complete monopoly of the American tea business. The terms thus granted would enable the giant corporation to sell the coveted leaves more cheaply than ever before, even with the three-pence tax added. But to many American consumers, principle was more important than price.

If British officials insisted on the letter of the law, violence would be inevitable, for the new

tea monopoly had many features that were hateful to the colonials. Above all, it seemed like a shabby attempt to trick the Americans, with the bait of cheaper tea, into acceptance of the detested tax. Fatefully, the British colonial authorities decided to enforce the law literally, and once more the colonials rose in their wrath. Not a single one of the several thousand chests of tea shipped by the company reached the hands of the consignees. At Annapolis, the Marylanders burned both the cargo and the vessel, while proclaiming "Liberty and Independence or death in pursuit of it." At Boston, which was host to the most famous tea party of all, a band of white townsfolk, disguised as Indians, boarded the three tea ships on ~~December 16, 1773~~. They smashed open 342 chests and dumped the "cursed weed" into the harbor, while a silent crowd watched approvingly from the wharves as salty tea was brewed for the fish.

Reactions varied. Extremists in America rejoiced; conservatives shuddered. This wanton destruction of private property was going too far. The British at home were outraged; even friends of America hung their heads. Punishment and coercion were the only possible responses of the London authorities, as long as the mercantilist philosophy prevailed and the colonials refused to accept responsibility. The granting of some kind of home rule to the Americans might have prevented rebellion, but not many Britons of that age were blessed with such vision. Edmund Burke, a friend of America in Parliament, stoically declared, "To tax and to please, no more than to love and be wise, is not given to men."

Josiah Quincy, a prominent Boston patriot and orator, lashed out against the Boston Port Act: "Blandishments will not fascinate us, nor will threats of a 'halter' [noose] intimidate. For, under God, we are determined that wheresoever, whensoever, or howsoever we shall be called to make our exit, we will die free men." He died at sea the next year while on a diplomatic mission to England.

Parliament Passes the "Intolerable Acts"

An outraged Parliament responded speedily to the Boston Tea Party with measures that brewed a revolution. By huge majorities in ~~1774~~

it passed a series of "Repressive Acts," which were designed to chastise Boston in particular, Massachusetts in general. They were branded in America as "the massacre of American Liberty."

Most drastic of all was the Boston Port Act. It closed the tea-stained harbor until damages were paid and order could be assured. By other "Intolerable Acts"—as they were called in America—many of the chartered rights of colonial Massachusetts were swept away. Restrictions were likewise placed on the precious town meetings. Contrary to previous practice, enforcing officials who killed colonials in the line of duty could now be sent to England for trial. There, suspicious Americans assumed, they would be likely to get off scot-free.

By a fateful coincidence, the "Intolerable Acts" were accompanied in 1774 by the Quebec Act. Passed at the same time, it was erroneously regarded in English-speaking America as one of the "repressive" measures. Actually, the Quebec Act was a good law in bad company. For many years the British government had debated how it should administer the sixty thousand or so conquered French subjects in Canada, and it had finally framed this farsighted and statesmanlike measure. The French were guaranteed their Catholic religion. They were also permitted to retain many of their old customs and institutions, which did not include a representative assembly or trial by jury in civil cases. In addition, the old boundaries of the Province of Quebec were now extended southward all the way to the Ohio River.

The Quebec Act, from the viewpoint of the French Canadians, was a shrewd and conciliatory measure. If England had only shown as much foresight in dealing with its English-speaking colonies, it might not have lost them.

But from the viewpoint of the American colonials as a whole, the Quebec Act was especially noxious. All the other "repressive" laws slapped directly at Massachusetts, but this one had a much wider range. It seemed to set a dangerous precedent in America against jury trials and popular assemblies. It alarmed land speculators, who were distressed to see the huge trans-Allegheny area snatched from their grasp. It aroused the host of anti-Catholics, who were shocked by the extension of Roman Catholic jurisdiction southward into a huge region that had once been earmarked for Protestantism—a region about as large as the thirteen original colonies. One angry Protestant cried that there ought to be a "jubilee in hell" over this enormous gain for "popery."

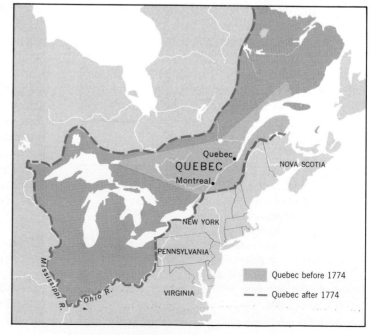

Quebec before and after 1774 *Young Alexander Hamilton voiced the fears of many colonists when he warned that the Quebec Act of 1774 would introduce "priestly tyranny" into Canada, making that country another Spain or Portugal. "Does not your blood run cold," he asked, "to think that an English Parliament should pass an act for the establishment of arbitrary power and Popery in such a country?"*

Quebec before 1774

Quebec after 1774

Samuel Adams (1722–1803)   *A second cousin of John Adams, he contributed a potent pen and tongue to the American Revolution as a political agitator and organizer of rebellion. He was the leading spirit in hosting the Boston Tea Party. A failure in the brewing business, he was sent by Massachusetts to the First Continental Congress of 1774. He signed the Declaration of Independence and served in Congress until 1781. (Museum of Fine Arts, Boston.)*

The Continental Congress and Bloodshed

American dissenters, outraged by the Quebec Act, responded sympathetically to the plight of Massachusetts. It had put itself in the wrong by the wanton destruction of the tea cargoes; now England had put itself in the wrong by brutal punishment that did not seem to fit the crime. Flags were flown at half-mast throughout the colonies on the day that the Boston Port Act went into effect, and sister colonies rallied to send food to the stricken city. Rice was shipped even from faraway South Carolina.

Most memorable of the responses to the "Intolerable Acts" was the summoning of a Continental Congress in 1774. It was to meet in Philadelphia to consider ways of redressing colonial grievances. Twelve of the thirteen colonies, with Georgia alone missing, sent fifty-five distinguished men, among them Samuel Adams, John Adams, George Washington, and Patrick Henry. Intercolonial frictions were partially melted away by social activity after working hours; in fifty-four days George Washington dined at his own lodgings only nine times.

The First Continental Congress deliberated for seven weeks, September 5 to October 26, 1774. It was not a legislative but a consultative body; it was a convention rather than a congress. John Adams played a stellar role. Eloquently swaying his colleagues to a revolutionary course, he helped defeat by the narrowest of margins a proposal by the moderates for a species of American home rule under British direction. After prolonged argument, the Congress drew up several dignified papers. These included a ringing Declaration of Rights, as well

Abigail Adams   *The wife of Revolutionary leader and future president John Adams, she was a prominent Patriot in her own right. She was also among the first Americans to see, however faintly, the implications of Revolutionary ideas for changing the status of women. (New York State Historical Association, Cooperstown, New York.)*

as solemn appeals to other British American colonies, to the king, and to the British people.

The most significant action of the Congress was the creation of The Association. Unlike previous nonimportation agreements, this one called for a *complete* boycott of British goods: nonimportation, nonexportation, and nonconsumption. A document known as The Association, by providing for concerted action, was the closest approach to a written constitution that the colonies as a unit had yet devised. But still there was no genuine drive toward independence—merely an effort to bring about a repeal of the offensive legislation and a return to the happy days before parliamentary taxation. If colonial grievances were redressed, well and good; if not, the Congress was to meet again in May 1775.

But the deadly drift toward war continued. The petitions of the Continental Congress were rejected, after considerable debate, by strong majorities in Parliament. In America chickens squawked and tar kettles bubbled as violators of The Association were tarred and feathered. Muskets were being collected, men were openly drilling, and a clash seemed imminent.

In April 1775, the British commander in Boston sent a detachment of troops to nearby Lexington and Concord. They were to seize stores of colonial gunpowder and also to bag the "rebel" ringleaders, Samuel Adams and John Hancock. At Lexington, the colonial "Minute Men" refused to disperse rapidly enough, and shots were fired that killed eight Americans and wounded several more. The affair was more the "Lexington Massacre" than a battle. The redcoats pushed on to Concord, whence they were forced to retreat by the homespun Americans, whom Emerson immortalized:

> By the rude bridge that arched the flood,
> Their flag to April's breeze unfurled,
> Here once the embattled farmers stood,
> And fired the shot heard round the world.[*]

The bewildered British, fighting off murderous fire from militiamen crouched behind thick stone walls, finally regained the sanctuary of Boston. Licking their wounds, they could count

---

[*]Ralph Waldo Emerson, "Concord Hymn."

Privately (1776) General Washington expressed his distrust of militia: "To place any dependence upon militia is assuredly resting on a broken staff. . . . The sudden change in their manner of living . . . brings on sickness in many, impatience in all, and such an unconquerable desire of returning to their respective homes that it not only produces shameful and scandalous desertions among themselves, but infuses the like spirit in others. . . . If I was called upon to declare upon oath whether the militia have been most serviceable or hurtful upon the whole, I should subscribe to the latter."

about three hundred casualties, including some seventy killed. England now had a war on its hands.

Imperial Strength and Weakness

Aroused Americans had brashly rebelled against a mighty empire. The population odds were about three to one against the rebels—some 7.5 million Britons to 2.5 million colonials. The odds in monetary wealth and naval power were overwhelmingly in favor of England.

Black people were only a partial asset to the American cause, for they could hardly be expected to fight for a society that had enslaved them. Still, about five thousand saw military service, whether as freemen or as slaves promised freedom, and in a number of engagements fought bravely. Even larger numbers, often guaranteed freedom with no strings attached, fled to enemy lines and left the country when the British departed.

Britain then boasted a professional army of some fifty thousand men, as compared with the numerous but wretchedly trained American militia. George III, in addition, had the money to hire foreign soldiers, and some thirty thousand Germans—so-called Hessians—were ultimately employed. The British enrolled about fifty thousand American Loyalists and enlisted the services of many Indians, who though unreliable fair-weather fighters, inflamed long stretches of the frontier. One British officer boasted that the war would offer no problems that could not be solved by an "experienced sheep herder."

Yet England was weaker than it seemed at first glance. Oppressed Ireland was a latent volcano, and British troops had to be detached to watch it. France, bitter from its recent defeat, was awaiting an opportunity to stab Britain in the back. The London government was confused and inept. There was no William Pitt, "Organizer of Victory," only the stubborn George III and his pliant Lord North.

Many earnest and God-fearing Britons had no desire whatever to kill their American cousins. William Pitt withdrew a son from the army rather than see him thrust his sword into fellow Anglo-Saxons struggling for liberty. The English Whig factions, opposed to Lord North's Tory factions, openly cheered American victories—at least at the outset. Aside from trying to embarrass the Tories politically, many Whigs believed that the battle for English freedom was

General Lafayette (1757–1834)   *He gave to America not only military services but some $200,000 of his private funds. He returned to France after the American Revolution to play a conspicuous but disappointing role in the French Revolution. (The Granger Collection.)*

being fought in America. If George III triumphed, his rule at home might become tyrannical. This outspoken sympathy in England, though plainly that of a minority, greatly encouraged the Americans. If they continued their resistance long enough, the Whigs might come into power and deal generously with them.

Britain's army in America had to operate under endless difficulties. The generals were second-rate; the soldiers, though on the whole capable, were brutally treated. There was one extreme case of eight hundred lashes on the bare back for striking an officer. Provisions were often scarce, rancid, and wormy. On one occasion a supply of biscuits, captured some fifteen years earlier from the French, was softened by dropping cannonballs on them.

Other handicaps loomed. The redcoats had to conquer the Americans; a draw would be a victory for the colonials. Britain was operating some 3,000 miles (4,800 kilometers) from its home base, and distance added greatly to the delays and uncertainties arising from storms and other mishaps. Military orders were issued in London that, when received months later, would not fit the changing situation.

America's geographical expanse was enormous: roughly 1,000 by 600 miles (1,600 by 970 kilometers). The united colonies had no urban nerve center, like France's Paris. British armies captured every city of any size, yet like a boxer punching a feather pillow, they made little more than a dent in the entire country. The Americans wisely traded space for time. Benjamin Franklin calculated that during the prolonged campaign in which the redcoats captured Bunker Hill and killed some 150 Yankees, about 60,000 American babies were born.

American Pluses and Minuses

The revolutionists were blessed with outstanding leadership. George Washington was a giant among men; Benjamin Franklin was a master among diplomats. Open foreign aid, theoretically possible from the start, eventually came from France. Numerous European officers, many of them unemployed and impoverished, volunteered their swords for pay. In a class by himself was a wealthy young French nobleman, the Marquis de Lafayette. Fleeing from boredom, loving glory and ultimately liberty, at age nineteen the "French gamecock" was made a major general in the colonial army. His commission was largely a recognition of his family influence and political connections, but the services of this teenage general in securing further aid from France were invaluable.

Other conditions aided the Americans. They were fighting defensively, with the odds, all things considered, favoring the defender. In agriculture, the colonies were mainly self-sustaining, like a kind of Robinson Crusoe's island. Colonial "buckskins," moreover, were a tough, self-reliant people. As marksmen, they far outshone the British, who often pointed rather than aimed their muskets. A competent American rifleman could hit a man's head at 200 yards (183 meters).

In addition, the Americans enjoyed the moral advantage that came from belief in a just cause. The historical odds were not impossible. Other peoples had triumphed in the face of greater obstacles: the Greeks against Persians, the Swiss against Austrians, the Dutch against Spaniards.

Yet the American rebels were badly organized for war. From the earliest days they had been almost fatally lacking in unity, and the new nation lurched forward uncertainly like an uncoordinated centipede. Even the Continental Congress, which directed the conflict, was hardly more than a debating society, and it grew feebler as the struggle dragged on. "Their Congress now is quite disjoint'd," jibed an English satirist, "Since Gibbits (gallows) [are] for them appointed." Disorganized colonials fought almost the entire war before adopting a written constitution—the Articles of Confederation—in 1781.

Jealousy everywhere raised its hideous head. Individual states, proudly regarding themselves as sovereign, resented the attempts of Congress to exercise its weak powers. Sectional jealousy boiled up over the appointment of military leaders; some distrustful New Englanders almost preferred British officers to Americans from other sections.

Economic difficulties were well-nigh insuperable. Metallic money had already been heavily drained away. A cautious Continental Congress, unwilling to raise anew the explosive issue of taxation, was forced to print "Continental" paper money in great amounts. As this currency poured from the presses, it depreciated until the expression became current, "not worth a Continental." One barber contemptuously papered his shop with the almost worthless dollars. The confusion worsened when the individual states were compelled to issue depreciated paper money of their own.

Inflation of the currency inevitably skyrocketed prices. Families of the soldiers at the fighting front were hard hit, and hundreds of anxious husbands and fathers deserted. Debtors easily acquired handfuls of the semiworthless money and gleefully paid their debts "without mercy"—sometimes with the bayonets of the authorities to back them up.

A Thin Line of Heroes

Basic military supplies in the colonies were dangerously scanty, especially firearms and powder. Benjamin Franklin seriously proposed going back to the bow and arrow. Even where food was accumulated, wagons were often not available to haul it. At Valley Forge, in the winter of 1777–1778, the shivering American soldiers were without bread for three successive days. In one southern campaign some men fainted for lack of food.

Manufactured goods were generally in short supply in agricultural America, and clothing and shoes were appallingly scarce. The path of the patriot fighting men was often marked by bloody snow. At frigid Valley Forge, during one anxious period, twenty-eight hundred men were barefooted or nearly naked. Woolens were desperately needed against the wintry blasts; and in general the only real uniform of the colonial army was uniform raggedness. During a grand parade at Valley Forge, some of the officers appeared wrapped in woolen bed covers. One Rhode Island unit was known as the "Ragged, Lousy, Naked Regiment."

American militiamen were numerous but also highly unreliable. Able-bodied American males—perhaps several hundred thousand of them—had received rudimentary training, and many of these recruits served for short terms in the rebel armies. But poorly trained plowboys, though better shots, could not stand up in the

General Washington's disgust is reflected in a diary entry for 1776: "Chimney corner patriots abound; venality, corruption, prostitution of office for selfish ends, abuse of trust, perversion of funds from a national to a private use, and speculations upon the necessities of the times pervade all interests."

open field against professional British troops advancing with bare bayonets. Many of these undisciplined warriors would, in the words of Washington, "fly from their own shadows."

A few thousand regulars—perhaps seven or eight thousand at war's end—were finally whipped into shape by stern drillmasters. Notable among these officers was an organizational genius, the salty German Baron von Steuben. He spoke no English when he reached America, but he soon taught his men that bayonets were not for broiling beefsteaks over open fires. As they gained experience, these soldiers of the Continental line could hold their own in open battle against crack British troops.

Morale in the Revolutionary army was badly undermined by American profiteers. These grasping gentry, putting profits before patriotism, sold to the British because the invader could pay in gold. Speculators forced prices sky-high; and some Bostonians made profits of 50 percent to 200 percent on army clothing while the American army was freezing at Valley Forge. Washington never had as many as twenty thousand effective troops in one place at one time, despite bounties of land and other inducements. Yet if the rebels had thrown themselves into the struggle with Revolutionary zeal, they could easily have raised many times that number.

The brutal truth is that only a select minority of the American colonials attached themselves to the cause of independence with a spirit of selfless devotion. These were the dedicated souls who bore the burden of battle and the risks of defeat; these were the freedom-loving patriots who deserved the gratitude and esteem of generations yet unborn. Seldom have so few done so much for so many.

CHRONOLOGY

1650	First Navigation Laws to control colonial commerce
1696	Board of Trade assumes governance of colonies
1763	French and Indian War (Seven Years' War) ends
1764	Sugar Act
1765	Quartering Act
	Stamp Act
	Stamp Act Congress
1766	Declaratory Act
1767	Townshend Acts passed
	New York legislature suspended
1768	British troops occupy Boston
1770	Boston Massacre
	All Townshend Acts except tea tax repealed
1772	Committees of correspondence formed
1773	British East India Company granted tea monopoly
	Boston Tea Party
1774	Intolerable Acts
	Quebec Act
	First Continental Congress
	The Association boycotts British goods
1775	Battle of Lexington and Concord

Varying Viewpoints

Historians once assumed that the Revolution was just another chapter in the unfolding story of human liberty—an important way station in a kind of divinely ordained progress toward perfection in human affairs. This approach is often called the Whig view of history. Around the beginning of the twentieth century, the concept was challenged by the so-called progressive historians, who argued that not God but a sharp struggle among different social groups brought about change. Progressive historians, among them Carl Becker, saw the Revolution as stemming from class conflict and ending in a truly transformed social order. As Becker put it, the Revolution centered on the question not only of home rule, but also of "who should rule at home."

Since World War II two broad interpretations of the Revolution have contended with one another. One view, advanced by scholars like Gary Nash and Edward Countryman, builds on Becker's work and emphasizes class conflict in both the urban seaports and the isolated countryside. Attacks by laborers on political elites and expressions of resentment toward wealth are taken as evidence of a society that was breeding revolutionary change from within, quite aside from British provocations.

A generally more influential view has been most prominently developed by Bernard Bailyn. His argument proceeds from the assumptions that the British imperial system was not outrageously burdensome to the colonists and that colonial society was *already* fairly democratic before 1776 (at least as regarded white people, especially males). Why then, asks Bailyn, did a revolution occur at all, and in what exactly did it consist?

Interestingly, Bailyn emphasizes neither British economic affronts nor domestic political friction but deep-seated ideological and even psychological factors. Inspired by their reading of mainly seventeenth-century English political theorists, the Americans grew extraordinarily (perhaps even exaggeratedly) suspicious of any attempts to tighten the imperial reins on the colonies. These hypersensitive colonists regarded the British moves to impose various taxes and commercial regulations in the 1760s as part of a conspiracy by a corrupt British government to deprive them of not just their livelihoods but their liberty. Opposition to this "ministerial plot" drove the Americans to armed insurrection and further inspired them to define the essence of the Revolution in terms of an ideology of liberty that has colored American thought and political action ever since.

Select Readings

Primary Source Documents

Adam Smith's *An Inquiry into the Nature and Causes of the Wealth of Nations** (1776) is a penetrating analysis of British mercantilism. Patrick Henry's "Speech before the Virginia House of Burgesses against the Stamp Act"* (1765) was an influential statement of colonial opposition to British policy, as was John Dickinson's response to the Townshend Acts, *Letters from a Farmer in Pennsyl-* *vania* (1768). For contemporary accounts of the beginning of hostilities, see Peter Force, ed., *American Archives,* Fourth Series, Vol. 2 (1839).*

Secondary Sources

Edmund S. Morgan, *The Birth of the Republic, 1763–1789* (1959), is among the best brief accounts of the Revolutionary era. It stresses the happy coincidence of the revolutionaries' principles and their interests. Lawrence Gipson, *The Coming of the Revolution, 1763–1775* (1954), summarizes his 15-volume masterwork (cited in Chapter 5). Merrill Jensen, *The Founding of a Nation* (1968), is a more recent effort at a general synthesis, as is Robert Middlekauff's *The Glorious Cause: The American Revolution, 1763–1789* (1982). Robert R. Palmer, *The Age of the Democratic Revolution: A Political History of Europe and America, 1760–1800* (2 vols., 1959, 1964), masterfully places American events in the larger context of Western history. Three enlightening collections of essays are Jack P. Greene, ed., *The Reinterpretation of the American Revolution, 1763–1789* (1968); Stephen Kurtz and James Hutson, eds., *Essays on the American Revolution* (1973); and Alfred F. Young, ed., *The American Revolution* (1976), which generally represents a "new left" revisionist view, a perspective also found in Edward A. Countryman, *The American Revolution* (1987). An interesting effort to blend British and American perspectives is Ian R. Christie and Benjamin W. Labaree, *Empire or Independence, 1760–1776* (1976). The sources of American dissatisfaction with the British imperial system can be traced in Carl Ubbelohde, *The American Colonies in the British Empire, 1607–1763* (1968), and Thomas C. Barrow, *Trade and Empire: The British Customs Service in Colonial America* (1967). Oliver M. Dickerson, *The Navigation Acts and the American Revolution* (1951), concludes that the navigation system did not put undue burdens on the colonies. Bernhard Knollenberg examines the effects of the British tightening of the imperial system in the 1760s in *Origin of the American Revolution, 1759–1766* (1960), as does Michael Kammen in *Empire and Interest* (1970). John Shy imaginatively explores an important aspect of the imperial system's effect on America in *Toward Lexington: The Role of*

the British Army in the Coming of the American Revolution (1965). A perceptive short account of the American reaction to British initiatives is Edmund S. Morgan and Helen M. Morgan, *The Stamp Act Crisis* (1953). Benjamin W. Labaree discusses another instance of American reaction in *The Boston Tea Party* (1964). P. Maier focuses on the crucial role of the "mob" in *From Resistance to Revolution: Colonial Radicals and the Development of American Opposition to Britain, 1765–1776* (1972). The British side is told in Peter D. G. Thomas, *British Politics and the Stamp Act Crisis* (1975). Clinton Rossiter, *Seedtime of the Republic* (1953), stresses the importance of ideas in pushing the Revolution forward, as does Bernard Bailyn's seminal *Ideological Origins of the American Revolution* (1967), which also emphasizes the colonists' fears of a conspiracy against their liberties. John Philip Reid, on the other hand, emphasizes legal ideas in *Constitutional History of the American Revolution: The Authority of Rights* (1987). Helpful biographies of key Revolutionary figures include John C. Miller, *Sam Adams* (1936); Robert D. Meade, *Patrick Henry* (1957); Merrill D. Peterson, *Thomas Jefferson and the New Nation* (1970); Dumas Malone, *Jefferson and His Time* (5 vols., 1948–1974); and Pauline Maier, *The Old Revolutionaries: Political Lives in the Age of Samuel Adams* (1980). Imaginative cultural history is found in Robert A. Gross, *The Minutemen and Their World* (1976). Edward A. Countryman emphasizes class conflict in *A People in Revolution: The American Revolution and Political Society in New York, 1760–1790* (1981). Two recent books take a psychological approach to the problem of the Revolutionary generation's assault on established authority: Kenneth S. Lynn, *A Divided People* (1977), and Jay Fliegelman, *Prodigals and Pilgrims: The American Revolution against Patriarchal Authority, 1750–1800* (1982).

7

America Secedes from the Empire, 1775–1783

These are the times that try men's souls. The summer soldier and the sunshine patriot will, in this crisis, shrink from the service of their country; but he that stands it now, deserves the love and thanks of man and woman.

Thomas Paine, December 1776

Congress Drafts George Washington

Bloodshed at Lexington and Concord, in April of 1775, was a clarion call to arms. About twenty thousand musket-bearing "Minute Men" swarmed around Boston, there to coop up the outnumbered British.

The Second Continental Congress met in Philadelphia the next month, on May 10, 1775; and this time the full slate of thirteen colonies was represented. The conservative element in Congress was still strong, despite the shooting in Massachusetts. There was no real sentiment for independence—merely a desire to continue, fighting in the hope that king and Parliament would consent to a redress of grievances. Congress hopefully drafted new appeals to the British people and king—appeals that were spurned. Anticipating a possible rebuff, the delegates also adopted measures to raise money and to create an army and navy.

Perhaps the most important single action of the Congress was to select George Washington, one of its members already in officer's uniform, to head the hastily improvised army besieging Boston. This choice was made with considerable misgivings. The tall, powerfully built, dignified, blue-eyed Virginia planter, then forty-three, had never risen above the rank of a colonel in the militia. His largest command had numbered only twelve hundred men, and that had been some twenty years earlier. Falling short of true military genius, Washington was actually destined to lose more pitched battles than he won.

But the distinguished Virginian was gifted with outstanding powers of leadership and immense strength of character. He radiated pa-

The Skirmish on Lexington Green, 1775 *Trained British troops won a swift victory in this first encounter with the green colonial militiamen, but by the end of the day the Americans inflicted heavy casualties on the Redcoats during the bloody British retreat from Concord. (New York Public Library, Picture Collection.)*

tience, courage, self-discipline, and a sense of justice. He was a ~~great moral force rather than~~ a ~~great military mind~~—a symbol and a rallying point. People instinctively trusted him; they sensed that when he put himself at the head of a cause, he was prepared, if necessary, to go down with the ship. He insisted on serving without pay, though he kept a careful expense account amounting to more than $100,000. Later he sternly reprimanded his steward at Mount Vernon for providing the enemy, under duress, with supplies. He would have preferred instead to see the enemy put the torch to his mansion.

The Continental Congress, though dimly perceiving Washington's qualities of leadership, chose more wisely than it knew. ~~His selection, in truth, was largely political. Americans in other sections, already jealous, were beginning to distrust the large New England army being collected around Boston.~~ Prudence suggested a commander from Virginia, the largest and most populous of the colonies. As a ~~man of wealth,~~ both by inheritance and by marriage, Washington ~~could not be accused of being a fortune~~ seeker. As an ~~aristocrat,~~ he could be counted on to ~~check the excesses of the masses.~~

Martha Washington (1732–1802) *Destined to be the first First Lady, she was the daughter of a prominent Virginia planter. Her first husband died, leaving her a wealthy young widow with two children. Two years later she married George Washington. Known as "Lady Washington" for her charm and aristocratic graciousness, she brought considerable status to the Patriot cause. She bore Washington no children. It was said that fate had ordained that he was to be only the Father of his Country.*

Bunker Hill and Hessian Hirelings

The clash of arms continued on a strangely contradictory basis. On the one hand, the Americans were emphatically affirming their loyalty to the king and earnestly voicing their desire to patch up existing difficulties. On the other hand, they were raising armies and shooting down His Majesty's soldiers. This curious war of inconsistency was fought for fourteen long months—from April 1775 to July 1776—before the fateful plunge into independence was taken.

Gradually the tempo of warfare increased. In May 1775 a tiny American force, under Ethan Allen and Benedict Arnold, surprised and captured the British garrisons at Ticonderoga and Crown Point, on the scenic lakes of upper New York. A priceless store of powder and artillery for the siege of Boston was thus secured. In June 1775 the colonials seized a hill, now known as Bunker Hill (actually Breed's Hill), from which they menaced the enemy in Boston. The British, instead of cutting off the retreat of their foes by flanking them, blundered bloodily when they launched a frontal attack with three thousand men. Sharpshooting Americans, numbering fifteen hundred and strongly entrenched, mowed down the advancing foe with frightful slaughter. But the colonials' scanty store of powder finally gave out, and they were forced to abandon the hill in disorder. With two more such victories, remarked the French foreign minister, the British would have no army left in America.

Following Bunker Hill, the king slammed the door on all hope of reconciliation. In August 1775 he formally proclaimed the colonies in rebellion, with all that this implied in the way of future hangings. The next month he further widened the chasm when he completed arrangements for hiring thousands of German troops (so-called Hessians) to help crush his rebellious subjects. Six German princes involved in the transaction needed the money (one reputedly had seventy-four children); George III needed the men.

News of the Hessian deal shocked the colonials. The quarrel, they felt, was within the family. Why bring in outside mercenaries, especially fiercely mustached foreigners, who had

an exaggerated reputation for butchery and bestiality?

Hessian hirelings proved to be good soldiers in a mechanical sense, but many of them were more interested in booty than in duty. For good reason they were dubbed "Hessian flies." Seduced by American promises of land, hundreds of them finally deserted and remained in the United States to become respected citizens.

The Abortive Conquest of Canada

The unsheathed sword continued to take its toll. In October 1775, on the eve of a cruel winter, the British burned Falmouth (Portland), Maine. In that same autumn the rebels daringly undertook a two-pronged invasion of Canada. American leaders believed, erroneously, that the conquered French were explosively restive under the British yoke. A successful assault on Canada would add a fourteenth colony, while depriving Britain of a valuable base for striking at the colonies in revolt. But this large-scale attack, involving some two thousand American troops, contradicted the claim of the colonials that they were merely fighting defensively for a redress of grievances. Invasion northward was undisguised offensive warfare.

This bold stroke for Canada narrowly missed success. One invading column under the Irish-born General Richard Montgomery, formerly of the British army, pushed up the Lake Champlain route and captured Montreal. He was joined at Quebec by the bedraggled army of General Benedict Arnold, whose men had been reduced to eating dogs and shoe leather during their grueling march through the Maine woods. An assault on Quebec, launched on the last day of 1775, was beaten off. The able Montgomery was killed; the dashing Arnold was wounded in one leg. Scattered remnants under his command retreated up the St. Lawrence River, reversing the way Montgomery had come. French-Canadian leaders, who had been generously treated by the British in the Quebec Act of 1774, showed no real desire to welcome the plundering anti-Catholic invaders.

Bitter fighting continued in the colonies, though the Americans still disclaimed all desire

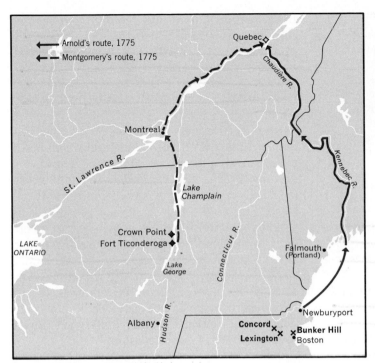

Revolution in the North, 1775–1776
Benedict Arnold's troops were described as "pretty young men" when they sailed from Massachusetts. They were considerably less pretty on their arrival in Quebec, after eight weeks of struggling through wet and frigid forests, often without food. "No one can imagine," one of them wrote, "the sweetness of a roasted shot-pouch [ammunition bag] to the famished appetite."

for independence. In ~~January 1776~~, the British set fire to the Virginia town of Norfolk. In March they were finally forced to evacuate Boston, taking with them the leading friends of the king. (Evacuation Day is still celebrated annually in Boston.) In the South the rebellious colonials won two victories in 1776—one in February against some fifteen hundred Loyalists at Moore's Creek Bridge, in North Carolina, and the other in June against an invading British fleet at Charleston harbor.

Thomas Paine Preaches Common Sense

Why did Americans continue to deny any ~~inten~~tion of independence? ~~Loyalty to the empire was deeply ingrained; colonial unity was poor;~~ and ~~open rebellion was dangerous~~, especially against a formidable Britain. Irish rebels of that day were customarily hanged, drawn, and quartered. American rebels might have fared no better. As late as January 1776—five months before independence was declared—the king's health was being toasted by the officers of

Washington's mess near Boston. "God save the king" had not yet been replaced by "God save the Congress."

Gradually the Americans were shocked into an awareness of their inconsistency. Their eyes were jolted open by harsh British acts like the burning of Falmouth and Norfolk, and especially by the hiring of the Hessians.

Then in ~~1776~~ came the ~~publication of Common Sense,~~ one of the most influential pamphlets ever written. Its author was the radical ~~Thomas Paine,~~ once an impoverished corsetmaker's apprentice, who had come over from England a year earlier. His tract became a whirlwind ~~best-seller~~ and within a few months reached the astonishing total of 120,000 copies.

Paine flatly branded the shilly-shallying of the colonials as contrary to "common sense." Why not throw off the cloak of inconsistency? ~~Nowhere in the physical universe did~~ the ~~smaller heavenly body control the larger one.~~ Then ~~why should the tiny island of England control the vast continent of America?~~ As for the king, whom the Americans professed to revere, he was nothing but "the Royal Brute of Great Britain." ~~America had a sacred mission—a~~

> Paine rose to heights of eloquence in **Common Sense:** *"O! ye that love mankind! Ye that dare oppose not only the tyranny but the tyrant, stand forth! Every spot of the Old World is overrun with oppression. Freedom hath been hunted round the globe. Asia and Africa have long expelled her. Europe regards her as a stranger and England hath given her warning to depart. O! receive the fugitive and prepare in time an asylum for mankind."*

moral obligation to the world—to set herself up as an independent, democratic republic, untainted by association with corrupt and monarchical Britain.

Paine's passionate protest was eloquent and radical—even doubly radical. It called not simply for independence, but for republicanism. Paine thus penned both persuasive propaganda and potent political theory. He helped thousands of American waverers, hesitant to make the break with Britain, to see that their cause embraced *both* self-determination and democracy. He also forcefully reminded them that they could not hope for open aid from France as long as they swore allegiance to the British king. The French crown was interested in destroying the British empire, not in helping to reconstruct it under a plan of reconciliation.

Jefferson's "Explanation" of Independence

Members of the Philadelphia Congress, instructed by their respective colonies, gradually edged toward a clean break. On June 7, 1776, fiery Richard Henry Lee of Virginia moved that "These United Colonies are, and of right ought to be, free and independent states. . . ." After considerable debate, the motion was adopted nearly a month later, on July 2, 1776.

The passing of Lee's resolution was the formal "declaration" of independence by the American colonies, and technically this was all that was needed to cut the British tie. John Adams wrote confidently that ever thereafter July 2 would be celebrated annually with fireworks.

But something more was required. An epochal rupture of this kind called for some formal explanation to "a candid world." An inspirational appeal was also needed to enlist other English colonies in the Americas, to invite assistance from foreign nations, and to rally resistance at home.

Shortly after Lee made his memorable motion on June 7, Congress appointed a committee to prepare an appropriate statement. The task of drafting it fell to Thomas Jefferson, a tall, freckled, sandy-haired Virginia lawyer of thirty-three. Despite his youth, he was already recognized as a brilliant writer, and he measured up splendidly to his opportunity. After some debate and amendment, the Declaration of Independence was formally approved by the Congress on July 4, 1776. It might better have been called "the Explanation of Independence" or, as one contemporary described it, "Mr. Jefferson's advertisement of Mr. Lee's resolution."

Jefferson's pronouncement, couched in a lofty style, was magnificent. He gave his appeal universality by invoking the "natural rights" of humankind—not just British rights. He argued persuasively that because the king had flouted these rights, the colonials were justified in cutting their connection. He then set forth a long list of the presumably tyrannous misdeeds of George III. The overdrawn bill of indictment included imposing taxes without consent, dispensing with trial by jury, abolishing valued laws, establishing a military dictatorship, maintaining standing armies in peacetime, cutting off trade, burning towns, hiring mercenaries, and inciting hostility among the Indians.[*]

Jefferson's withering blast was admittedly one-sided. But he was in effect the prosecuting attorney, and he took certain liberties with historical truth. He was not writing history; he was making it through what has been called "the world's greatest editorial." He owned many slaves, and his affirmation that "all men are created equal" was to haunt him and his fellow citizens for generations.

The formal declaration of independence cleared the air as a thundershower does on a

---

[*]For an annotated text of the Declaration of Independence, see the Appendix.

George III (1738–1820) *America's last king, he was a good man, unlike some of his scandal-tainted brothers and sons, but a bad king. Doggedly determined to regain arbitrary power for the crown, he antagonized and then lost the thirteen American colonies. During much of his sixty-year reign, he seemed to be insane, but recently medical science has found that he was suffering from a rare metabolic and hereditary disease called porphyria. (Reproduced by courtesy of the Trustees of the British Museum.)*

muggy day. Foreign aid could be solicited with greater hope of success. Those patriots who defied the king were now rebels, not loving subjects shooting their way into reconciliation. They must all hang together, Franklin is said to have grimly remarked, or they would all hang separately. Or, in the eloquent language of the great declaration, "We mutually pledge to each other our lives, our fortunes and our sacred honor."

Jefferson's defiant Declaration of Independence had a universal impact unmatched by any other American document. This "shout heard round the world" has been a source of inspiration to countless revolutionary movements against arbitrary authority. Lafayette hung a copy on a wall in his home, leaving beside it room for a future French Declaration of the Rights of Man—a declaration that was officially born thirteen years later.

Patriots and Loyalists

The War of Independence, strictly speaking, was a war within a war. Colonials loyal to the king (Loyalists) fought the American rebels (Patriots), while the rebels also fought the British redcoats. Loyalists were derisively called "Tories," after the dominant political factions in England, while Patriots were called "Whigs," after the opposition factions in England. A popular definition of a Tory among the Patriots betrayed bitterness: "A Tory is a thing whose head is in England, and its body in America, and its neck ought to be stretched."

Like many revolutions, the American Revolution was a minority movement. Many colonists were apathetic or neutral, including those Byrds of Virginia who sat on the fence. The opposing forces contended not only against each other but also for the allegiance and support of the civilian population. In this struggle for the hearts and minds of the people, the British proved fatally inept, and the Patriot militias played a crucial role. The British military proved able to control only those areas where it could maintain a massive military presence. Elsewhere, as soon as the redcoats had marched on, the rebel militiamen appeared and took up the task of "political education"—sometimes by coercive means. Often lacking bayonets but always loaded with political zeal, the ragtag militia units proved remarkably effective agents of Revolutionary ideas. They convinced many colonists, even those indifferent to indepen-

> The American signers had reason to fear for their necks. In 1802, twenty-six years later, George III approved this death sentence for seven Irish rebels: ". . . you are to be hanged by the neck, but not until you are dead; for while you are still living your bodies are to be taken down, your bowels torn out and burned before your faces, your heads then cut off, and your bodies divided each into four quarters, and your heads and quarters to be then at the King's disposal; and may the Almighty God have mercy on your souls."

New York Patriots Pull down the Statue of King George III *Erected after the repeal of the Stamp Act in 1766, this statue was melted down by the revolutionaries into bullets to be used against the king's troops. (Dr. Gilbert Darlington Collection.)*

dence, that the British army was an unreliable friend and that they had better throw in their lot with the Patriot cause. They also mercilessly harassed small British detachments and occupation forces. One British officer ruefully observed that "the Americans would be less dangerous if they had a regular army."

Loyalists, numbering perhaps 20 percent of the American people, remained true to their king. Families often split over the issue of independence: Benjamin Franklin supported the Patriot side, while his handsome illegitimate son, William Franklin (the last royal governor of New Jersey), upheld the Loyalist cause.

The Loyalists were tragic figures. For generations the English in the New World had been taught fidelity to their king. Loyalty is ordinarily regarded as a major virtue—loyalty to one's family, one's friends, one's country. If the king had triumphed, as he seemed likely to do, the Loyalists would have been acclaimed patriots, and defeated rebels like Washington would have been disgraced, severely punished, and probably forgotten.

Conservative Americans generally remained loyal—the people of education and wealth, of culture and caution. These moderate souls were satisfied with their lot and believed that any violent change would only be for the worse. They feared that the "dirty rabble," inflamed by violence, might break out of control. "If I must be devoured," moaned one aristocrat, "let me be devoured by the jaws of a lion, and not gnawed to death by rats and vermin." Loyalists were also more numerous among the older generation. Young people make revolutions, and from the outset energetic, purposeful, and militant young people surged forward—figures like the sleeplessly scheming Samuel Adams and the impassioned Patrick Henry. His flaming outcry before the Virginia Assembly—"Give me liberty or give me death!"—still quickens patriotic pulses.

Loyalists also included the king's officers and other beneficiaries of the crown—people who knew which side their daily bread came from. The same was generally true of the Anglican clergy and a large portion of their flocks, all of whom had long been taught obedience to the king.

Usually the Loyalists were most numerous where the Anglican church was strongest. A notable exception was Virginia, where the debt-burdened Anglican aristocrats flocked into the rebel camp. The king's followers were well entrenched in aristocratic New York City and Charleston, and also in Quaker Pennsylvania and New Jersey, where General Washington felt that he was fighting in "the enemy's country." While his men were starving at Valley Forge, nearby Pennsylvania farmers were selling their produce to the British for the king's gold.

Loyalists were least numerous in New England, where self-government was especially strong and mercantilism was especially weak. Rebels were the most numerous where Presbyterianism and Congregationalism flourished, notably in New England. Invading British armies vented their contempt and anger by using Yankee churches for pigsties.

The Loyalist Exodus

Before the Declaration of Independence in 1776, persecution of the Loyalists was relatively mild. Yet they were subjected to some brutality, including tarring and feathering and riding astride fence rails.

After the Declaration of Independence, which sharply separated Loyalists from Patriots, harsher methods prevailed. The rebels naturally desired a united front. Putting loyalty to the colonies first, they regarded their opponents, not themselves, as traitors. Loyalists were roughly handled; hundreds were imprisoned; and a few noncombatants were hanged. But there was no wholesale reign of terror comparable to that which later bloodied both France and Russia. For one thing, the colonials reflected Anglo-Saxon regard for order; for another, the leading Loyalists were prudent enough to flee to the British lines.

About eighty thousand loyal supporters of George III were driven out or fled, but several hundred thousand or so of the mild Loyalists were permitted to stay. The estates of many of the fugitives were confiscated and sold—a relatively painless way of helping to finance the war. Confiscation often worked great hardship, as, for example, when two aristocratic old ladies

Tory Suspended, While Goose Is Plucked for Coat of Feathers *(The Bettmann Archive, Inc.)*

were forced to live in their former chicken house.

Some fifty thousand Loyalist volunteers at one time or another bore arms for the British. They also helped the king's cause by serving as spies, by inciting the Indians, and by keeping Patriot soldiers at home to protect their families. Ardent Loyalists had their hearts in their cause, and a major blunder of the haughty British was not to make full use of them in the fighting.

General Washington at Bay

With Boston evacuated in March 1776, the British concentrated on New York as a base of operations. Here was a splendid seaport, centrally located, where the king could count on cooperation from the numerous Loyalists. An awe-inspiring British fleet appeared off New York in July 1776. It consisted of some five hundred ships and thirty five thousand men—the largest armed force to be seen in America until the Civil War. General Washington, dangerously outnumbered, could muster only eighteen thousand ill-trained troops with which to meet the crack army of the invader.

Disaster befell the Americans in the summer and fall of 1776. Outgeneraled and outmaneuvered, they were routed at the Battle of Long Island, where panic seized the raw recruits. By the narrowest of margins, and thanks to a favoring wind and fog, Washington escaped to Manhattan Island. Retreating northward, he crossed the Hudson River to New Jersey and finally reached the Delaware River with the British close at his heels. Tauntingly, enemy buglers sounded the fox-hunting call, so familiar to Virginians of Washington's day. The Patriot cause was at low ebb when the rebel remnants fled across the river, after collecting all available boats to forestall pursuit.

The wonder is that Washington's adversary, General William Howe, did not speedily crush the demoralized American forces. But he was no military genius, and he well remembered the horrible slaughter at Bunker Hill, where he had commanded. The country was rough, supplies were slow in coming, and as a professional soldier Howe did not relish the rigors of winter campaigning. He evidently found more agreeable the bedtime company of his mistress, the wife of one of his subordinates—a scandal with which American satirists had a good deal of ribald fun.

Washington, who was now almost counted out, stealthily recrossed the ice-clogged Delaware River. At Trenton, on December 26, 1776, he surprised and captured a thousand Hessians who were sleeping off the effects of their Christmas celebration. A week later, leaving his campfires burning as a ruse, he slipped away and inflicted a sharp defeat on a smaller British detachment at Princeton. This brilliant New Jersey campaign, crowned by these two lifesaving victories, revealed "Old Fox" Washington at his military best.

Burgoyne's Blundering Invasion

London officials adopted an intricate scheme for capturing the vital Hudson River Valley in 1777. If successful, the British would sever New England from the rest of the states and paralyze the American cause. The main invading force, under an actor-playwright-soldier, General ("Gentleman Johnny") Burgoyne, would push down the Lake Champlain route from Canada. General Howe's troops in New York, if needed, could advance up the Hudson River to meet Burgoyne near Albany. A third and much smaller British force, commanded by Colonel St. Leger, would come in from the west by way of Lake Ontario and the Mohawk Valley.

British planners did not reckon with General Benedict Arnold. After his repulse at Quebec in 1775, he had retreated slowly along the St. Lawrence River back to the Lake Champlain area, by heroic efforts keeping an army in the field. The British had pursued his tattered force to Lake Champlain in 1776. But they could not move farther south until they had won control of the lake, which, in the absence of roads, was indispensable for carrying their supplies.

Tireless, Arnold assembled a small fleet, and the British had to stop to construct a larger one. His tiny flotilla was finally destroyed after desperate fighting, but winter was descending and the British were forced to retire to Canada. General Burgoyne had to start anew from this base

New York and New Jersey, 1776–1777

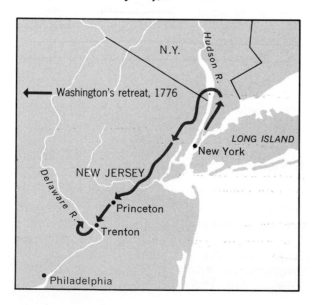

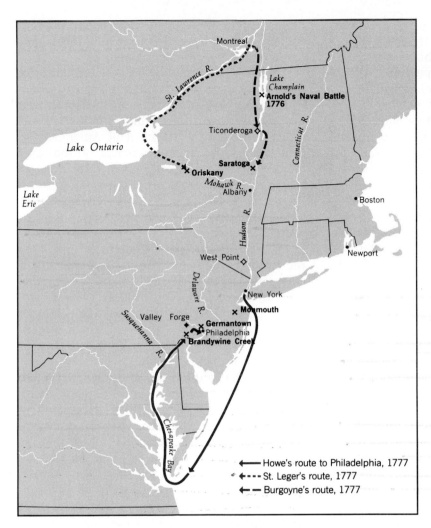

New York–Pennsylvania Theater, 1777–1778 *Distinguished members of the Continental Congress fled from Philadelphia in near-panic as the British army approached. Thomas Paine reported that at three o'clock in the morning the streets were "as full of Men, Women, and Children as on a Market Day." John Adams had anticipated that "I shall run away, I suppose, with the rest," since "we are too brittle ware, you know, to stand the dashing of balls and bombs." Adams got his chance to decamp with the others into the interior of Pennsylvania and tried to put the best face on things. "This tour," he commented, "has given me an opportunity of seeing many parts of this country which I never saw before."*

the following year. If Arnold had not contributed his daring and skill, the British invaders of 1776 almost certainly would have penetrated as far south as Fort Ticonderoga. If Burgoyne had started from this springboard in 1777, instead of Canada, he almost certainly would have succeeded in his venture. (At last the apparently futile American invasion of Canada in 1775 was beginning to pay rich dividends.)

General Burgoyne began his fateful invasion with seven thousand regular troops. He was encumbered by a heavy baggage train and a considerable number of women, many of whom were wives of his officers. Progress was painfully slow, for sweaty axmen had to chop a path through the forest, while American militiamen began to gather like hornets on Burgoyne's flanks.

~~General How~~e, meanwhile, was causing astonished eyebrows to rise. At a time when it seemed obvious that he ~~should be starting~~ up ~~the Hudson River from New York~~ to join his slowly advancing colleague, he ~~deliberately embarked with the main British~~ army for an attack ~~on Philadelphia,~~ the rebel capital. As scholars now know, he wanted ~~to force a general engagement with Washington's army, destroy it, and leave the path wide open for Burgoyne's thrust.~~ Howe apparently assumed that he had ample time to assist Burgoyne directly, should he be needed.

General Washington, keeping a wary eye on the British in New York, hastily transferred his army to the vicinity of Philadelphia. There, late in 1777, he was defeated in two pitched battles, at Brandywine Creek and Germantown. Pleasure-loving General Howe then settled down comfortably in the lively capital, leaving Burgoyne to flounder through the wilds of upper New York. Benjamin Franklin, recently sent to Paris as an envoy, truthfully jested that Howe had not captured Philadelphia but that Philadelphia had captured Howe. Washington finally retired to winter quarters at Valley Forge, a strong, hilly position some twenty miles northwest of Philadelphia, and there his frostbitten and hungry men were short of about everything except misery. This rabble was nevertheless whipped into a professional army by the recently arrived Prussian drillmaster, the profane but patient Baron von Steuben.

Burgoyne meanwhile had begun to bog down north of Albany, while a host of American militiamen, scenting the kill, swarmed about him. In a series of sharp engagements, in which General Arnold was again shot in the leg wounded at Quebec, the British army was trapped. Meanwhile the Americans had driven back St. Leger's force at Oriskany. Unable to advance or retreat, Burgoyne was forced to surrender his entire command at Saratoga, on October 17, 1777, to the American General Gates.

Saratoga ranks high among the decisive battles of both American and world history. The victory immensely revived the faltering colonial cause. Even more important, it made possible the urgently needed foreign aid from France which in turn helped ensure American independence.

Strange French Bedfellows

France, thirsting for revenge, was eager to inflame the quarrel that had broken out in America. The New World colonies were by far Britain's most valuable overseas possessions. If they could be wrested from Britain, it presumably would cease to be a front-rank power. France might then regain its former position and prestige, the loss of which in the recent Seven Years' War rankled deeply.

America's cause rapidly became something of a fad in France. The bored aristocracy, which had developed some interest in the writings of liberal French thinkers like Rousseau, was rather intrigued by the ideal of American liberty. Hardheaded French officials, on the other hand, were not prompted by a love for America but by a realistic concern for the interests of France. Any marriage with the United States would be strictly one of convenience.

After the shooting at Lexington, in April 1775, the French agents undertook to blow on the embers. They secretly provided the Americans with lifesaving amounts of powder and other munitions, chiefly through a sham company rigged up for that purpose. About 90 percent of all the gunpowder used by the Americans in the first two and a half years of the war came from French arsenals.

Secrecy enshrouded all these French schemes. Open aid to the American rebels might provoke England into a declaration of war; and France, still weakened by its recent defeat, was not ready to fight. It feared that the American rebellion might fade out, for the colonies were proclaiming their desire to patch up differences. But the Declaration of Independence in 1776 showed that the Americans really meant business; and the smashing victory at Saratoga seemed to indicate that they had an excellent chance of winning their freedom.

After the humiliation at Saratoga in 1777, the British Parliament belatedly passed a measure that in effect offered the Americans home rule within the empire. This was essentially all that the colonials had ever asked for—except independence. If the French were going to break up the British Empire, they would have to bestir themselves. Wily and bespectacled old Benjamin Franklin, whose simple fur cap and witty sayings had captivated the French public, played skillfully on France's fears of reconciliation.

The French king, Louis XVI, was reluctant to intervene. Although somewhat stupid, he was alert enough to see grave dangers in aiding the

Americans openly and incurring war with Britain. But his ministers at length won him over. They argued that hostilities were inevitable, sooner or later, to undo the victor's peace of 1763. If England should regain its colonies, it might join with them to seize the sugar-rich French West Indies and thus secure compensation for the cost of the recent rebellion. The French had better fight while they could have an American ally, rather than wait and fight both Britain and its reunited colonials.

So France, in 1778, offered the Americans a treaty of alliance. Their treaty promised everything that Britain was offering—plus independence. Both allies bound themselves to wage war until the United States had won its freedom and until both agreed to terms with the common foe.

This was the first entangling military alliance in the experience of the Republic and one that later caused prolonged trouble. The American people, with ingrained isolationist tendencies, accepted the French entanglement with distaste. They were painfully aware that it involved a hereditary foe that was also a Roman Catholic power. But when one's house is on fire, one does not inquire too closely into the background of those who carry the water buckets.

After concluding the alliance, France sent a minister to America, to the delight of one Patriot journalist: "Who would have thought that the American colonies, imperfectly known in Europe a few years ago and claimed by every pettifogging lawyer in the House of Commons, every cobbler in the beer-houses of London, as a part of their property, should to-day receive an ambassador from the most powerful monarchy in Europe."

The Colonial War Becomes a World War

England and France thus came to blows in 1778, and the shot fired at Lexington rapidly widened into a global conflagration. Spain entered the fray against Britain in 1779, as did Holland. Combined Spanish and French fleets outnumbered those of England, and on two occasions the British Isles seemed to be at the mercy of hostile warships.

The weak maritime neutrals of Europe, who had suffered from Britain's dominance over the seas, now began to demand more respect for

Britain against the World

BRITAIN AND ALLIES		ENEMY OR UNFRIENDLY POWERS
Great Britain Some Loyalists and Indians 30,000 hired Hessians *(Total population on Britain's side: c. 8 million)*	Belligerents *(Total population: c. 39.5 million)*	United States, 1775–1783 France, 1778–1783 Spain, 1779–1783 Holland, 1779–1783
		Ireland (restive)
	Members of the Armed Neutrality (with dates of joining)	Russia, 1780 Denmark-Norway, 1780 Sweden, 1780 Holy Roman Empire, 1781 Prussia, 1782 Portugal, 1782 Two Sicilies, 1783 (after peace signed)

their rights. ~~In 1780 the imperious Catherine the Great of Russia took the lead in organizing the Armed Neutrality,~~ which she later sneeringly called the "Armed Nullity." It lined up almost all the remaining European neutrals in an ~~attitude of passive hostility toward England.~~ The war was now being ~~fought not only in Europe and North America, but also in South America, the Caribbean, and Asia.~~

To say that America, with some French aid, defeated England is like saying, "Daddy and I killed the bear." ~~To England,~~ struggling for its very life, the ~~scuffle in the New World became secondary.~~ The Americans deserve credit for having kept the war going until 1778, with secret French aid. But they did not achieve their independence until the conflict erupted into a multipower world war that was too big for Britain to handle. From 1~~778 to 1783, France provided the rebels with large sums of money, immense amounts of equipment, about one-half of America's regular armed forces, and practically all of the new nation's naval strength.~~

France's entrance into the conflict ~~forced the British to change their basic strategy in America. Hitherto they could count on blockading the colonial coast and commanding the seas.~~

War in the South, 1780–1781

Now the ~~French had powerful fleets~~ in American waters, chiefly to protect their own valuable West Indian islands, but ~~in a position to jeopardize Britain's blockade and lines of supply.~~ The British therefore decided to ~~evacuate Philadelphia and concentrate their strength in New York City.~~

In June 1778 the withdrawing redcoats were attacked by General Washington at Monmouth, New Jersey, on a blisteringly hot day. Scores of men collapsed or died from sunstroke. But the battle was indecisive, and the British escaped to New York, although about one-third of their Hessians deserted. Henceforth, except for the Yorktown interlude of 1781, Washington remained in the New York area hemming in the British.

Blow and Counterblow

In the summer of 1780 a powerful French army of six thousand regular troops, commanded by the Comte de Rochambeau, arrived in Newport, Rhode Island. The Americans were somewhat suspicious of their former enemies; in fact, several ugly flare-ups, involving minor bloodshed, had already occurred between the new allies. But French gold and goodwill melted restraints. Dancing parties were arranged with the prim Puritan maidens; and one French officer related, doubtless with exaggeration, "The simple innocence of the Garden of Eden prevailed." No real military advantage came immediately from this French reinforcement, although preparations were made for a Franco-American attack on New York.

Improving American morale was staggered later in 1~~780, when General Benedict Arnold turned traitor.~~ A leader of undoubted dash and brilliance, he was ambitious, greedy, unscrupulous, and suffering from a well-grounded but petulant feeling that his valuable services were not fully appreciated. He plotted with the British to sell out the key stronghold of West Point, which commanded the Hudson River, for £6,300 and an officer's commission. By the sheerest accident the plot was detected in the nick of time, and Arnold fled to the British. "Whom can we trust now?" cried General Washington in anguish.

The British meanwhile had devised a plan to roll up the colonies, beginning with the South, where the Loyalists were numerous. The colony of Georgia was ruthlessly overrun in 1778–1779; Charleston, South Carolina, fell in 1780. The surrender of the city to the British involved the capture of five thousand men and four hundred cannon and was a heavier loss to the Americans, in relation to existing strength, than that of Burgoyne was to the British.

Warfare now intensified in the Carolinas, where Patriots bitterly fought their Loyalist neighbors. It was not uncommon for prisoners on both sides to be butchered in cold blood after they had thrown down their arms. A turn of the tide came later in 1780 and early in 1781, when American riflemen wiped out a British detachment at King's Mountain and then defeated a smaller force at Cowpens. In the Carolina campaign of 1781, General Nathanael Greene, a Quaker-reared tactician, distinguished himself by his strategy of delay. Standing and then retreating, he exhausted his foe, General Cornwallis, in vain pursuit. By losing battles but winning campaigns, the "Fighting Quaker" finally succeeded in clearing most of Georgia and South Carolina of British troops.

The Land Frontier and the Sea Frontier

The West was ablaze during much of the war. Indian allies of George III, hoping to protect their land, were busy with torch and tomahawk; they were egged on by British agents branded as "hair buyers" because they allegedly paid bounties for American scalps. Fateful 1777 was known as "the bloody year" on the frontier. Yet the human tide of westward-moving pioneers did not halt its flow. Eloquent testimony is provided by place names in Kentucky, such as Lexington (named after the battle) and Louisville (named after America's new ally, Louis XVI).

In the wild Illinois country the British were vulnerable to attack, for they held scattered posts which they had captured from the French. An audacious frontiersman, George Rogers Clark, conceived the idea of seizing

Joseph Brant, Mohawk Chief *Siding with the British, Brant led Indian frontier raids so ferocious that he was dubbed "monster Brant." When he later met King George III, he declined to kiss the king's hand, but asked instead to kiss the hand of the queen. (New York State Historical Association, Cooperstown, New York.)*

these forts by surprise. With the blessing of Virginia and £1,200 in depreciated currency, he floated down the Ohio River with about 175 men and captured in quick succession the forts Kaskaskia, Cahokia, and Vincennes. These daring forays no doubt helped quiet the Indians. But Clark's admirers have also assumed, without positive proof, that his occupation of the southwest corner of the great area north of the Ohio River forced the British to cede the whole region to the United States at the peace table in Paris.

America's infant navy had meanwhile been laying the foundations of a brilliant tradition. The naval establishment consisted of only a handful of nondescript ships, commanded by daring officers, the most famous of whom was a hard-fighting young Scotsman, John Paul Jones. As events turned out, this tiny naval

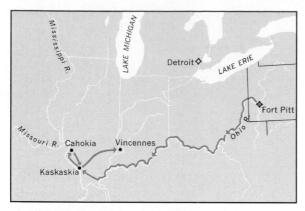

George Rogers Clark's Campaign, 1778–1779

force never made a real dent in Britain's thunderous fleets. Its chief contribution was in destroying British merchant shipping and thus carrying the war into the waters around the British Isles. An English song of the time, critical of the Royal Navy, began:

> The tradesmen stand still, and the merchant
>   bemoans
> The losses he meets with from such as Paul
>   Jones.

More numerous and damaging than ships of the regular American navy were swift privateers. These craft were privately owned armed ships—legalized pirates in a sense—specifically authorized by Congress to prey on enemy shipping. Altogether over a thousand American privateers, responding to the call of patriotism and profit, sallied forth with about seventy thousand men ("sailors of fortune"). They captured some six hundred British prizes, while British warships captured about as many American merchantmen and privateers.

Privateering was not an unalloyed asset. It had the unfortunate effect of diverting manpower from the main war effort and involving Americans, including Benedict Arnold, in speculation and graft. But the privateers brought in urgently needed gold, harassed the enemy, and raised American morale by providing victories at a time when victories were few. British shipping was so badly riddled by privateers and by the regular American navy that insurance rates skyrocketed. Merchant ships were compelled to

sail in convoy, and British shippers and manufacturers brought increasing pressure on Parliament to end the war on honorable terms.

Yorktown and the Final Curtain

One of the darkest periods of the war was 1780–1781, before the last decisive victory. Inflation of the currency was continuing at full gallop. Not only was the government virtually bankrupt but Congress had been forced to repudiate its financial obligations, in part, on a forty-to-one basis. Despair was prevalent; disunion was increasing among the states, and mutiny over back pay was spreading in the army.

Meanwhile the British General Cornwallis was blundering into a trap. After futile operations in Virginia, he had fallen back to Chesapeake Bay at Yorktown, there to await seaborne supplies and reinforcements. He assumed that Britain would continue to control the sea. But these few fateful weeks just happened to be one of the brief periods during the war in America when British naval superiority slipped away.

The French were now prepared to cooperate energetically in a brilliant stroke. Admiral de Grasse, operating with a powerful fleet in the West Indies, advised the Americans that he was free to join with them in an assault on Cornwallis at Yorktown. Quick to seize this opportunity, General Washington made a swift march of more than 300 miles (483 kilometers) to the Chesapeake from the New York area. Accompanied by Rochambeau's French army, he beset the British by land, while De Grasse blockaded them by sea after beating off the British fleet. Completely cornered, Cornwallis surrendered his entire force of seven thousand men, on October 19, 1781, as his band appropriately played "The World Turn'd Upside Down." The triumph was no less French than American: the French provided essentially all the seapower and about half of the regular troops in the besieging army of some sixteen thousand men.

Stunned by news of the disaster, Prime Minister Lord North cried, "Oh God! It's all over! It's all over!" But it was not. George III stubbornly planned to continue the struggle, for

> Lord George Germain, secretary of state for the colonies and a chief architect of war plans, swelled with confidence after Yorktown: "So very contemptible is the Rebel Force now in all Parts, and so vast is Our Superiority everywhere, that no resistance on their [Americans'] Part is to be apprehended, that can materially obstruct the Progress of the King's Army in the Speedy Suppression of the Rebellion."

England was far from being crushed. It still had fifty-four thousand troops in North America, including thirty-two thousand in the United States. Washington returned with his army to New York, there to continue keeping a vigilant eye on the British force of ten thousand men.

Fighting actually continued for more than a year after Yorktown, with Patriot-Loyalist warfare in the South especially savage. "No quarter for Tories" was the common battle cry. One of Washington's most valuable contributions was to keep the languishing cause alive, the army in the field, and the states together during these critical months. Otherwise a satisfactory peace treaty might never have been signed.

Peace at Paris

After Yorktown, the war-weary British were increasingly ready to come to terms. They had suffered heavy reverses in India and in the West Indies. The island of Minorca in the Mediterranean had fallen; the Rock of Gibraltar was tottering. Lord North's ministry collapsed in March 1782, temporarily ending the personal rule of George III. A Whig ministry, rather favorable to the Americans, replaced the Tory regime of Lord North.

Three American peace negotiators had meanwhile gathered at Paris: the aging but astute Benjamin Franklin; the flinty John Adams, vigilant for New England interests; and the impulsive John Jay of New York, deeply suspicious of Old World intrigue. The three envoys had explicit instructions from Congress to make no separate peace and to consult with their French allies at all stages of the negotiations. But the American representatives chafed under this directive. They well knew that it had been written by a subservient Congress, with the French Foreign Office indirectly guiding the pen.

France was in a painful position. It had induced Spain to enter the war on its side, in part by promising to deliver British-held Gibraltar. Yet the towering rock was defying frantic joint assaults by French and Spanish troops. Spain also coveted the immense trans-Allegheny area, on which restless American pioneers were already settling.

Benjamin Franklin (1706–1790) *He left school at age ten, and became a wealthy businessman, a journalist, an inventor, a scientist, a legislator, and preeminently a statesman-diplomatist. He was sent to France in 1776 as the American envoy at age seventy, and he remained there until 1785, negotiating the alliance with the French and helping to negotiate the treaty of peace. His fame had preceded him, and when he discarded his wig for the fur cap of a simple "American agriculturist," he took French society by storm. The ladies, with whom he was a great favorite, honored him by adopting the high coiffure à la Franklin in imitation of his cap. (C. W. Peale, Historical Society of Pennsylvania.)*

> *Blundering George III, a poor loser, wrote this of America: "Knavery seems to be so much the striking feature of its inhabitants that it may not in the end be an evil that they become aliens to this Kingdom."*

France, ever eager to smash Britain's empire, desired an independent United States, but one feebly independent. It therefore schemed to keep the new republic cooped up east of the Allegheny Mountains. A weak America—like a horse gentle enough to plow but not vigorous enough to kick—would be easier to manage in promoting French interests and policy. France was paying a heavy price in men and treasure to win America's independence, and it wanted to get its money's worth.

But John Jay was unwilling to play France's game. Suspiciously alert, he perceived that the French could not satisfy the conflicting ambitions of both Americans and Spaniards. He saw signs—or thought he did—that indicated that the Paris Foreign Office was about to betray America's trans-Allegheny interests to satisfy those of Spain. He therefore secretly made separate overtures to London, contrary to his instructions from Congress. The hard-pressed British, eager to entice one of their enemies from the alliance, speedily came to terms with the Americans. A preliminary treaty of peace was signed in 1782; the final peace, the next year.

By the Treaty of Paris of 1783, the British formally recognized the independence of the United States. In addition, they granted generous boundaries, stretching majestically to the Mississippi on the west, to the Great Lakes on the north, and to Spanish Florida on the south. (Spain had recently captured Florida from Britain.) The Yankees, though now divorced from the empire, were to retain a share in the priceless fisheries of Newfoundland. The Canadians, of course, were profoundly displeased.

The Reconciliation between Britannia and Her Daughter America *America (represented by an Indian) is invited to buss (kiss) her mother. (Detail from an English cartoon. New York Public Library.)*

The Americans, on their part, had to yield important concessions. Loyalists were not to be further persecuted, and Congress was to *recommend* to the state legislatures that confiscated Loyalist property be restored. As for the debts long owed to British creditors, the American states were bound to put no lawful obstacles in the way of their collection. Unhappily for future harmony, the assurances regarding both debts and Loyalists were not carried out in the manner hoped for by London.

A New Nation Legitimized

Britain's terms were liberal almost beyond belief. The enormous trans-Allegheny area was thrown in as a virtual gift, for George Rogers Clark had captured only a small segment of it. Why the generosity? Had the United States beaten England to its knees?

The key to the riddle may be found in the Old World. At the time the peace terms were drafted, England was trying to seduce America from its French alliance, so it made the terms as alluring as possible. The shaky Whig ministry, hanging on by its fingernails for only a few months, was more friendly to the Americans than were the Tories. It was determined, by a policy of liberality, to salve recent wounds, reopen old trade channels, and prevent future wars over the coveted trans-Allegheny region. This far-visioned policy was regrettably not followed by the successors of the Whigs.

In spirit, the Americans made a separate peace—contrary to the French alliance. In fact, they did not. The Paris Foreign Office formally approved the terms of peace, though disturbed by the lone-wolf course of its American ally. France was immensely relieved by the prospect of bringing the costly conflict to an end and of freeing itself from its embarrassing promises to the Spanish crown.

America alone gained from the world-girdling war. The British, though soon to stage a comeback, were battered and beaten. The French gained sweet revenge but plunged headlong down the slippery slope to bankruptcy and revolution. In truth, fortune smiled benignly on the Americans. Snatching their independence from the furnace of world conflict, they began their national career with a splendid territorial birthright and a priceless heritage of freedom. Seldom, if ever, have any people been so favored.

CHRONOLOGY

1775	Battle of Lexington and Concord
	Second Continental Congress
	Battle of Bunker Hill
	Failed invasion of Canada
1776	Paine's *Common Sense*
	Declaration of Independence
	Battle of Trenton
	Battle of Brandywine
	Battle of Saratoga
1778	Formation of French-American alliance
	Battle of Monmouth
1778–1779	Clark's victories in the West
1781	Battle of Yorktown
1782	North's ministry collapses in Britain
1783	Treaty of Paris

Varying Viewpoints

As the first colonial struggle for "national liberation," the Revolutionary War has long captured the attention of military historians. Early accounts concentrated on the engagements between British regulars and the Continental army, and the war's place in the context of European rivalries. The French alliance, the dramatic battles at Saratoga and Yorktown, and the terrible winter at Valley Forge receive the greatest emphasis in these studies.

During the period of the Cold War, the proliferation of guerrilla conflicts in the Third World prompted scholars to emphasize another distinctive feature of the War for American Independence—the "triangularity" of the Revolutionary struggle. Focusing on the efforts of the patriot militia to disrupt British supply lines and win the loyalty of the general public, recent accounts, most notably those of John Shy and Charles Royster, portray the conflict less as a battle between two armies than as a contest between the British and the militia for control of the civilian population. By forcing the apathetic majority to associate actively with the Patriot cause, the militia won this war for the hearts and minds of the people and made it unlikely that the British could have recovered the loyalty of the colonists, even had they achieved a military victory.

Select Readings

Primary Source Documents

Thomas Paine's fiery *Common Sense** (1776) is the manifesto of the Revolution. "The Declaration of Independence"* (1776) is one of the foundations of American political theory. See also the "Treaty of Peace with Great Britain" (1783), in Henry Steele Commager, *Documents of American History.*

Secondary Sources

The war is sketched in John R. Alden, *A History of the American Revolution* (1969), and in Don Higginbotham's excellent military history, *The War of American Independence: Military Attitudes, Policies and Practice, 1763–1789* (1971). On the implications of the Revolutionary conflict, see John Shy, *A People Numerous and Armed: Reflections on the Military Struggle for American Independence* (1976); E. Wayne Carp, *To Starve the Army at Pleasure: Continental Army Administration and American Political Culture, 1775–1783* (1984); and Charles Royster, *A Revolutionary People at War: The Continental Army and the American Character* (1980). The conflict is considered in its European setting in Piers Mackesy, *The War for America, 1775–1783* (1964). Carl Becker's classic *The Declaration of Independence* (1922) is masterful; on the same subject, see also Garry Wills, *Inventing America: Jefferson's Declaration of Independence* (1980). Propaganda is analyzed in Carl Berger, *Broadsides and Bayonets* (1961). The role of the Loyalists is treated in William H. Nelson, *The American Tory* (1961); Robert M. Calhoon, *The Loyalists in Revolutionary America* (1973); Mary Beth Norton, *The British-Americans: The Loyalist Exiles in England* (1972); and Bernard Bailyn's unusually sensitive biography of the governor of colonial Massachusetts, *The Ordeal of Thomas Hutchinson* (1974). A general treatment of an often neglected subject is Benjamin Quarles, *The Negro in the American Revolution* (1961). See also Duncan J. MacLeod, *Slavery, Race and the American Revolution* (1974), and David B. Davis, *The Problem of Slavery in the Age of Revolution, 1770–1823* (1975), an able, gracefully written book. International implications are developed in Samuel F. Bemis, *The Diplomacy of the American Revolution* (1935); James H. Hutson, *John Adams and the Diplomacy of the American Revolution* (1980); Jonathan R. Dull, *A Diplomatic History of the American Revolution* (1985); and Richard B. Morris, *The Peacemakers: The Great Powers and American Independence* (1965). Attention to the social history of the Revolution has been largely inspired by John F. Jameson's seminal *The American Revolution Considered as a Social Movement* (1926). Jackson T. Main, *The Social Structure of Revolutionary America* (1969), takes the exploration further along the same lines, with conclusions somewhat at variance with Jameson's. Local studies of this issue include Edward A. Countryman, *A People in Revolution: The American Revolution and Political Society in New York, 1760–1790* (1981); Gary Nash, *The Urban Crucible: Social Change, Political Consciousness and the Origins of the American Revolution* (1979); and Ronald Hoffman, *A Spirit of Dissension: Economics, Politics, and the Revolution in Maryland* (1973). Interesting biographies are Samuel E. Morison's swashbuckling *John Paul Jones* (1959); Eric Foner, *Tom Paine and Revolutionary America* (1976); James T. Flexner, *George Washington in the American Revolution, 1775–1783* (1968); and Charles Royster, *Light Horse Harry Lee and the Legacy of the American Revolution* (1981). British troubles are laid bare in Gerald S. Brown, *The American Secretary: The Colonial Policy of Lord George Germain, 1775–1778* (1963), and in William B. Willcox, *Portrait of a General: Sir Henry Clinton in the War of Independence* (1964). Women are the subject of Linda K. Kerber, *Women of the Republic: Intellect and Ideology in Revolutionary America* (1980), and Mary Beth Norton, *Liberty's Daughters: The Revolutionary Experience of American Women* (1980). Michael Kammen brilliantly evokes the ways that the Revolution has been enshrined in the national memory in *A Season of Youth: The American Revolution and the Historical Imagination* (1978).

8

The Confederation and the Constitution, 1776–1790

This example of changing the constitution by assembling the wise men of the state, instead of assembling armies, will be worth as much to the world as the former examples we have given it.

Thomas Jefferson

A Revolution of Sentiments

The American Revolution was not a revolution in the sense of a radical or total change. It did not suddenly and violently overturn the entire political and social framework, as later occurred in the French and Russian revolutions. What happened was accelerated evolution rather than outright revolution. During the conflict itself people went on working and praying, marrying and playing. Most of them were not seriously disturbed by the actual fighting, and many of the more isolated communities scarcely knew that a war was on.

Yet some striking changes were ushered in, affecting social customs, political institutions, and ideas about society, government, and even sexual roles. The exodus of some eighty thou-sand substantial Loyalists robbed the new ship of state of conservative ballast. This weakening of the aristocratic upper crust, with all its culture and elegance, paved the way for new, Patriot elites to emerge. It also cleared the field for the "leveling" ideas of unbridled democracy to sweep across the land.

Equality was everywhere the watchword. When a group of Continental Army officers in 1783 formed an exclusive military order, the Society of the Cincinnati, they were roundly denounced for their aristocratic pretensions. Most states reduced (but usually did not eliminate altogether) property-holding requirements for voting. Social democracy was further stimulated by the growth of trade organizations for artisans and laborers. Citizens in several states, flushed with republican fervor, also sawed off the remaining shackles of medieval inheritance laws, such as primogeniture, which awarded all of a father's property to the eldest son.

A protracted fight for separation of church and state resulted in notable gains. Although the well-entrenched Congregational church continued to be legally established in some New England states, the Anglican church, tainted by association with the British crown, was humbled. De-Anglicized, it re-formed as the Protestant Episcopal church and was everywhere disestablished. The struggle for divorce between religion and government proved to be bitterest in Virginia. It was prolonged to 1786, when free-thinking Thomas Jefferson and his co-reformers, including the lowly Baptists, won a complete victory with the passage of the Vir-

The impact of the American Revolution was worldwide. About 1783 a British ship stopped at some islands off the East African coast, where the natives were revolting against their Arab masters. When asked why they were fighting they replied: "America is free. Could not we be?"

ginia Statute for Religious Freedom. (See table of established churches, p. 74.

The egalitarian sentiments unleashed by the war likewise challenged the institution of slavery. Philadelphia Quakers in 1775 founded the world's first antislavery society. Hostilities hampered the noxious trade in "black ivory," and the

The Copley Family *Painting by John Singleton Copley, c. 1776–1777. The composition and use of light in this family portrait illustrate the importance of the mother in the era's ideal vision of the family. Mrs. Copley is here the visual center of the painting; the light falls predominantly on her, and she sits at the focus of activity in the family group. The artist thus powerfully expressed the sentiment of the age about "republican motherhood"—a sentiment that revered the role of women as homemakers and especially as mothers, responsible for the cultivation of good republican values in young citizens. (National Gallery of Art.)*

Continental Congress in 1774 called for the complete abolition of the slave trade, a summons to which most of the states responded positively. Several northern states went further and either abolished slavery outright or provided for the gradual emancipation of blacks.

These laws codified the Declaration's ringing concept that "all men are created equal," though laws against interracial marriage sprang up at the same time. Even in slave-burdened Virginia, a few idealistic masters freed their human chattels. In this still sadly incomplete revolution of sentiments, symbolized and inspired by the Declaration of Independence, were to be found the first frail sprouts of the later abolitionist movement.

But why in this dawning democratic age did abolition not go further and cleanly blot the evil of slavery from the fresh face of the new nation? The sorry truth is that the fledgling idealism of the Founding Fathers was sacrificed to political expediency. A fight over the slavery issue would have fractured the fragile national unity that was so desperately needed. Nearly a century later, the same issue did wreck the Union—temporarily.

Likewise incomplete was the extension of the doctrine of equality to women. Some women did serve (disguised as men) in the military, and New Jersey's new constitution in 1776 even temporarily enabled women to vote. But though Abigail Adams teased her husband John in 1776 that "the ladies" were determined "to foment a rebellion" of their own if they were not given political rights, most of the women in the Revolutionary era were still doing traditional women's work.

Yet women did not go untouched by Revolutionary ideals. Central to republican ideology was the concept of "civic virtue"—the idea that democracy depended on the unselfish commitment of each citizen to the public good. And who could better cultivate the habits of a virtuous citizenry than mothers, to whom society entrusted the moral education of the young? Indeed, the selfless devotion of a mother to her family was often cited as the very model of proper republican behavior. The idea of "republican motherhood" thus took root, elevating women to a newly prestigious role as the special keepers of the nation's conscience.

Constitution Making in the States

The Continental Congress in 1776 called upon the colonies to draft new constitutions. In effect, the Congress was asking the colonies to summon themselves into being as new states, whose sovereignty, according to the theory of republicanism, would rest on the authority of the people. For a period of time the manufacturing of governments was more pressing than the manufacturing of gunpowder. In Connecticut and Rhode Island the yellowing colonial charters were kept essentially intact but were retouched a bit to reflect the new vigor of republican thinking. Elsewhere, constitution writers worked tirelessly to capture the democratic spirit of the age on black-inked parchment.

Massachusetts contributed one especially noteworthy innovation when it called a special convention to draft its constitution and then submitted the final draft directly to the people for ratification. Once adopted in 1780, the Massachusetts constitution could be changed only by another specially called constitutional convention. This procedure was later imitated in the drafting and ratification of the federal Constitution.

The newly penned state constitutions enjoyed many features in common. Their similarity, as it turned out, made easier the drafting of a workable federal charter when the time was ripe. As *written* documents, the state constitutions were intended to represent a *fundamental* law, superior to the transient whims of ordinary legislation. Most of these documents included bills of rights, specifically guaranteeing long-prized liberties against later legislative encroachment. Most of them required the annual election of legislators, who were thus forced to stay in touch with the mood of the people. All of them deliberately created weak executive and judicial branches, at least by present-day standards. A generation of quarreling with His Majesty's officials had implanted a deep distrust of despotic governors and arbitrary judges.

In all the new state governments, the legislatures, as presumably the most democratic branch of government, were given sweeping powers. But as Thomas Jefferson warned, "173 despots [in a legislature] would surely be as op-

> *Thomas Jefferson, then minister to France, was not overjoyed by the prospect of much manufacturing. As he wrote (1784): "While we have land to labor then, let us never wish to see our citizens occupied at a work-bench, or twirling a distaff. . . . For the general operations of manufacture, let our workshops remain in Europe. . . . The mobs of great cities add just so much to the support of pure government, as sores do to the strength of the human body."*

pressive as one." Many Americans soon came to agree with him.

The democratic character of the new state legislatures was vividly reflected by the presence of many members from the recently enfranchised poorer western districts. Their influence was powerfully felt in their several successful movements to relocate state capitals from the haughty eastern seaports into the less pretentious interior. In the Revolutionary era, the capitals of New Hampshire, New York, Virginia, North Carolina, South Carolina, and Georgia were all moved westward. These geographical shifts portended political shifts with which many more conservative Americans grew increasingly uncomfortable.

Economic Crosscurrents

Economic changes begotten by the war were likewise noteworthy, but not overwhelming. States seized control of former crown lands, and although rich speculators had their day, many of the large Loyalist holdings were confiscated and eventually cut up into small farms. Roger Morris's huge estate in New York, for example, was sliced into 250 parcels—thus accelerating the spread of economic democracy. The frightful excesses of the French Revolution were avoided, partly because cheap land was easily available. People do not chop off heads so readily when they can chop down trees. It is highly significant that in the United States, economic democracy, broadly speaking, preceded political democracy.

A sharp stimulus was given to manufacturing by the prewar nonimportation agreements and later by the war itself. Goods that had formerly been imported from England were mostly cut off, and the ingenious Yankees were forced to make their own. Ten years after the Revolution the busy Brandywine Creek, south of Philadelphia, was turning the waterwheels of numerous mills along an eight-mile (thirteen-kilometer) stretch. Yet America remained overwhelmingly a nation of soil-tillers.

Economically speaking independence had drawbacks. Much of the coveted commerce of England was still reserved for the loyal parts of the empire; and now that the Americans were aliens, they were forced to find new customers. Fisheries were disrupted, and bounties for ships' stores had abruptly ended. In some respects, the hated British Navigation Laws were more disagreeable after independence than before.

New commercial outlets, fortunately, compensated partially for the loss of old ones. Americans could now trade freely with foreign nations, subject to local restrictions—a boon they had not enjoyed in the old days of mercantilism. Enterprising Yankee shippers ventured boldly—and profitably—into the Baltic and China seas. In 1784 the *Empress of China*, carrying a valuable weed (ginseng) that was highly prized by Chinese herb doctors as a cure for impotence, led the way into the East Asian markets.

Yet the general economic picture was far from rosy. War had spawned demoralizing extravagance, speculation, and profiteering, with profits as indecently high as 300 percent. Runaway inflation had been ruinous to many citizens, and Congress had failed in its feeble attempts to curb economic laws by fixing prices. The average citizen was probably worse off financially at the end of the shooting than before.

The whole economic and social atmosphere was unhealthy. A newly rich class of profiteers was noisily conspicuous, while many once-wealthy people were left destitute. The controversy leading to the war had bred a keen distaste for taxes; and the wholesale seizure of Loyalist estates had encouraged disrespect for private property and for the majesty of the law generally. John Adams had been shocked when gleefully told by a horse-jockey neighbor that the courts of justice were all closed—a plight that proved to be only temporary.

A Shaky Start Toward Union

What would the Americans do with the independence they had so dearly won? London had dumped the responsibility of creating and operating a new central government squarely into their laps.

Prospects for erecting a lasting regime were far from bright. It is always difficult to set up a new government, doubly difficult to set up a new type of government. The picture was further confused in America by leaders preaching "natural rights" and looking suspiciously at all persons clothed with authority. America was more a name than a nation, and unity ran little deeper than the color on the map.

Disruptive forces stalked the land. The departure of the conservative Tory element left the political system inclined toward experimentation and innovation. Patriots had fought the war with a high degree of disunity, but they had at least enjoyed the unifying cement of a common cause. Now even that was gone. It would have been almost a miracle if any government fashioned in all this confusion had long endured.

Hard times, the bane of all regimes, set in shortly after the war and hit bottom in 1786. As if other troubles were not enough, British manufacturers, with dammed-up surpluses, began flooding the American market with cut-rate goods. War-baby American industries, in particular, suffered industrial colic from such ruthless competition. One Philadelphia newspaper in 1783 urged the use of ill-fitting homespun cloth:

> Of foreign gewgaws let's be free,
> And wear the webs of liberty.

Yet hopeful signs could be discerned. The thirteen sovereign states were basically alike in governmental structure and functioned under similar constitutions. Americans enjoyed a rich political inheritance, derived partly from England and partly from their own homegrown devices for self-government. Finally, they were blessed with political leaders of a high order in men like George Washington, James Madison, John Adams, Thomas Jefferson, and Alexander Hamilton.

Creating a Confederation

The Second Continental Congress of Revolutionary days was little more than a conference of ambassadors from the thirteen states. It was totally without constitutional authority and in general did only what it dared to do, though it asserted some control over military affairs and foreign policy. In nearly all respects the states were sovereign, for they coined money, raised armies and navies, and erected tariff barriers. The legislature of Virginia even ratified separately the treaty of alliance of 1778 with France.

Shortly before declaring independence in 1776, the Congress appointed a committee to draft a written constitution for the new nation. The finished product was the Articles of Confederation. Adopted by Congress in 1777, it was translated into French after the battle of Saratoga so as to convince France that America had a genuine government in the making. In due course this new constitution was sent out to the states for their approval. But final action was delayed for four years, until 1781, less than eight months before the victory at Yorktown.

The chief apple of discord was western lands. Six of the jealous states, including Pennsylvania and Maryland, had no holdings beyond the Allegheny Mountains. Seven, notably New York and Virginia, were favored with enormous acreage, in most cases on the basis of earlier sea-to-sea charter grants. The six landless states argued that the more fortunate states would not have retained possession of this splendid prize if all the other states had not fought for it also. A major complaint was that the land-blessed states could sell their trans-Allegheny tracts and thus pay off pensions and other debts incurred in the common cause. States without such holdings would have to tax themselves heavily to defray these obligations. Why not turn the whole western area over to the central government?

Unanimous approval of the Articles of Confederation by the thirteen states was required,

Independence Hall *Originally built in the 1730s as a meeting place for the Pennsylvania colonial assembly, this building witnessed much history: Here Washington was given command of the Continental Army, the Declaration of Independence was signed, and the Constitution hammered out. The building began to be called "Independence Hall" only in the 1820s. (Historical Society of Pennsylvania.)*

and landless Maryland stubbornly held out until March 1, 1781. It at length gave in when New York surrendered its western claims and Virginia seemed about to do so. To sweeten the pill, Congress pledged itself to dispose of these vast areas for the "common benefit." It further agreed to carve from the new public domain not colonies but a number of "republican" states, which in time would be admitted to the Union on terms of complete equality with all the others. This extraordinary commitment faithfully reflected the anticolonial spirit of the Revolu-

Jefferson was never a friend of strong government (except when himself president), and he viewed with suspicion the substitute that was proposed for the Articles of Confederation: "Indeed, I think all the good of this new Constitution might have been couched in three or four new articles, to be added to the good, old, and venerable fabric."

tion, and the pledge was later fully redeemed in the famed Northwest Ordinance of 1787.

Fertile public lands thus transferred to the central government proved to be an invaluable bond of union. The states that had thrown their heritage into the common pot had to remain in the Union if they were to reap their share of the advantages from the land sales. An army of westward-moving pioneers purchased their farms from the federal government, directly or indirectly, and they learned to look to the national capital, rather than to the state capitals—with a consequent weakening of local influence. Finally, a uniform national land policy was made possible.

The Articles of Confederation: America's First Constitution

The Articles of Confederation—some have said "Articles of Confusion"—provided for a loose confederation or "firm league of friendship." Thirteen independent states were thus linked together for joint action in dealing with common problems, such as foreign affairs. A clumsy Congress was to be the chief agency of government. There was no executive branch—George III had left a bad taste—and the vital judicial arm was left almost exclusively to the states, which remained sovereign.

Congress, though dominant, was closely hobbled. Each state had a single vote, so that some 68,000 Rhode Islanders had the same voice as more than ten times that many Virginians. All bills dealing with specified subjects of importance required at least a two-thirds vote; any amendment of the Articles themselves required a unanimous vote. Unanimity was almost impossible, and this meant that the amending process, perhaps fortunately, was unworkable. If it had been workable, the Republic might have struggled along with a patched-up Articles of Confederation rather than adopting an effective new Constitution.

The shackled Congress was weak—and was purposely designed to be weak. Suspicious states, having just won control over taxation and commerce from Britain, had no desire to yield their newly acquired privileges to an American parliament—even one of their own making.

Two handicaps of the Congress were crippling. It had no power to regulate commerce, and this weakness left the states free to establish conflictingly different laws regarding tariffs and navigation. Nor could the Congress enforce its tax-collection program. It established a tax quota for each of the states and then asked them please to contribute their share on a voluntary basis. The central authority—a "government by supplication"—was lucky if in any year it received one-fourth of its requests.

The feeble national government in Philadelphia could advise and recommend and request. But in dealing with the independent states, it

Western Land Cessions to the United States, 1782–1802

could not command or coerce or enforce. It could not act directly upon the individual citizens of a sovereign state; it could not even protect itself against gross indignities. In 1783 a dangerous threat came from a group of mutinous Pennsylvania soldiers who demanded back pay. After Congress had appealed in vain to the state for protection, the members were forced to move in disgrace to Princeton College in New Jersey. The new Congress, with all its paper powers, was even less effective than the old Continental Congress, with no constitutional powers at all.

Yet the Articles of Confederation, weak though they were, proved to be a landmark in government. They were for those days a model of what a loose *con*federation ought to be. Thomas Jefferson enthusiastically hailed the new structure as the best one "existing or that ever did exist." To compare it with the European governments, he thought, was like comparing "heaven and hell." But although the Confederation was praiseworthy as confederations went, the troubled times demanded not a loose *con*federation but a tightly knit federation. This involved the yielding by the states of their sovereignty to a completely new federal government, which in turn would leave them free to control their local affairs.

In spite of their defects, the Articles of Confederation were a significant stepping-stone toward the present Constitution. They clearly outlined the general powers that were to be exercised by the central government, such as making treaties and establishing a postal service. As the first written constitution of the Republic, the Articles kept alive the flickering ideal of union and held the states together—until such time as they were ripe for the establishment of a strong constitution by peaceful, evolutionary methods. The anemic Articles represented what the states regarded as an alarming surrender of their power. Without this intermediary jump, they probably would never have consented to the breathtaking leap from the old boycott Association of 1774 to the Constitution of the United States.

Landmarks in Land Laws

Handcuffed though the Congress of the Confederation was, it succeeded in passing supremely farsighted pieces of legislation. These related to an immense part of the public domain recently acquired from the states and commonly known as the Old Northwest. This area of land lay northwest of the Ohio River, east of

Surveying the Old Northwest　*Sections of a township under Ordinance of 1785.*

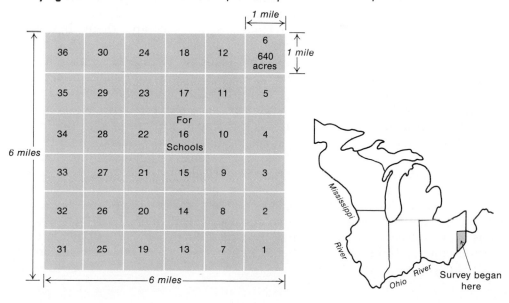

the Mississippi River, and south of the Great Lakes.

The first of these red-letter laws was the Land Ordinance of 1785. It provided that the acreage of the Old Northwest should be sold and that the proceeds should be used to help pay off the national debt. The vast area was to be surveyed before sale and settlement, thus forestalling endless confusion and lawsuits. It was to be divided into townships six miles square, each of which in turn was to be split into thirty-six sections of one square mile each. The sixteenth section of each township was set aside to be sold for the benefit of the public schools—a priceless gift to education in the Northwest. The orderly settlement of the Northwest Territory, where the land was methodically surveyed and titles duly recorded, contrasted sharply with the chaos south of the Ohio River, where uncertain ownership and fraud were rampant.

Even more noteworthy was the Northwest Ordinance of 1787, which related to governing of the Old Northwest. This law came to grips with the problem of how a nation should deal with its colonial peoples—the same problem that had bedeviled the king and Parliament in London. The solution provided by the Northwest Ordinance was a judicious compromise: temporary tutelage, then permanent equality. First, there would be two evolutionary territorial stages, during which the area would be subordinate to the federal government. Then, when a territory could boast sixty thousand inhabitants, it might be admitted by Congress as a state, with all the privileges of the thirteen charter members. (This is precisely what the Continental Congress had promised the states when they surrendered their lands in 1781.) The ordinance also forbade slavery in the Old Northwest—a pathbreaking gain for freedom.

The wisdom of Congress in handling this explosive problem deserves warm praise. If it had attempted to chain the new territories in permanent subordination, a second American Revolution almost certainly would have erupted in later years, fought this time by the West against the East. Congress thus neatly solved the seemingly insoluble problem of empire. The scheme

worked so well that its basic principles were ultimately carried over from the Old Northwest to other frontier areas.

The World's Ugly Duckling

Foreign relations, especially with London, continued troubled during these anxious years of the Confederation. England resented the stab in the back from its rebellious offspring and for eight years refused to send a minister to America's "backwoods" capital. It suggested, with barbed irony, that if it sent one, it would have to send thirteen.

Britain flatly declined to make a commercial treaty or to repeal its ancient Navigation Laws. Lord Sheffield, whose ungenerous views prevailed, argued persuasively in a widely sold pamphlet that England would win back America's trade anyhow. Commerce, he insisted, would naturally follow old channels. So why go to the Americans hat in hand? The British also officially shut off their profitable West Indian trade from the United States, though the Yankees, with their time-tested skill in smuggling, illegally shared some of it nonetheless.

Scheming British agents were also active along the far-flung northern frontier. They intrigued with the disgruntled Allen brothers of Vermont and sought to annex that troubled area to Britain. Along the northern border the redcoats continued to hold a chain of trading posts on United States soil, and there they maintained their profitable fur trade with the Indians. One plausible excuse for remaining was the failure of the American states to carry out the treaty of peace in regard to debts and Loyalists. But the main purpose of Britain in hanging on was probably to curry favor with the Indians and keep their tomahawks lined up on the side of the king as a barrier against future American attacks on Canada.

All these grievances against England were maddening to patriotic Americans. Some citizens demanded, with more heat than wisdom, that the United States force the British into line by imposing restrictions on their imports to

Main Centers of Spanish and British Influence after 1783 *This map shows graphically that the United States in 1783 achieved complete independence in name only, particularly in the area west of the Appalachian Mountains. Not until twenty years had passed did the new Republic, with the purchase of Louisiana from France in 1803, eliminate foreign influence from the area east of the Mississippi River.*

it held an important fort. It also intrigued with the neighboring Indians, grievously antagonized by the rapacious land policies of Georgia and North Carolina, to hem the Americans in east of the Alleghenies. Spain and England together, radiating their influence out among resentful Indian tribes, prevented America from exercising effective control over about half of its total territory.

Even America's French ally, now that it had humbled Britain, cooled off. It demanded the repayment of money loaned during the war; it restricted trade with its bustling West Indies and other ports.

Pirates of the North African states, including the arrogant Dey of Algiers, were ravaging America's Mediterranean commerce and enslaving Yankee sailors. The British purchased protection for their own subjects, and as colonials the Americans had enjoyed this shield. But as an independent nation the United States was too weak to fight and too poor to bribe. A few Yankee shippers engaged in the Mediterranean trade with forged British protection papers, but not all were so bold or so lucky.

John Jay, secretary for foreign affairs, derived some hollow satisfaction from these insults. He hoped they would at least humiliate the American people into framing a new government at home that would be strong enough to command respect abroad.

The Horrid Specter of Anarchy

Economic storm clouds continued to hang low in the mid-1780s. The requisition system of raising money was breaking down; some of the states refused to pay anything, while complaining bitterly about the tyranny of "King Congress." Interest on the public debt was piling up at home, while the nation's credit was evaporating abroad.

Individual states were getting out of hand. Several of them were quarreling over boundaries, which generated numerous minor pitched battles. Some of the states were levying duties on goods from their neighbors; New York, for example, taxed firewood from Con-

America. But Congress could not control commerce, and the states refused to adopt a uniform tariff policy. Some "easy states" deliberately lowered their tariffs in order to attract an unfair share of trade.

Spain, though recently an enemy of England, was openly unfriendly to the new Republic. It controlled the mouth of the all-important Mississippi, down which the pioneers of Tennessee and Kentucky were forced to float their produce. In 1784 Spain closed the river to American commerce, threatening the West with strangulation. Spain likewise claimed a large area north of the Gulf of Mexico, including Florida, granted to the United States by the British in 1783. At Natchez, on disputed soil,

necticut and cabbages from New Jersey. A number of the states were again starting to grind out depreciated paper currency, and a few of them had passed laws sanctioning the semi-worthless "rag money." As a contemporary rhymester put it:

> Bankrupts their creditors with rage pursue;
> No stop, no mercy from the debtor crew.

An alarming uprising, known as Shays's Rebellion, flared up in western Massachusetts in 1786. Impoverished backcountry farmers, many of them Revolutionary War veterans, were losing their farms through mortgage foreclosures and tax delinquencies. Led by Captain Daniel Shays, a veteran of the Revolution, these desperate debtors demanded cheap paper money, lighter taxes, and a suspension of mortgage foreclosures. Hundreds of angry agitators, again seizing their muskets, attempted to enforce their demands.

Massachusetts authorities responded with drastic action. Supported partly by contributions from wealthy citizens, they raised a small army under General Lincoln. Several skirmishes occurred—at Springfield three Shaysites were killed, and one was wounded—and the movement collapsed. Daniel Shays, who believed that he was fighting anew against tyranny, was condemned to death but was later pardoned.

Shays's followers were crushed—but the nightmarish memory lingered on. The outbursts of these and other distressed debtors struck fear in the hearts of the propertied class, who began to suspect that the Revolution had created a Frankenstein's monster of "mobocracy." "Good God!" burst out George Washington, who felt that only a Tory or a Briton could have predicted such disorders. There was obviously a crying need for a stronger central government. A few panicky citizens even talked of importing a European monarch to carry on where George III had failed.

How critical were conditions under the Confederation? Conservatives, anxious to safeguard their wealth and position, naturally exaggerated the seriousness of the nation's plight. They were eager to persuade their fellow citizens to scrap the Articles of Confederation, under which the states were sovereign, in favor of a muscular central government, in which the federal authority would be sovereign. But the poorer states' rights people, who favored at most a simple amending of the Articles, pooh-poohed the talk of anarchy. Many of them were debtors who feared that a powerful federal government would force them to pay their creditors.

Yet friends and critics of the Confederation agreed that it needed some strengthening. Popular toasts were "Cement to the Union" and "A hoop to the barrel." The chief differences arose over how this goal should be attained and how a maximum amount of states' rights could be reconciled with a strong central government. America probably could have muddled through somehow with amended Articles of Confederation. But the adoption of a completely new constitution certainly spared the Republic much costly indecision, uncertainty, and turmoil.

The nationwide picture was actually brightening before the Constitution was drafted. Nearly half the states had not issued semi-worthless paper currency; and some of the monetary black sheep showed signs of returning to the sound-money fold. Congressional control of commerce was in sight, specifically by means of an amendment to the Articles of Confederation. Prosperity was beginning to emerge from the fog of depression. By 1789 overseas shipping had largely regained its place in the commercial world. If conditions had been as grim in 1787 as painted by foes of the Articles of Confederation, the move for a new constitution would hardly have encountered such heated opposition.

A Convention of "Demi-Gods"

Control of commerce, more than any other problem, touched off the chain reaction that led to a constitutional convention. Interstate squabbling over this issue had become so alarming by 1786 that Virginia, taking the lead, issued a call for a convention at Annapolis, Maryland. Nine states appointed delegates, but only five were finally represented. With so feeble a showing, nothing could be done about the ticklish question of commerce. A classic-featured New Yorker, thirty-one-year-old Alexander Hamilton, brilliantly saved the convention from complete failure by engineering the adoption of his report. It called upon Congress to summon a convention to meet in Philadelphia the next year, not to deal with commerce alone but to bolster the entire fabric of the Articles of Confederation.

Congress, though slowly dying in New York City, was reluctant to take a step that might be the signing of its own death warrant. But after six of the states had seized the bit in their teeth and appointed delegates anyhow, Congress belatedly issued the call for a convention *"for the sole and express purpose of revising"* the Articles of Confederation.

Every state chose representatives, except independent-minded Rhode Island (still "Rogues' Island"), a stronghold of paper-moneyites. These leaders were all appointed by the state legislatures, whose members had been elected by voters who could qualify as property holders. This double distillation inevitably brought together a select group of propertied men—though it is a grotesque distortion to claim that they shaped the Constitution primarily to protect their personal financial interests. When one of them did suggest restricting federal office to major property owners, he was promptly denounced for the unwisdom of "interweaving into a republican constitution a veneration for wealth."

A quorum of the fifty-five emissaries from twelve states finally convened at Philadelphia on May 25, 1787, in the imposing red-brick statehouse. The smallness of the assemblage facilitated intimate acquaintance and hence compromise. Sessions were held in complete secrecy, with armed sentinels posted at the doors. Delegates knew that they would generate heated differences, and they did not want to advertise their own dissensions or put crippling arguments into the mouths of the opposition.

The caliber of the participants was extraordinarily high—"demi-gods," Jefferson called them. The crisis was such as to induce the ablest men to drop their personal pursuits and come to the aid of their country. Most of the

Regarding popular disorders, Jefferson wrote privately in 1787: "A little rebellion, now and then, is a good thing, and as necessary in the political world as storms in the physical. . . . It is a medicine necessary for the sound health of government."

members were lawyers, and most of them fortunately were old hands at constitution making in their own states.

George Washington, towering austere and aloof among the "demi-gods," was unanimously elected chairman. His enormous prestige, as "the Sword of the Revolution," served to quiet overheated tempers. Benjamin Franklin, then eighty-one, added the urbanity of an elder statesman, though he was inclined to be indiscreetly talkative in his declining years. James Madison, then thirty-six and a profound student of government, made contributions so notable that he has been dubbed "the Father of the Constitution." Alexander Hamilton, then only thirty-two, was present as an advocate of a super-powerful central government. His five-hour speech in behalf of his plan, though the most eloquent of the convention, left only one delegate convinced—himself.

Most of the flaming Revolutionary leaders of 1776 were absent. Thomas Jefferson, John Adams, and Thomas Paine were in Europe; Sa-

Alexander Hamilton clearly revealed his class-interest views of an aristocratic government in his Philadelphia speech (1787): "All communities divide themselves into the few and the many. The first are the rich and wellborn, the other the mass of the people... The people are turbulent and changing; they seldom judge or determine right. Give therefore to the first class a distinct, permanent share in the government. They will check the unsteadiness of the second, and as they cannot receive any advantage by change, they therefore will ever maintain good government."

The Chair in Which George Washington Sat During the Constitutional Convention *Pondering the symbol at the top of the chair, Benjamin Franklin observed that "I have the happiness to know it is a rising and not a setting sun." (Independence National Historic Park.)*

muel Adams and John Hancock were not elected by Massachusetts. Patrick Henry, ardent champion of states' rights, was chosen as a delegate from Virginia but declined to serve, declaring that he "smelled a rat." It was perhaps well that these architects of revolution were absent. The time had come to yield the stage to leaders interested in fashioning solid political systems.

Patriots in Philadelphia

The fifty-five delegates were a conservative, well-to-do body: lawyers, merchants, shippers, land speculators, and moneylenders. Not a single spokesperson was present from the poorer debtor groups. They were young (the average age was about forty-two) but experienced statesmen. Above all, they were nationalists, more interested in preserving and strengthening the young Republic than in further stirring the roiling cauldron of popular democracy.

The delegates hoped to crystallize the last evaporating pools of revolutionary idealism into a stable political structure that would endure. They strongly desired a firm, dignified, and respected government. They believed in republicanism but sought to protect the American democratic experiment from its weaknesses abroad and excesses at home. In a broad sense the piratical Dey of Algiers, who drove the delegates to their work, was a Founding Father. They aimed to clothe the central authority with genuine power, especially in controlling tariffs, so that the United States could wrest satisfactory commercial treaties from foreign nations. The shortsighted hostility of the British mercantilists spurred the constitution framers to their task, and in this sense the illiberal Lord Sheffield was a Founding Father.

Other motives were present in the stately Philadelphia hall. Delegates were determined to preserve the union, forestall anarchy, and ensure security of life and property against dangerous uprisings by the "mobocracy." Above all, they sought to curb the unrestrained democracy rampant in the various states. "We have, probably, had too good an opinion of human nature in forming our confederation," George Washington concluded. The specter of the recent outburst in Massachusetts was especially alarming, and in this sense Daniel Shays was a Founding Father. Grinding necessity extorted the Constitution from a reluctant nation. Fear occupied the fifty-sixth chair.

Hammering Out a Bundle of Compromises

Some of the travel-stained delegates, when they first reached Philadelphia, decided upon a daring step. They would completely *scrap* the old Articles of Confederation, despite explicit instructions from Congress to *revise*. Technically, these bolder spirits were determined to overthrow the existing government of the United

States by peaceful means. The sovereign states were in danger of losing their sovereignty.

A scheme proposed by populous Virginia, and known as "the large-state plan," was first pushed forward as the framework of the Constitution. Its essence was that representation in both houses of a bicameral Congress should be based on population—an arrangement that would naturally give the larger states an advantage.

Tiny New Jersey, suspicious of Virginia, countered with "the small-state plan." This provided for equal representation in a unicameral Congress by states, regardless of size and population, as under the existing Articles of Confederation. The weaker states feared that under the Virginia scheme the stronger states would band together and lord it over the rest. Angry debate, heightened by a stifling heat wave, led to deadlock. The danger loomed that the convention would break up in complete failure. Even skeptical old Benjamin Franklin seriously proposed that the daily sessions be opened with prayer by a local clergyman.

After bitter and prolonged debate, the "Great Compromise" of the convention was hammered out and agreed upon. A cooling of tempers came coincidentally with a cooling of the temperature. The larger states were conceded representation by population in the House of Representatives (Art. I, Sec. II, para. 3; see Appendix at the end of this book), and the smaller states were appeased by equal representation in the Senate (see Art. I, Sec. III, para. 1). Each state, no matter how poor or small, would have two senators. The big states, which would have to bear the major burden of taxation, obviously yielded more. As a sop to them, the delegates agreed that every tax bill or rev-

Gouverneur Morris (1752–1816) *A delegate from Pennsylvania to the Constitutional Convention of 1787, he spoke more frequently than any other member and served as principal draftsman of that superbly written document. A wealthy and rock-ribbed conservative, he had joined the Revolutionary movement with reluctance and to the end feared the "riotous mob." (National Portrait Gallery.)*

enue measure must originate in the House, where population counted more heavily (see Art. I, Sec. VII, para. 1). This critical compromise broke the log jam, and from then on success seemed within reach.

In a significant reversal of the arrangement most state constitutions had embodied, the new Constitution provided for a strong, independent executive in the presidency. The framers were here partly inspired by the example of Massachusetts, where a vigorous, popularly elected governor had suppressed Shays's Rebellion. The president was to be military commander in chief and to have wide powers of appointment to domestic offices—including judgeships. The president was also to have veto power over legislation.

The Constitution as drafted was a bundle of compromises; they stand out in every section. A vital compromise was the method of electing the president indirectly by the Electoral College, rather than by direct means (see Art. II, Sec. I, para. 2). One Virginia delegate insisted that to leave the choice to the people was like asking a blind person to choose colors.

Sectional jealousy also intruded. Should the voteless slave of the southern states count as a person in apportioning direct taxes and also representation in the House of Representatives? The South, not wishing to be deprived of

Jefferson, despite his high regard for the leaders at the Philadelphia convention, still was not unduly concerned about Shaysite rebellions. He wrote (November 1787): "What country before ever existed a century and a half without a rebellion?. . . The tree of liberty must be refreshed from time to time with the blood of patriots and tyrants. It is its natural manure."

influence, answered "yes." The North replied "no," arguing that the North might as logically have additional representation based on its horses. As a compromise between total representation and none at all, it was decided that a slave might count as three-fifths of a person. Hence the memorable, if somewhat illogical, "three-fifths compromise" (see Art. I, Sec. II, para. 3), an idea seriously discussed four years earlier.

Most of the states wanted to shut off the African slave trade. But South Carolina and Georgia, requiring slave labor in their rice paddies and malarial swamps, raised vehement protests. By way of compromise the convention stipulated that the slave trade might continue until the end of 1807, at which time Congress could turn off the spigot (see Art. I, Sec. IX, para. 1). It did so as soon as the prescribed interval had elapsed. Meanwhile all the new state constitutions except Georgia's forbade overseas slave trade.

Safeguards for Conservatism

Heated clashes among the delegates have been overplayed. The area of agreement was actually large; otherwise the convention would have speedily disbanded. Economically, the members generally saw eye to eye; they demanded sound money and the protection of private property. Politically, they were in basic agreement; they favored a stronger government, with three branches and with checks and balances among them—what critics called a "triple-headed mon-

ster." Finally, the convention was virtually unanimous in believing that manhood-suffrage democracy—government by "democratick babblers"—was something to be feared and fought.

Daniel Shays, the prime bogeyman, still frightened the conservative-minded delegates. They deliberately erected safeguards against the excesses of the "mob," and they made these barriers as strong as they dared. The awesome federal judges were to be appointed for life. The powerful president was to be elected *indirectly* by the Electoral College; the lordly senators were to be chosen *indirectly* by state legislatures (see Art. I, Sec. III, para. 1). Only in the case of one-half of one of the three great branches—the House of Representatives—were qualified (propertied) citizens permitted to choose their officials by *direct* vote (see Art. I, Sec. II, para. 1).

Yet the new charter also contained democratic elements. Above all, it stood foursquare on the two great principles of republicanism: that the only legitimate government was one based on the consent of the governed, and that the powers of government should be limited—in this case, specifically limited by a written constitution. The virtue of the people, not the authority of the state, was to be the ultimate guarantor of liberty, justice, and order. "We the people," the preamble began, in a ringing affirmation of these republican doctrines.

At the end of seventeen muggy weeks—May 25 to September 17, 1787—only forty-two of the original fifty-five members remained to sign the Constitution. Three of the forty-two, refusing to

Evolution of Federal Union

YEARS	ATTEMPTS AT UNION	PARTICIPANTS
1643–1684	New England Confederation	4 colonies
1686–1689	Dominion of New England	7 colonies
1754	Albany Congress	7 colonies
1765	Stamp Act Congress	9 colonies
1772–1776	Committees of Correspondence	13 colonies
1774	First Continental Congress (adopts The Association)	12 colonies
1775–1781	Second Continental Congress	13 colonies
1781–1789	Articles of Confederation	13 states
1789–1790	Federal Constitution	13 states

do so, returned to their states to resist ratification. The remainder, adjourning to the City Tavern, appropriately celebrated the occasion. They little suspected that one day an Eighteenth Amendment would be added forbidding the manufacture and sale of alcoholic beverages.

No members of the convention were completely happy about the result. They were too near their work—and too weary. Whatever their personal desires, they finally had to compromise and adopt what was acceptable to the entire body, and what presumably would be acceptable to the entire country.

The Clash of Federalists and Anti-Federalists

The Framing Fathers early foresaw that nationwide acceptance of the Constitution would not be easy to obtain. A formidable barrier was unanimous ratification by all thirteen states, as required for amendment by the still-existent Articles of Confederation. But since absent Rhode Island was certain to veto the Constitution, the delegates boldly adopted a different scheme. They stipulated that when *two-thirds* of the states—that is, nine—had registered their approval through specially elected conventions, the Constitution would become the supreme law of the land in those states ratifying (see Art. VII).

This was extraordinary, even revolutionary. It was in effect an appeal over the heads of the Congress that had called the convention, and over the heads of the legislatures that had chosen its members, to the people—or those of the people who could vote. In this way the framers could claim greater popular sanction for their handiwork. Congress reluctantly submitted the document to the states on this basis, without recommendation of any kind.

People were somewhat shocked, so well had the secrets of the convention been kept. The public had expected the old Articles of Confederation to be patched up; now it was handed a frightening document in which, many thought, the precious jewel of state sovereignty was swallowed up. One of the hottest debates of

One of the Philadelphia delegates recorded in his journal a brief episode involving Benjamin Franklin, who was asked by a lady when the convention ended, "Well, Doctor, what have we got, a republic or a monarchy?" He answered, "A republic, if you can keep it."

American history forthwith erupted. The anti-federalists, who opposed the stronger federal government, were arrayed against the federalists, who naturally favored it.

A motley crowd gathered in the anti-federalist camp. It consisted primarily, though not exclusively, of the states' rights devotees, the backcountry dwellers, the one-horse farmers, the work-soiled artisans, the ill-educated and illiterate—in general, the poorer classes. They were joined by paper-moneyites and debtors, many of whom feared that a potent central government would force them to pay off their debts—and at full value. Large numbers of anti-federalists suspected that something sinister was being put over on them by the aristocrats.

Silver-buckled federalists were more respectable; they generally embraced the cultured and propertied groups. Most of them lived in the settled areas along the seaboard, not in the raw backcountry. They were in outlook rather closely akin to the conservative Loyalist group of Revolutionary days. In fact, many of the remaining former Loyalists gave vigorous support to the Constitution; without them it might have failed of ratification.

Anti-federalists, their worst fears aroused, voiced vehement objections to the "gilded trap" known as the Constitution. They cried with much truth that it had been drawn up by the aristocratic elements and hence was antidemocratic. They likewise charged that the sovereignty of the states was being submerged and that the freedoms of the individual were jeopardized by the absence of a bill of rights. They decried the dropping of annual elections for congressional representatives, the setting up of a federal stronghold ten miles square (later the District of Columbia), the creation of a standing army, the omission of any reference to God, and the highly questionable procedure of ratifying with only two-thirds of the states. A Philadelphia newspaper added that Benjamin Franklin was "a fool from age" and George Washington "a fool from nature."

The Great Debate in the States

Special elections, some apathetic but others hotly contested, were held in the various states for members of the ratifying conventions. The candidates—federalist or anti-federalist—were elected on the basis of their pledges for or against the Constitution.

The newly forged document was quickly accepted by four small states, for they had come off much better than they could have expected. Pennsylvania, number two on the list of ratifiers, was the first large state to act, but not until high-handed irregularities had been employed by the federalist legislature in calling a convention. These included the forcible seating of two anti-federalist members, their clothes torn and their faces red with rage, in order to complete a quorum.

Massachusetts, the second most populous state, provided an acid test. If the Constitution

had failed there, the entire movement might easily have bogged down. The Boston ratifying convention at first contained an anti-federalist majority. It included weather-beaten Shaysites and the suspicious Samuel Adams, that aging "Engineer of Revolution" who now distrusted change. The assembly buzzed with dismaying talk of summoning another constitutional convention, as though the nation had not already shot its bolt. Clearly the choice was not between this Constitution and a better one, but between this Constitution and the creaking Articles of Confederation. The absence of a bill of rights alarmed the anti-federalists. But the federalists gave solemn assurances that the first Congress would add such a safeguard by amendment, and ratification was then secured in Massachusetts by the rather narrow margin of 187 to 168.

Three more states fell into line. The last of these was New Hampshire, whose convention at first had contained a strong anti-federalist majority. The federalists cleverly engineered a prompt adjournment and then won over enough waverers to secure ratification. Nine states—all but Virginia, New York, North Carolina, and Rhode Island—had now taken shelter under the "new federal roof," and the document was officially adopted on June 21, 1788. Francis

Strengthening the Central Government

UNDER ARTICLES OF CONFEDERATION	UNDER FEDERAL CONSTITUTION
A loose confederation of states	A firm union of people
1 vote in Congress for each state	2 votes in Senate for each state; representation by population in House (see Art. I, Secs. II, III)
$\frac{2}{3}$ vote (9 states) in Congress for all important measures	Simple majority vote in Congress, subject to presidential veto (see Art. I, Sec. VII, para. 2)
Laws executed by committees of Congress	Laws executed by powerful president (see Art. II, Secs. II, III)
No congressional power over commerce	Congress to regulate both foreign and interstate commerce (see Art. I, Sec. VIII, para. 3)
No congressional power to levy taxes	Extensive power in Congress to levy taxes (see Art. I, Sec. VIII, para. 1)
No federal courts	Federal courts, capped by Supreme Court (see Art. III)
Unanimity of states for amendment	Amendment less difficult (see Art. V)
No authority to act directly upon individuals and no power to coerce states	Ample power to enforce laws by coercion of individuals and to some extent of states

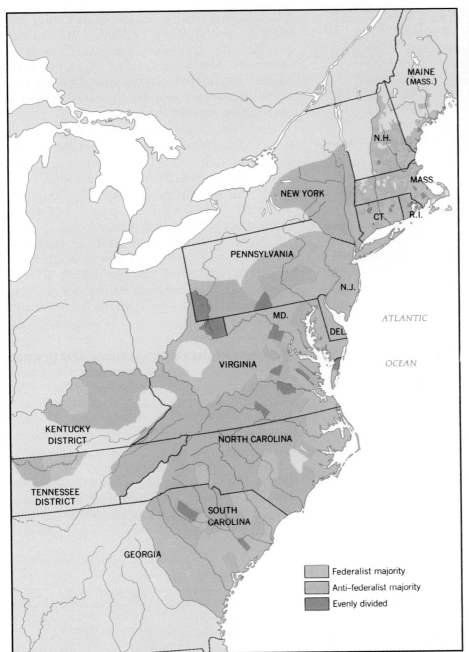

The Struggle over Ratification *This mottled map shows that federalist support tended to cluster around the coastal areas, which had enjoyed profitable commerce with the outside world, including the export of grain and tobacco. Impoverished frontiersmen, suspicious of a powerful new central government under the Constitution, were generally anti-federalists.*

Federalist majority

Anti-federalist majority

Evenly divided

Hopkinson exulted in his song "The New Roof":

> Huzza! my brave boys, our work is complete;
> The world shall admire Columbia's fair seat.

But such rejoicing was premature so long as the four dissenters, conspicuously New York and Virginia, remained outside the fold.

The Four Laggard States

Proud Virginia, the biggest and most populous state, provided fierce anti-federalist opposition. There the college-bred federalist orators, for once, encountered worthy antagonists, including the fiery Patrick Henry. He professed to see in the fearsome parchment the death warrant of

> *Richard Henry Lee, a prominent anti-federalist, attacked the proposed constitution in 1788: "'Tis really astonishing that the same people, who have just emerged from a long and cruel war in defense of liberty, should now agree to fix an elective despotism upon themselves and their posterity."*

liberty. George Washington, James Madison, and John Marshall, on the federalist side, lent influential support. With New Hampshire about to ratify, the new Union was going to be formed anyhow, and Virginia could not very well continue comfortably as an independent state. After a close and exciting debate in the state convention, ratification carried, 89 to 79.

New York, which also experienced an uphill struggle, was the only state that permitted a manhood-suffrage vote for the members of the ratifying convention. The result was a heavy anti-federalist majority. Alexander Hamilton at heart favored a much stronger central government than that under debate, but he contributed his sparkling personality and persuasive eloquence to whipping up support. He also joined John Jay and James Madison in penning a masterly series of articles for the New York newspapers. Though designed as propaganda, these essays remain the most penetrating commentary ever written on the Constitution and are still widely sold in book form as *The Federalist*. Probably the most famous of these is Madison's *"Federalist No. 10,"* which brilliantly refuted the conventional wisdom of the day that it was impossible to extend a republican form of government over a large territory.

New York finally yielded. Realizing that the state could not prosper apart from the Union, the convention ratified the document by the close count of 30 to 27. At the same time, it approved thirty-two proposed amendments and—vain hope—issued a call for yet another convention to modify the Constitution.

Last-ditch dissent developed in only two states. A hostile convention met in North Carolina, then adjourned without taking a vote. Rhode Island did not even summon a ratifying convention. The two most ruggedly individualist centers of the colonial era—homes of the "otherwise minded"—thus ran true to form. They were to change their course, albeit unwillingly, only after the new government had been in operation for some months.

The battle for ratification, despite much apathy, was close and extremely bitter in some localities. No lives were lost, but riotous disturbances broke out in New York, and Pennsylvania, involving bruises and bloodshed. There was much behind-the-scenes pressure on delegates who had solemnly promised their constituents to vote against the Constitution. The last four

Ratification of the Constitution

STATE	DATE	VOTE IN CONVENTION	RANK IN POPULATION	1790 POPULATION
1. Delaware	Dec. 7, 1787	Unanimous	13	59,096
2. Pennsylvania	Dec. 12, 1787	46 to 23	3	433,611
3. New Jersey	Dec. 18, 1787	Unanimous	9	184,139
4. Georgia	Jan. 2, 1788	Unanimous	11	82,548
5. Connecticut	Jan. 9, 1788	128 to 40	8	237,655
6. Massachusetts (incl. Maine)	Feb. 7, 1788	187 to 168	2	475,199
7. Maryland	Apr. 28, 1788	63 to 11	6	319,728
8. South Carolina	May 23, 1788	149 to 73	7	249,073
9. New Hampshire	June 21, 1788	57 to 46	10	141,899
10. Virginia	June 26, 1788	89 to 79	1	747,610
11. New York	July 26, 1788	30 to 27	5	340,241
12. North Carolina	Nov. 21, 1789	195 to 77	4	395,005
13. Rhode Island	May 29, 1790	34 to 32	12	69,112

REDEUNT SATURNIA REGNA.

On the erection of the Eleventh PILLAR of the great National DOME, we beg leave most sincerely to felicitate " OUR DEAR COUNTRY."

Rise it will.

The foundation good—it may yet be SAVED.

A Triumphant Cartoon *It appeared in the Massachusetts Centinel on August 2, 1788. Note the two laggards, especially the sorry condition of Rhode Island.*

states ratified, not because they wanted to but because they had to. They could not safely exist apart from the Union.

A Conservative Triumph

The minority had triumphed—doubly. A militant minority of American radicals had engineered the military Revolution that cast off the unwritten British constitution. A militant minority of conservatives—now embracing many of the earlier radicals—had engineered the peaceful revolution that overthrew the inadequate constitution known as the Articles of Confederation. Eleven states, in effect, had seceded from the Confederation, leaving two out in the cold.

A majority had not spoken. Only about one-fourth of the adult white males in the country, chiefly the propertied people, had voted for delegates to the ratifying conventions. Careful estimates indicate that if the new Constitution had been submitted to a manhood-suffrage vote, as in New York, it would have encountered much more opposition, probably defeat.

Conservatism was victorious. Safeguards had been erected against mob-rule excesses, and the democratic gains of the Revolution were conserved in the face of possible anarchy. Radicals like Patrick Henry, who had overthrown British rule, had in turn been overthrown by American conservatives. The result was a kind of peaceful counterrevolution. It restored the economic and political stability of colonial years and set the drifting ship of state on a more promising course.

Yet if the architects of the Constitution were conservative, it is worth emphasizing that what they conserved was the principle of popular, democratic government, made forever sacred in the fires of the Revolution. By ingeniously embedding the doctrine of self-rule in a self-limiting system of checks and balances, the Constitution reconciled the potentially conflicting principles of liberty and order. It represented a marvelous achievement; one that preserved the ideals of the Revolution even while setting boundaries to them. One of the distinctive—and enduring—paradoxes of American history was thus revealed: in the United States, conservatives and radicals alike have championed the heritage of democratic revolutionism.

Referring to the belief that self-government is better than good government, Fisher Ames of Massachusetts, a federalist member of the new Congress, is quoted as having said: "A monarchy is like a merchantman [merchant ship]. You get on board and ride the wind and tide in safety and elation but, by and by, you strike a reef and go down. But democracy is like a raft. You never sink, but, damn it, your feet are always in the water."

Hamiltonian Frigate   *A victory parade in New York City honoring Hamilton and the ratification of the Constitution. At the key New York ratifying convention at Poughkeepsie, Hamilton, by sheer eloquence and cogent argument, turned a two-thirds majority against the Constitution into a majority of three in favor of it. (The Granger Collection.)*

CHRONOLOGY

1774	Continental Congress calls for abolition of slave trade
1776	New Jersey constitution temporarily gives women the vote
1777	Articles of Confederation adopted by Congress
1780	Massachusetts adopts first constitution drafted in convention and ratified by popular vote
1781	Articles of Confederation put into effect
1783	Military officers form Society of the Cincinnati
1785	Land Ordinance of 1785
1786	Virginia Statute for Religious Freedom
	Shays's Rebellion
	Meeting of five states to discuss revision of the Articles of Confederation
1787	Northwest Ordinance
	Constitutional Convention in Philadelphia
1788	Ratification by nine states guarantees a new government under the Constitution

Varying Viewpoints

Charles Beard's book, *An Economic Interpretation of the Constitution of the United States* (1913), has long defined the area around which debate on the constitutional period has revolved. Beard described the Constitution as the "reactionary" phase of the Revolutionary era—a shrewd maneuver by conservative property owners to curtail the democratic excesses let loose in 1776. Most modern scholars, if they accept Beard's argument at all, accept it only with severe qualifications. The most recent discussions of the Constitution have been cast in terms of reflections on the ancient riddle of republicanism: Does republican self-government rest on the virtue of the people or on the formal political institutions that control human behavior? Seen in this light, the framers of the Constitution appear more "radical" than their opponents.

The anti-federalists who opposed the Constitution, in this view, so feared human weakness for corruption that they shuddered at the prospect of putting powerful political weapons in the hands of a central government. They saw small governments susceptible to local control as the only safeguard against tyranny. The federalists who made the Constitution, on the other hand, believed that a strong, balanced national government would rein in selfish human instincts and channel them toward the pursuit of the common good. Alarmed by the excesses of the state governments, the federalists developed the novel idea of an "extensive republic," a polity that would achieve stability by virtue of its great size and diversity. This conception, scholars such as Gordon S. Wood have concluded, challenged the conventional wisdom that a republic could only survive if it extended over a small area with a homogeneous population. In this sense, the Constitution represented a bold experiment—the fulfillment, rather than the repudiation, of the most advanced ideas of the Revolutionary era.

This appraisal of the making of the Constitution builds on Bernard Bailyn's interpretation of the "ideological origins" of the Revolution. Scholars following Bailyn's approach see disputes over the principles of republicanism—not economic and social conflict—as the force driving the evolution of American institutions. The federalists and their opponents, in this view, debated the proper application to American society of republican theory—a body of ideas Americans borrowed from the eighteenth-century English "country party" opposition to the power and alleged corruption of the court. "Country" politicians had emphasized the importance of public virtue, the preservation of an independent citizenry, and the election of government officials who would unselfishly serve the common good. All of these ideas seemed to apply with peculiar force in the rustic, egalitarian setting of democratic America. Indeed, many recent historians have cast the entire history of the pre–Civil War era in terms of a protracted debate over the extent to which American society conformed to republican ideals.

Select Readings

Primary Source Documents

A comparison of the text of the Articles of Confederation (1781), in Henry Steele Commager, *Documents of American History*, with the Constitution* makes an intriguing study. See also Madison, Hamilton, and Jay's explanations of the Constitution in *The Federalist* papers, especially "Federalist No. 10."*

Secondary Sources

John Fiske, in *The Critical Period of American History* (1888), portrayed America under the Articles of Confederation as a crisis-ridden country. His view has been sharply qualified by Merrill Jensen in *The New Nation* (1950). Jack N. Rakove's *The Beginnings of National Politics* (1979) offers a history of the Continental Congress that substantially revises Jensen's work. Especially learned is Gordon S. Wood's massive and brilliant study of the entire period, *The Creation of the American Republic, 1776–1787* (1969). An influential transatlantic perspective on the roots of American republicanism is J. G. A. Pocock, *The Machiavellian Moment: Florentine Political Thought and the Atlantic Republican Tradition* (1975). Edmund S. Morgan also looks at both England and America in *Inventing the People: The Rise of Popular Sovereignty in England and America* (1988). On the state constitutions, see Jackson T. Main, *The Sovereign States, 1775–1783* (1973), and Willi P. Adams, *The First American Constitutions* (1980). Peter S. Onuf carefully examines the Northwest Ordinance in *Statehood and Union: A History of the Northwest Ordinance* (1987). On the Constitutional Convention, see Clinton Rossiter, *1787: The Grand Convention* (1966), and Richard Bernstein's superb synthesis of current scholarship, *Are We to Be a Nation? The Making of the Constitution* (1987). Robert A. Rutland's *The Ordeal of the Constitution* (1966) describes the ratification struggle. Charles A. Beard shocked conservatives with *An Economic Interpretation of the Constitution of the United States* (1913). It is seriously weakened by two blistering attacks: Robert E. Brown, *Charles Beard and the Constitution* (1956), and Forrest McDonald, *We the People: The Economic Origins of the Constitution* (1958). See also McDonald's *E Pluribus Unum: The Formation of the American Republic, 1776–1790* (1965). Jackson T. Main, *The Anti-Federalists* (1961), partially rehabilitates Beard. Staughton Lynd explores another aspect of the topic in *Class Conflict, Slavery, and the United States Constitution* (1967). Sectionalism is discussed in William N. Chambers, *Political Parties in a New Nation* (1963). Finance is treated fully in Curtis P. Nettles, *The Emergence of a National Economy, 1775–1815* (1962). David Szatmary is perceptive on *Shays's Rebellion* (1980). Charles R. Kesler has edited a collection of essays on *The Federalist* papers, *Saving the Revolution: The Federalist Papers and the American Founding* (1987). Also see Morton White, *Philosophy, The Federalist, and the Constitution* (1987). Relevant biographical studies of merit are John C. Miller, *Alexander Hamilton: Portrait in Paradox* (1959); and Irving Brant, *James Madison* (6 vols., 1941–1961).

Launching the New Ship of State, 1789–1800

I shall only say that I hold with Montesquieu, that a government must be fitted to a nation, as much as a coat to the individual; and, consequently, that what may be good at Philadelphia may be bad at Paris, and ridiculous at Petersburg [Russia].

Alexander Hamilton, 1799

A New Ship on an Uncertain Sea

When the Constitution was launched in 1789, the Republic was continuing to grow at an amazing rate. Population was still doubling about every twenty-five years, and the first official census of 1790 recorded almost 4 million souls. Cities had blossomed proportionately: Philadelphia numbered 42,000; New York, 33,000; Boston, 18,000; Charleston, 16,000; and Baltimore, 13,000.

America's population was still about 90 percent rural, despite the flourishing cities; all but 5 percent of the people lived east of the mountains. The trans-Allegheny overflow was concentrated chiefly in Kentucky, Tennessee, and Ohio, all of which were welcomed as states within fourteen years. (Vermont had preceded them, becoming the fourteenth state in 1791.) Foreign travelers everywhere looked down their noses at the roughness and crudity resulting from ax-and-rifle pioneering life. Yet, critical though they might be, they were impressed by evidences of energy, self-confidence, and material well-being.

The new ship of state, despite these promising signs of fair weather, did not spread its sails to the most favorable breezes. Within twelve troubled years the American people had risen up and thrown overboard their first two constitutions: the British constitution and the Articles of Confederation. A decade of constitution smashing and law breaking was not the best training for government making. Americans had come to regard a central authority, replacing that of George III, as a necessary evil—something to be distrusted, watched, and curbed.

People of the western waters—in the stump-studded clearings of Kentucky, Tennessee, and Ohio—were restive and dubiously loyal. The mouth of the Mississippi, their life-giving outlet, lay in the hands of unfriendly Spaniards. Smooth-tongued Spanish and British agents, jingling gold, moved freely among the settlers and held out seductive promises of independence.

Finances of the infant government were likewise precarious. The revenue had declined to a trickle, while the public debt, with interest heavily in arrears, was mountainous. Worthless paper money, both state and national, was as plentiful as metallic money was scarce.

The Americans, moreover, were brashly trying to erect a republic on an immense scale, something that no other people had attempted and that traditional political theory held to be impossible. The eyes of a skeptical world were on the upstart United States, and the bejeweled monarchs of Europe in particular feared that the new republic would provide a dangerous example for their long-oppressed subjects.

Washington's Pro-Federalist Regime

General Washington, the esteemed war hero, was unanimously drafted as president by the Electoral College in 1789—the only presidential nominee ever to be honored by unanimity. His presence was imposing: 6 feet 2 inches, 175 pounds (1.88 meters, 79.5 kilograms), broad and sloping shoulders, strongly pointed chin, and pockmarks (from smallpox) on nose and

Washington Honored *This idealized portrait symbolized the reverential awe in which Americans held "the father of the country." (Metropolitan Museum of Art, Gift of Edgar and Bernice Garbisch, 1962.)*

cheeks. Much preferring the quiet of Mount Vernon to the turmoil of politics, he was perhaps the only president who did not in some way angle for this exalted office. Balanced rather than brilliant, he commanded his followers by strength of character rather than by the arts of the politician.

Washington's long journey from Mount Vernon to New York City, the temporary capital, was a triumphal procession. He was greeted by roaring cannon, pealing bells, flower-carpeted roads, and singing and shouting citizens. With appropriate ceremony, he solemnly and somewhat nervously took the oath of office on April 30, 1789, on a crowded balcony overlooking Wall Street, which some have regarded as a bad omen.

The Constitution does not mention a cabinet; it merely provides that the president "may require" written opinions of the heads of the executive-branch departments (see Art. II, Sec. II, para. 1). But this system proved so cumbersome, and involved so much homework, that cabinet meetings gradually evolved in the Washington administration.

At first only three full-fledged department heads served under the president: Secretary of State Thomas Jefferson, Secretary of the Trea-

> The French statesman Turgot had high expectations for a united America: *"This people is the hope of the human race. . . . The Americans should be an example of political, religious, commercial and industrial liberty. . . . But to obtain these ends for us, America . . . must not become . . . a mass of divided powers, contending for territory and trade."*

Evolution of the Cabinet

POSITION	DATE ESTABLISHED	COMMENTS
Secretary of state	1789	
Secretary of treasury	1789	
Secretary of war	1789	Loses cabinet status, 1947
Attorney general	1789	Not head of Justice Dept. until 1870
Secretary of navy	1798	Loses cabinet status, 1947
Postmaster general	1829	Loses cabinet status, 1970
Secretary of interior	1849	
Secretary of agriculture	1889	
Secretary of commerce and labor	1903	Office divided in 1913
Secretary of commerce	1913	
Secretary of labor	1913	
Secretary of defense	1947	Subordinate to this secretary, without cabinet rank, are secretaries of army, navy, and air force.
Secretary of health, education, and welfare	1953	Office divided in 1979
Secretary of housing and urban development	1965	
Secretary of transportation	1966	
Secretary of energy	1977	
Secretary of health and human services	1979	
Secretary of education	1979	
Secretary of veterans' affairs	1989	

sury Alexander Hamilton, and Secretary of War Henry Knox.

The Bill of Rights

Drawing up a bill of rights headed the list of tasks facing the new government. Many anti-federalists had sharply criticized the Constitution drafted at Philadelphia for its failure to provide guarantees of individual rights such as freedom of religion and trial by jury. Many states had ratified the federal Constitution on the understanding that it would soon be amended to include such guarantees.

Amendments to the Constitution could be proposed in either of two ways—by a new constitutional convention requested by two-thirds of the states or by a two-thirds vote of both houses of Congress. Fearing that a new convention might unravel the narrow federalist victory in the ratification struggle, James Madison determined to draft the amendments himself. He then guided them through Congress, where his

Confidence in the Constitution *This late eighteenth-century printer's cut caught the spirit of optimism and hope that prevailed in the infant Republic. (The Granger Collection.)*

scholarly and political skills were quickly making him the leading figure.

Adopted by the necessary number of states in 1791, the first ten amendments to the Constitution, popularly known as the Bill of Rights, safeguarded some of the most precious of American principles. Among these are protections for freedom of religion, speech, and the press; the right to bear arms and to be tried by a jury; and the right to assemble and petition the government for redress of grievances. The Bill of Rights also prohibited cruel and unusual punishments, and arbitrary government seizure of private property.

To guard against the danger that enumerating such rights might lead to the conclusion that they were the only ones protected, Madison inserted the crucial Ninth Amendment. It declared that specifying certain rights "shall not be construed to deny or disparage others retained by the people." In a gesture of reassurance to the states' righters, he included the equally significant Tenth Amendment, which reserved all rights not explicitly delegated or prohibited by the federal Constitution "to the States respectively, or to the people." By preserving a strong central government while specifying protections for minority and individual liberties, Madison's amendments partially swung the federalist pendulum back in an antifederalist direction. (See Amendments I–X, in the Appendix.)

The first Congress also nailed other newly sawed governmental planks into place. It created effective federal courts under the Judiciary Act of 1789. The act organized the Supreme Court, with a chief justice and five associates, as well as federal district and circuit courts, and established the office of attorney general. New Yorker John Jay, Madison's collaborator on *The Federalist* papers and one of the young Republic's most seasoned diplomats, became the first chief justice of the United States.

Hamilton Revives the Corpse of Public Credit

The key figure in the new government was smooth-faced Treasury Secretary Alexander Hamilton, a thirty-four-year-old native of the British West Indies. Hamilton's genius was unquestioned, but critics claimed he loved his adopted country more than his countrymen. Doubts about his character and his loyalty to the republican experiment always swirled about his head. Hamilton regarded himself as a kind of prime minister in Washington's cabinet and on occasion thrust his hands into the affairs of other departments, including that of his archrival, Thomas Jefferson.

A financial wizard, Hamilton set out immediately to correct the economic vexations that had crippled the Articles of Confederation. His plan was to shape the fiscal policies of the administration in such a way as to favor the wealthier groups. They, in turn, would gratefully lend the government monetary and moral support. The new federal regime would flourish, the propertied classes would grow fat, and prosperity would trickle down to the masses.

The youthful financier's first objective was to bolster the national credit. Without public confidence in the government, Hamilton could not secure the funds with which to float his risky schemes. He therefore boldly urged Congress to "fund" the entire national debt at par and to assume completely the debts incurred by the states during the recent war.

"Funding at par" meant that the federal government would pay off its debts at face value, plus accumulated interest—a then-enormous total of more than $54 million. So many people believed the infant Treasury incapable of meet-

Alexander Hamilton (1755–1804)   *He was one of the youngest and most brilliant of the Founding Fathers, who might have become president but for his ultraconservatism, an adulterous scandal, and a duelist's bullet. (National Portrait Gallery.)*

> *One of the most eloquent tributes to Hamilton came from Daniel Webster in the Senate (1831): "He smote the rock of the national resources, and abundant streams of revenue gushed forth. He touched the dead corpse of public credit, and it sprung upon its feet."*

ing those obligations that government bonds had depreciated to ten or fifteen cents on the dollar. Yet speculators held fistfuls of them, and when Congress passed Hamilton's measure in 1790, they grabbed for more. Some of them galloped into rural areas ahead of the news, buying for a song the depreciated paper holdings of farmers, war veterans, and widows.

Hamilton was willing, even eager, to have the new government shoulder additional obligations. While pushing the funding scheme, he urged Congress to assume the debts of the states, totaling some $21.5 million.

The secretary made a convincing case for "assumption." The state debts could be regarded as a proper national obligation, for they had been incurred in the war for independence. But foremost in Hamilton's thinking was the belief that assumption would chain the states more tightly to the "federal chariot." Thus, the secretary's maneuver would shift the attachment of wealthy creditors from the states to the federal government. The support of the rich for the national administration was a crucial link in Hamilton's political strategy of strengthening the central government.

States burdened with heavy debts, like Massachusetts, were delighted by Hamilton's proposal. States with small debts, like Virginia, were less happy. The stage was set for some old-fashioned horse trading. Virginia did not want the state debts assumed, but it did want the forthcoming federal district*—now the District of Columbia—to be located on the Potomac River. It would thus gain in commerce and prestige. Hamilton persuaded a reluctant Jefferson, who had recently come home from France, to line up enough votes in Congress for as-

---

*Authorized by the Constitution, Art. I, Sec. VIII, para. 17.

sumption. In return, Virginia would have the federal district on the Potomac. The bargain was carried through in 1790.

Customs Duties and Excise Taxes

The new ship of state thus set sail dangerously overloaded. The national debt had swelled to $75 million owing to Hamilton's insistence on honoring the outstanding federal and state obligations alike. Anyone less determined to establish such a healthy public credit could have sidestepped $13 million in back interest and could have avoided the state debts entirely.

But Hamilton, "Father of the National Debt," was not greatly worried. His objectives were as much political as economic. He believed that, within limits, a national debt was a "national blessing"—a kind of cement of union. The more creditors to whom the government owed money, the more people there would be with a personal stake in the success of his ambitious enterprise. His unique contribution was to make a debt—ordinarily a liability—an asset for vitalizing the financial system as well as the government itself.

Where was the money to come from to pay interest on this huge debt and run the government? Hamilton's first answer was customs duties, derived from a tariff. Tariff revenues, in turn, depended on a vigorous foreign trade, an-

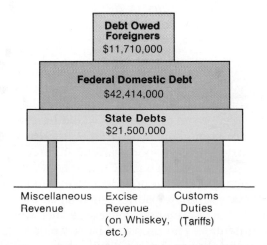

Hamilton's Financial Structure Supported by Revenues

other crucial link in Hamilton's overall economic strategy for the new Republic.

The first tariff law, imposing a low tariff of about 8 percent on the value of dutiable imports, was speedily passed by the first Congress in 1789, even before Hamilton was sworn in. Revenue was by far the main goal, but the measure was also designed to erect a low protective wall around infant industries, which bawled noisily for more shelter than they received. Hamilton had the vision to see that the industrial revolution would soon reach America, and he argued strongly in favor of more protection for the well-to-do manufacturing groups—another vital element in his economic program. But Congress was still dominated by the agricultural and commercial interests, and it voted only two slight increases in the tariff during Washington's presidency.

Hamilton, with characteristic vigor, sought additional internal revenue and in 1791 secured from Congress an excise tax on a few domestic items, notably whiskey. The new levy of seven cents a gallon was borne chiefly by the distillers who lived in the backcountry, where the wretched roads forced the farmer to reduce bulky bushels of grain to horseback proportions. Whiskey flowed so freely on the frontier that it was used for money.

Hamilton Battles Jefferson for a Bank

As the capstone of his financial system, Hamilton proposed a Bank of the United States. An enthusiastic admirer of most things English, he took as his model the Bank of England. Specifically, he proposed a powerful private institution, of which the government would be the major stockholder and in which the federal Treasury would deposit its surplus monies. The central government not only would have a convenient strongbox, but federal funds would stimulate business by remaining in circulation. The bank would also print urgently needed paper money and thus provide a sound and stable national currency, badly needed since the days when the Continental dollar was "not worth a Continental." The proposed bank would indeed be useful. But was it constitutional?

Jefferson, whose written opinion on this question Washington requested, argued vigorously against the bank. There was, he insisted, no specific authorization in the Constitution for such a financial octopus. He was convinced that all powers not specifically granted to the central government were reserved to the states, as provided in the about-to-be-ratified Bill of Rights (see Art. X). He therefore concluded that the states, not Congress, had the power to charter banks. Believing that the Constitution should be interpreted "literally" or "strictly," Jefferson and his states' rights disciples zealously embraced the theory of "strict construction."

Hamilton, also at Washington's request, prepared a brilliantly reasoned reply to Jefferson's arguments. Hamilton in general believed that what the Constitution did not forbid it permitted; Jefferson, in contrast, generally believed that what it did not permit it forbade. Hamilton boldly invoked that clause of the Constitution which stipulates that Congress may pass any laws "necessary and proper" to carry out the powers vested in the various governmental agencies (see Art. I, Sec. VIII, para. 18). The government was explicitly empowered to collect taxes and regulate trade. In carrying out these basic functions, Hamilton argued, a national bank would be not only "proper" but "necessary." By inference or implication—that is, by virtue of "implied powers"—Congress would be fully justified in establishing the Bank of the United States. In short, Hamilton contended for a "loose" or "broad" interpretation of the Constitution. He and his federalist followers thus evolved the theory of "loose construction" by invoking the "elastic clause" of the Constitution—a precedent for enormous federal powers.

Hamilton's financial views prevailed. His eloquent and realistic arguments were accepted by Washington, who reluctantly signed the bank measure into law. This explosive issue had been debated with much heat in Congress, where the old North-South cleavage again appeared ominously. The most enthusiastic support for the bank naturally came from the commercial and financial centers of the North, while the strongest opposition arose from the agricultural South.

The Bank of the United States, as created by

The Two Political Parties, 1793–1800

FEDERALIST FEATURES	DEMOCRATIC-REPUBLICAN (JEFFERSONIAN) FEATURES
Rule by the "best people"	Rule by the informed masses
Hostility to extension of democracy	Friendliness toward extension of democracy
A powerful central government at the expense of states' rights	A weak central government so as to conserve states' rights
Loose interpretation of Constitution	Strict interpretation of Constitution
Government to foster business; concentration of wealth in interests of capitalistic enterprise	No special favors for business; agriculture preferred
A protective tariff	No special favors for manufacturers
Pro-British (conservative Tory tradition)	Pro-French (radical Revolutionary tradition)
National debt a blessing, if properly funded	National debt a bane; rigid economy
An expanding bureaucracy	Reduction of federal officeholders
A powerful central bank	Encouragement to state banks
Restrictions on free speech and press	Relatively free speech and press
Concentration in seacoast area	Concentration in S. and S.W.; in agricultural areas and back country
A strong navy to protect shippers	A minimal navy for coast defense

Congress in 1791, was chartered for twenty years. Located in Philadelphia, it was to have a capital of $10 million, one-fifth of it owned by the federal government. Stock was thrown open to public sale. To the agreeable surprise of Hamilton, a milling crowd oversubscribed in less than two hours, pushing aside many would-be purchasers.

Mutinous Moonshiners in Pennsylvania

The Whiskey Rebellion, which flared up in southwestern Pennsylvania in 1794, sharply challenged the new national government. Hamilton's excise bore harshly on these home-spun pioneer folk. They regarded it not as a tax on a luxury but as a burden on an economic necessity and a medium of exchange. Even preachers of the gospel were paid in "Old Monongahela rye." Defiant distillers finally erected whiskey poles, similar to the liberty poles of anti–stamp tax days in 1765, and raised the cry "Liberty and No Excise." Boldly tarring and feathering revenue officers, they brought collections to a halt.

President Washington, once a revolutionist, was alarmed by what he called these "self-created societies." With the warm encouragement of Hamilton, he summoned the militia of several states. Anxious moments followed the call for there was much doubt as to whether men in other states would muster to crush a rebellion in a sister state. Despite some opposition, an army of about thirteen thousand rallied to the colors, and two widely separated columns marched briskly forth in a gorgeous, leaf-tinted Indian summer, until knee-deep mud slowed their progress.

When the troops reached the hills of western Pennsylvania, they found no insurrection. The "Whiskey Boys" were overawed, dispersed, or captured. Washington, with an eye to healing old sores, pardoned the two small-fry convicted culprits.

The Whiskey Rebellion was small—some three rebels were killed—but its consequences were large. George Washington's government, now substantially strengthened, commanded a new respect. Yet the numerous foes of the federalists condemned the administration for its brutal display of force—for having used a sledge hammer to crush a gnat.

The Emergence of Political Parties

Almost overnight, Hamilton's fiscal feats had established the government's sound credit rating. The Treasury could now borrow needed funds in the Netherlands on favorable terms.

But Hamilton's financial successes—funding, assumption, the excise, the bank, the suppression of the Whiskey Rebellion—created some political liabilities. All these schemes encroached sharply upon states' rights. Many Americans, dubious about the new Constitution in the first place, might never have approved it if they had foreseen how the states were going to be overshadowed by the federal colossus. Now, out of resentment against Hamilton's revenue-raising and centralizing policies, an organized opposition began to build. What once was a personal feud between Hamilton and Jefferson developed into a full-blown and often bitter political rivalry.

National political parties, in the modern sense, were unknown to America when George Washington took his inaugural oath. There had been Whigs and Tories, federalists and anti-federalists, but these groups were factions rather than parties. They had sprung into existence over hotly contested special issues; they had faded away when their cause had triumphed or had become hopelessly lost.

The Founders at Philadelphia had not envisioned the existence of permanent political parties. Organized opposition to the government—especially a democratic government based on popular consent—seemed tainted with disloyalty. It affronted the spirit of national unity that the glorious cause of the Revolution had inspired. The notion of a formal party apparatus was thus a novelty in the 1790s, and when Jefferson and Madison first organized their opposition to the Hamiltonian program, they confined their activities to Congress and did not anticipate creating a long-lived, popular party. But as their antagonism to Hamilton endured, and as the amazingly boisterous and widely read newspapers of the day spread their political message, and Hamilton's, among the people, primitive semblances of political parties emerged. The two-party system has existed in the United States since that time. Ironically, in light of early suspicions about the very legitimacy of parties, their competition for power has proved to be among the indispensable ingredients of a sound democracy. The party of the "outs"—"the loyal opposition"—traditionally plays the invaluable role of balance wheel on the machinery of government, ensuring that politics never drifts too far out of kilter with the wishes of the people.

The Impact of the French Revolution

When Washington's first administration ended, early in 1793, Hamilton's domestic policies had already stimulated the formation of two political

Republicanism Triumphant *Artists frequently relied on classical motifs to celebrate the triumph in America of republicanism—a form of government they traced back to ancient Greece and Rome. (Henry Francis du Pont Winterthur Museum.)*

camps—Jeffersonian Democratic-Republicans and Hamiltonian Federalists. As his second term began, foreign-policy issues brought the differences between them to a fever pitch.

Only a few weeks after Washington's inauguration in 1789, the curtain had risen on the first act of the French Revolution. Twenty-six years were to pass before the seething continent of Europe settled back into a peace of exhaustion. Few non-American events have left a deeper scar on American political and social life. In a sense, the French Revolution was misnamed: it was a *world* revolution that touched all civilized peoples.

In its early stages the upheaval was surprisingly peaceful, involving as it did a successful attempt to impose constitutional shackles on Louis XVI. The American people, loving liberty and deploring despotism, were pleased. They were flattered to think that the outburst in France was but the second chapter of their own glorious Revolution, as to some extent it was. Only a few ultraconservative Federalists—fearing change, reform, and "leveling" principles—were from the outset dubious or outspokenly hostile to the "despicable mobocracy." The more ardent Jeffersonians were overjoyed.

The French Revolution entered a more ominous phase in 1792, when France declared war on hostile Austria. Powerful ideals and powerful armies alike were on the march. Late in that year the electrifying news reached America that French citizen armies had hurled back the invading foreigners and that France had proclaimed itself a republic. Americans enthusiastically sang "The Marseillaise" and other rousing French Revolutionary songs and they renamed thoroughfares. King Street in New York, for example, became Liberty Street, while in Boston Royal Exchange Alley became Equality Lane.

But centuries of pent-up poison could not be purged without baleful results. The guillotine was set up, the king was beheaded in 1793, Christianity was abolished, and the head-rolling Reign of Terror was begun. Back in America, God-fearing Federalist aristocrats nervously fingered their tender white necks and eyed the Jeffersonian masses apprehensively. Lukewarm Federalist approval of the early Revolution turned, almost overnight, to heated opposition to "blood-drinking cannibals."

Sober-minded Jeffersonians regretted the bloodshed. But they felt, with Jefferson, that one could not expect to be carried from "despotism to liberty in a feather bed" and that a few thousand aristocratic heads were a cheap price to pay for human freedom.

Such gloating was shortsighted, for dire peril loomed ahead. The earlier battles of the French Revolution had not hurt America directly, but now Britain was sucked into the titanic conflict. The conflagration speedily spread to the New World, where it vitally affected the expanding young American Republic. Thus was repeated the familiar story of every major European war, beginning with 1689, that involved a death struggle for control of the Atlantic Ocean. (See table on p. 89.)

The Contrast *Adaptation of an English cartoon. C. C. Coffin,* Building a Nation, *1882. (Boston Public Library.)*

Washington's Neutrality Proclamation

Ominously, the Franco-American alliance of 1778 was still on the books. By its own terms it was to last "forever." It bound the United States to help the French defend their West Indies against future foes; and the booming British fleets were certain to attack these strategic islands.

Many Jeffersonian Democratic-Republicans favored honoring the alliance, though dubious about defending the French island outposts at the risk of war. Aflame with the liberal ideals of the French Revolution, red-blooded Jeffersonians were eager to enter the conflict against Britain, the recent foe, at the side of France, the recent friend. America owed France its freedom, they argued, and now was the time to pay the debt of gratitude.

But President Washington, levelheaded as usual, was not swayed by the clamor of the crowd. Backed by Hamilton, he perceived that war had to be avoided at all costs. Washington was coolly playing for enormous stakes. The nation in 1793 was militarily weak, economically wobbly, and politically disunited. But solid foundations were being laid, and American cradles were continuing to rock a bumper crop of babies. Washington sagaciously reasoned that if America could avoid the broils of Europe for a generation or so, it would then be populous enough and strong enough to assert its maritime rights with vigor and success. Otherwise, it might invite catastrophe. The strategy of delay—of playing for time while the birthrate fought America's battles—was a cardinal policy of the Founding Fathers. Hamilton and Jefferson, often poles apart on other issues, were in agreement here.

Accordingly, Washington boldly issued his Neutrality Proclamation in 1793, shortly after the outbreak of war between Britain and France. This epochal document not only proclaimed the government's official neutrality in the widening conflict but sternly warned American citizens to be impartial toward both armed camps. It was America's first formal declaration of aloofness from Old World quarrels and as such proved to be a major prop of the spreading isolationist tradition.

The pro-French Jeffersonians were enraged by the Neutrality Proclamation, especially by Washington's method of announcing it unilaterally, without consulting Congress. The pro-British Federalists were heartened. A few days earlier an impetuous, thirty-year-old representative of the French Republic, Citizen Edmond Genêt, had landed at Charleston, South Carolina. With unrestrained zeal, he undertook to fit out privateers and otherwise take advantage of the existing Franco-American alliance. The giddy-headed envoy—all sail and no anchor—was soon swept away by his enthusiastic reception by the Jeffersonian Republicans. He foolishly came to believe that the Neutrality Proclamation did not reflect the true wishes of the American people, and he consequently embarked upon unneutral activity not authorized by the French alliance—including the recruitment of armies to invade Spanish Florida and Louisiana, as well as British Canada. Even Madison and Jefferson were soon disillusioned by his conduct. After he had threatened to appeal over the head of "Old Washington" to the sovereign voters, the president demanded Genêt's withdrawal and the Frenchman was replaced by a less impulsive emissary.

Washington's Neutrality Proclamation clearly illustrates the truism that self-interest is the basic cement of alliances. In 1778, both France and America stood to gain; in 1793, only France. Technically, the Americans did not flout their obligation, because France never

William Cobbett wrote of the frenzied reaction in America to the death of Louis XVI: "Never was the memory of any man so cruelly insulted as that of this mild and humane monarch. He was guillotined in effigy, in the capital of the Union [Philadelphia], twenty or thirty times every day, during one whole winter and part of the summer. Men, women and children flocked to the tragical exhibition, and not a single paragraph appeared in the papers to shame them from it."

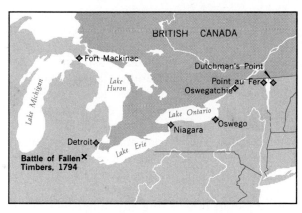

American Posts Held by the British After 1783

officially called upon them to honor it. Its homeland, and especially its blockaded West Indian islands, were urgently in need of Yankee foodstuffs. If the Americans had entered the war, the British fleets would have blockaded their coasts and cut off those desperately needed supplies. America was much more useful to France as a prosperous provider than as a prostrate partner.

Embroilments with Britain

President Washington's far-visioned policy of neutrality was sorely tried by the British. For ten long years they had been retaining the chain of northern frontier posts on U.S. soil, all in defiance of the peace treaty of 1783. The London government was reluctant to abandon the lucrative fur trade in the Great Lakes region and also hoped to build up an Indian buffer state to contain the ambitious Americans. British agents openly sold firearms and firewater to the Indians, who continued to attack palefaced pioneers invading their lands. When General "Mad Anthony" Wayne crushed the northwest Indians at the Battle of Fallen Timbers on August 20, 1794, the fleeing foe left on the field British-made arms, as well as the corpses of a few British-Canadians. In the Treaty of Greenville in 1795, the Indians, finally abandoned by their red-coated friends, ceded their claims to a vast virgin tract in the Ohio country.

On the sea frontier, the British were eager to starve out the French West Indies and naturally expected the United States to defend them under the Franco-American alliance. Hard-boiled commanders of the Royal Navy, acting under instructions from London in 1793, struck savagely. They seized about three hundred American merchant ships in the West Indies, impressed scores of seamen into service on English vessels, and threw hundreds of others into foul dungeons.

These actions outraged patriotic Americans. A mighty outcry arose, chiefly from Jeffersonians, that America should once again fight George III in defense of its liberties. At the very least, it should cut off all supplies to its oppressor through a nationwide embargo. But the Federalists stoutly resisted all demands for drastic action. War with Britain would be a lethal blow at the heart of the Hamiltonian financial system.

Jay's Treaty and Washington's Farewell

President Washington, in a last desperate gamble to avert war, decided to send Chief Justice John Jay to London in 1794. The Jeffersonians were acutely unhappy over the choice, partly because they feared that so notorious a Federalist and Britain-lover would sell out his country. Arriving in London, Jay gave the Jeffersonians further cause for alarm when, at the presentation ceremony, he routinely kissed the queen's hand.

Unhappily, Jay entered the negotiations with weak cards, which were further weakened by Hamilton. The latter, fearful of war with England, secretly supplied the British with the details of America's bargaining strategy. Not surprisingly, Jay won few concessions. The British did promise to evacuate the chain of posts on U.S. soil—a pledge that inspired little confidence, since it had been made before in Paris (to the same John Jay!) in 1783. In addition, Britain consented to pay damages for the recent seizures of American ships. But the British stopped short of pledging anything about *future* maritime seizures and impressments or about supplying arms to Indians. And they forced Jay to give ground by binding the United States to pay the debts still owed to British merchants on pre-Revolutionary accounts.

When the Jeffersonians learned of Jay's concessions, their rage was fearful to behold. The treaty seemed like an abject surrender to Britain, as well as a betrayal of the Jeffersonian South. Southern planters would have to pay the major share of the pre-Revolutionary debts, while rich Federalist shippers were collecting damages for recent British seizures. Jeffersonian mobs hanged, burned, and guillotined in effigy that "damn'd archtraitor, Sir John Jay." His unpopular pact, more than any other issue, vitalized the newborn Democratic-Republican party of Thomas Jefferson. Even George Washington's huge popularity was compromised by the controversy over the treaty.

Jay's Treaty had other unforeseen consequences. Fearing that the treaty foreshadowed an Anglo-American alliance, Spain moved hastily to strike a deal with the United States. Pinckney's Treaty of 1795 granted the Americans virtually everything they demanded, including free navigation of the Mississippi and the large disputed territory north of Florida. (See map on p. 151.)

Exhausted after the diplomatic and partisan battles of his second term, President Washington decided to retire. His choice contributed powerfully to establishing a two-term tradition for American presidents.* In his Farewell Address to the nation in 1796 (never delivered orally but printed in the newspapers), Washington strongly advised the avoidance of "permanent alliances" like the still-vexatious French Treaty of 1778. Contrary to general misunderstanding, Washington did not oppose all alliances, but favored only "temporary alliances" for "extraordinary emergencies." This was admirable advice for a weak and divided nation in 1796. But what is sound counsel for a growing youth may not apply later to a muscular giant.

Washington's contributions as president were enormous, even though the sparkling Hamilton at times seemed to outshine him. The central government, its fiscal feet now under it, was solidly established. The West was expanding. The merchant marine was plowing the seas. Above all, Washington had kept the nation out of both overseas entanglements and foreign wars. The experimental stage had passed, and the presidential chair could now be turned over to a less impressive figure. But republics are notoriously ungrateful. When Washington left office in 1797, he was showered with the brickbats of partisan abuse, quite in contrast with the bouquets that had greeted his coming.

"Bonny Johnny" Adams Becomes President

Who should succeed the exalted "Father of His Country"? Alexander Hamilton was the best-known member of the Federalist party, now that Washington had bowed out. But his financial policies, some of which had fattened

---

Evidently satirizing Jay's obeisance to the British queen, one American journal wrote "Hear the voice of truth, hear and believe! John Jay, ah! the arch traitor—seize him, drown him, hang him, burn him, flay him alive! Men of America, he betrayed you with a kiss!"

---

*Not broken until 1940 by Franklin D. Roosevelt and made a part of the Constitution in 1951 by the Twenty-second Amendment.

the speculators, had made him so unpopular that he could not hope to be elected president. The Federalists were forced to turn to Washington's vice-president, the experienced but ungracious John Adams, a rugged chip off old Plymouth Rock. The Democratic-Republicans naturally rallied behind their master organizer and leader, Thomas Jefferson.

Political passions ran feverishly high in the presidential canvass of 1796. The presence of Washington had hitherto imposed some re-

Thomas Paine, then in France and resenting George Washington's anti-French policies, addressed the president in an open letter (1796) that reveals his bitterness: "And as to you, sir, treacherous in private friendship (for so you have been to me, and that in the day of danger) and a hypocrite in public life, the world will be puzzled to decide, whether you are an apostate or an imposter; whether you have abandoned good principles, or whether you ever had any."

John Adams *Second president of the United States, Adams reflected the optimistic, forward-looking values of the eighteenth-century Enlightenment in his views on education: "I must study politics and war, that my sons may have liberty to study mathematics and philosophy. My sons ought to study mathematics and philosophy, geography, natural history and naval architecture, in order to give their children a right to study painting, poetry, music, architecture, statuary, tapestry and porcelain." (Harvard University Portrait Collection.)*

straints; now the lid was off. Cultured Federalists like Fisher Ames referred to the Jeffersonians as "fire-eating salamanders, poison-sucking toads." Federalists and Democratic-Republicans even drank their liquor in separate taverns. The issues of the campaign, as it turned out, focused heavily on personalities. But the Jeffersonians again assailed the too-forceful crushing of the Whiskey Rebellion and, above all, the negotiation of Jay's hated treaty.

John Adams, with most of his support in New England, squeezed through by the narrow margin of 71 votes to 68 in the Electoral College. Jefferson, as runner-up, became vice-president.* One of the ablest statesmen of his day, Adams at sixty-two was a stuffy figure. Sharp-featured, bald, short (5 feet 7 inches; 1.7 meters), and thickset ("His Rotundity"), he impressed observers as a man of stern principles who did his duty with stubborn devotion. Though learned and upright, he was a tactless and prickly intellectual aristocrat, with no appeal to the masses and with no desire to cultivate any. Many citizens regarded him with "respectful irritation."

The crusty New Englander suffered from other handicaps. He had stepped into Washington's shoes, which no successor could hope to

---

*The possibility of such an inharmonious two-party combination in the future was removed by the Twelfth Amendment to the Constitution in 1804. (See text in the Appendix.)

fill. In addition, Adams was hated by Hamilton, who had resigned from the Treasury in 1795 and who now headed the war faction of the Federalist party. The famed financier even secretly plotted with certain members of the cabinet against the president, who had a conspiracy rather than a cabinet on his hands. Adams regarded Hamilton as "the most ruthless, impatient, artful, indefatigable and unprincipled intriguer in the United States, if not in the world." Most ominous of all, Adams inherited a violent quarrel with France—a quarrel that foreshadowed blazing gunpowder.

Unofficial Fighting with France

The French were infuriated by Jay's Treaty. They condemned it as the initial step toward an alliance with England, their relentless foe. They further assailed the pact as a flagrant violation of the Franco-American Treaty of 1778. French warships, in retaliation, began to seize defenseless American merchant vessels, altogether about three hundred by mid-1797. Adding insult to outrage, the Paris regime haughtily refused to receive America's newly appointed envoy and even threatened him with arrest.

President Adams kept his head, temporarily, even though the nation was mightily aroused.

> Jefferson wrote privately of John Adams in 1787: "He is vain, irritable, and a bad calculator of the force and probable effect of the motives which govern men. This is all the ill which can possibly be said of him. He is as disinterested as the Being who made him."

True to Washington's policy of steering clear of war at all costs, he tried again to reach an agreement with the French and appointed a diplomatic commission of three men, including John Marshall, the future chief justice.

Adams's envoys, reaching Paris in 1797, hoped to meet Talleyrand, the crafty French foreign minister. They were secretly approached by three go-betweens, later referred to as X, Y, and Z in the published dispatches. The French spokesmen, among other concessions, demanded an unneutral loan of 32 million florins, plus what amounted to a bribe of $250,000, for the privilege of merely talking with Talleyrand.

These terms were intolerable. The American trio knew that bribes were standard diplomatic devices in Europe, but they gagged at paying a quarter of a million dollars for mere talk, without any assurances of a settlement. Negotia-

The XYZ Affair When President Adams's envoys to Paris were asked to pay a huge bribe as the price of doing diplomatic business, humiliated Americans rose up in wrath against France. Here an innocent young America is being plundered by Frenchmen as John Bull looks on in amusement. (The Lilly Library, Indiana University, Bloomington.)

tions quickly broke down, and John Marshall, on reaching New York in 1798, was hailed as a conquering hero for his steadfastness.

War hysteria swept the United States, catching up President Adams. The slogan of the hour became "Millions for defense, but not one cent for tribute." The Federalists were delighted at this unexpected turn of affairs, while all except the most rabid Jeffersonians hung their heads over the misbehavior of their French friends.

War preparations in America were pushed feverishly, despite considerable Jeffersonian opposition in Congress. The Navy Department was created; the three-ship navy was expanded; the United States Marine Corps was established. A new army of ten thousand men was authorized (but never fully raised).

Bloodshed was confined to the sea, and principally to the West Indies. In two and one-half years of undeclared hostilities (1798–1800), American privateers and men-of-war of the new navy captured over eighty armed vessels flying the French colors, though several hundred Yankee merchantmen were lost to the enemy. Evidently only a slight push would plunge both nations into a full-dress war.

Adams Puts Patriotism above Party

Embattled France, its hands full in Europe, wanted no war. An outwitted Talleyrand realized that to fight the United States would merely add one more foe to his enemies. The British, who were lending the Americans cannon and other war supplies, were actually driven closer to their wayward cousins than they were to be again for many years. Talleyrand therefore let it be known, through roundabout channels, that if the Americans would send a new minister, he would be received with proper respect.

This French furor brought to Adams a degree of personal acclaim that he had never known before—and was never to know again. He doubtless perceived that a full-fledged war, crowned by the conquest of the Floridas and Louisiana, would bring new plaudits to the Federalist party—and perhaps a second term to himself. But the heady wine of popularity did not sway his final judgment. He realized full well, like other Founding Fathers, that war must be avoided while the country was relatively weak.

Preparation for War to Defend Commerce
The building of the frigate Philadelphia. In 1803 this frigate ran onto the rocks near Tripoli harbor, and about three hundred officers and men were imprisoned by the Tripolitans. The ship was refloated for service against the Americans, but Stephen Decatur led a party of men that set it afire. (Prints Division, the New York Public Library, Astor, Lenox and Tilden Foundations.)

Adams unexpectedly exploded a bombshell when, early in 1799, he submitted to the Senate the name of a new minister to France. Hamilton and his war-hawk faction were enraged. But public opinion—Jeffersonian and reasonable Federalist alike—was favorable to one last try for peace.

America's envoys (now three) found the political skies brightening when they reached Paris early in 1800. The ambitious "Little Corporal," the Corsican Napoleon Bonaparte, had recently seized dictatorial power. He was eager to free his hands of the American squabble so that he might continue to redraw the map of Europe and perhaps create a New World empire in Louisiana. The distresses and ambitions of the Old World were again working to America's advantage.

After much haggling, a memorable treaty known as the Convention of 1800 was signed in Paris. France agreed to grant a divorce from the twenty-two-year-old marriage of (in)convenience, but as a kind of alimony the United States agreed to pay the damage claims of American shippers. So ended the nation's only peacetime military alliance for a century and a half. Its troubled history does much to explain the traditional antipathy of the American people to foreign entanglements.

Adams, flinty to the end, deserves immense credit for his belated push for peace, even though moved in part by jealousy of Hamilton. He not only avoided the hazards of war, but unwittingly smoothed the path for the peaceful purchase of Louisiana three years later. He should indeed rank high among the forgotten purchasers of this vast domain. If America had drifted into a full-blown war with France in 1800, Napoleon would not have sold Louisiana to Jefferson on any terms in 1803.

President Adams, the bubble of his popularity pricked by peace, was aware of his signal contribution to the nation. He later suggested as the epitaph for his tombstone (not used): "Here lies John Adams, who took upon himself the responsibility of peace with France in the year 1800."

The Federalist Witch Hunt

Exulting Federalists had meanwhile capitalized on the anti-French frenzy to drive through Congress in 1798 a sheaf of laws designed to reduce or gag their Jeffersonian foes.

The first of these oppressive laws was aimed at supposedly pro-Jeffersonian "aliens." Most European immigrants, lacking wealth, were scorned by the aristocratic Federalist party. But they were welcomed as voters by the less prosperous and more democratic Jeffersonians. The Federalist Congress, hoping to discourage the "dregs" of Europe, erected a disheartening barrier. They raised the residence requirements for aliens who desired to become citizens from a tolerable five years to an intolerable fourteen. This drastic new law violated the traditional American policy of open-door hospitality and speedy assimilation.

Two additional Alien Laws struck heavily at undesirable immigrants. The president was empowered to deport dangerous foreigners in time of peace and to deport or imprison them in time of hostilities. Though defensible as a war measure—and an officially declared war with France seemed imminent—this was an arbitrary grant of power contrary to American tradition and to the spirit of the Constitution—though the stringent Alien Laws were never enforced.

The "lockjaw" Sedition Act, the last of the harsh Federalist measures, was a direct slap at two priceless freedoms guaranteed in the Constitution by the Bill of Rights—freedom of speech and freedom of the press (First Amendment). This law provided that anyone who im-

> Adams's firmness was revealed in his message to Congress (June 1798): "I will never send another minister to France without assurances that he will be received, respected, and honored as the representative of a great, free, powerful, and independent nation."

In 1815 Adams wrote privately: *"I will defend my missions to France, as long as I have an eye to direct my hand, or a finger to hold my pen. They were the most disinterested and meritorious actions of my life. I reflect upon them with . . . satisfaction."*

peded the policies of the government or falsely defamed its officials, including the president, would be liable to a heavy fine and imprisonment. Severe though the measure was, the Federalists believed that it was justified. The verbal violence of the day was unrestrained, and foul-penned editors, some of them exiled aliens, assailed Adams's anti-French policy in vicious terms.

Many outspoken Jeffersonian editors were indicted under the Sedition Act, and ten were brought to trial. All of them were convicted, often by packed juries swayed by prejudiced Federalist judges. A few of the victims were harmless partisans, who should have been spared the notoriety of martyrdom. Among them was Congressman Matthew Lyon (the "Spitting Lion"), who had earlier gained fame by spitting in the face of a Federalist. He was sentenced to four months in jail for writing of President Adams's "unbounded thirst for ridiculous pomp, foolish adulation, and selfish avarice." Another culprit was lucky to get off with a fine of $100 after he had expressed the wish that the wad of a cannon fired in honor of Adams had landed in the seat of the president's breeches.

The Sedition Act, at least in spirit, was in direct conflict with the Constitution. But the Supreme Court, dominated by Federalists, was of no mind to declare this Federalist law unconstitutional. (The law expired, in March 1801, to much rejoicing from Jeffersonians.) This attempt by the Federalists to crush free speech and silence the opposition party, high-handed as it was, undoubtedly made many converts for the Jeffersonians.

Yet the Alien and Sedition Acts, despite pained outcries from the Jeffersonians, commanded widespread popular support. Anti-French hysteria played directly into the hands of witch-hunting conservatives. In the congressional elections of 1798–1799, the Federalists, riding a wave of popularity, scored the most sweeping victory of their entire history.

Congressional Pugilists
Satirical representation of Matthew Lyon's fight in Congress with the Federalist Representative Roger Griswold. (The Bettman Archive.)

In 1800 James Callender published a pamphlet that assailed the president in this language: "The reign of Mr. Adams has, hitherto, been one continued tempest of malignant passions. As president, he has never opened his lips, or lifted his pen, without threatening and scolding. The grand object of his administration has been to exasperate the rage of contending parties, to calumniate and destroy every man who differs from his opinions. . . . Every person holding an office must either quit it, or think and vote exactly with Mr. Adams." For such blasts Callender was prosecuted under the Sedition Act, fined $250, and sentenced to prison for nine months.

The Virginia (Madison) and Kentucky (Jefferson) Resolutions

Resentful Jeffersonians naturally refused to take the Alien and Sedition Laws lying down. Jefferson himself feared that if the Federalists managed to choke free speech and free press, they would then wipe out other precious constitutional guarantees. His own fledgling political party might even be stamped out of existence. If this had happened, the country might have drifted into a dangerous one-party dictatorship.

Fearing prosecution for sedition, Jefferson secretly penned a series of resolutions, which the Kentucky legislature approved in 1798 and 1799. His friend and fellow Virginian James Madison drafted a similar but less extreme statement, which was adopted by the legislature of Virginia in 1798.

Both Jefferson and Madison stressed the compact theory—a theory popular among English political philosophers in the seventeenth and eighteenth centuries. As applied to America by the Jeffersonians, this concept meant that the thirteen sovereign states, in creating the federal government, had entered into a "compact," or contract, regarding its jurisdiction. The national government was consequently the agent or creation of the states.

Since water can rise no higher than its source, the individual states were the final judges of whether their agent had broken the "compact" by overstepping the authority originally granted. Invoking this logic, Jefferson's Kentucky resolutions concluded that the federal regime had exceeded its constitutional powers and that with regard to the Alien and Sedition Acts "nullification" was the "rightful remedy."

No other state legislatures, despite Jefferson's hopes, fell into line. Some of them flatly refused to endorse the Virginia and Kentucky resolutions. Others, chiefly in Federalist states, added ringing condemnations. Many Federalists argued that the people, not the states, had made the original compact, and that it was up to the Supreme Court—not the states—to nullify unconstitutional legislation passed by Congress. This practice, though not specifically authorized by the Constitution, was finally adopted by the Supreme Court in 1803. (See p. 194.)

The Virginia and Kentucky resolutions were a brilliant formulation of the extreme states'-rights view regarding the Union. They were later used by southerners to support nullification—and ultimately secession. Yet neither Jefferson nor Madison, as Founding Fathers of the Union, had any intention of breaking it up: they were groping for ways to preserve it. Their resolutions were basically campaign documents designed to crystallize opposition to the Federalist party and to unseat it in the upcoming presidential election of 1800. The only real nullification that Jefferson had in view was the nullification of Federalist abuses.

Federalists versus Democratic-Republicans

As the presidential contest of 1800 approached, the differences between Federalists and Democratic-Republicans were sharply etched. As might be expected, federalists of the pre-Constitution period (1787–1789) became Federalists in the 1790s. Largely welded by Hamilton into an effective group by 1793, they openly advo-

Evolution of Major Parties*

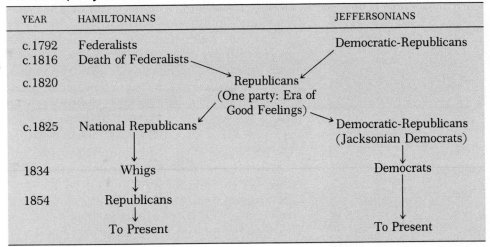

YEAR	HAMILTONIANS		JEFFERSONIANS
c.1792	Federalists		Democratic-Republicans
c.1816	Death of Federalists		
c.1820		Republicans (One party: Era of Good Feelings)	
c.1825	National Republicans		Democratic-Republicans (Jacksonian Democrats)
1834	Whigs		Democrats
1854	Republicans		
	To Present		To Present

*See Appendix (Presidential Elections) for third parties.

cated rule by the "best people." "Those who own the country," remarked Federalist John Jay, "ought to govern it." With their intellectual arrogance and Tory tastes, Hamiltonians distrusted full-blown democracy as the fountain of all mischiefs and feared the "swayability" of the untutored common folk.

Hamiltonian Federalists also advocated a strong central government with the power to crush democratic excesses like Shays's Rebellion, protect the lives and estates of the wealthy, and subordinate the sovereignty-loving states. They believed that government should support private enterprise, not interfere with it. This attitude came naturally to the seaboard merchants, manufacturers, and shippers who made up the majority of Federalist support. If a gunner could have fired a cannonball fifty miles (eighty kilometers) inland, it would have hit few Hamiltonians.

Federalists were also pro-British in foreign affairs. Many of them still harbored mildly Loyalist sentiments from Revolutionary days. All of them recognized that foreign trade, especially with England, was a key cog in Hamilton's fiscal machinery.

Leading the anti-Federalists, who came eventually to be known as Democratic-Republicans or sometimes simply Republicans, was Thomas Jefferson. Lanky and relaxed in appearance, lacking personal aggressiveness, weak-voiced, and unable to deliver a rabble-rousing speech, he became a master political organizer through his ability to lead people rather than drive them. His strongest appeal was to the middle class and to the underprivileged—the "dirt" farmers, the laborers, the artisans, and the small shopkeepers.

Liberal-thinking Jefferson, with his aristocratic head set on a farmer's frame, was a bundle of inconsistencies. By one set of tests he should have been a Federalist, for he was a Virginia aristocrat and slaveowner who lived in an imposing hilltop mansion at Monticello. A so-called traitor to his upper class, Jefferson cherished uncommon sympathy for the common people, especially the downtrodden, the oppressed, and the persecuted. As he wrote in 1800, "I have sworn upon the altar of God eternal hostility against every form of tyranny over the mind of man."

Jeffersonian Republicans demanded a weak central regime. They believed that the best government was the one that governed least. The bulk of the power, Jefferson argued, should be retained by the states. There the people, in inti-

Thomas Jefferson Among America's greatest statesmen, he wrote his own epitaph: "Here was buried Thomas Jefferson, Author of the Declaration of Independence, of the Statute of Virginia for Religious Freedom, and Father of the University of Virginia." (Alan P. Kirby Collection of Historical Paintings, LaFayette College.)

mate contact with local affairs, could keep a more vigilant eye on their public servants. Otherwise, a dictatorship might develop. Central authority—a kind of necessary evil—was to be kept at a minimum through a strict interpretation of the Constitution. The national debt, which Jefferson regarded as a curse illegitimately bequeathed to later generations, was to be paid off.

Jeffersonians, themselves primarily agrarians, insisted that there should be no special privileges for special classes, particularly manufacturers. Agriculture, to Jefferson, was the favored branch of the economy. He regarded farming as essentially ennobling; it kept people away from wicked cities, out in the sunshine and close to the sod—and God. Most of his followers naturally came from the agricultural South and Southwest.

Above all, Jefferson advocated the rule of the people. But he did not propose thrusting the ballot into the hands of *every* adult white male. He favored government *for* the people, but not by *all* the people—only by those men who were literate enough to inform themselves and wear the mantle of American citizenship worthily. Universal education would have to precede universal suffrage. The ignorant, he argued, were incapable of self-government. But he had profound faith in the reasonableness and teachableness of the masses and in their collective wisdom when taught. His enduring appeal was to America's better self.

The open-minded Jefferson championed free speech, because without free speech the misdeeds of tyranny could not be exposed. He even went so far as to say that as between "a government without newspapers" and "newspapers without a government," he would choose the latter. Yet no other American leader, except perhaps Abraham Lincoln, ever suffered more foul abuse from editorial pens; Jefferson might well have prayed for freedom *from* the Federalist press.

Jeffersonian Republicans, unlike the Federalist "British boot-lickers," were basically pro-French. They earnestly believed that it was to America's advantage to support the liberal ideals of the French Revolution, rather than applaud the reaction of the English Tories.

So as the young Republic's first full decade of nationhood came to a close, the Founders' hopes seemed already imperiled. Conflicts over domestic politics and foreign policy undermined the unity of the Revolutionary era and called into question the very survivability of the American experiment in democracy. As the presidential election of 1800 approached, the danger loomed that the fragile and battered American ship of state, like many another before it and after it, would founder on the rocks of controversy. The shores of history are littered with the wreckage of nascent nations torn asunder before they could grow to a stable maturity. Why should the United States expect to enjoy a happier fate?

Monticello, Jefferson's Self-Designed Architectural Marvel *A talented inventor, he installed a number of gadgets, including a device for pulling up chilled bottles of wine from the cellar to the dining table. (Robert Llewellyn.)*

CHRONOLOGY

1789	Constitution formally put into effect
	Judiciary Act of 1789
	Washington elected president
	French Revolution begins
1790	First official census
1791	Bill of Rights adopted
	Vermont becomes fourteenth state
	Bank of the United States created
	Excise tax passed
1792–1793	Federalist and Democratic-Republican parties formed
1793	Louis XVI beheaded; radical phase of French Revolution
	Washington's Neutrality Proclamation

1794	Whiskey Rebellion
	Battle of Fallen Timbers
	Jay's Treaty with Britain
1795	Treaty of Greenville: Indians cede Ohio
	Pinckney's Treaty with Spain
1796	Washington's Farewell Address
1797	Adams becomes president
	XYZ Affair
1798	Alien and Sedition Acts
1798–1799	Kentucky and Virginia resolutions
1798–1800	Undeclared war with France
1800	Convention of 1800: peace with France

Varying Viewpoints

Underlying all debates about the so-called Federalist era of the 1790s is one fundamental question: what allowed the United States, barely a nation in anything more than name at the conclusion of the Revolutionary War, to survive the explosive conflicts of its first decade and emerge as a coherent, viable polity? The earliest students of the period emphasized the philosophical differences between Hamiltonians and Jeffersonians and simply presumed that democratic (that is, Jeffersonian) ideas were destined to predominate. This interpretation, sometimes called the Whig view of history, proceeds from the premise that history is, essentially, the triumphal story of unfolding democracy and moral progress.

This high-minded approach was challenged in the early years of the twentieth century by historians who stressed the economic rivalries at the root of Federalist-age political debates. They saw the Hamiltonian-Jeffersonian dispute over political principles as a smokescreen for battles between creditors and debtors, commercial interests and agrarian interests, northern merchants and southern planters. In this view, it was not so much democracy, but capitalism, that inevitably triumphed.

More recent students have swung the pendulum back toward ideological factors. Scholars like Drew McCoy and Lance Banning see the turmoil of the Federalist era as a continuation of the debate over the meaning of republicanism that gave rise to the Revolution and the Constitution. But the recent scholarship emphasizes that virtually all participants in that debate believed in some version of republican values. Thus, in this view, the new nation survived the *apparent* divisiveness of the 1790s because *all* parties were, at bottom, republicans. Following this line of argument leads to a deeper question: what factors in the earlier Revolutionary era, or even before, had so "republicanized" American thinking?

Similar questions have been asked about Washington's and Adams's foreign policy, whose centerpiece was neutrality, or "isolation." Was this simply a realistic recognition of American weakness, or was it informed, as Felix Gilbert has argued, by the highest principles of Enlightenment thought about an ideal international order? This question—whether self-interest or idealism is the chief consideration in American foreign policy—has continued to be argued from Washington's day to the present.

Select Readings

Primary Source Documents

"The Report on Manufactures" (in Daniel Boorstin, ed., *American Primer*), the last of Alexander Hamilton's messages to Congress, presented the case for the development of American industry. Thomas Jefferson expounded his views in *Notes on the State of Virginia* (1784). For further study of the Hamiltonian-Jeffersonian debate, see Henry Cabot Lodge, ed., *The Works of Alexander Hamilton** (1904), and Paul L. Ford, ed., *The Writings of Thomas Jefferson** (1985). Important salvos in the battle between national power and state sovereignty, and between Federalists and Jeffersonians, were the Virginia and Kentucky resolutions* (1798) and the reply of Rhode Island* (1799). Washington's Farewell Address* (1796) established the foundation for American attitudes about party politics and foreign policy. See also Benjamin Franklin Bache's stinging editorial on Washington's retirement, Philadelphia *Aurora** (1797).

Secondary Sources

Perceptive introductions are provided by Marcus Cunliffe's succinct *The Nation Takes Shape, 1789–1837* (1959) and John C. Miller's more detailed *The Federalist Era, 1789–1801* (1960). On administration, consult Leonard D. White, *The Federalists* (1948); on finance, Curtis P. Nettles, *The Emergence of a National Economy, 1775–1815* (1962). On party politics, see William N. Chambers, *Political Parties in the New Nation* (1963), and Richard Hofstadter's thoughtful *The Idea of a Party System* (1969). Among the new interpretations of that subject, stressing the ideology of republicanism, are Drew McCoy, *The Elusive Republic: Political Economy in Jeffersonian America* (1980), and Lance Banning, *The Jeffersonian Persuasion* (1978). Charles G. Steffens examines the political beliefs of workers in *The Mechanics of Baltimore: Workers and Politics in the Age of Revolution, 1763–1812* (1984). For a trenchant analysis of Jeffersonianism, see Joyce Appleby, *Capitalism and a New Social Order: The Republican Vision* (1984). Also illuminating is Gerald Stourzh, *Alexander Hamilton and the Idea of Republican Government* (1970). Thomas P. Slaughter focuses on *The Whiskey Rebellion: Frontier Epilogue to the American Revolution* (1986). A comprehensive biography is James T. Flexner, *George Washington and the New Nation, 1783–1793* (1969). Consult also Forrest McDonald, *The Presidency of George Washington* (1974), and Garry Wills, *Cincinnatus: George Washington and the Enlightenment* (1984). Of special interest is Richard H. Kohn, *Eagle and Sword: The Federalists and the Creation of the Military Establishment in America, 1783–1802* (1975). On the rise of parties, consult Noble E. Cunningham, *The Jeffersonian Republicans* (1958). On aspects of foreign policy, see Alexander De Conde, *Entangling Alliance* (1958), and his *Quasi-War: The Politics and Diplomacy of the Undeclared War with France, 1797–1801* (1966); Gilbert Lycan, *Alexander Hamilton and American Foreign Policy* (1970); Jerald Combs, *The Jay Treaty* (1970); Lawrence S. Kaplan, *Colonies into Nation: American Diplomacy, 1763–1801* (1972); Louis M. Sears, *George Washington and the French Revolution* (1960); Paul A. Varg, *Foreign Policies of the Founding Fathers* (1963); Felix Gilbert, *To the Farewell Address* (1961); and Julian Boyd, *Number 7* (1964), on Hamilton's devious dealings with the British. For the view from across the Atlantic, see Charles R. Ritcheson, *Aftermath of Revolution: British Policy toward the United States, 1783–1795* (1969). On Adams, consult Page Smith, *John Adams* (2 vols.) (1962), and Stephen G. Kurtz, *The Presidency of John Adams* (1957). John C. Miller, *Crisis in Freedom* (1951), and James M. Smith, *Freedom's Fetters* (1956), treat the Alien and Sedition Acts, as does Leonard Levy, *Legacy of Suppression* (1960).

The Triumph of Jeffersonian Democracy, 1800–1809

Timid men . . . prefer the calm of despotism to the boisterous sea of liberty.

Thomas Jefferson, 1796

Federalist and Republican Mudslingers

In the critical presidential contest of 1800, Adams and Jefferson were again the standard-bearers of their respective parties. The Federalists labored under heavy handicaps. Their Alien and Sedition Acts had aroused a host of enemies, although most of these critics were dyed-in-the-wool Jeffersonians anyhow. The Hamiltonian wing of the Federalist party, robbed of its glorious war with France, split openly with President Adams. Hamilton, a victim of arrogance, was so indiscreet as to attack the president in a privately printed pamphlet. Jeffersonians soon got hold of the pamphlet and gleefully published it.

The most damaging blow to the Federalists was the refusal of Adams to give them a rousing fight with France. Their feverish war prepara-

tions had swelled the public debt and had required disagreeable new taxes, including a stamp tax. After all these unpopular measures, the war scare had petered out, and the country was left with an all-dressed-up-but-no-place-to-go feeling. The military preparations now seemed not only unnecessary but extravagant, as seamen for the "new navy" were called "John Adams's Jackasses." Adams himself was known as "the Father of the American Navy."

Thrown on the defensive, the Federalists concentrated their fire on Jefferson himself, who became the victim of one of the earliest "whispering campaigns." He was accused of having robbed a widow and her children of a trust fund and of having fathered numerous mulatto children by his own slave women. As a liberal in religion, he had earlier incurred the wrath of the orthodox clergy, largely through his successful struggle to separate church and

> The Reverend Timothy Dwight, president of Yale College, predicted that in the event of Jefferson's election "the Bible would be cast into a bonfire, our holy worship changed into a dance of [French] Jacobin phrensy, our wives and daughters dishonored, and our sons converted into the disciples of Voltaire and the dragoons of Marat."

The Jeffersonian "Revolution of 1800"

Jefferson won by a majority of 73 electoral votes to 65. But the colorless and presumably unpopular Adams polled more electoral strength than he had gained four years earlier—except for New York. The Empire State fell into the Jeffersonian basket, and with it the election, largely because Aaron Burr, a master wire-puller, turned New York to Jefferson by the narrowest of margins. The Virginian polled the bulk of his strength in the South and West, particularly in those states where manhood suffrage had been adopted.

Jeffersonians rejoiced wildly over the end of the "Federalist Reign of Terror." Some of them, with alcoholic enthusiasm, bawled the song

state in Virginia. From the New England stronghold of Federalism and Congregationalism, the preachers thundered against his atheism, although he did believe in God. Old ladies of Federalist families, fearing Jefferson's election, even buried their Bibles or hung them in wells.

The Providential Detection (Federalist Propaganda) The American eagle snatches the Constitution from Jefferson, who is about to burn it (together with the works of Voltaire, Paine, and others) on the altar to French Revolutionary despotism. (Massachusetts Historical Society.)

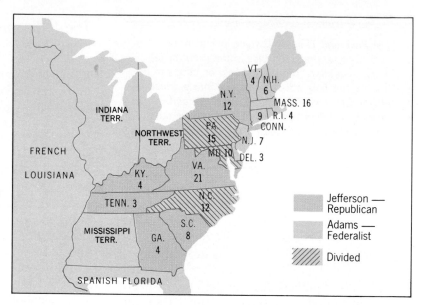

Presidential Election of 1800 (with electoral vote by state) New York was the key state in this election, and Aaron Burr helped swing it away from the Federalists with tactics that anticipated the political "machines" of a later day. Federalists complained that Burr "travels every night from one meeting of Republicans to another, haranguing ... them to the most zealous exertions. [He] can stoop so low as to visit every low tavern that may happen to be crowded with his dear fellow citizens." But Burr proved that the price was worth it. "We have beat you," Burr told kid-gloved Federalists after the election, "by superior Management."

"Jefferson and Liberty":

> Lord! how the Federalists will stare
> At Jefferson, in Adams's chair!

But Jeffersonian joy was dampened by an unexpected deadlock. Through a technicality Jefferson, the presidential candidate, and Burr, his vice-presidential running mate, received the same number of electoral votes for the presidency. Under the Constitution the tie could be broken only by the House of Representatives (see Art. II, Sec. I, para. 2). This body was controlled for several more months by the lame-duck Federalists, who had been swept into office during the French war scare and who were eager to elect Burr.*

Voting in the House moved slowly to a climax. As ballots were taken in wearisome succession, representatives snored in their seats; a sick member lay in an adjoining room. Historians used to think that Hamilton, bargaining secretly with Jefferson, played a decisive role. But the evidence indicates that the deadlock was broken when a few Federalists, despairing of electing Burr and hoping for moderation from Jefferson, refrained from voting. The election then went to the rightful candidate.

Jefferson later claimed that the election of 1800 was a "revolution" comparable to that of 1776. But it was no revolution in the sense of a massive popular upheaval or an upending of the political system. In truth, Jefferson had narrowly squeaked through to victory. A switch of some 250 votes in New York would have thrown the election to Adams. What *was* revolutionary was the peaceful and orderly transfer of power on the basis of an election whose results all parties accepted. This was a remarkable—indeed, even "revolutionary"—achievement for a raw young nation, especially after all the partisan bitterness that had agitated the country during Adams's presidency. It was particularly remarkable in that age; comparable developments would not take place in Britain for another generation. After a decade of division and doubt, Americans could take justifiable pride in the vigor of their experiment in democracy.

---

*A "lame duck" has been humorously defined as a politician whose political goose has been cooked at the recent elections. The possibility of another such tie was removed by the Twelfth Amendment in 1804 (for text, see the Appendix). Before then, each elector had two votes, with the second-place finisher becoming vice-president.

The Federalist Finale

John Adams, as fate would have it, was the last Federalist president of the United States. His party sank slowly into the mire of political oblivion and ultimately disappeared completely in the days of Andrew Jackson.

Whatever their shortcomings, the Federalists were a party of the elite. They boasted a much higher concentration of brains, talent, and ability than any other major American political party, past or present. Their political and financial leaders had built enduring foundations for the new government. Their diplomats, with a strong helping hand from Europe's distresses, had signed advantageous treaties with England, Spain, and France. Their leaders had kept the peace during a crucial period when peace had to be kept.

After all the turmoil of the American Revolution, a conservative party served a valuable function in preserving democratic gains and fending off anarchy. The Federalists provided a welcome breathing spell, a chance for the nation to get its bearings. They served, in the words of historian Henry Adams, great-grandson of John Adams, as the "half-way house between the European past and the American future."

But by 1800 the Federalists, blessed with more talent than wisdom, were out of place. The bustling new Republic knew instinctively where it was going. It was eager to take the high road over the mountains that would one day lead to the fulfillment of America's democratic experiment. The Federalists lost out because they were content to mark time and failed to get in step with the westward march of progress. They were unable or unwilling to unbend and appeal to the common people. They could not adapt—so they died, like the dinosaur. Distinguished though their past service had been, it was no substitute for a capacity to grapple democratically with future problems. The victorious Jeffersonians were prepared to keep the Federalist edifice while ousting the Federalist architects.

Responsibility Breeds Moderation

"Long Tom" Jefferson was inaugurated president on March 4, 1801, in the swampy village of Washington, the crude new national capital. Tall (6 feet 2.5 inches; 1.89 meters), with large

Jefferson's toleration was reflected in his inaugural address. "If there be any among us who would wish to dissolve this Union or to change its republican form, let them stand undisturbed as monuments of the safety with which error of opinion may be tolerated where reason is left free to combat it."

hands and feet, reddish hair ("The Red Fox"), and prominent cheekbones and chin, he was an arresting figure. Believing that the customary pomp did not befit his democratic ideals, he spurned a horse-drawn coach and simply walked over to the Capitol from his boardinghouse.

The inaugural address, beautifully phrased, was a classic statement of democratic principles. Seeking to allay Federalist fears of a bull-in-the-china-closet overturn, Jefferson blandly stated, "We are all Republicans, we are all Federalists." As for foreign affairs, he pledged "honest friendship with all nations, entangling alliances with none."

With its rustic setting, Washington lent itself admirably to the simplicity and frugality of the Jeffersonian Republicans. In this respect, it contrasted sharply with the elegant atmosphere of Federalist Philadelphia, the former temporary capital. Extending democratic principles to etiquette, Jefferson established the rule of pell-mell at official dinners—that is, seating without regard to rank. The resplendent British minister, who had enjoyed precedence among the pro-British Federalists, was insulted.

As a widower, Jefferson was shockingly unconventional. Having no wife to police his apparel, he would receive callers in sloppy attire—once in a dressing gown and heelless slippers. He started the precedent, unbroken for 112 years, of sending messages to Congress to be read by a clerk. Personal appearances, in the Federalist manner, suggested too strongly a monarchical speech from the throne. Besides, Jefferson was painfully conscious of his weak voice and unimpressive platform presence.

As if plagued by an evil spirit, Jefferson was forced to reverse many of the political principles

Washington and Jefferson Contrasted *This cartoon illustrates the centrality of the French issue in defining the differences between Washingtonian Federalists and Jeffersonian Democratic-Republicans. Here Washington, driving the federal chariot, tries to lead his troops against the French "cannibals," while Jefferson (at the far right) tries to stop the wheels of government. (New-York Historical Society.)*

he had so vigorously championed. There were in fact two Thomas Jeffersons. One was the private citizen, who had philosophized in his study. The other was the public official, who made the disturbing discovery that bookish theories worked out differently in the noisy arena of practical politics. The open-minded Virginian was therefore consistently inconsistent; it is easy to quote one Jefferson to refute the other.

The triumph of Jefferson's Democratic-Republicans and the eviction of the Federalists marked the first party overturn in American history. The vanquished naturally feared that the victors would grab all the spoils of office for themselves. But Jefferson, in line with his conciliatory inaugural address, showed unexpected moderation. To the dismay of his office-seeking friends, the new president dismissed few public servants for political reasons. Patronage-hungry Jeffersonians watched the Federalist appointees grow old in office and grumbled that "few die, none resign."

Jefferson quickly proved an able politician. He was especially effective in the informal atmosphere of a dinner party. There he wooed congressional representatives while personally pouring imported wines and serving the tasty dishes of his French cook.

In part, Jefferson had to rely on his personal charm because his party was so weak-jointed. Denied the power to dispense patronage, the Democratic-Republicans could not build a loyal political following. Opposition to the Federalists was the chief glue holding them together, and as the Federalists faded, so did Democratic-Republican unity. The era of well-developed, well-disciplined political parties still lay in the future.

Jeffersonian Restraint Helps to Further a "Revolution"

At the outset, Jefferson was determined to undo the Federalist abuses begotten by the anti-French hysteria. The hated Alien and Sedition Acts had already expired. The incoming president speedily pardoned the "martyrs" serving sentences under the Sedition Act, and the government returned many fines. Shortly after the Congress met, the Jeffersonians enacted the new naturalization law of 1802. The law reduced the unreasonable requirement of fourteen years of residence to the former and more reasonable requirement of five years.

Jefferson actually kicked away only one substantial prop of the Hamiltonian system. He hated the excise tax, which bred bureaucrats and bore heavily on his farmer following, and he early persuaded Congress to repeal it. His devotion to principle thus cost the federal government about a million dollars a year in urgently needed revenue.

Swiss-born and French-accented Albert Gallatin, "Watchdog of the Treasury," proved to be as able a secretary of the treasury as Hamilton. Gallatin agreed with Jefferson that a national debt was a bane rather than a blessing and by strict economy succeeded in reducing it substantially while balancing the budget.

Except for excising the excise tax, the Jeffersonians left the Hamiltonian framework essentially intact. They did not tamper with the Federalist programs for funding the national debt at par and assuming the Revolutionary War debts of the states. They launched no attack on the Bank of the United States, and they did not repeal the mildly protective Federalist tariff. In later years they embraced Federalism to such a degree as to recharter a bigger bank and to boost the protective tariff to higher levels.

Paradoxically, Jefferson's moderation thus further cemented the gains of the "Revolution of 1800." That revolution had consisted above all in the peaceful replacement of one governing party by another. By shrewdly absorbing the major Federalist programs, Jefferson showed that a change of regime need not be disastrous for the defeated group. His restraint pointed the way toward the two-party system that was later

to become a characteristic feature of American politics.

The "Dead Clutch" of the Judiciary

The "deathbed" Judiciary Act of 1801 was one of the last important laws passed by the expiring Federalist Congress. It created sixteen new federal judgeships and other judicial offices. President Adams remained at his desk until nine o'clock in the evening of his last day in office, allegedly signing the commissions of the Federalist "midnight judges." (Actually only three commissions were signed on his last day.)

This Federalist-sponsored Judiciary Act, though a long-overdue reform, aroused bitter resentment. "Packing" these lifetime posts with anti-Jeffersonian partisans was, in Republican eyes, a brazen attempt by the defeated party to entrench itself in one of the three powerful branches of government. Jeffersonians condemned the "midnight judges" in violent language. To them, the trickery of the Federalists was open defiance of the people's will, as recently expressed at the polls.

The newly elected Republican Congress bestirred itself to repeal the Judiciary Act of 1801 in the year after its passage. Jeffersonians thus swept sixteen benches from under the recently appointed "midnight judges." Frustrated Federalists, in turn, were acidly critical of this "assault" on the judicial arm.

Jeffersonians likewise had their knives sharpened for the scalp of Chief Justice John Marshall, whom Adams had appointed to the Supreme Court (as a fourth choice) in the dying days of his term. The lanky Marshall, with his rasping voice and steel-trap mind, was a cousin of Thomas Jefferson. As a Virginia Federalist, he was cordially disliked by the states' rights Jeffersonians. He served for about thirty days under a Federalist administration and thirty-four years under the administrations of the Jeffersonian Republicans and their successors. The Federalist party died out, but Marshall went on handing down Federalist decisions serenely for many more years. He probably did more than Hamilton to engraft the Hamiltonian concept of a powerful central government upon the American political and economic system.

> President John F. Kennedy later greeted a large group of Nobel Prize winners as "the most extraordinary collection of talent, of human knowledge, that has ever been gathered together at the White House, with the possible exception of when Thomas Jefferson dined alone."

One of the "midnight judges" of 1801 presented John Marshall with a historic opportunity. He was obscure William Marbury, whom President Adams had named a justice of the peace for the District of Columbia. When Marbury learned that his commission was being held up by the new secretary of state, James Madison, he sued for its delivery. Chief Justice Marshall knew that his Jeffersonian rivals, entrenched in the executive branch, would hardly spring forward to enforce a writ to deliver the commission to his fellow Federalist Marbury. He therefore dismissed Marbury's suit, avoiding a direct political showdown. But the wily Marshall snatched a victory from the jaws of this judicial defeat. In explaining his ruling, Marshall said that the part of the Judiciary Act of 1789 on which Marbury tried to base his appeal was unconstitutional. The act had attempted to assign to the Supreme Court powers that the Constitution had not foreseen.

In this self-denying opinion, Marshall greatly magnified the authority of the Court—and slapped at the Jeffersonians. Until the case of *Marbury* v. *Madison* (1803), controversy had clouded the question of who had the final authority to determine the meaning of the Constitution. Jefferson in the Kentucky resolutions (1798) had tried to assign that right to the individual states. But now his cousin on the Court had cleverly promoted the contrary principle of "judicial review"—that the black-robed tribunal of the Supreme Court alone had the last word on the question of constitutionality. In this epochal case, Marshall inserted the keystone into the arch that supports the tremendous power of the Supreme Court in American life.[*]

Jefferson Threatens the Supremacy of the Supreme Court

Marshall's decision regarding Marbury spurred the Jeffersonians in their desire to lay rough hands on the Supreme Court through impeachment. Certain Federalist judges had become highly offensive, especially in Sedition Act cases, by delivering harangues from the bench against the Republican "mobocracy." Jefferson favored free speech, but not this kind of free speech. Accordingly, he urged action against an arrogant Supreme Court justice, Samuel Chase, who was so unpopular that Republicans named vicious dogs after him.

Early in 1804 impeachment charges against Chase were voted by the House of Representatives, which then passed the question of guilt or innocence on to the Senate. The indictment by the House was based on "high crimes and misdemeanors," as specified in the Constitution.[†] Yet the evidence was plain that the intemperate judge had not been guilty of "high crimes" but of bad manners, injudicious statements, and unrestrained partisanship. The Senate, after a determined prosecution, failed to muster enough votes to convict and remove Chase. The precedent thus established was fortunate. From

---

In his decision in Marbury v. Madison, *Chief Justice Marshall vigorously asserted his view that the Constitution embodied a "higher" law than ordinary legislation, and that the Court must interpret the Constitution:*

"The Constitution is either a superior paramount law, unchangeable by ordinary means, or it is on a level with ordinary legislative acts, and, like other acts, is alterable when the legislature shall please to alter it.

"If the former part of the alternative be true, then a legislative act contrary to the constitution is not law; if the latter part be true, then written constitutions are absurd attempts, on the part of the people, to limit a power in its own nature illimitable . . .

"It is emphatically the province and duty of the judicial department to say what the law is . . .

"If, then, the courts are to regard the Constitution, and the Constitution is superior to any ordinary act of the legislature, the Constitution, and not such ordinary act, must govern the case to which they are both applicable."

---

[*]The next invalidation of a federal law by the Supreme Court came fifty-four years later, with the explosive Dred Scott decision (see p. 414).

[†]For impeachment, see Art. I, Sec. II, para. 5; Art. I, Sec. III, paras. 6, 7; Art. II, Sec. IV, in the Appendix.

Mad Tom in a Rage *A Federalist cartoon shows "Mad Tom" Jefferson, assisted by brandy and the Devil, trying to pull down the federal edifice erected by Washington and Adams. (Houghton Library, Harvard.)*

that day to this, no really serious attempt has been made to reshape the Supreme Court by the impeachment weapon.

John Marshall viewed the attack on Chase with deep misgivings. He suspected, not unreasonably, that if it succeeded, he would be next—and then his other Federalist colleagues. These fears were now laid to rest. Jefferson's ill-advised attempt at "judge breaking" was a reassuring victory for the independence of the judiciary and for the separation of powers among the three branches of the federal government.

The Pacifist Jefferson Turns Warrior

As a passionate champion of freedom, Jefferson distrusted large standing armies as a standing invitation to dictatorship. Navies, though also

suspect, were less to be feared: they could not march inland and "endanger liberties." Pinning his faith to the frail reed of an ill-trained militia, Jefferson reduced the military establishment to a mere police force of 2,500 officers and men. The Republicans, primarily agrarians, saw little point in protecting a few Federalist shippers with a costly navy that all the taxpayers would have to support. Pledged to rigid economy, Jefferson gladly reduced the navy to a peacetime footing, in accordance with legislation already passed by the outgoing Federalist Congress.

But harsh realities forced a penny-pinching Jefferson to change his tune on navies and war. Pirates of the North African states had long made a national industry of blackmailing and plundering merchant ships that ventured into the Mediterranean. Preceding Federalist administrations, in fact, had been forced to buy protection. At the time of the French crisis of 1798, when Americans were shouting, "Millions for defense, but not one cent for tribute," twenty-six barrels of blackmail dollars were being shipped to piratical Algiers.

At this price, war seemed cheaper than peace, and the showdown came in 1801. The Pasha of Tripoli, dissatisfied with his share of protection money, informally declared war on the United States by cutting down the flagstaff of the American consulate. A challenge was thus thrown squarely into the face of Jefferson—the noninterventionist, the pacifist, the critic of a big-ship navy, and the political foe of Federalist shippers. He reluctantly rose to the occasion by dispatching the infant navy to the "shores of Tripoli," as related in the song of the U.S. Marine Corps. After four years of intermittent fighting, marked by hair-raising exploits, Jefferson succeeded in extorting a treaty of peace from Tripoli in 1805. It was secured at the bargain price of only $60,000—a sum representing ransom payments for captured Americans.

With the pattern thus set, the punishment of other North African corsairs continued, off and on, until after the War of 1812. The navy reaped a rich harvest of experience, while strengthening its budding tradition. Foreign nations in general, and the Barbary cutthroats in particular, developed a wholesome respect for

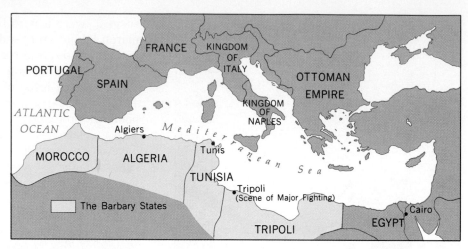

Four Barbary States of North Africa, c. 1805

the United States—a nation willing and able to defend its rights with blazing guns.

Small gunboats, which the navy had used with some success in the Tripolitan War, fascinated Jefferson. Pledged to tax reduction, he advocated a large number of tiny coastal craft—"Jeffs" or the "mosquito fleet," as they were contemptuously called. He believed that these frail vessels would prove valuable in guarding American shores, although not in defending Federalist merchantmen on the high seas.

About two hundred tiny gunboats were constructed, democratically in small shipyards where votes could be made for Jefferson. Often mounting only one unwieldy gun, they were sometimes more of a menace to the crew than to the prospective enemy. During a hurricane and tidal wave at Savannah, Georgia, one of them was deposited eight miles (12.9 kilometers) inland in a cornfield, to the derisive glee of the Federalists. They drank toasts to American gunboats as the best in the world—on land. Jefferson's pinchpenny economizing backfired badly when the War of 1812 broke out and the whole swarm of gunboats proved virtually stingless. The money could have been much more wisely invested in a few frigates of the *Constitution* class.

The Louisiana Godsend

A secret pact, fraught with peril for America, was signed in 1800. Napoleon Bonaparte induced the King of Spain to cede to France, for

attractive considerations, the immense trans-Mississippi region of Louisiana, which included the New Orleans area.

Rumors of the transfer were partially confirmed in 1802, when the Spaniards at New Orleans withdrew the right of deposit guaranteed America by the treaty of 1795. Deposit privileges were vital to frontier farmers who floated their produce down the Mississippi to its mouth, there to await oceangoing vessels. A roar of anger rolled up the mighty river and into its tributary valleys. American pioneers talked wildly of descending upon New Orleans, rifles in hand. Had they done so, the nation probably would have been involved in war with both Spain and France.

Thomas Jefferson, both pacifistic and anti-entanglement, was again on the griddle. Louisiana in the senile grip of Spain posed no real threat; America could seize the territory when the time was ripe. But Louisiana in the iron fist of Napoleon, the preeminent military genius of his age, foreshadowed a dark and blood-drenched future. The United States would probably have to fight to dislodge him; and because it alone was not strong enough to defeat

> *Explaining the western outburst over the closing of the river, James Madison wrote to Pinckney: "The Mississippi is to them every thing. It is the Hudson, the Delaware, the Potomac, and all the navigable rivers of the Atlantic States, formed into one stream."*

his armies, it would have to seek allies, contrary to the deepening anti-alliance policy.

Hoping to quiet the clamor of the West, Jefferson moved decisively. Early in 1803 he sent James Monroe to Paris to join forces with the regular minister there, Robert R. Livingston. The two envoys were instructed to buy New Orleans and as much land to the east as they could get for a maximum of $10 million. If these proposals should fail and the situation should become critical, negotiations were to be opened with England for an alliance. "The day that France takes possession of New Orleans," Jefferson wrote, "we must marry ourselves to the British fleet and nation."

Nothing could better illustrate Jefferson's concern. Though a passionate hater of war and an enemy of entangling alliances, he was proposing to make an alliance with his old foe, England, against his old friend, France, with the object of waging a defensive war.

At this critical juncture, Napoleon suddenly decided to sell all Louisiana and abandon his dream of a New World empire. Two developments prompted his change of mind. First, he had failed in his efforts to reconquer the sugar-rich island of Santo Domingo, for which Louisiana was to serve as a granary. Infuriated ex-slaves, ably led by a gifted black, Toussaint L'Ouverture, had put up a stubborn resistance that was ultimately broken. Then the island's second line of defense—mosquitoes carrying yellow fever—had swept away thousands of crack French troops. Santo Domingo could not be reconquered, except perhaps at a staggering cost; hence, there was no need for the granary. "Damn sugar, damn coffee, damn colonies!" burst out Napoleon. Second, Bonaparte was about to end the twenty-month lull in his deadly conflict with Britain. Because the British controlled the seas, he feared that he might be forced to make them a gift of Louisiana. Rather than drive America into the arms of England by attempting to hold the area, he decided to sell the huge wilderness to the Americans and pocket the money for his schemes nearer home. He hoped that the United States, strengthened by Louisiana, would one day grow up to be a military and naval power that would thwart the ambitions of the lordly British in the New World. The distresses of France in Europe were

Toussaint L'Ouverture (c. 1774–1803) *A self-educated ex-slave and military genius, L'Ouverture was finally betrayed by the French, who imprisoned him in a chilly dungeon in France, where he coughed his life away. By indirection he did much to set up the sale of Louisiana to the United States. (Library of Congress.)*

again paving the way for America's diplomatic successes.

Events now moved dizzily. The American Minister Livingston, pending the arrival of Monroe, was busily negotiating in Paris for a window on the Gulf of Mexico at New Orleans. Suddenly, out of a clear sky, the French foreign minister asked him how much he would give for all Louisiana. Scarcely able to believe his ears (he was partially deaf anyhow), Livingston nervously entered upon the negotiations. After about a week of haggling, while the fate of America trembled in the balance, treaties were signed, under the date April 30, 1803, ceding Louisiana to the United States for about $15 million.

Out-Federalizing the Federalists in Louisiana

When the news of the bargain reached America, Jefferson was startled. He had authorized his envoys to offer not more than $10 million for

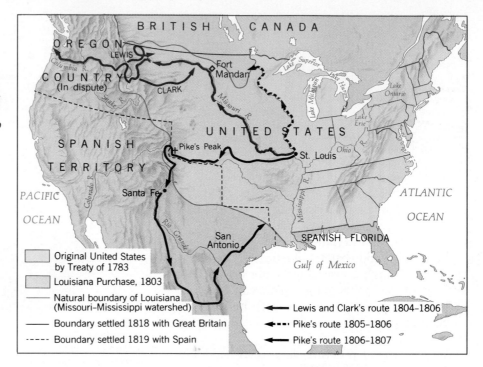

Exploring the Louisiana Purchase and the West
Seeking to avert friction with France by purchasing all of Louisiana, Jefferson bought trouble because of the vagueness of the boundaries. Among the disputants were Spain in the Floridas, Spain and Mexico in the Southwest, and Great Britain in Canada.

Original United States by Treaty of 1783
Louisiana Purchase, 1803
Natural boundary of Louisiana (Missouri–Mississippi watershed)
Boundary settled 1818 with Great Britain
Boundary settled 1819 with Spain

Lewis and Clark's route 1804–1806
Pike's route 1805–1806
Pike's route 1806–1807

New Orleans, and as much to the *east* in the Floridas as they could get. Instead, they had signed three treaties that pledged $15 million for New Orleans, plus a vast wilderness entirely to the *west*—an area that would more than double the United States. They had bought a wilderness to get a city.

Once again the two Jeffersons wrestled with each other in private: the theorist and former strict constructionist versus the realist and public official. Where in his beloved Constitution was the president authorized to negotiate treaties incorporating a huge new expanse into the union—an expanse containing some fifty thousand red, white, and black inhabitants? There was no such clause.

Conscience-stricken, Jefferson secretly proposed that a constitutional amendment be passed. But his friends pointed out in alarm that in the interval Napoleon, for whom thought was action, might suddenly change his mind. So Jefferson shamefacedly submitted the treaties to the Senate, while privately admitting that the purchase was unconstitutional.

The senators were less finicky than Jefferson. Reflecting enthusiastic public support, they registered their prompt approval of the transaction. Land-hungry Americans were not disposed to split constitutional hairs when confronted with perhaps the most magnificent real estate bargain in history—828,000 square miles (2,144,520 square kilometers) at about three cents an acre.

If Louisiana made Jefferson a loose constructionist, it made many Federalists strict constructionists. (Hamilton, to his credit, was a partial exception.) Federalists argued vehemently that there was no constitutional warrant for the transfer. (This argument hadn't bothered them when they had chartered the Bank of the United States!) Louisiana, so they claimed, was a worthless desert that would cost too

In accepting the Louisiana Purchase, Jefferson thus compromised with conscience in a private letter: "It is the case of a guardian, investing the money of his ward in purchasing an important adjacent territory; and saying to him when of age, I did this for your good; I pretend to no right to bind you: you may disavow me, and I must get out of the scrape as I can: I thought it my duty to risk myself for you."

much at a time when the Jeffersonians were pledged to rigid economy: $15 million in one pile of silver dollars would reach three miles into the air. (Shades of the Federalists who had cheerfully assumed Hamilton's debt of $75 million!)

What really worried the Federalists was that the signing of the Louisiana treaties was the signing of their own political death warrant. New states would be carved from the immense area—states that would outvote the thirteen charter members, including Federalist New England. The Jeffersonian agrarians would then become unassailable. At Williams College in Massachusetts, a debating group voted fifteen to one that the purchase of Louisiana was undesirable. A few Federalist extremists even threatened to secede from the Union.

The purchase of Louisiana—the most glorious achievement of Jefferson as president—was a triumph for which neither he nor anyone else could claim much direct credit. Napoleon, for reasons purely selfish, dumped this rich prize into the laps of Livingston, Monroe, and Jefferson. Louisiana was so desirable that Jefferson found it less embarrassing to reverse himself on strict construction than to lose the magnificent windfall.

Louisiana in the Long View

Jefferson's bargain with France was epochal. By scooping up Louisiana, America secured at one bloodless stroke the western half of the richest river valley in the world and further laid the foundations of a future major power. The ideal of a great agrarian democracy, as envisioned by Jefferson, would have elbowroom in the vast "Valley of Democracy." At the same time, the transfer established a precedent that was to be followed repeatedly: the acquisition of foreign territory and peoples by purchase.

The extent of the huge new area was more fully unveiled by a series of explorations under the direction of Jefferson. He was keenly interested in the natural treasures of his purchase, including an enormous (and nonexistent) mountain of salt. The expedition of Meriwether Lewis and William Clark ascended the "Great Muddy" Missouri River and struggled through

> The French minister who negotiated the Louisiana Purchase treaties recalled that Minister Livingston had remarked at the signing: "We have lived long, but this is the noblest work of our whole lives . . . From this day the United States take their place among the powers of the first rank. . . . The instruments which we have just signed will cause no tears to be shed: they prepare ages of happiness for innumerable generations of human creatures."

the Rockies to the mouth of the Columbia River. This hazardous venture into the uncharted western wilderness, from 1804 to 1806, bolstered America's claim to Oregon, while further opening the West to Indian trade and exploration. Zebulon M. Pike, in 1805–1806, explored the Louisiana territory near the headwaters of the Mississippi River and in 1806–1807 ventured into Colorado and New Mexico, sighting the peak that bears his name.

Jefferson's reluctant purchase of Louisiana proved to be a landmark in American foreign policy. Overnight he avoided a possible rupture with France and the consequent entangling alliance with England. The nation was thus able to continue the noninterventionist policies of the Founding Fathers, though it later quarreled with Spain and Britain over the vague boundaries of Louisiana, north, south, and west. Not needing the navy of the mother country, the United States drifted away and eventually fought England in 1812. But by that time, the Republic was bigger and stronger, and had Louisiana securely in its possession.

The Louisiana godsend likewise boosted national unity. Once-proud Federalists, now mere sectionalists, sank ever lower in public esteem as they were reduced to whining impotence. A few of their more extreme members attempted to plot with scheming Aaron Burr for the secession of New England and New York. But the intrigue failed, largely owing to the vigilance of Alexander Hamilton, who subsequently provoked Burr to a duel. The pistol that killed Hamilton in 1804 blew the brightest brain out of the Federalist party—and destroyed its one remaining hope of effective leadership.

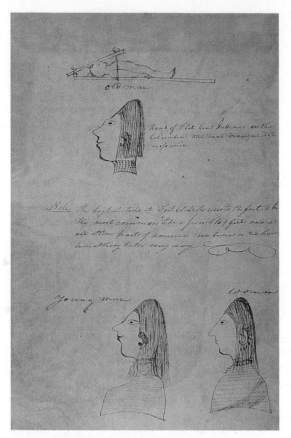

Flathead Indians, c. 1805   (left) William Clark served as the artist and cartographer of the Lewis and Clark Expedition. Here he has sketched the Flathead Indians of present-day Montana, showing the skull-molding practice from which they got their name. (Missouri Historical Society.) **Gifts from the Great White Chief**   (right) Among the objectives of the Lewis and Clark expedition was to establish good relations with the Indians in the newly acquired Louisiana Purchase territory. The American explorers presented all chiefs with copies of these medals, showing President Jefferson and the hands of an Indian and a white man clasped in "peace and friendship" under a crossed "peace pipe" and hatchet. All chiefs also received an American flag and a military uniform jacket, hat, and feather. (American Numismatic Society.)

A once-restive West, which now toasted the "immortal Jefferson," was more securely riveted to the Union by the purchase. People of the western waters were grateful to the federal government for having safeguarded their interests, particularly in securing the mouth of the Mississippi. A new spirit of unity surged through the West.

Aaron Burr, turning his disunionist plottings to the trans-Mississippi West, was arrested in 1806 for treason. Tried the next year at Richmond, Virginia, he was freed after the presiding judge, Chief Justice Marshall, had infuriated the Jeffersonians by what seemed to be bias in favor of the accused. The government's case collapsed when two witnesses to the same overt act of treason could not be found, as required by the Constitution (see Art. III, Sec. III). Burr's schemes are still somewhat shrouded in mystery, but he apparently planned to separate the western part of the United States from the eastern and unite it with to-be-conquered Spanish territory west of the Louisiana Purchase. The very fact that so dashing a figure as Burr could muster only threescore followers was quite significant. It indicated, among other things, that the West was developing a deeper sense of loyalty to the Washington government.

Meriwether Lewis *He is portrayed here as he looked on his return from the great expedition. (Charles Saint-Mémin, New-York Historical Society.)*

England (John Bull) Eats French Warships *Contemporary English caricature.*

America: A Nutcrackered Neutral

Jefferson was triumphantly reelected in 1804, with 162 electoral votes to only 14 for his Federalist opponent. His success was not so much due to Republicanizing the Federalists, as he fondly supposed, as to Federalizing the Republicans. The iron hand of reality gradually forced him, quite unintentionally, to kill off the opposition party by stealing many of its principles and embracing them as his own. He caught the Federalists in bathing, it was said, and made off with their clothes.

But the laurels of Jefferson's first administration soon withered under the blasts of the new storm that broke in Europe. After unloading

Louisiana in 1803, Napoleon deliberately provoked a renewal of his war with Britain—a conflict that crashed to an awesome close eleven long years later.

For two years a maritime United States—the number one neutral carrier since 1793—enjoyed juicy commercial pickings. But a setback came in 1805. At the Battle of Trafalgar, one-eyed Lord Nelson achieved immortality by smashing the combined French and Spanish fleets off the coast of Spain, thereby ensuring Britain's supremacy on the seas. At the Battle of Austerlitz in Austria—the Battle of the Three Emperors—Napoleon crushed the combined Austrian and Russian armies, thereby ensuring his mastery of the land. Like the tiger and the shark, France and Britain were supreme in their chosen elements.

Unable to hurt each other directly, the two antagonists were forced to strike indirect blows. England ruled the waves and waived the rules. The London government, beginning in 1806, issued a series of Orders in Council. These edicts closed the ports under French continental control to foreign shipping, including American, unless the vessels first stopped at a British port. There they would pay the necessary fees and, if acceptable, secure clearance papers. Napoleon struck back savagely in a series of decrees. In effect, they ordered the seizure of all merchant

Intercourse or Impartial Dealings A cartoon by "Peter Pencil" (1809) shows Jefferson being victimized by both England (left) and France (right). *(Houghton Library, Harvard.)*

ships, including American, that entered British ports.

Yankee skippers, like their predestined Calvinist ancestors, were seemingly damned if they did, damned if they did not. Even so, their trade prospered, because the greater the risk, the greater the profit. If only one vessel in three sailed over the reefs of French decrees and past the shoals of British Orders in Council, the owner could make a comfortable gain.

British Man-Stealing

Even more galling to American pride than the seizure of wooden ships was the seizure of flesh-and-blood American seamen. Impressment—the forcible enlistment of sailors—was a crude form of conscription which the British, among others, had employed for over four centuries. Clubs and stretchers (for men knocked unconscious) were standard equipment of press-gangs from His Majesty's man-hungry ships.

The London authorities themselves set limits to this ugly practice. They claimed the right to impress only British subjects on their own soil, in their own harbors, or on merchant ships on the high seas. But many fair-skinned Americans looked like Englishmen and the benefit of the doubt was seldom given to an experienced seaman in those shorthanded days. The result was that some six thousand bona fide United States citizens, according to the best estimates, were impressed by the "piratical man-stealers" of England from 1808 to 1811 alone. A number of these luckless souls died or were killed in the service, leaving their kinfolk and friends bereaved and embittered.

On their side, the British had countercomplaints. America's navy and merchant marine openly encouraged the enlistment of deserters from the "floating hells" of the British navy, where discipline was taught to the tune of the cat-o'-nine-tails. An expanding American merchant marine, also short of sailors, paid seductively high wages—"dollars for shillings." British deserters, conniving with ingenious Americans, would often secure fraudulent naturalization papers. (One resourceful female conniver had an oversized cradle in her shop so she could swear she had known the sailor "from the cradle.") His Majesty's press-gangs laughed aside such documents, whether genuine or not,

> Regarding the Chesapeake affair, the Washington Federalist reported: "We have never, on any occasion, witnessed the spirit of the people excited to so great a degree of indignation, or such a thirst for revenge, as on hearing of the late unexampled outrage on the Chesapeake. All parties, ranks, and professions were unanimous in their detestation of the dastardly deed, and all cried aloud for vengeance."

holding to the principle "Once an Englishman, always an Englishman." But the Americans, who had recently decided en masse to be English no longer, claimed that individuals had the right to choose their own country.

Britain had its back to the wall, and its desperate plight colored its views. If the Yankee "dollar grubbers" had not encouraged so much desertion, the British impressers might have been willing to make fewer mistakes in acquiring sailors. But England would not abandon its brutal practice of sailor-snatching at the behest of an upstart United States. Britons were making war; Americans were making money. The British feared that they would lose the war if they gave up their hoary method of conscription—and they would fight before they did.

Britain's determination was spectacularly highlighted in 1807. A royal frigate overhauled a United States frigate, the *Chesapeake*, about ten miles off the coast of Virginia. The British captain bluntly demanded the surrender of four alleged deserters. London had never claimed the right to seize sailors from a foreign warship, and the American commander, though totally unprepared to fight, refused the request. The British warship thereupon fired three devastating broadsides at close range, killing three Americans and wounding eighteen. Four deserters were dragged away, and the bloody hulk called the *Chesapeake* limped back to port.

An infuriated America—Federalists and Republicans alike—now joined in an outburst of national wrath. Nothing like it had been seen since the French XYZ insults of 1797. Jefferson, the peace lover, could easily have had war if he had wanted it. As the event proved, if America were going to fight at all, it should have fought when the country was united.

Britain was clearly in the wrong, as the London Foreign Office admitted. But Jefferson unwisely attempted to use the *Chesapeake* outrage as a lever to force the British to renounce impressment altogether. This they flatly refused to do. The affair rankled for five years; and when reparation was finally made, it came too late to salve old wounds.

Jefferson's Backfiring Embargo

National honor would not permit a slavish submission to British and French mistreatment. Yet a large-scale foreign war was contrary to the settled policy of the new Republic—and in addition it would be futile. The navy was weak, thanks largely to Jefferson's antinavalism; and the army was even weaker. A disastrous defeat would not improve America's plight.

The warring nations in Europe were heavily dependent upon the United States for raw materials and foodstuffs. In his eager search for an alternative to war, Jefferson seized upon this essential fact. He reasoned that if America voluntarily cut off its exports, the offending powers would be forced to come, hat in hand, and agree to respect its rights.

Responding to the presidential lash, Congress hastily passed the Embargo Act late in 1807. This rigorous law forbade the export of all goods from the United States, whether in American or in foreign ships. It was a compromise between submission and shooting.

Jefferson, the onetime strict constructionist, had once more flip-flopped into the camp of the loose constructionists. In the interests of the Federalist shippers, whom he disliked, he was rereading the Constitution with strange bifocals. To him, it now meant that Congress, under its authority to "regulate" commerce, could go so far as to stop foreign trade altogether. Regulation thus became strangulation.

Federalist New England could well have prayed for relief from its newly found Virginia friend, "Mad Tom" Jefferson. Forests of dead masts gradually filled once-flourishing harbors;

> A Federalist circular in Massachusetts against the embargo cried out: "Let every man who holds the name of America dear to him, stretch forth his hands and put this accursed thing, this Embargo from him. Be resolute, act like sons of liberty, of God, and your country; nerve your arm with vengeance against the Despot [Jefferson] who would wrest the inestimable germ of your independence from you—and you shall be Conquerors!!!"

docks that had once rumbled were deserted (except for illegal trade); and soup kitchens cared for some of the hungry unemployed. Jeffersonian Republicans probably hurt the commerce of New England, which they avowedly were trying to protect, far more than Old England and France together were doing.

Farmers of the South and West, the strongholds of Jefferson, suffered no less disastrously than New England. They were alarmed by the mounting piles of exportable cotton, grain, and tobacco. Tart-tongued John Randolph of Virginia remarked that enacting the embargo was like cutting off one's toes to cure one's corns. Jefferson in truth seemed to be waging war on his fellow citizens rather than on the offending belligerents.

The American people, from the days of the colonial Navigation Acts, have never submitted meekly to unpopular legislation. Though basically law-abiding, they habitually flout laws that are opposed by large numbers of the population. An enormous illicit trade mushroomed in 1808, especially along the Canadian border, where bands of armed Americans on loaded rafts overawed or overpowered federal agents. Irate citizens cynically transposed the letters of "Embargo" to read "O Grab Me," "Go Bar 'Em," and "Mobrage," while heartily denouncing the "Dambargo."

Jefferson nonetheless induced Congress to pass iron-toothed enforcing legislation. It was so inquisitorial and tyrannical as to cause some Americans to think more kindly of George III, whom Jefferson had berated in the Declaration of Independence. One indignant New Hampshire poet burst out in song:

> Our ships all in motion,
> Once whiten'd the ocean;
>   They sail'd and return'd with a Cargo;
> Now doom'd to decay
>   They are fallen a prey,
> To Jefferson, worms, and EMBARGO

New England seethed with talk of secession; and Jefferson later admitted that he felt the

The Embargo (Ograbme)   As a snapping turtle, it halts overseas shipments. (Prints Division, New York Public Library, Astor, Lenox and Tilden Foundations.)

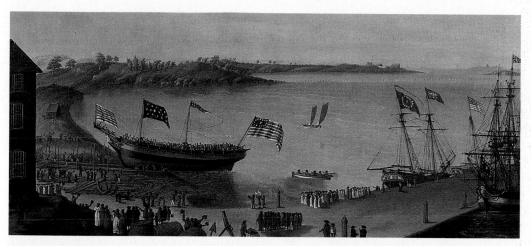

Launching of **Fame** *from Becket's Shipyard, Essex, Massachusetts, 1802* *Jefferson's embargo throttled thriving New England shipyards like this one, stirring bitter resentment. (Courtesy of the Essex Institute, Salem, MA.)*

foundations of government tremble under his feet.

An alarmed Congress, bowing to the storm of public anger, finally repealed the embargo, on March 1, 1809, three days before Jefferson's retirement. A half-loaf substitute was provided by the Non-Intercourse Act. This measure formally reopened trade with all the nations of the world, except the two most important, England and France. Though thus watered down, economic coercion continued to be the policy of the Jeffersonians from 1809 to 1812, when the nation finally plunged into war.

The Wooden-Gun Embargo: A Successful Failure

Why did the embargo, Jefferson's most daring act of statesmanship, collapse after fifteen dismal months? First of all, he underestimated the bulldog determination of the British, as others have, and overestimated their dependence on America's trade. Bumper grain crops blessed the British Isles during these years, and the revolutionary Latin American republics unexpectedly threw open their ports for compensating commerce.

The hated embargo was not continued long enough or tightly enough to achieve the desired results. But leaders must know the temper of their people, and Jefferson should have foreseen that such a self-crucifying weapon could not possibly command public support. The Americans, notoriously people of action, did not take kindly to the passive type of heroism. They much preferred commercial activity, with all its risks, to enforced inactivity, with no chance of profit.

A crestfallen Jefferson himself admitted that the embargo was three times more costly than war. The irony is that with only a fraction of its cost to the country, he could have built a fairly strong navy. Such a fighting force would have won more respect for American rights on the high seas and might well have prevented the War of 1812.

The embargo further embroiled relations with both Britain and France. It embittered the British, partly because it hit them more forcibly than it did Napoleon. The French despot naturally applauded the embargo, for it was an indirect American blockade of his foe. He cynically helped enforce it by seizing scores of Yankee merchant ships in his ports; by the terms of the Embargo Act, he argued, these vessels should have been tied up at home. His "cooperation" merely rubbed salt into old sores.

A stoppage of exports hurt Federalist shipping but temporarily revived the Federalist party. Gaining new converts, its leaders hurled their nullification of the embargo into the teeth of the "Virginia lordlings" in Washington. In 1804, the discredited Federalists had polled only 14 electoral votes out of 176; in 1808, the embargo year, the figure rose to 47 out of 175.

Curiously enough, New England plucked a new prosperity from the ugly jaws of the embargo. With shipping tied up and imported goods scarce, the resourceful Yankees reopened old factories and erected new ones. The real foundations of modern America's industrial might were laid behind the protective wall of the embargo, followed by nonintercourse and the War of 1812. Jefferson, the avowed critic of factories, may have unwittingly done more for American manufacturing than Alexander Hamilton, the outspoken friend of factories.

Jefferson's embargo, followed in modified form by nonintercourse, undeniably pinched England. Many British importers and manufacturers suffered severe losses, especially those dependent on American cotton. As thousands of factory workers were thrown out of jobs, agitation mounted for a repeal of the restrictions that had brought on the embargo. A petition to Parliament in 1812, from the city of Birmingham alone, bore twenty thousand names on a sheet of parchment 150 feet long. So strong was public pressure that two days before Congress declared war in June 1812, the British foreign secretary announced that the offensive Orders in Council would be immediately suspended. The supreme irony is that Jefferson's policy of economic coercion did win in the end, but America was not patient enough to reap the reward of its sacrifices.

The Living Jefferson

Thomas Jefferson retained much of his popularity, even though it was severely tarnished by the embargo. One public toast ran: "May he receive from his fellow citizens the reward of his merit, a halter, [hangman's noose]." But his grip on his party was such that he could easily have won a third nomination and election. The international crisis was still acute; and although Jefferson was sixty-five years old, he was mentally alert and physically vigorous. He lived eighteen

more years, glad to have escaped what he called the "splendid misery" of the presidential penitentiary.

Jefferson, rather than Washington, was the real father of the two-term tradition. Unlike the first president, who had no serious constitutional qualms, he feared that more than two terms might open the door to dictatorship. Yet Jefferson strongly favored the nomination and election of a kindred spirit, his friend and fellow Virginian, the quiet, intellectual, and unassuming James Madison.

Though bitterly assailed, Jefferson left office with the consolation that he had remained true to the guiding star of the other Founding Fathers. He had kept the country out of a serious foreign war. Despite numerous reversals of policy under the whiplash of practicality, he never lost his faith in democracy and in the common people. He brought a renovation rather than a revolution; the real revolution that did occur was in his own thinking. If the Federalists were the stepping-stone between monarchical Europe and republican America, then the Jeffersonians were the stepping-stone between aristocratic Federalism and democratic Jacksonianism.

Thomas Jefferson and John Adams died on the same day—appropriately the Fourth of July, 1826. The last words of Adams, then ninety-one, were: "Thomas Jefferson still survives." He was wrong, for three hours earlier Jefferson had breathed his last. But Thomas Jefferson still survives in the democratic ideals and liberal principles of the great nation that he risked his all to found and that he served so long and faithfully.

Early in 1805 Jefferson privately foresaw the two-term Twenty-Second Amendment (1951): "General Washington set the example of voluntary retirement after eight years. I shall follow it, and a few more precedents will oppose the obstacle of habit to anyone after a while who shall endeavor to extend his term. Perhaps it may beget a disposition to establish it by an amendment of the Constitution."

CHRONOLOGY

1800	Jefferson defeats Adams for presidency
1801	Jefferson inaugurated president
	Judiciary Act of 1801
1801–1805	Naval war with Tripoli
1802	Revised naturalization law
	Judiciary Act of 1801 repealed
1803	*Marbury* v. *Madison*
	Louisiana Purchase
1804	Jefferson reelected
	Impeachment of Justice Chase
1804–1806	Lewis and Clark expedition
1805	Peace treaty with Tripoli
1805–1806	Pike's explorations
1806	Burr treason trial
1807	*Chesapeake* affair
	Embargo Act
1809	Non-Intercourse Act replaces Embargo Act

Varying Viewpoints

The Jeffersonian era has long presented observers with a series of paradoxes, none greater than the question of how the man who proclaimed, "We are all Republicans, we are all Federalists," came to preside over one of the most bitterly partisan periods in American history.

Some scholars play down the importance of party conflict in this era. Stressing the early parties' lack of concern for organizing the electorate, these accounts note that the Jeffersonians and the Federalists distrusted parties; saw them only as temporary, necessary evils; and looked forward to their elimination. Thus, historians like James S. Young argue that the Jeffersonian era possessed no true party system.

Others, among them Noble E. Cunningham, see the organizations of the early na-

tional period as the prototypes of the modern American party system. Conceding that the Federalists and Jeffersonians never became mass-based organizations like the later Jacksonian parties, this interpretation emphasizes the innovations of the period. The Jeffersonians created a partisan press, maintained control of Congress by dominating committee chairmanships, and pioneered campaign tactics like stump speaking and door-to-door canvassing. Most important, the experiences of the Federalists and Jeffersonians, in the two decades after the ratification of the Constitution, led both groups to accept, grudgingly, the idea that party competition was inevitable and potentially beneficial in a republican society. This realization paved the way for the evolution of a full-blown two-party system in the 1830s.

Select Readings

Primary Source Documents

Jefferson's "First Inaugural Address" (1801), in Henry Steele Commager, *Documents of American History*, echoed the themes of Washington's Farewell and set the tone for his presidency. Reuben G. Thwaites, ed., *Original Journals of the Lewis and Clark Expedition** (1904), chronicles the explorers' adventures. For the political flavor of the age, see the debate over the Embargo Act* (1807); For Constitutional history, read the decision of John Marshall in *Marbury v. Madison** (1803).

Secondary Sources

A monument of American historical writing is Henry Adams, *History of the United States during the Administrations of Jefferson and Madison* (9 vols., 1889–1891), available in a one-volume abridgement edited by Ernest Samuels. Especially fascinating are Adams's epilogue and prologue on the United States in 1800 and 1817. A brief introduction is given in Marshall Smelser, *The Democratic Republic, 1801–1815* (1968). Problems with the judiciary can be traced in Albert J. Beveridge's still-respected *Life of John Marshall* (4 vols., 1919). A more recent and succinct analysis is Richard E. Ellis, *The Jeffersonian Crisis: Courts and Politics in the New Republic* (1971). Politics are treated in a broad, imaginative context in James S. Young, *The Washington Community, 1800–1829* (1966), and more traditionally in Noble E. Cunningham's rebuttal, *The Process of Government under Jefferson* (1979). See also the Joyce Appleby, Lance Banning, and Drew McCoy volumes cited in Chapter 9. The development of political parties is dissected in William N. Chambers, *Political Parties in a New Nation* (1963), and in Noble E. Cunningham, *The Jeffersonian Republicans: The Formation of Party Organization, 1789–1801* (1958). See also Richard Buel, Jr., *Securing the Revolution* (1972), and Robert E. Shalhope, *John Taylor of Carolina* (1980). The standard scholarly biography is Merrill D. Peterson, *Thomas Jefferson and the New Nation* (1970). Peterson has also scrutinized *The Jefferson Image in the American Mind* (1960). Leonard D. White brings administrative history to life in *The Jeffersonians* (rev. ed., 1959). Forrest McDonald is highly critical of his subject in *The Presidency of Thomas Jefferson* (1976). Leonard Levy debunks Jefferson's liberalism in *Jefferson and Civil Liberties* (1963), while Bernard W. Sheehan examines another important aspect of policy in *Seeds of Extinction: Jeffersonian Philanthropy and the American Indian* (1973). See also Reginald Horsman, *Expansion and American Indian Policy, 1783–1812* (1967). A first-class study of the negotiator of the Louisiana Purchase is George Dangerfield, *Chancellor Robert R. Livingston of New York* (1960). An expansionist thesis is fully developed in Alexander De Conde, *This Affair of Louisiana* (1976). The embargo is treated in Burton Spivak, *Jefferson's English Crisis: Commerce, Embargo and the Republican Revolution* (1979). Daniel Boorstin vividly evokes the intellectual climate of the age in *The Lost World of Thomas Jefferson* (1948). John C. Miller, *The Wolf by the Ears: Thomas Jefferson and Slavery* (1977), probes the third president's attitudes on an important question. Irving Brant looks at *James Madison, Secretary of State* (1953), and F. E. Ewing examines Jefferson's powerful treasury secretary in *America's Forgotten Statesman: Albert Gallatin* (1959).

James Madison and the Second War for Independence, 1809–1815

The Existing War—the Child of Prostitution. May no American Acknowledge it Legitimate.

A Federalist Toast during the War of 1812

Madison: Dupe of Napoleon

Scholarly James Madison took the presidential oath on March 4, 1809, as the awesome conflict in Europe was roaring to its climax. Small of stature (5 feet 4 inches; 1.62 meters), light of weight (about 100 pounds; 45 kilograms), bald of head, and weak of voice, he fell tragically short of providing vigorous executive leadership. Crippled also by factions within his cabinet, he was unable to dominate his party, as Jefferson had once done.

The Non-Intercourse Act of 1809—the limited substitute for the embargo aimed solely at Britain and France—would expire in about a year. Congress, desperately attempting to uphold American rights, adopted in 1810 a bar-gaining measure known as Macon's Bill No. 2. While permitting American trade with all the world, it dangled an attractive lure. If either England or France repealed its commercial restrictions, America would restore nonimportation against the nonrepealing nation. In short, the United States would bribe the belligerents into respecting its rights.

This opportunity was made to order for Napoleon, a past master of deceit. He was eager to have nonimportation clamped down once more on the British, because it would serve as a partial blockade, which he would not have to raise a finger to enforce. He was hopeful that such a boycott would embroil the Americans in war with Britain, for then they would be serving as his indirect allies to weaken his arch-enemy.

President James Madison (1751–1836) *Though an eminent constitutionalist, legislator, and diplomatist, he was not a strong Chief Executive. Foolishly, he was the only president ever to go directly to the fighting front, but he quickly rode away as the British advanced on Washington in 1814. (White House Historical Association.)*

Accordingly, he blandly announced, in August 1810, that his objectionable decrees had been repealed.

Responsible Americans, rising above self-delusion, should have examined the hollow-sounding French announcement with extreme caution. Napoleon, prince of liars, had no intention whatever of repealing his damaging de-

> *"The injuries received from France,"* insisted the editor of Niles's Weekly Register (June 27, 1812), *"do not lessen the enormity of those heaped upon us by England. . . . In this 'straight betwixt two' we had an unquestionable right to select our enemy. We have given the preference to Great Britain . . . on account of her more flagrant wrongs."*

crees. But Madison, frantically seeking to wrest a recognition of American rights from England, accepted French bad faith as good faith. He formally announced, in November 1810, that France had complied with the terms of Macon's Bill No. 2 and that nonimportation would consequently be reestablished against Britain.

Madison's decision was fateful. Britons were angered by America's apparent willingness to be the dupe and partner of Napoleon. Once Madison had aligned his nation against England commercially, he found himself gravitating toward France politically—and edging toward the whirlpool of war.

War Whoops Arouse the War Hawks

The complexion of the Twelfth Congress, which met late in 1811, differed markedly from that of its predecessor. Recent elections had swept away many of the older "submission men" and replaced them with young hotheads, chiefly from the South and West. The youthful newcomers—"the boys," John Randolph sneeringly called them—were on fire for a new war with the old enemy. Not having had a conflict in their own generation, these war hawks were weary of hearing how their fathers had "whipped" the British single-handedly. They won control of the House of Representatives and elevated to the speakership the tall (6 feet 2 inches; 1.88 meters), eloquent, and magnetic Henry Clay of Kentucky, the gallant "Harry of the West," then only thirty-four years old.

Western war hawks, first of all, were eager to wipe out the renewed Indian resistance against the white settlers streaming steadily into the western wilderness. As this white flood spread through the green forests, more and more Indians were pushed farther and farther toward the setting sun. Two remarkable Shawnee twin brothers, Tecumseh and the Prophet, knew that if this onrushing tide were ever to be stopped, that time had come. They began to weld together a far-flung confederacy of all the tribes east of the Mississippi. Their braves forswore firewater in order to be fit for the last-ditch battle with the "paleface" intruders. To make matters worse, the sturdy pioneers and their war

War Vote in House of Representatives, 1812,
Showing Western and Southwestern War Sentiment

STATES	REGIONS	FOR WAR	AGAINST WAR
N.H.	Frontier New England	3	2
Vt.		3	1
Mass.	Maritime and Federalist New England;	6	8
R.I.	Mass. (includes frontier Maine)	0	2
Conn.		0	7
N.Y.	Commercial and Federalist middle states	3	11
N.J.		2	4
Del.		0	1
Pa.	Jeffersonian middle states	16	2
Md.		6	3
Va.	Jeffersonian southern states	14	5
N.C.		6	3
S.C.		8	0
Ga.		3	0
Ohio	The trans-Allegheny West—nest of the war hawks	1	0
Ky.		5	0
Tenn.		3	0
		79	49

hawk representatives in Congress widely believed that the Indians' firearms and scalping knives were being furnished by British "hair buyers" in Canada.

Only a few days after the war hawk Congress convened in Washington, news of stirring events on the frontier further inflamed anti-Indian and anti-British feeling. General William H. Harrison, advancing with one thousand men upon the Indian headquarters, repelled a surprise attack at Tippecanoe, in present Indiana, on November 7, 1811. He then put the torch to the settlement.

Harrison's onslaught broke the back of the Indian rebellion. It also made the blood course faster in the veins of the impetuous war hawks. People like Representative Felix Grundy of Tennessee, three of whose brothers had been murdered, cried that there was only one way to remove the menace of the Indians: wipe out their Canadian base. Canada was a lush prize—so near, so desirable, and apparently so defenseless. "On to Canada, on to Canada" was the war hawks' ominous chant. Southern expansionists, less vocal, cast a covetous eye on Florida, then weakly held by Britain's ally Spain.

Henry Clay (1777–1852) *A glamorous, eloquent, and ambitious member of the House and Senate for many years, Clay was thrice an unsuccessful candidate for the highest office in the land. "Sir," he declared in the Senate in 1850, "I would rather be right than be President." Right or wrong, he never made the grade but his devotion to the Union was inspirational. (Library of Congress.)*

Tecumseh (1768?–1813) *A Shawnee Indian born in the Ohio country, he was probably the most gifted organizer and leader of his people in U.S. history. A noted warrior, he fought the tribal custom of torturing prisoners and opposed the practice of permitting any one tribe to sell land that, he believed, belonged to all Indians. (Field Museum of Natural History, Chicago.)*

The war hawks wanted "Free Trade and Sailors' Rights," as well as free land. It may seem strange that settlers beyond the mountains, many of whom had never seen a body of salt water larger than a salt lick, should want to fight for maritime rights. But the proud, nationalistic westerners were outraged by the manhandling of American sailors and by the British Orders in Council that dammed up their agricultural products from shipment to Europe. Westerners also joined many of their fellow citizens in believing that only a vigorous assertion of American rights could demonstrate the viability of American nationhood—and of democracy as a form of government. If America could not fight to protect itself, its experiment in republicanism would be discredited in the eyes of a scoffing world.

Militant war hawks, with scattered but essential support from other sections, finally engineered a declaration of war in June 1812. The vote in the House was 79 to 49, in the Senate 19 to 13. The close tally betrayed a dangerous degree of national disunity. Representatives from the pro-British maritime and commercial centers, as well as from the middle Atlantic states, almost solidly opposed hostilities. Thus, the West and Southwest, mostly landlocked, presented the sea-fronting East with a war for a free sea that the East vehemently resented.

Mr. Madison's War

But why fight Britain rather than France, which had committed nearly as many maritime offenses? The traditional Republican attachment to France partly explains the choice of foe, as does the visibility of British impressments and the British arming of the Indians, who were smashing into pioneer cabins on the frontier.

The choice prize of Canada also beckoned from the north. Americans fondly (but wrongly) believed that taking Canada would be absurdly simple, a "frontiersman's frolic." If this northern mirage had not been so inviting, the administration would have waited a few more months and thereby learned of London's intention to repeal the Orders in Council. In fact, the announcement of the intention to repeal was made two days *before* Congress voted for war. Had there been an Atlantic cable, the war hawks probably could not have forced a declaration of hostilities through the Senate.

Seafaring New England damned the war for a free sea. The news of the declaration of war was greeted with muffled bells, flags at half-mast, and public fasting.

Why the opposition? To New Englanders, impressment was an old and exaggerated wrong. New England shippers and manufacturers were still raking in money, and profits dull patriotism. Pro-British New England Federalists also sympathized with England and resented the Virginia dynasty's sympathy with Napoleon, whom they regarded as the "Corsican butcher" and "the anti-Christ of the age."

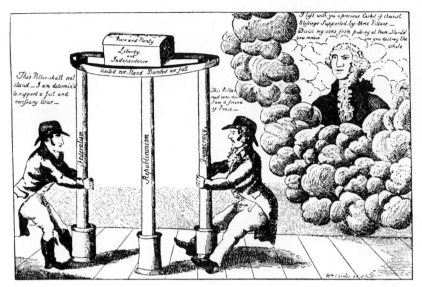

The Present State of Our Country
Partisan disunity over the War of 1812 threatens the nation's very existence. The prowar Jeffersonian at the left is attacking the pillar of federalism; the antiwar Federalist at the right is trying to pull down Democracy. The spirit of Washington warns that the country's welfare depends upon all three pillars, including Republicanism. (A cartoon by William Charles, New York Public Library.)

Federalists also condemned the War of 1812 because they opposed the acquisition of Canada, which would merely add more agrarian states from the wild Northwest. This, in turn, would increase the voting strength of the Jeffersonian Republicans. New England Federalists were determined, wrote one versifier:

> To rule the nation if they could,
> But see it damned if others should.

The bitterness of New Englanders against "Mr. Madison's War" led them to treason or near-treason. In a sense America fought two enemies simultaneously: old England and New England. New England gold holders probably lent more dollars to the British than to the federal treasury. New England farmers sent huge quantities of supplies and foodstuffs to Canada, enabling British armies to invade New York. New England governors stubbornly refused to permit their militia to serve outside their own states.

Fight over Canada on Land and Lakes

The War of 1812, largely because of widespread disunity, ranks as one of America's worst-fought wars. There was no burning national anger, as there had been in 1807, following the *Chesapeake* outrage. War hawks in Congress were no more than a zealous minority. President Madison, while supporting their aims, knew that there was serious disunity. The supreme lesson of this conflict was the folly of leading a divided and apathetic people into war.

The Republic was dangerously unprepared, despite warnings going back nineteen years to the outbreak of the European war in 1793. The nation was still suffering from its own embargo and nonintercourse, which it had partially enforced for the better part of four years. Congress had shortsightedly permitted the Bank of the United States to expire in 1811, at a time when a powerful financial institution was needed. It was knifed largely by the jealousies of the competing state banks.

The regular army was scandalously inadequate, for it was ill-trained, ill-disciplined, and widely scattered. It had to be supplemented by the even more poorly trained militia, who were sometimes distinguished by speed of foot in leaving the battlefield. Some of the ranking generals were semisenile heirlooms from the Revolutionary War, rusting on their laurels and lacking in vigor and vision.

The offensive strategy in Canada was poorly conceived. Had the Americans captured Montreal, the center of population and transportation, everything to the west would have died, just as the leaves of a tree wither when the

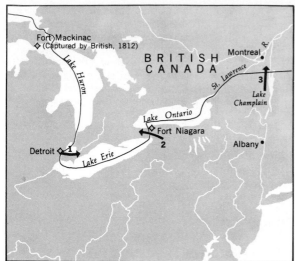

The Three U.S. Thrusts of 1812 *The thin red line delineates the Canadian border.*

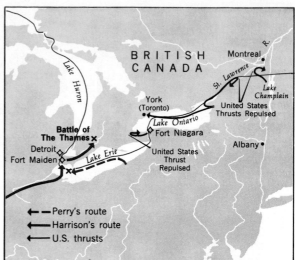

Campaigns of 1813 *The thin red line denotes the Canadian boundary.*

trunk is girdled. But instead of laying ax to the trunk, the Americans frittered away their strength in the three-pronged invasion of 1812. The trio of invading forces that set out from Detroit, Niagara, and Lake Champlain were all beaten back shortly after they had crossed the Canadian border.

By contrast, the British and Canadians displayed energy from the outset. Early in the war they captured the American fort of Mackinac, which commanded the upper Great Lakes and the Indian-inhabited area to the south and west. Their brilliant defensive operations were led by the inspired British general Isaac Brock and assisted (in the American camp) by "General Mud" and "General Confusion."

When several American land invasions of Canada were again hurled back in 1813, Americans looked for success on water. Control of the Great Lakes was vital, and an energetic American naval officer, Oliver Hazard Perry, managed to build a fleet of green-timbered ships on the shores of Lake Erie, manned by even greener seamen. When he captured a British fleet in a furious engagement on Lake Erie, he reported to his superior, "We have met the enemy and they are ours." Perry's victory and his slogan infused new life into the drooping American

cause. Forced to withdraw from Detroit and Fort Malden, the retreating redcoats were overtaken by General Harrison's army and beaten at the Battle of the Thames in October 1813. The gifted Indian leader Tecumseh, now a brigadier general in the British army, lost his life in the battle.

Despite these successes, the Americans by late 1814, far from invading Canada, were grimly defending their own soil against the invading British. In Europe, the diversionary power of Napoleon was destroyed in mid-1814, and the dangerous despot was marooned on the Mediterranean isle of Elba. The United States, which had so brashly provoked war behind the protective skirts of Napoleon, was now left to face the music alone. As thousands of red-coated veterans began to pour into Canada, Europe's distresses, for once, failed the Americans.

Assembling some ten thousand crack troops, the British prepared in 1814 for a crushing blow into New York, along the familiar lake-river route. In the absence of roads, the invader was forced to bring supplies over the Lake Champlain waterway. A weaker American fleet, commanded by the thirty-year-old Thomas Macdonough, challenged the British. The ensuing battle was desperately fought near Plattsburgh, on September 11, 1814, on floating slaughter-houses. The American flagship at one point was in grave trouble. But Macdonough, unexpectedly turning his ship about with cables, confronted the enemy with a fresh broadside and snatched victory from the fangs of defeat.

The results of this heroic naval battle were momentous. The invading British army was forced to retreat. Macdonough thus saved at least upper New York from conquest, New England from further disaffection, and the Union from possible dissolution. He also profoundly affected the concurrent negotiations of the Anglo-American peace treaty in Europe.

Washington Burned and New Orleans Defended

A second formidable British force, numbering about four thousand, landed in the Chesapeake Bay area in August 1814. Advancing rapidly on Washington, it easily dispersed some six thousand panicky militia at Bladensburg ("the Bladensburg races"). The invaders then entered the capital and set fire to most of the public buildings, including the Capitol and the White House ("the Yankee Palace"). President

Madison and his aides, chased into the surrounding hills like frightened rabbits, witnessed from afar the billowing smoke. The British fleet next appeared before Baltimore, a nest for privateers, but was beaten off by the doughty defenders at Fort McHenry, despite "bombs bursting in air." At the same time, the American land defenders, though driven back at first, caused the attacking army to withdraw. The memory of the Chesapeake campaign was further kept alive when Francis Scott Key, a detained American anxiously watching the bombardment at Baltimore from a British ship, was inspired to write the words of "The Star-Spangled Banner." Set to the tune of a saucy old English tavern refrain, the song quickly attained popularity.

A third British blow of 1814, aimed at New Orleans, menaced the entire Mississippi Valley. Gaunt and hawk-faced Andrew Jackson, fresh from crushing the southwest Indians at the Battle of Horseshoe Bend in what is now Alabama, was placed in command. His hodgepodge force consisted of seven thousand sailors, regulars, pirates, and Frenchmen, as well as militiamen from Louisiana, Kentucky, and Tennessee. Among the defenders were two Louisiana regiments of free black volunteers, numbering about four hundred men. The Americans threw

The Burning of Washington *America's military fortunes hit rock bottom on August 24, 1814, when British forces, having routed a ragtag American army on the outskirts of the capital, put the torch to Washington, D.C. (The Granger Collection.)*

The Southwest, 1814–1815

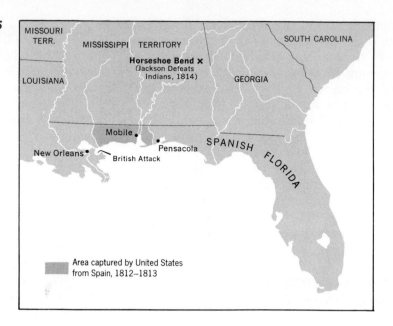

MISSOURI TERR.

MISSISSIPPI TERRITORY

SOUTH CAROLINA

Horseshoe Bend ✗
(Jackson Defeats Indians, 1814)

LOUISIANA

GEORGIA

Mobile •

New Orleans •
British Attack

Pensacola •

SPANISH FLORIDA

Area captured by United States from Spain, 1812–1813

up their entrenchment, and in the words of a popular song:

> Behind it stood our little force—
> None wished it to be greater;
> For ev'ry man was half a horse,
> And half an alligator.

The overconfident British, numbering some eight thousand battle-seasoned veterans, blundered badly. They made the mistake of launching a frontal assault, on January 8, 1815, on the entrenched American riflemen and cannoneers. The attackers suffered the most devastating defeat of the entire war, losing over two thousand, killed and wounded, in half an hour, as compared with some seventy for the Americans. This slaughter was as useless as it was horrible, for the treaty of peace had been signed at Ghent, in Europe, two weeks earlier. But Jackson became more than ever the hero of the West.

The "glorious news" from New Orleans reached Washington early in February 1815, and about two weeks later came the tidings of the treaty of peace. Naive citizens promptly concluded that the British, beaten to their knees by Jackson, had hastened to make terms.

Ship Duels and Privateer Prizes

Man for man and ship for ship the American navy did much better than the army. But the results of its heroism have been exaggerated.

Britain's navy in 1812 boasted more than 800 men of war. Of these oaken craft, 219 were ships of the line of the 74-gun class, and 296 were frigates of roughly the 44-gun class. America, by contrast, had only 16 ships in its entire navy, the largest of which were a few 44-gun frigates, unable to stand up to British ships of the line. There could obviously be no saltwater fleet engagements in the slam-bang Trafalgar tradition; the only fleet battles were fought on the interior lakes.

American frigates and smaller sloops did clash with the enemy in a series of spectacular duels. In the frigate class, the Americans won four out of five of the single-ship contests; and in the sloop class, eight out of nine. American craft on the whole were more skillfully handled, had better gunners, and were manned by non-press-gang crews who were burning to avenge numerous indignities. The American frigates were specially designed superfrigates, notably the *Constitution* ("Old Ironsides"). They had thicker sides, heavier firepower, and larger

Constitution and Guerrière, 1812 The Guerrière was heavily outweighed and outgunned, yet its British captain eagerly—and foolishly—sought combat. His ship was totally destroyed. Historian Henry Adams later concluded that this duel "raised the United States in one half hour to the rank of a first-class Power in the world." (Bettmann Archive.)

crews, of which one sailor in six was a free black.

The British were deeply humiliated by their naval defeats, all the more so because they had sneered at America's "few fir-built frigates, manned by a handful of bastards and outlaws." In a few months they lost more warships to the Yankees than the French and Spaniards together had captured in years of fighting.

Swift and annoying American privateers— the "militia of the sea"—numbered about 500. They were in fact much more damaging than the regular navy and had an important bearing on the coming of peace. Built to fly from stronger ships rather than fight them, these speedy craft captured or destroyed some 1,350 British merchantmen, even pursuing them into the English Channel and the Irish Sea. Assisted by fast-sailing sloops of the navy, Yankee privateers were so destructive that Lloyd's of London refused to insure unconvoyed British merchantmen crossing the Irish Sea. (At the same time, British warships and privateers were capturing hundreds of American merchant ships.)

Yet the American privateers were not an unmixed blessing. They lost scores of their own craft and diverted valuable manpower from the navy and army. But they brought urgently needed wealth into the country, boosted sagging morale, and slowed up British operations in Canada and elsewhere by capturing arms and supplies. More than that, the privateers brought the war home to British manufacturers, merchants, and shippers, who in turn exerted strong pressure on Parliament to end this costly conflict.

Its wrath aroused, the Royal Navy finally retaliated by throwing a ruinous naval blockade along America's coast and by landing raiding parties almost at will. American economic life, including fishing, was crippled. Customs rev-

Smarting from wounded pride on the sea, the London Times *urged chastisement for Americans: "The people—naturally vain, boastful, and insolent—have been filled with an absolute contempt of our maritime power, and a furious eagerness to beat down our maritime pretensions. Those passions, which have been inflamed by success, could only have been cooled by what in vulgar and emphatic language has been termed 'a sound flogging.'" (Dec. 30, 1814)*

Ive often heard of your Wasps and Harnets but little thought such diminutive Insects could giveme Such a Sting!!!

A Wasp on a Frolic   *U.S. sloops-of-war* Wasp *and Hornet* sting *John Bull's pride. The* Wasp *captured the* Frolic. *Contemporary American cartoon.*

enues were choked off, and near the end of the war the bankrupt Treasury was unable to meet its maturing obligations.

The Treaty of Ghent

Czar Alexander I of Russia, hard-pressed by Napoleon's army and not wanting his British ally to fritter away its strength in America, proposed mediation between the clashing Anglo-Saxon cousins in 1812. The czar's feeler eventually set in motion the machinery that brought five American peacemakers to the quaint Belgian city of Ghent in 1814. The bickering group was headed by early-rising, puritanical John Quincy Adams, son of John Adams, who deplored the late-hour card playing of his high-living colleague Henry Clay.

Confident after their military successes, Britain's envoys made sweeping demands for a neutralized Indian buffer state in the Great Lakes region, control of the Great Lakes, and a substantial part of conquered Maine. The Americans flatly rejected these terms, and the talks appeared stalemated. But news of British reverses in upper New York and at Baltimore, and increasing war-weariness in Britain, made London more willing to compromise. Preoccupied with the Congress of Vienna and still-dangerous France, the British lion resigned itself to licking its wounds. Revenge against its upstart American offspring would be sweet—but expensive. Once again European distress brought American diplomatic success, for the War of 1812 was "won" by the United States, so far as it was won at all, in Europe.

The Treaty of Ghent, signed on Christmas Eve in 1814, was essentially an armistice. Both sides simply agreed to stop fighting and to restore conquered territory. No mention was made of those grievances for which America had ostensibly fought: the Indian menace, search and seizure, Orders in Council, impressment, and confiscations. These maritime omissions have often been cited as further evidence of the insincerity of the war hawks. Rather, they are proof that the Americans did not defeat the British decisively. With neither side able to impose its will, the treaty negotiations—like the war itself—ended as a virtual draw.

The news from Ghent triggered an outburst of rejoicing in the United States. Many Americans had rather expected to lose some territory, so dark was the military outlook early in 1815. But when the treaty arrived, the public mood rocketed from gloom to glory. The popularity of the pact was so overwhelming that it was unanimously approved by the Senate. A slogan of the hour became "Not One Inch of Territory Ceded or Lost"—a watchword that contrasted strangely with "On to Canada" at the outset of the war.

Federalist Grievances and the Hartford Convention

Defiant New England remained a problem. It was by far the most prosperous section during the conflict, owing largely to illicit trade with the enemy in Canada and to the absence of a

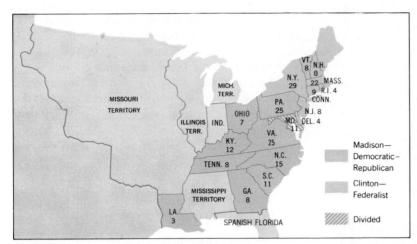

Presidential Election of 1812 (with electoral vote by state)　The Federalists showed impressive strength in the North and their presidential candidate, DeWitt Clinton, the future "father of the Erie Canal," almost won. If the 25 electoral votes of Pennsylvania had gone to the New Yorker, he would have won, 114 to 103.

British blockade until 1814. But the embittered opposition of the Federalists to the war continued unabated. Late in 1812, when the first wartime presidential election was held, unhappy Federalists combined with disaffected Republicans and almost unseated President Madison. If the state of Pennsylvania alone had been transferred to their electoral column, they would have won.

As the war dragged on, New England extremists became more vocal. A small minority of them proposed secession from the Union, or at least a separate peace with England. Ugly rumors were afloat about "Blue Light" Federalists—treacherous New Englanders who supposedly flashed lanterns on the shore so that blockading British cruisers would be alerted to the attempted escape of American ships.

The most spectacular manifestation of Federalist discontent was the ill-omened Hartford Convention. Late in 1814, when the capture of New Orleans seemed imminent, Massachusetts issued a call for a convention at Hartford, Connecticut. The states of Massachusetts, Connecticut, and Rhode Island dispatched full delegations, while New Hampshire and Vermont sent partial representation. This group of prominent men, twenty-six in all, met in complete secrecy for about three weeks—December 15, 1814, to January 5, 1815—to discuss their grievances and to seek redress for their wrongs.

In truth, the Hartford Convention was less radical than alarmists supposed. Its immediate goal was to secure financial assistance from Washington, because the shores of New England were then being menaced by British blockading squadrons. A minority of the delegates gave vent to much wild talk of secession, but they were outvoted by the moderate Federalists. The report and resolutions adopted by the convention, in fact, resemble a modern political platform.

The Hartfordites, resenting the war-bent policies of the administration, were eager to restore New England to its stellar role on the national stage. They recommended amendments to the Constitution aimed at hobbling Congress and restoring Federalist influence by a kind of minority veto. These proposals would require a two-thirds vote before an embargo could be imposed, before new western states could be admitted, and before war could be declared—except in case of invasion.

The War of 1812 won a new respect for America among many Britons. Michael Scott, a young lieutenant in the British navy, wrote: "I don't like Americans; I never did, and never shall like them. . . . I have no wish to eat with them, drink with them, deal with, or consort with them in any way; but let me tell the whole truth, nor fight with them, were it not for the laurels to be acquired, by overcoming an enemy so brave, determined, and alert, and in every way so worthy of one's steel, as they have always proved."

"Three Wise Men of Gotham Went to Sea in a Bowl—" *This satirical anti-Federalist cartoon shows three Massachusetts men sailing precariously for Washington in a large chamber pot bearing Hartfordite demands. They are quieting their fears of sinking by exchanging off-color remarks. (Massachusetts Historical Society.)*

Three special envoys from Massachusetts, bearing demands of the Hartford Convention for financial support to promote defense, journeyed to the burned-out capital of Washington. The trio arrived just in time to be overwhelmed by the glorious news from New Orleans, followed by that from Ghent. Pursued by the sneers and jeers of the press, they slunk away into obscurity and disgrace.

The Hartford resolutions, as it turned out, were the death song of the Federalist party. In 1816, the next year, the Federalists nominated their last presidential candidate. He was lopsidedly defeated by James Monroe, yet another Virginian.

Unhappily, the stench of treason has clung to the Hartford Convention. The taint was not justified by its formal resolutions. Yet if the war had not ended when it did, the convention might well have paved the way for treasonable courses.

Federalist doctrines of disunity, which long survived the party, blazed a fateful trail. Until 1815, there was far more talk of nullification and secession in New England than in any other section, including the South. The outright flouting of the Jeffersonian embargo and the later crippling of the war effort were the two most damaging acts of nullification in America prior to the events leading to the Civil War.

The Second War for American Independence

The War of 1812 was a small war, involving about 6,000 Americans killed or wounded. It was but a footnote to the mighty European conflagration. In 1812, when Napoleon invaded Russia with about 500,000 men, Madison tried to invade Canada with about 5,000 men. But if the American conflict was globally unimportant, its results were highly important to the United States.

Americans wrested no formal recognition of their rights on the high seas, but informally they did. No longer did British aristocrats jeer at the "striped bunting" over "American cockboats." The Republic had shown that it would resent, sword in hand, what it regarded as grievous wrongs. Other nations developed a new respect for American fighting men. Naval officers like Perry and Macdonough were the most effective type of negotiators; the hot breath of their broadsides spoke the most eloquent diplomatic language. America's diplomats abroad were henceforth treated with less scorn. In a diplomatic sense, if not in a military sense, the conflict could be called the Second War for American Independence.

A new nation, moreover, was welded in the fiery furnace of armed conflict. Sectionalism, now identified with discredited New England Federalists, was given a black eye. The painful events of the war glaringly revealed, as perhaps nothing else could have done, the folly of sectional disunity. In a sense, the most conspicuous casualty of the war was the Federalist party.

The nation thrilled to the victories of its warriors. A brilliant naval tradition, already well launched, was strengthened by the exploits of the gallant seamen. The ineptitude of insubordinate or fleeing militia was forgotten. The battle-singed regular army, which in the closing months of the war had fought bravely and well, had won its spurs. War heroes emerged, such as Andrew Jackson and William Henry Harrison, both of whom were to become president.

Hostile Indians in the South had been crushed by Jackson at Horseshoe Bend (1814) and those in the North by Harrison at the Battle of the Thames (1813). Left in the lurch by their British friends at Ghent, the Indians were forced to make such terms as they could. They reluctantly consented, in a series of treaties, to relinquish vast areas of forested land north of the Ohio River.

Manufacturing increased behind the fiery wooden wall of the British blockade. In an economic sense, as well as in a diplomatic sense, the War of 1812 may be regarded as the Second War for American Independence. The industries that were thus stimulated by the fighting rendered America less dependent on the workshops of Europe.

International Legacies

Regrettably, the war revived and intensified bitterness toward England. The uglier incidents of the conflict, notably the burning of Washington, added fuel to a century of Britain hating and Britain baiting. Mutual suspicion and hate were perhaps the most enduring heritages of this frustrating little war. Few Americans could have guessed in 1815 that it was to be the nation's last armed conflict with England.

Canadian patriotism and nationalism, no less than American patriotism and nationalism, received a powerful stimulus from the clash. The outnumbered Canadians, fighting bravely in defense of their homeland against the Yankee invaders, won their full share of the laurels. Their stirring song "The Maple Leaf" ringingly recalls these battles, including Chippewa and Lundy's Lane, which Americans regard as their victories.

Many Canadians felt betrayed by the treaty of Ghent. They were especially aggrieved by the failure to secure an Indian buffer state or even mastery of the Great Lakes. Canadians fully expected the frustrated Yankees to come again, and for a time the Americans and British engaged in a naval armaments race on the Great Lakes. But in 1817 the Rush-Bagot agreement between Britain and the United States severely limited naval armament on the lakes. Better relations brought the last border fortifications down in the 1870s, with the happy result that the United States and Canada came to share

The U.S.S. Constitution Today   *The oldest actively commissioned ship in the U.S. Navy, "Old Ironsides" is berthed in Boston harbor. (Richard Pasley/Stock, Boston.)*

the longest unfortified boundary in the world—5,527 miles (8,899 kilometers) long.

After Napoleon's final defeat at Waterloo in 1815, Europe slumped into a peace of exhaustion. Deposed monarchs returned to battered thrones, as the Old World took the rutted road back to conservatism, illiberalism, and reaction.

But the American people were largely unaffected by these European developments. Freed from the humiliating side blows of the belligerents, they no longer had to scan the Atlantic horizon for approaching sails—sails that might bring news of impending calamities. Americans thrilled to a new sense of nationality. They were like subject peoples attaining their majority and for the first time shaking off the shackles of colonialism. Turning their backs on the Old World, they faced resolutely toward the untamed West. Unlike monarchy-cursed Europe, Americans were ready to take the high road toward democracy, liberalism, and freedom. The steady tramp, tramp, tramp of the westward-moving pioneers came to be the giant drumbeat of a new destiny.

CHRONOLOGY

1810	Macon's Bill No. 2
	Napoleon supposedly repeals blockade decrees
	Madison declares boycott of British goods
1811	Battle of Tippecanoe
1812	United States declares war on Britain
	Madison reelected president
1812–1813	American invasions of Canada fail
1813	Battle of the Thames
	Battle of Lake Erie
1814	Battle of Plattsburgh
	British burn Washington
	Battle of Horseshoe Bend
	Treaty of Ghent signed
1814–1815	Hartford Convention
1815	Battle of New Orleans
1817	Rush-Bagot agreement

Varying Viewpoints

The causes and consequences of the War of 1812 have long sparked spirited debate. Was war the result of western war-hawk expansionism or of British provocations on the high seas? Most recent historians emphasize the naval issue. The young nation's pride and independence, they argue, could not tolerate John Bull's repeated affronts. The Jeffersonian Republicans accepted the need for war because they believed that the future of their party, and indeed of the entire American experiment in republican government, rested on the infant nation's ability to prove that it could meet external challenges.

Perhaps more interestingly, scholars also have seen the first vague outlines of an

American identity emerging from the smoke of the War of 1812. Henry Adams's magisterial *History* made this theme a central motif; Adams found evidence of a distinctive American character even in the tactics and techniques of Yankee seamen. The war does appear to have dissolved many localisms and to have begun the forging of a genuine national consciousness—thus paving the way for an upsurge of expansionism and nationalism in the so-called Era of Good Feelings.

Select Readings

Primary Source Documents

See James Madison's "War Message"* (1812), in James D. Richardson, ed., *Messages and Papers of the Presidents* (1896), Vol. I, pp. 500–504; and the protest of thirty-four Federalist congressmen, *Annals of Congress** 12 Cong., I sess., II cols. 2219–2221 (1812). Timothy Dwight offers a participant's view of the opposition to the war in *The History of the Hartford Convention** (1833).

Secondary Sources

An important recent work that sets the War of 1812 in a broad context of early American history is J. C. A. Stagg, *Mr. Madison's War: Politics, Diplomacy and Warfare in the Early American Republic* (1983). Also see Steven Watts, *The Republic Reborn: War and the Making of Liberal America, 1790–1820* (1987). On the causes of the war, Julius W. Pratt, *Expansionists of 1812* (1925), stresses western pressures; Bradford Perkins, *Prologue to War: England and the United States, 1805–1812* (1961), and Reginald Horsman, *The Causes of the War of 1812* (1962), discuss free seas; Roger H. Brown, *The Republic in Peril: 1812* (1964), emphasizes the need for saving the republican form of government. The relevant volumes of Henry Adams's nine-volume *History of the United States* (1889–1891) still contain magnificent reading, both on the war and on the peace. Federalist reaction to Republican foreign policy is vividly etched in David H. Fisher, *The Revolution of American Conservatism* (1965), and James M. Banner, *To the Hartford Convention: The Federalists and the Origins of Party Politics in Massachusetts* (1970). Consult also James H. Broussard, *The Southern Federalists, 1800–1816* (1979). Irving Brant continues his strong pro-Madison bias in the relevant volumes of his six-volume work, *James Madison: Commander in Chief, 1812–1836* (1961). See also Ralph Ketcham, *James Madison: A Biography* (1971). Other useful biographical studies are Bernard Mayo, *Henry Clay: Spokesman of the New West* (1937); Glyndon G. Van Deusen, *The Life of Henry Clay* (1937); and Marquis James's spirited *Andrew Jackson: The Border Captain* (1933).

12

The Postwar Upsurge of Nationalism, 1815–1824

The American continents . . . are henceforth not to be considered as subjects for future colonization by any European powers.

James Monroe, December 2, 1823

Nascent Nationalism

The most impressive by-product of the War of 1812 was a heightened nationalism—the spirit of nation-consciousness or national oneness. America may not have fought the war as one nation, but it emerged one nation. So exhilarating was the postwar era that President Madison, despite his blunders, enjoyed the unusual distinction of being more popular when he left the White House in 1817 than when he entered it in 1809.

A weak nationalism had existed since Revolutionary days, but the vibrant new nationalism was composed of many additional ingredients. It sprang partly from pride in recent victories,

partly from the setback to Federalist sectionalism and states' rightism, partly from a lessening of economic and political dependence on Europe, and partly from an exulting confidence in the future. Swelling numbers of citizens—although probably not yet a majority—were coming to regard themselves first of all as Americans and secondarily as citizens of their respective states.

The changed mood even manifested itself in the birth of a distinctively national literature. Washington Irving and James Fenimore Cooper attained international recognition in the 1820s, significantly as the nation's first writers of importance to use American scenes and themes. School textbooks, often British in an earlier era, were now being written by Americans for Americans. In the world of magazines, the highly intellectual *North American Review* began publication in 1815—the year of the triumph at New Orleans. Even American painters increasingly celebrated the glories of American landscapes on their canvases.

A fresh nationalistic spirit could be recognized in many other areas. A more handsome national capital began to rise from the ashes of Washington—a capital fit to symbolize America's prospective greatness. The army was expanded to ten thousand men. The navy further covered itself with glory in 1815 when it administered a thorough beating to the piratical plunderers of North Africa. These gratifying victories, inspired by the spirit of nationalism, further inflamed nationalism. Stephen Decatur, naval hero of the War of 1812 and the North African expeditions, pungently captured the nationalist mood in a famous toast made on his return from these Mediterranean triumphs: "Our

country! In her intercourse with foreign nations may she always be in the right; but our country, right or wrong!"

A rising tide of nation-consciousness also touched finance. The War of 1812 had demonstrated the folly of permitting the Bank of the United States to expire in 1811, on the very eve of hostilities. Weak state banks, responding to the vacuum, had seemingly sprung up beside every village tavern. The country was flooded with depreciated bank notes that, incidentally, had hampered the war effort.

A revived Bank of the United States, in response to these obvious needs, was voted by Congress in 1816. It was modeled on the first one but had a total capital of $35 million—three and one-half times that of the original. Jeffersonian Republicans, taught a bitter lesson during the war, supported the revived institution. In fact, they cleverly but inconsistently borrowed the same arguments for a bank that Hamilton had used against Jefferson back in 1791. The

Washington, D.C., 1824 *This view of the Capitol Building, much smaller than it is today, reveals the rustic conditions of the early days in the nation's capital. (Metropolitan Museum of Art, Purchase, 1942, Joseph Pulitzer Bequest.)*

Federalist minority in Congress, opposing the Republican measures with its dying gasps, no less inconsistently denounced the Federalist-spawned bank as being unconstitutional. The "moneyed monster," as it was branded by its enemies, further broadened nationalism as it thrust its numerous branches out across state boundaries.

"The American System"

Nationalism likewise manifested itself in manufacturing. Patriotic Americans took pride in the factories that had recently mushroomed forth, largely as a result of the self-imposed embargoes and the war.

When hostilities ended in 1815, British competitors undertook to recover lost ground. They began to dump the contents of their bulging warehouses on the United States, often cutting their prices below cost in an effort to strangle the American war-baby factories in the cradle. The infant industries bawled lustily for protection. To many red-blooded Americans it seemed as though the British, having failed on the battlefield to crush Yankee fighters, were now seeking to crush Yankee factories.

A nationalist Congress, out-Federalizing the old Federalists, responded by passing the path-breaking Tariff of 1816. The legislators were impressed with the desirability of saving the new industries for the national defense, while at the same time promoting the general welfare. The Tariff of 1816, significantly, was the first in American history with aims that were primarily protective. Its rates—roughly 20 to 25 percent on the value of dutiable imports—were not high enough to provide completely adequate safeguards, but the law was a bold beginning. A strongly protective trend was started that stimulated the appetites of the protected for more protection.

The battle in Congress over the Tariff of 1816 reflected North-South sectional crosscurrents. Thirty-four-year-old Representative John C. Calhoun of South Carolina—slender, handsome, black-haired, intense, and intellectual—played a stellar role in the debates. A recent war hawk and an ardent nationalist, he supported the tariff bill with all his eloquence and vigor. In 1816 there was some likelihood that the destiny of his native South lay in manufacturing, as well as in the intensive cultivation of cotton. But within a few years Calhoun became a relentless foe of a highly protective tariff. He sadly concluded that it was being used to enrich a few Yankee manufacturers rather than to build up the economic self-sufficiency and well-being of the entire nation.

Calhoun encountered a worthy adversary in Daniel Webster of New Hampshire, also thirty-four. Stocky, bushy-browed, and dark-haired, "Black Dan" Webster eloquently opposed the highly protective duties of the Tariff of 1816. He took this stand even though he was later to be a zealous nationalist and an ardent champion of high protection. The explanation is simple. Manufacturing in New England had not yet pushed shipping into a back seat, and the shippers of Webster's New Hampshire district feared that a tariff would interfere with their carrying trade. New England, though favoring some protection, was not yet completely willing to exchange the mainsail for the loom—but that day was slowly dawning.

Nationalism was further highlighted by a grandiose plan of Henry Clay for developing a profitable home market. Still radiating the nationalism of war hawk days, he threw himself behind an elaborate scheme known by 1824 as the American System. This system began with the protective tariff, behind which eastern manufacturing would flourish. Revenues gushing from the tariff would provide funds for roads and canals, especially in the fast-developing Ohio Valley. Through these new arteries of transportation would flow foodstuffs and raw materials from the South and West to the North and East. In exchange, a stream of manufactured goods would flow in the return direction.

House Vote on Tariff of 1816*

REGIONS	FOR	AGAINST
New England	17	10
Middle states	44	10
West (Ohio)	4	0
South and Southwest	23	34
TOTAL	88	54

* Even in South Carolina, Calhoun's state, the vote in favor of the bill was 4 to 3.

Conestoga Wagon on the Road
Painting by Thomas Birch, 1814. Henry Clay's "American System" envisioned a network of national roads like this one, paving the way for development of the West. (Shelburne Museum.)

Persistent and eloquent demands by Henry Clay and others for internal improvements struck a responsive chord with the public. The recent attempts to invade Canada had all failed partly because of oath-provoking roads—or no roads at all. People who have dug wagons out of hub-deep mud do not quickly forget their blisters and backaches. An outcry for better transportation, rising most noisily in the road-poor West, was one of the most striking aspects of the nationalism inspired by the War of 1812.

But attempts to secure federal funding for roads and canals stumbled on Republican constitutional scruples. Congress passed Calhoun's Bonus Bill in 1817, which would have parceled out $1.5 million to the states for internal improvements. But President Madison sternly vetoed this handout measure as unconstitutional. Madison's successor, James Monroe, generally followed the same line of negative reasoning. The individual states were thus forced to venture ahead with construction programs of their own, including the Erie Canal, triumphantly completed by New York in 1825. Jeffersonian Republicans, who had gulped down Hamiltonian loose constructionism on other important problems, choked on the idea of direct federal support of intrastate internal improvements.

The enfeebled Federalists, now turncoat strict constructionists, could grudgingly applaud the vetoes of the Jeffersonian Republican presidents. New England, in particular, strongly opposed federally constructed roads and canals, because such outlets would further drain away population and create competing states beyond the mountains.

The So-Called Era of Good Feelings

James Monroe—6 feet (1.83 meters) tall, somewhat stooped, courtly, and mild-mannered— was nominated for the presidency in 1816 by the Republicans. They thus undertook to continue the so-called Virginia dynasty of Washington, Jefferson, and Madison. The fading Federalists ran a candidate for the last time in their checkered history, and he was crushed by 183 electoral votes to 34.

The death of the once-proud Federalist party was due to various diseases, shortcomings, and misfortunes. A list would include its disgraceful war record, its inability to choke down the new nationalistic program, and the theft of its tenets by the Jeffersonians. Many Federalists followed their stolen principles into the opposition camp; others gradually crawled away to the political graveyard. The irony is that the original Hamiltonians, while the party of the "ins," had been conspicuously nationalistic; now, as the party of the "outs," they scorned the nationalism of the Republicans.

President James Monroe (1758–1831)
Monroe fought in the Revolution (suffering a wound), served as minister to France, became co-purchaser of Louisiana, and rose to the presidency in 1817. An excellent administrator, he presided over the Era of Good Feelings. His inaugural address declared: "National honor is national property of the highest value." His name is imperishably attached to the Monroe Doctrine and Monrovia, the capital city of Liberia in Africa. He had strongly backed the colonization there of ex-slaves. His wife and two daughters had expensive tastes, and like plantation owner Jefferson, he died deeply in debt. (The Granger Collection.)

In James Monroe, the man and the times auspiciously met. As the last president to wear an old-style cocked hat, he straddled two generations: the bygone age of the Founding Fathers and the emergent age of nationalism. Never brilliant, and perhaps not great, the serene Virginian with gray-blue eyes was in intellect and personal force the least distinguished of the first eight presidents. But the times called for sober administration, not heroics. And Monroe was an experienced, levelheaded executive, with an ear-to-the-ground talent for interpreting popular rumblings.

Emerging nationalism was further cemented by a goodwill tour that Monroe undertook early in 1817, ostensibly to inspect military defenses. He pushed northward deep into New England, and then westward to Detroit, viewing en route the Niagara Falls. Even in Federalist New England, "the enemy's country," he received a heartwarming welcome; a Boston newspaper was so far carried away as to announce that an "Era of Good Feelings" had been ushered in. This happy phrase since then has been commonly used to describe the administrations of Monroe.

The Era of Good Feelings, unfortunately, was something of a misnomer. Considerable tranquillity and prosperity did in fact smile upon the early years of Monroe, but the period was a troubled one. The acute issues of the tariff, the bank, internal improvements, and the sale of public lands were being hotly contested. Sectionalism was crystallizing, and the conflict over slavery was beginning to raise its hideous head.

A vanquished Federalist party was breathing its dying gasps, leaving the field to the triumphant Republicans and one-party rule. But where there is only one party, or where one of the parties enjoys a lopsided majority, the tendency is for factions to develop and fight among themselves. By the early 1820s an Era of Inflamed Feelings was dawning. Political giants—men like Clay, Calhoun, Jackson, and

> Boston's Columbian Centinel *was not the only newspaper to regard President Monroe's early months as the Era of Good Feelings. The* Washington National Intelligencer *observed in July 1817: "Never before, perhaps, since the institution of civil government, did the same harmony, the same absence of party spirit, the same national feeling, pervade a community. The result is too consoling to dispute too nicely about the cause."*

John Quincy Adams—elbowed for power and aggressively promoted the clashing economic interests of their respective sections.

The Panic of 1819 and the Curse of Hard Times

Much of the goodness went out of the good feelings in 1819, when a paralyzing economic panic descended. It brought deflation, depression, bankruptcies, bank failures, unemployment, soup kitchens, and overcrowded pesthouses known as debtors' prisons.

This was the first national financial panic since President Washington took office. It was to be followed by a succession of others every twenty or so years, in what seemed an inevitable cycle. Many factors contributed to the catastrophe of 1819, but looming large was overspeculation in frontier lands. The Bank of the United States, through its western branches, had become deeply involved in this popular type of outdoor gambling.

Financial paralysis from the panic, which lasted in some degree for several years, gave a rude setback to the nationalistic ardor. Various parts of the country tended to drift back toward the old sectionalism, as they concentrated on bailing themselves out. The West was especially hard hit. When the pinch came, the Bank of the United States forced the speculative ("wildcat") western banks to the wall and foreclosed mortgages on countless farms. All this was technically legal but politically unwise. In the eyes of the western debtor, the bank soon became a kind of financial devil.

A more welcome child of the panic was fresh legislation to govern the sale of public lands. The plight of the western farmer, combined with the evils of land speculation, laid bare the defects of the Land Act of 1800, as amended in 1804. By its terms, the pioneer could buy a minimum of 160 acres at $2 an acre over a period of four years, with a down payment of $80. When hard times came, entire communities would default on their installments. An improved Land Act of 1820 lightened the burden somewhat. It permitted the buyer to secure 80 virgin acres at a minimum of $1.25 an acre in cash—for a total cost of $100. There was less acreage but less outlay.

The panic of 1819 also created backwashes in the political and social world. It hit especially hard at the poorer classes—the one-suspender men—and hence helped cultivate the seedbed of Jacksonian democracy. It also directed attention to the inhumanity of imprisoning debtors. In extreme cases, often overplayed, mothers were torn from their infants for owing a few dollars. Mounting agitation against imprisonment for debt bore fruit in remedial legislation in an increasing number of states.

Growing Pains of the West

Beyond doubt the West, out of which had swooped the war hawks of 1812, was by far the most nationalistic of the sections. Being new, it had no long-established states' rights tradition. Moreover, it had early learned to lean on the national government, from which it had secured most of its land, directly or indirectly. It was a mixing bowl within the huge American melting pot, for people from all the sections rubbed elbows on the frontier.

Marvelous indeed had been the onward march of the West; nine frontier states had joined the original thirteen between 1791 and 1819. With an eye to preserving the North-South sectional balance, most of these commonwealths had been admitted alternately, free or slave. (See Admission of States in the Appendix.)

Why this explosive expansion? In part, it was simply a continuation of the generations-old westward movement, which had been going on since early colonial days. In addition, the siren call of cheap land—"the Ohio fever"—had a special appeal to European immigrants. Quaintly garbed newcomers from abroad were beginning to shuffle down the gangplanks in impressive numbers, especially after the war of embargoes and bullets. Land exhaustion in the older tobacco states, where the soil was "mined" rather than cultivated, likewise drove people westward. Glib-tongued speculators, accepting small down payments, made easier the purchase of new holdings.

The western boom was stimulated by additional developments. Acute distress during the embargo years turned many saddened faces toward the setting sun. The crushing of the Indi-

A Frontier Log Cabin, 1826 *Pioneers in the fast-filling West were at first too busy (and too poor) to build elegant residences. (The Granger Collection.)*

ans in the Northwest and South, by Generals Harrison and Jackson, pacified the frontier and opened up vast virgin tracts of land. The building of highways improved the land routes to the Ohio Valley. Noteworthy was the Cumberland Road, begun in 1811, which ran ultimately from western Maryland to Illinois. The use of the first steamboat on western waters, also in 1811, heralded a new era of upstream navigation.

But the West, despite the inflow of settlers, was still weak in population and influence. Not potent enough politically to make its voice heard, it was forced to ally itself with other sections. Thus strengthened, it demanded cheap acreage and partially achieved its goal in the Land Act of 1820. It demanded cheap transportation and slowly got it, despite the constitutional qualms of the presidents and the hostility of easterners. Finally, the West demanded cheap money, issued by its own "wildcat" banks, and fought the powerful Bank of the United States to attain its goal.

Wagons West *This busy scene on the Frederick Road, leading westward from Baltimore, was typical as pioneers flooded into the newly secured West in the early 1800s. (Maryland Historical Society.)*

Slavery and the Sectional Balance

Sectional tensions were nakedly revealed in 1819, when the territory of Missouri knocked on the doors of Congress for admission as a slave state. This fertile and well-watered area contained sufficient population to warrant statehood. But the House of Representatives threw a monkey wrench into the plans of the Missourians by passing the incendiary Tallmadge amendment. It stipulated that no more slaves should be brought into Missouri and also provided for the gradual emancipation of children born to slave parents already there. A mounting roar of anger burst from slaveholding southerners. They were joined by many depression-cursed pioneers who favored unhampered expansion of the West and by many northerners, especially diehard Federalists, who were eager to use the issue to break the back of the "Virginia dynasty."

Southerners saw in the Tallmadge amendment, which was defeated in the Senate, an ominous threat to the sectional balance. When the Constitution was adopted in 1788, the North and South were running neck and neck in wealth and population. But with every passing decade the North was becoming wealthier and also more thickly settled—an advantage reflected in an increasing northern majority in the House of Representatives. Yet in the Senate, with eleven states free and eleven slave, the southerners had maintained equality. They were therefore in a good position to thwart any northern effort to interfere with the expansion of slavery, and they did not want to lose this veto.

The future of the slave system caused southerners profound concern. Missouri was the first state entirely west of the Mississippi River to be carved out of the Louisiana Purchase, and the Missouri emancipation amendment might set a damaging precedent for all the rest of the area. Even more disquieting was another possibility. If Congress could abolish the "peculiar institution" in Missouri, might it not attempt to do likewise in the older states of the South? The wounds of the Constitutional Convention of 1787 were once more ripped open.

Burning moral questions also protruded,

Contemporary Antislavery Propaganda   *This also appeared as "Am I Not a Woman and a Sister?"*

even though the main issue was political and economic balance. A small but growing group of antislavery agitators in the North seized the occasion to raise an outcry against the evils of slavery. They were determined that the plague of human bondage should not spread further into the virgin territories.

The Uneasy Missouri Compromise

Deadlock in Washington was at length broken in 1820 by the time-honored American solution of compromise—actually a bundle of three compromises. Courtly Henry Clay of Kentucky, gifted conciliator, played a leading role. Congress, despite abolitionist pleas, agreed to admit Missouri as a slave state. But at the same time, free-soil Maine, which until then had been a part of Massachusetts, was admitted as a separate state. The balance between North and South was thus kept at twelve states each and remained there for fifteen years. Although Missouri was permitted to retain slaves, all future bondage was prohibited in the remainder of the

While the debate over Missouri was raging, Thomas Jefferson wrote to a correspondent: "The Missouri question . . . is the most portentous one which ever yet threatened our Union. In the gloomiest moment of the revolutionary war I never had any apprehensions equal to what I feel from this source." He also wrote that the "question, like a firebell in the night, awakened and filled me with terror." With slavery, the aging ex-president declared, "we have the wolf by the ears, and we can neither hold him nor safely let him go." John Quincy Adams confided to his diary: "I take it for granted that the present question is a mere preamble—a title-page to a great, tragic volume."

Louisiana Purchase north of the line of 36° 30′—the southern boundary of Missouri.

This horse-trading adjustment was politically evenhanded, though denounced by extremists on each side as a "dirty bargain." Both North and South yielded something; both gained something. The South won the prize of Missouri as an unrestricted slave state. The North won the concession that Congress could forbid slavery in the remaining territories. More gratifying to many northerners was the fact that the

immense area north of 36° 30′, except Missouri, was forever closed to the blight of slavery. Yet the restriction on future slavery in the territories was not unduly offensive to the slaveowners, partly because the northern prairie land did not seem adapted to slave labor. Even so, a majority of southern congressmen voted against the compromise.

Neither North nor South was acutely displeased, although neither was completely happy. Fortunately, the Missouri Compromise lasted thirty-four years—a vital formative period in the life of the young Republic—and during that time it preserved the shaky compact of the states. Yet the embittered dispute over slavery heralded the future breakup of the Union. Ever after, the morality of the South's "peculiar institution" was an issue that could not be swept under the rug. The Missouri Compromise only ducked the question—it did not resolve it. Sooner or later, Thomas Jefferson predicted, it will "burst on us as a tornado."

The Missouri dispute proved to be another serious setback to nationalism and a tremendous stimulus to sectionalism—in the North, South, and West. From this time forward the embattled South began to develop a nationalism of its own—a kind of sectional nationalism. Needing sectional reinforcements, it cast flirtatious eyes upon the adolescent West, which in turn was seeking allies.

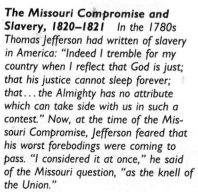

The Missouri Compromise and Slavery, 1820–1821 *In the 1780s Thomas Jefferson had written of slavery in America: "Indeed I tremble for my country when I reflect that God is just; that his justice cannot sleep forever; that . . . the Almighty has no attribute which can take side with us in such a contest." Now, at the time of the Missouri Compromise, Jefferson feared that his worst forebodings were coming to pass. "I considered it at once," he said of the Missouri question, "as the knell of the Union."*

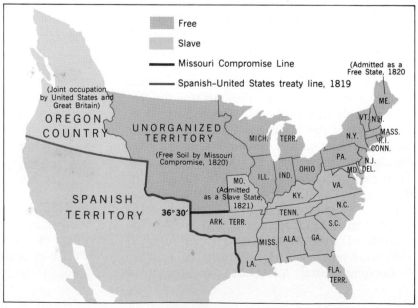

Hotheads in both the North and South, numbering only a tiny minority, clamored for secession or a shooting showdown in 1820. But fortunately for the Union, hostilities were postponed. With every passing decade the North was becoming stronger in population, wealth, industry, and transportation—all of which added up to military strength.

Admittedly, the Missouri solution was a compromise—a partial surrender on both sides. Subsequent generations have tended to sneer at Henry Clay and the other architects of the settlement as weak—as "appeasers." Yet the fact should not be overlooked that compromise and statesmanship are often Siamese twins. In a free and peaceful association of once-sovereign states, no group of them could lord it over the others—that is, if they were all going to live together under the same roof. Without compromise there could have been no Constitution in 1787. Compromise made the Union in 1789; compromise saved the Union until 1860. When compromise broke down, the Union broke up.

The Missouri Compromise and the concurrent panic of 1819 should have dimmed the political star of President Monroe. Certainly both unhappy events had a dampening effect on the Era of Good Feelings. But smooth-spoken James Monroe was so popular, and the Federalist opposition so weak, that in the presidential election of 1820 he received every electoral vote except one. Unanimity was an honor reserved for George Washington. Monroe, as it turned out, was the only president in American history to be reelected after a term in which a major financial panic began.

John Marshall and Judicial Nationalism

Upsurging nationalism of the post-Ghent years, despite setbacks, was further reflected and strengthened by the Supreme Court.

The august tribunal was dominated by the tall, thin, and aggressive Chief Justice John Marshall, a "deathbed" Federalist appointee of John Adams's expiring administration. He had served at Valley Forge during the Revolution and while suffering from cold and hunger had

John Marshall (1755–1835) *Born in a log cabin on the Virginia frontier, he attended law lectures for just a few weeks at the college of William and Mary—his only formal education. (Bettmann Archive.)*

been painfully impressed with the drawbacks of feeble central authority. Before Marshall mounted the supreme bench in 1801, the judiciary had been the weakest and most timid of the three arms of the federal government. But he boldly asserted the doctrine of judicial review of congressional legislation in the case of *Marbury* v. *Madison* (1803).* And long before the end of his thirty-four years of service, he had made the judiciary, in some respects, the strongest branch of the national government.

Marshall, whose formal legal schooling had lasted only six weeks, was a judicial statesman rather than a strictly impartial judge. He examined a case through the colored lenses of his Federalist philosophy and then undertook to find legal precedents to support his Hamiltonian preconceptions. Sure of his ground, he

*See p. 194.

wrote some of his most important decisions even before the lawyers had concluded their arguments.

In the vain hope of offsetting Marshall's Federalism, President Jefferson and his successors appointed Republicans to the Supreme Court. But by this time many Republicans had come to accept the Federalist ideal of a strong central government, and the masterful Marshall found it easy to lead his colleagues the rest of the way. The Jeffersonians raged, while Jefferson himself privately condemned the "twistifications" of his cousin, "the crafty chief judge." But Marshall pushed ahead inflexibly on his Federalist course, though bending slightly in his final years before the rising popular demands for a more democratic control of government.

For over three decades, the ghost of Alexander Hamilton spoke through the lanky, black-robed judge. As a shaper of the Constitution in the direction of a more potent central government, Marshall ranks as the foremost of the Molding Fathers. As a wealthy businessman and land speculator, he instinctively shared Hamilton's preference for the propertied class. As a Virginia aristocrat, he deplored democratic excesses and opposed manhood suffrage and the rule of the unwashed masses.

The Supreme Court Curbs States' Rights

One group of Marshall's decisions—perhaps the most famous—resulted in bolstering the power of the federal government at the expense of the states. A notable case in this category was *McCulloch* v. *Maryland* (1819). The suit involved an attempt by the state of Maryland to destroy a branch of the Bank of the United States by imposing a tax on its notes. John Marshall, speaking for the Court, declared the bank constitutional by invoking the Hamiltonian doctrine of implied powers (see p. 170). At the same time, he strengthened federal authority and slapped at state infringements when he denied the right of Maryland to tax the bank. With ringing emphasis, he affirmed "that the power to tax involves the power to destroy" and "that a power to create implies a power to preserve."

Marshall's ruling in this case gave the doctrine of "loose construction" its most famous formulation. The Constitution, he said, derived from the consent of the people and thus permitted the government to act for their benefit. He further argued that the Constitution was "intended to endure for ages to come and, consequently, to be adapted to the various crises of human affairs." Finally, he declared: "Let the end be legitimate, let it be within the scope of the Constitution, and all means which are appropriate, which are plainly adapted to that end, which are not prohibited, but consist with the letter and spirit of the Constitution, are constitutional."

Two years later (1821) the case of *Cohens* v. *Virginia* gave Marshall one of his greatest opportunities. The Cohens, found guilty by the Virginia courts of illegally selling lottery tickets, appealed to the highest tribunal. Virginia won, in that the conviction of the Cohens was upheld. But it lost, in that Marshall resoundingly asserted the right of the Supreme Court to review the decisions of the state supreme courts in all questions involving powers of the federal government. The states' rights people were aghast.

Hardly less significant in Marshall's career was the celebrated "steamboat case," *Gibbons* v. *Ogden* (1824). The suit grew out of an attempt by the state of New York to grant to a private concern a monopoly of waterborne commerce between New York and New Jersey. Marshall sternly reminded the upstart state that the Constitution conferred on Congress alone the control of interstate commerce (see Art. I, Sec. VIII, para. 3). He thus struck another blow at states' rights, while upholding the sovereign powers of the federal government. Interstate streams were thus cleared of this judicial snag, while the departed spirit of Hamilton may have applauded.

Judicial Dikes against Democratic Excesses

Another sheaf of Marshall's decisions bolstered judicial barriers against democratic or demagogic attacks on property rights.

The notorious case of *Fletcher* v. *Peck* (1810) arose when a Georgia legislature, swayed by bribery, granted 35 million acres in the Yazoo River country (Mississippi) to private speculators. The next legislature, yielding to an angry public outcry, canceled the crooked transaction. But the Supreme Court, with Marshall presiding, decreed that the legislative grant was a contract (even though fraudulently secured) and that the Constitution forbids state laws "impairing" contracts (Art. I, Sec. X, para. 1). The decision is perhaps most noteworthy as further protecting property rights against popular pressures. It is also one of the earliest clear assertions of the right of the Supreme Court to invalidate state laws conflicting with the federal Constitution.

A similar principle was upheld in the case of *Dartmouth College* v. *Woodward* (1819), perhaps the best remembered of Marshall's decisions. The college had been granted a charter by King George III in 1769, but the democratic New Hampshire state legislature had seen fit to change it. Dartmouth appealed the case, employing as counsel its most distinguished alumnus, Daniel Webster ('01). The "Godlike Daniel" reportedly pulled out all the stops of his tear-inducing eloquence when he declaimed, "It is, sir, as I have said, a small college. And yet there are those who love it."

Marshall needed no dramatics in the Dartmouth case. He put the states firmly in their place when he ruled that the original charter must stand. It was a contract—and the Constitution protected contracts against state encroachments. The Dartmouth decision had the fortunate effect of safeguarding business enterprise from domination by the states. But it had the unfortunate effect of creating a precedent that enabled chartered corporations, in later years, to escape the handcuffs of needed public control.

If John Marshall was a Molding Father of the Constitution, Daniel Webster was an Expounding Father. Time and again he left his seat in the Senate, stepped downstairs to the Supreme Court chamber (then located in the Capitol Building), and there expounded his Federalistic and nationalistic philosophy before the supreme bench. The eminent chief justice, so Webster

> *When Supreme Court Chief Justice John Marshall died, a New York newspaper rejoiced that "the chief place in the supreme tribunal of the Union will no longer be filled by a man whose political doctrines led him always . . . to strengthen government at the expense of the people."*

reported, approvingly drank in the familiar arguments as a baby sucks in its mother's milk. The two men dovetailed with each other. Webster's classic speeches in the Senate, challenging states' rights and nullification, were largely repetitious of the arguments that he had earlier presented before a sympathetic Supreme Court.

Marshall's decisions are felt even today. In this sense his nationalism was the most tenaciously enduring of the era. He buttressed the federal Union and helped to create a stable, na-

Daniel Webster (1782–1852) *Premier orator and statesman, he served many years in both Houses of Congress and also as secretary of state. Often regarded as presidential timber, he was somewhat handicapped by an overfondness for good food and drink and was frequently in financial difficulties. His devotion to the Union was inflexible. "One country, one constitution, and one destiny," he declaimed in 1837. (The Metropolitan Museum of Art, Gift of I. N. Phelps Stokes, Edward S. Hawes, Alice Mary Hawes, Marion Augusta Hawes, 1937.)*

U.S.-British Boundary Settlement, 1818 Note that the United States gained considerable territory by securing a treaty boundary rather than the natural boundary of the Missouri River watershed. The line of 49° was extended westward to the Pacific Ocean under the Treaty of 1846 with Britain (see p. 371).

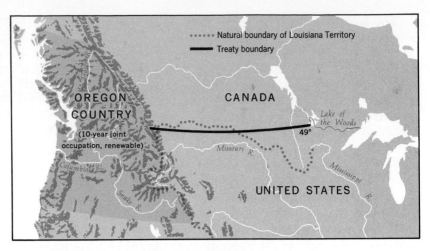

tionally uniform environment for business. At the same time, Marshall checked the excesses of popularly elected state legislatures. In an age when white manhood suffrage was flowering and America was veering toward stronger popular control, Marshall almost single-handedly shaped the Constitution along conservative, centralizing lines that ran somewhat counter to the dominant spirit of the new century. Through him the conservative Hamiltonians triumphed from the tomb.

Sharing Oregon and Acquiring Florida

The yeasty nationalism of the years after the War of 1812 was likewise reflected in the shaping of foreign policy. To this end, the nationalistic President Monroe teamed with his nationalistic secretary of state, John Quincy Adams, the cold and scholarly son of the frosty and bookish ex-president. The younger Adams, a statesman of the first rank, happily rose above the ingrown Federalist sectionalism of his native New England and proved to be one of the great secretaries of state.

To its credit, the Monroe administration negotiated the much-underrated Treaty of 1818 with England. It permitted Americans to share the coveted Newfoundland fisheries with their Canadian cousins. This multisided agreement also fixed the vague northern limits of Louisiana along the forty-ninth parallel from the Lake

of the Woods to the Rocky Mountains. The treaty further provided for a ten-year joint occupation of the untamed Oregon country, without a surrender of the rights or claims of either America or Britain.

To the south lay semitropical Spanish Florida, which many Americans believed geography and providence had destined to become part of the United States. Americans already claimed West Florida, where uninvited American settlers had torn down the hated Spanish flag in 1810. Congress ratified this grab in 1812, and during the War of 1812 against Spain's ally, Britain, a small American army seized the Mobile region. But the bulk of Florida remained, tauntingly, under Spanish rule.

Acquiring the Floridas, 1810–1819

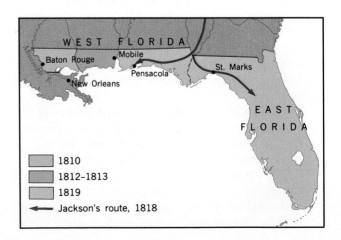

When an epidemic of revolutions broke out in South America, notably in Argentina (1816), Venezuela (1817), and Chile (1818), Spain was forced to denude Florida of troops to fight the rebels. A chaotic situation rapidly developed in the swampy peninsula. Bands of Indians, runaway slaves, and white outcasts poured across the border into American territory, burning and scalping, and then fled to safety behind the surveyor's line.

General Andrew Jackson, idol of the West and scourge of the Indians, reappeared in 1817. The Monroe administration formally commissioned him to punish the Indians, and, if necessary, to pursue them into Florida. But he was to respect all posts under the Spanish flag.

Early in 1818 Jackson swept across the Florida border with all the fury of an avenging angel. He hanged two Indian chiefs without ceremony and, after hasty military trials, executed two British subjects for assisting the Indians. He also seized the two most important Spanish posts in the area, St. Marks and then Pensacola, where he deposed the Spanish governor, who was lucky enough to escape Jackson's jerking noose.

Jackson had clearly exceeded his instructions from Washington. Alarmed, President Monroe consulted his cabinet. Its members were for disavowing or disciplining the overzealous Jackson—all except the lone wolf John Quincy Adams, who refused to howl with the pack. An ardent patriot and nationalist, the flinty New Englander finally won the others over to his point of view. Far from apologizing, he took the offensive and emphatically informed Spain that it had violated the Spanish-American Treaty of 1795 by not suppressing the outlaws of Florida.

Warrior Andrew Jackson, 1814 A self-taught and popularly elected major general of the militia, Andrew Jackson became a major general of the U.S. Army in 1814. He was noted for his stern discipline, iron will ("Old Hickory"), and good luck. (National Gallery of Art, Washington, Andrew W. Mellon Collection.)

The successful invasion of Spain, so Secretary of State Adams recorded in his diary, caused panic in official Washington: "I find him [President Monroe] . . . alarmed, far beyond anything that I could have conceived possible, with the fear that the Holy Alliance [of European powers] are about to restore immediately all South America to Spain."

He then insisted that the alternatives were for the Spaniards to control the area (a task that they admitted was impossible) or cede it to the United States (a course that was galling to their pride).

Distressed in Latin America and at home, and believing that they were going to lose Spanish Florida in any case, the Spanish decided to dispose of the alligator-infested area while they could still get something for it. In the mislabeled Florida Purchase Treaty of 1819, Spain ceded Florida, as well as shadowy Spanish claims to Oregon, in exchange for America's abandonment of equally shadowy claims to Texas, soon to become part of independent Mexico. The hitherto vague western boundary of Louisiana was made to run zigzag along the Rockies to the forty-second parallel and then to turn due west to the Pacific, dividing Oregon from Spanish holdings.

The Menace of Monarchy in America

After the Napoleonic nightmare, the rethroned autocrats of Europe banded together in a kind of monarchical protective association. Determined to restore the good old days, they undertook to stamp out the democratic tendencies that had sprouted from soil richly manured by the ideals of the French Revolution. The world must be made safe *from* democracy.

The crowned despots acted promptly. With complete ruthlessness, they smothered the embers of rebellion in Italy (1821) and in Spain (1823). According to the European rumor factory, they were also gazing across the Atlantic. Russia, Austria, Prussia, and France, acting in partnership, would presumably send powerful fleets and armies to the revolted colonies of Spanish America and there restore the autocratic Spanish king to his ancestral domains.

Many Americans were alarmed. Sympathetic to democratic revolutions everywhere, they had cheered when the Latin American republics rose from the ruins of monarchy. Americans feared that if the European powers intervened in the New World, the cause of republicanism would suffer irreparable harm. The physical security of the United States—the mother lode of democracy—would be endangered by the proximity of powerful and unfriendly forces.

The southward push of the Russian bear, from the chill region now known as Alaska, had already publicized the menace of monarchy to North America. In 1821 the czar of Russia issued a decree extending Russian jurisdiction over 100 miles (161 kilometers) of the open sea down to the line of 51°, an area that embraced most of the coast of present-day British Columbia. The energetic Russians had already established trading posts almost as far south as the entrance to San Francisco Bay, and the fear prevailed in the United States that they were planning to cut the Republic off from California, its prospective window on the Pacific.

Great Britain, still Mistress of the Seas, was now beginning to play a lone-hand role on the complicated international stage. In particular, it recoiled from joining hands with the continental European powers in crushing the newly won liberties of the Spanish-Americans. These

The West and Northwest, 1819–1824   *The British Hudson's Bay Company moved to secure its claim to the Oregon country in 1824, when it sent a heavily armed expedition led by Peter Skene Ogden into the Snake River country. In May 1825, Ogden's party descended the Bear River "and found it discharged into a large Lake of 100 miles in length"—one of the first documented sightings by white explorers of Great Salt Lake. (The mountain man Jim Bridger is usually credited with being the first white man to see the lake.)*

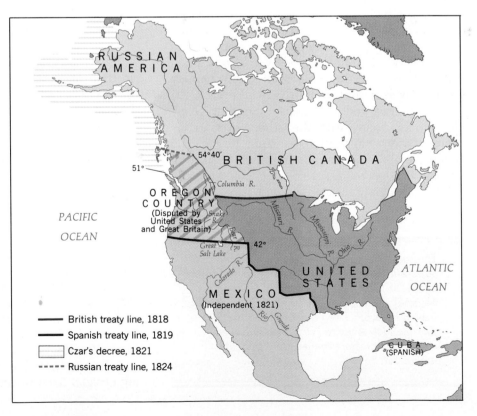

revolutionists had thrown open their monopoly-bound ports to outside trade, and British shippers, as well as Americans, had found the profits sweet.

Accordingly, in August 1823, George Canning, the haughty British foreign secretary, approached the American minister in London with a startling proposition. Would not the United States combine with Britain in a joint declaration, renouncing any interest in acquiring Latin American territory, and specifically warning the European despots to keep their harsh hands off the Latin American republics? The American minister, lacking instructions, referred this fateful scheme to his superiors in Washington.

Mr. Monroe and His Doctrine

Reactions in America to the Canning proposal varied. The intimate advisers of President Monroe, including the aged Jefferson and Madison, recommended that the Republic lock arms with the hitherto distrusted mother country. The one notable exception was again the lone-wolf nationalist, Secretary Adams, who was hard-headed enough to beware of Britons bearing gifts. Why should the lordly British, with the mightiest navy afloat, need America as an ally—an America that had neither naval nor military strength? Such a union, argued Adams, was undignified—like a tiny American "cockboat" sailing "in the wake of the British man-of-war."

Adams, ever alert, thought that he detected the joker in the Canning proposal. The British feared that the aggressive Yankees would one day seize Spanish territory in the Americas—perhaps Cuba—which would jeopardize England's possessions in the Caribbean. If Canning could seduce the United States into joining with him in support of the territorial integrity of the New World, America's own hands would be morally tied.

A self-denying alliance with Britain would not only hamper American expansion, concluded Adams, but it was unnecessary. He suspected—correctly—that the European powers had not agreed upon any definite plans for invading the Americas. In any event, the British navy would not permit hostile fleets to come,

because the South American markets had to be kept open at all costs for English merchants. It was presumably safe for Uncle Sam, behind the protective wooden petticoats of the British navy, to blow a defiant, nationalistic blast at all Europe. The distresses of the Old World again set the stage for another American diplomatic coup.

The Monroe Doctrine was born late in 1823, when the nationalistic Adams won the nationalistic Monroe over to his way of thinking. The president, in his regular annual message to Congress on December 2, 1823, incorporated a stern warning to the European powers. Its two basic features were (1) noncolonization and (2) nonintervention.

Monroe first directed his verbal blast primarily at the lumbering Russian bear in the Northwest. With emphatic tones he proclaimed, in effect, that the era of colonization in the Americas had ended and that henceforth there would be a permanently closed season. What the great powers had they might keep, but neither they nor any other Old World powers could seize or otherwise acquire more. This lofty declaration was later resented by those nations, notably Germany and Italy, that were not unified and hence unable to take out colonial hunting licenses until late in the century.

At the same time, Monroe sounded a trumpet blast against foreign intervention. He was clearly concerned with regions to the south, where fears were felt for the newly fledged Spanish-American republics. Monroe bluntly warned the crowned heads of Europe to keep their hated monarchical systems out of this hemisphere. For its part, the United States would not intervene in the war that the Greeks were then fighting against the Turks for their independence.

Monroe's Dictum Abroad

Monroe's ringing declaration quickened the patriotic pulse of nationalistic young America. The American people were thrilled, even though they had no effective army or navy, to shake their collective fists at all the European despots and loudly warn them to stay away. While gratifying national pride and striking a blow for democratic rule, Monroe was also striking a blow for the "Almighty Dollar," as represented by the freshly opened Latin American markets.

Reactions in England were mixed. The British press, likewise savoring the juicy Latin American markets, was generally favorable to Monroe's forceful warning. But Canning was irked, for he perceived that the Monroe Doctrine was aimed at possible land-grabbing by Britain, as well as by Europe. "Hands off" applied to all outside powers, including proud Britain.

The ermined monarchs of Europe were angered. Having resented the incendiary American experiment from the beginning, they were now deeply offended by Monroe's high-flown pronouncement—all the more so because of the gulf between America's loud pretensions and her weak military strength. But though offended by the upstart Yankees, the European powers found their hands tied, and their frustration increased their annoyance. Even if they had worked out plans for invading the Americas, they would have been helpless before the booming broadsides of the British navy.

Monroe's solemn warning, when issued, made little splash in the newly hatched republics to the south. Anyone could see that Uncle Sam was only secondarily concerned about his neighbors, because he was primarily concerned about defending himself against future invasion. Only a relatively few educated Latin Americans knew of the message, and they generally recognized that the British navy—not the paper pronouncement of James Monroe—stood between them and a hostile Europe.

In truth, Monroe's message did not have much contemporary significance. Americans applauded it and then forgot it as they turned back to such activities as felling trees and fighting Indians. Not until 1845 did President Polk revive it, and not until midcentury did it become an important national dogma.

> *Prince Metternich, the Austrian chancellor, wrote bitterly of the "dangerous" new manifesto with its "unprovoked attacks . . . indecent declarations . . . evil doctrines and pernicious examples."*

The new doctrine was not even necessary, in a narrow sense, when given to the world. Secretary Adams, in firm diplomatic notes, had already warned Russia against trespassing on the northwest coast. Even before Monroe's stiff message, the czar had decided to retreat. This he formally did in the Russo-American Treaty of 1824, which fixed his southernmost limits at the line of 54° 40′—the present southern tip of the Alaska panhandle.

Monroe's Doctrine Appraised

The Monroe Doctrine might more accurately have been called the Self-Defense Doctrine. President Monroe was concerned basically with the security of his own country—not of Latin America. The United States has never willingly permitted a powerful foreign nation to secure a foothold near its stragetic Caribbean vitals. Yet in the absence of the British navy or other allies, the strength of the Monroe Doctrine has never been greater than America's power to eject the trespasser. The doctrine, as often noted, was just as big as the nation's armed forces—and no bigger. But attaching Monroe's name to the Self-Defense Doctrine has given it the prestige that comes from a distinguished personage.

Monroe and Adams must share about equally the credit for the authorship of the so-called Monroe Doctrine. But its basic principles, in one form or another, had been set forth earlier by Washington, Jefferson, Hamilton, and others. Monroe and Adams merely collected and codified existing ideas, giving them a new emphasis and slant.

The Monroe Doctrine has had a long career of ups and downs. It was never law—domestic or international. It was not, technically speaking, a pledge or an agreement. It was merely a simple, personalized statement of the policy of President Monroe. What one president says, another may unsay. And Monroe's successors have ignored, revived, distorted, or expanded the original version, chiefly by adding interpretations. Like ivy on a tree, it has grown with America's growth.

But the Monroe Doctrine in 1823 was largely an expression of the post-1812 nationalism energizing the United States. Although directed at a specific menace in 1823, and hence a kind of period piece, the doctrine proved to be the most famous of all the long-lived offspring of that nationalism. While giving vent to a spirit of patriotism, it simultaneously deepened the illusion of isolationism. Many Americans falsely concluded, then and later, that the Republic was in fact isolated from European dangers simply because it wanted to be and because, in a nationalistic outburst, Monroe had publicly warned the Old World powers to stay away.

CHRONOLOGY

1810	*Fletcher* v. *Peck* case
1815	*North American Review* founded
	Battle of New Orleans
1816	Second Bank of the United States founded
	Protectionist Tariff of 1816
	Monroe elected president
1817	Madison vetoes Calhoun's Bonus Bill
1818	Treaty of 1818 with Britain
	Jackson invades Florida
1819	Panic of 1819
	Spain cedes Florida to United States
	McCulloch v. *Maryland* case
	Dartmouth College v. *Woodward* case
1820	Missouri Compromise
	Land Act of 1820
	Monroe reelected
1821	*Cohens* v. *Virginia* case
1823	Secretary Adams proposes Monroe Doctrine
1824	Russo-American Treaty of 1824
	Gibbons v. *Ogden* case
1825	Erie Canal completed

Varying Viewpoints

The Era of Good Feelings, at first, generated little ill feeling among historians. They generally agreed in seeing the period in terms not of conflict but of consolidation. There were then few irreconcilable controversies, but rather a remarkable consensus on laying the new nation's institutional base. In effect, the era set up a political program for the future; defined the power of the Supreme Court and its relation to the other branches of government; stabilized national boundaries; and established basic elements of foreign policy in the Monroe Doctrine.

Recently, historians have uncovered the smoldering tensions seething under the calm surface of the period. One-party rule masked deep divisions over economic and sectional issues that would soon erupt into bitter struggles over the tariff, expansion, and especially, slavery. The tenuous Missouri Compromise revealed the fragility of the era's buoyant nationalism.

Select Readings

Primary Source Documents

Charles F. Adams, ed., *Memoirs of John Quincy Adams** (1875), offers a behind-the-scenes portrait of the creation of the Monroe Doctrine. See also the text of Monroe's public statement in James D. Richardson, ed., *Messages and Papers of the Presidents** (1896), vol. II, pp. 207 ff. John Marshall's decision in *McCulloch v. Maryland**, 4 Wheaton 316 (1819), is a leading statement of the era's surging nationalism. "The Missouri Compromise" (1819–1820), in Henry Steele Commager, *Documents of American History*, reveals the dangerous sectional animosities underlying such national pride.

Secondary Sources

An excellent introduction is George Dangerfield, *The Awakening of American Nationalism, 1815–1828* (1965), which supplements his *Era of Good Feelings* (1952). See also Robert H. Wiebe's ambitious *Opening of American Society: From the Adoption of the Constitution to the Eve of Disunion* (1984). Perry Miller, *The Life of the Mind in America* (1965), contains suggestive insights on legal thought and the role of the legal profession in the Marshall era. This and other topics are astutely placed in context by Lawrence Friedman in *A History of American Law*

(1973). R. Kent Newmyer, *The Supreme Court under Marshall and Taney* (1968), briefly charts constitutional development. More comprehensive is Alfred H. Kelly, Winfred A. Harbison, and Herman Belz, *The American Constitution: Its Origin and Development* (6th ed., 1983). George R. Taylor's classic *Transportation Revolution* (1955) remains a valuable source on that subject. Glover Moore, *The Missouri Controversy, 1819–1821* (1953), and Charles S. Sydnor, *The Development of Southern Sectionalism, 1819–1848* (1948), place the Missouri Compromise in a broader context. On the Monroe Doctrine, the best single volume is Dexter Perkins, *A History of the Monroe Doctrine* (1955). More recently, Ernest R. May has somewhat unconvincingly tied the doctrine to domestic politics, especially the impending election of 1824, in *The Making of the Monroe Doctrine* (1975). Related to the doctrine is John A. Logan, Jr., *No Transfer: An American Security Principle* (1961). See also Harry Ammon, *James Monroe: The Quest for National Identity* (1971). On Calhoun consult Margaret L. Coit, *John C. Calhoun* (1950); Gerald M. Capers, *John C. Calhoun, Opportunist* (1960); Richard N. Current, *John C. Calhoun* (1963); and John Niven, *John C. Calhoun and the Price of Union* (1988). See also Samuel F. Bemis, *John Quincy Adams and the Foundations of American Foreign Policy* (1949).

The Rise of Jacksonian Democracy, 1824–1830

In the full enjoyment of the gifts of Heaven and the fruits of superior industry, economy, and virtue, every man is equally entitled to protection by law; but when the laws undertake to add to those natural and just advantages artificial distinctions . . . and exclusive privileges . . . the humble members of society—the farmer, mechanics, and laborers . . . have a right to complain of the injustice of their government.

Andrew Jackson, 1832

Politics for the People

Democracy was something of a taint in the days of the lordly Federalists. Martha Washington, the first First Lady, was shocked after a presidential reception to find a greasy smear on the wallpaper—left there, she was sure, by an uninvited "filthy democrat."

But by the 1820s, if not before, aristocracy was becoming a taint, and democracy was becoming respectable. Politicians were now forced to unbend and curry favor with the ·voting masses. Lucky indeed was the aspiring office seeker who could boast of birth in a log cabin. In 1840 Daniel Webster publicly apologized for not being able to claim so humble a birthplace,

though quickly adding that his brothers could. Fatally handicapped was the candidate who appeared to be too clean, too well dressed, too grammatical, too high-browishly intellectual. In the West, especially, the belief was spreading that a man was well qualified for high office if he was a superior militia commander or a victorious Indian fighter, like Andrew Jackson, or even an outstanding hunter, like Davy Crockett. The semiliterate Crockett was elected to Congress mainly on the basis of his prowess with a rifle. He once killed 105 bears in a season, and his Tennessee constituents began to talk of running him for the presidency. Yet colorful characters like Crockett were exceptions. Most high political offices continued to be filled by

David ("Davy") Crockett (1786–1836) *A semiliterate Tennesseean, he failed at farming but won distinction as a rifleman, soldier, scout, humorist, and three-time congressman. Rejected in politics, he left Tennessee to fight for Texas against the Mexicans and fell, bullet-riddled, in the final assault on the Alamo.*

"leading citizens." But now these wealthy and prominent men had to forsake all social pretensions and cultivate the common touch if they hoped to win elections.

Jeffersonian democracy had proclaimed that the people should be governed as little as possible; Jacksonian democracy now added that whatever governing was to be done should be done directly by the people. The common man was at last moving to the center of the national political stage: the sturdy American who donned plain trousers rather than silver-buckled knee breeches, who besported a plain haircut and a coonskin cap rather than a powdered wig, and who wore no man's collar, often not even one of his own. Instead of the old divine right of kings, America was now witnessing the divine right of the people.

The New Democracy, so called, was based on universal white manhood suffrage rather than the old property qualifications. The frontier state of Vermont, admitted to the Union in 1791, was the first to place the ballot in the hands of all adult white males. This trend continued, notably in the West, where land was so easily obtained as to render almost meaningless the old property qualifications. Property tests for officeholding were also widely abolished, and even judges were now being popularly elected. The South trailed other regions in giving up property requirements, but it, too, eventually extended suffrage and the right to hold office to all white men.

Snobbish bigwigs, unhappy over the change, sneered at "coonskin congressmen" and at the newly enfranchised "bipeds of the forest." To them, the tyranny of King Numbers was no less offensive than that of King George. But they protested in vain. The masses marched unswervingly toward a fuller measure of control over the Republic's political affairs. If they made mistakes, they made them themselves and were not the victims of aristocratic domination. If at times they stumbled, they stumbled forward. The New Democracy had arrived to stay.

Nourishing the New Democracy

What caused this lush flowering of political democracy? In part it was simply the logical outgrowth of the egalitarian ideas that had taken root in colonial days and been lavishly fertilized during the Revolutionary era. More immediately, the panic of 1819 and the Missouri Compromise of 1820 rank high on the list of the New Democracy's nutrients.

The economic downturn was blamed by many workers and farmers on banking irregularities and speculation. In particular, the panic nurtured burning resentment at the government-granted privileges of the banks. Farmers unable to pay their debts usually lost their farms; overextended bankers unable to fulfill their obligation to redeem their paper bank notes in coin simply suspended payment and escaped any further threat to their property. Holders of bank notes were left with worthless paper and might next find their own property under foreclosure, as the bank called in its debts. These kinds of practices reeked of favoritism and seemed to mock the democratic principles of equality and fair play. The desire to purge the land of this sort of "corruption" and restore the republican ideals of Jefferson's day invigorated the interest of many Americans in politics—especially the followers of Andrew Jackson. They sought control of the government in order to tear the banks from its protective embrace, to substitute hard money for bank notes, and even to abolish the banks altogether. Opposed to the Jacksonians were those persons who favored the current banking system and, more generally, who believed that the federal government had a legitimate role to play in promoting economic growth.

The Missouri Compromise likewise awakened many Americans, especially white southerners, to the importance of politics. The spectacle of organized northern resistance to admission of Missouri as a slave state aroused fears in the white South about further federal aggressions against states' rights—especially the right to perpetuate slavery. Controlling the federal government in order to prevent that result thus became a prime goal of white southerners, stimulating heightened involvement in politics.

Economic distress and the slavery issue together raised the political stakes in the 1820s, ushering in a whole new chapter in the history of American politics. The deference, apathy, and virtually nonexistent party organizations of the Era of Good Feelings gave way to the boisterous democracy, frenzied vitality, and strong political parties of the Jacksonian era. Voter turnout rose dramatically; only about one-quarter of eligible voters cast a ballot in the presidential election of 1824, but that proportion doubled in 1828, and in the election of 1840 it reached 78 percent. A new style of politicking emerged, as candidates made increasing use of banners, badges, parades, barbecues, free drinks, and baby kissing in an effort to "get out the vote." The old suspicion of political parties as illegitimate disrupters of society's natural harmony was replaced by an acceptance of the sometimes wild contentiousness of political life. Vigorous political conflict even came to be celebrated as necessary for the health of democracy.

Everywhere the people flexed their political muscles. To an increasing degree, members of

The New Politics *Politicians in the Jacksonian era had to take their message to the common man, as shown in this painting by George Caleb Bingham. (Nelson-Atkins Museum of Art, Kansas City, Missouri, Nelson Fund.)*

An Election Day Scene in the Age of Jackson   *Though politics was serious business in the Jacksonian era, it also provided the occasion for much socializing and merriment. This election-day crowd in Philadelphia appears in an especially festive mood. (Historical Society of Pennsylvania.)*

the Electoral College were being chosen directly by the people rather than by state legislatures. Presidential nominations by a congressional caucus, meeting secretly, took on a bad odor. This procedure was now condemned as furtive, elitist, and subversive of democracy. The delicate checks and balances among the three federal branches were thought to be weakened when the president was indirectly indebted to Congress for his exalted office.

New and more democratic methods of nominating presidential candidates were devised. In 1824 the voters, crying "The People Must Be Heard" and "Down with King Caucus," turned against the candidate (Crawford) who had been selected by the congressional clique. For a brief period nominations were made by some of the state legislatures. But these did not seem democratic either, and in 1831 the first of the circus-like national nominating conventions was held (by the short-lived but significant Anti-Masonic party). Here the people appeared to exercise greater control, though their will was often thwarted by paunchy bosses in smoke-filled rooms.

The Adams-Clay "Corrupt" Bargaining

The woods were full of presidential timber in 1824. Four candidates towered above the others: Andrew Jackson of Tennessee, the tall, silver-maned, and hollow-cheeked "Old Hero" of New Orleans; Henry Clay of Kentucky, the gamy and gallant "Harry of the West"; William H. Crawford of Georgia, a giant of a man, able though ailing; and John Quincy Adams of Massachusetts, highly intelligent, experienced, and aloof.

All four rivals professed to be "Republicans." Well-organized parties had not yet emerged, as illustrated by the fact that John C. Calhoun appeared as the vice-presidential candidate on both the Adams and the Jackson tickets.

The results of the noisy campaign were interesting but confusing. Jackson, the war hero, clearly had the strongest personal appeal, especially in the West. Foreshadowing the themes that would later shape the historical identity of his presidency, his campaign appealed for the salvation of republicanism from the forces of corruption and privilege in government, especially as embodied in "King Caucus." He polled almost as many popular votes as his next two rivals combined, but he failed to win a majority of the electoral vote. In such a deadlock the House of Representatives, as directed by the Twelfth Amendment (see the Appendix), must choose among the top three candidates. Clay was thus eliminated, yet he still presided over the very chamber that had to pick the winner. Since he enjoyed all the influence of a popular Speaker of the House, he was in a position to throw the election to the candidate of his choice.

Clay reached his fateful decision by a process of elimination. Crawford, recently felled by a paralytic stroke, was out of the picture. Clay hated the "military chieftain" Jackson, his archrival for the allegiance of the West. Jackson, in turn, bitterly resented Clay's public denunciation of his Florida foray in 1818. The only candidate left was the puritanical Adams, with whom Clay—a free-living gambler and duelist—had never established cordial personal relations. But the two men had much in common politically: both were fervid nationalists and advocates of the American System. Shortly before the final balloting in the House, Clay met privately with Adams and assured him of his support.

Decision day came early in 1825. The House of Representatives met amid tense excitement, with sick members being carried in on stretchers. On the first ballot, thanks largely to Clay's behind-the-scenes influence, Adams was elected president. A few days later, the victor announced that Henry Clay would be the new secretary of state.

The secretaryship of state was then the prize plum, even more so than today. Three of the four preceding secretaries had reached the

> *Suspicions of a "corrupt bargain" have been strengthened by entries in Adams's diary. On January 1, 1825, after a public dinner, he wrote: "He [Clay] told me [in a whisper] that he should be glad to have with me soon some confidential conversation upon public affairs. I said I should be happy to have it whenever it might suit his convenience." The diary entry for January 9 reads in part: "Mr. Clay came at six, and spent the evening with me in a long conversation explanatory of the past and prospective of the future." Exactly a month later, with Clay's backing, Adams was elected.*

presidency, and the high cabinet office was regarded as an almost certain runway to the White House. By allegedly dangling the secretaryship as a bribe before Clay, Adams, the second choice of the people, apparently defeated the first choice of the people, Andrew Jackson.

Masses of angered Jacksonians, most of them common folk, raised a roar of protest against the "corrupt bargain." The clamor continued for nearly four years. Jackson condemned Clay as the "Judas of the West," and John Randolph of Virginia publicly assailed the alliance between "the Puritan [Adams] and the black-leg [Clay]," who, he added "shines and stinks like rotten mackerel by moonlight." Clay, outraged, challenged Randolph to a duel, the bloodless outcome of which proved nothing, except perhaps shaky nerves and poor marksmanship.

No positive evidence has yet been unearthed to prove that Adams and Clay entered into a formal bargain, corrupt or otherwise. But appearances were so damning as to render denials unconvincing. Even if a bargain had been struck,

Election of 1824

CANDIDATES	ELECTORAL VOTE	POPULAR VOTE	POPULAR PERCENTAGE
Jackson	99	153,544	42.16%
Adams	84	108,740	31.89
Crawford	41	46,618	12.95
Clay	37	47,136	12.99

it was not necessarily corrupt, for "deals" of a similar nature are the stock-in-trade of politicians. But this "bargain" differed from others in its apparent flouting of the popular will by both Adams and Clay. Both men erred, the one by offering the post in circumstances sure to arouse suspicion, the other by accepting it. The best that can be said of them is that neither avoided the appearance of evil.

A Yankee Misfit in the White House

John Quincy Adams was a chip off the old family glacier. Short (5 feet 7 inches; 1.7 meters), thickset, and billiard-bald, he was even more frigidly austere than his presidential father, John Adams. Shunning people, he often went for early morning swims, sometimes stark naked, in the then-pure Potomac River. Essentially a closeted thinker rather than a politician, he was irritable, sarcastic, and tactless. Yet few individuals have ever come to the presidency

President John Quincy Adams (1767–1848) Adams wrote in his diary, in June 1819, nearly six years before becoming president, "I am a man of reserved, cold, austere, and forbidding manners: my political adversaries say, a gloomy misanthropist, and my personal enemies an unsocial savage." (Metropolitan Museum of Art.)

with a more brilliant record in statecraft, especially in foreign affairs. He ranks as one of the most successful secretaries of state, yet one of the least successful presidents.

A man of puritanical honor, Adams entered upon his four-year "sentence" in the White House smarting under charges of "bargain," "corruption," and "usurpation." Fewer than one-third of the voters had voted for him. As the first "minority president," he would have found it difficult to win popular support even under the most favorable conditions. Possessing almost none of the arts of the politician, he had achieved high office by commanding respect rather than by courting popularity. In an earlier era, an aloof John Adams could win the votes of propertied men by sheer ability. But with the raw New Democracy in the driver's seat, his cold-fish son could hardly hope for success at the polls.

Political spoilsmen annoyed Adams. Whether through high-mindedness or ineptitude, he resolutely declined to oust efficient officeholders in order to create vacancies for political supporters. During his entire administration he removed only twelve public servants from the federal payroll. Such stubbornness caused countless Adams followers to throw up their hands in despair. If the president would not reward party workers with political plums, why should they labor to keep him in office?

Adams's nationalistic views involved him in further woes. The old Jeffersonian Republican party was breaking into fragments, most of which tended to coalesce around a common hatred of the Adams-Clay partnership. The flinty president refused to recognize that the popular tide was turning away from the post-Ghent nationalism toward states' rights and sectionalism. Confirmed nationalist that he was, Adams urged upon Congress in his first annual message the construction of roads and canals. He renewed George Washington's proposal for a national university and went so far as to advocate federal support for an astronomical observatory, similar to Europe's more than 130 "lighthouses of the skies."

The public reaction to some of these proposals was prompt and unfavorable. To many workaday Americans grubbing out stumps, astronomical observatories seemed like a scandalous waste of public funds. The South in particular bristled. If the federal government should take on such heavy financial burdens, it would have to continue the hated tariff duties. If it could meddle in local concerns like education and roads, it might even try to lay its hand on the "peculiar institution" of black slavery.

Adams's land policy likewise antagonized the westerners. They clamored for wide-open expansion and were angered by the president's well-meaning attempts to curb feverish speculation in the public domain. The fate of the Cherokee Indians, who were about to be evicted from their holdings in Georgia, generated additional bitterness. Ruggedly honest Adams attempted to deal fairly with the friendless Indians, further offending the West in general and the state of Georgia in particular. The governor, who threatened a resort to arms, successfully resisted the efforts of the Washington government to interpose federal authority on behalf of the Indians. Another fateful chapter was thus written in the nullification of the national will.

The Tricky "Tariff of Abominations"

The touchy tariff issue became one of Adams's biggest headaches. Congress had increased the general tariff in 1824, from about 23 percent on dutiable goods to about 37 percent. But wool manufacturers, dissatisfied with their share of protection, bleated for still-higher barriers.

Ardent Jacksonites, seeking to unhorse Adams, seized this opportunity to play politics with the Tariff of 1828. They rigged up a bill that was seemingly more concerned with manufacturing a president than with protecting manufacturers. A part of their scheme was to push the duties as high as about 45 percent on the value of certain manufactured items. At the same time, they would impose a heavy tariff on certain raw materials, notably wool. These materials were so urgently needed for manufacturing, especially in New England, that even this industrial section would presumably vote against the entire measure. Adams, whose stronghold was New England, would thus be given another political black eye, and Jackson

would receive a boost, especially in the middle states. There many voters were politically uncertain but protection-prone.

But the New Englanders spoiled this clever little game. Though disliking the proposed duties, they were anxious to continue the principle of protection. As a consequence, enough of them choked down the dishonest Tariff of 1828, as amended, to force its passage. Daniel Webster, who had earlier fought the mild Tariff of 1816, and John C. Calhoun, who had sponsored it, had by this time completely reversed their positions. They and others now clearly saw that the future of New England lay in the factory, rather than on the waves, while the destiny of the South lay in the cotton fields.

Southerners, as heavy consumers of manufactured goods, were shocked by what they regarded as the outrageous rates of the Tariff of 1828. Hotheads promptly branded it the "Black Tariff" or the "Tariff of Abominations." Several southern states adopted formal protests; in South Carolina flags were lowered to half-mast. "Let the *New* England beware how she imitates the *Old*," cried one eloquent Carolinian who remembered 1776.

Why did the South, especially South Carolina, react so angrily against the tariff? Underlying the southern outcry were growing anxieties about possible federal interference with the institution of slavery. The congressional debate on the Missouri Compromise had kindled those anxieties, and they were further fed by an ominous slave rebellion in Charleston in 1822, led by a free black, Denmark Vesey. The South Carolinians, still closely tied to the British West

House Vote on Tariff of 1828 ("Tariff of Abominations")*

REGIONS	FOR	AGAINST
New England	16	23
Middle states	57	11
West (Ohio, Ind., Ill., Mo.)	17	1
South (incl. La.)	3	50
Southwest (Tenn., Ky.)	12	9
TOTAL	105	94

*Compare 1816 tariff, p. 226.

Indies, also knew full well how their slaveowning West Indian cousins were feeling the mounting pressure of British abolitionism on the London government. Abolitionism in America might similarly use the power of the government in Washington to suppress slavery in the South. If so, now was the time, and the tariff was the issue, for taking a strong stand on principle against all federal encroachments on states' rights.

Nearer the surface was the real economic distress of the Old South—the seaboard area first settled. It was now the least flourishing of all the sections. The bustling Northeast was experiencing a boom in manufacturing; the developing West was prospering from rising property values and a multiplying population; and the energetic Southwest was expanding into virgin cotton lands. Overcropped acres of the Old South were petering out, and the price of cotton was falling sharply. John Randolph of Virginia grimly quipped that masters would soon cease to advertise for their fugitive slaves, and slaves would advertise for their fugitive masters. So the Old South was seeking a scapegoat, and the tariff proved to be a convenient and plausible one.

The Tariff Yoke in the South

Southerners believed, not illogically, that the "Yankee tariff" discriminated against them. They sold their cotton and other farm produce in a world market completely unprotected by tariffs and were forced to buy their manufactured goods in an American market heavily protected by tariffs.

The plight of the South may be illustrated by a hypothetical case. Suppose that in 1828 an English manufacturer sold shoes in South Carolina at $1.25 a pair, whereas a Massachusetts shoemaker, paying higher wages, would have to charge $1.50 for a pair of equal quality. South Carolinians would naturally buy the British footwear. But if a tariff of $0.50 a pair were levied on foreign shoes at the Charleston customshouse, the British shoes would cost $1.75 a pair. The Massachusetts shoemaker could now safely raise the price to anything less than $1.75—say, $1.74—and still undercut the British competitor by selling the cheapest shoes in South Carolina. South Carolinians would thus be forced to pay higher prices, while the profits of the Yankee manufacturer were commensurately fattened. This artificial inflation of prices

Tariff Inequalities, North and South   *The protective tariff under which the North grows fat and prosperous brings economic hardship to the South. (United States Weekly Telegram, 1832.)*

has always been among the most objectionable features of high tariffs.

The South also objected to other consequences of towering tariffs. Higher prices generally lead to a reduced volume of purchases. And if Americans bought fewer English textiles, the British would in turn buy less southern cotton with which to make the textiles. Southerners thus would suffer both as consumers and as producers, as importers and as exporters. Little wonder that southern leaders regarded the protective tariff as a foe of their economic development. On the other hand, many failed to appreciate that in the long run a prosperous manufacturing economy in the Northeast could itself contribute to their prosperity by consuming their cotton and other farm products.

South Carolinians took the lead in protesting against the "Tariff of Abominations." Their legislature went so far as to publish in 1828, though without formal endorsement, a pamphlet known as "The South Carolina Exposition." It had been secretly written by John C. Calhoun, one of the few topflight political theorists ever produced by America. (As vice-president, he was forced to conceal his authorship.) "The Exposition" boldly denounced the recent tariff as unjust and unconstitutional. Going a stride beyond the Kentucky and Virginia resolutions of 1798, it bluntly and explicitly proposed that the states should nullify the tariff—that is, they should declare it null and void within their borders.

Calhoun found himself caught in an awkward straddle. Still a Unionist and a nationalist, he was also a southern sectionalist. He therefore desperately sought a formula that would protect the minority in the South from the "tyranny of the majority" in the North and West. Seizing upon nullification, he undertook by this explosive device to preserve the Union and prevent secession. Calhoun's aim was not to destroy the Union but to salvage it by quieting the fears of those forces that might one day destroy it.

Calhoun's "Exposition," at least immediately, was a false alarm. No other state joined South Carolina in its heated antitariff protest. But the disruptive theory of nullification was further publicized, while the even more dangerous doc-

John C. Calhoun (1782–1850)   *Calhoun was a South Carolinian, educated at Yale. Beginning as a strong nationalist and Unionist, he reversed himself and became the ablest of the sectionalists and disunionists in defense of the South and slavery. As a foremost nullifier, he died trying to reconcile strong states' rights with a strong Union. In his last years he advocated a Siamese-twin presidency, probably unworkable, with one president for the North and one for the South. His former plantation home is now the site of Clemson University. (National Archives.)*

trine of secession was foreshadowed. South Carolina was not then prepared to force the controversy to a showdown. The election of Carolina-born Andrew Jackson to the presidency had occurred two weeks earlier, and the "Old Hero"—a fellow cotton planter and slaveowner—was expected to sympathize with the plight of the South.

Going "Whole Hog" for Jackson in 1828

The presidential campaign for Andrew Jackson had started early. It began on February 9, 1825, the day of John Quincy Adams's controversial election by the House, and continued noisily for nearly four years.

Even before the election of 1828, the temporarily united Republicans of the Era of Good Feelings had split into two camps. One was the National Republicans, with the ultranationalistic Adams as their standard-bearer. The other was the Democratic-Republicans, with the fiery Jackson heading their ticket. Rallying cries of the Jackson zealots were "Bargain and Corruption," "Huzza for Jackson," and "All Hail Old Hickory." Jacksonites planted hickory poles for their hickory-tough hero; "Adamites" adopted the oak as the symbol of their oakenly independent candidate.

"Shall the people rule?" was the chief issue of 1828, at least to Jacksonians. They argued that the will of the voters had been thwarted in 1825 by the backstairs "bargain" of Adams and Clay. The only way to right the wrong was to seat Jackson, who would then bring about "reform" by sweeping out the "dishonest" Adams gang. "Jackson and Reform" was a widely mouthed

Mrs. Andrew Jackson *A devoted wife who did not live to become First Lady, she had unwittingly, and hence innocently, involved herself and her husband in scandal. (The Granger Collection.)*

> One anti-Jackson newspaper declared, "General Jackson's mother was a Common Prostitute, brought to this country by the British soldiers! She afterwards married a MULATTO MAN with whom she had several children, of which number GENERAL JACKSON is one."

slogan, while hickory brooms were brandished as tokens of a forthcoming "clean sweep." Seldom has the public mind been so successfully poisoned against an honest and high-minded president.

Mudslinging reached a disgraceful level, partly as a result of the taste of the new mass electorate for bare-knuckle politics. Adams would not stoop to gutter tactics, but many of his backers were less squeamish. They described Jackson's mother as a prostitute; they printed black-bordered handbills, shaped like coffins, recounting his numerous duels and brawls and trumpeting his hanging of six mutinous militiamen. The "Old Hero" was also branded an adulterer. He had married an estimable woman, Rachel Robards, confident that her divorce had been granted. To the consternation of both, they discovered two years later that it had not been, and they made haste to correct the marital miscue.

Rachel Jackson was crushed by the vicious charges of bigamy and adultery. She lived to see her husband win the presidency, but she died—supposedly of a broken heart—before she could become First Lady. Jackson, devotedly attached to his wife, was convinced that his enemies had killed her. He never forgave them.

Jackson men also hit below the belt. President Adams had purchased, with his own money and for his own use, a billiard table and a set of chessmen. In the mouths of rabid Jacksonites, these items became "gaming tables" and "gambling furniture" for the "presidential palace." Criticism was also unfairly directed at the large sums that Adams had received over the years in federal salaries, well earned though they had been. He was even accused of having procured a servant girl for the lust of a Russian nobleman while minister to Russia—in short, of having served as a pimp.

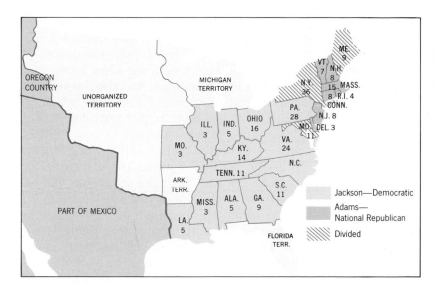

Presidential Election of 1828 (with electoral vote by state) *Jackson swept the South and West, while Adams retained the old Federalist stronghold of the Northeast. Yet Jackson's inroads in the Northeast were decisive. He won twenty of New York's electoral votes, and all twenty-eight of Pennsylvania's. If those votes had gone the other way, Adams would have been victorious—by a margin of one vote.*

The Jacksonian "Revolution of 1828"

General Jackson, victorious on the battlefields, was no less victorious at the ballot boxes. The popular tally was 647,286 votes for him to 508,064 for Adams, with an electoral count of 178 to 83. Support for Jackson came mainly from the West and South, and to a considerable extent from the sweat-stained laborers of the eastern seaboard. Generally speaking, the common people—though by no means all of them—voted for the Hero of New Orleans. Adams won the backing of his own New England, as well as the propertied "better elements" of the Northeast.

The election of 1828 has often been called the "Revolution of 1828." Actually, as in 1800, there was no upheaval or landslide that swept out the incumbent. Adams, in fact, polled a respectable 44 percent of the popular vote. A considerable part of Jackson's support, moreover, was lined up by machine politicians, especially in New York and Pennsylvania, and not entirely among the leather-aproned artisans and other manual workers.

But the concept of a *political* revolution in 1828 is not completely farfetched. The increased turnout of voters proved that the common people, especially in the universal-white-manhood-suffrage states, now had the vote and the will to use it for their ends. A discontented

West, with its numerous rustics and debtors, generally voted for Jackson. The results show that the political center of gravity was continuing to shift away from the conservative seaboard East toward the emerging states across the mountains.

So in a broader sense the election *was* a "revolution," comparable to that of 1800. It was a peaceful revolution, achieved by ballots instead of bullets, by counting heads instead of crushing them. "Shall the people rule?" cried the Jacksonians. The answering roar seemed to say, "The people *shall* rule!" In the struggle between the poorer masses and the entrenched classes, the homespun folk scored a resounding triumph, befuddling some members of the elite establishment. "I never saw anything like it," a puzzled Daniel Webster mused about Jackson's inaugural. "Persons have come five hundred miles to see General Jackson, and they really seem to think that the country is rescued from some dreadful danger."

America hitherto had been ruled by an elite of brains and wealth, whether aristocratic Federalist shippers or aristocratic Jeffersonian planters. Jackson's victory accelerated the transfer of national power from the counting-house to the farmhouse, from the East to the West, and from the snobs to the mobs. If Jefferson had been the hero of the gentleman farmer, Jackson was the hero of the dirt farmer. The plowholders were now ready to take over the government—their government.

Adams, though president-reject, was still destined for an enviable public career. Ever high-minded, he did not deem it beneath his dignity as an ex-president to accept election to the House of Representatives from Massachusetts. ("No person can be degraded by serving the people," he declared.) There he served with conspicuous success for seventeen fruitful years. Affectionately known as "Old Man Eloquent," he fought stalwartly for free government, free speech, free soil, and free people. A rough and savage debater, he finally was stricken on the floor of the House in 1848, at age eighty. His funeral was the greatest pageant of its kind that Washington had yet seen. Ironically, the popularity that had escaped him in life came to him in death.

The Advent of "Old Hickory" Jackson

Andrew Jackson cut a striking figure—tall (6 feet 1 inch; 1.86 meters), gaunt, and with bushy iron-gray hair brushed high above a prominent forehead, craggy eyebrows, and blue eyes. His irritability and emaciated condition (140 pounds; 64 kilograms) probably had resulted in part from long-term bouts with dysentery, malaria, tuberculosis, and lead poisoning from two bullets that he carried in his body from near-fatal duels. His autobiography was largely written in his lined face.

To a considerable degree, Jackson personified the new West. He reflected its individualism, its jack-of-all-trades versatility, its opportunism, its energy, its directness, and its prejudices. He was a genuine folk hero—an uncommon common man. The backwoods preacher who cried that Jesus was "just another Andrew Jackson" reflected a sentiment that did not seem out of place to some.

Jackson's upbringing was not of the best. Born in the Carolinas and early orphaned, "Mischievous Andy" grew up without parental restraints. As a youth, he displayed much more interest in brawling and cockfighting than in his scanty opportunities for reading and spelling. Although he ultimately learned to express himself in writing with vigor and clarity, his

grammar was always rough-hewn, and his spelling was often original, like that of many contemporaries. He sometimes misspelled a word two different ways in the same letter.

The youthful Carolinian had the foresight to emigrate "up West" to Tennessee, where a fighting man was more highly regarded than a writing man. There—through native intelligence, force of personality, and powers of leadership—he became a judge and a member of Congress. His passions were so terrible that on occasion he would choke into silence when he tried to speak. He won his greatest fame as a commander of militia troops, who dubbed him "Old Hickory" in honor of his toughness. Afflicted with a violent temper, he early became involved in numerous duels, stabbings, and other bloody frays. But, rough and forthright as democracy itself, he made things move.

The first president from the West, the first nominated at a formal party convention (in 1832), and the first without a college education (except Washington), Jackson was unique. His university was adversity. He had risen from the masses, but he was not one of them, except insofar as he shared many of their prejudices. Essentially a frontier aristocrat, he owned many slaves, cultivated broad acres, and lived in one of the finest mansions in America—the Hermitage, near Nashville, Tennessee. More westerner than easterner, more country gentleman than common clay, more courtly than crude, he was hard to fit into a neat category:

> He's none of your old New England stock,
> Or your gentry-proud Virginians,
> But a regular Western fighting-cock
> With Tennessee opinions.*

As befitted an authentic man of the people and hero of the one-suspender man, Jackson's political ideas had a stark simplicity. Like the anti-federalists of an earlier day, he was suspicious of the federal government as a bastion of privilege, an institution dangerously remote from popular scrutiny. He was therefore deter-

---

*"Andrew Jackson," from *A Book of Americans*, by Rosemary & Stephen Vincent Benét. Copyright, 1933, by Rosemary & Stephen Vincent Benét. Copyright renewed ©, 1961, by Rosemary Carr Benét. Reprinted by permission of Brandt & Brandt Literary Agency, Inc.

mined to reduce it "to that simple machine which the Constitution created," which meant, among other things, hostility to the active federal economic role envisioned in Henry Clay's American System. Conversely, he and especially his followers were generally friendly toward the frothy democracy bubbling up in the states and looked with some favor on economic activism on the part of state governments. Yet Jackson was destined to disappoint some of his states' rights supporters in the South by his insistence on the sacredness of the Union and the ultimate supremacy of federal power over that of the states.

While president, Jackson proved to be a storm center. As a former military man, he demanded prompt and loyal support from his subordinates. If one was not for him, one was against him. Cherishing strong ideas as to his constitutional prerogatives, he ignored the Supreme Court on several conspicuous occasions. He likewise defied or dominated Congress as few presidents have done. His six predecessors had wielded the veto ten times; during his two terms he employed it twelve times, sometimes on grounds of personal distaste rather than constitutional principle. Jackson's modest use of the veto ax was perfectly legitimate, but his numerous enemies condemned him as "King Andrew the First."

Jackson's inauguration symbolized the newly won ascendancy of the masses. "Hickoryites" poured into Washington from far places, sleeping on hotel floors or in hallways. They were curious to see their hero take office and perhaps to pick up a well-paying office for themselves. Nobodies mingled with notables as the White House, for the first time, was thrown open to the multitude. A milling crowd of clerks, shopkeepers, hobnailed artisans, and grimy laborers

"King Andrew the First"   *Jackson is here assailed as a tyrant who tramples underfoot the Constitution, the courts, and domestic welfare. (Houghton Library, Harvard.)*

surged in, wrecking the china and furniture, and threatening the "people's champion" with cracked ribs. Jackson was hastily spirited through a side door, and the White House miraculously emptied itself when the word was passed that huge bowls of well-spiked punch had been placed on the lawns. Such was "the inaugural brawl."

To conservatives, this orgy seemed like the end of the world. "King Mob" reigned triumphant as Jacksonian vulgarity replaced Jeffersonian simplicity. Old ladies of both sexes shuddered, drew their blinds, and recalled the opening scenes of the French Revolution.

In 1824, Jefferson said of Jackson: "When I was President of the Senate he was a Senator; and he could never speak on account of the rashness of his feelings. I have seen him attempt it repeatedly, and as often choke with rage. His passions are no doubt cooler now . . . but he is a dangerous man."

Jackson Nationalizes the Spoils System

Under Jackson the spoils system—that is, rewarding political supporters with public office—was introduced into the federal government on a large numerical scale. On a percentage basis, Jefferson, with reluctance and discrimination, had already made about as large a beginning. Jackson, with more ruthlessness, extended it to more people, while complaining about those "clamoring for a public tit from which to suck the treasury."

The basic idea was as old as politics. Its name came later from Senator Marcy's classic remark in 1832, "To the victor belong the spoils of the enemy." The system had already secured a firm hold in New York and Pennsylvania, where well-greased machines were operating. Professional politicians, by ladling out the "gravy" of office, had been able to make politics a full-time business rather than a sideline. The emphasis was more on spoils than on responsibilities.

A housecleaning of some sort in Washington was clearly needed. No party overturn had occurred since the defeat of the Federalists in 1800, and even that had not produced wholesale evictions. During the ensuing twenty-eight years, festering evils had developed in the civil service. The old colonial-system ideal of holding office during good behavior had bred some incompetence and corruption, as well as considerable indifference and insolence ("uncivil servants"). A few officeholders, their commissions signed by President Washington, were lingering on into their eighties, drawing breath and salary but doing little else.

Jackson fully shared the view of the New Democracy that "every man is as good as his neighbor"—perhaps "equally better." As this was believed to be so, and as the routine of office was also thought to be simple enough for any upstanding American to learn quickly, why encourage the development of an aristocratic, bureaucratic, officeholding class? Experience, of course, had some value. But alertness and new blood had more—at least in the eyes of Jacksonians.

The New Democracy also trumpeted the ideal of "rotation in office"—or "a turn about is fair play." Since experience was discounted, and since officeholding provided valuable training for citizenship, let as many citizens as possible feed at the public trough for at least a short time. This was a polite way of saying "Throw the rascals out and put our rascals in."

More Victors Than Spoils

Elected as a reformer, Jackson believed that the swiftest road to reform was to sweep out the Adams-Clay gang and bring in his own trusted henchmen. Furiously aroused against his foes, he agreed that the old Adams "barnacles" must "be scraped clean from the Ship of State."

The spoilsmen now had their inning. Office seekers hounded Jackson at every turn and even invaded his privacy: for every appointee there were seemingly ten disappointees. In view of such pressures, one may marvel that he removed so few incumbents rather than so many. During his eight years, only about one-fifth of the old civil servants were dismissed, leaving more than nine thousand out of the original eleven thousand. The "clean sweeps" were to come in later administrations.

Even so, a demoralizing practice was begun on a national scale. Insecurity replaced security and discouraged many able citizens from entering the public service. Terrible hardships were worked on poor men with large families. One discharged employee cut his throat from ear to ear; another went raving mad. Fitness, merit, and the ideal of public service were subordinated, while offices were prostituted to political ends. The questions were not "What can he do for the country?" but "What has he done for the party?" or "Is he loyal to Jackson?"

Scandal inevitably accompanied the new system. Men were appointed to high office who had openly bought their posts by campaign contributions. Illiterates, incompetents, and plain crooks were given positions of public trust; they lusted for the spoils of office rather than the toils of office. Samuel Swartwout, despite ample warnings of his untrustworthiness, was awarded the high-salaried post of collector

One elderly postmaster, a Revolutionary War veteran, while personally appealing to Jackson not to evict him from office, removed his coat to display his war wounds. Jackson later exclaimed: "By the eternal! I will not remove the old man. Do you know that he carries a pound of British lead in his body?"

of the customs of the port of New York. Nearly nine years later he "Swartwouted out" for England, leaving his accounts more than a million dollars short—the first person to steal a million from the Washington government.

Finally, the spoils system built up a potent, personalized political machine. Its delicate gears were lubricated by gifts from expectant party members and by percentage levies on the salaries of officeholders—a kind of political job insurance. The system at length secured such a tenacious hold that more than half a century passed before its grip could be even partially loosened.

Cabinet Crises and Nationalistic Setbacks

Jackson's cabinet was mediocre; its members were used primarily as executive clerks. The only person of conspicuous ability was the smooth-tongued and keen-witted secretary of state, Dutch-descended Martin Van Buren of New York, who shone as a gifted conciliator and wire-puller. A balding, sharp-featured little man, he was affectionately addressed by Jackson as "Matty." But he was known to his enemies as the "Little Magician."

The official cabinet of six was privately supplemented by an extraofficial cabinet of about thirteen ever-shifting members. It grew out of Jackson's informal meetings with his advisers, some of whom were newspaper people who kept him in touch with the fickle winds of public opinion. The enemies of the president branded these shirt-sleeved cronies "the Kitchen Cabinet." Subsequent generations have retained the picture of an uncouth clique gathering in the kitchen and spitting tobacco juice in the general direction of grimy spittoons. Actually, the group did not gather in the kitchen; it never met officially; its overall influence has been grossly exaggerated; and it was not unconstitutional. Presidents are free to consult with such unofficial advisers as they desire.

The regular cabinet was wrecked in 1831, as a result of the "Eaton malaria." Secretary of War Eaton had married the daughter of a Washington boardinghouse keeper, pretty Peggy O'Neal, whom the tongue of scandal had perhaps unfairly linked with the male boarders. She was consequently snubbed by the ladies of Jackson's official family, conspicuously by the blue-blooded wife of Vice-President Calhoun. The president, whose own spouse had been victimized by scandalmongers, was chivalrously aroused in behalf of Mrs. Eaton's chastity. With a zeal worthy of a better cause, he tried to force the social acceptance of the black-haired beauty. But the all-conquering general finally had to acknowledge defeat in the "Petticoat War" at the hands of the female phalanx.

The Eaton scandal played directly into the hands of Secretary Van Buren. As a fancy-free widower, he further curried favor with Jackson by paying marked attention to Mrs. Eaton, whose physical charms helped to lighten this self-imposed task. Jackson turned increasingly against Calhoun, and finally broke with him completely. Followers of the South Carolinian were purged from the cabinet in 1831. Calhoun himself, resigning the vice-presidency the next year, entered the Senate as a champion of South Carolina.

It would be absurd to say that Peggy Eaton caused the Civil War. But up to this time Calhoun had publicly been a strong nationalist, de-

Peggy Eaton (1796–1879) *Though scandal raised her to notoriety, she retained Jackson's favor. After her husband left the cabinet, the president appointed him minister to Spain. For four years she basked in a brilliant Madrid society that had no prejudice against a woman with a past. (Library of Congress.)*

spite his secret espousal of nullification in "The South Carolina Exposition" of 1828. As vice-president, he thought himself in line for the presidency after Jackson had served one term. The open break with the incumbent, though foreshadowed earlier, blighted his hopes. He gradually abandoned his weakening national-ism and became an inflexible defender of south-ern sectionalism. Seeking extreme medicines for protecting the states and preserving the Union, the "Great Nullifier" contributed to the almost fatal illness of the Union.

Jackson himself, consistent with his Jefferso-nian principles, dealt nationalism a body blow by his hostility to localized roads and canals. It is true that he signed a number of measures that appropriated federal funds for ambitious in-ternal improvements. But his states' rights prin-ciples rebelled against spending money from the pinched Washington Treasury for roads built entirely within individual states and unre-lated to an interstate network. He headlined his antagonism in 1830, when he vigorously vetoed a bill for improving the Maysville Road, which lay completely within Henry Clay's Kentucky (but which was connected with an interstate artery). This setback slapped at the internal im-provements aspect of the American System, so ardently championed by Clay, the "corrupt bar-gainer" whom Jackson never forgave. "Old Hickory's" veto was also a signal victory for eastern and southern states' rightism in its struggle with Jackson's own West.

The Webster-Hayne Forensic Duel

Sectional jealousies found a spectacular outlet in the Senate during 1829–1830. Hidebound New England, resenting the marvelous expan-sion of the West, was determined to call a halt. The lavish distribution of western acreage was draining off eastern population while further upsetting the political balance. Late in 1829, therefore, a New England senator introduced a resolution designed to curb the sale of public lands.

Sectional passions flared angrily in the Sen-ate, as the western senators sprang furiously to the defense of their interests. The South, seek-ing sectional allies in its controversies with the Northeast, promptly sided with the West. Its most persuasive spokesman was Robert Y. Hayne, of South Carolina, one of the silver-tongued orators of his generation.

Hayne's oratorical effort in the Senate was impressive. He roundly condemned the obvious disloyalty of New England during the War of 1812, as well as its selfish inconsistency on the protective tariff. Airing in detail the grievances of the South, he reserved his heavy fire for the "Tariff of Abominations" (1828). He then ac-claimed Calhoun's dangerous doctrine of nulli-fication as the only means of safeguarding the minority interests of his section. Hayne, like Calhoun, did not advocate a breakup of the Union; rather, he was seeking to protect south-ern rights within the Union and under the Con-stitution. But his arguments were carefully stored up by nullifiers and secessionists for fu-ture use.

The "Godlike Daniel" Webster, spokesman for New England, now took the floor. Matchless orator and leader of the American bar, he awed audiences by his majestic presence, including craglike brows, flashing eyes, a sonorous voice, a noble head, and a well-chested frame. His life up to this point, including his frequent appear-ances before Chief Justice Marshall, had been a preparation for this nine-day running debate with Hayne in January of 1830.

After defending New England with vigor, if not complete candor, Webster, the ex-Federal-ist, passed on to the larger issue of Union. In-sisting that the *people* and not the *states* had framed the Constitution (here he was on shaky historical ground*), he decried the insidious doctrine of nullification. Either the Supreme Court would judge the constitutionality of laws, or the Republic would be torn by revolution. If each of the twenty-four states were free to go its separate way in obeying or rejecting federal statutes, there would be no union but only a "rope of sand." Webster's concluding outburst,

---

*The original preamble of the Constitution of 1787 had read: "We the people of the states of"—and then they were listed by name. But when it was objected that all the states might not ratify, the formula "We the people of the United States" was adopted. (For the text of the preamble, see the Appendix.)

In 1839 Daniel Webster visited England, where his distinguished bearing and intellectual power made a great impression. The Reverend Sydney Smith, a merciless critic of America, reportedly remarked, "Daniel Webster struck me much like a steam-engine in trousers." He was also a "living lie, because no man on earth could be so great as he looked."

which brought tears to listeners' eyes, was a magnificent tribute to the Union, ending with those imperishable words: "Liberty and Union, now and forever, one and inseparable."

Websterian Cement for the Union

Webster did not overpower Hayne with his thunderous oratory; Hayne did not defeat Webster with his seductive eloquence. There were no official judges. The polished southerner was sounder on historical and economic grounds; the impassioned New Englander was sounder on constitutional practicalities and common sense—on things as they were rather than as

Webster challenged Hayne in these words: "The proposition that, in case of a supposed violation of the Constitution by Congress, the states have a constitutional right to interfere and annul the law of Congress is the proposition of the gentleman. I do not admit it. If the gentleman had intended no more than to assert the right of revolution for justifiable cause, he would have said only what all agree to. But I cannot conceive that there can be a middle course, between submission to the laws, when regularly pronounced constitutional, on the one hand, and open resistance, which is revolution or rebellion, on the other" (January 26, 1830). Webster and Hayne thus clashed over the same question that had vexed Jefferson in the Kentucky resolutions and Marshall in Marbury v. Madison. Where did final authority to interpret the Constitution lie?

they had been. Each section was satisfied with its champion.

The impact of Webster's reply was spectacular. About forty thousand copies were printed in three months, and arguments for the Union were seared into the minds of countless northerners. Among them was young Abraham Lincoln, just turning twenty-one and moving from Indiana to the Illinois frontier. Webster's inspirational peroration was printed in the school readers and was memorized by tens of thousands of impressionable lads—the Boys in Blue who in 1861–1865 were willing to lay down their lives for the Union.

Webster, beyond a doubt, had a large hand in winning the Civil War. He probably did more than any other person to arouse the oncoming generation of northerners to fight for the ideal of Union. His admirers have claimed that the nation was saved hardly less by the thunder of Webster's replies to Hayne than by the thunder

A Jackson Campaign Poster, 1832 Note the emphasis on *democracy* and *union*. (Tennessee State Library and Archives.)

"The man who has filled the measure of his Country's Glory."
JEFFERSON.

Jackson,

DEMOCRACY,

And our Country.

"The Union must be Preserved."

of General Grant's replies to the cannonading of General Lee.

Hot-tempered "Old Hickory" had meanwhile been keeping strangely silent on southern grievances. States' rights leaders, at a Jefferson Day banquet in 1830, schemed to smoke him out. Their strategy was to devise a series of toasts in honor of Jefferson, onetime foe of centralization, that would lean toward states' rights and nullification. The plotters assumed that the "Old Hero"—a fellow southerner—would be swept along by the tenor of the toasts and speak up in favor of states' rights.

Jackson, forewarned and inwardly fuming, had carefully prepared his response. At the proper moment he rose to his full height, fixed his eyes on Calhoun, and with dramatic intensity proclaimed:

> "Our Union: It must be preserved!"

The southerners were dumbfounded, and Calhoun haltingly replied, in part:

> "The union, next to our liberty, most dear!"

Some seventy other anticlimactic toasts followed this exchange, but in effect the party was over.

Jackson's military ire was aroused. As commander in chief, he would stand for no back talk from the states or particularly from the hated Calhoun. But, as fate decreed, the showdown with defiant South Carolina was postponed for over two years.

CHRONOLOGY

1822	Vesey slave rebellion in South Carolina
1824	Lack of electoral majority for presidency throws election into the House of Representatives
1825	House elects John Quincy Adams president
1828	Tariff of 1828 ("Tariff of Abominations")
	Jackson elected president
1830	Webster-Hayne debate
1831	Anti-Masonic party holds first national convention
	Eaton affair
1832	Calhoun resigns as vice-president

Varying Viewpoints

Aristocratic nineteenth-century historians damned Jackson as a backwoods barbarian. They criticized Jacksonianism as democracy run riot—an irresponsible, backcountry outburst that overturned the electoral system and raised hob with the national financial structure. Early twentieth-century "progressive" historians followed the lead of Frederick Jackson Turner in his famous 1893 essay "The Significance of the Frontier in American History." They saw the frontier as the fount of democratic virtue, and they hailed Jackson as a popular hero sprung from the forests of the West. But with the publication of Arthur M. Schlesinger, Jr.'s *The Age of Jackson* in 1945, the focus of the debate on Jacksonianism shifted. Contending that the urban working people of the Northeast formed the backbone of Jackson's support, Schlesinger argued that its identification with a social class, rather than a geographic section, was the most important characteristic of Jacksonianism.

Soon after Schlesinger's book appeared,

the discussion again shifted ground. The "ethnocultural" school, led by Lee Benson, argued that social class was less important than ethnic and religious conflict in determining political alignments. Local issues such as temperance, this argument ran, were far more influential in shaping political life than were the national financial questions analyzed by Schlesinger.

In the 1980s, however, Sean Wilentz and other scholars began to reclaim some of Schlesinger's interpretation. Wilentz maintains that Jacksonian politics cannot be properly understood without reference to the changing national economy. Artisans during this period, he suggests, watched in horror as new manufacturing techniques put many of them out of business and replaced them with low-skilled wage laborers. To these anxious small producers, big, impersonal institutions and dependence on large-scale employers threatened the very existence of a republic founded on the principle that its citizens were virtuously self-sufficient. Thus Jackson's attack on the Bank of the United States symbolized the antagonism these individuals felt toward the emergent corporate economy and determined their strong allegiance to Jackson.

Select Readings

Primary Source Documents

Davy Crockett's *Exploits and Adventures in Texas** (1836) is a lively description of the democratic political order of Jacksonian America. C.W. Janson, *The Stranger in America, 1793–1806** (1807), exposes the seamier aspects of American egalitarianism. On the Tariff of Abominations and its implications, see the "Webster-Hayne Debate"* (1830). Webster's reply to Hayne is one of the greatest specimens of American political oratory.

Secondary Sources

A still-living classic treatise on the Jacksonian period is Alexis de Tocqueville, *Democracy in America* (1835, 1840). General introductions are Glyndon G. Van Deusen, *The Jacksonian Era* (1959), and Edward Pessen, *Jacksonian America: Society, Personality and Politics* (rev. ed., 1978). The latter volume sharply disputes Tocqueville's findings. Marvin Meyers, *The Jackson Persuasion* (1957), and John William Ward, *Andrew Jackson: Symbol for an Age* (1955), examine the broader cultural significance of Old Hickory and his supporters. Arthur M. Schlesinger, Jr., in his seminal *The Age of Jackson* (1945), stresses the support of eastern labor for Jackson, a view that has come under attack in Lee Benson, *The Concept of Jacksonian Democracy: New York as a Test Case* (1961). Daniel Feller links political turmoil to land and labor disputes in *The Public Lands in Jacksonian Politics* (1984). On the evolution of mass-based political parties, see Richard P. McCormick, *The Second American Party System* (1966), and two books by Ronald P. Formisano, *The Birth of Mass Political Parties: Michigan, 1827–1861* (1971) and *The Transformation of Political Culture: Massachusetts Parties, 1790s–1840s* (1983). McCormick has also authored a general survey of party politics from Jackson into the twentieth century, *The Party Period and Public Policy: American Politics from the Age of Jackson to the Progressive Era* (1986). Three works that consider Jacksonian politics in the South are William J. Cooper, *The South and the Politics of Slavery, 1828–1856* (1978); J. Mills Thornton III, *Politics and Power in a Slave Society: Alabama, 1800–1860* (1978); and Harry L. Watson, *Jacksonian Politics and Community Conflict: The Emergence of the Second American Party System in Cumberland County, North Carolina* (1981), which discusses the opponents of Jackson. Samuel Flagg Bemis, *John Quincy Adams and the Union* (1956), is the second volume of a distinguished biography, as is Robert V. Remini, *Andrew Jackson and the Course of American Freedom, 1822–1832* (1981). A masterful analysis of the period's most celebrated statesmen is Merrill D. Peterson, *The Great Triumvirate: Webster, Clay and Calhoun* (1987). See also Sydney Nathans, *Daniel Webster and Jacksonian Democracy* (1973). The standard work on tariffs is Frank W. Taussig, *The Tariff History of the United States* (1931).

14

Jacksonian Democracy at Flood Tide, 1830–1840

The vain threats of resistance by those who [in South Carolina] have raised the standard of rebellion shew their madness and folly. . . . In forty days, I can have within the limits of So. Carolina fifty thousand men. . . . The Union will be preserved.

Andrew Jackson, 1832

"Nullies" in South Carolina

The "abominable" Tariff of 1828 continued to rankle hot-blooded South Carolinians. They persisted in seeing it not only as economically punitive in the short run, but as a possible entering wedge for later federal interference with slavery in the southern states. In protest, some South Carolinians took to wearing ill-fitting garments of homespun, untaxed by the hated Yankee tariff, while their slaves sported discarded broadcloth. The nullifiers—"nullies," they were called—tried strenuously to muster the necessary two-thirds vote for nullification in the South Carolina legislature. But they were blocked by a determined minority of Unionists, scorned as "submission men."

Back in Washington, Congress touched off the fuse by passing the new Tariff of 1832,

which fell far short of meeting all southern demands. The measure did pare away the worst of the "abominations" of 1828, and it did lower the imposts to about the level of the moderate Tariff of 1824—roughly 35 percent, or a reduction of 10 percent. Yet the new law was still frankly protective, and to many southerners it had a disquieting air of permanence.

South Carolina was now nerved for drastic action. Nullifiers and Unionists clashed head-on in the state election of 1832. "Nullies," defiantly wearing palmetto ribbons on their hats, emerged with more than a two-thirds majority. The state legislature then called for a special convention. Several weeks later the delegates, meeting in Columbia, solemnly declared the existing federal tariff to be null and void within South Carolina. The hotheaded assemblage also called upon the state legislature to undertake any necessary military preparations. As a final act of defiance, the convention threatened to take South Carolina out of the Union if the Washington regime attempted to collect the customs duties by force.

President-General Jackson, his military instincts rasped, reacted violently. Hating Calhoun and pledged to uphold the Union, he privately threatened to hang the nullifiers. But fortunately for compromise, he was much less pugnacious in public. He dispatched modest naval and military reinforcements to the Palmetto State, while quietly preparing a sizable army. He also issued a ringing proclamation against nullification, to which the governor of South Carolina, ex-Senator Hayne, responded with a counterproclamation. If civil war were to be avoided, one side would have to surrender, or both would have to compromise.

Conciliatory Henry Clay of Kentucky, now in the Senate, stepped forward. An unforgiving foe of Jackson, he had no desire to see his old enemy win new laurels by crushing the Carolinians and returning with the scalp of Calhoun dangling from his belt. The gallant Kentuckian therefore threw his influence behind a compromise bill that would gradually reduce the Tariff of 1832 by about 10 percent over a period of eight years. By 1842 the rates would be at approximately the mildly protective level of 1816—that is, 20 percent to 25 percent on the value of dutiable goods.*

The compromise Tariff of 1833 finally squeezed through Congress. Debate was bitter,

Calhoun Commands the Sun to Stand Still This cartoon mocks Calhoun's efforts to snuff out abolitionist ideas and protect the institution of slavery in South Carolina. "Sun of Intellectual light & liberty, stand ye still, in Masterly inactivity," Calhoun says in the cartoon, "that the Nation of Carolina may continue to hold Negroes & plant Cotton till the day of Judgment!" Note that the sun he commands to stand still is a printing press, representing the power of ideas and of the printed word to convey them. (New York State Historical Association.)

---

*For the history of tariff rates, see the Appendix.

House Vote on Tariff of 1832*

REGIONS	FOR	AGAINST	EXPLANATIONS
New England	17	17	Divided on moderate tariff
Middle states	52	18	Pa., N.Y., protectionist strongholds
West (Ohio, Ind., Ill., Mo.)	18	0	Undeveloped West for tariff to support improvements
South (incl. La.)	27	27	Note division on moderate tariff
Southwest (Tenn., Ky.)	18	3	West favorable to tariff
TOTAL	132	65	

*The vote was badly divided because the bill was really a compromise between extreme protection and free trade. Compare the vote on the 1828 tariff, p. 249.

House Vote on Compromise Tariff of 1833

REGIONS	FOR	AGAINST	EXPLANATIONS
New England	10	28 ⎫	Opposition in manufacturing centers to
Middle states	24	47 ⎭	lowered tariff
West	10	8	Divided on moderate tariff
South and Southwest	75	2	Strong southern support for compromise
TOTAL	119	85	

with most of the opposition naturally coming from protectionist New England and the middle states. Calhoun and the South favored the compromise, so it was evident that Jackson would not have to use firearms and rope. But at the same time, and partly as a face-saving device, Congress passed the Force Bill, known among Carolinians as the "Bloody Bill." It authorized the president to use the army and navy, if necessary, to collect federal tariff duties.

Militant South Carolinians welcomed this opportunity to extricate themselves without loss of face from a dangerously tight corner. To the consternation of the Calhounites, no other southern states had sprung to their support, though Georgia and Virginia toyed with the idea. Moreover, an appreciable Unionist minority within South Carolina was gathering guns, organizing militia, and nailing the Stars and Stripes to flagpoles. Faced with civil war within and invasion from without, the Columbia convention met again and repealed the ordinance of nullification. As a final but futile gesture of fist-shaking, it nullified the unnecessary Force Act and adjourned.

A Victory for Both Union and Nullification

Neither Jackson nor the "nullies" won a clear-cut triumph. Admirers of "Old Hickory" insisted that he had avoided an armed clash, induced the South Carolinians to repeal their ordinance of nullification, and preserved the Union. On the other hand, the danger of disunion seems to have been exaggerated.

South Carolina actually emerged with colors flying. Although confronted with overwhelming odds, it had forced a reduction of the tariff to as reasonable a level as it could have expected. It

had not only saved face but it had surrendered no principle. Unrepentant and defiant, it felt that it had won; and the people of Charleston—the "Cradle of Secession"—gave a gala "victory ball" for the volunteer troops. But ominously the South Carolinians gradually abandoned nullification in favor of the more extreme remedy of secession.

Later generations, gazing back through the smoke of the Civil War, have condemned the "appeasement" of South Carolina in 1833 as sheer folly. Unbloody and unbowed, it could have been voted the state most likely to secede. (In 1860 it was the first to go.) If Jackson had only strangled the serpent of secession in the cradle, so the argument runs, there might have been no costly Civil War. During the crisis of 1832 medals were struck off in honor of Calhoun bearing the words, "First President of the Southern Confederacy."

Yet force was the risky solution. The flare-up in South Carolina was no mere Whiskey Rebellion, and the nation was not yet ready to drink the cup of blood. Violence tends to beget violence. Armed invasion might have aroused other southern states and touched off a civil war, at a time when the Unionists were even worse prepared for fighting than in 1861. Force is a confession that statesmanship has failed. Reasonable compromise was in the American tradition, and in 1833 any other course seemed unwise.

The Bank as a Political Football

President Jackson did not hate all banks and all businesses, but he distrusted monopolistic banking and overbig business, as did his followers. A man of violent dislikes, he came to share the prejudices of his own West against the

In his message vetoing the bill to recharter the Bank of the United States, President Andrew Jackson summarized the basic principles of "Jacksonian democracy": "Distinctions in society will always exist under every just government. Equality of talents, of education, or of wealth can not be produced by human institutions. . . . But when the laws undertake to add to these natural and just advantages artificial distinctions . . . the humble members of society—the farmers, mechanics, and laborers—who have neither the time nor the means of securing like favors to themselves, have a right to complain of the injustice of their government." Jackson's words constituted a virtual manifesto of what came to be known as the "populist" strain in American political culture, with its notorious hostility to "privilege."

"moneyed monster" known as the Bank of the United States (BUS). He might have tolerated a renewal of its charter in 1836, with adequate safeguards. But hated Henry Clay aroused his ire by throwing himself behind a premature move in the Senate to recharter the bank in 1832—four years early. "Gallant Harry" was the leading candidate of the National Republicans for the presidency, and with fateful blindness he looked upon the bank issue as a surefire winner.

Clay's scheme was to ram a recharter bill through Congress and then send it on to the White House. If Jackson signed it, he would alienate his worshipful western followers. If he vetoed it, as seemed certain, he would pre-

Banker Nicholas Biddle wrote to Henry Clay (August 1, 1832) expressing his satisfaction: "I have always deplored making the Bank a party question, but since the President will have it so, he must pay the penalty of his own rashness. As to the veto message, I am delighted with it. It has all the fury of a chained panther biting the bars of his cage. It is really a manifesto of anarchy . . . and my hope is that it will contribute to relieve the country of the domination of these miserable [Jackson] people."

sumably lose the presidency in the forthcoming election by alienating the wealthy and influential groups in the East. Clay seems not to have fully realized that the "best people" were now only a minority and that they generally feared Jackson anyhow. The president growled privately, "The Bank . . . is trying to kill me, but I will kill it."

The recharter bill slid through Congress on greased skids, as planned, but was killed by a scorching veto from Jackson. The "Old Hero" assailed the plutocratic and monopolistic bank as unconstitutional. Of course, the Supreme Court had earlier declared it constitutional in the case of *McCulloch* v. *Maryland* (1819), but Jackson acted as though he regarded the executive branch as superior to the judicial branch. He had taken an oath to uphold the Constitution as he understood it, not as his foe John Marshall understood it.

Jackson's veto message went on to condemn the bank as not only antiwestern but anti-American. A substantial minority of its stockholders were foreigners, chiefly Britons, for whom Americans still harbored a war-born hate. Thus, at one bold stroke, Jackson succeeded in mobilizing the prejudices of the West against the East. He was setting the log cabin against the business office, the apprehensive debtor against the steely-eyed creditor. More than that, the president was arousing the "native" American against the foreigner, the states' righter against the centralizer.

Jackson's veto message was epochal. It not only squashed the bank bill but vastly amplified the power of the presidency. In more than four decades under the Constitution, previous presidents had used the veto only ten times; Jackson was to use it twelve times, or more than all his predecessors combined. Besides, all previous vetoes had rested almost exclusively on questions of constitutionality. But though Jackson invoked the Constitution in his bank-veto message, he essentially argued that he was vetoing the bill because he personally found it harmful to the nation. In effect, he was claiming for the president alone a power equivalent to two-thirds of the votes in Congress. If the legislative and judicial branches were partners in government, he implied, the president was unmistakably the senior partner.

Nicholas Biddle (1786–1844)   *A precociously brilliant linguist, writer, magazine editor, diplomat, legislator, and financier, he entered the University of Pennsylvania at age ten and completed the requirements for graduation at age thirteen. Drawn into high finance, he mastered the business and became president of the Bank of the United States. (Historical Society of Pennsylvania.)*

The gods continued to misguide Henry Clay. Delighted with the financial fallacies of Jackson's message but blind to its political appeal, he arranged to have thousands of copies printed as a campaign document. The president's sweeping accusations may indeed have seemed demagogic to the moneyed people of the country, but they made good sense to the common people. The bank issue was now thrown into the noisy arena of the Clay-Jackson presidential canvass of 1832.

Brickbats and Bouquets for the Bank

What of Jackson's vigorous charges? The bank was undeniably antiwestern in its strong hostility to the wobbly "wildcat banks" that provided financial fuel—often volatile paper—for western expansion. It had foreclosed on many western farms and had thus drained "tribute" into eastern coffers. For that era, it was a mammoth superbank—a "monster monopoly"—and hence out of touch with the sweaty New Democracy. It was undeniably plutocratic, run by an elite moneyed aristocracy, headed by the able but high-handed Nicholas Biddle (dubbed "Czar Nicholas I"). The bank was also in some degree autocratic and tyrannical, especially when it turned the screws on the weak "rag money" banks.

The charge that the bank was a "hydra of corruption" contained much truth. Biddle cleverly lent funds where they would make influential friends. In 1831 alone, a total of fifty-nine members of Congress borrowed sums from "Biddle's Bank" totaling about a third of a million dollars. Even a dog does not ordinarily bite the hand that feeds it. During one period Daniel Webster was a director of the bank, its chief paid counsel, its debtor in the sum of thousands of dollars, and a member of the Senate, where he eloquently battled for his employer's interests. Judicious loans by Biddle to newspaper editors likewise ensured a "good press" and led to the sneer, "Emperor Nick of the Bribery Bank." Whomever he could not corrupt, it was believed, he crushed.

Yet the bank had much to commend it. A financially sound organization, it imposed some restraint on fly-by-night banks—banks that often consisted of little more than a few chairs and a suitcase full of printed notes. It reduced bank failures and, at a time when the country was flooded with depreciated paper money, issued sound bank notes ("Old Nick's Money"). It promoted economic expansion by making credit and sound currency reasonably abundant. It was a safe depository for the funds of the Washington government, which it also served by transferring and disbursing money. But paradoxically, the bank's enormous economic power made it politically vulnerable.

The bank, in short, was a highly important and useful institution, but one whose very existence seemed to sin against the egalitarian credo of American democracy. Its officers were not only arrogant but were also not fully aware of their responsibilities to society in the management of what amounted to a public trust.

"Old Hickory" Crushes Clay in 1832

Clay, as a National Republican, and Jackson, as a Democrat, were the chief gladiators in the presidential contest of 1832. The gaunt old general, who had earlier favored one term for a president and rotation in office, was easily persuaded by his cronies not to rotate himself out of office. Presidential power is a heady brew—and habit-forming.

The ensuing campaign was colorful and noisy. The "Old Hero's" adherents again raised the hickory pole and bellowed, "Jackson Forever: Go the Whole Hog." Admirers of Clay shouted, "Freedom and Clay," while his foes harped on his dueling, gambling, cockfighting, and fast living.

Novel features made the campaign of 1832 especially memorable. For the first time, a third party entered the field—the newborn Anti-Masonic party, which opposed the fearsome secrecy of the Masonic order. Energized by the mysterious disappearance and probable murder in 1826 of a New Yorker who was threatening to expose the secret rituals of the Masons, the Anti-Masonic party quickly became a potent political force in New York and spread its influence throughout the middle Atlantic and New England states. The Anti-Masons appealed to long-standing American suspicions of secret

societies, which they condemned as citadels of privilege and monopoly—a note that harmonized with the democratic chorus of the Jacksonians. But since Jackson himself was a Mason, and publicly gloried in his membership, the Anti-Masonic party was also an anti-Jackson party. Moreover, the Anti-Masons attracted support from many evangelical Protestant groups seeking to use political power to effect moral and religious reforms, such as prohibiting mail deliveries on Sunday and otherwise keeping the Sabbath holy. This moral busybodiness was anathema to the Jacksonians, who were generally opposed to all government meddling in social and economic life.

A further novelty of the presidential contest in 1832 was the calling of national nominating conventions (three of them) to name candidates. The Anti-Masons and a group of National Republicans added still another innovation when they adopted formal platforms, publicizing their positions on the issues.

Henry Clay and his overconfident National Republicans enjoyed impressive advantages. Ample funds flowed into their campaign chest, including $50,000 in "life insurance" from the BUS. Most of the newspaper editors, some of them "bought" with Biddle's bank loans, dipped their pens in acid when they wrote of Jackson. Oratorical big guns, including the incomparable

"Race Over Uncle Sam's Course" Clay, with his American System, is supposed to gain the White House as Jackson, with his veto club and Van Buren as running mate, falls on the bank issue in 1832. A falsely optimistic Whig cartoon. (Boston Public Library.)

Webster, were lined up on the side of Clay, as was true of the middle- and upper-income groups.

Yet Jackson won easily over the sparkling Kentuckian. The popular count stood at 687,502 to 530,189; the electoral count, 219 to 49. The Anti-Masons carried only Vermont. A Jacksonian wave swept over the West and South, washed into Pennsylvania and New York, and even broke into rock-ribbed New England.

Henry Clay, long bitten by the presidential bug, was crushed. Himself magnetically appealing, he had enlisted on his side the big money, the brilliant oratory, the "solid" citizenry, and the sound financial reasoning. But the peppery president, the idol of the masses, won because he had the votes. The poor always outnumber the rich—and in 1832, as in 1824 and 1828, the poor voted for "Old Andy" Jackson.

Badgering Biddle's Bank

A vindictive Jackson was not one to let the financial octopus die in peace. He was convinced that he now had a "mandate" from the voters, and he had good reason to fear that the slippery Biddle might try to manipulate the bank (as he did) so as to force its recharter. Jackson therefore decided to weaken the bank by "removing" federal deposits from its vaults. He proposed depositing no more funds with Biddle and gradually shrinking existing deposits by using them to defray the day-to-day expenses of the government. By slowly siphoning off the government's funds, he would bleed the bank dry and ensure its demise when its charter expired in four years.

"Removing" the deposits involved nasty complications. Jackson, his dander up, was forced to reshuffle his cabinet before he could find a secretary of the treasury who would bend to his iron will. Surplus federal funds henceforth were placed in several dozen state institutions—the so-called pet banks or Jackson's pets. These new depositories were selected partly because of their pro-Jackson sympathies, but in general they were not nearly so weak as pictured by the president's enemies.

Biddle, for his part, was compelled to retrench after losing the federal deposits. But he called in loans with unnecessary severity and evidently for the purpose of forcing a reconsideration of the charter by Congress. A number of the wobblier banks were driven to the wall by "Biddle's Panic," and the vengeful conduct of the dying "monster" seemed to justify the earlier accusations of its foes.

The teetering financial structure of the country received an additional shock in 1836, the year the bank breathed its last. "Wildcat" currency had become so unreliable, especially in the West, that Jackson authorized the Treasury to issue a Specie Circular—a decree that required all public lands to be purchased with "hard," or metallic, money. This drastic step was overdue, but coming at that time it gave the speculative bubble another sharp prick. Hard money brought hard feelings and hard times for the West.

Yet inflationary pressure continued. By 1835 the national debt was finally liquidated for the first time, but additional funds still poured into the federal Treasury. This revenue flowed principally from the customshouses, which were benefiting from the high tariff duties and the heavy imports resulting from flush times. In 1836 a scheme passed Congress for distributing the surplus above $5 million to the states. When this transfer began, early in 1837, the risky speculative spiral was given another boost. Later that year the panic broke, and the bothersome problem of the surplus became the even more bothersome problem of a deficit.

Transplanting the Tribes

Wondrous indeed was the continued expansion of the American population. The unflagging fertility of the people, reinforced by immigration, brought the total figure to nearly 13 million by 1830—or more than three times that of 1790.*

Henry Clay expressed sentiments typical of his time when he said in the 1820s that Indians were "essentially inferior to the Anglo-Saxon race . . . and their disappearance from the human family will be no great loss to the world."

---

*For population figures since 1790, see the Appendix.

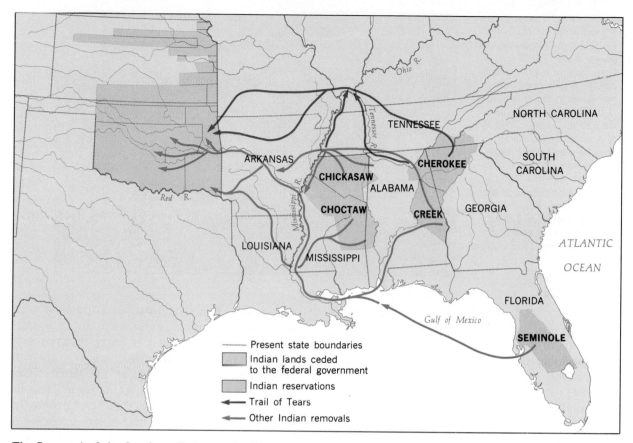

The Removal of the Southern Tribes to the West

Most of the states east of the Mississippi had been admitted, leaving islands of Indians marooned on lands coveted by their white neighbors.

President Jackson, the veteran Indian fighter known as "Big Knife," was convinced of the folly of continuing to regard the tribes as separate nations within the individual states. When Georgia attempted to exercise control over the Cherokees, and the Supreme Court thrice upheld the rights of the Indians, Jackson viewed continued defiance by the state with unaccustomed composure. A state might flout federal law if whites thereby profited at the Indians' expense. In a callous sneer at the Indians' defender, Jackson reportedly snapped, "John Marshall has made his decision; now let him enforce it."

Yet Jackson, who had raised an adopted Indian boy from infancy, also harbored protective feelings toward the Indians. Their present condition, he told Congress in 1829, "contrasted with what they once were, makes a most powerful appeal to our sympathies." Could not something be done, he implored, to preserve "this much injured race"? Jackson proposed a bodily removal of the remaining eastern tribes—chiefly Cherokee, Creek, Choctaw, Chickasaw, and Seminole—beyond the Mississippi. Individual Indians might remain if they adopted white society's ways. Emigration should be voluntary, since it would be "cruel and unjust to compel the aborigines to abandon the graves of their fathers."

Jackson's policy was high-sounding, but it led to the more or less forcible uprooting of more than 100,000 Indians in the 1830s. Many died on the "Trail of Tears" to the newly established Indian Territory (present Oklahoma), where they were to be "permanently" free of white encroachments. The Bureau of Indian Affairs was established in 1836 to administer relations with America's original inhabitants. But as the land-hungry "palefaces" pushed west faster

The Trail of Tears In the fall and winter of 1838–1839, the U.S. Army forcibly removed about 15,000 Cherokees, some of them in manacles, from their ancestral homelands in the southeastern United States and marched them to the "Indian Territory" of present-day Oklahoma. Freezing weather and inadequate food supplies led to unspeakable suffering. The escorting troops refused to slow the forced march so that the ill could recover, and some 4,000 Cherokees died on the 116-day journey. (The Granger Collection.)

than anticipated, the government's guarantees went up in smoke. The "permanent" frontier lasted about fifteen years.

Suspicious of white intentions from the start, braves from Illinois and Wisconsin, ably led by Black Hawk, resisted eviction. They were bloodily crushed in 1832 by regular troops, including Lieutenant Jefferson Davis of Mississippi, and by volunteers, including Captain Abraham Lincoln of Illinois.

In Florida the Seminole Indians, joined by runaway black slaves, retreated to the swampy Everglades. For seven years (1835–1842) they waged a bitter guerrilla war that took the lives of some fifteen hundred soldiers and proved to be the costliest Indian conflict in American experience. The spirit of the Seminoles was at last broken in 1837, when the American field commander treacherously seized their half-breed leader, Osceola, under a flag of truce. The war dragged on fitfully for five more years, but the Seminoles were doomed. Some fled deeper into the Everglades, where their descendants now live, but about four-fifths of them were moved to present Oklahoma, where about three thousand of the tribe survive.

The Lone Star of Texas Flickers

Americans, greedy for land, continued to covet the vast expanse of Texas, which the United States had abandoned to Spain when acquiring

Florida in 1819. The Spanish authorities were desirous of populating this virtually unpeopled area, but before they could carry through their contemplated plans, the Mexicans won their independence. A new regime in Mexico City thereupon concluded arrangements in 1823 for granting a huge tract of land to Stephen Austin, with the understanding that he would bring in three hundred American families. Immigrants

Proud in Defeat Chief Black Hawk and his son are here depicted in captivity. After their surrender in the Black Hawk War in 1832, they were put on public display throughout the United States. (Thomas Gilcrease Institute, Tulsa, Oklahoma.)

Samuel ("Sam") Houston (1793–1863) *After a promising career in Tennessee as a soldier, lawyer, congressman, and governor, Houston became the chief leader and hero of the Texas rebels. Elected to the U.S. Senate and the governorship of Texas, he was forced into retirement when his love for the Union caused him to spurn the Confederacy in the Civil War.*

were to be of the established Roman Catholic faith and in addition were to become properly Mexicanized.

These two restrictions were largely ignored. Hardy Texan pioneers remained Americans at heart, resenting the trammels imposed by a "foreign" government. They were especially annoyed by the presence of Mexican soldiers, many of whom were ragged ex-convicts.

Virile and prolific, Texas-Americans numbered about thirty thousand by 1835 (see "Makers of America," pp. 272–273). Most of them were law-abiding, God-fearing people, but some of them had left the "states" only one or two jumps ahead of the sheriff. "G. T. T." (Gone to Texas) became current descriptive slang. Among the adventurers were Davy Crockett, the fabulous rifleman, and James Bowie, the presumed inventor of the murderous knife that bears his name. It was widely known in the Southwest as the "genuwine Arkansas toothpick." A distinguished latecomer and leader was an ex-governor of Tennessee, Sam Houston. His life had been temporarily shattered in 1829 when his bride of a few weeks left him and he took up transient residence with the Arkansas Indians, who dubbed him "Big Drink." He subsequently took the pledge of temperance.

The pioneer individualists who came to Texas were not easy to push around. Friction

The Alamo As It Looks Today *When Moses Austin, father of famed Texas pioneer Stephen Austin, first saw this building on December 23, 1820, it was an abandoned mission, founded by Franciscan friars in 1718 as San Antonio de Valero. Renamed The Alamo, from the Spanish word for cottonwood tree, it was made into a fortress and became famous in 1836 when Santa Anna's armies wiped out its garrison of Americans. (Bob Daemmrich/Stock, Boston.)*

Mexican or Texican?

Moses Austin, born a Connecticut Yankee in 1761, was determined to be Spanish—if that's what it took to acquire cheap land and freedom from pesky laws. In 1798 he tramped into untracked Missouri, still part of Spanish Louisiana, and pledged his allegiance to the king of Spain. He was not pleased when the Louisiana Purchase of 1803 restored him to American citizenship. In 1820, his old Spanish passport in his saddlebag, he rode into Spanish Texas and asked for permission to establish a colony of three hundred families.

Austin's request posed a dilemma for the Texas governor. The Spanish authorities had repeatedly stamped out the bands of American horse thieves and squatters who periodically splashed across the Red and Sabine rivers from the United States into Spanish territory. Yet the

Sam Maverick   *(Courtesy the Texas State Library, Archives Division, Austin.)*

Spanish had lured only some three thousand Mexican settlers into Texas during their three centuries of rule. If the land were ever to be wrested from the Indians and "civilized," maybe Austin's plan could do it. Hoping that this band of the "right sort" of Americans might prevent the further encroachment of buckskinned border ruffians, the governor reluctantly agreed to Austin's proposal.

Upon Moses Austin's death in 1821, the task of realizing his dream fell to his twenty-seven-year-old son, Stephen. "I bid an everlasting farewell to my native country," Stephen Austin said, and he crossed into Texas on July 15, 1821, "determined to fulfill rigidly all the duties and obligations of a Mexican citizen." Soon he learned fluent Spanish and was signing his name as "Don Estévan F. Austin." In his new colony between the Brazos and Colorado rivers, he allowed "no drunkard, no gambler, no profane swearer, no idler"—and sternly enforced these rules. Not only did he banish several families as "undesirables," but he ordered the

José Antonio Navarro (1795–1871)   *A native of San Antonio, Navarro signed the Texas Declaration of Independence in 1836. (Courtesy the Texas State Library, Archives Division, Austin.)*

public flogging of unwanted interlopers.

Austin fell just three families short of recruiting the three hundred households that his father had contracted to bring to Texas. The original settlers were nevertheless dubbed "the Old Three Hundred," the Texas equivalent of New England's Mayflower Pilgrims or the "First Families of Virginia." Mostly Scotch-Irish southerners from the transappalachian frontier, the Old Three Hundred were cultured folk by frontier standards; all but four of them were literate. Other settlers followed, from Europe as well as America. Within ten years the "Anglos" (many of them French and German) outnumbered the Mexican residents, or *tejanos*, ten to one. They soon evolved a distinctive "Texican" culture. The wide-ranging horse patrols that they organized to attack Indian camps eventually became the Texas Rangers; Samuel Maverick, whose unbranded calves roamed freely on the limitless prairies, left his name in the language to describe rebellious loners who refuse to run with the herd; and Jared Groce, an Alabama planter whose caravan of fifty covered wagons and one hundred slaves rumbled up to the Brazos in 1822, etched the original image of the larger-than-life, big-time Texas operator.

The original Anglo-Texans brought with them the old Scotch-Irish frontiersman's hostility to officialdom and authority. When the Mexican government tried to impose its will on the Anglo-Texans in the 1830s, they protested. Like the American revolutionaries of the 1770s, who at first demanded only the rights of Englishmen, the Texans began by asking simply for Mexican recognition of their rights as guaranteed by the Mexican constitution of 1824. But bloodshed at the Alamo in 1836, like that at Lexington in 1775, transformed protest into rebellion.

Texas lay—and still lies—along the frontier where Hispanic and Anglo-American cultures met, mingled, and clashed. In part, the Texas Revolution was a contest between those two cultures. But it was also a contest about philosophies of government, pitting liberal frontier ideals of freedom against the conservative concept of centralized control. Stephen Austin sincerely tried to "Mexicanize" himself and his followers—until the Mexican government grew too arbitrary and authoritarian. And not all the Texan revolutionaries were "Anglos." Seven *tejanos* perished defending the Alamo. Among the fifty-nine signers of the Texas declaration of independence were several Hispanics, including the *tejanos* José Antonio Navarro and Francisco Ruiz. Lorenzo de Zavala, an ardent Mexican liberal who had long resisted the centralizing tendencies of Mexico's dominant political party, was designated vice-president of the Texas Republic's interim government in 1836. Like Moses and Stephen Austin, these *tejanos* and Mexicans had sought in Texas an escape from the fetters of overbearing governmental authority. Their role in the Texas revolution underscores the fact that the uprising constituted a struggle of liberalism against tyranny—or of frontier individualism against central authority—as much as it did a fight between Anglo and Mexican cultures.

Texas Rangers in 1844 *(Courtesy the Barker Texas History Center, University of Texas, Austin.)*

rapidly increased between Mexicans and Texans over such issues as slavery, immigration, and local rights. Slavery was a particularly touchy issue. Mexico emancipated its slaves in 1830 and prohibited their further importation into Texas, as well as further settlement by troublesome Americans. The Texans refused to honor this decree. They kept their slaves in bondage, and new American settlers kept bringing more slaves into Texas. When Stephen Austin went to Mexico City in 1833 to negotiate these differences with the Mexican government, dictator Santa Anna clapped him in jail for eight months. The explosion finally came in 1835, when Santa Anna wiped out all local rights and started to raise an army to suppress the upstart Texans.

Early in 1836 the Texans declared their independence and unfurled their Lone Star flag—with Sam Houston as commander in chief. Santa Anna, at the head of about six thousand men, swept ferociously into Texas. Trapping a band of nearly two hundred pugnacious Texans at the Alamo in San Antonio, he wiped them out to a man after a thirteen-day siege. Their commander, Colonel W. B. Travis, had heroically declared, "I shall never surrender nor retreat. . . . Victory or Death." The victims included Jim Bowie, who was shot as he lay sick and crippled on his cot, and Davy Crockett, whose body was found riddled with bullets and surrounded by enemy corpses. But the Mexican losses were extremely heavy. A short time later a band of about four hundred surrounded and defeated American volunteers, having thrown down their arms at Goliad, were butchered as "pirates." All these operations further delayed the Mexican advance.

Texan war cries—"Remember the Alamo!" "Remember Goliad!" and "Death to Santa Anna!"—swept up into the United States. Scores of vengeful Americans seized their rifles and rushed to the aid of relatives, friends, and compatriots. But despite their efforts, the Lone Star was in grave danger of being dimmed forever as General Sam Houston's small army continued its thirty-seven-day eastward retreat.

But Houston proved equal to the occasion. A commanding figure of a man and a natural leader of the Texans, he lured the pursuers onward to San Jacinto, near the site of the city that now bears his name. The invaders numbered about thirteen hundred men; the Texans, about nine hundred. Suddenly, on April 21, 1836, Houston turned. Taking full advantage of the Mexican siesta hour, he wiped out the invading force and captured Santa Anna, who was found cowering in the tall grass near the battlefield. Confronted with thirsty bowie knives, the quaking dictator was speedily induced to sign two treaties. By their terms he agreed to withdraw Mexican troops and to recognize the Rio Grande as the extreme southwestern boundary of Texas. When released, he repudiated the whole agreement as illegal and as extorted under duress.

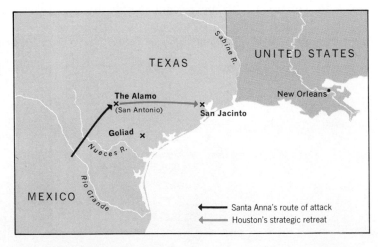

The Texas Revolution, 1835–1836 *General Houston's strategy was to retreat and use defense in depth. His line of supply from the United States was shortened as Santa Anna's lengthened. The Mexicans were forced to bring up supplies by land because the Texas navy controlled the sea. This force consisted of only four small ships, but it was big enough to do the job.*

Texas: An International Derelict

Mexico no doubt had a genuine grievance against the United States. The Texans, though courageous, could hardly have won their independence without unneutral help in men and supplies from their American cousins. The Washington government, as the Mexicans bitterly complained, had a solemn obligation under international law to enforce its leaky neutrality statutes. But American public opinion, overwhelmingly favorable to the Texans, openly nullified the existing legislation. The federal authorities were powerless to act.

Jackson's heart was torn by the Texas issue. He disliked the Mexican overlords and admired the heroism of Sam Houston, his old comrade-in-arms against the Indians. But Jackson was in no haste to recognize Texas formally as an independent republic. To do so would touch off the whole explosive issue of slavery, at a time when he was trying to engineer the election of his handpicked successor, Martin Van Buren. But after Van Buren had come safely under the wire, Jackson extended the right hand of recognition, on the day before he left office in 1837.

Texas had every reason to expect a union with the United States, for what nation in its right mind would refuse so princely a dowry? The radiant Texan bride, officially petitioning for annexation in 1837, presented herself for marriage. But the expectant groom, Uncle Sam, was jerked back by the black hand of the slavery issue. Antislavery crusaders in the North were opposing annexation with increasing vehemence; they contended that the whole scheme was merely a conspiracy cooked up by the southern "slavocracy" to bring new slave pens into the Union.

At first glance, a "slavery plot" charge seemed plausible. Most of the early settlers in Texas, as well as American volunteers during the revolution, had come from the states of the South and Southwest. But scholars have concluded that the settlement of Texas was merely the normal and inexorable march of the westward movement. Most of the immigrants came from the South and Southwest simply because these states were closer. The explanation was proximity rather than conspiracy. Yet the fact remained that many Texans were slaveholders, and admitting Texas to the Union inescapably meant enlarging American slavery.

Texas was left in a dangerous predicament. Fearing the return of the "villain," Santa Anna, it understandably went so far as to send feelers out to Britain and France for support. An ugly situation, involving balance-of-power politics, began to develop below the underbelly of the United States. It could not be allowed to go on indefinitely.

The Birth of the Whigs and the Election of 1836

New political parties were gelling as the 1830s lengthened. As early as 1828, the Democratic-Republicans of Andrew Jackson had unashamedly adopted the once-tainted name of "Democrats." Jackson's opponents, fuming at his ironfisted exercise of presidential power, condemned him as "King Andrew I" and began to coalesce as the *Whigs*—a name deliberately chosen to recollect eighteenth-century British and Revolutionary American opposition to the monarchy.

The Whig party contained so many diverse elements that it was mocked at first as "an organized incompatibility." Hatred of Jackson and his "executive usurpation" was its only apparent cement in its formative days. The Whigs first emerged as an identifiable group in the Senate, where Clay and Calhoun joined forces in 1834 to pass a motion censuring Jackson for his single-handed removal of federal deposits from the Bank of the United States. Thereafter, the Whigs rapidly evolved into a potent national political force by attracting other groups alienated by Jackson: supporters of Clay's American System; southern states' righters offended by Jackson's stand on nullification; the larger northern industrialists and merchants; and eventually, many of the evangelical Protestants associated with the Anti-Masonic party.

As the presidential election of 1836 neared, the still-ramshackle organization of the Whigs showed in their inability to nominate a single presidential candidate. Their long-shot strategy was instead to run several prominent "favorite sons," who would so scatter the vote that no candidate would win a majority. The deadlock would then have to be broken by the House of Representatives, where the Whigs might have a chance. With Henry Clay rudely elbowed aside, the leading "favorite son" was heavy-jawed General William Henry Harrison of Ohio, hero of the Battle of Tippecanoe.

Martin Van Buren of New York, a smooth-as-silk politician, was Jackson's choice for "appointment" as his successor. The hollow-cheeked Jackson, now nearing seventy, was too old and ailing to consider a third term. But he was not loath to try to serve a third term through Van Buren, something of a "yes man." Leaving nothing to chance, the general carefully rigged the nominating convention and rammed his favorite down the throats of the delegates. Van Buren was supported by the Jacksonites without wild enthusiasm, even though he had promised "to tread generally" in the military-booted footsteps of his predecessor.

The finespun schemes of the Whigs availed nothing. Van Buren, the dapper "Little Van," squirmed into office by the close popular vote of 765,483 to 739,795, but by the comfortable margin of 170 votes to 73 in the Electoral College. Jackson could now step down.

In retrospect, the Jackson years were yeasty ones. It is true that they were marred by noise and bluster, as well as by bull-in-the-china-closet financial policies. Yet the rough-hewn general—through forthrightness, energy, and strength of character—left a lasting imprint on the presidency. He bolstered the power of the executive branch; he led the common people into national politics; he united them into the powerful and long-lived Democratic party; and he proved that they could be trusted with the vote. Reasserting the prestige of the presidency, he amazed weak-kneed politicians by showing that the courageous course often wins the most votes.

The other side of the ledger is less satisfying. Jackson cannot escape blame for his encouragement of the spoils system and of unsound finance, with its heartbreaking legacy of a century of thousands of bank failures. No one can

Martin Van Buren (1782–1862)   *He has been generally underrated as a president because of his skill as a politician. It was said of him that he rowed toward his objectives "with muffled oars." Yet he eventually took a strong stand against the expansion of slavery by his hopeless run for the presidency as the candidate of the Free-Soil Party in 1848. (Library of Congress.)*

deny that the BUS was a powerful and ultimately a corrupting monopoly, which needed to have its wings clipped. But chopping off its head instead of its wings was of dubious benefit to the entire nation.

Big Woes for the "Little Magician"

Martin Van Buren, eighth president, was the first to be born under the American flag. Bland of face, bald of head, slender of figure, the adroit little New Yorker has been described as "a first-class second-rate man." An accomplished wire-puller and spoilsman—"the wizard of Albany"—he was also a statesman of wide experience in both legislative and administrative life. In intelligence, education, and training, he was above the average of the presidents since Jackson. The myth of his complete mediocrity sprouted from a series of misfortunes over which he had no control.

From the outset, the new politician-president labored under severe handicaps. As a machine-made candidate, he incurred the resentment of many Democrats—those who objected to having a "bastard politician" smuggled into office beneath the tails of the old general's military coat. Jackson, the master showman, had been the dynamic type of executive whose administration had resounded with furious quarrels and cracked heads. Easygoing Martin Van Buren seemed to rattle about in the military boots of his testy predecessor. The people felt let down. Inheriting Andrew Jackson's mantle without his popularity, the polished New Yorker also inherited the ex-president's numerous and vengeful enemies.

Van Buren's four years overflowed with toil and trouble. A rebellion in Canada in 1837 stirred up ugly incidents along the northern frontier and threatened to trigger war with Britain. The president's attempt to play a neutral game led to the cry "Woe to Martin Van Buren!" The antislavery agitators in the North were in full cry and among other grievances were condemning the prospective annexation of Texas.

Worst of all, Van Buren inherited the making of a searing depression from Jackson. Much of his energy had to be devoted to the purely negative task of battling the panic, and there were not enough rabbits in the "Little Magician's" tall silk hat. Hard times ordinarily blight the reputation of a president—and Van Buren was no exception.

Depression Doldrums and the Independent Treasury

The panic of 1837 was a symptom of the financial sickness of the times. Its basic cause was evidently overspeculation, prompted by a mania of get-rich-quickism. Gamblers in western lands were doing a "land-office business" on borrowed capital, much of it in the shaky currency of "wildcat banks." The speculative craze spread to canals, roads, railroads, and slaves.

But speculation alone did not cause the crash. Jacksonian finance, including the Bank War and the Specie Circular, gave an additional jolt to an already teetering structure. Failures of wheat crops, ravaged by the Hessian fly, deepened the distress. Grain prices were forced so high that mobs in New York City, three weeks before Van Buren took the oath, stormed warehouses and broke open flour barrels. The panic really began before Jackson left, but its full fury burst about Van Buren's bewildered head.

Financial stringency abroad likewise left its imprint on America. Late in 1836, while Jackson was still president, the failure of two prominent British banks created tremors, and these in turn caused English investors to call in foreign loans. The resulting pinch in the United States, combined with other setbacks, heralded the beginning of the panic. Europe's economic distresses have often been America's distresses, for every major American financial panic has been affected by conditions overseas.

Hardship was acute and widespread. American banks collapsed by the hundreds, including some "pet banks," which carried down with them several millions in government funds. Commodity prices drooped, sales of public lands fell off, and customs revenues dried to a rivulet.

> *Philip Hone, a New York businessman, described in his diary (May 10, 1837) a phase of the financial crisis: "The savings-bank also sustained a most grievous run yesterday. They paid 375 depositors $81,000. The press was awful; the hour for closing the bank is six o'clock, but they did not get through the paying of those who were in at that time till nine o'clock. I was there with the other trustees and witnessed the madness of the people—women nearly pressed to death, and the stoutest men could scarcely sustain themselves; but they held on as with a death's grip upon the evidences of their claims, and, exhausted as they were with the pressure, they had strength to cry 'Pay! Pay!'"*

Factories closed their doors; unemployed workers darkened the streets.

Increasingly, the Whigs were coming forward with proposals for active government remedies for the economy's ills. They called for the expansion of bank credit, higher tariffs, and subsidies for internal improvements. But Van Buren, shackled by the Jacksonian philosophy of keeping the government's paws off the economy, scorned all such ideas.

The beleaguered Van Buren tried to apply vintage Jacksonian medicine to the ailing economy through his controversial "Divorce Bill." Convinced that some of the financial fever was fed by the injection of federal funds into private banks, he championed the principle of "divorcing" the government from banking altogether. By establishing a so-called independent treasury, the government could lock its surplus money in vaults in several of the larger cities. Government funds would thus be safe, but they would also be denied to the banking system as reserves, thereby shriveling available credit resources. Van Buren's desire for political purity triumphed over enlightened economics.

Van Buren's "divorce" scheme was never highly popular. It was supported only lukewarmly by his fellow Democrats, many of whom longed for the risky but lush days of the "pet banks." The new policy was condemned by the Whigs, primarily because it would dampen their hopes for a revived Bank of the United States. After a prolonged struggle, the Independent Treasury Bill passed Congress in 1840. Repealed the next year by the victorious Whigs, the scheme was reenacted by the triumphant Democrats in 1846 and then continued until merged with the Federal Reserve System in the next century.

President William Henry Harrison (1773–1841)
Harrison can claim several distinctions. At sixty-eight, he was the oldest man to be sworn in until Ronald Reagan's inauguration 140 years later; he delivered the longest inaugural address (two hours); dying of pneumonia, he served the shortest term (thirty-one days); he obviously accomplished the least of any president; and he was responsible for the most progeny: 10 children, 48 grandchildren, 106 great-grandchildren. One of his grandchildren, Benjamin Harrison, became the twenty-third president. (National Portrait Gallery, Smithsonian Institution, Washington, D.C.)

"Tippecanoe" Versus "Little Van"

Martin Van Buren, though panic-tainted, was renominated by the Democrats in 1840, albeit without terrific enthusiasm. The party had no acceptable alternative to what the Whigs called "Martin Van Ruin."

The Whigs, hungering for the spoils of office, scented victory in the breeze. Pangs of the panic were still being felt; and voters blindly blamed their woes on the party in power. The Whigs turned again not to their ablest statesman—Clay or Webster—but to their presumably ablest vote-getter: General Harrison, a coarse-featured military chieftain, with a long, thin face and medium build (5 feet 8 inches; 1.72 meters).

The aging hero, nearly sixty-eight when the

campaign ended, was a small-bore candidate. Despite an inflated reputation, he had been only moderately successful in civilian and military life, notably at the Battles of Tippecanoe (1811) and the Thames (1813). "Old Tippecanoe" was then living quietly in a sixteen-room mansion, located on a three-thousand-acre farm near North Bend, Ohio. His views on current issues were only vaguely known. He was nominated primarily because he was issueless and enemyless—and a most unfortunate precedent was thus set. John Tyler of Virginia, an afterthought, was selected as his vice-presidential running mate.

The Whigs benefited from the economic distresses of Van Buren's term, and they were generally perceived as advocates of positive governmental steps to revive the economy. But

The Hard Cider Campaign, 1840 *An almanac cover promoting Harrison's candidacy. (The Granger Collection.)*

officially, the Whigs played the political game with the cards close to their vests. They published no platform, because they feared making bothersome commitments and were unwilling to reveal the deep divisions within their own patchwork party. They hoped to sweep their hero into office with a frothy huzza-for-Harrison campaign.

A dull-witted Democratic editor played directly into Whig hands. Stupidly insulting the West, he sneered at Harrison as an impoverished old farmer who would be content with a pension, a log cabin, and a barrel of hard cider—the poor westerner's champagne. Whigs gleefully took up the challenge and, stressing the hard cider and log cabin theme, turned the campaign into a huge political revival meeting. Harrisonites portrayed their hero as the poor "Farmer of North Bend," who had been called from his plow and his log cabin to drive corrupt Jackson spoilsmen from the "presidential palace."

A nonexistent candidate rapidly began to take shape in the hands of Whig mythmakers. The real Harrison was not lowborn, but from one of the FFVs (first families of Virginia). He was not poverty-stricken; he did not live in a one-room log cabin; he did not swill down gallons of hard cider (he evidently preferred whiskey); and he did not plow his fields with his own "huge paws."

Whig propagandists made merry with little "Matty" Van Buren, the "Flying Dutchman." Although reared in poverty, he was denounced as a supercilious aristocrat, who wore corsets and ate French food with golden teaspoons from golden plates. Jackson's rough-timbered Democratic party, deeply rooted in the West, was thus saddled with a simpering dandy from the aristocratic East. The aristocratic Whig party of Webster and Biddle, no less inconsistently, had come up with a backwoods nominee from the Democratic West—a reasonably good facsimile of wrinkled old General Jackson. As a jeering Whig campaign song proclaimed:

Old Tip, he wears a homespun shirt,
　He has no ruffled shirt, wirt, wirt.
But Matt, he has the golden plate,
　And he's a little squirt, wirt, wirt.

The Log Cabins and Hard Cider of 1840

Eager Democrats, who had hurrahed Jackson into the White House, now discovered to their chagrin that this was a game two could play. Acres of Whig audiences and miles of Whig marchers shouted such slogans as: "Harrison, Two Dollars a Day and Roast Beef" and "With Tip and Tyler We'll Bust Van's Biler." Log cabins were dished up in every conceivable form. Bawling Whigs, stimulated by fortified cider, rolled huge inflated balls from village to village and state to state—balls that represented the snowballing majority for "Tip and Ty." As they pushed, they sang:

> Tippecanoe, and Tyler too.
> And with them we'll beat little Van, Van, Van,
> Oh! Van is a used-up man.

Claptrap was king, as the electoral debauch reached an all-time intellectual low. There was little sober discussion of solid issues. Democrats inquired earnestly about the bank, internal improvements, and the tariff. The replies were "log cabin," "hard cider," and "Harrison is a poor man." Van Burenites, protesting futilely, were drowned in a tidal wave of apple juice as America experienced its first mass-turnout election.

Harrison won by the surprisingly close margin of 1,274,624 popular votes to 1,127,781, but by the overwhelming electoral count of 234 to 60. The hard-ciderites had seemingly received a mandate to go to Washington, tear down the White House, and erect a log cabin.

Basically, the vote was a protest against hard times—a thunderous shout of "Out with the old and in with the new." But the blatant bunkum and silly slogans set an unfortunate example for future campaigns. Democracy calls for hard thinking, not hard cider; for dignity, not delirium. Yet an able, well-organized, and well-entrenched political party, committed to solid principles, was hooted out of office by an inane hoopla campaign.

The Democrats were baffled. They complained with much bitterness and no little truth that they had been shouted down, sung down,

A Hard Road to Hoe!   *Jackson urges Van Buren toward the White House over a road littered with log cabins and hard cider. Van Buren, handicapped also by his unpopular subtreasury policy, would evidently prefer the smoother road back to his Kinderhook home. Van Buren's campaign may have contributed the slang expression "O.K." to the language. A campaign cartoon of 1840. (Library of Congress.)*

lied down, and drunk down. Yet, though out-sloganed, they had kept their ranks intact. Even in defeat they were a stronger party than the Whigs. Though temporarily overdosed with hard cider, the Democrats would be heard from again.

The Two-Party System Emerges

The Jeffersonians of an earlier day had been so successful in absorbing the programs of their Federalist opponents that a full-blown two-party system had never truly emerged in the subsequent Era of Good Feelings. The idea had prevailed that parties of any sort smacked of conspiracy and "faction" and were injurious to the health of the body politic in a virtuous republic.

But the American political world changed dramatically in the era of the New Democracy.

One of Andrew Jackson's most lasting legacies was the impetus he gave to the formation of a vigorous and durable two-party system, which had fully come of age by 1840.

Both parties, the Democrats as well as the Whigs, grew out of the rich soil of Jeffersonian republicanism, and each laid claim to different aspects of the republican inheritance. Jacksonians glorified the liberty of the individual and were fiercely on guard against the inroads of "privilege" into government. Whigs trumpeted the natural harmony of society and the value of community, and were willing to use government to realize their objectives. Whigs also berated those leaders—and they considered Jackson to be one—whose appeals to self-interest fostered conflict among individuals, classes, or sections.

Democrats clung to states' rights and federal restraint in social and economic affairs as their

Politics for the Common Man *Artist George Caleb Bingham here gently satirizes the drinking and wheeler-dealing that sometimes marred the electoral process in the boisterous age of Jacksonian politics. (Boatman's National Bank of St. Louis.)*

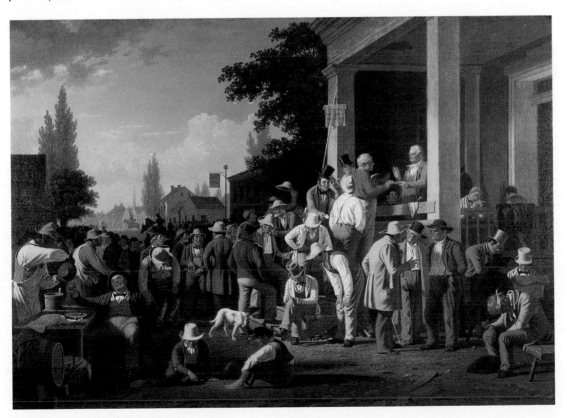

Andrew Jackson advised a supporter in 1835 on how to tell the difference between Democrats and "Whigs, nullies, and blue-light federalists." In doing so, he neatly summarized the Jacksonian philosophy: "The people ought to inquire [of political candidates]—are you opposed to a national bank; are you in favor of a strict construction of the Federal and State Constitutions; are you in favor of rotation in office; do you subscribe to the republican rule that the people are the sovereign power, the officers their agents, and that upon all national or general subjects, as well as local, they have a right to instruct their agents and respresentatives, and they are bound to obey or resign; in short, are they true Republicans agreeable to the true Jeffersonian creed?"

basic doctrines. Whigs, on the other hand, tended to favor a renewed national bank; protective tariffs; internal improvements; public schools; and increasingly, moral reforms such as the prohibition of liquor and eventually the abolition of slavery.

The two parties were thus separated by real differences of philosophy and policy. But they also had much in common. Both were mass-based, "catchall" parties that tried deliberately to mobilize as many voters as possible for their cause. Though it is true that Democrats tended to be more humble folk and Whigs more prosperous, both parties nevertheless commanded the loyalties of all kinds of Americans, from all social classes and in all sections. The social diversity of the two parties had important implications. It fostered horse-trading compromises *within* each party that prevented either from assuming extreme or radical positions. By the same token, the geographical diversity of the two parties retarded the emergence of purely sectional political parties—temporarily suppressing, through compromise, the ultimately uncompromisable issue of slavery. When the two-party system began to creak in the 1850s, the Union was mortally imperiled.

CHRONOLOGY

1823	Mexico opens Texas to American settlers
1832	Jackson defeats Clay for presidency
	"Bank War" over rechartering Bank of the United States
	Tariff of 1832
	Black Hawk War
1833	South Carolina nullification crisis
	Compromise Tariff of 1833
	Jackson removes federal deposits from Bank of the United States
1836	Bank of the United States expires
	Specie Circular issued
	Southeastern Indians removed on "Trail of Tears"
	Bureau of Indian Affairs established
	Texas wins independence from Mexico
	Van Buren elected president
1837	Seminole Indians defeated and removed from Florida
	United States recognizes Texas but refuses annexation
	Panic of 1837
1840	Independent Treasury established
	Harrison defeats Van Buren for presidency

Varying Viewpoints

As the debate over Jacksonianism shifted from a concern with geography to a consideration of social class, and later to an analysis of religion and ethnicity, historical evaluations of the rival parties have also changed. Patrician historians of the nineteenth century made the Whigs the champions of enlightened civilization against the excesses of the Jacksonian rabble. The progressive historians of the early years of this century reversed those assessments. They praised the Jacksonians as the representatives of freedom and equality and damned the Whigs as self-serving, aristocratic snobs. That view held sway until recent times, when historians began exploring the operation of the party system on a local level and the variations in party positions from state to state. Studies such as those by Ronald Formisano and Michael Holt stress the two parties' connections with various religious and immigrant groups and have encouraged a more balanced assessment of the merits of both parties.

Select Readings

Primary Source Documents

An incisive commentary on Jacksonian politics is novelist James Fenimore Cooper's *The American Democrat** (1838). On the Bank War, see Andrew Jackson's "Veto Message" (July 10, 1832), in James D. Richardson, ed., *Messages and Papers of the Presidents* (1896), vol. II, pp. 576 ff,* and Daniel Webster's "Speech on Jackson's Veto of the U.S. Bank Bill" (1832), in Richard Hofstadter, ed., *Great Issues in American History.*

Secondary Sources

Glyndon G. Van Deusen, *The Jacksonian Era, 1828–1848* (1959), is an excellent introduction. More thorough is the concluding volume of Robert V. Remini's biography, *Andrew Jackson and the Course of American Democracy, 1833–1845* (1984). On Van Buren, see John Niven, *Martin Van Buren: The Romantic Age of American Politics* (1983). Incisive analysis can be found in Richard Hofstadter's essay on Jackson in *The American Political Tradition* (1948). A superior monograph is William W. Freehling, *Prelude to Civil War: The Nullification Controversy in South Carolina* (1966). Also see Richard E. Ellis, *The Union at Risk: Jacksonian Democracy, States' Rights and the Nullification Crisis* (1987).

Jacksonians are charged with ignorance and hypocrisy in Bray Hammond, *Banks and Politics in America from the Revolution to the Civil War* (1957), and Thomas P. Govan defends *Nicholas Biddle: Nationalist and Public Banker* (1959). John McFaul looks at the broader picture in *The Politics of Jacksonian Finance* (1972). Robert V. Remini focuses on political questions in *Andrew Jackson and the Bank War* (1967). Jackson's Indian policies are scrutinized in Ronald N. Satz, *American Indian Policy in the Jacksonian Era* (1975), and Michael P. Rogin's heavily psychoanalytic *Fathers and Children: Andrew Jackson and the Subjugation of the American Indians* (1975). Important political transformations are handled in the Ronald P. Formisano and Richard P. McCormick volumes cited in Chapter 13. See also the opening chapters of Michael F. Holt's *The Political Crisis of the 1850s* (1978) and Amy Bridges, *A City in the Republic: Antebellum New York and the Origins of Machine Politics* (1984). Daniel W. Howe provides a stimulating analysis of Jackson's opponents in *The Political Culture of the American Whigs* (1980). Also see Thomas Brown, *Politics and Statesmanship: Essays on the American Whig Party* (1985). Peter Temin interprets *The Jacksonian Economy* (1969). The color of the frothy presidential campaign of 1840 comes through in Robert G. Gunderson, *The Log-Cabin Campaign* (1957).

Forging the National Economy, 1790–1860

The Westward Movement

The rise of Andrew Jackson, the first president from beyond the Appalachian Mountains, exemplified the inexorable westward march of the American people. The West, with its raw frontier, was the most typically American part of America. As Ralph Waldo Emerson wrote in 1844, "Europe stretches to the Alleghenies; America lies beyond."

The Republic was young and so were the people—as late as 1850, half of Americans were under the age of thirty. They were also restless and energetic, seemingly always on the move, and always westward. One "tall tale" of the frontier described chickens that voluntarily crossed their legs every spring, waiting to be tied for the annual move west. By 1840 the "demographic center" of the American population map had crossed the Alleghenies. By the eve of the Civil War, it had marched across the Ohio River.

Legend portrays an army of muscular axmen triumphantly carving civilization out of the western woods. But in reality life was downright grim for most pioneer families. Poorly fed, ill clad, housed in hastily erected shanties (Abraham Lincoln's family lived for a year in a three-sided lean-to made of brush and sticks), they were perpetual victims of disease, depression, and premature death. Above all, unbearable loneliness haunted them, especially the women, who sometimes cracked under the strain. These women settlers were often cut off from human contact, even their neighbors, for days or even weeks, while confined to the cramped orbit of a dark cabin in a secluded clearing. Breakdowns and even madness were all too frequently the "opportunities" that the frontier offered to pioneer women.

A Frontier Cabin *This crude shelter, standing simple and lonely in a rough clearing, was typical of many pioneer dwellings in frontier days. (The Buffalo and Erie County Historical Society.)*

Frontier life could be tough and crude for men as well. No-holds-barred wrestling, which permitted such niceties as the biting off of noses and the gouging out of eyes, was a popular entertainment. Pioneering Americans, marooned by geography, were often ill informed, superstitious, provincial, and fiercely individualistic. Emerson's popular lecture-essay "Self-Reliance" struck a deeply responsive chord. Popular literature of the period abounded with portraits of heroically unique, isolated figures like James Fenimore Cooper's Natty Bumppo and Herman Melville's Captain Ahab—just as Jacksonian politics aimed to emancipate the lone-wolf, enterprising businessperson. Yet even in this heyday of "rugged individualism" there were important exceptions. Pioneers, in tasks clearly beyond their own individual resources, would call upon neighbors for logrolling and barnraising and upon their governments for help in building internal improvements.

The March of the Millions

As the American people moved west, they also multiplied at an amazing rate. By midcentury the population was still doubling approximately every twenty-five years, as in fertile colonial days.

By 1860 the original thirteen states had more than doubled in number: thirty-three stars graced the American flag. The United States was the fourth most populous nation in the western world, exceeded only by three European countries—Russia, France, and Austria.

Urban growth continued explosively. In 1790 there had been only two cities that could boast 20,000 or more souls: Philadelphia and New York. By 1860 there were forty-three; and about three hundred other places claimed over 5,000 inhabitants apiece. New York was the metropolis; New Orleans, the "Queen of the South"; and Chicago, the swaggering lord of the Midwest, destined to be "hog butcher for the world."

Such overrapid urbanization unfortunately brought undesirable by-products. It intensified the problems of smelly slums, feeble street lighting, inadequate policing, impure water, foul sewage, ravenous rats, and improper garbage disposal. Hogs poked their scavenging snouts about many city streets as late as the 1840s. Boston in 1823 pioneered with a sewage system; and New York in 1842 abandoned wells and cisterns for a piped-in water supply. The

YEAR	WHITE	NONWHITE	PERCENT NONWHITE	TOTAL POPULATION	
1790	3,172,000	757,000	19	3,929,000	
1800	4,306,000	1,002,000	19	5,308,000	
1810	5,862,000	1,378,000	19	7,240,000	
1820	7,867,000	1,772,000	18	9,639,000	
1830	10,537,000	2,329,000	18	12,866,000	
1840	14,196,000	2,874,000	17	17,070,000	
1850	19,553,000	3,639,000	16	23,192,000	
1860	26,922,000	4,521,000	14	31,443,000	

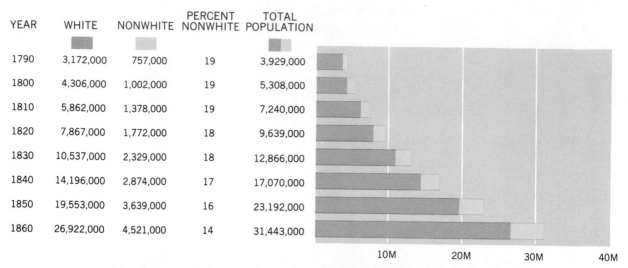

10M   20M   30M   40M

Population Increase, Including Slaves and Indians, 1790–1860 *Increasing European immigration and the closing of the slave trade gradually "whitened" the population beginning in 1820. This trend continued into the early twentieth century.*

city thus unknowingly eliminated the breeding places of many disease-carrying mosquitoes.

A continuing high birthrate accounted for most of the increase in population, but by the 1840s the tides of immigration were adding hundreds of thousands more. Before this decade, immigrants had been flowing in at a rate of about 60,000 a year, but suddenly the influx was tripled in the 1840s and then quadrupled in the 1850s. During these two

Cincinnati in 1843 *Famous as a processor of hogs, this "Queen City of the West" was a town of 2,540 people in 1800 and 161,044 in 1860, 45 percent of them foreign-born. Though tied to the South by downriver commerce on the Ohio and Mississippi rivers, it remained loyal to the North during the Civil War. (Cincinnati Public Library.)*

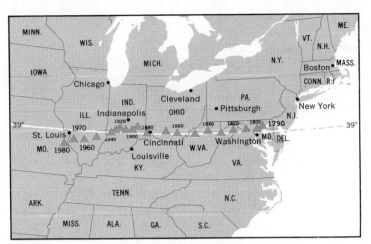

Westward Movement of Center of Population, 1790–1980 *Note the remarkable equilibrium of the north-south pull from 1790 onward and the strong spurt west and south after 1940. The 1980 census revealed that the nation's center of population had at last moved west of the Mississippi River.*

feverish decades, over a million and a half Irish, and nearly as many Germans, swarmed down the gangplanks. Why did they come?

The immigrants came partly because Europe seemed to be running out of room. The population of the Old World more than doubled in the nineteenth century, and Europe began to generate a great seething pool of apparently "surplus" people. They were displaced and footloose in their homelands before they felt the tug of the American magnet. Indeed, at least as many people moved about *within* Europe as crossed the Atlantic. America benefited from these people-churning changes but did not set them all in motion. Nor was the United States the sole beneficiary of the process: of the nearly 60 million persons who abandoned Europe in the century after 1840, about 25 million went somewhere other than the United States.

Yet America still beckoned most strongly to the struggling masses of Europe, and the majority of migrants headed for the "land of freedom and opportunity." There was freedom from aristocratic caste and state church; there was

Irish and German Immigration by Decade

YEARS	IRISH	GERMANS
1831–1840	207,381	152,454
1841–1850	780,719	434,626
1851–1860	914,119	951,667
1861–1870	435,778	787,468
1871–1880	436,871	718,182
1881–1890	655,482	1,452,970
1891–1900	388,416	505,152

abundant opportunity to secure broad acres and better one's condition. Much-read letters sent home by immigrants—"America letters"—often described in glowing terms the richer life: low taxes, no compulsory military service, and "three meat meals a day." The introduction of transoceanic steamships also meant that the immigrants could come speedily, in a matter of ten or twelve days instead of ten or twelve weeks. They were still jammed into unsanitary quarters, thus suffering an appalling death rate, but the nightmare was more endurable because it was shorter.

The Emerald Isle Moves West

Ireland, already groaning under the heavy hand of British overlords, was prostrated in the mid-1840s. A terrible rot attacked the potato crop, on which the people had become dangerously dependent, and about one-fourth of them were swept away by disease and hunger. Starved bodies were found dead by the roadsides with grass in their mouths. All told, about 2 million perished.

Tens of thousands of destitute souls, fleeing the Land of Famine for the Land of Plenty, flocked to America in the "Black Forties." Ireland's great export has been population; and the Irish take their place beside the Jews as a dispersed people (see "Makers of America," pp. 288–289).

These uprooted newcomers—too poor to move west and buy the necessary land, live-

The Irish

For a generation, from 1793 to 1815, war raged across Europe. Ruinous as it was on the continent, the fighting brought unprecedented prosperity to the long-suffering landsmen of Ireland, groaning since the twelfth century under the yoke of British rule. For as Europe's fields lay fallow, irrigated only by the blood of its farmers, Ireland fed the hungry armies that ravened for food as well as territory. Irish farmers planted every available acre, interspersing the lowly potato amongst their fields of grain. With prices for food products ever mounting, tenant farmers reaped a temporary respite from their perpetual struggle to remain on the land. Most landlords were satisfied by the prosperity and so relaxed their pressure on tenants; others, stymied by the absence of British police forces that had been stripped of manpower to fight in Europe, had little means to enforce eviction notices.

But the peace that brought solace to battle-scarred Europe changed all this. After 1815 war-inflated wheat prices plummeted by half. Hard-pressed landlords resolved to leave vast fields unplanted. Assisted now by a strengthened British constabulary, they vowed to sweep the pesky peasants from the retired acreage. Many of those forced to leave sought work in England itself; some went to America. Then in 1845, a blight that ravaged the potato crop sounded the final knell for the Irish peasantry. The resultant famine spread desolation throughout the island. In five years, more than a million people died. Another million sailed for America.

Of the emigrants, most were young and literate in English, the majority under thirty-five years old. Families typically pooled money to send strong young sons to the New World, where they would earn wages to pay the fares for those who remained behind. These "famine Irish" mostly remained in the port cities of the Northeast, abandoning the farmer's life for the squalor and congestion of the urban metropolis.

The Irish newcomers had poor preparation indeed for urban life. They found progress up the economic ladder painfully slow. Their work as domestic servants or construction laborers was dull and arduous, and mortality rates were astoundingly high. Escape from the potato famine hardly guaranteed a long life to an Irish-

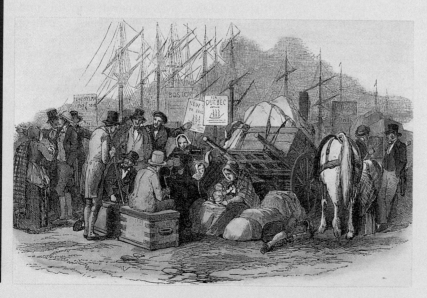

Irish Emigrants Preparing to Leave from Cork, Ireland, c. 1850 (The Granger Collection.)

Irish Pipe-Laying Gang in New Jersey in the 1890s *(Drilling Magazine.)*

Anti-Irish Cartoon Harper's Weekly *published this cartoon in 1883, protesting the British government's practice of "exporting" paupers to America. (Culver Pictures.)*

trust and resentment of their native-born, Protestant American neighbors. The cornerstone of social and religious life for Irish immigrants was the parish. Worries about safeguarding their children's faith inspired the construction of parish schools, financed by the pennies of struggling working-class Irish parents.

If Ireland's green fields scarcely equipped her sons and daughters for the scrap and scramble of economic life in America's cities, life in the old country nevertheless had instilled in them an aptitude for politics. Irish-Catholic resistance against centuries of British Anglican domination had instructed many old-country Irish in the ways of mass politics. That political experience readied them for the boss system of the political "machines" in America's northeastern cities. The boss's local representatives met each newcomer soon after landing in America. Asking only for votes, the machine supplied coal in wintertime, food, and help with the law. Irish voters soon became a bulwark of the Democratic party, reliably supporting the party of Jefferson and Jackson in cities like New York and Boston. As Irish Americans like New York's "Honest John" Kelly themselves became bosses, white-collar jobs in government service opened up to the Irish. They became building inspectors, aldermen, and even policemen—an astonishing irony for a people driven from their homeland by the nightsticks and bayonets of the British police.

American; a gray-bearded Irishman was a rare sight in nineteenth-century America. Most of the new arrivals toiled as day laborers. A fortunate few owned boardinghouses or saloons, where their disspirited countrymen sought solace in the bottle. For Irish-born women, opportunities were still scarcer; they worked mainly as domestic servants.

But it was their Roman Catholicism, more even than their penury or their perceived fondness for alcohol, that earned the Irish the dis-

An early-nineteenth-century French traveler recorded his impressions of America and Ireland: "I have seen the Indian in his forests and the Negro in his chains, and thought, as I contemplated their pitiable condition, that I saw the very extreme of human wretchedness; but I did not then know the condition of unfortunate Ireland."

stock, and equipment—swarmed into the larger seaboard cities. Noteworthy were Boston and particularly New York, which rapidly became the largest Irish city in the world. Before many decades had passed, more people of Hibernian blood lived in America than on the "ould sod" of Erin's Isle.

The luckless Irish received no red-carpet treatment. Forced to live in squalor, they worsened already vile slum conditions. They were scorned by the older American stock, especially "proper" Protestant Bostonians, who regarded the scruffy Catholic newcomers as a social menace. Barely literate "Biddies" (Bridgets) took jobs as kitchen maids. Broad-shouldered "Paddies" (Patricks) were pushed into pick-and-shovel drudgery on canals and railroads, where thousands left their bones as victims of disease and accidental explosions. It was said that an Irishman lay buried under every railroad tie. As wage-depressing competitors for jobs, the Irish were hated by native workers. "No Irish Need Apply" was a sign commonly posted at factory gates and was often abbreviated to NINA. The Irish, for similar reasons, fiercely resented the blacks, with whom they shared society's basement. Race riots between black and Irish dockworkers flared up in several port cities, and the Irish were generally cool to the abolitionist cause.

The friendless "Famine Irish" were forced to fend for themselves. The Ancient Order of Hibernians, a semisecret society founded in Ireland to fight rapacious landlords, served in

Ragged Irish Immigrants Arriving in America   *Bewildered Irish newcomers were often whisked to "boardinghouses"—filthy hovels above a "grog shop" where whiskey flowed and a saucer of free tobacco sat on the bar. The hard-drinking Irish scandalized old-stock Americans, but Boston's Orestes Brownson predicted in 1852: "Out from these . . . dirty streets will come forth some of the noblest sons of our country, whom she will delight to own and honor." (The Granger Collection.)*

America as a benevolent society, aiding the downtrodden. It also helped to spawn the "Molly Maguires," a shadowy Irish miners' union that rocked the Pennsylvania coal districts in the 1860s and 1870s.

The Irish tended to remain in low-skill occupations but gradually improved their lot, usually by acquiring modest amounts of property. The education of children was cut short as families struggled to save money to purchase a home. But for humble Irish peasants, cruelly cast out of their homeland, property ownership counted as a grand "success."

Politics quickly attracted these gregarious Gaelic newcomers. They soon began to gain control of powerful city machines, notably New York's Tammany Hall, and reaped the patronage rewards. Before long, beguilingly brogued Irishmen dominated police departments in many big cities, where they now drove the "Paddy wagons" that had once carted their brawling forebears to jail.

American politicians made haste to cultivate the Irish vote, especially in the politically potent state of New York. Irish hatred of the British lost nothing in the transatlantic transplanting. As the Irish-Americans increased in number—nearly 2 million arrived between 1830 and 1860—officials in Washington glimpsed political gold in those Hibernian hills. Politicians often found it politically profitable to fire verbal volleys at London—a process vulgarly known as "twisting the British lion's tail."

The German Forty-Eighters

The influx of refugees from Germany between 1830 and 1860 was hardly less spectacular than that from Ireland. During these troubled years, over a million and a half Germans stepped onto American soil. (See "Makers of America," pp. 292–293). The bulk of them were uprooted farmers, displaced by crop failures and other hardships. But a strong sprinkling were liberal political refugees. Saddened by the collapse of the democratic revolutions of 1848, they had decided to leave the autocratic fatherland and flee to America—the one brightest hope of democracy.

Germany's loss was America's gain. Zealous German liberals like the lanky and public-spirited Carl Schurz, a relentless foe of slavery and public corruption, contributed richly to the elevation of American political life.

Many of the Germanic newcomers, unlike the Irish, possessed a modest amount of this world's goods. Most of them pushed out to the lush lands of the Middle West, notably Wisconsin, where they settled and established model farms. Like the Irish, they formed an influential body of voters whom American politicians shamelessly wooed. But the Germans were less potent politically because their strength was more widely scattered.

The hand of Germans in shaping American life was widely felt in still other ways. The Conestoga wagon, the Kentucky rifle, and the Christmas tree were all German contributions to American culture. Germans had fled from the militarism and wars of Europe and consequently came to be a bulwark of isolationist sentiment in the upper Mississippi Valley. Better educated on the whole than the stump-grubbing Americans, they warmly supported public schools, including their *Kindergarten* (children's garden). They likewise did much to stimulate art and music. As outspoken champions of freedom, they became relentless enemies of slavery during the fevered years before the Civil War.

Yet the Germans—often dubbed "damned Dutchmen"—were occasionally regarded with suspicion by their old-stock American neighbors. Seeking to preserve their language and culture, they sometimes settled in compact "colonies" and kept aloof from the surrounding community. Accustomed to the "Continental Sunday" and uncurbed by Puritan tradition, they made merry on the Sabbath and drank huge quantities of an amber beverage called *Bier* (beer), which dates its real popularity in America to their coming. Their Old World drinking habits, like those of the Irish newcomers, spurred advocates of greater temperance in the use of alcohol to redouble their reform efforts.

Flare-Ups of Antiforeignism

The invasion by this so-called immigrant "rabble" in the 1840s and 1850s inflamed the hates of American "nativists." They feared that

The Germans

Between 1820 and 1920, a sea of Germans lapped at America's shores and seeped into its very heartland. Their numbers surpassed those of any other immigrant group, even the prolific and detested Irish. Yet this Germanic flood, unlike its Gaelic equivalent, stirred little panic in the hearts of native-born Americans, because the Germans largely stayed to themselves, far from the madding crowds and nativist fears of northeastern cities. They prospered with astonishing ease, building towns in Wisconsin, agricultural colonies in Texas, and religious communities in Pennsylvania. They added a decidedly Germanic flavor to the heady brew of reform and community building that so animated antebellum America.

These "Germans" actually hailed from many different Old World lands, because there was no unified nation of Germany until 1871, when the ruthless and crafty Prussian Otto von Bismarck assembled the German state out of a mosaic of independent principalities, kingdoms, and duchies. Until that time, "Germans" came to America as Prussians, Bavarians, Hessians, Rhinelanders, Pomeranians, and Westphalians. They arrived at different times and for many different reasons. Some, particularly the so-called Forty-Eighters—the refugees from the failed democratic revolution of 1848—hungered for the democracy they had failed to win in Germany. Others, particularly Jews, Pietists, and Anabaptist groups like the Amish and the Mennonites, coveted religious freedom. And they came not only to America. Like the Italians later, many Germans sought their new life in Brazil, Argentina, or Chile. But the largest number ventured into the United States.

Typical German immigrants arrived with fatter purses than their Irish counterparts. Small landowners or independent artisans in their native countries, they did not have to settle for bottom-rung industrial employment in the grimy factories of the Northeast and instead

A German Homestead in Wisconsin *This settler's Germanic heritage is evident in the architecture of the log cabin. Traditional log cabins used log walls right up to the roofline, but the Germans closed their gables with vertical board-and-batten siding. (State Historical Society of Wisconsin.)*

could afford to push on to the open spaces of the American West.

In Wisconsin these immigrants found a home away from home, a place with a climate, soil, and geography much like central Europe's. Milwaukee, a crude frontier town before the Germans' arrival, became the "German Athens." It boasted a German theater, German beer gardens, a German volunteer fire company, and a German-English academy. In distant Texas, German settlements like New Braunfels and Friedrichsburg flourished. When the famous landscape architect and writer Frederick Law Olmsted stumbled upon these prairie outposts of Teutonic culture in 1857, he was shocked to

Amish Country near Lancaster, Pennsylvania
Spurning the modern technologies represented by the gas station behind them, these Amish folk hold fast to their traditional horse-and-buggy ways. (Fred Wilson.)

be "welcomed by a figure in a blue flannel shirt and pendant beard, quoting Tacitus." These German colonies in the frontier Southwest mixed high European elegance with Texas ruggedness. Olmsted described a visit to a German household where the settlers drank "coffee in tin cups upon Dresden saucers" and sat upon "barrels for seats, to hear a Beethoven symphony on the grand piano."

These Germanic colonizers of America's heartland also formed religious communities, none more distinctive or durable than the Amish settlements of Pennsylvania, Indiana, and Ohio. The Amish took their name from their founder and leader, the Swiss Anabaptist Jacob Amman. Like other Anabaptist groups, they shunned extravagance and reserved baptism for adults, repudiating the tradition of infant baptism practiced by most Europeans. For this they were persecuted, even imprisoned, in Europe. Seeking escape from their oppression, a handful of Amish—some five hundred—ventured to Pennsylvania in the 1700s, followed by three thousand in the years from 1815 to 1865.

In America they formed enduring religious communities—isolated enclaves where they could shield themselves from the corruption and the conveniences of the modern world. To this day the German-speaking Amish still travel in horse-drawn carriages and farm without heavy machinery. No electric lights brighten the darkness that nightly envelops their tidy farmhouses; no ringing telephones punctuate the reverent tranquillity of their mealtime prayer; no ornaments relieve the austere simplicity of their black garments. The Amish remain a stalwart, traditional community in a rootless, turbulent society, a living testament to the religious ferment and social experiments of the antebellum era.

Crooked Voting A bitter "nativist" cartoon charging Irish and German immigrants with "stealing" elections. (The Granger Collection.)

these foreign hordes would outbreed, outvote, and overwhelm the old "native" stock. Not only did the newcomers take jobs from "native" Americans, but the bulk of the displaced Irish were Roman Catholics, as were a substantial minority of the Germans. The Church of Rome was still widely regarded by many old-line Americans as a "foreign" church; convents were commonly referred to as "Popish brothels."

Roman Catholics were now on the move. Seeking to protect their children from Protestant indoctrination in the public schools, they began in the 1840s to construct an entirely separate Catholic educational system—an enormously expensive undertaking for a poor immigrant community, but one that revealed the strength of its religious commitment. They had formed a negligible minority during colonial days, and their numbers had increased gradually. But with the enormous influx of the Irish and Germans in the 1840s and 1850s, the Catholics became a powerful religious group. In 1840 they had ranked fifth, behind the Baptists, Methodists, Presbyterians, and Congregationalists. By 1850, with some 1.8 million communicants, they had bounded into first place—a position they have never lost.

"Native" Americans were alarmed by these mounting figures. They professed to believe that in due time the "alien riffraff" would "establish" the Catholic church at the expense of Protestantism and would introduce "Popish idols." The noisier American "nativists" rallied for political action. In 1849 they formed the Order of the Star-Spangled Banner, which soon developed into the formidable American, or "Know-Nothing," party—a name derived from its secretiveness. "Nativists" agitated for rigid restrictions on immigration and naturalization and for laws authorizing the deportation of alien paupers. They also promoted a lurid literature of exposure, much of it pure fiction. The authors, sometimes posing as escaped nuns, described sin as they imagined it behind brick convent walls, including the secret burial of babies. One of these books—Maria Monk's *Awful Disclosures* (1836)—sold over 300,000 copies.

Even uglier was occasional mass violence. As early as 1834 a Catholic convent near Boston was burned by a howling mob, and in ensuing

Strong antiforeignism was reflected in the platform of the American (Know-Nothing) party in 1856: "Americans must rule America; and to this end, native-born citizens should be selected for all state, federal, or municipal offices of government employment, in preference to naturalized citizens."

years there were a few scattered attacks on Catholic schools and churches. The most frightful flare-up occurred during 1844 in Philadelphia, where the Irish Catholics fought back against the threats of the "nativists." The City of Brotherly Love did not quiet down until two Catholic churches had been burned and some thirteen citizens had been killed and fifty wounded in several days of fighting. These outbursts of intolerance, though infrequent and generally localized in the larger cities, remain an unfortunate blot on the record of America's treatment of minority groups.

Immigrants were undeniably making America a more pluralistic society—one of the most ethnically and racially varied in the history of the world—and perhaps it was small wonder that cultural clashes would occur. Why, in fact, were such episodes not even more frequent and more violent? Part of the answer lies in the robustness of the American economy. The vigorous growth of the economy in these years both attracted immigrants in the first place and ensured that, once arrived, they could claim their share of American wealth without decreasing the wealth of others. Their hands and brains, in fact, helped fuel economic expansion. Immigrants and the American economy, in short, needed one another. Without the newcomers, a preponderantly agricultural United States might well have been condemned to watch in envy as the industrial revolution swept through nineteenth-century Europe.

The March of Mechanization

A gifted group of British inventors, beginning about 1750, perfected a series of machines for the mass production of textiles. This enslavement of steam multiplied the power of human muscles some ten thousandfold and ushered in the modern factory system—and with it, the so-called industrial revolution. It was accompanied by a no less spectacular transformation in agricultural production and in the methods of transportation and communication.

The factory system gradually spread from England—"the world's workshop"—to other lands. It took a generation or so to reach western Europe, and then the United States. Why was the youthful American Republic, destined to be an industrial giant, so slow to embrace the machine?

For one thing, virgin soil in America was cheap. Land-starved descendants of land-starved peasants were not going to coop themselves up in smelly factories when they might till their own acres in God's fresh air and sunlight. Labor was therefore generally scarce, and enough nimble hands to operate the machines were hard to find—until immigrants began to pour ashore in the 1840s. Money for capital investment, moreover, was not plentiful in pioneering America. Raw materials lay undeveloped, undiscovered, or unsuspected. The Republic was one day to become the world's leading coal producer, but much of the coal burned in colonial times was imported all the way from England.

Just as labor was scarce, so were consumers. The young country at first lacked a domestic market large enough to make factory-scale manufacturing profitable.

Long-established British factories, which provided cutthroat competition, posed another problem. Their superiority was attested by the fact that a few unscrupulous Yankee manufacturers, out to make a dishonest dollar, learned to stamp their own products with faked English trademarks.

The British also enjoyed a monopoly of the textile machinery, whose secrets they were anxious to hide from foreign competitors. Parliament enacted laws, in harmony with the mercantilistic system, forbidding the export of the machines or the emigration of mechanics able to reproduce them.

Although a number of small manufacturing enterprises existed in the early Republic, the future industrial colossus was still snoring. Not until well past the middle of the nineteenth century did the value of the output of the factories exceed that of the farms.

Whitney Ends the Fiber Famine

Samuel Slater has been acclaimed the "Father of the Factory System" in America, and seldom can the paternity of a movement more properly be ascribed to one person. A skilled British mechanic of twenty-one, he was attracted by bounties being offered to English workers familiar

Eli Whitney (1765–1825) *Few men have been so pivotal in American history. His cotton gin revolutionized southern agriculture, ushering in the Cotton-and-Slave Kingdom of the early nineteenth century. His system of interchangeable parts revolutionized northern industry, giving the North economic and technological superiority in the Civil War that ultimately extinguished slavery. (Yale University Art Gallery, Gift of George Hoadley, B. A. 1801.)*

Whitney's Cotton Gin *Shown here as it was pictured in Whitney's application for a U.S. patent, the gin was artfully simple. Wire brushes on a rotating wheel pulled the cotton fibers through slots too narrow to allow seeds to pass. A second set of brushes removed the fibers. Whitney's gin made possible the mass cultivation of upland or short-staple cotton, which was unprofitable to raise when its seeds had to be laboriously removed by hand. Before Whitney's invention, cotton-growing had been largely confined to long-staple or Sea Island cotton, which could only grow in hot, humid coastal areas; now short-staple cotton cultivation spread across the southern interior and so did slavery. (Eli Whitney Museum.)*

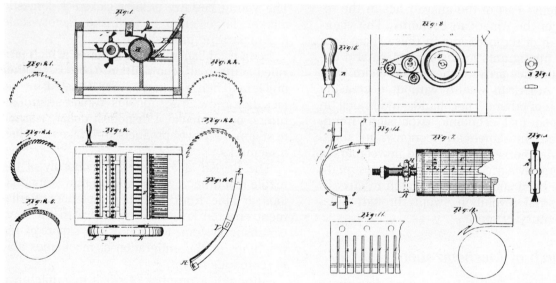

with the textile machines. After memorizing the plans for the machinery, he escaped in disguise to America, where he won the backing of Moses Brown, a Quaker capitalist in Rhode Island. Laboriously reconstructing the essential apparatus with the aid of a blacksmith and a carpenter, he put into operation in 1791 the first efficient American machinery for spinning cotton thread.

The ravenous mechanism was now ready, but where was the cotton fiber? Handpicking 1 pound (0.45 kilogram) of lint from 3 pounds

(1.36 kilograms) of seed was a full day's work for one slave, and this process was so expensive that cotton cloth was relatively rare.

Another mechanical genius, Massachusetts-born Eli Whitney, now made his mark. After graduating from Yale College, he journeyed to Georgia to serve as a private tutor while preparing for the law. There he was told that the poverty of the South would be relieved if someone could only invent a workable device for separating the seed from the short-staple cotton fiber. Within ten days, in 1793, he constructed a crude machine called the cotton gin (short for en*gine*) that was fifty times more effective than the handpicking process.

Few machines have ever wrought so wondrous a change. The gin affected not only the history of America but that of the world. Almost overnight the raising of cotton became highly profitable, and the South was tied hand and foot to the throne of King Cotton. Human bondage had been dying out, but the insatiable demand for cotton reriveted the chains on the limbs of the luckless southern blacks.

South and North both prospered. Slave-driving planters cleared more acres for cotton, pushing the Cotton Kingdom westward off the depleted tidewater plains, over the Piedmont, and onto the black loam bottomlands of Alabama and Mississippi. Humming gins poured out avalanches of snowy fiber for the spindles of the Yankee machines, though for decades to come the mills of England bought the lion's share of southern cotton. The American phase of the industrial revolution, which first blossomed in cotton textiles, was well on its way.

Factories at first flourished most actively in New England, though branching out into the more populous areas of New York, New Jersey, and Pennsylvania. The South, increasingly wedded to the production of cotton, could boast of comparatively little manufacturing. Its capital was bound up in slaves; its local consumers for the most part were desperately poor.

New England was singularly favored as an industrial center for several reasons. Its narrow belt of stony soil discouraged farming and hence made manufacturing more attractive than elsewhere. A relatively dense population provided labor and accessible markets; shipping brought in capital; and snug seaports made easy the import of raw materials and the export of the finished products. Finally, the rapid rivers—notably the Merrimack in Massachusetts—provided abundant water power to turn the cogs of the machines. By 1860, more than 400 million pounds (182,000 metric tons) of southern cotton poured annually into the gaping maws of over a thousand mills, mostly in New England.

America's First Textile Mill   This rude "factory," established by Samuel Slater in the 1790s at Pawtucket, Rhode Island, drew its power from the falls of the Blackstone River. The mill at first only produced yarn, which was then distributed to home weavers who turned it into cloth. (Slater Mill Historic Site.)

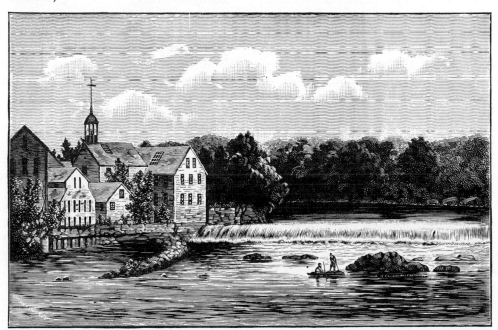

One observer in 1836 published a newspaper account of conditions in some of the New England factories: "The operatives work thirteen hours a day in the summer time, and from daylight to dark in the winter. At half past four in the morning the factory bell rings, and at five the girls must be in the mills. . . . So fatigued . . . are numbers of girls that they go to bed soon after receiving their evening meal, and endeavor by a comparatively long sleep to resuscitate their weakened frames for the toil of the coming day."

Marvels in Manufacturing

America's factories spread slowly until about 1807, when there began the fateful sequence of the embargo, nonintercourse, and the War of 1812. Stern necessity dictated the manufacture of substitutes for normal imports, while the stoppage of European commerce was temporarily ruinous to Yankee shipping. Both capital and labor were driven from the waves onto the factory floor, as New England, in the striking phrase of John Randolph, exchanged the trident for the distaff. Generous bounties were offered by local authorities for homegrown goods; "Buy American" and "Wear American" became popular slogans; and patriotism prompted the wearing of baggy homespun garments. President Madison donned some at his inauguration, where he was said to have been a walking argument for the better processing of native wool.

But the manufacturing boomlet broke abruptly with the peace of Ghent in 1815. British competitors unloaded their dammed-up surpluses at ruinously low prices, and American newspapers were so full of British advertisements for goods on credit that little space was left for news. In one Rhode Island district, all 150 mills were forced to close their doors, except the original Slater plant. Responding to pained outcries, Congress provided some relief when it passed the mildly protective Tariff of 1816—among the earliest political contests to control the shape of the economy.

As the factory system flourished, it embraced numerous other industries in addition to textiles. Prominent among them was the manufacturing of firearms, and here the wizardly Eli Whitney again appeared with an epochal contribution. Frustrated in his earlier efforts to monopolize the cotton gin, he turned to the mass production of muskets for the U.S. Army. Up to this time each part of a firearm had been hand-tooled, and if the trigger of one broke, the trigger of another might or might not fit. About 1798 Whitney seized upon the idea of having machines make each part, so that all the triggers, for example, would be as much alike as the successive imprints of a copperplate engraving. Journeying to Washington, he reportedly dismantled ten of his new muskets in the presence of skeptical officials, scrambled the parts together, and then quickly reassembled ten different muskets.

The principle of interchangeable parts was widely adopted by 1850, and it ultimately became the basis of modern mass-production, assembly-line methods. It gave to the North the vast industrial plant that ensured military preponderance over the South. The Yankee Eli Whitney, by perfecting the cotton gin, gave slavery a renewed lease on life and perhaps made inevitable the Civil War. The same Whitney, by popularizing the principle of interchangeable parts, caused factories to flourish in the North and contributed heavily to the winning of that war by the Union.

The sewing machine, invented by Elias Howe in 1846 and perfected by Isaac Singer, gave another strong boost to northern industrialization. The sewing machine became the foundation of the ready-made clothing industry, which took root about the time of the Civil War. It drove many a seamstress from the shelter of the private home to the factory where, like a human robot, she tended the clattering mechanisms.

Each momentous new invention seemed to stimulate still more imaginative inventions. For the decade ending in 1800 only 306 patents were registered in Washington, but the decade ending in 1860 saw the amazing total of 28,000. Yet in 1838 the clerk of the Patent Office had resigned in despair, complaining that all worthwhile inventions had been discovered.

Technical advances spurred equally important changes in the form and legal status of business organizations. The principle of limited liability aided the concentration of capital by permitting the individual investor, in cases of legal claims or bankruptcy, to risk no more than his own share of the corporation's stock. Laws of "free incorporation," first passed in New York in 1848, meant that businessmen could create corporations without applying for individual charters from the legislature.

Samuel F. B. Morse's telegraph was among the inventions that tightened the sinews of an increasingly complex business world. A distinguished but poverty-stricken portrait painter, Morse finally secured from Congress, to the accompaniment of the usual jeers, an appropriation of $30,000 to support his experiment with "talking wires." In 1844 Morse strung a wire 40 miles (64 kilometers) from Washington to Baltimore, and tapped out the historic message, "What hath God wrought?" The invention brought fame and fortune to Morse, as he put distantly separated people in almost instant communication with one another.

Workers and "Wage Slaves"

One ugly offspring of the factory system was an increasingly acute labor problem. Hitherto manufacturing had been done in the home, or in the small shop, where the master craftsman and his apprentice, rubbing elbows at the same bench, could maintain an intimate and friendly relationship. The industrial revolution submerged this personal association in the impersonal ownership of stuffy factories in "spindle cities." Around these, like tumors, the slumlike hovels of the "wage slaves" tended to cluster.

Clearly the early factory system did not shower its benefits evenly on all. While many owners waxed fat, workingpeople often wasted away at their workbenches. Hours were long, wages were low, and meals were skimpy and hastily gulped. Workers were forced to toil in

> "The patent system," said Abraham Lincoln in a lecture in 1859, ". . . secured to the inventor for a limited time exclusive use of his invention, and thereby added the fuel of interest to the fire of genius in the discovery and production of new and useful things." Ten years earlier Lincoln had received patent No. 6469 for a scheme to buoy steamboats over shoals. It was never practically applied, but he remains the only president ever to have secured a patent.

unsanitary buildings that were poorly ventilated, lighted, and heated. They were forbidden by law to form labor unions to raise wages, for such cooperative activity was regarded as a criminal conspiracy. Not surprisingly, only twenty-four recorded strikes occurred before 1835.

Especially vulnerable to exploitation were child workers. In 1820, half the nation's indus-

Elias Howe's First Sewing Machine *The young Republic often lacked the money to match the genius of its inventors, and Howe had to travel to England to secure the financial backing necessary to turn his revolutionary invention to practical use. (National Museum of History and Technology, Smithsonian Institution, Washington, D.C.)*

The Master Craftsman *Dignity and pride of workmanship are evident in this tidy wheelwright's shop. Small-scale, intimate workplaces like this were eventually overshadowed by the mass-production, impersonal factory system, as in the illustration on p. 304. (Collection of E. F. Fisher.)*

trial toilers were children under ten years of age. Victims of factory labor, many children were mentally blighted, emotionally starved, physically stunted, and even brutally whipped in special "whipping rooms." In Samuel Slater's mill of 1791, the first machine tenders were seven boys and two girls, all of whom were under twelve years of age.

By contrast, the lot of most adult wage workers improved markedly in the 1820s and 1830s. In the full flush of Jacksonian democracy, many of the states granted the laboring man the vote. Brandishing the ballot, he first strove to lighten his burden through workingmen's parties. Aside from such goals as the ten-hour day, higher wages, and tolerable working conditions, he demanded public education for his children and an end to the inhuman practice of imprisonment for debt.

Employers, abhorring the rise of the "rabble" in politics, fought the ten-hour day to the last

ditch. They argued that reduced hours would lessen production, increase costs, and demoralize the workers. Laborers would have so much leisure time that the Devil would lead them into mischief. A red-letter gain was at length registered for labor in 1840, when President Van Buren established the ten-hour day for federal employees on public works. In ensuing years a number of states gradually fell into line by reducing the hours of workingpeople.

Day laborers at last learned that their strongest weapon was to lay down their tools, even at the risk of prosecution under the law. Dozens of strikes erupted in the 1830s and 1840s, most of them for higher wages, some for the ten-hour day, and a few for such unusual goals as the right to smoke on the job. The workers usually lost more strikes than they won, for the employer could resort to such tactics as the importing of strikebreakers—often derisively called "scabs" or "rats," and often

Textile Workers of Lawrence (Massachusetts) *Engraving by Winslow Homer, a famous painter. Born in Boston in 1836, Homer first became famous as a magazine illustrator. His drawings of battlefield scenes for* Harper's Weekly *during the Civil War made the conflict come to life for thousands of home-bound readers. He abandoned illustration in 1876 and gained even greater renown as a painter in oils and watercolors, especially with his depictions of marine scenes and life among blacks. (*Harper's Weekly, *1868.)*

fresh off the boat from the Old World. Labor long raised its voice against the unrestricted in-pouring of wage-depressing and union-busting immigrant workers.

Labor's early and painful efforts at organization had netted some 300,000 trade unionists by 1830. But such encouraging gains were dashed

Violence broke out along the New York water-front in 1836 when laborers striking for higher wages attacked "scabs." "The Mayor," Philip Hone's diary records, "who acts with vigour and firmness, ordered out the troops, who are now on duty with loaded arms. . . . These measures have restored order for the present, but I fear the elements of disorder are at work; the bands of Irish and other foreigners, instigated by the mischievous councils of the trades-union and other combinations of discontented men, are acquiring strength and importance which will ere long be difficult to quell."

on the rocks of hard times following the severe depression of 1837. As unemployment spread, union membership shriveled. Yet toilers won a hope-giving legal victory in 1842. The supreme court of Massachusetts ruled in the case of *Commonwealth* v. *Hunt* that labor unions were not illegal conspiracies, provided that their methods were "honorable and peaceful." This enlightened decision did not legalize the strike overnight throughout the country, but it was a significant signpost of the times. Trade unions still had a rocky row to hoe, stretching ahead for about a century, before they could meet man-agement on relatively even terms.

Women and the Economy

Women were also sucked into the clanging mechanism of factory production. They typi-cally toiled six days a week, earning a pittance for dreary stints of twelve or thirteen hours—"from dark to dark." The Boston Associates pridefully pointed to their textile mill at Lowell,

Massachusetts, as a showplace factory. The workers were virtually all New England farm girls, carefully supervised on and off the job by watchful matrons. Escorted regularly to church from their company boardinghouses, forbidden to form unions, they were as disciplined and docile a labor force as any employer could wish.

But factory jobs of any kind were still unusual for women. Opportunities for women to be economically self-supporting were scarce and consisted mainly of nursing, domestic service, and especially teaching. The dedicated Catharine Beecher, unmarried daughter of a famous preacher and sister of Harriet Beecher Stowe, tirelessly urged women to enter the teaching profession. She eventually succeeded beyond her dreams, as men left teaching for other lines of work and schoolteaching became a thoroughly "feminized" occupation. Other work "opportunities" for women beckoned in household service. Perhaps one white family in ten employed servants at midcentury, most of whom were poor white, immigrant, or black women. About 10 percent of white women were

working for pay outside their own homes in 1850, and estimates are that about 20 percent of all women had been employed at some time prior to marriage.

The vast majority of working women were single. Upon marriage, they left their paying jobs and took up their new work (without wages) as wives and mothers. In the home they were enshrined in a "cult of domesticity," a widespread cultural creed that glorified the traditional functions of the homemaker. From their pedestal, married women commanded immense moral power, and they increasingly made decisions that altered the character of the family itself.

Women's changing roles and the spreading industrial revolution brought some important changes in the life of the nineteenth-century home—the traditional "women's sphere." Love, not parental "arrangement," more and more frequently determined the choice of a spouse—yet parents often retained the power of veto. Families thus became more closely knit and affectionate, providing the emotional refuge that

The Woman's Sphere   *This 1845 sketch of life on a Virginia plantation suggests the clear division of labor between men and women in the nineteenth-century American family. (Kennedy Gallery, New York.)*

made the threatening impersonality of big-city industrialism tolerable to many people.

Most striking, families grew smaller. The average household had nearly six members at the end of the eighteenth century but fewer than five members a century later. The "fertility rate," or number of births among women aged 14 to 45, dropped sharply among white women in the years after the Revolution and, in the course of the nineteenth century as a whole, fell by half. Birth control was still a taboo topic for polite conversation, and contraceptive technology was primitive, but clearly some form of family limitation was being practiced quietly and effectively in countless families, rural and urban alike. Women undoubtedly played a large part—perhaps the leading part—in decisions to have fewer children. This newly assertive role for women has been called "domestic feminism," because it signified the growing power and independence of women, even while they remained trapped in the "cult of domesticity."

Smaller families, in turn, meant child-centered families, since where children are fewer, parents can lavish more care on them individually. European visitors to the United States in the nineteenth century often complained about the unruly behavior of American "brats." But though American parents may have increasingly spared the rod, they did not spoil their children. Lessons were enforced by punishments other than the hickory stick. When the daughter of novelist Harriet Beecher Stowe neglected to do her homework, her mother sent her from the dinner table and gave her "only bread and water in her own apartment." What Europeans saw as permissiveness was in reality the consequence of an emerging new idea of child rearing, in which the child's will was not to be simply broken, but shaped. In the little republic of the family, as in the Republic at large, good citizens were raised not to be meekly obedient to authority, but to be independent individuals who could make their own decisions on the basis of internalized moral standards. Thus, the outlines of the "modern" family were clear by midcentury: it was small, affectionate, child-centered, and provided a special arena for the talents of women. Feminists of a later day might decry the stifling atmosphere of the Vic-

torian home, but to many women of the time it seemed a big step upward from the conditions of grinding toil—often alongside men in the fields—in which their mothers had lived.

Western Farmers Reap a Revolution in the Fields

As smoke-belching factories altered the eastern skyline, flourishing farms were changing the face of the West. The trans-Allegheny region—especially the Ohio-Indiana-Illinois tier—was fast becoming the nation's breadbasket. Before long, it would become a granary to the world.

Pioneer farmers first hacked a clearing out of the forest and then planted their painfully furrowed fields to corn. The yellow grain was amazingly versatile. It could be fed to hogs ("corn on the hoof") or distilled into liquor ("corn in the bottle"). Both these products could be more easily transported than the bulky grain itself, and they became the early western farmer's staple market items. So many hogs were butchered, traded, or shipped at Cincinnati that the city was known as the "Porkopolis" of the West.

Most western produce was at first floated down the Ohio-Mississippi river system, to feed the lusty appetite of the booming Cotton Kingdom. But western farmers were as hungry for profits as southern slaves and planters were for food. These soil-tillers, spurred on by the easy availability of seemingly boundless acres, sought ways to bring more and more land into cultivation.

Ingenious inventors came to their aid. One of the first obstacles that frustrated the farmers was the thickly matted soil of the West, which snagged and snapped fragile wooden plows. John Deere of Illinois in 1837 finally produced a steel plow that broke the virgin soil. Sharp and effective, it was also light enough to be pulled by horses, rather than oxen.

In the 1830s Virginia-born Cyrus McCormick contributed the most wondrous contraption of all: a mechanical mower-reaper. The clattering cogs of McCormick's horse-drawn machine were to the western farmers what the cotton gin was to the southern planters. Seated on his red-

McCormick Reaper Works, 1850s *Contrast this scene of "Mass Production" with the workplace depicted in "The Master Craftsman" on p. 300. (McCormick Collection, State Historical Society of Wisconsin.)*

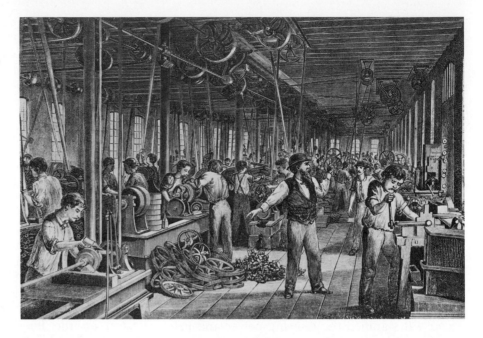

chariot reaper, a single husbandman could do the work of five men with sickles and scythes.

No other American invention cut so wide a swath. It made ambitious capitalists out of humble plowmen, who now scrambled for more acres on which to plant more fields of billowing wheat. Subsistence farming gave way to production for the market, as large-scale ("extensive"), specialized, cash-crop agriculture came to dominate the trans-Allegheny West.

With it followed mounting indebtedness, as farmers bought more land and more machinery to work it. Soon hustling farmer-businesspeople were annually harvesting a larger crop than the South—which was becoming self-sufficient in food production—could devour. They began to dream of markets elsewhere—in the mushrooming factory towns of the East, or across the faraway Atlantic. But they were still largely landlocked. Commerce moved north and south

McCormick's Miraculous Reaper *This illustration shows an early test of Cyrus McCormick's mechanical reaper near his home in Virginia in 1831. The reaper was best suited, however, to the horizonless fields of wheat on the rolling prairies of the Midwest; by the 1850s McCormick's Chicago factory was cranking out more than 20,000 reapers a year for midwestern farmers. (Chicago Historical Society.)*

on the river systems. Before it could begin to move east-west in bulk, a transportation revolution would have to occur.

Highways and Steamboats

In 1789, when the Constitution was launched, primitive methods of travel were still in use. Waterborne commerce, whether along the coast or on the rivers, was slow, uncertain, and often dangerous. Stagecoaches and wagons lurched over bone-shaking roads. Passengers would be routed out to lay nearby fence rails across muddy stretches, and occasionally horses would drown in muddy pits while wagons sank slowly out of sight.

Cheap and efficient carriers were imperative if raw materials were to be transported to the factories and if the finished product were to be delivered to the consumer. On December 3, 1803, a firm in Providence, Rhode Island, sent a shipment of yarn to a point 60 miles (97 kilometers) away, notifying the purchaser that the consignment could be expected to arrive in "the course of the winter."

A promising change for the better came in the 1790s, when a private company completed the Lancaster turnpike in Pennsylvania. It was a broad, hard-surfaced highway that thrust 62 miles (100 kilometers) westward, from Philadelphia to Lancaster. As drivers approached the toll gate, they were confronted with a barrier of sharp pikes, which were turned aside when they paid their toll. Hence, the term *turnpike*.

The Lancaster Pike proved to be a highly successful venture, returning as high as 15 percent annual dividends to its stockholders. It attracted a rich trade to Philadelphia and touched off a turnpike-building boom that lasted about twenty years. It also stimulated western development. The turnpikes beckoned to the canvas-covered Conestoga wagons, whose creakings heralded a westward advance that would know no real retreat.

Western road building, always expensive, encountered many obstacles. Looming large among them were the noisy states' righters, who opposed federal aid to local projects. Eastern states also protested against being bled of their populations by the westward-reaching arteries.

Westerners scored a notable triumph in 1811 when the federal government began to construct the elongated National Road, or Cumberland Road. This highway ultimately stretched from Cumberland, in western Maryland, to Vandalia, in Illinois, a distance of 591 miles (952 kilometers). The War of 1812 interrupted construction, and states' rights shackles on internal improvements hampered federal grants. But the thoroughfare was belatedly brought to its destination, in 1852, by a combination of aid from the states and the federal government.

The steamboat craze, which overlapped the turnpike craze, was touched off by an ambitious painter-engineer named Robert Fulton. He installed a powerful steam engine in a vessel that posterity came to know as the *Clermont* but that a dubious public dubbed "Fulton's Folly." On a

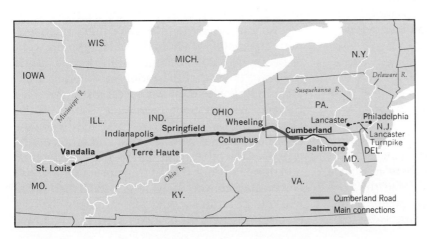

Cumberland (National) Road and Main Connections

historic day in 1807, the quaint little ship, belching sparks from its single smokestack, churned steadily from New York City up the Hudson River toward Albany. It made the run of 150 miles (242 kilometers) in 32 hours.

The success of the steamboat was sensational. People could now in large degree defy wind, wave, tide, and downstream current. Within a few years Fulton had changed all of America's navigable streams into two-way arteries, thereby doubling their carrying capacity. Hitherto keelboats had been pushed up the Mississippi, with quivering poles and raucous profanity, at less than one mile an hour—a process that was prohibitively costly. Now the steamboats could churn rapidly against the current, ultimately attaining speeds in excess of 10 miles (16 kilometers) an hour. The mighty Mississippi had now met its master.

By 1820 there were some sixty steamboats on the Mississippi and its tributaries; by 1860, about one thousand, some of them luxurious river palaces. Keen rivalry among the swift and gaudy steamers led to memorable races. Excited passengers would urge the captain to pile on wood at the risk of bursting the boilers, which all too often exploded with tragic results for the floating firetraps.

Chugging steamboats played a vital role in the opening of the West and South, both of which were richly endowed with navigable rivers. Like bunches of grapes on a vine, population clustered along the banks of the broad-flowing streams. Cotton growers and other farmers made haste to take up the now-profitable virgin soil. Not only could they float their produce out to market but, hardly less important, they could ship in at low cost their shoes, hardware, and other manufactured necessities.

"Clinton's Big Ditch" in New York

A canal-cutting craze paralleled the boom in turnpikes and steamboats. A few canals had been built around falls and elsewhere in colonial days, but ambitious projects lay in the future. Resourceful New Yorkers, cut off from federal aid by states' righters, themselves dug

the Erie Canal, linking the Great Lakes with the Hudson River. They were blessed with the driving leadership of Governor DeWitt Clinton, whose grandiose project was scoffingly called "Clinton's Big Ditch" or "the Governor's Gutter."

Begun in 1817, the canal eventually ribboned 363 miles (585 kilometers). On its completion in 1825, a garland-bedecked canal boat glided from Buffalo, on Lake Erie, to the Hudson River and on to New York harbor. There, with colorful ceremony, Governor Clinton emptied a cask of water from the lake to symbolize "the marriage of the waters."

The water from Clinton's cask baptized an Empire State. Mule-drawn passengers and bulky freight could now be handled with cheapness and dispatch, at the dizzy speed of 5 miles (8 kilometers) an hour. The cost of shipping a ton of grain from Buffalo to New York City fell from $100 to $5, and the time of transit from about twenty days to six.

Ever-widening economic ripples followed the completion of the Erie Canal. The value of land along the route skyrocketed, and new cities—such as Rochester and Syracuse—blossomed. Industry in the state boomed. The new profitableness of farming in the Old Northwest —notably in Ohio, Michigan, Indiana, Illinois— attracted thousands of European immigrants to the unaxed and untaxed lands now available. Flotillas of steamships soon plied the Great Lakes, connecting with canal barges at Buffalo. Interior waterside villages like Cleveland, Detroit, and Chicago exploded into mighty cities.

Other profound economic and political changes followed the completion of the canal. The price of potatoes in New York City was cut in half, and many dispirited New England farmers, no longer able to face this ruinous competition, abandoned their rocky holdings and went elsewhere. Some became mill hands, thus speeding the industrialization of America. Others, finding it easy to go west over the Erie Canal, took up new farmlands south of the Great Lakes, where they were joined by countless thousands of New Yorkers and other northerners. Still others shifted to fruit, vegetable, and dairy farming. These transformations in the Northeast showed how long-established local market structures could be swamped by the emerging behemoth of a continental economy.

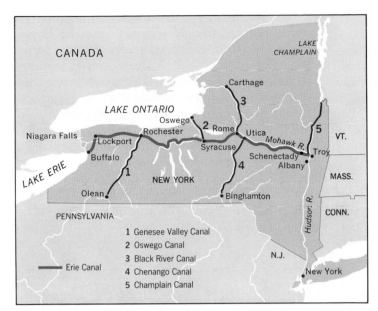

Erie Canal and Main Branches *The Erie Canal system, and others like it, tapped the fabulous agricultural potential of the Midwest, while canal construction and maintenance provided employment for displaced eastern farmers squeezed off the land by competition from their more productive midwestern cousins. The transportation revolution thus simultaneously expanded the nation's acreage under cultivation and speeded the shift of the work force from agricultural to manufacturing and "service" occupations. In 1820 more than three-quarters of American workers labored on farms; by 1850 only a little more than half of them were so employed.*

A Set of Locks on the Erie Canal *An engineering marvel, it had to raise boats 571 feet (174 meters) from the Hudson to Lake Erie. Thousands of laborers died of afflictions ranging from malaria to snakebite—conspicuously Irish immigrant laborers, some of whom worked for $37\frac{1}{2}$ cents an hour plus whiskey. (Courtesy of the New-York Historical Society, New York City.)*

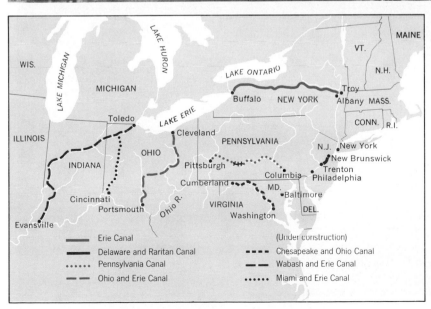

Principal Canals in 1840 *Note that the canals mainly facilitated east-west traffic, especially along the great Lake Erie artery. No comparable network of canals existed in the South—a disparity that helps to explain Northern superiority in the Civil War that came two decades later.*

Pioneer Railroad Promoters

The most significant contribution to the development of such an economy proved to be the railroad. It was fast, reliable, cheaper than canals to construct, and not frozen over in winter. Able to go almost anywhere, even through the Allegheny barrier, it defied terrain and weather. The first railroad appeared in the United States in 1828. By 1860, only thirty-two years later, the United States boasted 30,000 miles (48,000 kilometers) of railroad track, three-fourths of it in the rapidly industrializing North.

At first the railroad faced strong opposition from vested interests, especially canal backers. Anxious to protect its investment in the Erie Canal, the New York legislature in 1833 prohibited the railroads from carrying freight—at least temporarily. Early railroads were also considered a dangerous public menace, for sparks set fire to haystacks and houses, and appalling accidents turned the wooden "miniature hells" into flaming funeral pyres for their riders.

Railroad pioneers had to overcome other obstacles as well. Brakes were so feeble that the engineer might miss the station twice, both arriving and backing up. Arrivals and departures were conjectural, and numerous differences in gauge (the distance between the rails) meant frequent changes of trains for passengers. In 1840 there were seven transfers between Philadelphia and Charleston. But gauges gradually became standardized, safety devices were adopted, and the Pullman "sleeping palace" was introduced in 1859. America at long last was being bound together with ribs of iron, later to be made of steel.

The Transport Web Binds the Union

More than anything else, the desire of the East to tap the West stimulated the "transportation revolution." Until about 1830, the produce of the western region drained southward to the

The Stourbridge Lion *On August 8, 1829, at Honesdale, Pennsylvania, this smoke-belching beast made the first successful trip in America by a steam locomotive. (The Bettmann Archive.)*

Railroads in Operation in 1850

Railroads in Operation in 1860 Note concentration in North.

cotton belt or to the heaped-up wharves of New Orleans. The steamboat vastly aided the reverse flow of finished goods up the watery western arteries and helped bind West and South together. But the truly revolutionary changes in commerce and communication came in the three decades before the Civil War, as canals and railroad tracks radiated out from the East, across the Alleghenies and into the blossoming heartland. The ditchdiggers and tie-layers were attempting nothing less than a conquest of nature itself. They would offset the "natural" flow of trade on the interior rivers by laying down an impressive grid of "internal improvements."

The builders succeeded beyond their wildest dreams. The Mississippi was increasingly robbed of its traffic, as goods moved eastward on chugging trains, puffing lake boats, and mule-tugged canal barges. Governor Clinton had in effect picked up the mighty Father of Waters and flung it over the Alleghenies, forcing it to empty into the sea at New York City. By the 1840s the city of Buffalo handled more western produce than New Orleans. Between 1836 and 1860, grain shipments through Buffalo increased a staggering sixtyfold. New York City became the seaboard queen of the nation, a gigantic port through which a vast hinterland

poured its wealth and to which it daily paid economic tribute.

By the eve of the Civil War, a truly continental economy had emerged. The principle of division of labor, which spelled productivity and profits in the factory, applied on a national scale as well. Each region now specialized in a particular type of economic activity. The South raised cotton for export to New England and old England; the West grew grain and livestock to feed factory workers in the East and in Europe; the East made machines and textiles for the other two regions.

The economic pattern thus woven had fateful political and military implications. Many southerners regarded the Mississippi as a silver chain that naturally linked together the upper valley states and the Cotton Kingdom. They were convinced, as secession approached, that some or all of these states would have to secede with them or be strangled. But they overlooked the man-made links that now bound the upper Mississippi Valley to the East in intimate commercial union. Southern rebels would have to fight not only Northern armies but the tight bonds of an interdependent continental economy. Economically, the two northerly sections were Siamese twins.

The Levee at New Orleans With the expansion of cotton-growing into the new states of the trans-Appalachian Southwest, and the coming of the steamboat, the entire Cotton Kingdom paid economic tribute to New Orleans, Queen City of the South. (The Granger Collection.)

The emergence of a specialized, continental-scale economy also had far-reaching social effects. As more and more Americans—mill hands as well as farmers, women as well as men—linked their economic fate to the burgeoning market economy, the self-sufficient households of colonial days were transformed. Most families had once raised all their own food, spun their own wool, and bartered with their neighbors for the few necessities they could not make themselves. In growing numbers, they now scattered to work for wages in the mills, or they planted just a few crops for sale at market and used the money to buy goods made by strangers in far-off factories. As store-bought fabrics, candles, and soap replaced homemade products, a quiet revolution occurred in the household division of labor and status. Traditional women's work was rendered superfluous and devalued. The home itself, once a center of economic production in which all family members cooperated, grew into a place of refuge from the world of work, a refuge that became increasingly the special and separate sphere of women.

Wealth and Poverty

Revolutionary advances in manufacturing and transportation brought increased prosperity to all Americans, but they also widened the gulf between the rich and the poor. Millionaires had been rare in the early days of the Republic, but by the eve of the Civil War several specimens of colossal financial success were strutting across the national stage. Spectacular was the case of fur trader and real estate speculator John Jacob Astor, who left an estate of $30 million on his death in 1848.

Cities bred the greatest extremes of economic inequality. Unskilled workers, then as always, fared worst. Many of them came to make up a floating mass of "drifters," buffeted from

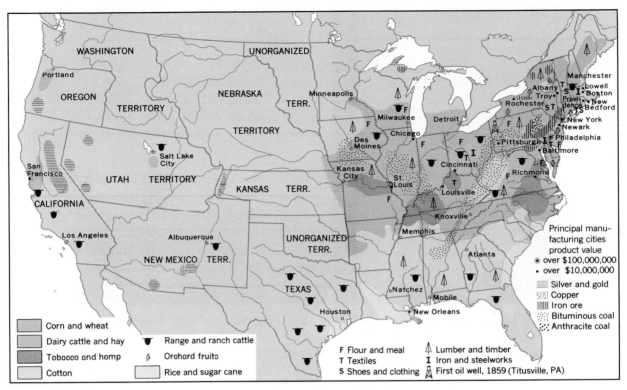

Industry and Agriculture, 1860 *Still a nation of farmers on the eve of the Civil War, Americans had nevertheless made an impressive start on their own industrial revolution, especially in the Northeast.*

town to town by the shifting prospects for menial jobs. These wandering workers accounted at various times for up to half the population of the brawling industrial centers. Though their numbers were large, they left little behind them but the homely fruits of their transient labor. Largely unstoried and unsung, they are among the forgotten men and women of American history.

Many myths about "social mobility" grew up over the buried memories of these unfortunate day laborers. Mobility did exist in industrializing America—but not in the proportions that legend often portrays. Rags-to-riches success stories were relatively few.

Yet America, with its dynamic society and wide-open spaces, undoubtedly provided more "opportunity" than did the contemporary countries of the Old World—which is why millions of immigrants packed their bags and headed for New World shores. Moreover, a rising tide lifts all boats, and the improvement in overall standards of living was real. Wages for unskilled workers in a labor-hungry America rose about 1 percent a year from 1820 to 1860. This general prosperity helped defuse the potential class conflict that might otherwise have exploded—and that did explode in many European countries.

Cables, Clippers, and Pony Riders

A new pattern of American foreign trade also emerged in the antebellum years, though businessmen concentrated on developing the wondrously rewarding domestic market. (Foreign commerce seldom added up to more than 7 percent of the national product.) Abroad as at home, cotton was king and regularly accounted for more than half the value of all American exports. After the repeal of the British exclusionary Corn Laws in 1846, the wheat gathered by McCor-

A Clipper Ship *(The Peabody Museum of Salem, Massachusetts, photo by Mark Sexton.)*

Fur Traders Descending the Missouri, 1844 *Missourian George Caleb Bingham captured in this painting a moment of calm in the usually strenuous life of the rough-and-tumble fur traders. The fragile dugout canoe on the ominously placid water, the tethered animal in the bow, and the recently shot duck (contrasted with the flock on the wing in the distant sky) evoke the pioneer's relentless battle with nature. (The Metropolitan Museum of Art, Morris K. Jesup Fund, 1933.)*

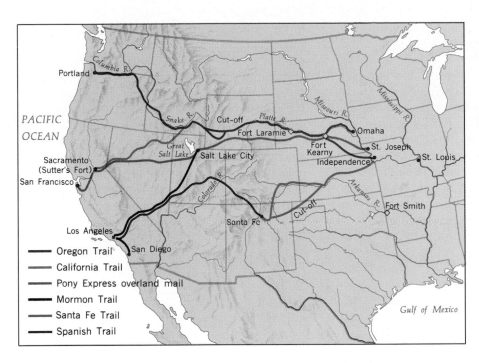

Main Routes West Before the Civil War *Mark Twain described his stagecoach trip to California in the 1860s:*

We began to get into country, now, threaded here and there with little streams. These had high, steep banks on each side, and every time we flew down one bank and scrambled up the other, our party inside got mixed somewhat. First we would all be down in a pile at the forward end of the stage, . . . and in a second we would shoot to the other end, and stand on our heads. And . . . as the dust rose from the tumult, we would all sneeze in chorus, and the majority of us would grumble, and probably say some hasty thing, like: "Take your elbow out of my ribs!—can't you quit crowding?"

mick's reapers began to play an increasingly important role in trade with Great Britain. Americans generally exported agricultural products and imported manufactured goods—and they generally imported more than they exported.

A crucial step came in 1858 when Cyrus Field, called "the greatest wire puller in history," finally stretched a cable under the deep North Atlantic waters from Newfoundland to Ireland. Although this initial cable went dead after three weeks of public rejoicing, a heavier cable laid in 1866 permanently linked the American and European continents.

The United States merchant marine encountered rough sailing during much of the early nineteenth century. American vessels had been repeatedly laid up by the embargo, the War of 1812, and the panics of 1819 and 1837. American naval designers made few contributions to

As late as 1877 stagecoach passengers were advised in print: "Never shoot on the road as the noise might frighten the horses. . . . Don't point out where murders have been committed, especially if there are women passengers. . . . Expect annoyances, discomfort, and some hardships."

maritime progress. A pioneer American steamer, the *Savannah*, had crept across the Atlantic in 1819, but it used sail most of the time and was pursued for a day by a British captain who thought it afire.

In the 1840s and 1850s a golden age dawned for American shipping. Yankee naval yards, notably Donald McKay's at Boston, began to send down the ways sleek new craft called clipper ships. Long, narrow, and majestic, they glided across the sea under towering masts and clouds of canvas. In a fair breeze they could outrun any steamer.

The stately clippers sacrificed cargo space for speed, and their captains made killings by hauling high-value cargoes in record times. They wrested much of the tea-carrying trade between the Far East and England from their slower-moving British competitors, and they sped thousands of impatient adventurers to the gold fields of California and Australia.

But the hour of glory for the clipper was relatively brief. On the eve of the Civil War the British had clearly won the world race for maritime ascendancy with their iron tramp steamers ("tea-kettles"). Though slower and less romantic than the clipper, these vessels were steadier, more capacious, more reliable, and hence more profitable.

No story of rapid American communication would be complete without including the Far West. By 1858 horse-drawn overland stages, immortalized by Mark Twain's *Roughing It*, were a familiar sight. Their dusty tracks stretched into California from the bank of the muddy Missouri River clear to California.

Even more dramatic was the Pony Express, established in 1860 to carry mail speedily the 2,000 lonely miles (3,220 kilometers) from St. Joseph, Missouri, to Sacramento, California. Daring, lightweight riders, leaping onto wiry ponies saddled at stations approximately 10 miles (16 kilometers) apart, could make the trip in an amazing ten days. These unarmed horsemen galloped on, summer or winter, day or night, through dust or snow, past red Indians and white bandits. The speeding postmen missed only one trip, though the whole enterprise lost money heavily and folded after only eighteen legend-leaving months.

Just as the clippers had succumbed to steam, so were the express riders unhorsed by Morse's clacking keys, which began tapping messages to California in 1861. The swift ships and the fleet ponies ushered out a dying technology of wind and muscle. In the future, machines would be in the saddle.

CHRONOLOGY

c.1750	Industrial revolution begins in Britain
1791	Samuel Slater builds first U.S. factory
1793	Eli Whitney invents cotton gin
1798	Whitney develops interchangeable parts
1807	Robert Fulton's first steamboat
	Embargo spurs American manufacturing
1811	Cumberland Road construction begins
1817	Erie Canal construction begins
1828	First railroad in United States appears
1830s	Cyrus McCormick invents mechanical mower-reaper
1834	Anti-Catholic riot in Boston
1837	John Deere develops steel plow
1840–1848	Potato famine in Ireland
1840	President Van Buren establishes ten-hour day for federal employees
1842	Massachusetts declares labor unions legal in *Commonweath* v. *Hunt*
1844	Samuel Morse invents telegraph
	Anti-Catholic riot in Philadelphia
1846	Elias Howe patents sewing machine
1848	First general incorporation laws in New York
	Democratic revolutions collapse in Germany
1849	Order of the Star-Spangled Banner (Know-Nothings) formed
1858	Cyrus Field lays first transatlantic cable
1860	Pony Express established
1861	First transcontinental telegraph
1866	Permanent transatlantic cable established

Varying Viewpoints

Economic history was once simply a tale of industrious inventors and inventive industrialists. But economics has become a sophisticated science, and so has the story of the material past. Historians now seek to know just why economic growth occurred. Many scholars emphasize the plentiful resources of the United States. These resources, especially the abundance of arable land in the trans-Appalachian West, led to high agricultural productivity and stimulated advances in transportation and communication that raised land values. The availability of land, this view holds, in turn limited the industrial labor supply, driving up wages and inducing manufacturers to adopt laborsaving machinery. Thus, the natural plenty of the continent set off a chain reaction that unleashed explosive economic growth.

Other historians stress the contribution of human resources to America's economic progress. They focus on the large population of natives and immigrants to till the soil and fill the factories, the exploitation of slaves, legal and political innovations like the tariff and the general incorporation laws, and the technical genius of the American people, which by 1860 had become the envy of the entire Atlantic world.

Historians are also increasingly interested in the question: Which people benefited most from economic growth? This is known as the "welfare" question, as distinct from the fact of growth alone. Recently, labor historians, such as Sean Wilentz, have described the emergence of an increasingly self-conscious working class in antebellum America. These studies reveal the efforts of urban workers to protect themselves against the dislocations of industrialization and to secure a fair share of the benefits of economic development.

Select Readings

Primary Source Documents

Seth Luther, *An Address to the Working-Men of New-England* * (1833), is the eloquent appeal of an uneducated working-class labor reformer. On the transportation revolution, see John H. B. Latrobe's *Western Waters* * (1871) and Mark Twain's classic *Life on the Mississippi* (1883). Lemuel Shaw's decision of 1842 in *Commonwealth* v. *Hunt*, 4 Metc. III (in Henry Steele Commager, *Documents of American History*) is regarded as the "Magna Carta of American labor organization."

Secondary Sources

On immigration, see Maldwyn Jones, *American Immigration* (1960), Carl Wittke, *We Who Built America* (rev. ed., 1964), and *Refugees of Revolution: The German Forty-Eighters in America* (1952) and *The Irish in America* (1956). Solid introductions are George R. Taylor, *The Transportation Revolution, 1815–1860* (1951); Clarence H. Danhoff, *Change in Agriculture: The Northern United States, 1820–1870* (1969); and Douglas C. North, *Economic Growth in the United States, 1790–1860* (1961). See also North's *Growth and Welfare in the American Past* (rev. ed., 1974). The events of the period are placed in a larger context of economic history in Stuart Bruchey, *The Roots of American Economic Growth, 1607–1861* (1965), and in Walt W. Rostow, *The Stages of Economic Growth* (rev. ed., 1971). Richard A. Easterlin analyzes *Population, Labor Force, and Long Swings in Economic Growth: The American Experience* (1968). Thomas C. Cochran, *Frontiers of Change: Early Industrialism in America* (1981), sees industrialization as culturally inspired change. Two fascinating case studies of the coming of industrialism are Alan Dawley, *Class and Community: The Industrial Revolution in Lynn* (1977), and Anthony F. C. Wallace, *Rockdale: The Growth of an American Village in the Early Industrial Revolution* (1978). The laboring classes are chronicled in Joseph Rayback, *History of American Labor* (1966). Consult also Herbert Gutman's path-breaking *Work, Culture, and Society in Industrializing America* (1976) and Sean Wilentz's insightful *Chants Democratic: New*

York City and the Rise of the American Working Class, 1788–1850 (1984). The experiences of women workers are the focus of Thomas Dublin, *Women at Work: The Transformation of Work and Community in Lowell, Massachusetts, 1826–1860* (1979). On the introduction of technology, see the provocative anthology edited by S. B. Saul, *Technological Change: The U.S. and Britain in the Nineteenth Century* (1970) and David H. Hounshell, *From the American System to Mass Production, 1800–1932: The Development of Manufacturing Technology in the United States* (1984). Ideological aspects of this process are described in John F. Kassen, *Civilizing the Machine: Technology and Republican Values in America, 1776–1900* (1976). The canal era is comprehensively described in Carter Goodrich, *Government Promotion of American Canals and Railroads, 1800–1890* (1960). See also H. N. Schreiber, *The Ohio Canal Era* (1968). On railroads, consult Robert Fogel, *Railroads and American Economic Growth* (1964), which presents the startling thesis that the iron horse in fact did little to promote growth. For a different view, see Albert Fishlow, *American Railroads and the Transformation of the Ante-Bellum Economy* (1965). Steven Hahn and Jonathan Prude, eds., *The Countryside in the Age of Capitalist Transformation: Essays in the Social History of Rural America* (1985) is a provocative look at the impact of the transportation and industrial revolutions on the countryside. The clipper ships are lovingly described in Carl C. Cutler, *Greyhounds of the Sea* (1930), and Samuel E. Morison, *By Land and By Sea* (1953). An excellent introduction to the romance of the tall ships is Richard H. Dana Jr.'s personal narrative, *Two Years before the Mast* (1840).

16

The Ferment of Reform and Culture, 1790–1860

We [Americans] will walk on our own feet; we will work with
our own hands; we will speak our own minds.

Ralph Waldo Emerson,
"The American Scholar," 1837

Reviving Religion

Church attendance was still a regular ritual for about three-fourths of the 23 million Americans in 1850. Alexis de Tocqueville declared that there was "no country in the world where the Christian religion retains a greater influence over the souls of men than in America." Yet the religion of these years was not the old-time religion of colonial days. The austere Calvinist rigor had long been seeping out of the American churches. The rationalist ideas of the French Revolutionary era had done much to soften the older orthodoxy. Thomas Paine's widely circulated book *The Age of Reason* (1794) had shockingly declared that all churches were "set up to terrify and enslave mankind, and monopolize power and profit." American anticlericalism was seldom that virulent, but many of the Founding Fathers, including Jefferson and Franklin, embraced the liberal doctrines of Deism that Paine promoted. Deists relied on reason rather than revelation, on science rather than the Bible. They rejected the concept of original sin and denied Christ's divinity. Yet Deists believed in a Supreme Being who had created a knowable universe and endowed human beings with a capacity for moral behavior.

Deism helped to inspire an important spin-off from the severe Puritanism of the past—the Unitarian faith, which began to gather momentum in New England at the end of the eigh-

In his lecture "Hindrances to Revivals," delivered in the 1830s, Charles Grandison Finney proposed the excommunication of drinkers and slaveholders: "Let the churches of all denominations speak out on the subject of temperance, let them close their doors against all who have anything to do with the death-dealing abomination, and the cause of temperance is triumphant. A few years would annihilate the traffic. Just so with slavery. . . . It is a great national sin. It is a sin of the church. The churches by their silence, and by permitting slaveholders to belong to their communion, have been consenting to it. . . . The church cannot turn away from this question. It is a question for the church and for the nation to decide, and God will push it to a decision."

Charles Grandison Finney, 1792–1875   *(New-York Historical Society.)*

teenth century. Unitarians held that God existed in only *one* person (hence *uni*tarian), and not in the orthodox Trinity. Although denying the divinity of Jesus, Unitarians stressed the essential goodness of human nature rather than its vileness; they proclaimed their belief in free will and the possibility of salvation through good works; they pictured God not as a stern Creator but as a loving Father. Embraced by many leading thinkers (including Ralph Waldo Emerson), the Unitarian movement appealed mostly to intellectuals whose rationalism and optimism contrasted sharply with the hellfire doctrines of Calvinism, especially predestination and human depravity.

A boiling reaction against the growing liberalism in religion set in about 1800. A fresh wave of roaring revivals, beginning on the southern frontier but soon rolling even into the cities of the Northeast, sent a Second Great Awakening surging across the land. Sweeping up even more people than the First Great Awakening almost a century earlier, the Second Awakening was one of the most momentous episodes in the history of American religion. This tidal wave of spiritual fervor left in its wake countless converted souls, many shattered and reorganized churches, and numerous new sects. It also encouraged an effervescent evangelicism that bubbled up into innumerable areas of American life—including prison reform, the

temperance cause, the women's movement, and the crusade to abolish slavery.

The Second Great Awakening was spread to the masses on the frontier by huge "camp meetings." As many as twenty-five thousand persons would gather for an encampment of several days to drink the hellfire gospel as served up by an itinerant preacher. Thousands of spiritually starved souls "got religion" at these gatherings and in their ecstasy engaged in orgies of rolling, dancing, barking, and jerking. Many of the "saved" soon backslid into their former sinful ways, but the revivals massively stimulated church membership and a variety of humanitarian reforms. Easterners were moved to engage in missionary work in the Indian backwoods, in Hawaii, and in faraway Asia.

Methodists and Baptists reaped the biggest harvest of souls from the fields fertilized by revivalism. Both sects stressed personal conversion (contrary to predestination), a relatively democratic control of church affairs, and a rousing emotionalism. As a frontier jingle ran:

> The devil hates the Methodist
> Because they sing and shout the best.

Powerful Peter Cartwright (1785–1872) was the best known of the Methodist "circuit riders," or traveling frontier preachers. This ill-educated but sinewy servant of the Lord ranged for a

A Camp Meeting at Sing Sing, New York   Note the preacher with uplifted hands under the canopy at the left. A British visitor wrote in 1839 of a revival meeting: "In front of the pulpit there was a space railed off and strewn with straw, which I was told was the anxious seat, and on which sat those who were touched by their consciences." (Library of Congress.)

half-century from Tennessee to Illinois, calling upon sinners to repent. With bellowing voice and flailing arms, he converted thousands of souls to the Lord. Not only did he lash the Devil with his tongue, but with his fists he knocked out rowdies who tried to break up his meetings. His Christianity was definitely muscular.

Bell-voiced Charles Grandison Finney was the greatest of the revival preachers. Trained as a lawyer, Finney abandoned the bar to become an evangelist after a deeply moving conversion experience as a young man. Tall and athletically built, Finney held huge crowds spellbound with the power of his oratory and the pungency of his message. He led massive revivals in Rochester and New York City in 1830 and 1831. Finney preached a version of the old-time religion, but he was also an innovator. He devised the "anxious bench," where repentant sinners could sit in full view of the congregation, and he encouraged women to pray aloud in public. Holding out the promise of a perfect Christian kingdom on earth, Finney denounced both alcohol and slavery. He eventually served

as president of Oberlin College in Ohio, which he helped to make a hotbed of revivalist activity and abolitionism.

The Circuit Preacher   (From the drawing by A. R. Waud in Harper's Weekly, October 12, 1867.)

Denominational Diversity

Revivals also furthered the fragmentation of religious faiths. Western New York, where many descendants of New England Puritans had settled, was so blistered by sermonizers preaching "hellfire and damnation" that it came to be known as the "Burned-Over District."

Millerites, or Adventists, who mustered several hundred thousand adherents, rose from the superheated soil of the Burned-Over region in the 1830s. Named after the eloquent and commanding William Miller, they interpreted the Bible to mean that Christ would return to earth on October 22, 1844. Donning their go-to-meeting clothes, they gathered in prayerful assemblies to greet their Redeemer. The failure of Jesus to descend on schedule dampened but did not destroy the movement.

Like the First Great Awakening, the Second Great Awakening tended to widen the lines between classes and regions. The more prosperous and conservative denominations in the East were little touched by revivalism, while Episcopalians, Presbyterians, Congregationalists, and Unitarians continued to rise mostly from the wealthier, better-educated levels of society. Methodists, Baptists, and the members of the other new sects spawned by the swelling evangelistic fervor tended to come from less prosperous, less "learned" communities in the rural South and West.

Religious diversity further reflected social cleavages when the churches faced up to the slavery issue. By 1844–1845 both the southern Baptists and the southern Methodists had split with their northern brethren over human bondage. The Methodists came to grief over the case of a slaveowning bishop in Georgia, whose second wife added several household slaves to his estate. In 1857 the Presbyterians, North and South, parted company. The secession of the southern churches foreshadowed the secession of the southern states. First the churches split, then the political parties split, and then the Union split.

A Desert Zion in Utah

The smoldering spiritual embers of the Burned-Over District kindled one especially ardent flame in 1830. In that year Joseph Smith—a tall, powerfully built visionary, proud of his prowess at wrestling—reported that he had received some golden plates from an angel. When deciphered, they constituted the Book of Mormon, and the Church of Jesus Christ of Latter-

Mormon Pioneers
Determined Mormons tamed some of the most forbidding and inhospitable terrain in America, including the "Desert Zion" of Utah. Their polygamous practices, apparent in this photograph, created much friction with non-Mormon "gentiles" in early days. (Oakland Museum.)

Day Saints (Mormons) was launched. It was a native American product, a new religion, destined to spread its influence worldwide.

After establishing a religious oligarchy, Smith ran into serious opposition from his non-Mormon neighbors, first in Ohio, and then in Missouri and Illinois. His cooperative sect rasped rank-and-file Americans, who were individualistic and dedicated to free enterprise. The Mormons aroused further antagonism by voting as a unit and by openly but understandably drilling their militia for defensive purposes. Accusations of polygamy likewise arose and increased in intensity, for Joseph Smith was reputed to have several wives.

Continuing hostility finally drove the Mormons to desperate measures. In 1844 Joseph Smith and his brother were murdered and mangled by a mob in Carthage, Illinois, and the movement seemed near collapse. The falling torch was seized by a remarkable Mormon Moses named Brigham Young. Stern and austere in contrast to Smith's charm and affability, the barrel-chested Brigham Young had received only eleven days of formal schooling. But he quickly proved to be an aggressive leader, an eloquent preacher, and a gifted administrator. Determined to escape further persecution, Young in 1846–1847 led his oppressed and despoiled Latter-Day Saints over vast rolling plains to Utah as they sang "Come, Come, Ye Saints."

Overcoming pioneer hardships, the Mormons soon made the desert bloom like a new Eden by means of ingenious and cooperative methods of irrigation. The crops of 1848, threatened by

Polygamy was an issue of such consequence that it was bracketed with slavery in the Republican national platform of 1856: "It is both the right and the imperative duty of Congress to prohibit in the Territories those twin relics of barbarism—Polygamy and Slavery."

hordes of crickets, were saved when flocks of gulls appeared, as if by a miracle, to gulp down the invaders. (A monument to the sea gulls stands in Salt Lake City today.)

Semiarid Utah grew remarkably. By the end of 1848 some five thousand settlers had arrived, and other large bands were to follow them. Many dedicated Mormons in the 1850s actually made the 1,300-mile (2,090-kilometer) trek across the plains pulling two-wheeled carts.

Under the rigidly disciplined management of Brigham Young, the community became a prosperous frontier theocracy and a cooperative commonwealth. Young married as many as twenty-seven women—some of them wives in name only—and begot fifty-six children. The population was further swelled by thousands of immigrants from Europe, where the Mormons had established a flourishing missionary movement.

A crisis developed when the Washington government was unable to control the hierarchy of Brigham Young, who had been made territorial governor in 1850. A federal army marched in 1857 against the Mormons, who harassed its lines of supply and rallied to die in their last

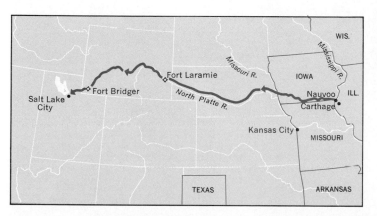

The Mormon Trek, 1846–1847 *Accompanied by livestock, the first pioneer band, led by Brigham Young, set out for Utah in 1846. The party consisted of 146 young men and women driving seventy-three wagons.*

dusty ditch. Fortunately, the quarrel was finally adjusted without serious bloodshed. The Mormons later ran afoul of the antipolygamy laws passed by Congress in 1862 and 1882, and their unique marital customs delayed statehood for Utah until 1896.

Free Schools for a Free People

Tax-supported primary schools were scarce in the early years of the Republic. They had the odor of pauperism about them, since they existed chiefly to educate the children of the poor—the so-called ragged schools. Advocates of "free" public education met stiff opposition. A middlewestern legislator cried that he wanted only this simple epitaph when he died: "Here lies an enemy of public education."

Well-to-do, conservative Americans gradually saw the light. If they did not pay to educate "other folkses brats," the brats might grow up into a dangerous, ignorant rabble—armed with the vote. Taxation for education was an in-

Lincoln wrote of his education (1859): "There were some schools so-called [in Indiana], but no qualification was ever required of a teacher beyond 'readin', writin' and cipherin'' to the rule of three. . . . There was absolutely nothing to excite ambition for education. Of course, when I came of age I did not know much. Still, somehow, I could read, write and cipher to the rule of three, but that was all. I have not been to school since. The little advance I now have upon this store of education, I have picked up from time to time under the pressure of necessity. I was raised to work, which I continued till I was twenty-two."

surance premium that the wealthy paid for stability and democracy.

Tax-supported public education, though miserably lagging in the slavery-cursed South, triumphed between 1825 and 1850. Grimy-handed laborers wielded increased influence and demanded instruction for their children.

The Country School   *Stark and simple by latter-day standards, the one-room schoolhouse nevertheless contributed richly to the development of the young Republic. From a painting by Winslow Homer. (St. Louis Art Museum, Museum Purchase.)*

Most important was the gaining of manhood suffrage for whites in Jackson's day. A free vote cried aloud for free education. A civilized nation that was both ignorant and free, declared Thomas Jefferson, "never was and never will be."

The famed little red schoolhouse—with one room, one stove, one teacher, and often eight grades—became the shrine of American democracy. Regrettably, it was an imperfect shrine. Early free schools stayed open only a few months of the year. Schoolmasters were too often ill trained, ill tempered, and ill paid. They frequently put more stress on "lickin'" (with a hickory stick) than on "larnin'." These knights of the blackboard often "boarded around" in the community, and some knew scarcely more than their older pupils. They usually taught only the "three Rs"—"readin', 'ritin', and 'rithmetic." To many rugged Americans, suspicious of "book larnin'," this was enough.

Reform was urgently needed. Into the breach stepped Horace Mann (1796–1859), a brilliant and idealistic graduate of Brown University. As secretary of the Massachusetts Board of Education, he campaigned effectively for more and better schoolhouses, longer school terms, higher pay for teachers, and an expanded curriculum. His influence radiated out to other states, and impressive improvements were chalked up. Yet education remained an expensive luxury for many communities. As late as 1860 the nation counted only about a hundred public secondary schools—and nearly a million white adult illiterates. Black slaves in the South were legally forbidden to receive instruction in reading or writing, and even free blacks, in the North as well as the South, were usually excluded from the schools.

Educational advances were aided by improved textbooks, notably those of Noah Webster (1758–1843), a Yale-educated Connecticut Yankee who was known as the "Schoolmaster of the Republic." His "reading lessons," used by millions of children in the nineteenth century, were partly designed to promote patriotism. He devoted twenty years to his famous dictionary, published in 1828, which helped to standardize the American language.

Equally influential was Ohioan William H. McGuffey (1800–1873), a teacher-preacher of rare power. His grade-school readers, first published in the 1830s, sold 122 million copies in the following decades. *McGuffey's Readers* hammered home lasting lessons in morality, patriotism, and idealism. One copy-exercise ran:

> Beautiful hands are they that do
> Deeds that are noble good and true;
> Beautiful feet are they that go
> Swiftly to lighten another's woe.

Higher Goals for Higher Learning

Higher education was likewise stirring. The religious zeal of the Second Great Awakening, beginning about 1800, led to the planting of many small, denominational, liberal arts colleges, chiefly in the South and West. Too often they were educationally anemic, established more to satisfy local pride than genuinely to advance the cause of learning. Like their more venerable, ivy-draped brethren, the new colleges offered a narrow, tradition-bound curriculum of Latin, Greek, mathematics, and moral philosophy. On new and old campuses alike there was little intellectual vitality and much boredom.

The first state-supported universities sprang up in the South, beginning with North Carolina in 1795. Federal land grants nourished the growth of state institutions of higher learning. Conspicuous among the early group was the University of Virginia, founded in 1819. It was largely the brainchild of Thomas Jefferson, who designed its beautiful architecture and who at times watched its construction through a telescope from his hilltop home. He dedicated the university to freedom from religious or political shackles, and modern languages and the sciences received unusual emphasis.

Women's higher education was frowned upon in the early decades of the nineteenth century. A woman's place was in the home, and

> *Horace Mann deplored indolence when he said, "Lost, yesterday, somewhere between sunrise and sunset, two golden hours, each set with sixty diamond minutes. No reward is offered, for they are gone forever."*

training in needlecraft seemed more important than training in algebra. In an era when the clinging-vine bride was the ideal, coeducation was regarded as frivolous. Prejudices also prevailed that too much learning injured the feminine brain, undermined health, and rendered a young lady unfit for marriage. The teachers of Susan B. Anthony, the future feminist, refused to instruct her in long division.

Women's schools at the secondary level began to attain some respectability in the 1820s, thanks in part to the dedicated work of Emma Willard (1787–1870). In 1821 she established the Troy (New York) Female Seminary. Oberlin College, in Ohio, jolted traditionalists in 1837 when it opened its doors to women as well as men. (Oberlin had already created shock waves

Mary Lyon (1797–1849) *An intrepid pioneer in the field of higher education for women, Mary Lyon was a gifted teacher who achieved an important breakthrough when, in the face of much antagonism, she managed to raise enough money to launch her "Female Seminary," now Mount Holyoke College. The year after it opened in 1837, she had to turn away some four hundred applicants. She served as principal for twelve years.*

by admitting black students.) In the same year, Mary Lyon established an outstanding women's school, Mount Holyoke Seminary (later College), in South Hadley, Massachusetts. Mossback critics scoffed that "they'll be educatin' cows next."

Adults who craved more learning satisfied their thirst for knowledge at private subscription libraries or, increasingly, at tax-supported libraries. House-to-house peddlers also did a lush business in feeding the public appetite for culture. Traveling lecturers helped to carry learning to the masses through the lyceum lecture associations, which numbered about three thousand by 1835. The lyceums provided platforms for speakers in such areas as science, literature, and moral philosophy. Talented talkers like Ralph Waldo Emerson journeyed thousands of miles on the lyceum circuits, casting their pearls of civilization before appreciative audiences.

Magazines flourished in the pre–Civil War years, but most of them withered after a short life. The *North American Review*, founded in 1815, was the long-lived leader of the intellectuals. *Godey's Lady's Book*, founded in 1830, survived until 1898 and attained the enormous circulation (for those days) of 150,000. It was devoured devotedly by countless millions of women.

An Age of Reform

As the young Republic grew, reform campaigns of all types flourished in sometimes bewildering abundance. There was not "a reading man" who was without some scheme for a new utopia in his "waistcoat pocket," claimed Ralph Waldo Emerson. Reformers promoted rights for women as well as miracle medicines, communal living, polygamy, celibacy, rule by prophets, and guidance by spirits. Societies were formed against alcohol, tobacco, profanity, and the transit of mail on the Sabbath. Fad diets proved popular, including the whole-wheat bread and crackers regimen of Sylvester Graham. Eventually overshadowing all other reforms was the crusade against slavery.

Many reformers were simply crackbrained

cranks. But most were intelligent, inspired idealists, usually touched by the fire of evangelical religion then licking through the pews and pulpits of American churches. The optimistic promises of the Second Great Awakening inspirited countless souls to do battle against earthly evils. These modern idealists dreamed anew the old Puritan vision of a perfected society: free from cruelty, war, intoxicating drink, discrimination, and—ultimately—slavery. Women were particularly prominent in these reform crusades, especially in their own struggle for suffrage. For many middle-class women, the reform campaigns provided a unique opportunity to escape the confines of home and enter the arena of public affairs.

In part, the practical, activist Christianity of these reformers resulted from their desire to reaffirm traditional values as they plunged ever further into a world disrupted and transformed by the turbulent forces of a market economy.

Dorothea Dix (1802–1887) *A tireless reformer, she worked mightily to improve the treatment of the mentally ill. At the outbreak of the Civil War she was appointed superintendent of women nurses for the Union forces. (National Portrait Gallery, Smithsonian Institution, Washington, D.C.)*

Mainly middle-class descendants of pioneer farmers, they were often blissfully unaware that they were witnessing the dawn of the industrial era, which posed unprecedented problems and called for novel ideas. They either ignored the factory workers, for example, or blamed their problems on bad habits. With naive single-mindedness, reformers sometimes applied conventional virtue to refurbishing an older order—while events hurtled them headlong into the new.

Imprisonment for debt continued to be a nightmare, though its extent has been exaggerated. As late as 1830 hundreds of penniless persons were languishing in filthy holes, sometimes for owing less than one dollar. The poorer working classes were especially hard hit by this merciless practice. But as the embattled laborer won the ballot and asserted himself, state legislatures gradually abolished debtors' prisons.

Criminal codes in the states were likewise being softened, in accord with more enlightened European practices. The number of capital offenses was being reduced, and brutal punishments, such as whipping and branding, were being slowing eliminated. A refreshing idea was taking hold that prisons should reform as well as punish—hence "reformatories," "houses of correction," and "penitentiaries" (for penance).

Sufferers from so-called insanity were still being treated with incredible cruelty. The medieval concept had been that the mentally deranged were cursed with unclean spirits; the nineteenth-century idea was that they were willfully perverse and depraved—to be treated only as beasts. Many crazed persons were chained in jails or poorhouses with sane people.

Into this dismal picture stepped a quiet New England teacher-author, Dorothea Dix (1802–1887). A physically frail woman afflicted with persistent lung trouble, she possessed infinite compassion and willpower. Never raising her voice to a screech, she traveled some 60,000 miles (97,000 kilometers) in eight years and assembled her damning reports on insanity from firsthand observations. Her classic petition of 1843 to the Massachusetts legislature, describing cells so foul that visitors were driven back by the stench, turned legislative stomachs and hearts. Her persistent prodding resulted in improved conditions and in a gain for the concept that the demented were not willfully perverse but mentally ill.

Agitation for peace also gained some momentum in the pre–Civil War years. In 1828 the American Peace Society was formed, with a ringing declaration of war on war. A leading spirit was William Ladd, who orated when his legs were so badly ulcerated that he had to sit on a stool. His ideas were finally to bear some fruit in the international organizations for collective security of the twentieth century. The American peace crusade, linked with the European crusade, was making promising progress by midcentury, when it was set back by the bloodshed of the Crimean War in Europe and the Civil War in America.

Demon Rum—The "Old Deluder"

The ever-present drink problem attracted dedicated reformers. Custom, combined with a hard and monotonous life, led to the excessive drinking of hard liquor, even among women, clergymen, and members of Congress. Weddings and funerals all too often became disgraceful brawls, and occasionally a drunken mourner would fall into the open grave with the corpse. Heavy drinking decreased the efficiency of labor, while the introduction of poorly safeguarded machinery increased the danger of accidents occuring at work. Drunkenness also fouled the sanctity of the family, threatening the spiritual welfare—and physical safety—of women and children.

After earlier and feebler efforts, the American Temperance Society was formed at Boston in 1826. Within a few years about a thousand local groups sprang into existence. They implored drinkers to sign the temperance pledge and organized children's clubs, known as the "Cold Water Army." Temperance crusaders also made effective use of pictures, pamphlets, and lurid lecturers, some of whom were reformed drunkards. A popular temperance song ran:

> We've done with our days of carousing,
> Our nights, too, of frolicsome glee;
> For now with our sober minds choosing,
> We've pledged ourselves never to spree.

The most popular antialcohol tract of the era was T. S. Arthur's melodramatic novel, *Ten Nights in a Barroom and What I Saw There* (1854). It described in shocking detail how a once-happy village was ruined by Sam Slade's tavern. The book was second only to Stowe's *Uncle Tom's Cabin* as a best-seller in the 1850s, and it enjoyed a highly successful run on the stage. Its touching theme song began with the words of a little girl:

> Father, dear father, come home with me now,
> The clock in the belfry strikes one.

Early foes of Demon Drink adopted two major lines of attack. One was to stiffen the individual's will to resist the wiles of the little brown jug. The moderate reformers thus stressed "temperance" rather than "teetotalism," or the

The Perils of Drink   *Among the many evils of alcohol, reformers fulminated especially against its corrupting effects on family life, as shown in this prohibitionist tract of the 1820s, entitled* The Drunkard's Progress. *(American Antiquarian Society, Worcester, Massachusetts.)*

total elimination of intoxicants. But less patient zealots came to believe that temptation should be removed by legislation. Prominent among this group was Neal S. Dow of Maine, a bluenosed reformer who, as a mayor of Portland and an employer of labor, had often witnessed the debauching effect of alcohol.

Dow—the "Father of Prohibition"—sponsored the so-called Maine Law of 1851. This drastic new statute, hailed as "the law of Heaven Americanized," prohibited the manufacture and sale of intoxicating liquor. Other states in the North followed Maine's example, and by 1857 about a dozen had passed various prohibitory laws. But these figures are deceptive, for within a decade some of the statutes were repealed or declared unconstitutional, if not openly flouted.

It was clearly impossible to legislate thirst out of existence, especially in localities where public sentiment was hostile. Yet on the eve of the Civil War the prohibitionists had registered inspiriting gains. There was much less drinking among women than earlier in the century and probably much less per capita consumption of hard liquor.

Women in Revolt

It was still a man's world, in America and Europe, when the nineteenth century opened. A wife was supposed to immerse herself in her home and subordinate herself to her lord and master. Like black slaves, she could not vote; like black slaves, she could be legally beaten by her overlord "with a reasonable instrument." When she married, she could not retain title to her property; it passed to her husband.

Yet American women, though legally regarded as perpetual minors, fared better than their European cousins, partly because of their scarcity in frontier communities. A western woman could warn her spouse to be respectful, for "if you don't there's plenty will." Few American husbands were brutes; and women always had quiet ways of protecting themselves, regardless of law.

Despite these relative advantages, women were still "the submerged sex" in America in the early part of the century. But as the decades unfolded, women increasingly emerged to breathe the air of freedom and self-determination. In contrast to colonial times, many women avoided marriage altogether—about 10 percent of adult women remained "spinsters" at the time of the Civil War.

Sexual differences were strongly emphasized in nineteenth-century America—largely because the burgeoning market economy was increasingly separating women and men into sharply distinct economic roles. Women were thought to be physically and emotionally weak, but also artistic and refined. Endowed with finely tuned moral sensibilities, they were the keepers of society's conscience, with special responsibility to teach the young how to be good and productive citizens of the Republic. Men were considered strong but crude, always in danger of slipping into some savage or beastly way of life if not guided by the gentle hands of their loving ladies.

But if sexual roles were sharply separated, men and women could still be regarded as equals. As a sign of the prestigious position of American women, French visitor Alexis de Toc-

Stellar Suffragists *Elizabeth Cady Stanton (left) and Susan B. Anthony (right) were two of the most persistent battlers for women's rights. (Brown Brothers.)*

queville noted that in his native France rape was punished only lightly, while in America it was one of the few crimes punishable by death.

The home was a woman's special sphere. Even reformers like Catharine Beecher, who urged her sisters to seek employment as teachers, endlessly celebrated the role of the good homemaker. But some women increasingly felt that the glorified sanctuary of the home was in fact a gilded cage. They yearned to tear down the bars that separated the private world of women from the public world of men.

Clamorous female reformers began to gather strength as the century neared its halfway point. Most of them were broad-gauge battlers; while demanding rights for women, they participated in the general reform movement of the age, fighting for temperance and the abolition of slavery. Like men, they had been touched by the evangelical spirit that offered the alluring promise of earthly reward for human endeavor. Neither foul eggs nor foul words, when hurled by disapproving men, could halt women heartened by these doctrines.

The woman's rights movement was mothered by some arresting characters. Prominent among them was Lucretia Mott, a sprightly Quaker whose ire had been aroused when she and her fellow female delegates to the London

antislavery convention of 1840 were not recognized. Elizabeth Cady Stanton, a mother of seven who had insisted on leaving "obey" out of her marriage ceremony, shocked fellow feminists by going so far as to advocate suffrage for women. Quaker-reared Susan B. Anthony, a militant lecturer for women's rights, fearlessly exposed herself to rotten garbage and vulgar epithets. She became such a conspicuous advocate of female rights that progressive women everywhere were called "Suzy Bs."

Other feminists challenged the man's world. Dr. Elizabeth Blackwell, a pioneer in a previously forbidden profession for women, was the first female graduate of a medical college. Precocious Margaret Fuller edited a transcendentalist journal, *The Dial,* and took part in the struggle to bring unity and republican government to Italy. She died in a shipwreck off New York's Fire Island while returning to the United States in 1850. The talented Grimké sisters, Sarah and Angelina, championed antislavery. Lucy Stone retained her maiden name after marriage—hence, the latter-day "Lucy Stoners," who follow her example. Amelia Bloomer revolted against the current "street sweeping" female attire by donning a semimasculine short skirt with Turkish trousers—"bloomers," they were called—amid much bawdy ridicule about

What It Would Be If Some Ladies Had Their Own Way
The men are sewing, tending the baby, and washing clothes. This scene seemed absurd then, but not a century later. (Historical Pictures Service, Chicago.)

"Bloomerism" and "loose habits." A jeering male rhyme of the times jabbed:

> Gibbey, gibbey gab
> The women had a confab
> And demanded the rights
> To wear the tights
> Gibbey, gibbey gab.

Fighting feminists met at Seneca Falls, New York, in a memorable Woman's Rights Convention (1848). The defiant Stanton read a "Declaration of Sentiments," which in the spirit of the Declaration of Independence declared that "all men *and women* are created equal." One resolution formally demanded the ballot for females. Amidst scorn and denunciation from press and pulpit, the Seneca Falls meeting launched the modern women's rights movement.

The crusade for woman's rights was eclipsed by that against slavery in the decade before the Civil War. Male idiots could still vote; women could not. Yet women were being gradually admitted to colleges, and some states, beginning with Mississippi in 1839, were even permitting wives to own property after marriage.

Wilderness Utopias

Bolstered by the utopian spirit of the age, various reformers, ranging from the high-minded to the "lunatic fringe," set up more than forty communities of a cooperative, communistic, or "communitarian" nature. Seeking human betterment, a wealthy and idealistic Scottish textile manufacturer, Robert Owen, established in 1825 a communal society of about a thousand persons at New Harmony, Indiana. Little harmony prevailed in the colony, which, in addition to hardworking visionaries, attracted a sprinkling of radicals, work-shy theorists, and outright scoundrels. The enterprise sank in a morass of contradiction and confusion.

Brook Farm in Massachusetts, comprising two hundred acres of grudging soil, was started in 1841 with the brotherly and sisterly cooperation of about twenty intellectuals. They prospered reasonably well until 1846, when they lost by fire a large new communal building shortly before its completion. The whole venture in "plain living and high thinking" then collapsed in debt. The Brook Farm experiment inspired Nathaniel Hawthorne's classic novel

Shaker Businesspeople *The radical Quakers known as Shakers were skilled craftsmen and businessmen who made and marketed high-quality furniture and woolens. The elegant simplicity of the "Shaker style" in furniture, as in the chairs and desks shown here, made their wares popular not only with contemporaries, but with later collectors. The sect's strict observance of celibacy forced it to rely on conversions to sustain its numbers; as religious ardor waned, the Shakers slowly died out. (Lightfoot Collection.)*

The Blithedale Romance (1852), whose main character was modeled on Margaret Fuller.

A more radical experiment was the Oneida Colony, founded in New York in 1848. It practiced free love ("complex marriage"), birth control, and the eugenic selection of parents to produce superior offspring. The leader finally fled to Canada to escape prosecution for adultery. This curious enterprise flourished for more than thirty years, largely because its craftsmen made superior steel traps and Oneida Community (silver) Plate. In 1879–1880 the group embraced monogamy and abandoned communism.

Various communistic experiments, mostly small-scale, have been attempted since Jamestown. But in competition with democratic free enterprise and free land, virtually all of them sooner or later failed or changed their methods. Among the longest-lived sects were the Shakers. Led by Mother Ann Lee, they began in the 1770s to set up the first of a score or so of religious communities. They attained a membership of about six thousand in 1840, but since their monastic customs prohibited both marriage and free love, they were virtually extinct by 1940.

The Dawn of Scientific Achievement

Early Americans, confronted with pioneering problems, were more interested in practical gadgets than in pure science. Thomas Jeffer-

Passenger Pigeons, by John Audubon (left) *An astute naturalist and a gifted artist, Audubon drew the birds of America in loving detail. Ironically, he had to go to England in the 1820s to find a publisher for his pioneering depictions of the unique beauty of American wildlife. (New-York Historical Society.)* **John J. Audubon** (right) *Born in Haiti and educated in France, he achieved fame as America's greatest ornithologist. (American Museum of Natural History.)*

son, for example, was a gifted amateur inventor, who won a gold medal for a new type of plow. Noteworthy were the writings of the mathematician Nathaniel Bowditch (1733–1838) on practical navigation and of the oceanographer Matthew F. Maury (1806–1873) on ocean winds and currents. All these writers promoted safety, speed, and economy. But as far as basic science was concerned, Americans were best known for borrowing and adapting the findings of Europeans.

Yet the Republic was not without scientific talent. The most influential American scientist

Early Advertising *Hawkers of patent medicines pioneered the techniques of modern advertising. Here a pain killer is promoted by invoking the totally irrelevant image of Molly Pitcher. The legendary subject of a poem by John Greenleaf Whittier, Pitcher reputedly took her fallen husband's place at a cannon during the Revolutionary War Battle of Monmouth in 1778. What this exploit had to do with anaesthetics is by no means clear, but it supposedly sold the product. (The Granger Collection.)*

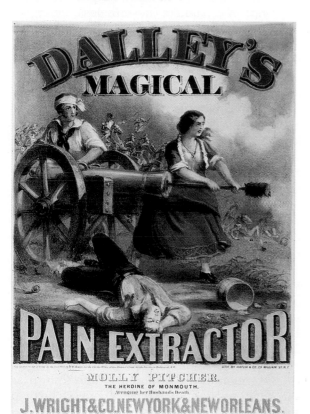

of the first half of the nineteenth century was Professor Benjamin Silliman (1779–1864), a pioneer chemist and geologist who taught and wrote brilliantly at Yale College for more than fifty years. Professor Louis Agassiz (1807–1873), a distinguished French-Swiss immigrant, served for a quarter of a century at Harvard College. A path-breaking student of biology who sometimes carried snakes in his pockets, he insisted on original research and deplored the overemphasis on memory work. Professor Asa Gray (1810–1888) of Harvard College, the Columbus of American botany, published over 350 books, monographs, and papers. His textbooks set new standards for clarity and interest.

Lovers of American bird lore owed much to the French-descended John J. Audubon (1785–1851), who painted wild fowl in their natural habitat. His magnificently illustrated *Birds of America* attained considerable popularity. The Audubon Society for the protection of birds was named after him, although as a young man he shot much feathered game for sport.

Medicine in America, despite a steady growth of medical schools, was still primitive by modern standards. Bleeding remained a common remedy. Plagues of smallpox were still dreaded, and the terrible yellow fever epidemic of 1793 in Philadelphia took several thousand lives. "Bring out your dead!" was the daily cry of the drivers of the death wagons.

People everywhere complained of ill health—malaria, the "rheumatics," the "miseries," and the chills. Illness often resulted from improper diet, hurried eating, perspiring and cooling off

An outbreak of cholera occurred in New York City in 1832, and a wealthy businessman, Philip Hone, wrote in his diary for the Fourth of July: "The alarm about the cholera has prevented all the usual jollification under the public authority. . . . The Board of Health reports to-day twenty new cases and eleven deaths since noon yesterday. The disease is here in all its violence and will increase. God grant that its ravages may be confined, and its visit short."

too rapidly, and ignorance of germs and sanitation. "We was sick every fall, regular," wrote the mother of the future President Garfield. Life expectancy was still dismayingly short—about forty years for a white person born in 1850, and less for blacks. The suffering from decayed or ulcerated teeth was enormous; tooth extraction was often practiced by the muscular village blacksmith.

Self-prescribed patent medicines were common (one dose for people, two for horses) and included Robertson's Infallible Worm Destroying Lozenges. Among home remedies was the rubbing of tumors with dead toads. The use of medicine by the regular doctors was often harmful, and Dr. Oliver Wendell Holmes declared in 1860 that if the medicines, as then employed, were thrown into the sea, humans would be better off and the fish worse off.

Victims of surgical operations were ordinarily tied down, often after a stiff drink of whiskey. The surgeon then sawed or cut with breakneck speed, undeterred by the piercing shrieks of the patient. A priceless boon for medical progress came in the early 1840s, when several American doctors and dentists, working independently, successfully employed laughing gas and ether as anesthetics.

Artistic Achievements

Architecturally, America contributed little of note in the first half of the century. The rustic Republic, still under pressure to erect shelters in haste, was continuing to imitate European models. Public buildings and other important structures followed Greek and Roman lines, which seemed curiously out of place in a wilderness setting. A remarkable Greek revival came between 1820 and 1850, partly stimulated by the heroic efforts of the Greeks in the 1820s to wrest independence from the "terrible Turk." About midcentury strong interest developed in a revival of Gothic forms, with their emphasis on pointed arches and large windows.

Talented Thomas Jefferson, architect of revolution, was probably the ablest American architect of his generation. He brought a classical design to his Virginia hilltop home, Monticello—perhaps the most stately mansion in the nation (see p. 185). The quadrangle of the University of Virginia at Charlottesville, another creation of Jefferson, remains one of the finest examples of classical architecture in America.

The art of painting continued to be handicapped. It suffered from the dollar grabbing of a raw civilization; from the hustle, bustle, and absence of leisure; from the lack of a wealthy class to sit for portraits—and then pay for them. Some of the earliest painters were forced to go to England, where they found both training and patrons. America exported artists and imported art.

Painting, like the theater, also suffered from the Puritan prejudice that art was a sinful waste of time—and often obscene. John Adams boasted that "he would not give a sixpence for a bust of Phidias or a painting by Raphael." When Edward Everett, the eminent Boston scholar and orator, placed a statue of Apollo in his home, he had its naked limbs draped.

Competent painters nevertheless emerged. Gilbert Stuart (1755–1828), a spendthrift Rhode Islander and one of the most gifted of the early group, wielded his brush in England in competition with the best artists. He produced several portraits of Washington, all of them somewhat idealized and dehumanized. Truth to tell, the famous general had by then lost his natural teeth and some of the original shape of his face. Charles Willson Peale (1741–1827), a Marylander, painted some sixty portraits of Washington, who patiently sat for about fourteen of them. John Trumbull (1756–1843), who had fought in the Revolutionary War, recaptured its scenes and spirit on scores of striking canvases.

During the nationalistic upsurge after the War of 1812, American painters of portraits turned increasingly from human landscapes to romantic mirrorings of local landscapes. The Hudson River school excelled in this type of art. At the same time, portrait painters gradually encountered some unwelcome competition from the invention of a crude photograph known as the daguerreotype, perfected about 1839 by a Frenchman, Louis Daguerre.

Autumn—On the Hudson River   *Painting by Jasper Francis Cropsey (1823–1900). This romantic, heroic, sumptuous, mythic rendering of a brooding and beautiful American landscape was typical of the so-called Hudson River School, which flourished in the mid-nineteenth century. Other prominent artists in this group included Thomas Doughty, Asher Brown Durand, Thomas Cole, and George Inness. (National Gallery of Art.)*

Music was slowly shaking off the restraints of colonial days, when the prim Puritans had frowned upon nonreligious singing. Rhythmic and nostalgic "darky" tunes, popularized by whites, were becoming immense hits by mid-century. Special favorites were the uniquely American minstrel shows, featuring white actors with blackened faces. "Dixie," later adopted by the Confederates as their battle hymn, was written in 1859, ironically in New York City by an Ohioan. The most famous black songs, also ironically, came from a white Pennsylvanian, Stephen C. Foster (1826–1864). His one excursion into the South occurred in 1852, after he had published "Old Folks at Home." Foster made a valuable contribution to American folk music by capturing the plaintive spirit of the slaves. An odd and pathetic figure, he finally lost both his art and his popularity and died in a charity ward after drowning his sorrows in drink.

The Blossoming of a National Literature

"Who reads an American book?" sneered a British critic in 1820. The painful truth was that the nation's rough-hewn, pioneering civilization gave little encouragement to "polite" literature. Much of the reading matter was imported or plagiarized from England.

Busy conquering a continent, the Americans poured most of their creative efforts into practical outlets. Praiseworthy were political essays, like *The Federalist* of Hamilton, Jay, and Madison, pamphlets, like Tom Paine's *Common Sense;* and political orations, like the masterpieces of Daniel Webster. In the category of nonreligious books published before 1820, Benjamin Franklin's *Autobiography* (1818) is one of the few that achieved genuine distinction. His narrative is a classic in its simplicity, clarity, and inspirational quality. Even so, it records only a fragment of "Old Ben's" long, fruitful, and amorous life.

A genuinely American literature received a strong boost from the wave of nationalism that followed the War of Independence and especially the War of 1812. By 1820 the older seaboard areas were sufficiently removed from tree-chopping so that literature could be supported as a profession. The Knickerbocker Group in New York blazed brilliantly across the literary heavens, thus enabling America for the first time to boast of a literature to match its magnificent landscapes.

Washington Irving (1783–1859), born in New York City, was the first American to win international recognition as a literary figure. Steeped in the traditions of New Netherland, he published in 1809 his *Knickerbocker's History of New York,* with its amusing caricatures of the Dutch. When the family business failed, Irving was forced to turn to the goose-feather pen. In 1819–1820 he published *The Sketch Book,* which brought him immediate fame at home and abroad. Combining a pleasing style with delicate charm and quiet humor, he used English as well as American themes and included such immortal Dutch-American tales as "Rip Van Winkle" and "The Legend of Sleepy Hollow." Europe was amazed to find at last an American with a feather in his hand, not in his hair. Later turning to Spanish locales and biography, Irving did much to interpret America to Europe and Europe to America. He was, said the Englishman William Thackeray, "the first ambassador whom the New World of letters sent to the Old."

James Fenimore Cooper (1789-1851) was the first American novelist, as Washington Irving was the first general writer, to gain world fame and to make New World themes respectable. Marrying into a wealthy family, he settled down on the frontier of New York. Reading one day to his wife from an insipid English novel, Cooper remarked in disgust that he could write a better book himself. His wife challenged him to do so—and he did.

After an initial failure, Cooper launched out upon an illustrious career in 1821 with his second novel, *The Spy*—an absorbing tale of the American Revolution. His stories of the sea were meritorious and popular, but his fame rests most enduringly on the *Leatherstocking Tales.* A deadeye rifleman named Natty Bumppo, one of nature's noblemen, meets with Indians in stirring adventures like *The Last of the Mohicans.* James Fenimore Cooper's novels had a wide sale among Europeans, some of whom came to think of all American people as born with tomahawk in hand. Actually Cooper was exploring the viability and destiny of America's republican experiment, by contrasting the values of "natural men," children of the wooded wilderness, with the artificiality of modern civilization.

A third member of the Knickerbocker group in New York was the belated Puritan William Cullen Bryant (1794–1878), transplanted from Massachusetts. At age sixteen he wrote the meditative and melancholy "Thanatopsis" (published in 1817), which was one of the first high-quality poems produced in the United States. Critics could hardly believe that it had been written on "this side of the water." Although Bryant continued with poetry, he was forced to make his living by editing the influential New York *Evening Post.* For over fifty years he set a model for journalism that was dignified, liberal, and high-minded.

Trumpeters of Transcendentalism

A golden age in American literature dawned in the second quarter of the nineteenth century, when an amazing outburst shook New England. One of the mainsprings of this literary flowering was transcendentalism, especially in the Boston area, which preened itself as "the Athens of America."

The transcendentalist movement of the 1830s resulted in part from a liberalizing of the straitjacket Puritan theology. It also owed much to foreign influences, including the German romantic philosophers and the religions of the Orient. The transcendentalists rejected the prevailing theory, derived from John Locke, that all knowledge comes to the mind through the senses. Truth, rather, "transcends" the senses: it cannot be found by observation alone. Every person possesses an inner light that can illuminate the highest truth and put him or her in direct touch with God, or the "Oversoul."

These mystical doctrines of transcendentalism defied precise definition, but they underlay concrete beliefs. Foremost was a stiff-backed individualism in matters religious as well as social. Closely associated was a commitment to self-reliance, self-culture, and self-discipline. These traits naturally bred hostility to authority and to formal institutions of any kind, as well as to all conventional wisdom. Finally came exaltation of the dignity of the individual, whether black or white—the mainspring of a whole array of humanitarian reforms.

In 1849 Thoreau published On the Duty of Civil Disobedience, *asserting "I heartily accept the motto, 'That government is best which governs least'; and I should like to see it acted up to more rapidly and systematically. Carried out, it finally amounts to this, which also I believe— 'That government is best which governs not at all'; and when men are prepared for it, that will be the kind of government which they will have. Government is at best an expedient; but most governments are sometimes, inexpedient."*

Ralph Waldo Emerson (1803–1882) *Emerson's philosophical observations include such statements as: "The less government we have, the better—the fewer laws, and the less confided power"; "To be great is to be misunderstood"; "Every hero becomes a bore at last"; "Shallow men believe in luck"; "When you strike a king, you must kill him." (Courtesy, Concord Free Public Library, gift of Mrs. Arthur Holland.)*

Best known of the transcendentalists was Boston-born Ralph Waldo Emerson (1803–1882). Tall, slender, and intensely blue-eyed, he mirrored serenity in his noble features. Trained as a Unitarian minister, he early forsook his pulpit and ultimately reached a wider audience by pen and platform. He was a never-failing favorite as a lyceum lecturer and for twenty years took a western tour every winter. Perhaps his most thrilling public effort was a Phi Beta Kappa address, "The American Scholar," delivered at Harvard College in 1837. This brilliant appeal was an intellectual Declaration of Independence, for it urged American writers to throw off European traditions and delve into the riches of their own backyards.

Hailed as both a poet and a philosopher, Emerson was not of the highest rank as either. He was more influential as a practical philosopher and through his fresh and vibrant essays enriched countless thousands of humdrum lives. Catching the individualistic mood of the Republic, he stressed self-reliance, self-improvement, self-confidence, optimism, and freedom. The secret of Emerson's popularity lay largely in the fact that his ideals reflected those of an expanding America. By the 1850s he was an outspoken critic of slavery, and he ardently supported the Union cause in the Civil War.

Henry David Thoreau (1817–1862) was Emerson's close associate—a poet, a mystic, a transcendentalist, and a nonconformist. Condemning a government that supported slavery, he refused to pay his Massachusetts poll tax

Walt Whitman   *This portrait of the young poet appeared in the first edition of* Leaves of Grass *(1855). (Rare Book Division, New York Public Library, Astor, Lenox and Tilden Foundations.)*

(1819–1892). In his famous collection of poems *Leaves of Grass* (1855), he gave free rein to his gushing genius with what he called a "barbaric yawp." Highly romantic, emotional, and unconventional, he dispensed with titles, stanzas, rhymes, and at times even regular meter. He handled sex with shocking frankness, although he laundered his verses in later editions, and his book was banned in Boston.

Whitman's *Leaves of Grass* was at first a financial failure. The only three enthusiastic reviews that it received were written by the author himself—anonymously. But in time the once-withered *Leaves of Grass*, revived and honored, won for Whitman an enormous following in both America and Europe. His fame increased immensely among "Whitmaniacs" after his death.

Leaves of Grass gained for Whitman the informal title "Poet Laureate of Democracy." Singing with transcendental abandon of his love for the masses, he caught the exuberant enthusiasm of an expanding America that had turned its back on the Old World:

> All the Past we leave behind;
> We debouch upon a newer, mightier world,
>   varied world;
> Fresh and strong the world we seize—world
>   of labor and the march—
> Pioneers! O Pioneers!

Here at last was the native art for which critics had been crying.

and was jailed for a night.* A gifted prose writer, he is well known for *Walden: Or Life in the Woods* (1854). The book is a record of Thoreau's two years of simple existence in a hut that he built on the edge of Walden Pond, near Concord, Massachusetts. A stiff-necked individualist, he believed that he should reduce his bodily wants so as to gain time for a pursuit of truth through study and meditation. Thoreau's *Walden* and his essay on *Civil Disobedience* exercised a strong influence in furthering idealistic thought, both in America and abroad. His writings later encouraged Mahatma Gandhi to resist British rule in India and, still later, inspired the development of American civil rights leader Martin Luther King, Jr.'s thinking about nonviolence.

Bold, brassy, and swaggering was the open-collared figure of Brooklyn's Walt Whitman

---

*The story (probably apocryphal) is that Emerson visited Thoreau at the jail and asked, "Why are you here?" The reply came, "Why are you *not* here?"

> In 1876 the London Saturday Review referred to Whitman as the author of a volume of "so-called poems which were chiefly remarkable for their absurd extravagances and shameless obscenity, and who has since, we are glad to say, been little heard of among decent people." In 1888 Whitman wrote: "I had my choice when I commenced. I bid neither for soft eulogies, big money returns, nor the approbation of existing schools and conventions. . . . I have had my say entirely my own way, and put it unerringly on record—the value thereof to be decided by time."

Glowing Literary Lights

Certain other literary giants were not actively associated with the transcendentalist movement, though not completely immune to its influences. Professor Henry Wadsworth Longfellow (1807–1882), who for many years taught modern languages at Harvard College, was one of the most popular poets ever produced in America. Handsome and urbane, he lived a generally serene life, except for the tragic deaths of two wives, the second of whom perished before his eyes when her dress caught fire. Writing for the genteel classes, he was adopted by the less cultured masses. His wide knowledge of European literature supplied him with many themes, but some of his most admired poems were based on American traditions—"Evangeline," "Hiawatha," and "The Courtship of Miles Standish." Immensely popular in Europe, Longfellow was the only American ever to be honored with a bust in the Poets' Corner of Westminster Abbey.

A fighting Quaker, John Greenleaf Whittier (1807–1892), with piercing dark eyes and swarthy complexion, was the uncrowned poet laureate of the antislavery crusade. Less talented as a craftsman than Longfellow, he was vastly more important in influencing social action. His poems cried aloud against inhumanity, injustice, and intolerance, against

> The outworn rite, the old abuse,
> The pious fraud transparent grown.

Undeterred by insults and the stonings of mobs, Whittier helped arouse a calloused America on the slavery issue. A great conscience rather than a great poet or intellect, Whittier was one of the moving forces of his generation, whether moral, humanitarian, or spiritual. Gentle and lovable, he was preeminently the poet of human freedom.

Many-sided James Russell Lowell (1819–1891), who succeeded Professor Longfellow at Harvard, ranks as one of America's better poets. He was also a distinguished essayist, literary critic, editor, and diplomat—a diffusion of talents that hampered his poetical output. He is remembered as a political satirist in his *Biglow Papers,* especially those of 1846 dealing with the Mexican War. Written partly as poetry in the Yankee dialect, the *Papers* condemned in blistering terms the alleged slavery-expansion designs of the Polk administration.

Slender Dr. Oliver Wendell Holmes (1809–1894), who taught anatomy with a sparkle at Harvard Medical School, was a prominent poet, essayist, novelist, lecturer, and wit. A nonconformist and a fascinating conversationalist, he shone among a group of literary lights who regarded Boston as "the hub of the universe." His poem "The Last Leaf," in honor of the last "white Indian" of the Boston Tea Party, came to apply to himself. Dying at age eighty-five, he was the "last leaf" among his distinguished contemporaries.*

The most noteworthy literary figure produced by the South before the Civil War, unless Edgar Allan Poe is regarded as a southerner, was novelist William Gilmore Simms (1806–1870). Quantitatively, at least, he was great: eighty-two books flowed from his ever-moist pen, winning for him the title "the Cooper of the South." His themes dealt with the southern frontier in colonial days and with the South during the Revolutionary War. But he was neglected by his own section, even though he married into the socially elite and became a slaveowner. The high-toned planter aristocracy would never accept the son of a poor Charleston storekeeper.

Literary Individualists and Dissenters

Not all writers in these years believed so keenly in human goodness and social progress. Edgar Allan Poe (1809–1849), who spent much of his youth in Virginia, was an eccentric genius. Orphaned at an early age, cursed with ill health, and married to a child-wife of fourteen who fell fatally ill of tuberculosis, he suffered hunger, cold, poverty, and debt. Failing at suicide, he took refuge in the bottle and dissipated his talent early. Poe was a gifted lyric poet, as "The Raven" attests. A master stylist, he also excelled

---

*Oliver Wendell Holmes had a son with the same name who became a distinguished justice of the Supreme Court (1902–1932) and who lived to be ninety-four, less two days.

in the short story, especially of the horror type, in which he shared his alcoholic nightmares with fascinated readers. If he did not invent the modern detective novel, he at least set new high standards in tales like "The Gold Bug."

Poe was fascinated by the ghostly and ghastly, as in "The Fall of the House of Usher" and other stories. He reflected a morbid sensibility distinctly at odds with the usually optimistic tone of American culture. Partly for this reason, Poe has perhaps been even more prized by Europeans than by his own countrymen. His brilliant career was cut short when he was found drunk in a Baltimore gutter and shortly thereafter died.

Two other writers reflected the continuing Calvinist obsession with original sin and with the never-ending struggle between good and evil. In somber Salem, Massachusetts, writer Nathaniel Hawthorne (1804–1864) grew up in an atmosphere heavy with the memories of his Puritan forebears and the tragedy of his father's premature death on an ocean voyage. His masterpiece was *The Scarlet Letter* (1850), which described the Puritan practice of forcing an adultress to wear a scarlet *A* on her clothing. The tragic tale chronicles the psychological effects of sin on the guilty heroine and her secret lover (the father of her baby), a minister of the gospel in Puritan Boston. In *The Marble Faun* (1860), Hawthorne dealt with a group of young American artists who witness a mysterious murder in Rome. The book explored the concepts of the omnipresence of evil and the dead hand of the past weighing upon the present.

Herman Melville (1819–1891), an orphaned and ill-educated New Yorker, went to sea as a youth and served eighteen adventuresome months on a whaler. "A whale ship was my Yale College and my Harvard," he wrote. Jumping ship in the South Seas, he lived among cannibals, from whom he providentially escaped uneaten. His fresh and charming tales of the South Seas were immediately popular, but his masterpiece, *Moby Dick* (1851), was not. This epic novel was a complex allegory of good and evil, told in terms of the conflict between a whaling captain, Ahab, and a giant white whale, Moby Dick. Captain Ahab, who lost a leg to the marine monster, swore revenge. His pursuit finally ended when Moby Dick rammed and sank Ahab's ship, leaving only one survivor. The whale's exact identity and Ahab's motives remained obscure. In the end the sea, like the terrifyingly impersonal and unknowable universe of Melville's imagination, simply rolled on.

Hazardous Whaling *Moby Dick gives a vivid firsthand picture of whaling which proved to be an important industry from colonial times to the end of the nineteenth century. (From* Etchings of a Whaling Cruise, *by John Ross Browne, 1846. Stanford University Libraries.)*

Moby Dick was widely ignored at the time of its publication; people were accustomed to more straightforward and upbeat prose. A disheartened Melville continued to write unprofitably for some years, part of the time eking out a living as a customs inspector, and then died in relative obscurity and poverty. Ironically, his brooding masterpiece about the mysterious white whale had to wait until the more jaded twentieth century for readers and for proper recognition.

Portrayers of the Past

A distinguished group of American historians was emerging at the same time that other writers were winning distinction. Energetic George Bancroft (1800–1891), who as secretary of the navy helped found the Naval Academy at Annapolis in 1845, has deservedly received the title "Father of American History." He published a spirited, superpatriotic history of the United States to 1789 in six (originally ten) volumes (1834–1876), a work that grew out of his vast researches in dusty archives in Europe and America.

Two other historians are read with greater pleasure and profit today. William H. Prescott (1796–1859), who accidentally lost the sight of an eye while in college, conserved his remaining weak vision and published classic accounts of the conquest of Mexico (1843) and Peru (1847). Francis Parkman (1823–1893), whose eyes were so defective that he wrote in darkness with the aid of a guiding machine, penned a brilliant series of volumes, beginning in 1851. In epic style he chronicled the struggle between France and England in colonial times for the mastery of North America.

Early American historians of prominence were almost without exception New Englanders, largely because the Boston area provided well-stocked libraries and a stimulating literary tradition. These writers numbered abolitionists among their relatives and friends and hence were disposed to view unsympathetically the slavery-cursed South. The writing of American history for generations to come was to suffer from an antisouthern bias perpetuated by this early "made in New England" interpretation.

CHRONOLOGY

1770s	First Shaker communities formed
1794	Thomas Paine publishes *The Age of Reason*
1795	University of North Carolina founded
1800	Second Great Awakening begins
1819	Jefferson founds University of Virginia
1821	Cooper publishes *The Spy*
	Emma Willard establishes Troy (New York) Female Seminary
1825	New Harmony commune established
1826	American Temperance Society founded
1828	American Peace Society founded
1830	Joseph Smith founds Mormon church
1830–1831	Finney conducts revivals in eastern cities
1837	Emerson delivers "The American Scholar" address
	Mary Lyon establishes Mount Holyoke Seminary
	Oberlin College admits female students
1841	Brook Farm commune established

1843	Dorothea Dix petitions Massachusetts legislature on behalf of the insane
1846–1847	Mormon migration to Utah
1848	Seneca Falls Women's Rights Convention held
	Oneida commune established
1850	Hawthorne publishes *The Scarlet Letter*
1851	Melville publishes *Moby Dick*
	Maine passes first law prohibiting liquor
1855	Whitman publishes *Leaves of Grass*

Varying Viewpoints

Early chronicles of the antebellum period universally lauded the era's reformers, portraying them as idealistic crusaders intent on improving American society. After World War II, however, some historians began to detect selfish and even conservative motives underlying the apparent benevolence of the reformers. This view described the advocates of reform as anxious, upper-class men and women threatened by the ferment of life in antebellum America. The pursuit of reforms like prohibition, asylums, and mandatory education represented a means of asserting "social control." In this vein, David H. Donald identified one reform movement as "the anguished protest of an aggrieved class against a world they never made."

The wave of reform activity in the 1960s prompted a reevaluation of the reputations of the antebellum reformers. Recent interpretations find much to admire in the authentic religious commitments of reformers and especially in the participation of women, who sought various social improvements as an extension of their function as protectors of the home and family.

The role of women has been particularly scrutinized in recent years, as scholars animated by the modern feminist movement seek to reconstruct the feminine past. Here the work of Nancy Cott has been especially influential, with its stress on women's efforts to create and nurture networks of strong, affective human associations that would sustain communitarian values.

Select Readings

Primary Source Documents

Alexis de Tocqueville's *Democracy in America* (1835, 1840) has stood for a century and a half as the classic analysis of the American character. Joseph Smith, *The Pearl of Great Price** (1829), contains an account of the Mormon leader's religious visions, which capture the religious restiveness of the age. William H. McGuffey, *Fifth Eclectic Reader** (1879), was the most popular school text of the age. On the women's movement, see the "Seneca Falls Manifesto"* (1848), which laid the foundations of the feminist movement. Catharine Beecher and Harriet Beecher Stowe, *The American Woman's Home** (1869), discusses the role of women. Stowe's classic novel, *Uncle Tom's Cabin* (1852), offers an emotional appeal against slavery and a fascinating portrait of slavery, religion, and family life in antebellum America.

Secondary Sources

A magisterial synthesis is Daniel Boorstin, *The Americans: The National Experience* (1965). Satisfying detail is found in two Russell B. Nye books: *The Cultural Life of the New Nation, 1776–1830* (1960), and *Society and Culture in America, 1830–1860* (1974). Alexis de Tocqueville's classic account of life in the young Republic is brilliantly analyzed by James R. Schlieffer in *The Making of Tocqueville's "Democracy in America"* (1980). Sydney E. Ahlstrom, *Religious History of the American People* (1972), is sweeping. On revivalism, see William G. McLoughlin, *Modern Revivalism: Charles Grandison Finney to Billy Graham* (1959); Whitney Cross's absorbing *The Burned-Over District* (1950); and Michael Barkun's *Crucible of the Millennium: The Burned-Over District of New York in the 1840s* (1986). Richard L. Bushman describes the origins of Mormonism in *Joseph Smith and the Beginnings of Mormonism* (1984), and Leonard J. Arrington analyzes the most celebrated Mormon leader in *Brigham Young: American Moses* (1984). On reformers, see Ronald Walters, *American Reformers, 1815–1860* (1978), and Alice F. Tyler, *Freedom's Ferment* (1944). For particular subjects, consult David Rothman, *The Discovery of the Asylum* (1971), and Gerald Grob, *Mental Institutions in America: Social Policy to 1875* (1973); on the development of hospitals, see Charles Rosenberg, *The Care of Strangers: The Rise of America's Hospital System* (1987); on juvenile delinquency, Joseph Hawes, *Children in Urban Society* (1971); and on prohibition, Ian Tyrrell, *Sobering Up: From Temperance to Prohibition in Antebellum America* (1979). On education, see Lawrence A. Cremin, *American Education: The National Experience, 1789–1860* (1980); David Nasaw, *Schooled to Order: A Social History of Public Schooling in the United States* (1979); and Carl F. Kaestle and Maris A. Vinovskis, *Education and Social Change in Nineteenth-Century Massachusetts* (1980). An alternative interpretation of the rise of public education can be found in Michael Katz, *The Irony of Early School Reform* (1968), and in Samuel Bowles and Herbert Gintis, *Schooling in Capitalist America* (1976). Vinovskis offers a critique of these "revisionist" authors in *The Origins of Public High Schools: A Reexamination of the Beverly High School Controversy* (1985). Women's history for this period has recently blossomed in a number of studies, including Ellen Carol DuBois, *Feminism and Suffrage* (1978); Barbara J. Berg, *The Remembered Gate: Origins of American Feminism—The Woman and the City, 1800–1860* (1977); Ruth Bordin, *Women and Temperance* (1981); Estelle B. Freedman, *Their Sisters' Keepers: Women's Prison Reform in America, 1830–1930* (1981); Christine Stansell, *City of Women: Sex and Class in New York, 1789–1860* (1986); Keith E. Melder, *The Beginnings of Sisterhood* (1977); and, emphasizing intellectual and literary history, Ann Douglas, *The Feminization of American Culture* (1977). Family history is covered in Steven Mintz and Susan Kellogg, *Domestic Revolutions: A Social History of American Family Life* (1988); Joseph F. Kett, *Rites of Passage: Adolescence in America* (1976); Lewis Perry, *Childhood, Marriage, and Reform: Henry Clarke Wright, 1797–1870* (1980); Carl N. Degler, *At Odds: Women and the Family in America from the Revolution to the Present* (1980); and Mary P. Ryan, *Cradle of the Middle Class: The Family in Oneida County, New York* (1981). See also Kathryn Kish Sklar, *Catharine Beecher: A Study in Domesticity* (1973). Suzanne Lebsock, *The Free Women of Petersburg* (1984), discusses these issues in a southern context. Special topics are treated in Lewis D. Saum, *The Popular Mood of Pre–Civil War America* (1980); Morton J. Horowitz, *The Transformation of American Law, 1780–1860* (1977); James W. Hurst, *Law and Social Order in the United States* (1977); and James H. Kettner, *The Development of American Citizenship, 1608–1870* (1978).

17

The South and the Slavery Controversy, 1793–1860

If you put a chain around the neck of a slave, the other end fastens itself around your own.

Ralph Waldo Emerson, 1841

"Cotton Is King!"

When George Washington first took the presidential oath, the economic wheels of the South were creaking badly. The region was burdened with depressed prices, unmarketable products, overcropped lands, and the dead weight of an unprofitable slave system. Some southern statesmen, including Thomas Jefferson, were talking openly of freeing their slaves and confidently predicting that slavery would gradually die of economic anemia.

But the introduction of Whitney's cotton gin in 1793 changed the scene. The newly popularized short-staple cotton, which brought a premium price, gradually became the dominant southern crop, eclipsing tobacco, rice, and sugar. Slavery was reinvigorated, with the slave

being chained to the gin, and the planter being chained to the slave.

As time passed, the Cotton Kingdom developed into a huge agricultural factory, pouring out avalanches of the fluffy fiber. Quick profits drew planters to the virgin bottomlands of the gulf states. As long as the soil was still vigorous, the yield was bountiful and the rewards were high. Caught up in an economic spiral, the planters bought more slaves and land to grow more cotton, so as to buy still more slaves and land.

Northern shippers reaped a large part of the profits from the cotton trade. They would load bulging bales of cotton at southern ports, transport them to England, sell them for pounds sterling, and buy needed manufactured goods for sale in the United States. To a large degree

Cotton as King *In this Northern Civil War cartoon, the Confederacy appears as a lighted bomb.*

the prosperity of both North and South rested on the bent backs of southern slaves.

Cotton accounted for half the value of all American exports after 1840. The South produced more than half of the entire world's supply of cotton—a fact that held foreign nations in partial bondage. Britain was then the leading industrial power. Its most important single manufacture in the 1850s was cotton cloth, from which about one-fifth of its population, directly or indirectly, drew its livelihood. About 75 percent of this precious supply of fiber came from the white-carpeted acres of the South.

Southern leaders were fully aware that England was tied to them by cotton threads, and this dependence gave them a heady sense of power. In their eyes "Cotton was King," the gin was his throne, and the black bondsmen were his henchmen. If war should ever break out between North and South, northern warships would presumably cut off the outflow of cotton. Fiber-famished British factories would then

close their gates, starving mobs would force the London government to break the blockade, and the South would triumph. Cotton was a powerful monarch indeed.

The Planter "Aristocracy"

Before the Civil War the South was in some respects not so much a democracy as an oligarchy—or a government by the few, in this case heavily influenced by a planter aristocracy. In 1850 only 1,733 families owned more than 100 slaves each, and this select group provided the cream of the political and social leadership of the section and nation. Here was the mint-julep South of the tall-columned and white-painted plantation mansion—the "big house," where dwelt the "cottonocracy."

The planter aristocrats, with their blooded horses and Chippendale chairs, enjoyed a lion's share of southern wealth. They could educate their children in the finest schools, often in the North or abroad. Their money provided the leisure for study, reflection, and statecraft, as was notably true of men like John C. Calhoun (a Yale graduate) and Jefferson Davis (a West Point graduate). They felt a keen sense of obligation to serve the public. It was no accident that Virginia and its southern sisters produced a higher proportion of front-rank statesmen be-that Virginia and the other southern states produced a higher proportion of front-rank statesmen before 1860 than the "dollar-grubbing" North.

But even in its best light, dominance by a favored aristocracy was basically undemocratic. It widened the gap between rich and poor. It ham-

Thomas Jefferson wrote in 1782: "The whole commerce between master and slave is a perpetual exercise of the . . . most unremitting despotism on the one part, and degrading submissions on the other. . . . Indeed I tremble for my country when I reflect that God is just; that his justice cannot sleep forever." Unlike Washington, Jefferson did not free his slaves in his will; he had fallen upon distressful times.

Harvesting Cotton *This Currier and Ives print shows slaves of both sexes harvesting cotton, which is then "ginned," baled, carted to the riverbank, and taken by paddlewheeler downriver to New Orleans. (The Granger Collection.)*

pered tax-supported public education, because the rich planters could and did send their children to private institutions.

A favorite author of southerners was Sir Walter Scott, whose manors and castles, graced by brave Ivanhoes and fair Rowenas, roughly mirrored their own semifeudal society. Southern aristocrats, who sometimes staged jousting tournaments, strove to perpetuate a type of medievalism that had died out in Europe—or was rapidly dying out.* Mark Twain later accused Sir Walter Scott of having had a hand in starting the Civil War. The British novelist, Twain said, aroused the southerners to fight for a decaying social structure—"a sham civilization."

The plantation system also shaped the lives of southern women. The mistress of a great plantation commanded a sizable household staff of mostly female slaves. She gave daily orders to her cooks, maids, seamstresses, laundresses, and body servants. Relationships between mistresses and slaves ranged from affectionate to atrocious. Some mistresses showed tender re-

gard for their bondswomen, and some slave women took pride in their status as "members" of the household. But slavery stressed even the bonds of womanhood. Virtually no slaveholding women believed in abolition, and relatively few protested when the husbands and children of their slaves were sold. One plantation mistress harbored a special affection for her slave Annica but noted in her diary that "I whipt Annica" for insolence.

Slaves of the Slave System

Unhappily the moonlight-and-magnolia tradition concealed much that was worrisome, distasteful, and sordid. Plantation agriculture was wasteful, largely because King Cotton and his money-hungry subjects despoiled the good earth. Quick profits led to excessive cultivation, or "land butchery," which in turn caused a heavy leakage of population to the West and Northwest.

The economic structure of the South became increasingly monopolistic. As the land wore thin, many small farmers sold their holdings to

---

*Oddly enough, by legislative enactment jousting became the official state sport of Maryland in 1962.

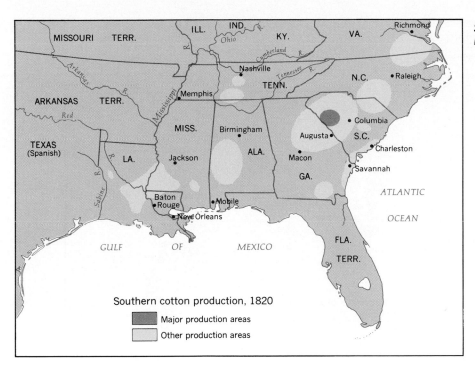

Southern cotton production, 1820

■ Major production areas

□ Other production areas

more prosperous neighbors and went north or west. The big got bigger and the small smaller. When the Civil War finally broke, a large percentage of southern farms had passed from the hands of the families that had originally cleared them.

Another cancer in the bosom of the South was the financial instability of the plantation

---

Basil Hall, an Englishman, visited part of the cotton belt on a river steamer (1827–1828). Noting the preoccupation with cotton, he wrote: "All day and almost all night long, the captain, pilot, crew, and passengers were talking of nothing else; and sometimes our ears were so wearied with the sound of cotton! cotton! cotton! that we gladly hailed a fresh inundation of company in hopes of some change—but alas! . . . 'What's cotton at?' was the first eager inquiry. 'Ten cents [a pound].' 'Oh, that will never do!' From the cotton in the market they went to the crops in the fields—the frost which had nipped their shoots—the hard times—the overtrading—and so round to the prices and prospects again and again."

---

system. The temptation to overspeculate in land and slaves caused many planters, including Andrew Jackson in his later years, to plunge in beyond their depth. Although the black slaves might in extreme cases be fed for as little as ten cents a day, there were other expenses. The slaves represented a heavy investment of capital, perhaps $1,200 each in the case of prime field hands; and they might deliberately injure themselves or run away. An entire slave quarter might be wiped out by disease or even by lightning, as happened in one instance to twenty ill-fated blacks.

Dominance by King Cotton likewise led to a dangerous dependence on a one-crop economy, whose price level was at the mercy of world conditions. The whole system discouraged a healthy diversification of agriculture and particularly of manufacturing.

Southern planters resented watching the North grow fat at their expense. They were pained by the heavy outward flow of commissions and interest to northern middlemen, bankers, agents, and shippers. True sons of the South, especially by the 1850s, deplored the fact that when born they were wrapped in Yankee-made swaddling clothes and that they spent the rest of their lives in servitude to Yankee

Southern Cotton Production, 1860

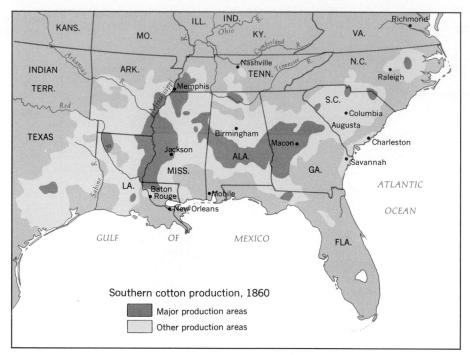

Southern cotton production, 1860

▮ Major production areas
▯ Other production areas

manufacturing. When they died, they were laid in coffins held together with Yankee nails and were buried in graves dug with Yankee shovels. The South furnished the corpse and the hole in the ground.

The Cotton Kingdom also repelled large-scale European immigration, which added so richly to the manpower and wealth of the North. In 1860 only 4.4 percent of the southern population was foreign-born, as compared with 18.7 percent for the North. German and Irish immigration to the South was generally discouraged by the competition of slave labor, by the high cost of fertile land, and by European ignorance of cotton growing. The diverting of non-English immigration to the North caused the white South to become the most Anglo-Saxon section of the nation.

The White Majority

Only a handful of southern whites lived in Grecian-pillared mansions. Below those 1,733 families in 1850 who owned a hundred or more

Slaveowning Families, 1850   *The philosopher Ralph Waldo Emerson, a New Englander, declared in 1856: "I do not see how a barbarous community and a civilized community can constitute a state. I think we must get rid of slavery or we must get rid of freedom."*

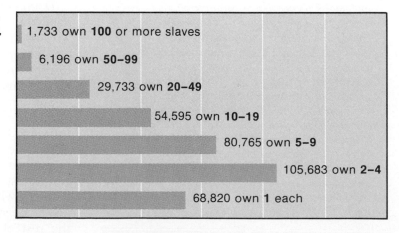

1,733 own **100** or more slaves
6,196 own **50–99**
29,733 own **20–49**
54,595 own **10–19**
80,765 own **5–9**
105,683 own **2–4**
68,820 own **1 each**

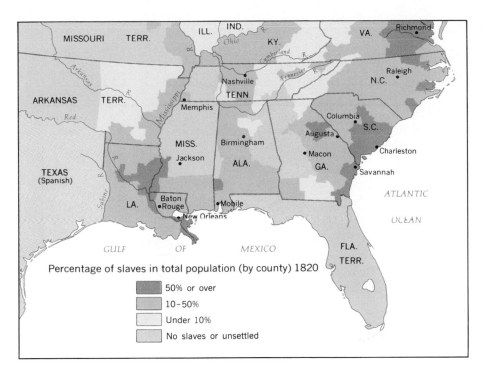

MISSOURI TERR.
ILL.
IND.
KY.
VA.
Richmond
Raleigh
N.C.
Columbia
S.C.
Augusta
Charleston
Savannah
ARKANSAS TERR.
Memphis
TENN.
Nashville
MISS.
Birmingham
Jackson
ALA.
Macon
GA.
TEXAS (Spanish)
LA.
Baton Rouge
Mobile
New Orleans
ATLANTIC OCEAN
GULF OF MEXICO
FLA. TERR.

Percentage of slaves in total population (by county) 1820

- 50% or over
- 10–50%
- Under 10%
- No slaves or unsettled

slaves were the less wealthy slaveowners. They totaled in 1850 some 345,000 families, representing about 1,725,000 white persons. Over two-thirds of these families—255,268 in all—owned fewer than ten slaves each. All told, only about one-fourth of white southerners owned slaves or belonged to a slaveowning family.

The smaller slaveowners did not own a majority of the slaves, but they made up a majority of masters. These lesser masters were typically small farmers. With the striking exception that their household contained a slave or two, or perhaps an entire slave family, the style of their lives probably resembled that of small farmers in the North more than it did that of the southern planter aristocracy. They lived in modest farmhouses and sweated beside their bondsmen in the cotton fields, laboring callus for callus just as hard as their slaves.

Beneath the slaveowners was the great body of whites who owned no slaves at all. By 1860 their numbers had swelled to 6,120,825 persons—three-quarters of the southern white population. Shouldered off the richest bottomlands by the mighty planters, they scratched a simple living from the thinner soils of the backcountry

and the mountain valleys. To them, the riches of the Cotton Kingdom were a distant dream, and they often sneered at the lordly pretensions of the cotton "snobocracy." These red-necked yeomen participated in the market economy scarcely at all. As subsistence farmers, they raised corn and hogs, not cotton, and often lived isolated lives, punctuated periodically by extended socializing and sermonizing at religious camp meetings.

Some of the least prosperous nonslaveholding whites were scorned even by slaves as "poor white trash." Known also as "hillbillies," "crackers," or "clay eaters," they were often described as listless, shiftless, and misshapen. Later investigations have revealed that many of them were not simply lazy, but sick, suffering from malnutrition and parasites, especially hookworm.

All these whites without slaves had no direct stake in the preservation of slavery, yet they were among the stoutest defenders of the slave system. Why? The answer is not far to seek.

The carrot on the stick ever dangling before their eyes was the hope of buying a slave or two and of parlaying their holdings into riches—all

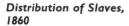

Distribution of Slaves, 1860

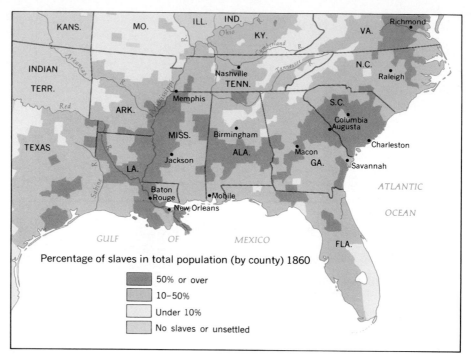

Percentage of slaves in total population (by county) 1860

- 50% or over
- 10–50%
- Under 10%
- No slaves or unsettled

in accord with the "American dream" of upward social mobility. They also took fierce pride in their presumed racial superiority, which would be watered down if the slaves were freed. Many of the poorer whites were hardly better off economically than the slaves; some, indeed, were not so well off. But even the most wretched whites could take perverse comfort from the knowledge that they outranked someone in status: the still more wretched African-American slave. Thus did the logic of economics join with the illogic of racism in buttressing the slave system.

In a special category among white southerners were the mountain whites, more or less marooned in the valleys of the Appalachian range that stretched from western Virginia to northern Georgia and Alabama. Civilization had largely passed them by, and they still lived under spartan frontier conditions. They were a kind of living ancestry, for some of them retained Elizabethan speech forms and habits that had long since died out in England.

As independent small farmers, hundreds of miles distant from the heart of the cotton kingdom and rarely if ever in sight of a slave, these mountain whites had little in common with the whites of the flatlands. Many of them, including future president Andrew Johnson of Tennessee, hated both the haughty planters and their gangs of blacks. They looked upon the impending strife between North and South as "a rich man's war but a poor man's fight."

When the war came, the tough-fibered mountain whites constituted a vitally important peninsula of Unionism jutting down into the secessionist Southern sea. They ultimately played a significant role in crippling the Confederacy. Their attachment to the Union party of Abraham Lincoln was such that, for generations after the Civil War, the only concentrated Republican strength in the solid South was to be found in the southern highlands.

Free Blacks: Slaves Without Masters

Precarious in the extreme was the standing of the South's free blacks, who numbered about 250,000 by 1860. In the upper South, the free black population traced its origins to a wavelet of emancipation inspired by the idealism of Revolutionary days. In the deeper South, many free blacks were mulattoes, usually the emancipated children of a white planter and his black mistress. Throughout the South were some free blacks who had purchased their freedom with earnings from labor after hours. Many free blacks owned property, especially in New Orleans, where a sizable mulatto community prospered. Some, such as William T. Johnson, the "barber of Natchez," even owned slaves. He was the master of fifteen bondsmen; his diary records that in June 1848 he flogged two slaves and a mule.

The free blacks in the South were a kind of "third race." They were prohibited from certain occupations and forbidden from testifying against whites in court. They were always vulnerable to being highjacked back into slavery by unscrupulous slave traders. As free men and women they were walking examples of what might be achieved by emancipation and hence were resented and detested by defenders of the slave system.

Free blacks were also unpopular in the North, where about another 250,000 of them lived. Several states forbade their entrance, most denied them the right to vote, and some barred blacks from public schools. In 1835 New Hampshire farmers hitched their oxen to a small schoolhouse that had dared to enroll fourteen black children and dragged it into a swamp. Northern blacks were especially hated by the pick-and-shovel Irish immigrants, with whom they competed for menial jobs. Much of the agitation in the North against the spread of slavery into the new territories in the 1840s and 1850s grew out of race prejudice, not humanitarianism.

Antiblack feeling was in fact frequently stronger in the North than in the South. The gifted and eloquent former slave Frederick Douglass, an abolitionist and self-educated orator of rare power, was several times mobbed and beaten by northern rowdies. It was sometimes observed that white southerners, who were often suckled and reared by black nurses, liked the black as an individual but despised the race. The white northerner, on the other hand, often professed to like the race but disliked individual blacks.

Plantation Slavery

In society's basement in the South of 1860 were nearly 4 million black human chattels. Their numbers had quadrupled since the dawn of the century, as the booming cotton economy created a seemingly unquenchable demand for slave labor. Legal importations of African slaves into America ended in 1808, when Congress nailed up the bars. But the price of "black ivory" was so high in the years before the Civil War that uncounted thouands of blacks were smuggled into the South, despite the death penalty for slavers. Though several were captured, Southern juries repeatedly acquitted them. Only one slave trader was ever executed, N. P. Gordon, and this took place in New York in 1862, the second year of the Civil War. Yet the huge bulk of the increase in the slave population came not from imports but instead from natural reproduction—a fact that distinguished slavery in America from other New World soci-

Slave Nurse and Young White Master *Southern whites would not allow slaves to own property or exercise civil rights but, paradoxically, they often entrusted them with the raising of their own precious children. Many a slave "mammy" served as a surrogate mother for the offspring of the planter class. (Missouri Historical Society.)*

The Cruelty of Slavery (left) *Held captive in a net, a slave sits on the Congo shore, waiting to be sold and shipped (Collection Photothèque Musée de 'Homme) (above) The device was riveted around a slave's neck. Its attached bells, like a cow bell, made it impossible for the wearer to hide from his or her owner.*

eties and that implied much about the tenor of the slave regime and the conditions of family life under slavery.

Above all, the planters regarded the slaves as investments, into which they had sunk nearly $2 billion of their capital by 1860. Slaves were the primary form of wealth in the South, and as such they were cared for as any asset is cared for by a prudent capitalist. Accordingly, they were sometimes, though by no means always, spared dangerous work, like putting a roof on a house. If a neck was going to be broken, the master preferred it to be that of a wage-earning Irish laborer rather than that of a prime field hand, worth $1,800 by 1860 (a price that had quintupled since 1800). Tunnel blasting and swamp draining were often consigned to itinerant gangs of expendable Irishmen because the labor was "death on niggers and mules."

Slavery was profitable for the great planters, though it hobbled the economic development of the region as a whole. The profits from the cotton boom sucked ever more slaves from the upper to the lower South, so that by 1860 the Deep South states of South Carolina, Florida,

Mississippi, Alabama, and Louisiana each had a majority or near-majority of blacks and accounted for about half of all slaves in the South.

Breeding slaves in the way that cattle are bred was not openly encouraged. But thousands of blacks from the soil-exhausted slave states of the Old South, especially tobacco-depleted Virginia, were "sold down the river" to toil as field-gang laborers on the cotton frontier of the lower Mississippi Valley. Women who bore thirteen or fourteen babies were prized as "rattlin' good breeders," and some of these fecund females were promised their freedom when they had produced ten. White masters, all too frequently, would force their attentions on female slaves, fathering a sizable mulatto population, most of which remained enchained.

Slave auctions were brutal sights. The open selling of human flesh under the hammer, sometimes with cattle and horses, was among the most revolting aspects of slavery. On the auction block families were separated with distressing frequency, usually for economic reasons such as bankruptcy or the division of "property" among heirs. The sundering of families in this fashion was perhaps slavery's greatest psychological horror. Abolitionists decried the practice, and Harriet Beecher Stowe seized on the emotional power of this theme by putting it at the heart of the plot of *Uncle Tom's Cabin*.

Life Under the Lash

White southerners often romanticized about the happy life of their singing, dancing, banjo-strumming, joyful "darkies." But how did the slaves actually live? There is no simple answer to this question. Conditions varied greatly from region to region, from large plantation to small farm, and from master to master. Everywhere, of course, slavery meant hard work, ignorance, and oppression. The slaves—both men and women—usually toiled from dawn to dusk in the fields, under the watchful eyes and ready whip-hand of a white overseer or black "driver." They had no civil or political rights, other than minimal protection from arbitrary murder or unusually cruel punishment. Some states offered further protections, such as banning the sale of a child under the age of ten away from his or her mother. But all such laws were difficult to enforce, since slaves were forbidden to testify in court or even to have their marriages legally recognized.

CASH!

All persons that have SLAVES to dispose of, will do well by giving me a call, as I will give the HIGHEST PRICE FOR Men, Women, & CHILDREN.

Any person that wishes to sell, will call at Hill's tavern, or at Shannon Hill for me, and any information they want will be promptly attended to.

Thomas Griggs.

Charlestown, May 7, 1835.

PRINTED AT THE FREE PRESS OFFICE, CHARLESTOWN.

A Slave Auction *Abraham Lincoln said in 1865, "Whenever I hear anyone arguing for slavery, I feel a strong impulse to see it tried on him personally." (above The Library of Congress; below The Chicago Historical Society.)*

Floggings were common, for the whip was the substitute for the wage-incentive system and the most visible symbol of the planter's mastery. Strong-willed slaves were sometimes sent to "breakers," whose technique consisted mostly in lavish laying on of the lash. As an abolitionist song of the 1850s lamented:

> To-night the bond man, Lord
> Is bleeding in his chains;
> And loud the falling lash is heard
> On Carolina's plains!

But savage beatings made sullen laborers, and lash marks hurt resale values. There are, to be sure, sadistic monsters in any population, and the planter class contained its share. But for financial as well as humane reasons, the typical planter did not customarily go out and beat to death a valuable field hand before breakfast.

By 1860 most slaves were concentrated in the "black belt" of the Deep South that stretched from South Carolina and Georgia into the new southwest states of Alabama, Mississippi, and Louisiana. This was the region of the southern frontier, into which the explosively growing Cotton Kingdom had burst in a few short decades. As on all frontiers, life was often rough and raw, and in general the lot of the

Flogging Slaves   *An example of antislavery propaganda, 1838. (Courtesy, American Antiquarian Society.)*

slave was harder here than in the more settled areas of the Old South.

A majority of blacks lived on larger plantations that harbored communities of twenty or more slaves. In some counties of the Deep South, especially along the lower Mississippi River, blacks accounted for more than 75 percent of the population. There the family life of slaves tended to be relatively stable, and a distinctive African-American slave culture developed. Forced separations of spouses, parents, and children were evidently more common on smaller plantations and in the upper South.

The Slave Quarters   *This Civil War–era photograph shows the stark simplicity of black family life in the South. South Carolina Senator Hammond declared in 1858: "In all social systems there must be a class to do the mean duties. . . . It constitutes the very mudsills of society. . . . Fortunately for the South, she found a race adapted to that purpose. . . . We use them for that purpose and call them slaves." (Library of Congress.)*

Slave marriage vows sometimes proclaimed, "Until death or *distance* do you part."

With impressive resilience, blacks managed to sustain family life in slavery, and most slaves were raised in stable two-person households. Continuity of family identity across generations was evidenced in the widespread practice of naming children for grandparents or adopting the surname not of a current master, but of a forebear's master. African-Americans also displayed their African cultural roots when they avoided marriage between first cousins, in contrast to the frequent intermarriage of close relatives among the ingrown planter aristocracy.

African roots were also visible in slave religious practices. Though heavily Christianized by the itinerant evangelists of the Second Great Awakening, blacks in slavery molded their own distinctive religious forms from a mixture of Christian and African elements. They emphasized those aspects of the Christian heritage that seemed most pertinent to their own situation—especially the captivity of the Israelites in Egypt. One of their most haunting spirituals implored:

> Tell old Pharaoh
> "Let my people go."

And another lamented:

> Nobody knows de trouble I've had
> Nobody knows but Jesus

African practices also persisted in the "responsorial" style of preaching, in which the congregation frequently punctuates the minister's remarks with assents and *amen*s—an adaptation of the give-and-take between caller and dancers in the African ringshout dance.

The Burdens of Bondage

Slavery was intolerably degrading to the victims. They were deprived of the dignity and sense of responsibility that come from independence and the right to make choices. They were denied an education, because reading brought ideas, and ideas brought discontent. Many states passed laws forbidding their instruction, and perhaps nine-tenths of adult slaves at the beginning of the Civil War were totally illiterate. For all slaves—indeed for virtually all blacks, slave or free—the "American dream" of bettering one's lot through study and hard work was a cruel and empty mockery.

Not surprisingly, victims of the "peculiar institution" devised countless ways to throw sand in its gears. When workers are not voluntarily hired and adequately compensated, they can hardly be expected to work with alacrity. Accordingly, slaves often slowed the pace of their labor to the barest minimum that would spare them the lash, thus fostering the myth of black "laziness" in the minds of whites. They filched food from the "big house" and pilfered other goods that had been produced by their labor. They sabotaged expensive equipment, stopping the work routine altogether until repairs were accomplished. Occasionally, they even put poison in their master's food.

The slaves also universally pined for freedom. Many took to their heels as runaways, frequently in search of a separated family member. A black girl, asked if her mother was dead, replied, "Yassah, massah, she is daid, but she's free." Others rebelled, though never successfully. In 1800 an armed insurrection led by a slave named Gabriel in Richmond, Virginia, was foiled by informers, and its leaders were hanged. Denmark Vesey, a free black, led another ill-fated rebellion in Charleston in 1822. Also betrayed by informers, Vesey and more than thirty followers were publicly strung from the gallows. In 1831 the semiliterate Nat Turner, a visionary black preacher, led an uprising that slaughtered about sixty Virginians, mostly women and children. Reprisals were swift and bloody.

The dark taint of slavery also left its mark on the whites. It fostered the brutality of the whip, the bloodhound, and the branding iron. White southerners increasingly lived in a state of imagined siege, surrounded by potentially rebellious blacks inflamed by abolitionist propaganda from the North. Their fears bolstered an intoxicating theory of biological racial superiority and turned the South into a reactionary backwater in an era of progress—one of the last bastions of

Early Emancipation in the North

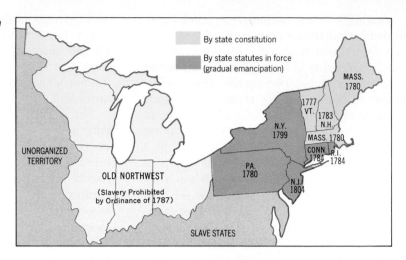

slavery in the Western world. The defenders of slavery were forced to degrade themselves, along with their victims. As Booker T. Washington, a distinguished black leader and former slave, later observed, whites could not hold blacks in a ditch without getting down there with them.

Early Abolitionism

The inhumanity of the "peculiar institution" gradually caused antislavery societies to sprout forth. The first stirrings of abolitionist sentiment occurred at the time of the Revolution, especially among Quakers. Because of the widespread loathing of blacks, some of the earliest abolitionist efforts focused on transporting the blacks bodily back to Africa. The American Colonization Society was founded for this purpose in 1817, and in 1822 the Republic of Liberia, on the fever-stricken West African coast, was established for former slaves. Its capital, Monrovia, was named after President Monroe. Some 15,000 freed blacks were transported over the next four decades. But most blacks had no wish to be transplanted into a strange civilization after becoming partially Americanized. By 1860 virtually all southern slaves were no longer Africans, but native-born African-Americans, with their own distinctive history and culture. Yet the colonization idea appealed to some anti-

slaveryites, including Abraham Lincoln, down to the time of the Civil War.

In the 1830s the abolitionist movement took on new energy and momentum, mounting to the proportions of a crusade. American abolitionists took heart in 1833 when their British counterparts unchained the slaves in the West Indies. Most important, the religious spirit of the Second Great Awakening now inflamed the hearts of many abolitionists against the sin of slavery. Prominent among them was lanky, tousle-haired Theodore Dwight Weld, who had been evangelized by Charles Grandison Finney in New York's Burned-Over District in the 1820s. Self-educated and simple in manner and speech, Weld appealed with special power and directness to his rural audiences of untutored farmers.

Spiritually inspired by Finney, Weld was materially aided by two wealthy and devout New York merchants, the brothers Arthur and Lewis Tappan. In 1832 they paid his way to Lane Theological Seminary in Cincinnati, Ohio, which was presided over by the formidable Lyman Beecher, father of a remarkable brood, including novelist Harriet Beecher Stowe, reformer Catharine Beecher, and preacher-abolitionist Henry Ward Beecher. Expelled along with several other students in 1834 for organizing an eighteen-day debate on slavery, Weld and his fellow "Lane Rebels"—full of the energy and idealism of youth—fanned out across the Old

Northwest preaching the antislavery gospel. Humorless and deadly earnest, Weld also assembled a potent propaganda pamphlet, *American Slavery As It Is* (1839). It was among the most effective abolitionist tracts and greatly influenced Harriet Beecher Stowe's *Uncle Tom's Cabin.*

Radical Abolitionism

On New Year's Day, 1831, a shattering abolitionist blast came from the bugle of William Lloyd Garrison, a mild-looking reformer of twenty-six. The emotionally high-strung son of a drunken father and a spiritual child of the

"Am I Not a Woman and a Sister?" *A popular appeal. (Garrison's* Liberator.*)*

William Lloyd Garrison (1805–1879) *The most conspicuous and most vilified of the abolitionists, Garrison was a nonresistant pacifist and a poor organizer. He favored northern secession from the South and antagonized both sections with his intemperate language. (The Bettman Archive.)*

Second Great Awakening, Garrison published in Boston the first issue of his militantly antislavery newspaper *The Liberator.* With this mighty paper broadside Garrison triggered a thirty-year war of words and in a sense fired one of the opening guns of the Civil War.

Stern and uncompromising, Garrison nailed his colors to the masthead of his weekly. He proclaimed in strident tones that under no circumstances would he tolerate the poisonous weed of slavery but would stamp it out at once, root and branch:

> I will be as harsh as truth and as uncompromising as justice . . . I am in earnest—I will not equivocate—I will not excuse—I will not retreat a single inch—and I WILL BE HEARD!

Other dedicated abolitionists rallied to Garrison's standard, and in 1833 they founded the American Anti-Slavery Society. Prominent among them was Wendell Phillips, a Boston patrician and renowned orator who came to be known as "abolition's golden trumpet." A man of strict principle, he would eat no cane sugar and wear no cotton cloth, since both were produced by southern slaves.

Black abolitionists distinguished themselves as living monuments to the cause of African-American freedom. Their ranks included David

Walker, whose incendiary *Appeal to the Colored Citizens of the World* (1829) advocated a bloody end to white supremacy. Also noteworthy were Sojourner Truth, a freed black woman in New York who fought tirelessly for black emancipation and women's rights, and Martin Delaney, one of the few black leaders to take seriously the notion of mass recolonization of Africa. In 1859 he visited West Africa's Niger Valley seeking a suitable site for relocation.

The greatest of the black abolitionists was Frederick Douglass. Escaping from bondage in 1838 at the age of twenty-one, Douglass was "discovered" by the abolitionists three years later when he gave a stunning impromptu speech at an antislavery meeting in Massachusetts. Thereafter he lectured widely for the

Frederick Douglass (c. 1817–1895) *Born a slave in Maryland, Douglass escaped to the North and became the most prominent black abolitionist. Gifted as an orator, writer, and editor, he continued to battle for the civil rights of his people after emancipation. Near the end of a distinguished career, he served as U.S. minister to Haiti. (Library of Congress.)*

Sojourner Truth *Also known simply as "Isabella," she held audiences spellbound with her deep, resonant voice and the religious passion with which she condemned the sin of slavery. This photo was taken about 1870. (National Portrait Gallery, Smithsonian Institution, Washington, D.C.)*

cause, despite frequent beatings and threats against his life. In 1845 he published his classic autobiography, *Narrative of the Life of Frederick Douglass*. It depicted his remarkable origins as the son of a black slave woman and a white father, his struggle to learn to read and write, and his eventual escape to the North.

Douglass was as flexibly practical as Garrison was stubbornly principled. Garrison often appeared to be more interested in his own righteousness than in the substance of the slavery evil itself. He repeatedly demanded that the "virtuous" North secede from the "wicked" South. Yet he did not explain how the creation of an independent slave republic would bring an end to the "damning crime" of slavery. Renouncing politics, on the Fourth of July, 1854, he publicly burned a copy of the Constitution as "a covenant with death and an agreement with hell" (a phrase he borrowed from a Shaker

> *Frederick Douglass, the remarkable ex-slave, told of Mr. Covey, a white owner who bought a single female slave "as a breeder." She gave birth to twins at the end of the year. "At this addition to the human stock Covey and his wife were ecstatic with joy. No one dreamed of reproaching the woman or finding fault with the hired man, Bill Smith, the father of the children, for Mr. Covey himself had locked the two up together every night, thus inviting the result."*

condemnation of marriage). Critics, including some of his former supporters, charged that Garrison was cruelly probing the moral wound in America's underbelly but offering no acceptable balm to ease the pain.

Douglass, on the other hand, along with other abolitionists, increasingly looked to politics to end the blight of slavery. These political abolitionists backed the Liberty party in 1840, the Free-Soil party in 1848, and eventually the Republican party in the 1850s. In the end, most abolitionists, including even the pacifistic Garrison himself, followed out the logic of their beliefs and supported a frightfully costly fratricidal war as the price of emancipation.

High-minded and courageous, the abolitionists were men and women of goodwill and various colors who faced the cruel choice that people in many ages have had thrust upon them: When is evil so enormous that it must be denounced, even at the risk of precipitating bloodshed and butchery?

The South Lashes Back

Antislavery sentiment was not unknown in the South, and in the 1820s antislavery societies were more numerous south of Mason and Dixon's line than north of it. But after about 1830 the voice of white southern abolitionism was silenced. In a last gasp of southern questioning of slavery, the Virginia legislature debated and eventually defeated various emancipation proposals in 1831–1832. That debate marked a turning point. Thereafter all the slave states tightened their slave codes and moved to prohibit emancipation of any kind, voluntary or compensated. Nat Turner's rebellion in 1831 sent a wave of hysteria sweeping over the snowy cotton fields, and planters in growing numbers slept with pistols by their pillows. Although Garrison had no demonstrable connection with the Turner conspiracy, his *Liberator* appeared at about the same time, and he was bitterly condemned as a terrorist and an inciter of murder. The state of Georgia offered $5,000 for his arrest and conviction.

The nullification crisis in 1832 further implanted haunting fears in white southern minds, conjuring up nightmares of black incendiaries and abolitionist devils. Jailings, whippings, and lynchings now greeted rational efforts to discuss the slavery problem in the South.

Pro-slavery whites responded by launching a massive defense of slavery as a positive good. In doing so, they forgot their own section's previous doubts about the morality of the "peculiar institution." Slavery, they claimed, was supported by the authority of the Bible and the wisdom of Aristotle. It was good for the Africans, who were lifted from the barbarism of the jungle and clothed with the blessings of Christian civilization. Slavemasters did indeed encourage religion in the slave quarters. A catechism for blacks contained such passages as:

Q. Who gave you a master and a mistress?
A. God gave them to me.
Q. Who says that you must obey them?
A. God says that I must.

White apologists also pointed out that master-slave relationships really resembled those of a family. On many plantations, especially those in the Old South of Virginia and Maryland, this argument had a certain plausibility. A slave's tombstone bore this touching inscription:

JOHN:
A faithful servant
 and true friend:
Kindly, and considerate:
Loyal, and affectionate:
The family he served
Honours him in death:
But, in life they gave him love:
For he was one of them

A Two-Way Proslavery Cartoon *Published in New York, the cartoon shows a chilled and rejected free black in the North* (left) *disconsolately passing a grogshop, while* (right) *a happy southern slave enjoys life with a fishing rod in the company of a white youth.*

Southern whites were quick to contrast the "happy" lot of their "servants" with that of the overworked northern wage slaves, including sweated women and stunted children. The blacks mostly toiled in the fresh air and sunlight, not in dark and stuffy factories. They did not have to worry about slack times or unemployment, as did the "hired hands" of the North. Provided with a jail-like form of Social Security, they were cared for in sickness and old age, unlike northern workers, who were turned adrift.

These curious proslavery arguments only widened the chasm between a backward-looking South and a forward-looking North—and indeed much of the rest of the Western world. The southerners reacted to the pressure of their own fears and the merciless nagging of the northern abolitionists. Increasingly the white South turned in upon itself and grew hotly intolerant of any embarrassing questions about the status of slavery.

Regrettably, also, the controversy over free people endangered free speech in the entire country. Piles of petitions poured in upon Congress from the antislavery reformers; and in 1836 sensitive southerners drove through the House the so-called gag resolution. It required all such antislavery appeals to be tabled without debate. This attack on the right of petition aroused the sleeping lion in an aged ex-president, Representative John Quincy Adams, and he waged a successful eight-year fight for its repeal.

Southern whites likewise resented the flooding of their mails with incendiary abolitionist literature. Even if the blacks could not read, they could interpret the inflammatory drawings, such as those that showed masters knocking the teeth out of their slaves with clubs. In 1835 a mob in Charleston, South Carolina, looted the local post office and burned a pile of abolitionist propaganda. Capitulating to southern pressures, the Washington government in the 1830s ordered southern postmasters to destroy abolitionist material and called on southern state officials to arrest federal postmasters who did not comply. Such was "freedom of the press" as guaranteed by the Constitution.

William Lloyd Garrison Mobbed in Boston, 1835 *Garrison and the visiting English abolitionist George Thompson were roughly treated by a mob that mocked and feared their abolitionist ideals. Yet within a generation many Bostonians, perhaps even a majority, would embrace Garrison's cause, and he would eventually be lionized as a heroic keeper of the nation's conscience. (New-York Historical Society.)*

The Abolitionist Impact in the North

Abolitionists—especially the extreme Garrisonians—were for a long time unpopular in many parts of the North. Northerners had been brought up to revere the Constitution and to regard the clauses on slavery as a lasting bargain. The ideal of Union, hammered home by the thundering eloquence of Daniel Webster and others, had taken deep root; and Garrison's wild talk of secession grated harshly on northern ears.

The North also had a heavy economic stake in Dixieland. By the late 1850s the southern planters owed northern bankers and other creditors about $300 million, and much of this immense sum would be lost—as, in fact, it later was—should the Union dissolve. New England textile mills were fed with cotton raised by the slaves, and a disrupted labor system might cut off this vital supply and bring unemployment. The Union during these critical years was partly bound together with cotton threads, tied by lords of the loom in collaboration with the so-called lords of the lash. It was not surprising that strong hostility developed in the North against the boat-rocking tactics of the radical antislaveryites.

Repeated tongue-lashings by the extreme abolitionists provoked many mob outbursts in the North, some led by respectable gentlemen. A gang of young toughs broke into Lewis Tappan's New York house in 1834 and demolished its interior, while a crowd in the street cheered. In 1835 Garrison, with a rope tied around him, was dragged through the streets of Boston by the so-called Broadcloth Mob but escaped almost miraculously. Reverend Elijah P. Lovejoy, of Alton, Illinois, not content to assail slavery, impugned the chastity of Catholic women. His printing press was destroyed four times, and in 1837 he was killed by a mob, thus becoming "the martyr abolitionist." So unpopular were the antislavery zealots that ambitious politicians, like Lincoln, usually avoided the taint of Garrisonian abolition like the plague.

Yet by the 1850s the abolitionist outcry had made a deep dent in the northern mind. Many citizens had come to see the South as the land of the unfree and the home of a hateful institution. Few northerners were prepared to abolish slavery outright, but a growing number, including Abraham Lincoln, opposed extending it to the territories in the West. People of this stamp, commonly called "free-soilers," swelled their ranks as the Civil War approached.

CHRONOLOGY

1793	Whitney's cotton gin transforms southern economy
1800	Gabriel slave rebellion in Virginia
1808	Congress outlaws slave trade
1817	American Colonization Society formed
1822	Republic of Liberia established in Africa Vesey slave rebellion in Charleston
1829	Walker publishes *Appeal to the Colored Citizens of the World*
1831	Garrison publishes *The Liberator* Turner slave rebellion in Virginia
1831–1832	Virginia lesiglature debates slavery and emancipation
1833	British abolish slavery in the West Indies American Anti-Slavery Society founded
1834	Abolitionist students expelled from Lane Seminary
1835	U.S. Post Office orders destruction of abolitionist mail "Broadcloth Mob" attacks Garrison
1836	House of Representatives passes "Gag Resolution"
1837	Mob kills abolitionist Lovejoy in Alton, Illinois
1839	Weld publishes *American Slavery As It Is*
1840	Liberty party organized
1845	Douglass publishes *Narrative of the Life of Frederick Douglass*
1848	Free-Soil party organized

Varying Viewpoints

Ulrich Bonnell Phillips made three key arguments in his landmark study *American Negro Slavery* (1918). First, he claimed that slavery was a dying economic institution, unprofitable to the slaveowner and an obstacle to the economic development of the South as a whole. Second, he contended that slavery was a rather benign institution and that the planters, contrary to abolitionist charges of ruthless exploitation, treated their chattels with kindly paternalism. Third, he reflected the dominant racial attitudes of his time in his belief that slaves were passive and dim by nature and did not abhor the institution.

For nearly a century, historians have debated these assertions, sometimes heatedly. More sophisticated economic analysis has refuted Phillips's claim that slavery would have withered away without a war. Economic historians have demonstrated that slavery was a viable, profitable, expanding economic system and that slaves constituted a good investment. The price of a prime field hand rose dramatically, even in the 1850s.

No such definitive conclusion has yet been reached in the disputes over slave treatment and slave personality. Beginning in the late 1950s, historians came increasingly to emphasize the harshness of the slave system. One study, Stanley Elkins' *Slavery,* went so far as to compare the "peculiar institution" to the Nazi concentration camps. Both were "total institutions," Elkins contended, which "infantilized" their victims. Recently, scholars such as Eugene Genovese have criticized both views. Without diminishing the deprivations and pains of slavery, these students of the "peculiar institution" concede that slavery embraced a strange form of paternalism, a system that reflected not the benevolence of southern slaveholders but their need to protect and coax work out of their often recalcitrant "investment."

The revised conceptions of the master-slave relationship also spilled over into the debate over slave personality. Some histori

ans, like Kenneth Stampp, denied Phillips's portrait of the slave as a passive "Sambo." They stressed the frequency and variety of violent and peaceful slave resistance. Others, like Elkins, accepted the Sambo stereotype but saw it as a consequence of slavery rather than a natural attribute of the slave. A third view sees the Sambo character as an act, an image that slaves used to confound their masters without incurring punishment. Adherents of the latter view, conspicuously including Herbert Gutman and Lawrence Levine, also emphasize the tenacity with which slaves maintained their own culture, despite the hardships of bondage.

The reputation of the abolitionists, both moderate and extreme, has greatly improved, reflecting the changed atmosphere generated by the civil rights struggles of the 1960s and 1970s. Once vilified as irresponsible provokers of a needless war, they are now commonly hailed as champions of human rights.

Select Readings

Primary Source Documents

Two influential abolitionist documents are Theodore Dwight Weld, *American Slavery As It Is** (1839), and the inaugural editorial of William Lloyd Garrison's *The Liberator** (1831). Roy P. Basler, ed., *The Collected Works of Abraham Lincoln* (1933), contains the Great Emancipator's assessment of abolitionism in 1854. For southern perspectives, see James Henry Hammond's famous "Cotton Is King" speech, *Congressional Globe,* 36 Cong., 1 sess. p 961 (March 3, 1858).*

Secondary Sources

A good introduction to southern history is Clement Eaton, *A History of the Old South: The Emergence of a Reluctant Nation* (1975). Wilbur J. Cash, *The Mind of the South* (1941), is an engagingly written classic. Always incisive is C. Vann Woodward, *The Burden of Southern History* (1960) and *American Counterpoint* (1971). Frank L. Owsley, *Plain Folk of the Old South* (1949), illuminates the lives of non-

slaveholding whites. Owsley's views are challenged in Eugene Genovese, *The Political Economy of Slavery* (1965), and Genovese and Elizabeth Fox-Genovese, *Fruits of Merchant Capital* (1983). Genovese also discusses *The World the Slaveholders Made* (1970), which should be supplemented by James Oakes, *The Ruling Race: A History of American Slaveholders* (1982). Gavin Wright, *The Political Economy of the Cotton South* (1978), is particularly thoughtful. Catherine Clinton examines *The Plantation Mistress* (1982) while Elizabeth Fox-Genovese discusses southern women more generally in *Within the Plantation Household: Black and White Women of the Old South* (1988). The literature on slavery and African-Americans is enormous; the best place to start is John Hope Franklin, *From Slavery to Freedom* (5th ed., 1980). Consult also Nathan Irving Huggins's sometimes lyrical *Black Odyssey* (1977). The modern debate on slavery began with Ulrich B. Phillips's classic *American Negro Slavery* (1918); a darker view of the same subject is found in Kenneth M. Stampp, *The Peculiar Institution* (1956). Consult also Stanley Elkins's stimulating essay, *Slavery* (2d ed., 1968), which also has interesting observations on the abolitionists. More recently, considerable furor has surrounded the publication of Robert Fogel and Stanley Engerman, *Time on the Cross: The Economics of American Slavery* (2 vols., 1974). For contrasting views and rebuttals, see John W. Blassingame, *The Slave Community* (rev. ed., 1979); Herbert Gutman, *Slavery and the Numbers Game* (1975) and *The Black Family in Slavery and Freedom, 1750–1925* (1976); Paul David, *Reckoning with Slavery* (1976); Eugene Genovese, *Roll, Jordan, Roll* (1974); Sterling Stuckey, *Slave Culture: Nationalist Theory and the Foundations of Black America* (1987); and Carl N. Degler's comparison of slavery and race relations in Brazil and the United States, *Neither Black nor White* (1971). Two studies also compare the development of race relations in South Africa and the United States: George M. Frederickson, *White Supremacy: A Comparative Study in American and South African History* (1981), and John Cell, *The Highest Stage of White Supremacy: The Origins of Segregation in South Africa and the American South* (1981). Robert Starobin examines *Industrial Slavery in the Old South* (1970), and Ira Berlin tells the story of free blacks in *Slaves without Masters* (1975), which should be supplemented by Michael P. Johnson and James L. Roark, *Black Masters: A Free Family of Color in the Old South* (1984), and their *No Chariot Let Down: Charleston's Free People of Color on the Eve of the Civil War* (1984). See also Leon Litwack, *North of Slavery* (1961), for the situation of blacks outside the South. David B. Davis provides indispensable background to the history of abolitionism in *The Problem of Slavery in Western Culture* (1966) and *The Problem of Slavery in the Age of Revolution* (1975). The best brief history of the abolitionists is James B. Stewart, *Holy Warriors* (1976). Ronald E. Walters emphasizes the constraints that American culture placed on the abolitionists in *The Antislavery Appeal: American Abolitionism After 1830* (1976), while James B. Stewart focuses on *Wendell Phillips: Liberty's Hero* (1987). Aileen Kraditor is favorably disposed toward Garrison in *Means and Ends in American Abolitionism: Garrison and His Critics* (1967). Consult also Lewis Perry, *Radical Abolitionists* (1973). Benjamin Quarles examines *Black Abolitionists* (1969), as do Jane H. and William H. Pease in *They Who Would Be Free: Blacks Search for Freedom, 1830–1861* (1974). Arna Bontemps presents the life of Frederick Douglass, the most prominent black abolitionist, in *Free at Last* (1971). Also see Waldo E. Martin, Jr., *The Mind of Frederick Douglass* (1984). White attitudes can be studied in Winthrop Jordan's masterful *White over Black* (1968) and George Frederickson's insightful *The Black Image in the White Mind* (1971).

Manifest Destiny and Its Legacy, 1841–1848

Our manifest destiny [is] to overspread the continent allotted by Providence for the free development of our yearly multiplying millions.

John L. O'Sullivan, 1845*

The Accession of "Tyler Too"

A horde of hard-ciderites descended upon Washington early in 1841, clamoring for the spoils of office. Newly elected President Harrison, bewildered by the uproar, was almost hounded to death by Whig spoilsmen.

The real leaders of the Whig party regarded "Old Tippecanoe" as little more than an impressive figurehead. Daniel Webster, as secretary of state, and Henry Clay, the uncrowned king of the Whigs and their ablest spokesman in the Senate, would grasp the helm. The aging general was finally forced to rebuke the overzealous Clay and pointedly remind him that William

Henry Harrison was president of the United States.

Unluckily for Clay and Webster, their schemes soon hit a fatal snag. Before the new term had fairly started, Harrison came down with pneumonia. Wearied by official functions and plagued by office seekers, the enfeebled old warrior died after only four weeks in the White House—the shortest administration by far in American history, following by far the longest inaugural address.

The "Tyler too" part of the Whig ticket, hitherto only a rhyme, now claimed the spotlight. What manner of man did the nation now find in the presidential chair? Six feet (1.83 meters) tall, slender, blue-eyed, and fair-haired, with classical features and a high forehead, Tyler was a Virginia gentleman of the old school—gracious and kindly, yet stubbornly attached to

*Earliest known use of the term *Manifest Destiny,* sometimes called "manifest desire."

principle. He had earlier resigned from the Senate, quite unnecessarily, rather than accept distasteful instructions from the Virginia legislature. Still a lone wolf, he had forsaken the Jacksonian Democratic fold for that of the Whigs, largely because he could not stomach the dictatorial tactics of Jackson.

Tyler's enemies accused him of being a Democrat in Whig clothing, but this charge was only partially true. The Whig party, like the Democratic party, was something of a catchall, and the accidental president belonged to the minority wing, which embraced a number of Jeffersonian states' righters. Tyler had in fact been put on the ticket partly to attract the vote of this influential group, many of whom were southern gentry.

Yet Tyler, high-minded as he was, should never have consented to run on the ticket. Though the dominant Clay-Webster group had published no platform, every alert politician knew what the unpublished platform contained. And on virtually every major issue the obstinate Virginian was at odds with the majority of his Whig party, which was pro-bank, pro–protective tariff, and pro–internal improvements. "Tyler too" rhymed with "Tippecanoe," but there the harmony ended. As events turned out, President Harrison, the Whig, served for only four weeks, while Tyler, the ex-Democrat who was still largely a Democrat at heart, served for 204 weeks.

President John Tyler (1790–1862) *The first "accidental president," he was faithful to his states' rights convictions until death. A member of the Virginia secession convention in 1861, he served in the provisional congress of the Confederacy and was elected to a seat in the Confederate house of representatives. Invading Northern troops vengefully despoiled his beautiful Virginia estate, Sherwood Forest. (Chicago Historical Society.)*

John Tyler: A President without a Party

After their hard-won, hard-cider victory, the Whigs brought their not-so-secret platform out of Clay's waistcoat pocket. To the surprise of no one, it outlined a strongly nationalistic program.

Financial reform came first. The Whig Congress hastened to pass a law ending the independent treasury system, and President Tyler, disarmingly agreeable, signed it. Clay next drove through Congress a bill for a "Fiscal Bank," which would establish a new Bank of the United States.

Tyler's hostility to a centralized bank was notorious, and Clay—the "Great Compromiser"

—would have done well to conciliate him. But the Kentuckian, robbed repeatedly of the presidency by lesser men, was in an imperious mood and riding for a fall. When the bank bill reached the presidential desk, Tyler flatly vetoed it on both practical and constitutional grounds. A drunken mob gathered late at night near the White House and shouted insultingly, "Huzza for Clay!" "A Bank! A Bank!" "Down with the Veto!"

The stunned Whig leaders tried once again. Striving to meet Tyler's objections to a "Fiscal Bank," they passed another bill providing for a

"Fiscal Corporation." But the president, still unbending, vetoed the offensive substitute. Democrats were jubilant: they had been saved from another financial "monster" only by the pneumonia that had felled Harrison.

Whig extremists, boiling with indignation, condemned Tyler as "His Accidency" and as an "Executive Ass." Widely burned in effigy, he received numerous letters threatening him with death. A wave of influenza then sweeping the country was called the "Tyler grippe." To the delight of Democrats, the stiff-necked Virginian was formally expelled from his party by a caucus of Whig congressmen, and a serious attempt to impeach him was made in the House of Representatives. His entire cabinet resigned in a body, except Secretary of State Webster, who was then in the midst of delicate negotiations with England.

The proposed Whig tariff also felt the prick of the president's well-inked pen. Tyler appreciated the necessity of bringing additional revenue to the Treasury. But old Democrat that he was, he looked with a frosty eye on the major tariff scheme of the Whigs, because it provided, among other features, for a distribution among the states of revenue from the sale of public lands in the West. Tyler could see no point in squandering federal money when the federal Treasury was not overflowing, and he again wielded an emphatic veto.

Chastened Clayites redrafted their tariff bill. They chopped out the offensive dollar-distribution scheme and pushed down the rates to about the moderately protective level of 1832, roughly 32 percent on dutiable goods. Tyler had no fondness for a protective tariff, but realizing the need for additional revenue, he reluctantly signed the law of 1842. In subsequent months, the pressure for higher customs duties slackened as the country gradually edged its way out of the depression. The Whig slogan, "Harrison, Two Dollars a Day and Roast Beef," was rewritten by unhappy Democrats to read, "Ten Cents a Day and Bean Soup."

A War of Words with England

Hatred of England during the nineteenth century came to a head periodically and had to be lanced by treaty settlement or by war. The poison had festered ominously by 1842.

"Life In An American Hotel" *An English caricature of American rudeness and readiness with the pistol. (Punch, 1856.)*

Anti-British passions were compounded of many ingredients. At bottom lay the bitter, red-coated memories of the two Anglo-American wars. In addition, the genteel pro-British Federalists had died out, eventually yielding to the boisterous Jacksonian Democrats. British travelers, sniffing with aristocratic noses at the crude scene, wrote acidly of American tobacco spitting, slave auctioneering, lynching, eye gouging, and other unsavory features of the rustic civilization. Travel books penned by these critics, whose views were avidly read on both sides of the Atlantic, stirred up angry outbursts in America.

But the literary fireworks did not end here. British magazines added fuel to the flames when, enlarging on the travel books, they launched sneering attacks on Yankee shortcomings. American journals struck back with "you're another" arguments, thus touching off the "Third War with England." Fortunately, this British-American war was fought with paper broadsides, and only ink was spilled. British authors, including Charles Dickens, entered the fray with gall-dipped pens, for they were being denied rich royalties by the absence of an American copyright law.*

Sprawling America, with expensive canals to dig and railroads to build, was a borrowing nation in the nineteenth century. Imperial Britain, with its overflowing coffers, was a lending nation. The tightfisted creditor is never popular with the debtor, and the phrase "bloated British bondholder" rolled bitterly from many an American tongue. When the panic of 1837 broke, and several states defaulted on their bonds or repudiated them openly, honest Englishmen assailed Yankee trickery. One of them offered a new stanza for an old song:

> Yankee Doodle borrows cash,
> Yankee Doodle spends it,
>   And then he snaps his fingers at
> The jolly flat [simpleton] who lends it.

Troubles of a more dangerous sort came closer to home in 1837, when a short-lived insurrection erupted in Canada. It was supported by such a small minority of Canadians that it never had a real chance of success. Yet hundreds of hot-blooded Americans, hoping to strike a blow for freedom against the hereditary enemy, furnished military supplies or volunteered for armed service. The Washington regime tried arduously, though futilely, to uphold its weak neutrality regulations. But again, as in the case of Texas, it simply could not enforce unpopular laws in the face of popular opposition.

A provocative incident on the Canadian frontier brought passions to boil in 1837. An American steamer, the *Caroline*, was engaged in carrying supplies to the insurgents across the swift Niagara River. It was finally attacked on the New York shore by a determined British force, which set the vessel on fire. Lurid American illustrators showed the flaming ship, laden with shrieking souls, plunging over the Niagara Falls. The craft in fact sank short of the falls, and only one American was killed.

This unlawful invasion of American soil—a counterviolation of neutrality—had alarming aftermaths. The Washington officials lodged vigorous but ineffective protests. Three years later, in 1840, the incident was dramatically revived in the state of New York. A Canadian named McLeod, after allegedly boasting in a tavern of his part in the *Caroline* raid, was arrested and indicted for murder. The London Foreign Office, which regarded the *Caroline* raiders as members of an armed force and not as criminals, made clear that his execution would mean war. Fortunately, McLeod was freed after establishing an alibi. It must have been airtight, for it was good enough to convince a New York jury. The tension forthwith eased, but it snapped taut again in 1841, when British officials in the Bahamas offered asylum to 130 Virginia slaves who had rebelled and captured the American ship *Creole*.

Manipulating the Maine Maps

An explosive controversy of the early 1840s involved the Maine boundary dispute. The St. Lawrence River is icebound several months of

---

*Not until 1891 did Congress extend copyright privileges to foreign authors.

the year, as the British, remembering the War of 1812, well knew. They were determined, as a defensive precaution against the Yankees, to build a road westward from the seaport of Halifax to Quebec. But the proposed route ran through disputed territory—claimed also by Maine under the misleading peace treaty of 1783. Tough-knuckled lumberjacks from both Maine and Canada entered the disputed no-man's-land of the tall-timbered Aroostook River Valley. Ugly fights flared up and both sides summoned the local militia. The small-scale lumberjack clash, which was dubbed the "Aroostook War," threatened to widen into a full-dress shooting war.

As the crisis deepened in 1842, the London Foreign Office took an unusual step. It sent to Washington a nonprofessional diplomat, the conciliatory financier Lord Ashburton, who had married a wealthy American woman. He speedily established cordial relations with Secretary Webster, who had recently been lionized during a visit to England.

The two statesmen, their nerves frayed by protracted negotiations in the heat of a Washington summer, finally agreed to compromise on the Maine boundary. On the basis of a rough, split-the-difference arrangement, the Americans were to retain some 7,000 square miles (18,130 square kilometers) of the 12,000 square miles (31,080 square kilometers) of wilderness in dispute. The British got less land

> *The* London Morning Chronicle *greeted the Webster-Ashburton treaty thusly:* "See the feeling with which the treaty has been received in America; mark the enthusiasm it has excited. What does this mean? Why, either that the Americans have gained a great diplomatic victory over us, or that they have escaped a great danger, as they have felt it, in having to maintain their claim by war."

but won the desired Halifax-Quebec route. During the negotiations the *Caroline* affair, dragged out since 1837, was patched up by an exchange of diplomatic notes.

The surrender of 5,000 square miles (12,950 square kilometers) of allegedly American soil to the British proved highly unpopular, especially among loyal Maine citizens. One irate U.S. senator branded the treaty a "solemn bamboozlement." But Webster had obtained an ancient map which indicated, ironically, that the British were entitled to the entire area in dispute. When he secretly displayed his find in Washington, the treaty quickly slipped through the Senate on greased skids.

British imperialists likewise condemned Lord Ashburton for his "capitulation." But their opposition also evaporated when the London officials turned up with another yellowing map: it proved that the *Americans* were entitled to the entire area in contention. Thus each party to the negotiation secretly held the other's trump card in the historic "Battle of the Maps."

Historians have since proved that the United States had a valid claim to the entire territory. This fact was not known at the time, perhaps fortunately, for the British were in no mood to give up the Halifax route. The yielding of 5,000 square miles (12,950 square kilometers) of pine-forested land, at least in 1842, seemed like a cheap price to pay for avoiding a senseless war.

An overlooked bonus was won in the same treaty when the British, in adjusting the boundary to the west, surrendered 6,500 square miles (16,835 square kilometers). The area was later found to contain the priceless Mesabi iron ore of Minnesota.

Maine Boundary Settlement, 1842

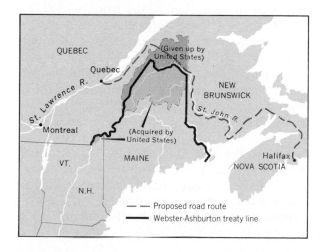

The Lone Star of Texas Shines Alone

During the uncertain eight years since 1836, Texas had led a precarious existence. Mexico, refusing to recognize its independence, regarded the Lone Star Republic as a province in revolt, to be reconquered in the future. Mexican officials loudly threatened war if the American eagle should gather the fledgling republic under its protective wings.

The Texans were forced to maintain a costly military establishment. Vastly outnumbered by their Mexican foe, they could not tell when he would strike again. Mexico actually did make two halfhearted raids that, though ineffectual, foreshadowed more fearsome efforts. Confronted with such perils, Texas was driven to open negotiations with England and France, in the hope of securing the defensive shield of a protectorate. In 1839 and 1840, the Texans concluded treaties with France, Holland, and Belgium.

Britain was intensely interested in an independent Texas. Such a republic would check the southward surge of the American colossus, whose bulging biceps posed a constant threat to nearby British possessions in the New World. A puppet Texas, dancing to strings pulled by Britain, could be turned upon the Yankees. Subsequent clashes would create a smoke-screen diversion, behind which foreign powers could move into the Americas and challenge the insolent Monroe Doctrine. French schemers were likewise attracted by the hoary game of divide and conquer. These actions would result, they hoped, in the fragmentation and militarization of America.

Dangers threatened from other foreign quarters. British abolitionists were busily intriguing for a foothold in Texas. If successful in freeing the few blacks there, they presumably would inflame the nearby slaves of the South. In addition, British merchants regarded Texas as a potentially important free-trade area—an offset to the tariff-walled United States. British manufacturers likewise perceived that those vast Texan plains constituted one of the great cotton-producing areas of the future. An independent Texas would relieve British looms of their fatal dependence on American fiber—a supply that might be cut off in time of crisis by embargo or war.

The Belated Texas Nuptials

Partly because of the fears aroused by British schemers, Texas became a leading issue in the presidential campaign of 1844. The foes of expansion assailed annexation, while southern hotheads cried, "Texas or Disunion." The proexpansion Democrats under James K. Polk finally triumphed over the Whigs under Henry Clay, the hardy perennial candidate. Lame-duck President Tyler thereupon interpreted the narrow Democratic victory, with dubious accuracy, as a "mandate" to acquire Texas.

Eager to crown his troubled administration with this splendid prize, Tyler deserves much of the credit for shepherding Texas into the fold. Many "conscience Whigs" feared that Texas in the Union would be red meat to nourish the lusty "slave power." Aware of their opposition, Tyler despaired of securing the needed two-thirds vote for a treaty in the Senate. He therefore arranged for annexation by a joint resolution. This solution required only a simple majority in both houses of Congress. After a spirited debate, the resolution passed early in 1845, and Texas was formally invited to become the twenty-eighth star on the American flag.

Mexico angrily charged that the Americans had despoiled it of Texas. This was to some extent true in 1836, but hardly true in 1845, for the area was no longer Mexico's to be despoiled of. As the years stretched out, realistic observers could see that the Mexicans would not be able to reconquer their lost province. Yet Mexico left the Texans dangling by denying their right to dispose of themselves as they chose.

By 1845, the Lone Star Republic had become a danger spot, inviting foreign intrigue that menaced the American people. Its continued existence as an independent nation threatened to involve the United States in a series of ruinous wars, both in America and in Europe. Americans were in a "lick all creation" mood when they sang "Uncle Sam's Song to Miss Texas":

> If Mexy back'd by secret foes,
>   Still talks of getting you, gal;
> Why we can lick 'em all you know
>   And then annex 'em too, gal.

What other power would have spurned the imperial domain of Texas? The bride was so near, so rich, so fair, so willing. Whatever the peculiar circumstances of the Texas revolution, the United States can hardly be accused of unseemly haste in achieving annexation. Nine long years were surely a decent wait between the beginning of the courtship and the consummation of the marriage.

Oregon Fever Populates Oregon

The so-called Oregon Country was an enormous wilderness. It sprawled magnificently west of the Rockies to the Pacific Ocean, and north of California to the line of 54° 40′—the present southern tip of the Alaska panhandle. All or substantial parts of this immense area were claimed at one time or another by four nations: Spain, Russia, Britain, and the United States.

Two claimants dropped out of the scramble. Spain, though the first to raise its banner in Oregon, bartered away its claims to the United States in the so-called Florida Treaty of 1819. The Russian bear retreated to the line of 54° 40′ by the treaties of 1824 and 1825 with America and Britain. These two remaining rivals now had the field to themselves.

British claims to Oregon were strong—at least to that portion north of the Columbia River. They were based squarely on prior discovery and exploration, on treaty rights, and on actual occupation. The most important colonizing agency was the far-flung Hudson's Bay Company, which was trading profitably with the Indians of the Pacific Northwest for their furs.

Americans, for their part, could also point pridefully to exploration and occupation. Cap-

Oregon Fever *Thousands of pioneers like these pulling away from St. Louis said farewell to civilization as they left the Mississippi River and headed across the untracked plains to Oregon in the 1840s. (St. Louis Art Museum, Eliza McMillan Purchase Fund.)*

tain Robert Gray in 1792 had stumbled upon the majestic Columbia River, which he named after his ship; and the famed Lewis and Clark expedition of 1804–1806 had ranged overland through the Oregon Country to the Pacific. This shaky American toehold was ultimately strengthened by the presence of missionaries and other settlers, a sprinkling of whom reached the grassy Willamette River Valley, south of the Columbia, in the 1830s. These men and women of God, in saving the soul of the Indian, were instrumental in saving the soil of Oregon for the United States. They stimulated interest in a faraway domain that countless Americans had earlier assumed would not be settled for centuries.

Scattered American and British pioneers in Oregon continued to live peacefully side by side. At the time of negotiating the Treaty of 1818, the United States had sought to divide the vast domain at the forty-ninth parallel. But the British, who regarded the Columbia River as the St. Lawrence of the West, were unwilling to yield this vital artery. A scheme for peaceful "joint occupation" was thereupon adopted, pending future settlement.

The handful of Americans in the Willamette Valley was suddenly multiplied in the early 1840s, when "Oregon fever" seized hundreds of restless pioneers. In increasing numbers their creaking covered wagons jolted over the 2,000-mile (3,200-kilometer) Oregon Trail as the human rivulet widened into a stream.* By 1846 about five thousand Americans had settled south of the Columbia River, some of them tough "border ruffians," expert with bowie knife and "revolving pistol."

The British, in the face of this rising torrent of humanity, could muster only seven hundred or so subjects north of the Columbia. Losing out lopsidedly in the population race, they were beginning to see the wisdom of arriving at a

In winning Oregon the Americans had great faith in their procreative powers. "Our people are spreading out," boasted one congressman in 1846, "with the aid of the American multiplication table. Go to the West and see a young man with his mate of eighteen; after the lapse of thirty years, visit him again, and instead of two, you will find twenty-two. That is what I call the American multiplication table."

peaceful settlement before being engulfed by their neighbors.

A curious fact is that only a relatively small segment of the Oregon Country was in actual controversy by 1845. The area in dispute consisted of the rough quadrangle between the Columbia River on the south and east, the forty-ninth parallel on the north, and the Pacific Ocean on the west. Britain had repeatedly offered the line of the Columbia; America had repeatedly offered the forty-ninth parallel. The whole fateful issue was now tossed into the presidential election of 1844, where it was largely overshadowed by the question of annexing Texas.

A Mandate (?) for Manifest Destiny

The two major parties nominated their presidential standard-bearers in May 1844. Ambitious but often frustrated Henry Clay, easily the most popular man in the country, was enthusiastically chosen by the Whigs at Baltimore. The Democrats, meeting later in the same city, seemed hopelessly deadlocked. Finally the expansionists, dominated by the pro-Texas southerners, trotted out and nominated James K. Polk of Tennessee, the nation's first "dark horse" or "surprise" presidential candidate.

Polk may have been a dark horse, but he was hardly an unknown or decrepit nag. Speaker of the House of Representatives for four years and governor of Tennessee for two terms, he was a determined, industrious, ruthless, and intelligent public servant. Sponsored by Andrew Jack-

---

*The average rate of progress in covered wagons was 1 to 2 miles an hour. This amounted to about 100 miles (161 kilometers) a week, or about five months for the entire journey. Thousands of humans, in addition to horses and oxen, died en route. One estimate is seventeen deaths a mile for men, women, and children.

Westward the Course of Empire Takes Its Way
This romantic tribute to the spirit of Manifest Destiny was commissioned by Congress in 1860 and may still be seen in the Capitol. (National Museum of American Art.)

son, his friend and neighbor, he was rather implausibly built up by Democrats as yet another "Young Hickory." Whigs attempted to jeer him into oblivion with the taunt, "Who is James K. Polk?" They soon found out.

The campaign of 1844 was in part an expression of the mighty emotional upsurge known as Manifest Destiny. Countless citizens in the 1840s and 1850s, feeling a sense of mission, believed that Almighty God had "manifestly" destined the American people for a hemispheric career. They would irresistibly spread their uplifting and ennobling democratic institutions over at least the entire continent, and possibly over South America as well. Land greed and ideals—"empire" and "liberty"—were thus conveniently conjoined.

Expansionist Democrats were strongly swayed by the intoxicating spell of Manifest Destiny. They came out flat-footedly in their platform for the "Reannexation of Texas"* and the "Reoccupation of Oregon," all the way to 54° 40′. Out-bellowing the Whig log-cabinites in

the game of slogans, they shouted "All of Oregon or None." They also condemned Clay as a "corrupt bargainer," a dissolute character, and a slaveowner. (Their own candidate, Polk, also owned slaves—a classic case of the pot calling the kettle black.)

The Whigs, as noisemakers, took no back seat. They countered with such slogans as "Hooray for Clay" and "Polk, Slavery, and Texas, or Clay, Union, and Liberty." They also spread the lie that a gang of Tennessee slaves had been seen on their way to a southern market with the initials J.K.P. (James K. Polk) branded on them.

On the crucial issue of Texas, the acrobatic Clay tried to ride two horses at once. The "Great Compromiser" appears to have compromised away the presidency when he wrote a series of confusing letters. They seemed to say that while he personally favored annexing slaveholding Texas (an appeal to the South), he also favored postponement (an appeal to the North). He might have lost more ground if he had not "straddled," but he certainly alienated the more ardent antislaveryites.

In the stretch drive, "Dark Horse" Polk nipped Henry Clay at the wire, 170 to 105 votes in the Electoral College and 1,338,464 to

---

*The United States had given up its claims to Texas in the so-called Florida Purchase Treaty with Spain in 1819 (see p. 237). The slogan "Fifty-four forty or fight" was evidently not coined until two years later, in 1846.

1,300,097 in the popular column. Clay would have won if he had not lost New York State by a scant 5,000 votes. There the tiny antislavery Liberty party absorbed nearly 16,000 votes, many of which would otherwise have gone to the unlucky Kentuckian. Ironically, the anti-Texas Liberty party, by helping to ensure the election of pro-Texas Polk, hastened the annexation of Texas.

Land-hungry Democrats, flushed with victory, proclaimed that they had received a mandate from the voters to take Texas. But a presidential election is seldom, if ever, a clear-cut mandate on anything. The only way to secure a true reflection of the voters' will is to hold a special election on a given issue. The picture that emerged in 1844 is not one of mandate but of muddle. What else could there have been when the results were so close, the personalities so colorful, and the issues so numerous—including Oregon, Texas, the tariff, slavery, the bank, and internal improvements? Yet this unclear "mandate" was interpreted by President Tyler as a clear mandate to annex Texas—and he signed the joint resolution three days before leaving the White House.

James K. Polk (1795–1849) *Distinguished for both determination and deviousness, Polk added more territory to the United States (by questionable means) than any other president. In tenaciously pursuing his goals, he broke himself down with overwork and died 103 days after his single term ended. His somewhat priggish wife (and secretary) banned all drinking and dancing in the White House. (National Archives.)*

Polk the Purposeful

"Young Hickory" Polk, unlike "Old Hickory" Jackson, was not an impressive figure. Of middle height (5 feet 8 inches; 1.72 meters), lean, white-haired (worn long), gray-eyed, and stern-faced, he took life seriously and drove himself mercilessly into a premature grave. His burdens were increased by an unwillingness to delegate authority. Methodical and hardworking but not brilliant, he was shrewd, narrow, conscientious, and persistent. "What he went for he fetched," wrote a contemporary. Purposeful in the highest degree, he developed a positive four-point program and with remarkable success achieved it completely in less than four years.

One of Polk's goals was a lowered tariff. His secretary of the treasury, wispy Robert J. Walker, devised a tariff-for-revenue bill that reduced the average rates of the Tariff of 1842 from about 32 percent to 25 percent. With the strong support of low-tariff southerners, Walker lobbied the measure through Congress, though not without loud complaints from the Clayites, especially in New England and the middle states, that American manufacturing would be ruined. But these prophets of doom missed the mark. The Walker Tariff of 1846 proved to be an excellent revenue producer, largely because it was followed by boom times and heavy imports.

A second objective of Polk was the restoration of the independent treasury, unceremoniously dropped by the Whigs in 1841. Pro-bank Whigs in Congress raised a storm of opposition, but victory at last rewarded the president's efforts in 1846.

The third and fourth points on Polk's "must list" were the acquisition of California and the settlement of the Oregon dispute.

"Reoccupation" of the "whole" of Oregon had been promised northern Democrats in the campaign of 1844. But southern Democrats, once they had annexed Texas, rapidly cooled off. Polk, himself a southerner, had no intention of

House Vote on Tariff of 1846*

REGIONS	FOR	AGAINST
New England	9	19
Middle states	18	44
West and Northwest	29	10
South and Southwest	58	20
TOTAL	114	93

*Compare vote on 1832 tariff, p. 263.

insisting on the 54° 40′ pledge of his own platform. But feeling bound by the three offers of his predecessors to London, he again proposed the compromise line of 49°. The British minister in Washington, on his own initiative, brusquely spurned this olive branch.

The next move on the Oregon chessboard was up to Britain. Fortunately for peace, the ministry began to experience a change of heart. British antiexpansionists ("Little Englanders") were now persuaded that the Columbia River after all was not the St. Lawrence of the West and that the turbulent American hordes might one day seize the Oregon Country. Why fight a hazardous war over this wilderness on behalf of an unpopular monopoly, the Hudson's Bay Company, which had already "furred out" much of the area anyhow?

Early in 1846 the British, hat in hand, came

around and themselves proposed the line of 49°. President Polk, irked by the previous rebuff, threw the decision squarely into the lap of the Senate. The senators speedily accepted the offer and approved the subsequent treaty, despite a few diehard shouts of "fifty-four forty forever!" and "Every foot or not an inch!" The fact that the United States was then a month deep in a war with Mexico doubtless influenced the Senate's final vote.

Satisfaction with the Oregon settlement among Americans was not unanimous. The northwestern states, hotbed of Manifest Destiny and "fifty-four fortyism," joined the antislavery forces in condemning what they regarded as a base betrayal by the South. Why *all* of Texas and not *all* of Oregon? Because, sneered the expansionist Senator Benton of Missouri, "Great Britain is powerful and Mexico is weak."

So Polk, despite all the campaign bluster, got neither "fifty-four forty" nor a fight. But he did get something that in the long run was better: a reasonable compromise without shedding a drop of blood.

Misunderstandings with Mexico

Faraway California was another worry of Polk's. He and other disciples of Manifest Destiny had long coveted its verdant valleys, and especially

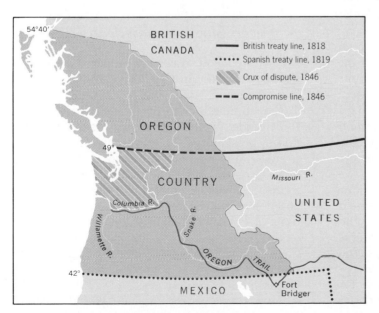

The Oregon Controversy

Britain Mocks American Claims in Oregon *This British cartoon makes sport of American pretensions to sovereignty in the Oregon country. "What, you young Yankee-Noodle," says an imperious John Bull, "strike your own father?" (Bettmann Archive.)*

the spacious bay of San Francisco. This splendid harbor was widely regarded as America's future gateway to the Pacific Ocean.

The population of California in 1845 was curiously mixed. It consisted of some seven thousand sun-blessed Spanish-Mexicans, plus more than ten times as many dispirited Indians. There were fewer than a thousand foreigners, mostly Americans, some of whom had "left their consciences" behind them as they rounded Cape Horn. Given time, these transplanted Yankees might yet bring California into the Union by "playing the Texas game."

Polk was eager to buy California from Mexico, but relations with Mexico City were dangerously embittered. Among other friction points, the United States had claims against the Mexicans for some $3 million in damages to American citizens and their property. The revolution-riddled regime in Mexico had formally agreed to assume most of this debt but had been forced to default on its payments.

A more serious bone of contention was Texas. The Mexican government, after threatening war if the United States should acquire the Lone Star Republic, had recalled its minister from Washington following annexation. Diplomatic relations were completely severed.

Deadlock with Mexico over Texas was further tightened by a question of boundaries. During the long era of Spanish-Mexican occu-

pation, the southwestern boundary of Texas had been the Nueces River. But the expansive Texans, on rather farfetched grounds, were claiming the more southerly Rio Grande instead. Polk, for his part, felt a strong moral obligation to defend Texas in its claim, once it was annexed.

The Mexicans were far less concerned about this boundary quibble than the United States. In their eyes all of Texas was still theirs, although temporarily in revolt, and a dispute over the two rivers seemed pointless. Yet Polk was careful to keep American troops out of virtually all of the explosive no-man's-land between the Nueces and the Rio Grande, as long as there was any real prospect of peaceful adjustment.

The golden prize of California continued to cause Polk much anxiety. Disquieting rumors (now known to have been ill-founded) were circulating that the British lion was about to buy or seize California—a grab that Americans could not tolerate under the Monroe Doctrine. In a last desperate throw of the dice, Polk dispatched John Slidell to Mexico City as minister late in 1845. The new envoy, among other alternatives, was instructed to offer a maximum of $25 million for California and territory to the east. But the proud Mexican people would not even permit Slidell to present his "insulting" proposition.

American Blood on American (?) Soil

A frustrated Polk was now prepared to force a showdown. On January 13, 1846, he ordered four thousand men, under General Zachary Taylor, to march from the Nueces River to the Rio Grande, provocatively near Mexican forces. Polk's presidential diary reveals that he expected at any moment to hear of a clash. When none occurred after an anxious wait, he informed his cabinet on May 9, 1846, that he proposed to ask Congress to declare war on the basis of (1) unpaid claims and (2) Slidell's rejection. These, at best, were rather flimsy pretexts. Two cabinet members spoke up and said that they would feel better satisfied if Mexican troops should fire first.

That very evening, as fate would have it, news of bloodshed arrived. On April 25, 1846,

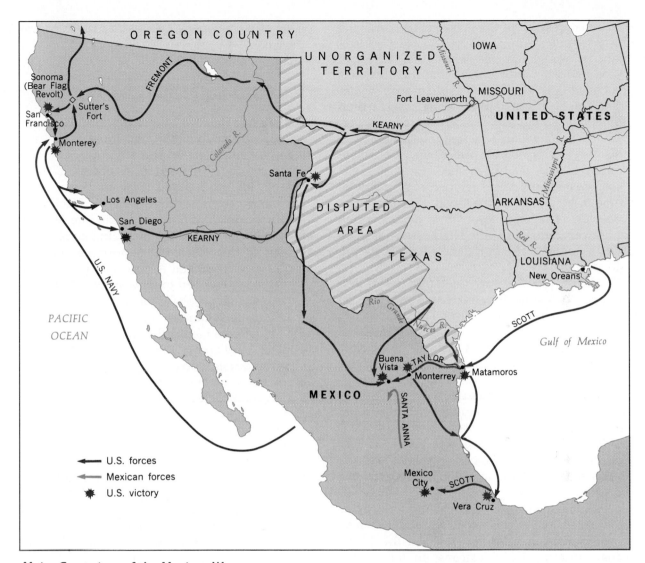

Major Campaigns of the Mexican War

Mexican troops had crossed the Rio Grande and attacked General Taylor's command, with a loss of sixteen Americans killed or wounded.

Polk, further aroused, sent a vigorous war message to Congress. He declared that despite "all our efforts" to avoid a clash, hostilities had been forced upon the country by the shedding of "American blood on the American soil." A patriotic Congress overwhelmingly voted for war, and enthusiastic volunteers cried, "Ho for the Halls of the Montezumas!" and "Mexico or Death!" Inflamed by the war fever, even antislavery Whig centers joined with the rest of the nation, though they later condemned "Jimmy

Polk's war." As James Russell Lowell of Massachusetts lamented,

> Massachusetts, God forgive her,
> She's akneelin' with the rest.

Less than a year before he became president, Lincoln wrote that "the act of sending an armed force among the Mexicans was unnecessary, inasmuch as Mexico was in no way molesting or menacing the United States or the people thereof; and that it was unconstitutional, because the power of levying war is vested in Congress, and not in the President" (June 1, 1860).

In his message to Congress Polk was making history—not writing it. If he had been a historian, he would have explained that American blood had been shed on soil that the Mexicans had good reason to regard as their own. A gangling, rough-featured Whig congressman from Illinois, one Abraham Lincoln, introduced certain resolutions that requested information as to the precise "spot" on American soil where American blood had been shed. He pushed his "spot" resolutions with such persistence that he came to be known as the "spotty Lincoln," who could die of "spotted fever." The more extreme antislavery agitators of the North, many of them Whigs, branded the president a liar—"Polk the Mendacious."

Did Polk provoke war? California was an imperative point in his program, and Mexico would not sell it at any price. The only way to get it was to use force or wait for an internal American revolt. Yet delay seemed dangerous, for the claws of the British lion might snatch the ripening California fruit from the talons of the American eagle. Grievances against Mexico were annoying yet tolerable; in later years America endured even worse ones. But in 1846 patience had ceased to be a virtue, as far as Polk was concerned. Determined to grasp California by fair means or foul, he pushed the quarrel to a bloody showdown.

Both sides, in fact, were spoiling for a fight. Hotheaded Americans, especially southwestern expansionists, were eager to teach the Mexicans a lesson. The Mexicans, in turn, were burning to humiliate the "Bullies of the North." Possessing a considerable standing army, heavily overstaffed with generals, they boasted of invading the United States, freeing the black slaves, and lassoing whole regiments of Americans. They were hoping that the quarrel with Britain over Oregon would blossom into a full-dress war, as it came near doing, and further pin down the hated *yanquis*. A conquest of Mexico's vast and arid expanses seemed fantastic, especially in view of the bungling American invasion of Canada in 1812.

Both sides were fired by moral indignation. The Mexican people could fight with the flaming sword of righteousness, for had not the "insolent" Yankee picked a fight by polluting their soil? Many earnest Americans, on the other hand, sincerely believed that Mexico was the aggressor.

The Mastering of Mexico

Polk wanted California—not war. But when war came, he hoped to fight it on a limited scale and then pull out when he had won the prize. The dethroned Mexican dictator Santa Anna, then exiled with his teenage bride in Cuba, let it be known that if the American blockading squadron would permit him to slip into Mexico, he would sell out his country. Incredibly, Polk agreed to this discreditable intrigue. But the double-crossing Santa Anna, once he returned to Mexico, proceeded to rally his countrymen to a desperate defense of their soil.

American operations in the Southwest and in California were completely successful. In 1846 General Stephen W. Kearny led a detachment of seventeen hundred troops over the famous Santa Fe trail from Fort Leavenworth to Santa Fe. This sunbaked outpost, with its drowsy plazas, was easily captured. But before Kearny could reach California, the fertile province was won. When war broke out, Captain John C. Frémont, the dashing explorer, just "happened" to be there with several dozen well-armed men. In helping to overthrow Mexican rule in 1846, he collaborated with American naval officers and with the local Americans, who had hoisted the banner of the short-lived California Bear Flag Republic.

General Zachary Taylor meanwhile had been spearheading the main thrust. Known as "Old Rough and Ready" because of his iron constitution and incredibly unsoldierly appearance—he sometimes wore a Mexican straw hat—he fought his way across the Rio Grande into Mexico. After several gratifying victories, he reached Buena Vista. There, on February 22–23, 1847, his weakened force of five thousand men was attacked by some twenty thousand march-weary troops under Santa Anna. The Mexicans were finally repulsed with extreme difficulty, and overnight Zachary Taylor became the "Hero of Buena Vista." One Kentuckian was heard to say that "Old Zack" would be elected president in 1848 by "spontaneous combustion."

Sound American strategy now called for a crushing blow at the enemy's vitals—Mexico City. General Taylor, though a good leader of modest-sized forces, could not win decisively in the semideserts of northern Mexico. The command of the main expedition, which pushed inland from the coastal city of Vera Cruz early in 1847, was entrusted to General Winfield Scott. A handsome giant of a man, Scott had emerged as a hero from the War of 1812 and had later earned the nickname of "Old Fuss and Feathers" because of his resplendent uniforms and strict discipline. He was severely handicapped in the Mexican campaign by inadequate numbers of troops, by expiring enlistments, by a more numerous enemy, by mountainous terrain, by disease, and by political backbiting at home. Yet he succeeded in battling his way up to Mexico City by September 1847 in one of the most brilliant campaigns in American military annals. He proved to be the most distinguished general produced by his country between 1783 and 1861.

Fighting Mexico for Peace

Polk was anxious to end the shooting as soon as he could secure his territorial goals. Accordingly, he sent along with Scott's invading army the chief clerk of the State Department, Nicholas P. Trist, who among other weaknesses was afflicted with an overfluid pen. Trist and Scott arranged for an armistice with Santa Anna, at a cost of $10,000. The wily dictator pocketed the bribe and then used the time to bolster his defenses.

Negotiating a treaty with a sword in one hand and a pen in the other was ticklish business. Polk, disgusted with his blundering envoy, abruptly recalled Trist. The wordy diplomat then dashed off a sixty-five-page letter explaining why he was not coming home. The president was furious. But Trist, grasping a fleeting opportunity to negotiate, signed the Treaty of Guadalupe Hidalgo on February 2, 1848, and forwarded it to Washington.

The terms of the treaty were breathtaking. They confirmed the American title to Texas and yielded the enormous area stretching westward to Oregon and the ocean and embracing coveted California. This total expanse, including Texas, was about one-half of Mexico. The United States agreed to pay $15 million for the land and to assume the claims of its citizens against Mexico in the amount of $3,250,000 (see "Makers of America," pp. 380–381).

Polk submitted the treaty to the Senate. Although Trist had proved highly annoying, he had generally followed his original instructions. And speed was imperative. The antislavery Whigs in Congress—dubbed "Mexican Whigs" or "Conscience Whigs"—were condemning this "damnable war" with increasing heat. Having secured control of the House in 1847, they were even threatening to vote down supplies for the armies in the field. If they had done so, Scott probably would have been forced to retreat, and the fruits of victory might have been tossed away.

Another peril impended. A swelling group of expansionists, intoxicated by Manifest Destiny, was clamoring for all of Mexico. If America had seized it, the nation would have been saddled with an expensive and vexatious policing problem. Farseeing southerners like Calhoun, alarmed by the mounting anger of antislavery agitators, realized that the South would do well not to be too greedy. The treaty was finally approved by the Senate, 38 to 14. Oddly enough, it was condemned both by those opponents who wanted all of Mexico and by opponents who wanted none of it.

Victors rarely pay an indemnity, especially after a costly conflict has been "forced" on them. Yet Polk, who had planned to offer $25 million before the war, arranged to pay $18,250,000 after winning the war. Cynics have charged that the Americans were pricked by guilty consciences; apologists have pointed proudly to the "Anglo-Saxon spirit of fair play." A decisive factor was the need for haste, while there was still a responsible Mexican government to carry out

Early in 1848 the New York *Evening Post* demanded: *"Now we ask, whether any man can coolly contemplate the idea of recalling our troops from the [Mexican] territory we at present occupy . . . and . . . resign this beautiful country to the custody of the ignorant cowards and profligate ruffians who have ruled it for the last twenty-five years? Why, humanity cries out against it. Civilization and Christianity protest against this reflux of the tide of barbarism and anarchy."* Such was one phase of Manifest Destiny.

the treaty and before political foes in the United States, notably the antislavery zealots, sabotaged Polk's expansionist program.

Profit and Loss in Mexico

As wars go, the Mexican War was a small one. It cost some thirteen thousand American lives, most of them taken by disease. But the fruits of the fighting were enormous.

America's total expanse, already vast, was increased by about one-third (counting Texas)—an addition even greater than that of the Louisiana Purchase. A sharp stimulus was given to the spirit of Manifest Destiny, for as the proverb has it, the appetite comes with eating.

As fate ordained, the Mexican War was the blood-splattered schoolroom of the Civil War. The campaigns provided priceless field experience for most of the officers destined to become leading generals in the forthcoming conflict, including Captain Robert E. Lee and Lieutenant U. S. Grant. The Military Academy at West Point, founded in 1802, fully justified its existence through the well-trained officers. Useful also was the navy, which did valuable work in throwing a crippling blockade around Mexican ports. The Marine Corps, in existence since 1798, won new laurels, and to this day sings in its stirring hymn about the Halls of Montezuma.

The army waged war without defeat and without a major blunder, despite formidable obstacles and a half-dozen or so achingly long marches. Chagrined British critics, as well as

PLUCKED:

THE MEXICAN EAGLE BEFORE THE WAR!   THE MEXICAN EAGLE AFTER THE WAR!

A Cartoon from Yankee Doodle, 1847 *This satiric drawing was symbolic of the "lick all creation" spirit of the times.*

other foreign skeptics, reluctantly revised upward their estimate of Yankee military prowess. Opposing armies, moreover, emerged with increased respect for each other. The Mexicans, though poorly led, fought heroically. At Chapultepec, near Mexico City, the teenage lads of the military academy there (*los niños*) perished to a boy.

Long-memoried Mexicans have never forgotten that their northern enemy tore away about half of their country. The argument that they were lucky not to lose all of it, and that they had been paid something for their land, did not lessen their bitterness. The war also marked an ugly turning point in the relations between the United States and Latin America as a whole. Hitherto, Uncle Sam had been regarded with some complacency, even friendliness. Henceforth, he was increasingly feared as the "Colossus of the North." Suspicious neighbors to the south condemned him as a greedy and untrustworthy bully, who might next despoil them of their soil.

Most ominous of all, the war rearoused the snarling dog of the slavery issue, and the beast did not stop yelping until drowned in the blood of the Civil War. Abolitionists assailed the Mexican conflict as one provoked by the southern "slavocracy" for its own evil purposes. As James Russell Lowell had Hosea Biglow drawl in his Yankee dialect:

> They jest want this Californy
> So's to lug new slave-states in
> To abuse ye, an' to scorn ye,
> An' to plunder ye like sin.

In line with Lowell's charge, the bulk of the American volunteers were admittedly from the South and Southwest. But, as in the case of the Texan revolution, the basic explanation was proximity rather than conspiracy.

Quarreling over slavery extension also erupted on the floors of Congress. In 1846, shortly after the shooting started, Polk had requested an appropriation of $2 million with which to buy a peace. Representative David Wilmot of Pennsylvania, fearful of the southern "slavocracy," introduced a fateful amendment. It stipulated that slavery should never exist in any of the territory to be wrested from Mexico.

The disruptive Wilmot amendment twice passed the House, but not the Senate. Southern members, unwilling to be robbed of prospective slave states, fought the restriction tooth and nail. Antislavery men in Congress and out, battled no less bitterly for the exclusion of slaves. The "Wilmot Proviso," eventually endorsed by the legislatures of all but one of the free states, soon came to symbolize the burning issue of slavery in the territories.

In a broad sense, the opening shots of the Mexican War were the opening shots of the

The Californios

In 1848 the United States, swollen with the spoils of war, reckoned the costs and benefits of the conflict with Mexico. Nearly two thousand Americans had fallen in battle, and millions of dollars had been invested in a war machine. For this expenditure of blood and money, the nation was repaid with ample land—and with people, the former citizens of Mexico who now became, whether willingly or not, Americans. The largest single addition to American territory in history, the Mexican Cession stretched the United States from sea to shining sea. It secured Texas, brought in vast tracts of the desert Southwest, and included the great prize—the fruited valleys and port cities of California. There, at the conclusion of the Mexican War, dwelled some thirteen thousand Californios—descendants of the Spanish and Mexican conquerors who had once ruled California.

The Spanish had first arrived in California in 1769, extending their New World empire and outracing Russian traders to bountiful San Francisco Bay. Father Junipero Serra, an enterprising Franciscan friar, soon established twenty-one missions along the California coast. Indians in the iron grip of the missions found themselves forced to adopt Christian and European ways and to toil endlessly as farmers and herders, in the process suffering disease and degradation. These maltreated mission Indians occupied the lowest rungs on the ladder of Spanish colonial society.

Upon the loftiest rungs perched the Californios. Pioneers from the Mexican heartland of New Spain, they had trailed Serra to California, claiming land and civil offices in their new home. Yet even the proud Californios had deferred to the all-powerful Franciscan missionaries until Mexico threw off the Spanish colonial yoke in 1826, whereupon the infant Mexican government turned an anxious eye toward its frontier outpost.

Mexico now emptied its jails to send settlers to the sparsely populated north, built and gar-

risoned fortresses, and, most important, transferred authority from the missions to secular, (that is, governmental) authorities. This "secularization" program attacked and eroded the immense power of the missions and of their Franciscan masters—with their bawling herds of cattle, degraded Indian workers, millions of acres of land, and lucrative foreign trade. The frocked friars had commanded their fiefdoms so

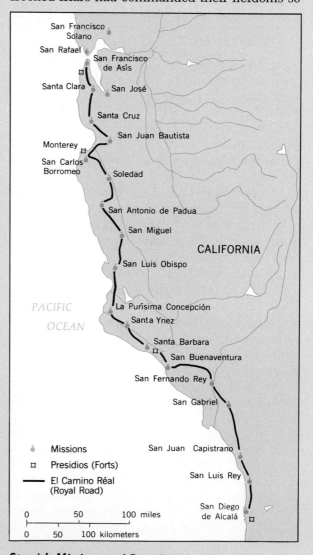

Spanish Missions and Presidios

self-confidently that earlier reform efforts had dared to go no further than levying a paltry tax on the missions and politely requesting that the missionaries limit their floggings of Indians to fifteen lashes per week. But during the 1830s, the power of the missions weakened, and much of their land and their assets were confiscated by the Californios. Vast *ranchos* (ranches) formed, and from those citadels the Californios ruled in their turn until the Mexican war.

The Californios' glory faded in the wake of the American victory, even though in some isolated places they clung to their political offices for a decade or two. Overwhelmed by the inrush of Anglo golddiggers—some eighty-seven thousand after the discovery at Sutter's Mill in 1848—and by the waning of the pastoral economy, the Californios saw their recently acquired lands and their recently established political power slip through their fingers. When the Civil War broke out in 1861, so harshly did the word *Yankee* ring in their ears that many Californios supported the South.

By 1870 the Californios' brief ascendancy had utterly vanished—a short and sad tale of riches to rags in the face of the Anglo onslaught. Half a century later, beginning in 1910, hundreds of thousands of young Mexicans would swarm into California and the Southwest. They would enter a region liberally endowed with Spanish architecture and artifacts, bearing the names of Spanish missions and Californio *ranchos*. But they would find it a land dominated by Anglos, a place far different from that which their Californio ancestors had settled so hopefully in earlier days.

Civil War. President Polk left the nation the splendid physical heritage of California and the Southwest but also the ugly moral heritage of an embittered slavery dispute. "Mexico will poison us," said the philosopher Ralph Waldo Emerson. Even the great champion of the South, John C. Calhoun, had prophetically warned that "Mexico is to us the forbidden fruit . . . the penalty of eating it would be to subject our institutions to political death." Mexicans could later take some satisfaction in knowing that the territory wrenched from them had proved to be a frightful apple of discord that could well be called Santa Anna's revenge.

CHRONOLOGY

1837	Canadian rebellion and *Caroline* incident
1841	Harrison dies after four weeks in office
	Tyler assumes presidency
1842	Aroostook War over Maine boundary
	Webster-Ashburton treaty
1844	Polk defeats Clay in "Manifest Destiny" election
1845	United States annexes Texas
1846	United States settles Oregon dispute with Britain
	United States and Mexico clash over Texas boundary
	Kearny takes Santa Fe
	Frémont conquers California
	Wilmot Proviso passes House of Representatives
1846–1848	Mexican War
1847	Battle of Buena Vista
	Scott takes Mexico City
1848	Treaty of Guadalupe Hidalgo

Varying Viewpoints

Historians have long probed for the real meaning behind the pulse-stirring phrase *Manifest Destiny*. Some have emphasized the idealistic impulses behind continental expansion. Others have stressed the supposed "superiority" of Anglo-Saxon culture over Indian and Spanish civilizations. Still other writers have seen American expansion as simply another chapter in the familiar story of territorial conquest. In recent years, many historians, no doubt influenced by the general reappraisal of America's relations with the rest of the world, have stressed the "imperialistic" forces behind America's territorial growth. These writers identify economic considerations—the quest for markets, the desire for cheap land, the demands for the expansion of slavery—as the motivations for conquest. Scholars have also begun to show more interest in, and sympathy for, the people displaced or absorbed in America's sweep to the western sea. They condemn the racial doctrines that had earlier been used to justify expansionism.

Select Readings

Primary Source Documents

The colorful reminiscences of the pioneers are collected in Dale Morgan, ed., *Overland in 1846: Diaries and Letters of the California-Oregon Trail** (1963). The outbreak and conduct of the Mexican War come alive in the fascinating *Diary of James K. Polk*, edited by Milo Milton Quaife (1910).

Secondary Sources

A brief introduction is Ray A. Billington, *The Far Western Frontier, 1830–1860* (1956); more comprehensive is his *Westward Expansion* (rev. ed. 1974). Still useful is Albert K. Weinberg, *Manifest Destiny* (1935), though it should be supplemented by two works of Frederick Merk, *Manifest Destiny and Mission in American History* (1963) and *Monroe Doctrine and Expansionism, 1843–1849* (1966). Paul Horgan, *Great River* (1954), is a magnificent history of the Southwest and the Rio Grande. *The Texas Revolution* is the subject of William C. Binkley's 1952 study. It should be supplemented by Frederick W. Merk, *Slavery and the Annexation of Texas* (1972). For the Pacific region, see Francis Parkman's classic *The California and Oregon Trail* (1849) and Norman A. Graebner's general account, *Empire on the Pacific* (1955). On the conflict with Mexico, see K. Jack Bauer, *The Mexican-American War, 1846–1848* (1974). The other side's perspective is given in Gene M. Brack, *Mexico Views Manifest Destiny, 1821–1846* (1976). John H. Schroeder analyzes an important aspect of the conflict in *Mr. Polk's War: American Opposition and Dissent, 1846–1848* (1973), while Paul H. Bergeron scrutinizes Polk's administration in *The Presidency of James K. Polk* (1987). David M. Pletcher gives an overall view in *The Diplomacy of the Annexation of Texas, Oregon, and the Mexican War* (1973). Robert W. Johansen uses the war to investigate American culture in *To the Halls of the Montezumas: The Mexican War in the American Imagination* (1985). See also Bernard DeVoto's popular *Year of Decision, 1846* (1943). William H. Goetzmann brings to life *Army Exploration in the American West, 1803–1863* (1959). Unusually colorful social history of the westward movement is provided in John Mack Faragher, *Women and Men on the Overland Trail* (1979), and John D. Unruh, Jr., *The Plains Across: The Overland Emigrants and the Trans-Mississippi West, 1840–1860* (1979). Julie Roy Jeffrey focuses on *Frontier Women* (1979), while William R. Brock summarizes the politics of the 1840s in *Parties and Political Conscience: American Dilemmas, 1840–1850* (1979).

19

Renewing the Sectional Struggle, 1848–1854

Secession! Peaceable secession! Sir, your eyes and mine are never destined to see that miracle.

Daniel Webster,
Seventh of March speech, 1850

The Popular Sovereignty Panacea

The year 1848, highlighted by a rash of revolutions in Europe, was filled with unrest in America. The Treaty of Guadalupe Hidalgo had officially ended the war with Mexico, but it had initiated a new and perilous round of political warfare in the United States. The vanquished Mexicans had been forced to relinquish an enormous tract of real estate, including Texas, California, and all the area between. The acquisition of this huge domain raised anew the burning issue of extending slavery into the territories. Northern antislaveryites had rallied behind the Wilmot Proviso, which flatly prohibited slavery in any territory acquired in the Mexican War. Southern senators had blocked the passage of the proviso, but the issue would not die.

Ominously, debate over slavery in the area of the Mexican Cession threatened to disrupt the ranks of both Whigs and Democrats and split national politics along North-South sectional lines.

Each of the two great political parties was a vital bond of national unity, for each enjoyed powerful support in both North and South. If they should be replaced by two purely sectional groupings, the Union would be in peril. To politicians, the wisest strategy seemed to be to sit on the lid of the slavery issue and ignore the boiling beneath. Even so, the cover bobbed up and down ominously in response to the agitation of zealous northern abolitionists and impassioned southern "fire-eaters."

Anxious Democrats were forced to seek a new standard-bearer in 1848. President Polk, broken in health by overwork and chronic diarrhea, had pledged himself to a single term. The Democratic National Convention at Baltimore turned to an aging leader, General Lewis Cass, a veteran of the War of 1812. Though a senator and diplomat of wide experience and considerable ability, he was sour-visaged and somewhat pompous. His enemies dubbed him General "Gass" and quickly noted that *Cass* rhymed with *jackass*. The Democratic platform, in line with the lid-sitting strategy, was silent on the burning issue of slavery in the territories.

But Cass himself had not been silent. His views on the extension of slavery were well known, because he was the reputed father of "popular sovereignty." This was the doctrine that stated that the sovereign people of a territory, under the general principles of the Constitution, should themselves determine the status of slavery.

Popular sovereignty had a persuasive appeal. The public liked it because it accorded with the democratic tradition of self-determination. Politicians liked it because it seemed a comfortable compromise between a ban on slavery in the territories and southern demands that Congress protect slavery in the territories. Popular sovereignty tossed the slavery problem into the laps of the people in the various territories. Advocates of the doctrine thus hoped to dissolve the most stubborn national issue of the day into a series of local issues. Yet popular sovereignty had one fatal defect: it might serve to spread the blight of slavery.

Political Triumphs for General Taylor

The Whigs, meeting in Philadelphia, cashed in on the "Taylor fever." They nominated frank and honest Zachary Taylor, the "Hero of Buena Vista," who had never held civil office or even voted for president. Henry Clay, the living embodiment of Whiggism, should logically have been nominated. But he had made too many speeches—and too many enemies.

As usual, the Whigs pussyfooted in their platform. Eager to win at any cost, they dodged all troublesome issues and merely extolled the homespun virtues of their candidate. The self-reliant old frontier fighter had not committed himself on the issue of slavery extension. But as a wealthy resident of Louisiana, living on a sugar plantation, he owned scores of slaves.

Ardent antislavery men in the North, distrusting both Cass and Taylor, organized the Free-Soil party. Aroused by the conspiracy of silence in the Democratic and Whig platforms, the Free-Soilers made no bones about their own stand. They came out foursquare for the Wilmot Proviso and against slavery in the territories. Going beyond other antislavery groups, they broadened their appeal by advocating federal aid for internal improvements and by urging free government homesteads for settlers.

The new party assembled a strange assortment of people in the same political bed. It attracted industrialists miffed at Polk's reduction

General Zachary Taylor   *This Democratic campaign cartoon of 1848 charges that Taylor's reputation rested on Mexican skulls. (Courtesy of The New-York Historical Society, New York City.)*

of protective tariffs. It appealed to Democrats resentful of Polk's settling for part of Oregon while insisting on all of Texas—a disparity that suggested a menacing southern dominance in the Democratic party. It harbored many northerners whose hatred was directed not so much at slavery as at blacks and who gagged at the prospect of sharing the virgin western territories with African-Americans. It also contained a large element of "conscience Whigs," heavily influenced by the abolitionist crusade, who condemned slavery on moral grounds. The Free-Soilers trotted out wizened former President Van Buren and marched into the fray, shouting "Free soil, free speech, free labor, and free men." As the first widely inclusive party organized around the issue of slavery and confined to a single section, the Free-Soil party foreshadowed the emergence of the Republican party six years later.

With the slavery issue officially shoved under the rug by the two major parties, the politicians on both sides opened fire on personalities. The amateurish Taylor had to be carefully watched, lest his indiscreet pen puncture the reputation won by his sword. His admirers puffed him up as a gallant knight and a Napoleon, and sloganized his remark, allegedly uttered during the Battle of Buena Vista, "General Taylor never surrenders." Taylor's wartime popularity pulled him through. He harvested 1,360,967 popular and 163 electoral votes, as compared with Cass's 1,222,342 popular and 127 electoral votes. Free-Soiler Van Buren, although winning no state, polled 291,263 ballots and apparently diverted enough Democratic strength from Cass in the crucial state of New York to throw the election to Taylor.

"Californy Gold"

Tobacco-chewing President Taylor—with his stumpy legs, rough features, heavy jaw, black hair, ruddy complexion, and squinty gray eyes—was a military square peg in a political

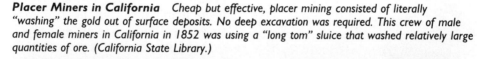

Placer Miners in California Cheap but effective, placer mining consisted of literally "washing" the gold out of surface deposits. No deep excavation was required. This crew of male and female miners in California in 1852 was using a "long tom" sluice that washed relatively large quantities of ore. (California State Library.)

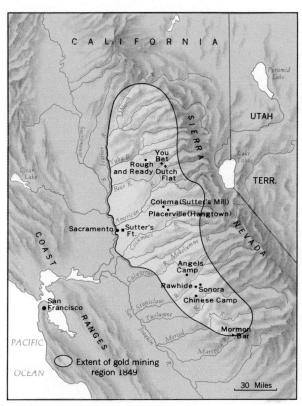

California Gold Rush Country *Miners from all over the world swarmed over the rivers that drained the western slope of California's Sierra Nevada mountains. Their nationalities and religions, their languages and their ways of life, are recorded in the colorful place names they left behind.*

ing was even sent as far away as the Hawaiian Islands for washing.

The overnight inpouring of tens of thousands of people into the future Golden State completely overwhelmed the one-horse government of California. A distressingly high proportion of the newcomers were lawless men, accompanied or followed by virtueless women. A contemporary song ran:

> Oh what was your name in the States?
> Was it Thompson or Johnson or Bates?
> Did you murder your wife,
> And fly for your life?
> Say, what was your name in the States?

An outburst of crime inevitably resulted from the presence of so many outcasts. Robbery, claim jumping, and murder were commonplace; and such violence was only partly discouraged by rough vigilante justice. In San Francisco, from 1848 to 1856, there were scores of lawless killings but only three semilegal hangings.

A majority of the Californians, as decent and law-abiding citizens needing protection, grappled earnestly with the problem of erecting an adequate state government. Privately encouraged by President Taylor, they drafted a constitution in 1849 that excluded slavery and then boldly applied to Congress for admission. California would thus bypass the usual territorial stage, thwarting southern congressmen seeking to block free soil. Southern politicians, alarmed by this "impertinent" stroke for freedom, arose in violent opposition. Would California prove to be the golden straw that broke the back of the Union?

Sectional Balance and the Underground Railroad

The South of 1850 was relatively well off. It then enjoyed, as it had from the beginning, more than its share of the nation's leadership. It had seated in the White House the war hero Zachary Taylor, a Virginia-born, slaveowning planter from Louisiana. It had a majority in the cabinet and on the supreme bench. If outnumbered in the House, the South had equality in

round hole. He would have been spared much turmoil if he could have continued to sit on the slavery lid. But the discovery of gold in California, early in 1848, blew the cover off.

A horde of adventurers poured into the valleys of California. Singing "O Susannah!" and shouting "Gold! Gold! Gold!" they began tearing frantically at the yellow-graveled streams and hills. A fortunate few of the bearded miners "struck it rich" at the "diggings." But the luckless many, who netted blisters instead of nuggets, probably would have been money well ahead if they had stayed at home unaffected by the "gold fever," which was often followed by more deadly fevers. The most reliable profits were made by those who mined the miners, notably by charging outrageous rates for laundry and other personal services. Some soiled cloth-

Blacksmith Shop *Completed in the last third of the nineteenth century, this painting is attributed to Francis A. Beckett. This blacksmith shop in gold rush California was exceptionally well outfitted. The leather-aproned owner sports a stovepipe hat, while his assistants wear mere derbies. Note the massive bellows suspended from the high ceiling. It could heat the fire to blast-furnace temperatures. (National Gallery of Art, Washington, Gift of Edgar William and Bernice Chrysler Garbisch.)*

the Senate, where it could hope to exercise a veto voice. Its cotton fields were expanding, and the price of the snowy fiber was profitably high. Few sane people, North or South, believed that slavery was seriously threatened where it already existed below the Mason-Dixon line.* The fifteen slave states could easily veto any proposed constitutional amendment.

Yet the South was deeply worried, as it had been for several decades, by the ever-tipping political balance. There were then fifteen slave states and fifteen free states. The admission of California would destroy the delicate equilibrium in the Senate, perhaps forever. Potential

slave territory under the American flag was running short, if it had not already disappeared. Agitation had already developed in the territories of New Mexico and Utah for admission as nonslave states. The fate of California might well establish a precedent for the rest of the Mexican Cession territory—an area purchased largely with southern blood.

> The idea that many ne'er-do-wells went west is found in Ralph Waldo Emerson's Journals (January 1849): "If a man is going to California, he announces it with some hesitation; because it is a confession that he has failed at home."

---

*Originally the southern boundary of colonial Pennsylvania.

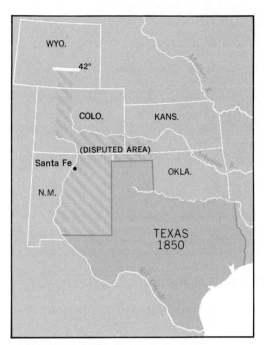

Texas and the Compromise of 1850

Texas nursed an additional grievance of its own. It claimed a huge area east of the Rio Grande and north to the forty-second parallel, embracing in part about half the territory of present New Mexico. The federal government was proposing to detach this prize, while hot-blooded Texans were threatening to descend upon Santa Fe and seize what they regarded as rightfully theirs. The explosive quarrel fore-shadowed shooting.

Many southerners were also angered by the nagging agitation in the North for the abolition of slavery in the District of Columbia. They looked with alarm on the prospect of a ten-mile-square oasis of free soil, thrust between slave-holding Maryland and slaveholding Virginia.

Even more disagreeable to the South was the loss of runaway slaves, many of whom were assisted north by the Underground Railroad. It consisted of an informal chain of "stations" (antislavery homes), through which scores of "passengers" (runaway slaves) were spirited by "conductors" (usually white and black abolition-ists) from the slave states to the free-soil sanctuary of Canada.

The most amazing of these "conductors" was an illiterate runaway slave from Maryland, fear-less Harriet Tubman. During nineteen forays into the South, she rescued more than three hundred slaves, including her aged parents, and deservedly earned the title "Moses." Lively imaginations later exaggerated the role of the Underground Railroad and its "station masters," but its existence was a fact.

Resurrection of Henry Box Brown *Brown, a slave, was shipped to Philadelphia abolition-ists from Virginia in a box. (Library of Congress.)*

Harriet Tubman, Premier Assistant of Runaway Slaves   *John Brown called her "General Tubman" for her effective work in helping slaves escape to Canada. During the Civil War she served as a Union spy behind Confederate lines. Herself illiterate, she worked after the war to bring education to the freed slaves in North Carolina. (Library of Congress.)*

By 1850 southerners were demanding a new and more stringent fugitive-slave law. The old one, passed by Congress in 1793, had proved inadequate to cope with runaways, especially since unfriendly state authorities failed to provide needed cooperation. Unlike cattle thieves, the abolitionists who ran the Underground Railroad did not gain personally from their lawlessness. But to the slaveowners the loss was infuriating, whatever the motives. The moral judgments of the abolitionists seemed, in some ways, more galling than outright theft. They reflected not only a holier-than-thou atti-

tude but a refusal to obey the laws solemnly passed by Congress.

Estimates indicate that the South in 1850 was losing perhaps 1,000 runaways a year, out of its total of some 4 million slaves. In fact, more blacks probably gained their freedom by self-purchase or voluntary emancipation than ever escaped. But the principle weighed heavily with the slavemasters. They rested their argument on the Constitution, which protected slavery, and on the laws of Congress, which provided for slave-catching. "Although the loss of property is felt," said a southern senator, "the loss of honor is felt still more."

Twilight of the Senatorial Giants

Southern fears were such that Congress was confronted with catastrophe in 1850. Free-soil California was banging on the door for admission, and "fire-eaters" in the South were voicing ominous threats of secession. The crisis brought into the congressional forum the most distinguished assemblage of statesmen since the Constitutional Convention of 1787—the Old Guard of the dying generation and the young gladiators of the new. That "immortal trio"—Clay, Calhoun, and Webster—appeared together for the last time on the public stage.

Henry Clay, now seventy-three years of age, played a crucial role. The "Great Pacificator" had come to the Senate from Kentucky to engineer his third great compromise. The once-glamorous statesman—though disillusioned, enfeebled, and racked by a cruel cough—was still eloquent, conciliatory, captivating. He proposed and skillfully defended a series of compromises. He was ably seconded by thirty-seven-year-old Senator Stephen A. Douglas of Illinois, the "Little Giant" (5 feet 4 inches; 1.62 meters), whose role was less spectacular but even more important. Clay urged with all his persuasiveness that the North and South both make concessions and that the North partially yield by enacting a more effective fugitive-slave law.

Senator John C. Calhoun, then sixty-eight and dying of tuberculosis, championed the South in his last formal speech. Too weak to deliver it himself, he sat bundled up in the Senate chamber, his eyes glowing within a stern face, while a younger colleague read his fateful words. Although approving the purpose of Clay's proposed concessions, Calhoun rejected them as not providing adequate safeguards. His impassioned plea was to leave slavery alone, return runaway slaves, give the South its rights as a minority, and restore the political balance. He had in view, as was later revealed, an utterly unworkable scheme of electing two presidents, one from the North and one from the South, each wielding a veto.

Calhoun died in 1850, before the debate was over, uttering the sad words, "The South! The South! God knows what will become of her!" Appreciative fellow citizens in Charleston erected to his memory an imposing monument, which bore the inscription "Truth, Justice, and the Constitution." Calhoun had labored to preserve the Union and had taken his stand on the Constitution, but his proposals in their behalf almost undid both.

Daniel Webster next took the Senate spotlight to uphold Clay's compromise measures in his last great speech, a three-hour effort. Now sixty-eight years old and suffering from a liver complaint aggravated by high living, he had lost some of the fire in his magnificent voice. Speaking deliberately and before overflowing galleries, he urged all reasonable concessions to the South, including a new fugitive-slave law with teeth.

As for slavery in the territories, asked Webster, why legislate on the subject? To do so was an act of sacrilege, for Almighty God had already passed the Wilmot Proviso. The good Lord had decreed—through climate, topography, and geography—that a plantation economy, and hence a slave economy, could not profitably exist in the Mexican Cession territory.* Webster sanely concluded that compromise, concession, and sweet reasonableness would provide the only solutions. "Let us not be pygmies," he pleaded, "in a case that calls for men."

---

*Webster was wrong here; within one hundred years California had become one of the great cotton-producing states of the Union.

> *Ralph Waldo Emerson, the philosopher and moderate abolitionist, was outraged by Webster's support of concessions to the South in the Fugitive Slave Act. In February 1851 he wrote in his Journal: I opened a paper to-day in which he [Webster] pounds on the old strings [of liberty] in a letter to the Washington Birthday feasters at New York. 'Liberty! liberty!' Pho! Let Mr. Webster, for decency's sake, shut his lips once and forever on this word. The word liberty in the mouth of Mr. Webster sounds like the word love in the mouth of a courtesan."*

Webster's famed Seventh of March speech, 1850, was his finest, if measured by its immediate effects. It helped turn the tide in the North toward compromise. The clamor for printed copies became so great that Webster mailed out more than 100,000, remarking that 200,000 would not satisfy the demand. His tremendous effort visibly strengthened Union sentiment. It was especially pleasing to the banking and commercial centers of the North, which stood to lose millions of dollars by secession. One prominent Washington banker canceled two notes of Webster's, totaling $5,000, and sent him a personal check for $1,000 and a message of congratulations.

But the abolitionists, who had regarded Webster as one of themselves, upbraided him as a traitor, worthy of bracketing with Benedict Arnold. The poet Whittier lamented.

> So fallen! so lost! the light withdrawn
> Which once he wore!
> The glory from his gray hairs gone
> For evermore!

These reproaches were most unfair. Webster, who had long regarded slavery as evil but disunion as worse, despised the abolitionists and never joined their ranks.

Deadlock and Danger on Capitol Hill

The stormy congressional debate of 1850 was not finished, for the Young Guard from the North were yet to have their say. This was the group of newer leaders who, unlike the aging Old Guard, had not grown up with the Union. They were more interested in purging and purifying it than in patching and preserving it.

William H. Seward, the wiry and husky-throated freshman senator from New York, was the able spokesman for many of the younger northern radicals. A strong antislaveryite, he came out flat-footedly against concession. He seemed not to realize that compromise had brought the Union together and that when the sections could no longer compromise, they would have to part company.

Seward argued earnestly that Christian legislators must obey God's moral law as well as man's mundane law. He therefore appealed, with reference to excluding slavery in the territories, to an even "higher law" than the Constitution. This alarming phrase, wrenched from its context, may have cost him the presidential nomination and the presidency in 1860.

As the great debate in Congress ran its heated course, deadlock seemed certain. Blunt old President Taylor, who had allegedly fallen under the influence of men like "Higher Law" Seward, seemed bent on vetoing any compromise passed by Congress. His military ire was aroused by the threats of Texas to seize Santa Fe. He appeared to be doggedly determined to "Jacksonize" the dissenters, if need be, by leading an army against the Texans in person and hanging all "damned traitors." If troops had begun to march, the South probably would have rallied to the defense of Texas, and the Civil War might have erupted in 1850.

A Seward Caricature *He later became Lincoln's foremost rival for the presidency, and still later his secretary of state.*

Compromise of 1850

CONCESSIONS TO THE NORTH	CONCESSIONS TO THE SOUTH
California admitted as a free state	The remainder of the Mexican Cession area to be formed into the territories of New Mexico and Utah, without restriction on slavery, hence open to popular sovereignty
Territory disputed by Texas and New Mexico to be surrendered to New Mexico	Texas to receive $10 million from the federal government as compensation
Abolition of the slave trade (but not slavery) in the District of Columbia	A more stringent Fugitive Slave Law, going beyond that of 1793

an Johnson brilliantly evokes
lyn O.L. Conkling.)

itself. A movement in the
rthern goods gained some
end the southern Union-
warm glow of prosperity,

ssemblage of southern ex-
Nashville, Tennessee, ironi-
place of Andrew Jackson.
nly took a strong position in
ondemned the compromise
g hammered out in Con-
later in the year after the
convention proved to be a
outhern opinion had reluc-
erdict of Congress.
er a storm, a second Era of
ed. Disquieting talk of se-
Peace-loving people, both
were determined that the
be a "finality" and that the
very should be buried. But
reason proved all too brief.

mpromise Scales

f the compromise of 1850?
arly the North. California,
d the Senate balance per-
e South. The territories of
ah were open to slavery on

**lavery after the Compromise
of 1850**

ed
oia)

g wedge toward complete eman-
nation's capital.
g of all, the drastic new Fugitive
e Bloodhound Bill"—stirred up a
ition in the North. The fleeing
t testify in their own behalf, and
d a jury trial. These harsh prac-
l to create dangerous precedents
The federal commissioner who
e of a fugitive would receive five
naway were freed and ten dol-
arrangement that strongly re-
be. Freedom-loving northerners
slave to escape were liable to
jail sentences. They might even
oin the slave-catchers, and this
ed salt into old sores.
s this "Man-Stealing Law" that

A Ride for Liberty   *This famous painting by New England artist Eastm*
the anxiety of fleeing slaves. (The Brooklyn Museum. Gift of Miss Gwend

the basis of popular sovereignty. But the iron law of nature—the "highest law" of all—had loaded the dice in favor of free soil. The southerners urgently needed more slave territory to restore the "sacred balance." If they could not carve new states out of the recent conquests from Mexico, where else would they get them? In the Caribbean, was one answer.

Even the apparent gains of the South rang hollow. Disgruntled Texas was to be paid $10 million toward discharging its indebtedness, but in the long run this was a modest sum. The immense area in dispute had been torn from the side of slaveholding Texas and was almost certain to be free. The South had halted the drive toward abolition in the District of Columbia, at least temporarily, by permitting the outlawing of the slave traffic. But even this move

was an enterin
cipation in the

Most alarmi
Slave Law—"tl
storm of oppo
slaves could n
they were deni
tices threatene
for the whites.
handled the ca
dollars if the r
lars if not—an
sembled a bri
who aided the
heavy fines an
be ordered to
possibility rubl

So savage w

Breaking the Congressional Logjam

At the height of the controversy in 1850, President Taylor unknowingly helped the cause of concession by dying suddenly, probably of an acute intestinal disorder. Portly, round-faced Vice-President Millard Fillmore, a colorless and conciliatory New York lawyer-politician, took over the reins. As presiding officer of the Senate, he had been impressed with the arguments for conciliation, and he gladly signed the series of compromise measures that passed Congress after seven long months of stormy debate. The balancing of interests in the Compromise of 1850 was delicate in the extreme.

The struggle to get these measures accepted by the country was hardly less heated than in Congress. In the northern states, "Union savers" like Senators Clay, Webster, and Douglas orated on behalf of the compromise. The ailing Clay himself delivered more than seventy speeches, as a powerful sentiment for acceptance gradually crystallized in the North. It was strengthened by a growing spirit of goodwill, which sprang partly from a feeling of relief and partly from an upsurge of prosperity enriched by California gold.

But the "fire-eaters" of the South were still violently opposed to concessions. One extreme South Carolina newspaper avowed that it loathed the Union and hated the North as much as it did Hell itself. A movement in the South to boycott northern goods gained some headway, but in the end the southern Unionists, assisted by the warm glow of prosperity, prevailed.

In mid-1850 an assemblage of southern extremists had met in Nashville, Tennessee, ironically near the burial place of Andrew Jackson. The delegates not only took a strong position in favor of slavery but condemned the compromise measures then being hammered out in Congress. Meeting again later in the year after the bills had passed, the convention proved to be a dud. By that time southern opinion had reluctantly accepted the verdict of Congress.

Like the calm after a storm, a second Era of Good Feelings dawned. Disquieting talk of secession subsided. Peace-loving people, both North and South, were determined that the compromises should be a "finality" and that the explosive issue of slavery should be buried. But this placid period of reason proved all too brief.

Balancing the Compromise Scales

Who got the better of the compromise of 1850?

The answer is clearly the North. California, as a free state, tipped the Senate balance permanently against the South. The territories of New Mexico and Utah were open to slavery on

Slavery after the Compromise of 1850

OREGON TERR.

CALIF.

UTAH TERR.

NEW MEXICO TERR.

MINNESOTA TERR.

UNORGANIZED TERR.

IOWA

WIS.

MICH.

ILL. IND. OHIO

MO.

KY.

INDIAN TERR.

ARK.

TENN.

MISS. ALA. GA.

TEX.

LA.

FLA.

S.C.

N.C.

VA.

PA.

N.Y.

N.J.

MD. DEL.

(Slave trade prohibited in District of Columbia)

ME.

VT. N.H. MASS. R.I. CONN.

Free

Slave

Decision left to territory

A Ride for Liberty *This famous painting by New England artist Eastman Johnson brilliantly evokes the anxiety of fleeing slaves. (The Brooklyn Museum. Gift of Miss Gwendolyn O.L. Conkling.)*

the basis of popular sovereignty. But the iron law of nature—the "highest law" of all—had loaded the dice in favor of free soil. The southerners urgently needed more slave territory to restore the "sacred balance." If they could not carve new states out of the recent conquests from Mexico, where else would they get them? In the Caribbean, was one answer.

Even the apparent gains of the South rang hollow. Disgruntled Texas was to be paid $10 million toward discharging its indebtedness, but in the long run this was a modest sum. The immense area in dispute had been torn from the side of slaveholding Texas and was almost certain to be free. The South had halted the drive toward abolition in the District of Columbia, at least temporarily, by permitting the outlawing of the slave traffic. But even this move

was an entering wedge toward complete emancipation in the nation's capital.

Most alarming of all, the drastic new Fugitive Slave Law—"the Bloodhound Bill"—stirred up a storm of opposition in the North. The fleeing slaves could not testify in their own behalf, and they were denied a jury trial. These harsh practices threatened to create dangerous precedents for the whites. The federal commissioner who handled the case of a fugitive would receive five dollars if the runaway were freed and ten dollars if not—an arrangement that strongly resembled a bribe. Freedom-loving northerners who aided the slave to escape were liable to heavy fines and jail sentences. They might even be ordered to join the slave-catchers, and this possibility rubbed salt into old sores.

So savage was this "Man-Stealing Law" that

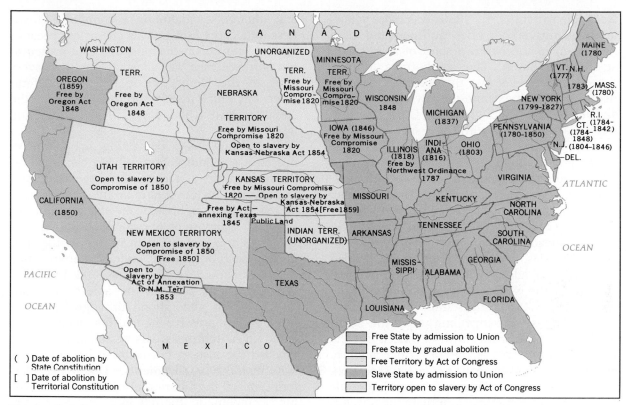

The Legal Status of Slavery, from the Revolution to the Civil War

it touched off an explosive chain reaction in the North. Many shocked moderates, hitherto passive, were driven into the swelling ranks of the antislaveryites. When a runaway slave from Virginia was captured in Boston in 1854, he had to be removed from the city under heavy federal guard through streets lined with sullen Yankees and shadowed by black-draped buildings festooned with flags flying upside down. One prominent Bostonian who witnessed this grim spectacle wrote that "we went to bed one night old-fashioned, conservative, Compromise Union Whigs and waked up stark mad Abolitionists."

The Underground Railroad stepped up its timetable, while infuriated northern mobs rescued slaves from their pursuers. Massachusetts, in a move toward nullification suggestive of South Carolina in 1832, made it a penal offense for any state official to enforce the new federal statute. Other states passed "personal liberty laws," which denied local jails to federal officials and otherwise hampered enforcement. The abolitionists rent the heavens with their protests against the man-stealing statute. A meeting presided over by Garrison in 1851 declared, "We execrate it, we spit upon it, we trample it under our feet."

Beyond question, the Fugitive Slave Law was an appalling blunder on the part of the South.

Regarding the Fugitive Slave Act of 1850, Ralph Waldo Emerson declared (May 1851) at Concord, Massachusetts: "The act of Congress . . . is a law which every one of you will break on the earliest occasion—a law which no man can obey, or abet the obeying, without loss of self-respect and forfeiture of the name of gentleman." Privately he wrote in his Journal: "This filthy enactment was made in the nineteenth century, by people who could read and write. I will not obey it, by God" (July 1851).

No single irritant of the 1850s was more persistently galling to both sides, and none did more to awaken in the North a spirit of antagonism against the South. The southerners in turn were embittered because the northerners would not in good faith execute the law—the one real and immediate "gain" from the Great Compromise. Slave-catchers, with some success, redoubled their efforts.

Should the shooting showdown have come in 1850? From the standpoint of the secessionists, yes; from the standpoint of the Unionists, no. Time was fighting for the North. With every passing decade this huge section was forging further ahead in population and wealth—in crops, factories, foundries, ships, and railroads.

Delay also added immensely to the moral strength of the North—to its will to fight for the Union. In 1850 countless thousands of northern moderates were unwilling to pin the South to the rest of the nation with bayonets. But the inflammatory events of the 1850s did much to bolster the Yankee will to resist secession, whatever the cost. This one feverish decade gave the North time to accumulate the physical and moral strength that provided the margin of victory. Thus, the Compromise of 1850, from one point of view, won the Civil War for the Union.

Defeat and Doom for the Whigs

Meeting in Baltimore, the Democratic nominating convention of 1852 startled the nation. Hopelessly deadlocked, it finally stampeded to the second "dark horse" candidate in American history, an unrenowned lawyer politician, Franklin Pierce, from the hills of New Hampshire. The Whigs tried to jeer him back into obscurity with the cry, "Who is Frank Pierce?" Democrats replied, "The Young Hickory of the Granite Hills."

Pierce, though handsome, was a weak and indecisive figure. Youngish, militarily erect, smiling, and convivial, he had served without real distinction in the Mexican War. As a result of a painful groin injury that caused him to fall off a horse, he was known as the "Fainting General," though scandalmongers pointed to a fondness for alcohol. But he was enemyless because he had been inconspicuous, and as a prosouthern northerner he was acceptable to the slavery wing of the Democratic party. His platform came out emphatically for the finality of the compromise of 1850, Fugitive Slave Law and all.

The Whigs, also convening in Baltimore, missed a splendid opportunity to capitalize on their record in statecraft. Able to boast of a praiseworthy achievement in the Compromise of 1850, they might logically have nominated President Fillmore or Senator Webster, both of whom were associated with it. But having won in the past only with military heroes, they turned to another, "Old Fuss and Feathers" Winfield Scott, perhaps the ablest American general of his generation. Although he was a huge and impressive figure, his manner bordered on haughtiness. His personality not only repelled the masses but eclipsed his genuinely statesmanlike achievements. The Whig platform praised the Compromise of 1850 as a lasting arrangement, though less enthusiastically than the Democrats.

With slavery and sectionalism to some extent soft-pedaled, the campaign again degenerated into a dull and childish attack on personalities. Democrats ridiculed Scott's pomposity; Whigs charged that Pierce was the hero of "many a well-fought *bottle*." Democrats cried exultantly, "We Polked 'em in '44; we'll Pierce 'em in '52."

Luckily for the Democrats, the Whig party was hopelessly split. Antislavery Whigs of the North swallowed Scott as their standard-bearer but deplored his platform, which endorsed the hated Fugitive Slave Law. The current phrase ran, "We accept the candidate but spit on the platform." Southern Whigs, who doubted Scott's loyalty to the Compromise of 1850 and especially to the Fugitive Slave Law, accepted the platform but spat on the candidate. More than five thousand Georgia Whigs—"finality men"—futilely voted for Webster, although he had died nearly two weeks before the election.

General Scott, victorious on the battlefield, met defeat at the ballot box. His friends remarked whimsically that he was not used to "running." Actually, he was stabbed in the back by his fellow Whigs, notably in the South. The pliant Pierce won in a landslide, 254 electoral votes to 42, though the popular count was closer, 1,601,117 to 1,385,453.

The election of 1852 was fraught with frightening significance, though it may have seemed tame at the time. It marked the effective end of the disorganized Whig party and, within a few years, its complete death. The Whigs' demise foreshadowed the eclipse of *national* parties and the ominous rise of purely *sectional* political alignments. The Whigs were governed at times by the crassest opportunism, and they won only two presidential elections (1840, 1848) in their colorful career, both with war heroes. They finally choked to death trying to gag down the Fugitive Slave Law. But their great contribution—and a noteworthy one indeed—was to help uphold the ideal of Union through their electoral strength in the South and through the eloquence of leaders like Clay and Webster. Both of these statesmen, by unhappy coincidence, died during the campaign. But the good they had done lived after them and contributed powerfully to the eventual preservation of a united United States.

President Pierce the Expansionist

At the outset the Pierce administration displayed vigor. The new president, standing confidently before some fifteen thousand people on inauguration day, delivered from memory a clear-voiced inaugural address. His cabinet contained aggressive southerners, including as secretary of war one Jefferson Davis, future president of the Confederacy. The people of Dixie were determined to acquire more slave territory, and the compliant Pierce was prepared to be their willing tool.

The intoxicating victories of the Mexican War stimulated the spirit of Manifest Destiny. The conquest of a Pacific frontage, and the discovery of gold on it, aroused lively interest in the trans-isthmian land routes of Central America, chiefly in Panama and Nicaragua. Many Americans were looking even further ahead to potential canal routes and to the islands flanking them, notably Spain's Cuba.

These visions especially fired the ambitions of the "slavocrats." They lusted for new territory after the Compromise of 1850 seemingly closed most of the lands of the Mexican Cession to the "peculiar institution." In 1856 a Texan proposed

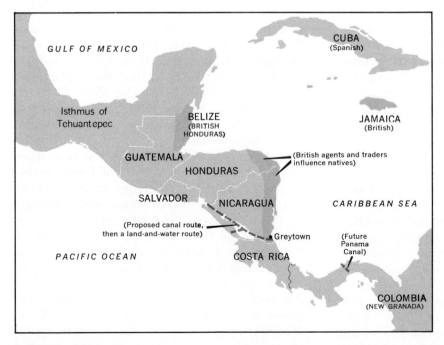

Central America, c. 1850, Showing British Possessions and Proposed Canal Routes *Until President Theodore Roosevelt swung into action with his big stick in 1903, a Nicaraguan canal, closer to the United States, was generally judged more desirable than a canal across Panama.*

William Walker (1824–1860) *This military adventurer, backed both by slaveowners seeking new slave territory and by northern commercial interests seeking a route for a transisthmian canal in Central America, briefly installed himself as dictator of Nicaragua in the 1850s. He was eventually executed by a Honduran firing squad in 1860. (The Bettmann Archive.)*

a toast that was drunk with gusto: "To the Southern republic bounded on the north by the Mason and Dixon line and on the South by the Isthmus of Tehuantepec [southern Mexico], including Cuba and all other lands on our Southern shore."

Southerners took a special interest in Nicaragua. A brazen American adventurer, William Walker, tried repeatedly to grab control of this Central American country in the 1850s. (He had earlier attempted and failed to seize Baja California from Mexico and turn it into a slave state.) Backed by an armed force largely recruited in the South, he installed himself as president in July 1856 and promptly legalized slavery. One southern newspaper proclaimed to the planter aristocracy that Walker—the "grey-eyed man of destiny"—"now offers Nicaragua to you and your slaves, at a time when you have not a friend on the face of the earth." But a coalition of Central American nations formed an alliance to overthrow him. President Pierce withdrew diplomatic recognition, and the grey-

eyed man's destiny was to crumple before a Honduran firing squad in 1860.

Nicaragua was also of vital concern to Great Britain, the world's leading maritime and commercial power. Fearing that the grasping Yankees would monopolize the trade arteries there, the British made haste to secure a solid foothold at Greytown, the eastern end of the proposed Nicaraguan canal route. This challenge to the Monroe Doctrine forthwith raised the ugly possibility of an armed clash. The crisis was surmounted in 1850 by the Clayton-Bulwer Treaty, which stipulated that neither America nor Britain would fortify or secure exclusive control over any future isthmian waterway. This agreement, at the time, seemed necessary to halt the British, but to American canal promoters in later years, it proved to be a ball and chain.

America had become a Pacific power with the acquisition of California and Oregon, both of which faced the Orient. The prospects of a rich trade with the Far East now seemed rosier. Americans had already established contacts with China, and shippers were urging Washington to push for commercial intercourse with Japan. The mikado's empire, after some disagreeable experiences with the European world, had withdrawn into a cocoon of isolationism and had remained there for over two hundred years. The Japanese were so protective of their insularity that they prohibited shipwrecked foreign sailors from leaving and refused to readmit to Japan their own sailors who had been washed up on the West Coast of North America. But by 1853, as events proved, Nippon was ready to emerge, partly because of the Russian menace.

The Washington government was now eager to pry open the bamboo gates of Japan. It dispatched a fleet of awesome, smoke-belching warships, commanded by Commodore Matthew C. Perry, brother of the hero of the Battle of Lake Erie in 1813. By a judicious display of force and tact, he persuaded the Japanese in 1854 to sign a memorable treaty. It provided for only a commercial foot in the door, but it was the beginning of an epochal relationship between the Land of the Rising Sun and the Western world. Ironically, this achievement attracted little notice at the time, partly because Perry devised no memorable slogan.

Coveted Cuba: Pearl of the Antilles

Sugar-rich Cuba, lying off the nation's southern doorstep, was the prime objective of Manifest Destiny in the 1850s. Supporting a large population of enslaved blacks, it was coveted by the South as the most desirable slave territory available. Carved into several states, it would once more restore the political balance in the Senate.

Cuba was a kind of heirloom—the most important remnant of Spain's once-mighty New World empire. Polk, the expansionist, had taken steps to offer $100 million for it, but the sensitive Spaniards had replied that they would see it sunk into the ocean before they would sell it to the Americans at any price. With purchase completely out of the question, seizure was apparently the only way to pluck the ripening fruit.

Private adventurers from the South now undertook to shake the tree of Manifest Destiny. During 1850–1851 two "filibustering" expeditions (from the Spanish "filibustero," meaning freebooter or pirate), each numbering several hundred armed men, descended upon Cuba. Both feeble efforts were repelled, and the last one ended in tragedy when the leader and fifty followers—some of them from the "best families" of the South—were summarily shot or strangled. So outraged were the southerners that an angry mob sacked Spain's consulate in New Orleans.

Spanish officials in Cuba rashly forced a showdown in 1854, when they seized an American steamer, *Black Warrior,* on a technicality. Now was the time for President Pierce, dominated as he was by the South, to provoke a war with Spain and seize Cuba. The major powers of Europe—England, France, and Russia— were about to become bogged down in the Crimean War and hence were unable to aid Spain.

An incredible cloak-and-dagger episode followed. The secretary of state instructed the American ministers in Spain, England, and France to prepare confidential recommendations for the acquisition of Cuba. Meeting initially at Ostend, Belgium, the three envoys drew up a top-secret dispatch, soon known as the Ostend Manifesto. This startling document urged that the administration offer $120 million for Cuba. If Spain refused, and if its continued ownership endangered American interests, the United States would "be justified in wresting" the island from the Spanish.

The secret Ostend Manifesto quickly leaked out. Northern free-soilers, already angered by the Fugitive Slave Law and other gains for slavery, rose in an outburst of wrath against the "manifesto of brigands." Confronted with disruption at home, the red-faced Pierce administration was forced to drop its brazen schemes for Cuba.

Clearly the slavery issue, like a two-headed snake with the heads at cross purposes, deadlocked territorial expansion in the 1850s. The North, flushed with Manifest Destiny, was developing a renewed appetite for Canada. The South coveted Cuba. Neither section would permit the other to get the apple of its eye, so neither got either. The shackled black hands of Harriet Beecher Stowe's Uncle Tom, who had already aroused the North, held the South back from Cuba. The internal distresses of the United States were such that, for once, it could not take advantage of Europe's distresses—in this case the Crimean War.

Pacific Railroad Promoters and the Gadsden Purchase

Acute transportation problems were another legacy of the Mexican War. The newly acquired prizes of California and Oregon might just as well have been islands some eight thousand miles (thirteen thousand kilometers) west of the nation's capital. The sea routes to and from the isthmus of Panama, to say nothing of those

> The first platform of the newly born (antislavery) Republican party in 1856 lashed out at the Ostend Manifesto, with its transparent suggestion that Cuba be seized. The plank read: Resolved, *That the highwayman's plea, that 'might makes right,' embodied in the Ostend Circular, was in every respect unworthy of American diplomacy, and would bring shame and dishonor upon any Government or people that gave it their sanction."*

Gadsden Purchase, 1853 *Future Southern Pacific Railroad (completed 1882) is shown.*

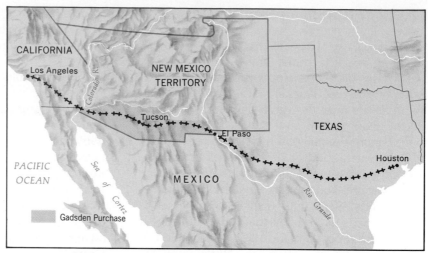

around South America, were too long. Covered-wagon travel past bleaching animal bones was possible, but slow and dangerous. A popular song recalled:

> They swam the wide rivers and crossed the tall peaks,
> And camped on the prairie for weeks upon weeks.
> Starvation and cholera and hard work and slaughter,
> They reached California spite of hell and high water.

Feasible land transportation was imperative—or the newly won possessions on the Pacific Coast might break away. Camels were even proposed as the answer. Several score of these temperamental beasts—"ships of the desert"—were imported from the Near East, but mule-driving Americans did not adjust to them. A transcontinental railroad was clearly the only real solution to the problem.

Railroad promoters, both North and South, had projected many drawing-board routes to the Pacific Coast. But the estimated cost in all cases was so great that for many years there could obviously be only one line. Should its terminus be in the North or in the South? The favored section would reap rich rewards in wealth, population, and influence. The South, losing the economic race with the North, was eager to extend a railroad through adjacent southwestern territory all the way to California.

Another chunk of Mexico now seemed desirable, because the campaigns of the recent war had shown that the best railway route ran slightly south of the Mexican border. Secretary of War Jefferson Davis, a Mississippian, arranged to have James Gadsden, a prominent South Carolina railroad man, appointed minister to Mexico. Finding Santa Anna in power for the sixth and last time, and as usual in need of money, Gadsden made gratifying headway. He negotiated a treaty in 1853, which ceded to the United States the Gadsden Purchase area for $10 million. The transaction aroused much criticism among northerners, who objected to paying a huge sum for a cactus-strewn desert nearly the size of Gadsden's South Carolina. Undeterred, the Senate approved the pact after shortsightedly eliminating a window on the Gulf of California.

No doubt the Gadsden Purchase enabled the South to claim the coveted railroad with even greater insistence. A southern track would be easier to build, because the mountains were less high and because the route, unlike the proposed northern lines, would not pass through unorganized territory. Texas was already a state at this point, and New Mexico (with the Gadsden Purchase added) was a formally organized territory, with federal troops available to provide protection against marauding tribes of Indians. Any northern or central railroad line would have to be thrust through the unorganized territory of Nebraska, where the buffalo and Indians roamed.

Northern railroad boosters quickly replied that if organized territory were the test, then Nebraska should be organized. Such a move was not premature, because thousands of land-hungry pioneers were already poised on the Nebraska border. But all schemes proposed in Congress for organizing the territory were greeted with apathy or hostility by many southerners. Why should the South help create new free-soil states and thus cut its own throat by facilitating a northern railroad?

Douglas's Kansas-Nebraska Scheme

At this point in 1854 Senator Stephen A. Douglas of Illinois delivered a counterstroke to offset the Gadsden thrust for southern expansion westward. A squat, bull-necked, and heavy-chested figure, the "Little Giant" radiated the energy and breezy optimism of the self-made man. An ardent booster for the West, he longed to break the North-South deadlock over westward expansion and stretch a line of settlements across the continent. He had also invested heavily in Chicago real estate and in railway stock and was eager to have the Windy City become the eastern terminus of the proposed Pacific railroad. He would thus endear himself to the voters of Illinois, benefit his section, and enrich his own purse.

A veritable "steam engine in breeches," Douglas threw himself behind a legislative scheme that would enlist the support of a reluctant South. The proposed Territory of Nebraska would be carved into two territories, Kansas and Nebraska. Their status regarding slavery would be settled by popular sovereignty—a democratic concept to which Douglas and his western constituents were deeply attached. Kansas, which lay due west of slaveholding Missouri, would presumably choose to become a slave state. But Nebraska, lying west of free-soil Iowa, would presumably become a free state.

Douglas's Kansas-Nebraska scheme ran headlong into a formidable political obstacle. The Missouri Compromise of 1820 had forbidden slavery in the proposed Nebraska Territory, which lay north of the sacred 36°30′ line; and

Stephen A. Douglas (1813–1861) *Despite having stirred up sectional bitterness, Douglas was so devoted to the Union that he warmly supported his rival, Lincoln, when war broke out. He attended the inauguration and reportedly held Lincoln's stovepipe hat while the president spoke. (National Portrait Gallery, Smithsonian Institution, Washington, D.C.)*

the only way to open the region to popular sovereignty was to repeal the ancient compact outright. This bold step Douglas was prepared to take, even at the risk of shattering the uneasy truce patched up by the Great Compromise of 1850.

Many southerners, who had not conceived of Kansas as slave soil, rose to the bait. Here was a chance to gain one more slave state. The pliable President Pierce, under the thumb of southern advisers, threw his full weight behind the Kansas-Nebraska Bill.

But the Missouri Compromise, now thirty-four years old, could not be brushed aside lightly. Whatever Congress passes it can repeal, but by this time the North had come to regard the sectional pact as almost as sacred as the Constitution itself. Free-soil members of Congress struck back furiously. They met their match in the violently gesticulating Douglas, who was the ablest rough-and-tumble debater of his generation. Employing twisted logic and oratorical fireworks, he rammed the bill through Congress, with strong support from many southerners. So heated were political passions that bloodshed was barely averted. Some members carried a concealed revolver or a bowie knife—or both.

Douglas's motives in prodding anew the snarling dog of slavery have long puzzled historians. His personal interests have already been mentioned. In addition, his foes accused him of angling for the presidency in 1856. Yet his admirers have argued plausibly in his defense that if he had not championed the ill-omened bill, someone else would have.

The truth seems to be that Douglas acted somewhat impulsively and recklessly. His heart did not bleed over the issue of slavery, and he declared repeatedly that he did not care whether it was voted up or down in the territories. What he failed to perceive was that hundreds of thousands of his fellow citizens in the North *did* feel deeply on this moral issue. They regarded the repeal of the Missouri Compromise as an intolerable breach of faith, and they would henceforth resist to the last trench all future Southern demands for slave territory. As Abraham Lincoln said, the North wanted to give to pioneers in the West "a clean bed, with no snakes in it."

Genuine leaders, like skillful chess players, must foresee the possible effects of their moves. Douglas predicted a "hell of a storm," but he grossly underestimated its proportions. His critics in the North, branding him a "Judas" and a "traitor," greeted his name with frenzied boos, hisses, and "three groans for Doug." But he still enjoyed a high degree of popularity among his following in the Democratic party, especially in Illinois, a stronghold of popular sovereignty.

Douglas Hatches a Slavery Problem *Note the already hatched Missouri Compromise, Squatter Sovereignty, and Filibustering (in Cuba), and the about-to-hatch Free Kansas and Dred Scott decision. So bitter was the outcry against Douglas at the time of the Kansas-Nebraska controversy that he claimed with exaggeration that he could have traveled from Boston to Chicago at night by the light from his burning effigies. (Republican cartoon.)*

Congress Legislates a Civil War

The Kansas-Nebraska Act—a curtain raiser to a terrible drama—was one of the most momentous measures ever to pass Congress. By one way of reckoning, it led directly down the slippery slope to Civil War.

Antislavery northerners were angered by what they condemned as an act of bad faith by

The Massachusetts senator Charles Sumner described the Kansas-Nebraska Bill as "at once the worst and the best Bill on which Congress ever acted." It was the worst because it represented a victory for the slave power in the short run. But it was the best, he said prophetically, because "it annuls all past compromises with slavery, and makes all future compromises impossible. Thus it puts freedom and slavery face to face, and bids them grapple. Who can doubt the result?"

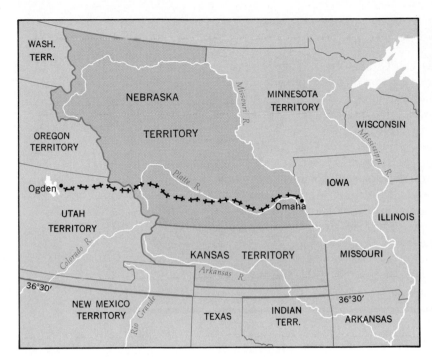

Kansas and Nebraska, 1854 *Future Union Pacific Railroad (completed 1869) is shown. Note the Missouri Compromise line of 36°30′ (1820).*

the "Neb-rascals" and their "Nebrascality." All future compromise with the South would be immeasurably more difficult, and without compromise there was bound to be conflict.

Henceforth the Fugitive Slave Law of 1850, previously enforced in the North only halfheartedly, was a dead letter. The Kansas-Nebraska Act wrecked two compromises: that of 1820, which it repealed specifically, and that of 1850, which northern opinion repealed indirectly. Emerson wrote, "The Fugitive [Slave] Law did much to unglue the eyes of men, and now the Nebraska Bill leaves us staring." Northern abolitionists and southern "fire-eaters" alike were stirred to new outbursts. The growing legion of antislaveryites gained numerous recruits, who resented the grasping move by the "slavocracy" for Kansas. The southerners, in turn, became inflamed when the free-soilers tried to control Kansas, contrary to the presumed "deal."

The proud Democrats—a party now over half a century old—were shattered by the Kansas-Nebraska Act. They managed to elect a president two years later, but he was the last one they were to boost into the White House for twenty-eight long years.

Undoubtedly the most durable offspring of the Kansas-Nebraska blunder was the new Republican party. It sprang up spontaneously in the Middle West, notably in Wisconsin and Michigan, as a mighty moral protest against the gains of slavery. Gathering together dissatisfied elements, it soon included disgruntled Whigs (among them Abraham Lincoln), Democrats, Free-Soilers, Know-Nothings, and other foes of the Kansas-Nebraska Act. The hodgepodge party spread eastward with the rapidity of a prairie fire and with the zeal of a religious crusade. Unheard of and unheralded at the beginning of 1854, it elected a Republican Speaker of the House of Representatives within two years. Never really a third-party movement, it erupted with such force as to become almost overnight the second major political party—and a purely sectional one at that.

At long last the dreaded sectional rift had appeared. The new Republican party would not be allowed south of the Mason-Dixon line. Countless southerners subscribed wholeheartedly to the sentiment that it was "a nigger stealing, stinking, putrid, abolition party." The Union was in dire peril.

CHRONOLOGY

1848	Treaty of Guadalupe Hidalgo
	Taylor defeats Cass for presidency
1849	California gold rush
1850	Compromise of 1850
	Fugitive Slave Law
	Clayton-Bulwer Treaty with Britain
	Fillmore assumes presidency after Taylor's death
1852	Pierce defeats Scott for presidency
1853	Gadsden Purchase from Mexico
1854	Commodore Perry opens Japan
	Ostend Manifesto proposes seizure of Cuba
	Kansas-Nebraska Act
	Republican party organized
1856	William Walker becomes president of Nicaragua and legalizes slavery

Varying Viewpoints

Historical analysts of the 1850s have long been preoccupied with the mounting controversy over slavery. Why, they have asked, did the long-simmering slavery issue finally boil to a head in the decade of the 1850s, eventually exploding in the Civil War of 1861–1865? Many scholars, most notably David M. Potter, have argued that the irreconcilable differences between free and slave societies—moral, political, economic, and social—increasingly eroded the ties between the sections and inexorably set the United States on the road to the Civil War. In this process, no event was more important than the breakdown of the Jacksonian party system. When the slavery issue tore apart both the Democratic and Whig parties, the last ligaments binding the nation together were dissolved, and the war inevitably came.

In recent years, historians of the "ethnocultural" school, especially Michael Holt, have challenged this traditional view. They note that the two great national parties had focused attention on issues like the tariff, banking, and internal improvements, thereby muting sectional differences over slavery. In this view, the demise of the "second-party system" is blamed not on growing differences over slavery but on a temporary *consensus* between the two parties on almost all national issues *other* than slavery. In this peculiar political atmosphere, the slavery issue was shoved to the fore, encouraging the emergence of Republicans in the North and secessionists in the South. In the absence of regular, national, two-party conflict over economic issues, purely regional parties (like the Republicans) coalesced. They identified their opponents not simply as competitors for power but as threats to their way of life, even to the life of the Republic itself. This approach thus suggests an answer to the question of why the Civil War came when it did: sectional strife had existed at least since the Missouri Compromise, but, paradoxically, it was only with the collapse of traditional partisan conflict in the 1850s that it led to war.

Select Readings

Primary Source Documents

The *Congressional Globe* for 1850 contains the dramatic orations of a dying generation of American statesmen on the Compromise of 1850. See the speeches by Webster,* Calhoun,* and Clay (in Richard Hofstadter, ed., *Great Issues in American History*). The debate on the Kansas-Nebraska Bill can be found in the 1854 volume of the same source, which includes addresses by Stephen A. Douglas* and his Republican opponent, Salmon P. Chase.*

Secondary Sources

The best account of the events of the 1850s is David M. Potter's masterful *The Impending Crisis, 1848–1861* (1976). A concise summary of the events leading to the war is also available in the opening chapters of James M. McPherson, *Battle Cry of Freedom: The Civil War Era* (1988). Sketchy but penetrating is Roy F. Nichols, *The Stakes of Power, 1845–1877* (1961); see also his more detailed *The Disruption of American Democracy* (1948). Comprehensive treatments may be found in James G. Randall and David Donald, *The Civil War and Reconstruction* (rev. ed., 1969), and Allan Nevins, *Ordeal of the Union* (2 vols., 1947). See also Avery O. Craven, *The Coming of the Civil War* (2d ed., 1957), his *Civil War in the Making* (1959), and his *Growth of Southern Nationalism* (1953). David Potter also offers illuminating insights in *The South and the Sectional Conflict* (1968). The standard work is Holman Hamilton, *Prologue to Conflict: The Crisis and Compromise of 1850* (1964). The emergence of the Republican party can be studied in Eric Foner's brilliant discussion of ideology, *Free Soil, Free Labor, Free Men* (1970); William Gienapp, *The Origins of the Republican Party, 1852–1856* (1987); and Michael Holt's perceptive *Forging a Majority: The Formation of the Republican Party in Pittsburgh* (1969). Foner's ideas can be pursued further in his *Politics and Ideology in the Age of the Civil War* (1980), while Holt has developed his views in *The Political Crisis of the 1850s* (1978), an unusually provocative book. Party politics are treated in Thomas B. Alexander, *Sectional Stress and Party Strength: A Computer Analysis of Roll-Call Voting Behavior in the United States House of Representatives, 1836–1860* (1967), and two books by Joel H. Silbey, *The Shrine of Party: Congressional Voting Behavior, 1841–1852* (1967) and his unorthodox *Partisan Imperative: The Dynamics of American Politics Before the Civil War* (1985). Richard H. Sewell, *Ballots for Freedom: Antislavery Politics in the United States, 1837–1860* (1976), is a standard work.

20

Drifting Toward Disunion, 1854–1861

A house divided against itself cannot stand. I believe this government cannot endure permanently half slave and half free.

Abraham Lincoln, 1858

Stowe and Helper: Literary Incendiaries

Sectional tensions were further strained in 1852, and later, by an inky phenomenon. Harriet Beecher Stowe, a wisp of a woman and the mother of a half-dozen children, published her heartrending novel *Uncle Tom's Cabin*. Dismayed by the passage of the Fugitive Slave Law, she was determined to awaken the North to the wickedness of slavery by laying bare its terrible inhumanity, especially the cruel splitting of families. Her wildly popular book relied on powerful imagery and touching pathos. "God wrote it," she explained in later years—a reminder that the deeper sources of her antislavery sentiments lay in the evangelical religious crusades of the Second Great Awakening.

The success of the novel at home and abroad was sensational. Several hundred thousand copies were published in the first year, and the totals soon ran into the millions as the tale was translated into more than a score of languages. It was also put on the stage in "Tom shows" for lengthy runs. No other novel in American history—perhaps in all history—can be compared with it as a political force. To millions of people it made slavery appear almost as evil as it really was.

When Mrs. Stowe was introduced to President Lincoln in 1862, he reportedly remarked with twinkling eyes, "So you're the little woman who wrote the book that made this great war." The truth is that *Uncle Tom's Cabin* did help start the Civil War—and win it. The South condemned that "vile wretch in petticoats" when it

Harriet Beecher Stowe (1811–1896) She was a re-markable woman whose pen helped to change the course of history. (The Metropolitan Museum of Art, gift of I. N. Phelps Stokes, Edward S. Hawes, Alice Mary Hawes, and Marion Augusta Hawes, 1937.)

135,000 SETS, 270,000 VOLUMES SOLD.

UNCLE TOM'S CABIN

FOR SALE HERE.

AN EDITION FOR THE MILLION, COMPLETE IN 1 Vol., PRICE 37 1-2 CENTS.
" " IN GERMAN, IN 1 Vol., PRICE 50 CENTS.
" " IN 2 Vols., CLOTH, 6 PLATES, PRICE $1.50.
SUPERB ILLUSTRATED EDITION, IN 1 Vol., WITH 153 ENGRAVINGS,
PRICES FROM $2.50 TO $5.00.

The Greatest Book of the Age.

"The Book that Made this Great War" Lincoln's celebrated remark to author Harriet Beecher Stowe reflected the enormous emotional impact of her impassioned novel. (The Granger Collection.)

learned that hundreds of thousands of fellow Americans were reading and believing her "unfair" indictment. Mrs. Stowe had never witnessed slavery at first hand in the Deep South, but she had seen it briefly during a visit to Kentucky, and she had lived for many years in Ohio, a center of Underground Railway activity.

Uncle Tom, endearing and enduring, left a profound impression on the North. Uncounted thousands of readers swore that henceforth they would have nothing to do with the enforcement of the Fugitive Slave Law. The tale was devoured by millions of impressionable youths in the 1850s—the later Boys in Blue who volunteered to fight the Civil War through to its grim finale. The memory of a beaten and dying Uncle Tom helped sustain them in their determination to wipe out the plague of slavery.

The novel was immensely popular abroad, especially in England and France. Countless readers wept over the kindly Tom and the angelic Eva, while deploring the brutal Simon Legree. When the guns in America finally be-

> In the closing scenes of Stowe's novel, Uncle Tom's brutal master, Simon Legree, orders the $1,200 slave savagely beaten (to death) by two fellow slaves. Through tears and blood Tom exclaims: "No! no! no! my soul an't yours Mas'r! You haven't bought it—ye can't buy it! It's been bought and paid for by One that is able to keep it. No matter, no matter, you can't harm me!" "I can't" said Legree, with a sneer; "we'll see—we'll see! Here, Sambo, Quimbo, give this dog such a breakin' in as he won't get over this month!"

gan to boom, the common people of England sensed that the triumph of the North would spell the end of the black curse. The governments in London and Paris seriously considered intervening in behalf of the South, but they were sobered by the realization that many of their own people, aroused by the "Tom-mania," might not support them.

Another trouble-brewing book appeared in 1857, five years after the debut of Uncle Tom. Entitled *The Impending Crisis of the South,* it was written by Hinton R. Helper, a nonaristocratic white from North Carolina. Hating both slavery and blacks, he attempted to prove by an array of statistics that indirectly the nonslaveholding whites were the ones who suffered most from the millstone of slavery. Unable to secure a publisher in the South, he finally managed to find one in the North.

Helper's influence was negligible among the poorer whites to whom he addressed his message. His book, with its "dirty allusions," was banned in the South, where book-burning parties were held. But in the North untold thousands of copies, many in condensed form, were distributed as campaign literature by the Republicans. Southerners were further embittered when they learned that their northern brethren were spreading these wicked "lies." Thus did southerners, reacting much as they did to *Uncle Tom's Cabin,* become increasingly unwilling to sleep under the same federal roof with their hostile Yankee bedfellows.

The North-South Contest for Kansas

The rolling plains of Kansas had meanwhile been providing a horrible example of the workings of popular sovereignty, although admittedly under abnormal conditions.

Newcomers who ventured into Kansas were a motley lot. Most of the northerners were just ordinary westward-moving pioneers in search of richer lands beyond the sunset. But a small part of the inflow was financed by groups of northern abolitionists or free-soilers. The most famous of these antislavery organizations was the New England Emigrant Aid Company, which sent about two thousand persons to the troubled area to forestall the South—and also to make a profit. Shouting "Ho for Kansas," many of them carried the deadly new breech-loading Sharps rifles, nicknamed "Beecher's Bibles" after the Reverend Henry Ward Beecher (Harriet Beecher Stowe's brother), who had helped raise money for their purchase. Many of the Kansas-bound pioneers sang Whittier's marching song (1854):

> We cross the prairie as of old
> The pilgrims crossed the sea,
> To make the West, as they the East,
> The homestead of the free!

Southern spokesmen, now more than ordinarily touchy, raised furious cries of betrayal. They had supported the Kansas-Nebraska

Bleeding Kansas, 1854–1860
"Enter every election district in Kansas . . . and vote at the point of a bowie knife or revolver," one proslavery agitator exhorted a St. Joseph, Missouri, crowd. Proslavery Missouri senator David Atchison declared that "there are 1,100 men coming over from Platte County to vote, and if that ain't enough we can send 5,000—enough to kill every Goddamned abolitionist in the Territory."

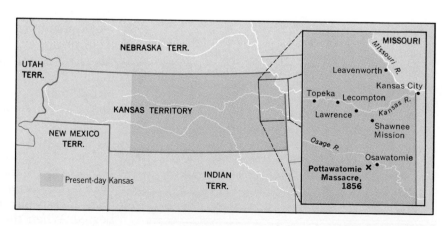

scheme of Douglas with the informal understanding that Kansas would become slave and Nebraska free. The northern "Nebrascals," allegedly by foul means, were now apparently out to "abolitionize" *both* Kansas and Nebraska.

A few southern hotheads, quick to respond in kind, attempted to "assist" small groups of well-armed slaveowners to Kansas. Some carried banners proclaiming:

> Let Yankees tremble, abolitionists fall,
> Our motto is, "Give Southern Rights to All."

But planting blacks on Kansas soil was a losing game. Slaves were valuable and volatile property, and foolish indeed were owners who would take them where bullets were flying and where the soil might be voted free under popular sovereignty. The census of 1860 found only 2 slaves among 107,000 souls in all the territory

John Brown (1800–1859) *A militant abolitionist, Brown became perhaps the most sung-about man up to that time, except Jesus. From a primitive photograph (daguerreotype) taken in 1856. (Courtesy Kansas Historical Society.)*

and only 15 in Nebraska. There was much force in the charge that the whole quarrel over slavery in the territories revolved around "an imaginary Negro in an impossible place."

Crisis conditions in Kansas rapidly worsened. When the day came in 1855 to elect members of the first territorial legislature, proslavery "border ruffians" poured in from Missouri to vote early and often. The slavery supporters triumphed and then set up their own puppet government at Shawnee Mission. The free-soilers, unable to stomach this fraudulent conspiracy, established an extralegal regime of their own in Topeka. The confused Kansans thus had their choice between two governments—one based on fraud, the other on illegality.

Tension mounted as settlers also feuded over conflicting land claims. The breaking point came in 1856 when a gang of proslavery raiders, alleging provocation, shot up and burned a part of the free-soil town of Lawrence. This outrage was but the prelude to a bloodier tragedy.

Kansas in Convulsion

The fanatical figure of John Brown now stalked upon the Kansas battlefield. Spare, gray-bearded, iron-willed, and narrowly ignorant, he was dedicated to the abolitionist cause. The power of his glittering gray eyes was such, so he claimed, that his stare could force a dog or cat to slink out of a room. Becoming involved in dubious dealings, including horse stealing, he moved to Kansas from Ohio with a part of his large family. Brooding over the recent attack on Lawrence, "Old Brown" of Osawatomie led a band of his followers to Pottawatomie Creek, in May 1856. There they literally hacked to pieces five surprised men, allegedly proslaveryites. This fiendish butchery, clearly the product of a deranged mind, besmirched the free-soil cause and brought vicious retaliation from the proslavery forces.

Civil war in Kansas, which thus flared forth in 1856, continued intermittently until it merged with the large-scale Civil War of 1861–1865. Altogether, the Kansas conflict de-

> *John Brown, an avid reader of the Old Testament, evidently believed in the principle of an eye for an eye, and a hand for a hand. A surviving son of one of his victims later testified under oath that "I found my father and one brother, William, lying dead in the road . . . I saw my other brother lying dead on the ground . . . in the grass, near a ravine, his fingers were cut open; there was a hole in his breast. William's head was cut open, and a hole in his jaw . . . and a hole was also in his side. My father was shot in the forehead and stabbed in the breast."*

stroyed millions of dollars' worth of property, paralyzed agriculture in certain areas, and cost scores of lives.

Yet by 1857 Kansas had enough people, chiefly free-soilers, to apply for statehood on a popular-sovereignty basis. The proslavery forces, then in the saddle, devised a tricky document known as the Lecompton Constitution. The people were not allowed to vote for or against the constitution as a whole, but for the constitution either "with slavery" or "with no slavery." If they voted against slavery, one of the remaining provisions of the constitution would protect the owners of slaves already in Kansas. So whatever the outcome, there would still be black bondage in Kansas. Many free-soilers, infuriated by this trick, boycotted the polls. Left to themselves, the slaveryites approved the constitution with slavery late in 1857.

The scene next shifted to Washington. President Pierce had been succeeded by the no-less-pliable James Buchanan, who was also strongly under southern influence. Blind to sharp divisions within his own Democratic party, Buchanan threw the weight of his administration behind the notorious Lecompton Constitution. But Senator Douglas, who had championed true popular sovereignty, would have none of this semipopular fraudulency. Deliberately tossing away his strong support in the South for the presidency, he fought courageously for fair play and democratic principles. The outcome was a compromise that, in effect, submitted the

entire Lecompton Constitution to a popular vote. The free-soil voters thereupon thronged to the polls and snowed it under. Kansas remained a territory until 1861, when the southern secessionists left Congress.

President Buchanan, by antagonizing the numerous Douglas Democrats in the North, hopelessly divided the once-powerful Democratic party. Until then, it had been the only remaining *national* party, for the Whigs were dead and the Republicans were sectional. With the disruption of the Democrats came the snapping of one of the last important strands in the rope that was barely binding the Union together.

"Bully" Brooks and His Bludgeon

"Bleeding Kansas" also splattered blood on the floor of the Senate in 1856. Senator Charles Sumner of Massachusetts, a tall and imposing figure, was a leading abolitionist—one of the few prominent in political life. Highly educated but cold, humorless, intolerant, and egotistical, he had made himself one of the most disliked men in the Senate. Brooding over the turbulent miscarriage of popular sovereignty, he delivered a blistering speech entitled "The Crime against Kansas." Sparing few epithets, he condemned the proslavery men as "hirelings picked from the drunken spew and vomit of an uneasy civilization." He also referred insultingly to South Carolina and to her white-haired Senator Butler, one of the best-liked members of the Senate.

Hot-tempered Congressman Preston S. Brooks of South Carolina now took vengeance into his own hands. Ordinarily gracious and gallant, he resented the insults to his state and to her senator, a distant cousin. His code of honor called for a duel, but in the South one fought only with one's social equals. And had not the coarse language of the Yankee, who probably would reject a challenge, dropped him to a lower order? To Brooks, the only alternative was to chastise the senator as one would beat an unruly dog. On May 22, 1856, he approached Sumner, then sitting at his Senate desk, and pounded the orator with an eleven-ounce cane

SOUTHERN CHIVALRY — ARGUMENT versus CLUB'S.

Sumner Beaten by Brooks *Note that the cartoonist has two of the senators smiling or laughing and one of them preventing interference with his cane. Note also that Sumner is defending himself with a quill pen while Brooks is wielding a club. (Courtesy the New York Public Library, Astor, Lenox, and Tilden Foundations.)*

until it broke. The victim fell bleeding and unconscious to the floor, while several nearby senators refrained from interfering.

Sumner had been provocatively insulting, but this counteroutrage put Brooks in the wrong. The House of Representatives could not muster enough votes to expel the Carolinian, but he resigned and was triumphantly reelected. Southern admirers deluged Brooks with

Regarding the Brooks assault on Sumner, one of the more moderate antislavery journals (Illinois State Journal) declared, "Brooks and his Southern allies have deliberately adopted the monstrous creed that any man who dares to utter sentiments which they deem wrong or unjust, shall be brutally assailed. . . . " One of the milder southern responses came from the Petersburg (Virginia) Intelligencer: "Although Mr. Brooks ought to have selected some other spot for the altercation than the Senate chamber, if he had broken every bone in Sumner's carcass it would have been a just retribution upon this slanderer of the South and her individual citizens."

canes, some of them gold-headed, to replace the one that had been broken. The injuries to Sumner's head and nervous system were serious. He was forced to leave his seat for three and a half years and go to Europe for treatment that was both painful and costly. Meanwhile Massachusetts defiantly reelected him, leaving his seat eloquently empty. Bleeding Sumner was thus joined with bleeding Kansas as a political issue.

The free-soil North was mightily aroused against the "uncouth" and "cowardly" "Bully" Brooks. Copies of Sumner's abusive speech, otherwise doomed to obscurity, were sold by the tens of thousands. Every blow that struck the senator doubtless made thousands of Republican votes. The South, although not unanimous in approving Brooks, was angered not only because Sumner had made such an intemperate speech but because it had been so extravagantly applauded in the North.

The Sumner-Brooks clash and the ensuing reactions revealed how dangerously inflamed passions were becoming, North and South. It was ominous that the cultured Sumner should have used the language of a barroom bully and that the gentlemanly Brooks should have employed the tactics and tools of a thug. Emotion was displacing thought. The blows rained on

Sumner's head were, broadly speaking, among the first blows of the Civil War.

"Old Buck" versus "The Pathfinder"

With bullets whining in Kansas, the Democrats met in Cincinnati to nominate their presidential standard-bearer of 1856. They shied away from both the weak-kneed President Pierce and the dynamic Douglas. Each was too heavily blackened by the Kansas-Nebraska Act. The delegates finally chose James Buchanan (pronounced by many *Buck*-anan), who was muscular, white-haired, and tall (6 feet; 1.83 meters), with a short neck and a protruding chin. Because of an eye defect, he carried his head cocked to one side. A well-to-do Pennsylvania lawyer, he had been serving as minister to London during the recent Kansas-Nebraska uproar. He was therefore "Kansasless," and hence relatively enemyless. But in a crisis that called for giants, "Old Buck" Buchanan was mediocre, irresolute, and confused.

Delegates of the fast-growing Republican party met in Philadelphia with bubbling enthusiasm. "Higher Law" Seward was their most conspicuous leader, and he probably would have arranged to win the nomination had he been confident that this was a "Republican year." The final choice was Captain John C. Frémont, the so-called Pathfinder of the West—a dashing but erratic explorer-soldier-surveyor who was supposed to find the path to the White House. The black-bearded and flashy young adventurer was virtually without political experience, but like Buchanan he was not tarred with the Kansas brush. The Republican platform came out vigorously against the extension of slavery into the territories, while the Democrats declared no less emphatically for popular sovereignty.

An ugly dose of antiforeignism was injected into the campaign, even though slavery extension loomed largest. The recent horde of immigrants from Ireland and Germany had alarmed "nativists," as many old-stock Protestants were called. They organized the American party,

A Know-Nothing Rally *These armed ruffians were campaigning in Baltimore for their ultranationalistic, anti-immigrant, anti-Catholic candidate. (Maryland Historical Society.)*

known also as the Know-Nothing party because of its secretiveness, and in 1856 nominated the lackluster ex-president Fillmore. Antiforeign and anti-Catholic, these superpatriots adopted the slogan "Americans Must Rule America." Remnants of the dying Whig party likewise endorsed Fillmore, and they and the Know-Nothings threatened to cut into Republican strength.

Republicans fell in behind Frémont with the zeal of crusaders. Shouting "We Follow the Pathfinder" and "We Are Buck Hunting," they organized glee clubs which sang (to the tune of the "Marseillaise"):

> Arise, arise ye brave!
> And let our war-cry be,
> Free speech, free press, free soil, free men,
> Fré-mont and victory!

"And free love," sneered the Buchanan supporters ("Buchaneers").

Mudslinging bespattered both candidates. "Old Fogy" Buchanan was assailed because he was a bachelor: the fiancée of his youth had died after a lovers' quarrel. Frémont was reviled because of his illegitimate birth, for his young mother had left her elderly husband, a Virginia planter, to run away with a French adventurer. In due season she gave birth to John in Savannah, Georgia—further to shame the South. More harmful to Frémont was the allegation,

Spiritual overtones developed in the Frémont campaign, especially over slavery. The Independent, a foremost religious journal, saw in Frémont's nomination "the good hand of God." As election day neared it declared: "Fellow-Christians! Remember it is for Christ, for the nation, and for the world that you vote at this election! Vote as you pray! Pray as you vote!"

which alienated many bigoted Know-Nothings and other "nativists," that he was a Roman Catholic.

The Electoral Fruits of 1856

A bland Buchanan, although polling less than a majority of the popular vote, won handily. His tally in the Electoral College was 174 to 114 for Frémont, with Fillmore garnering 8. The popular vote was 1,832,955 for Buchanan to 1,339,932 for Frémont, with 871,731 for Fillmore.

Why did the aroused Republicans go down to defeat? Frémont lost much ground because of grave doubts as to his honesty, capacity, and sound judgment. Perhaps more damaging were the violent threats of the southern "fire-eaters"

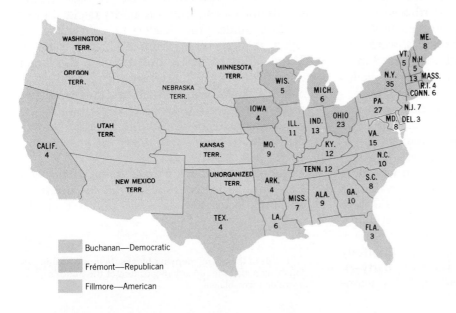

Presidential Election of 1856 (electoral vote by state) *The fateful split of 1860 was here foreshadowed. The regional polarization in 1856, shown here, was to be even sharper four years later, as illustrated by the maps on p. 422.*

Dred Scott *This lone slave's long legal battle for his freedom, culminating in the Dred Scott decision by the U.S. Supreme Court in 1857, helped to start the Civil War. (The Bettmann Archive.)*

ishing showing against the well-oiled Democratic machine. Whittier exulted:

> Then sound again the bugles,
> Call the muster-roll anew;
> If months have well-nigh won the field,
> What may not four years do?

The election of 1856 cast a long shadow forward, and politicians, North and South, peered anxiously toward 1860.

The Dred Scott Bombshell

The Dred Scott decision, handed down by the Supreme Court on March 6, 1857, abruptly ended the two-day presidential honeymoon of the unlucky bachelor, James Buchanan. This pronouncement was one of the opening paper-gun blasts of the Civil War.

Basically, the case was simple. Dred Scott, a black slave, had lived with his master for five years in Illinois and Wisconsin Territory. Backed by interested abolitionists, he sued for freedom on the basis of his long residence on free soil.

The Supreme Court proceeded to turn a simple legal case into a complex political issue. It ruled, not surprisingly, that Dred Scott was a black slave and not a citizen, and hence could not sue in federal courts.* The tribunal could then have thrown out the case on these technical grounds alone. But a majority decided to go further, under the leadership of emaciated Chief Justice Taney from the slave state of Maryland. A sweeping judgment on the larger issue of slavery in the territories seemed desirable, particularly to forestall arguments by two free-soil members who were preparing dissenting opinions. The prosouthern majority evidently hoped in this way to lay the vexed question to rest.

Taney's thunderclap rocked the free-soilers back on their heels. A majority of the Court decreed that because a slave was private property,

that the election of a sectional "Black Republican" would be a declaration of war on them, forcing them to secede. Many northerners, anxious to save both the Union and their profitable business connections with the South, were thus intimidated into voting for Buchanan. Innate conservatism triumphed, assisted by so-called southern bullyism.

It was probably fortunate for the Union that secession and civil war did not come in 1856, following a Republican victory. Frémont, an ill-balanced and second-rate figure, was no Abraham Lincoln. And in 1856 the North was more willing to let the South depart in peace than in 1860. Dramatic events from 1856 to 1860 were to arouse hundreds of thousands of still-apathetic northerners to a fighting pitch.

Yet the Republicans in 1856 could rightfully claim a "victorious defeat." The new party—a mere two-year-old infant—had made an aston-

---

*This part of the ruling, denying blacks their citizenship, seriously menaced the precarious position of the South's quarter-million free blacks.

he or she could be taken into *any* territory and legally held there in slavery. The reasoning was that the Fifth Amendment clearly forbade Congress to deprive persons of their property without due process of law. The Court, to be consistent, went further. The Missouri Compromise, banning slavery north of 36°30′, had been repealed three years earlier by the Kansas-Nebraska Act. But its spirit was still venerated in the North. Now the Court ruled that the Compromise of 1820 had been unconstitutional all along: Congress had no power to ban slavery from the territories, regardless even of what the territorial legislatures themselves might want.

A cry of delight broke from southern throats over this unexpected victory. Champions of popular sovereignty were aghast, including Senator Douglas and a host of northern Democrats. Another lethal wedge was thus driven between the northern and southern wings of the once-united Democratic party.

Taney's decision, in the case of Dred Scott, referred to the status of slaves when the Constitution was adopted: "They had for more than a century before been regarded as beings of an inferior order; and altogether unfit to associate with the white race, either in social or political relations; and so far inferior that they had no rights which the white man was bound to respect. . . . This opinion was at that time fixed and universal in the civilized portion of the white race." Taney's statement accurately described historical attitudes, but it deeply offended antislaveryites when applied to conditions in 1857.

Foes of slavery extension, especially the Republicans, were infuriated by the Dred Scott setback. Their chief rallying cry had been the banishing of bondage from the territories. They now insisted that the ruling of the Court was merely an opinion, not a decision, and no more binding than the views of a "southern debating society." Republican defiance of the exalted tribunal was intensified by an awareness that a majority of its members were southerners and by the conviction that it had debased itself—"sullied the ermine"—by wallowing in the gutter of politics.

Southerners in turn were inflamed by all this defiance. They began to wonder anew how much longer they could remain married to a section that refused to honor the Supreme Court, to say nothing of the constitutional compact that had established it.

Wall Street During the Panic of 1857 *The financial crisis further burdened President Buchanan, already reeling from the armed clashes in Kansas and the controversy over the Dred Scott decision. (Museum of the City of New York.)*

The Financial Crash of 1857

Bitterness caused by the Dred Scott decision was deepened by hard times, which dampened a period of feverish prosperity. Late in 1857 a panic burst about Buchanan's harassed head. The storm was not so bad economically as the panic of 1837, but psychologically it was probably the worst of the nineteenth century.

What caused the crash? Inpouring California gold played its part by helping to inflate the currency. The demands of the Crimean War had overstimulated the growing of grain, while frenzied speculation in land and railroads had further ripped the economic fabric. When the collapse came, over five thousand businesses failed within a year. Unemployment, accompanied by hunger meetings in urban areas, was widespread. "Bread or Death" stated one desperate slogan.

The North, including the grain growers, was hardest hit. The South, enjoying favorable cotton prices abroad, rode out the storm with flying colors. Panic conditions seemed further proof that cotton *was* king and that its economic kingdom was stronger than that of the North. This fatal delusion helped drive the overconfident southerners closer to a shooting showdown.

Financial distress in the North, especially in agriculture, gave a new vigor to the demand for free farms of 160 acres from the public domain. For several decades interested groups had been urging the federal government to abandon its ancient policy of selling the land for revenue. Instead, the argument ran, acreage should be given outright to the sturdy pioneers as a reward for risking health and life to develop it.

A scheme to make outright gifts of homesteads encountered two-pronged opposition. Eastern industrialists had long been unfriendly to free land; some of them feared that their underpaid workers would be drained off to the West. The South was even more bitterly opposed, partly because gang-labor slavery could not flourish on a mere 160 acres. Free farms would merely fill up the territories more rapidly with free-soilers and further tip the political balance against the South. In 1860, after years of debate, Congress finally passed a homestead act—one that made public lands available at a nominal sum of twenty-five cents an acre. But it was stabbed to death by the veto pen of Buchanan, near whose elbow sat leading southern sympathizers.

The panic of 1857 also created a clamor for higher tariff rates. Several months before the crash, Congress, embarrassed by a large Treasury surplus, had enacted the Tariff of 1857. The new law, responding to pressures from the South, reduced duties to about 20 percent on dutiable goods—the lowest point since the War

of 1812. Hardly had the revised rates been placed on the books when financial distress descended like a black pall. Northern manufacturers, many of them Republicans, noisily blamed their misfortunes on the low tariff. As the surplus melted away in the Treasury, industrialists in the North pointed to the need for higher duties. But what really concerned them was their desire for increased protection. Thus, the panic of 1857 gave the Republicans two surefire economic issues for the election of 1860: protection for the unprotected and farms for the farmless.

An Illinois Rail-Splitter Emerges

The Illinois senatorial election of 1858 now claimed the national spotlight. Senator Douglas's term was about to expire, and the Republicans decided to run against him a rustic Springfield lawyer, one Abraham Lincoln. The candidate—6 feet 4 inches (1.93 meters) in height and 180 pounds (81.7 kilograms) in weight—presented an awkward but arresting figure. Lincoln's legs, arms, and neck were grotesquely long; his head was crowned by coarse, black, and unruly hair; and his face was sad, sunken, and weather-beaten.

Lincoln was no silver-spoon child of destiny. Born in 1809 in a Kentucky log cabin to impoverished parents, he attended a frontier school for not more than a year; being an avid reader, he was mainly self-educated. All his life he said,

In 1832, when Lincoln became a candidate for the Illinois legislature, he delivered a speech at a political gathering: "I presume you all know who I am. I am humble Abraham Lincoln. I have been solicited by many friends to become a candidate for the Legislature. My [Whiggish] politics are short and sweet, like the old woman's dance. I am in favor of a national bank. I am in favor of the internal-improvement system, and a high protective tariff. These are my sentiments and political principles. If elected, I shall be thankful; if not, it will be all the same." He was elected two years later.

"git," "thar," "heered." Though narrow-chested and somewhat stoop-shouldered, he shone in his frontier community as a wrestler and weight lifter, and spent some time, among other pioneering pursuits, as a splitter of logs for fence rails. A superb teller of earthy and amusing stories, he would oddly enough plunge into protracted periods of melancholy.

Lincoln's private and professional life was not especially noteworthy. He married "above himself" socially, into the influential Todd family of Kentucky; and the temperamental outbursts of his high-strung wife, known by her enemies as the "she wolf," helped to school him in patience and forbearance. After reading a little law, he gradually emerged as one of the dozen or so better-known trial lawyers in Illinois, although still accustomed to carrying important papers in his stovepipe hat. He was widely referred to as "Honest Abe," partly because he would refuse cases that he could not conscientiously defend.

Abraham Lincoln, a Most Uncommon Common Man   *Early photograph (daguerreotype) by Matthew B. Brady, distinguished photographer of the era.*

The rise of Lincoln as a political figure was less than rocketlike. After making his mark in the Illinois legislature as a Whig politician of the logrolling variety, he served one undistinguished term in Congress, 1847–1849. Until 1854, when he was forty-five years of age, he had done nothing to establish a claim to statesmanship. But the passage of the Kansas-Nebraska Act in that year lighted within him unexpected fires. After mounting the Republican bandwagon, he emerged as one of the foremost politicians and orators of the Northwest. At the Philadelphia convention of 1856, where John Frémont was nominated, Lincoln actually received 110 votes for the vice-presidential nomination.

The Great Debate: Lincoln versus Douglas

Lincoln, as Republican nominee for the Senate seat, boldly challenged Douglas to a series of joint debates. This was a rash act, because the stumpy senator was probably the nation's most devastating debater. Douglas promptly accepted the challenge, and seven meetings were arranged from August to October 1858.

At first glance, the two contestants seemed ill matched. The well-groomed and polished Douglas, with stocky figure and bullish voice, presented a striking contrast to the lanky Lincoln, with his baggy clothes and unshined shoes. Moreover, "Old Abe," as he was called in both affection and derision, had a piercing, high-pitched voice and was often ill at ease when he began to speak. But as he threw himself into an argument, he seemed to grow in height, while his glowing eyes lighted up a rugged face. He relied on logic rather than on table-thumping.

The most famous of the forensic clashes came at Freeport, Illinois, where Lincoln nearly impaled his opponent on the horns of a dilemma. Suppose, he queried, the people of a territory should vote slavery down? The Supreme Court in the Dred Scott decision had decreed that they could not. Who would prevail, the Court or the people?

Legend to the contrary, Douglas and some

Lincoln and Douglas Debate, 1858 *Thousands attended each of the seven Lincoln-Douglas debates. Douglas is shown here sitting to Lincoln's right in the debate at Charleston, Illinois, in September. On one occasion, Lincoln quipped that Douglas's logic would prove that a horse chestnut was a chestnut horse. (Illinois State Historical Library.)*

southerners had already publicly answered the Freeport question. The "Little Giant" therefore did not hesitate to meet the issue head on, honestly and consistently. He replied that no matter how the Supreme Court ruled, slavery would stay down if the people voted it down. Laws to protect slavery would have to be passed by the territorial legislatures. These would not be forthcoming in the absence of popular approval, and black bondage would soon disappear. Douglas, in truth, had American history on his side. Where public opinion does not support the federal government, as in the case of Jefferson's embargo, the law is almost impossible to enforce.

The upshot was that Douglas defeated Lincoln for the Senate seat. The "Little Giant's" loyalty to popular sovereignty, which still had a powerful appeal in Illinois, probably was decisive. Senators were then chosen by state legislatures; and in the general election that followed the debates, more pro-Douglas members were

Lincoln expressed his views on the relation of the black and white races in 1858, in a debate with Stephen A. Douglas: "I, as well as Judge Douglas, am in favor of the race to which I belong, having the superior position. I have never said anything to the contrary, but I hold that notwithstanding all this, there is no reason in the world why the negro is not entitled to all the natural rights enumerated in the Declaration of Independence, the right to life, liberty, and the pursuit of happiness. I hold that he is as much entitled to those rights as the white man. I agree with Judge Douglas he is not my equal in many respects—certainly not in color, perhaps not in moral or intellectual endowment. But in the right to eat the bread, without leave of anybody else, which his own hand earns, he is my equal and the equal of Judge Douglas, and the equal of every living man." (First Lincoln-Douglas Debate, Ottawa, Illinois, August 21, 1858.)

John Brown Going to His Execution   This painting may have been inspired by the journalist Horace Greeley, who was not present but wrote that "a black woman with a little child stood by the door. He stopped for a moment, and stooping, kissed the child." That scene never took place, as Brown was escorted from the jail only by a detachment of soldiers. But this painting has become famous as a kind of allegorical expression of the pathos of Brown's martyrdom for the abolitionist cause. (Metropolitan Museum of Art.)

elected than pro-Lincoln members. Yet thanks to inequitable apportionment, the districts carried by Douglas supporters represented a smaller population than those carried by the Lincoln supporters. "Honest Abe" thus won a clear moral victory.

Lincoln possibly was playing for larger stakes than just the senatorship. Although defeated, he had shambled into the national limelight in company with the most prominent northern politicians. Newspapers in the East published detailed accounts of the debates, and Lincoln began to emerge as a potential Republican nominee for president. But Douglas, in winning Illinois, hurt his chances of winning the presidency, while further splitting his splintering party. After his opposition to the Lecompton Constitution for Kansas and his further defiance of the Supreme Court at Freeport, southern Democrats were determined to break up the party (and the Union) rather than accept him. The Lincoln-Douglas debate platform thus proved to be one of the preliminary battlefields of the Civil War.

John Brown: Murderer or Martyr?

The gaunt, grim figure of John Brown of Kansas fame now appeared again in a more terrible way. His crackbrained scheme was to invade the South secretly with a handful of followers, call upon the slaves to rise, furnish them with arms, and establish a kind of black free state as a sanctuary. Brown secured several thousand dollars for firearms from northern abolitionists and finally arrived in hilly western Virginia with some twenty men, including several blacks. At scenic Harpers Ferry he seized the federal arsenal in October 1859, incidentally killing seven innocent people, including a free black, and injuring ten or so more. But the slaves, largely ignorant of Brown's strike, failed to rise, and the wounded Brown and the remnants of his tiny band were quickly captured.

"Old Brown" was convicted of murder and treason, after a hasty but legal trial. His presumed insanity was supported by affidavits from seventeen friends and relatives, who were trying to save his neck. Actually thirteen of his

> Sentenced to be hanged, John Brown wrote to his brother: "I am quite cheerful in view of my approaching end, being fully persuaded that I am worth inconceivably more to hang than for any other purpose. . . . I count it all joy. 'I have fought the good fight,' and have, as I trust, 'finished my course.' "

near relations were regarded as insane, including his mother and grandmother. Governor Wise of Virginia would have been most wise, so his critics say, if he had only clapped the culprit into a lunatic asylum.

But Brown—"God's angry man"—was given every opportunity to pose and to enjoy martyrdom. Though probably of unsound mind, he was clever enough to see that he was worth much more to the abolitionist cause dangling from a rope than in any other way. His demeanor during the trial was dignified and courageous, his last words ("this *is* a beautiful country") were to become legendary, and he marched up the scaffold steps without flinching. His conduct was so exemplary, his devotion to freedom so inflexible, that he took on an exalted character, however deplorable his previous record may have been. So the hangman's trap was sprung, and Brown plunged not into oblivion but into world fame. A memorable marching song of the impending Civil War ran:

> John Brown's body lies a-mould'ring in the grave,
> His soul is marching on.

The effects of Harpers Ferry were calamitous. In the eyes of the South, already embittered, "Osawatomie Brown" was a wholesale murderer and an apostle of treason. Many southerners asked how they could possibly remain in the Union while a "murderous gang of abolitionists" were financing armed bands to "Brown" them. Moderate northerners, including Republican leaders, openly deplored this mad exploit. But the South naturally concluded that the violent abolitionist view was shared by the entire North, dominated by "Brown-loving" Republicans.

Abolitionists and other ardent free-soilers were infuriated by Brown's execution. Many of them were ignorant of his bloody past and his even more bloody purposes, and they were outraged because the Virginians had hanged so earnest a reformer who was working for so righteous a cause. On the day of his execution, free-soil centers in the North tolled bells, fired guns, half-masted flags, and held mass meetings. Some spoke of "Saint John" Brown, while the serene Ralph Waldo Emerson compared the new martyr-hero with Jesus. The gallows became a cross. E. C. Stedman wrote:

> And Old Brown,
> Osawatomie Brown,
> May trouble you more than ever,
>   when you've nailed his coffin down!

The ghost of the martyred Brown would not be laid to rest.

The Disruption of the Democrats

Beyond question the presidential election of 1860 was the most fateful in American history. On it hung the issue of peace or civil war.

Deeply divided, the Democrats met in Charleston, South Carolina, with Douglas the leading candidate of the northern wing of the party. But the southern "fire-eaters" regarded him as a traitor, as a result of his unpopular stand on the Lecompton Constitution and the Freeport Doctrine. After a bitter wrangle over the platform, the delegates from most of the cotton states walked out. When the remainder could not scrape together the necessary two-thirds vote for Douglas, the entire body dissolved in confusion. The first tragic secession was the secession of southerners from the Democratic National Convention. It became habit-forming.

The Democrats tried again in Baltimore. This time the Douglas Democrats, chiefly from the North, were firmly in the saddle. Many of the cotton-state delegates again took a walk, and the rest of the convention enthusiastically nominated their hero. The platform came out squarely for popular sovereignty and, as a sop to

> Alexander H. Stephens, destined the next year to become vice-president of the new Confederacy, wrote privately in 1860 of the anti-Douglas Democrats who seceded from the Charleston convention: "The seceders intended from the beginning to rule or ruin; and when they find they cannot rule, they will then ruin. They have about enough power for this purpose; not much more; and I doubt not but they will use it. Envy, hate, jealousy, spite . . . will make devils of men. The secession movement was instigated by nothing but bad passions."

the South, against obstruction of the Fugitive Slave Law by the states.

Angered southern Democrats promptly organized a rival convention in Baltimore, in which many of the northern states were unrepresented. They selected as their leader the stern-jawed vice-president, John C. Breckinridge, a man of moderate views from the border state of Kentucky. The platform favored the extension of slavery into the territories and the annexation of slave-populated Cuba.

A middle-of-the-road group, fearing for the Union, hastily organized the Constitutional Union party, sneered at as the "Do Nothing" or "Old Gentleman's" party. It consisted mainly of former Whigs and Know-Nothings, a veritable "gathering of graybeards." Desperately anxious to elect a compromise candidate, they met in Baltimore and nominated for the presidency John Bell of Tennessee. They went into battle ringing hand bells for Bell and voicing the slogan "The Union, the Constitution, and the Enforcement of the Laws."

A Rail-Splitter Splits the Union

Elated Republicans were presented with a heaven-sent opportunity. Scenting victory in the breeze as their opponents split hopelessly, they gathered in Chicago in a huge, boxlike wooden structure called the Wigwam. William H. Seward was by far the best known of the contenders. But his radical utterances, includ-

ing his "irrepressible conflict" speech at Rochester in 1858, had fatally injured his prospects.* His numerous enemies coined the slogan "Success Rather than Seward." Lincoln, the favorite son of Illinois, was definitely a "Mr. Second Best," but he was a stronger candidate because he had made fewer enemies. Overtaking Seward on the third ballot, he was nominated amid scenes of the wildest excitement.

The Republican platform had a seductive appeal for just about every important nonsouthern group. For the free-soilers, nonextension of slavery; for the northern manufacturers, a protective tariff; for the immigrants, no abridgment of rights; for the Northwest, a Pacific railroad; for the West, internal improvements at federal expense; and for the farmers, free homesteads from the public domain. Seductive slogans were "Vote Yourselves a Farm" and "Land for the Landless."

Southern secessionists promptly served notice that the election of the "baboon" Lincoln—the "abolitionist" rail-splitter—would split the Union. In fact, "Honest Abe," though hating slavery, was no outright abolitionist. But he saw fit, perhaps mistakenly, to issue no statements to quiet southern fears. He had already put himself on record; and fresh statements might stir up fresh antagonisms.

As the election campaign ground noisily forward, Lincoln enthusiasts staged roaring rallies and parades, complete with pitch-dripping torches and oilskin capes. They extolled "High Old Abe," the "Woodchopper of the West," and the "Little Giant Killer," while groaning dismally for "Poor Little Doug." Enthusiastic "Little Giants" and "Little Dougs" retorted with "We want a statesman, not a rail-splitter, as President." Douglas himself waged a vigorous speaking campaign, even in the South, and threatened to put the hemp with his own hands around the neck of the first secessionist.

The returns, breathlessly awaited, proclaimed a sweeping victory for Lincoln (see the table on page 423).

---

*Seward had referred to an "irrepressible conflict" between slavery and freedom, though not necessarily a bloody one.

The Electoral Upheaval of 1860

Awkward "Abe" Lincoln had run a curious race. To a greater degree than any other holder of the nation's highest office (except J. Q. Adams), he was a minority president. Sixty percent of the voters preferred some other candidate. He was also a sectional president, for in ten southern states, where he was not allowed on the ballot, he polled no popular votes. The election of 1860 was virtually two elections: one in the North, the other in the South. South Carolinians rejoiced over Lincoln's victory; they now had their excuse to secede. In winning the North the "rail-splitter" had split off the South.

Douglas, though scraping together only twelve electoral votes, made an impressive showing. Boldly breaking with tradition, he campaigned energetically for himself. (Presidential candidates customarily maintained a dignified silence.) He drew important strength from all sections and ranked a fairly close second in the popular-vote column. In fact, the Douglas Democrats and the Breckinridge Democrats together amassed 366,484 more votes than did Lincoln.

Presidential Election of 1860 (electoral vote by state) *It is a surprising fact that Lincoln, often rated among the greatest presidents, ranks near the bottom in percentage of popular votes. In all the eleven states that seceded, he received only a scattering of one state's votes—about 1.5 percent in Virginia.*

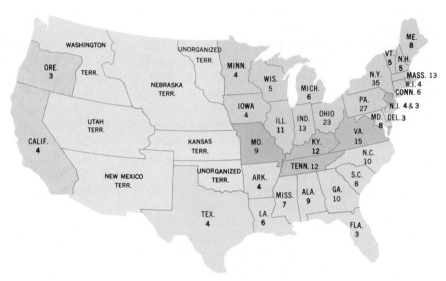

- Lincoln—Republican
- Breckinridge—Democratic
- Bell—Constitutional Union
- Douglas—Democratic
- No votes cast

Presidential Election of 1860 (showing popular vote by county) *Note that the vote by counties for Lincoln was virtually all cast in the North. The northern Democrat, Douglas, was also nearly shut out in the South, which divided its votes between Breckinridge and Bell. (Note that only citizens of states could vote; inhabitants of territories could not.)*

Election of 1860

CANDIDATE	POPULAR VOTE	PERCENTAGE OF POPULAR VOTE	ELECTORAL VOTE
Lincoln	1,865,593	39.79%	180 (every vote of the free states except for 3 of New Jersey's 7 votes)
Douglas	1,382,713	29.40	12 (only Missouri and 3 of New Jersey's 7 votes)
Breckinridge	848,356	18.20	72 (all the cotton states)
Bell	592,906	12.61	39 (Virginia, Kentucky, Tennessee)

A myth persists that if the Democrats had only united behind Douglas, they would have triumphed. Yet the cold figures tell a different story. Even if the "Little Giant" had received all the electoral votes cast for all three of Lincoln's opponents, the "rail-splitter" would have won, 169 to 134, instead of 180 to 123. Lincoln still would have carried the populous states of the North and the Northwest. On the other hand, if the Democrats had not broken up, they could have entered the campaign with higher enthusiasm and better organization and might have won.

Significantly, the verdict of the ballot box did not indicate a strong sentiment for secession. Breckinridge, while favoring the extension of slavery, was no disunionist. Although the candidate of the "fire-eaters," in the slave states he polled fewer votes than the combined strength of his opponents, Douglas and Bell. He even failed to carry his own Kentucky.

Yet the South, despite its electoral defeat, was not badly off. It still had a five-to-four majority on the supreme bench. Although the Republicans had elected Lincoln, they controlled neither the Senate nor the House of Representatives. The federal government could not touch slavery in those states where it existed except by a constitutional amendment, and such an amendment could be defeated by one-fourth of the states. The fifteen slave states numbered nearly one-half of the total—a fact not fully appreciated by southern firebrands.

The Secessionist Exodus

A tragic chain reaction of secession now began to explode. South Carolina, which had threatened to go out if the "sectional" Lincoln came in, was as good as its word. Four days after the election of the "Illinois baboon" by "insulting" majorities, its legislature voted unanimously to call a special convention. Meeting at Charleston in December 1860, it unanimously voted to secede. During the next six weeks, six other states of the lower South, though somewhat less united, followed South Carolina over the precipice. Four more were to join them later, bringing the total to eleven.

With the eyes of destiny upon them, the seven seceders, formally meeting at Montgomery, Alabama, created a government known as the Confederate States of America. As their president they chose Jefferson Davis, a dignified and austere recent member of the U.S. Senate from Mississippi. He was a West Pointer and a former cabinet member with wide military and administrative experience; but he suffered from chronic ill-health, as well as from a frustrated ambition to be a Napoleonic strategist.

The crisis, already critical enough, was deepened by the "lame duck"* interlude. Lincoln, al-

---

*The "lame duck" period was shortened to ten weeks in 1933 by the Twentieth Amendment (see the Appendix).

President Jefferson Davis (1808–1889) Faced with grave difficulties, he was probably as able a man for the position as the Confederacy could have chosen. The Davis family had moved south from Kentucky; the Lincoln family, north. If the migrations had been reversed, the presidential roles might have been reversed, as some have speculated. (Library of Congress.)

Three days after Lincoln's election, Horace Greeley's influential New York Tribune *(November 9, 1860) had declared: "If the cotton States shall decide that they can do better out of the Union than in it, we insist on letting them go in peace. The right to secede may be a revolutionary one, but it exists nevertheless. . . . Whenever a considerable section of our Union shall deliberately resolve to go out, we shall resist all coercive measures designed to keep it in. We hope never to live in a republic, whereof one section is pinned to the residue by bayonets." After the secession movement got well under way, Greeley's* Tribune *changed its tune.*

though elected president in November 1860, could not take office until four months later, March 4, 1861. During this period of protracted uncertainty, when he was still a private citizen in Illinois, seven of the eleven deserting states pulled out of the Union.

President Buchanan, the aging incumbent, has been blamed for not holding the seceders in the Union by sheer force—for wringing his hands instead of secessionist necks. Never a vigorous man and habitually conservative, he was now nearly seventy, and although devoted to the Union, he was surrounded by prosouth-

Southern Opposition to Secession, 1860–1861 (showing vote by county) This county vote shows the opposition of the antiplanter, antislavery mountain whites in the Appalachian region. There was also considerable resistance to secession in Texas, where Governor Sam Houston, who led the Unionists, was deposed by secessionists.

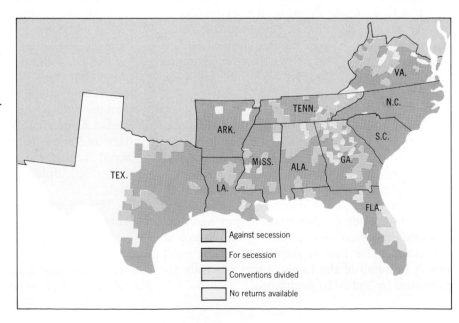

Against secession

For secession

Conventions divided

No returns available

WASHINGTON
ORE.
TERR.
UNORG. TERR.
NEBRASKA TERR.
UTAH TERR.
CALIF.
36°30'
KANSAS TERR.
NEW MEXICO TERR.
UNORG. TERR.
36°30'
TEXAS

Proposed Crittenden Compromise, 1860 *Stephen A. Douglas claimed that "If the Crittenden proposition could have been passed early in the session [of Congress], it would have saved all the States, except South Carolina." But Crittenden's proposal was doomed—Lincoln opposed it, and Republicans cast not a single vote in its favor.*

Slavery prohibited during territorial status, thereby virtually assuring free-soil states

Slavery protected during territorial status; states might be either slave or free

ern advisers. As an able bachelor-lawyer wedded to the Constitution, he did not believe that the southern states could legally secede. Yet he could find no authority in the Constitution for stopping them with guns.

"Oh for one hour of Jackson!" cried the advocates of strong-arm tactics. But "Old Buck" Buchanan was not "Old Hickory," and he was faced with a far more complex and serious problem. One important reason why he did not resort to force was that the tiny standing army of some fifteen thousand men, then widely scattered, was urgently needed to control the Indians in the West. Public opinion in the North, at that time, was far from willing to unsheathe the sword. Fighting would merely shatter all prospects of adjustment, and until the guns began to boom, there was still a flickering hope of reconciliation rather than a contested divorce. The weakness lay not so much in Buchanan as in the Constitution and in the Union itself. Ironically, when Lincoln became president, he continued essentially Buchanan's wait-and-see policy.

The Collapse of Compromise

Impending bloodshed spurred final and frantic attempts at compromise—in the American tradition. The most promising of these efforts was

sponsored by Senator Crittenden of Kentucky, on whose shoulders had fallen the mantle of a fellow Kentuckian, Henry Clay.

The proposed Crittenden amendments to the Constitution were designed to appease the South. Slavery in the territories was to be prohibited north of 36°30', but south of that line it was to be given federal protection in all territories existing or "hereafter to be acquired" (such as Cuba). Future states, north or south of 36°30', could come into the Union with or without slavery, as they should choose. In short, the slavery supporters were to be guaranteed full rights in the southern territories, as long as they

One reason why the Crittenden Compromise failed in December 1860 was the prevalence of an attitude reflected in a private letter of Senator Hammond of South Carolina on April 19: "I firmly believe that the slave-holding South is now the controlling power of the world—that no other power would face us in hostility. Cotton, rice, tobacco, and naval stores command the world; and we have sense to know it, and are sufficiently Teutonic to carry it out successfully. The North without us would be a motherless calf, bleating about, and die of mange and starvation."

were territories, regardless of the wishes of the majority under popular sovereignty. Federal protection in a territory south of 36°30′ might conceivably, though improbably, turn the entire area permanently to slavery.

Lincoln flatly rejected the Crittenden scheme, which offered some slight prospect of success, and all hope of compromise fled. For this refusal he must bear a heavy responsibility. Yet he had been elected on a platform that opposed the extension of slavery, and he felt that as a matter of principle he could not afford to yield, even though gains for slavery in the territories might be only temporary. Larger gains might come later in Cuba and Mexico. Crittenden's proposal, said Lincoln, "would amount to a perpetual covenant of war against every people, tribe, and state owning a foot of land between here and Tierra del Fuego."

As for the supposedly spineless "Old Fogy" Buchanan, how could he have prevented the Civil War by starting a civil war? No one has yet come up with a satisfactory answer. If he had used force on South Carolina in December 1860, the fighting almost certainly would have erupted three months sooner than it did, and under less favorable circumstances for the Union. The North would have appeared as the heavy-handed aggressor. And the crucial Border States, so vital to the Union, probably would have been driven into the arms of their "wayward sisters."

Farewell to Union

Secessionists who parted company with their sister states left for a number of avowed reasons, mostly relating in some way to slavery. They were alarmed by the inexorable tipping of the political balance against them—"the despotic majority of numbers." The "crime" of the North, observed James Russell Lowell, was the census returns. Southerners were also dismayed by the triumph of the new sectional Republican party, which seemed to threaten their rights as a slaveholding minority. They were weary of free-soil criticism, abolitionist nagging, and northern interference, ranging from the Underground Railroad to John Brown's raid. "All we ask is to be let alone," declared president Jefferson Davis in an early message to his congress.

Many southerners supported secession because they felt sure that their departure would be unopposed, despite "Yankee yawp" to the contrary. They were confident that the clodhopping and codfishing Yankee would not or could not fight. They believed that northern manufacturers and bankers, so heavily dependent on southern cotton and markets, would not dare to cut their own economic throats with their own swords. But should war come, the immense debt owed to northern creditors by the South—happy thought—could be promptly repudiated, as it later was.

The Folly of Secession *This northern cartoon expressed the sentiment of many people north of the Mason-Dixon line that secession was a self-defeating move, doomed to failure. (From* Pictorial History of the Confederacy, *1951.)*

> Regarding the Civil War, the London Times (November 7, 1861) editorialized: "The contest is really for empire on the side of the North, and for independence on that of the South, and in this respect we recognize an exact analogy between the North and the Government of George III, and the South and the Thirteen Revolted Provinces."

> James Russell Lowell, the northern poet and essayist, wrote in the Atlantic Monthly shortly after the secessionist movement began: "The fault of the free States in the eyes of the South is not one that can be atoned for by any yielding of special points here and there. Their offence is that they are free, and that their habits and prepossessions are those of freedom. Their crime is the census of 1860. Their increase in numbers, wealth, and power is a standing aggression. It would not be enough to please the Southern States that we should stop asking them to abolish slavery: what they demand of us is nothing less than that we should abolish the spirit of the age. Our very thoughts are a menace."

Southern leaders regarded secession as a golden opportunity to cast aside their generations of "vassalage" to the North. An independent Dixieland could develop its own banking and shipping, and trade directly with Europe. The low Tariff of 1857, passed largely by southern votes, was not in itself menacing. But who could tell when the "greedy" Republicans would win control of Congress and drive through their own oppressive protective tariff? For decades this fundamental friction had pitted the North, with its manufacturing plants, against the South, with its agrarian economy.

Worldwide impulses of nationalism—then stirring in Italy, Germany, Poland, and elsewhere—were fermenting in the South. This huge area, with its distinctive culture, was not so much a section as a subnation. It could not view with complacency the possibility of being lorded over, then or later, by what it regarded as a hostile nation of northerners.

The principles of self-determination—of the Declaration of Independence—seemed to many southerners to apply perfectly to them. Few, if any, of the seceders felt that they were doing anything wrong or immoral. The thirteen original states had voluntarily entered the Union, and now seven—ultimately eleven—southern states were voluntarily withdrawing from it.

Historical parallels ran even deeper. In 1776, thirteen American colonies, led by the rebel George Washington, had seceded from the British Empire by throwing off the yoke of King George. In 1860–1861, eleven American states, led by the rebel Jefferson Davis, were seceding from the Union by throwing off the yoke of "King" Abraham Lincoln. With that burden gone, the South was confident that it could work out its own peculiar destiny more quietly, happily, and prosperously.

CHRONOLOGY

1852	Harriet Beecher Stowe publishes *Uncle Tom's Cabin*
1854	Kansas-Nebraska Act
1856	Buchanan defeats Frémont and Fillmore for presidency
	Sumner beaten by Brooks in Senate chamber
	Brown's Osawatomie massacre
1856–1860	Civil war in "bleeding Kansas"
1857	Dred Scott decision
	Lecompton Constitution rejected
	Panic of 1857

	Hinton R. Helper publishes *The Impending Crisis of the South*
1858	Lincoln-Douglas debates
1859	Brown raids Harpers Ferry
1860	Lincoln wins four-way race for presidency
	South Carolina secedes from the Union
	Crittenden Compromise fails
1861	Seven seceding states form the Confederate States of America

Varying Viewpoints

Few issues have generated as much heat among American historians as the causes of the War for Southern Independence. The very names chosen to describe the conflict—notably *Civil War* or *War Between the States*—reveal much about various authors' points of view. Opinions have naturally differed according to section, but in general the appraisals of the war have gone through four phases.

The so-called nationalist school in the late nineteenth century found slavery and Union to be the fundamental causes of the bloodletting and approved the war because it ended slavery and preserved the Union. In the early twentieth century, some writers, notably Charles Beard, argued that the war was not about slavery per se but about the basic economic conflict between an industrial North and an agricultural South.

After the disappointing results of World War I, some historians argued that the Civil War itself had been a great mistake, traceable not to any fundamentally "irreconcilable conflict," whether racial or economic, but to the breakdown of political institutions and the ineptitude of a blundering generation of leaders. But since World War II, a "neonationalist" view has generally prevailed. It pictures the Civil War as an all-but-inevitable clash between two cultures and two sets of social values, ending in victory for the forces of virtue and progress.

Select Readings

Primary Source Documents

Harriet Beecher Stowe's *Uncle Tom's Cabin* (1852) and Hinton R. Helper's *The Impending Crisis of the South** (1852) are vivid and important. The Lincoln-Douglas debates* (1858) frame the issues of the 1850s and remain classics of American oratory.

Secondary Sources

Refer to Chapter 19 for the titles by Roy F. Nichols, James G. Randall and David Donald, and Avery O. Craven. Richly detailed is Allan Nevins, *The Emer-* gence of Lincoln (2 vols., 1950). David Donald, *Charles Sumner and the Coming of the Civil War* (1960), is an outstanding biography. See also his able *Charles Sumner and the Rights of Man* (1970). Lincoln's rise is developed in Don E. Fehrenbacher's *Prelude to Greatness* (1962) and in Carl Sandburg's *Abraham Lincoln: The Prairie Years* (2 vols., 1926). On Mary Todd Lincoln, see Jean H. Baker, *Mary Todd Lincoln: A Biograhy* (1987). The explosive Kansas issue is dealt with in James A. Rawley, *Race and Politics: "Bleeding Kansas" and the Coming of the Civil War* (1969). On the Lincoln-Douglas debates see Harry V. Jaffa, *Crisis of the House Divided* (1959). Don E. Fehrenbacher brilliantly and thoroughly dissects *The Dred Scott Case* (1978). The final moments before fighting began are scrutinized in David M. Potter, *Lincoln and His Party in the Secession Crisis* (1942), and in Kenneth M. Stampp, *And the War Came* (1950). The southern side of the question appears in Steven A. Channing, *Crisis of Fear: Secession of South Carolina* (1970); William L. Barney, *The Secessionist Impulse: Alabama and Mississippi* (1974); William J. Evitts, *A Matter of Allegiances: Maryland from 1850 to 1861* (1974); and Ralph A. Wooster, *The Secessionist Convention of the South* (1962). See also Michael P. Johnson, *Toward a Patriarchal Republic: The Secession of Georgia* (1977); J. Mills Thornton III, *Power and Politics in a Slave Society: Alabama 1820–1860* (1978); and Marc W. Kruman, *Parties and Politics in North Carolina, 1836–1865* (1983). Stephen B. Oates paints a vivid portrait of John Brown in *To Purge This Land with Blood* (1970). Thomas J. Pressley reviews the copious literature about the war in *Americans Interpret Their Civil War* (1954). George Forgie offers a psychoanalytic explanation of the coming of the war in *Patricide in the House Divided: A Psychological Interpretation of Lincoln and IIis Age* (1979).

21

Girding for War: The North and the South, 1861–1865

I consider the central idea pervading this struggle is the necessity that is upon us, of proving that popular government is not an absurdity. We must settle this question now, whether in a free government the minority have the right to break up the government whenever they choose. If we fail it will go far to prove the incapability of the people to govern themselves.

Abraham Lincoln, May 7, 1861

President of the Disunited States of America

Abraham Lincoln solemnly took the oath of office on March 4, 1861, after having slipped into Washington at night, partially disguised to thwart assassins. He thus became president, not of the *United* States of America, but of the disunited states of America. Seven had departed; eight more were teetering on the edge. The girders of the unfinished Capitol dome loomed nakedly in the background, as if to symbolize the imperfect state of the Union.

Lincoln's inaugural address was firm yet conciliatory: there would be no conflict unless the South provoked it. Secession, the president declared, was wholly impracticable, because "Physically speaking, we cannot separate."

Here Lincoln put his finger on a profound geographical truth. The North and South were Siamese twins, bound inseparably together. If they had been divided by the Pyrenees Mountains or the Danube River, a sectional divorce would have been more feasible. But the Appalachian Mountains and the mighty Mississippi River both ran the wrong way.

Uncontested secession would create new controversies. What share of the national debt should the South be forced to take with it? What portion of the jointly held federal territories, if any, should the Confederate states be allotted—areas so largely purchased with Southern blood? How would the fugitive-slave issue be dealt with? The Underground Railroad would certainly redouble its activity, and it would have to transport its passengers only across the Ohio River, not all the way to Canada. Was it conceivable that all such problems could have been solved without ugly armed clashes?

A united United States had hitherto been the paramount republic in the Western Hemisphere. If this powerful democracy should break into two hostile parts, the European nations would be delighted. They could gleefully transplant to America their hoary concept of the balance of power. Playing the no less hoary game of divide and conquer, they could incite one snarling fragment of the dis-United States against the other. The colonies of the European powers in the New World, notably those of Britain, would thus be made safer against the rapacious Yankees. And European imperialists, with no unified republic to stand across their path, could more easily defy the Monroe Doctrine and seize territory in the Americas.

South Carolina Assails Fort Sumter

The issue of the divided Union came to a head over the matter of federal forts in the South. As the seceding states left, they had seized the United States arsenals, mints, and other public property within their borders. When Lincoln took office, only two significant forts in the South still flew the Stars and Stripes. The more

Secretary William H. Seward (1801–1872) *Seward was a senator, a secretary of state, and the purchaser of Alaska ("Seward's Folly"), where both a peninsula and a city were named after him. (National Archives.)*

important of the pair was square-walled Fort Sumter, in Charleston Harbor, with fewer than 100 men.

Ominously, the choices presented to Lincoln by Fort Sumter were all bad. This stronghold had provisions that would last only a few weeks—until the middle of April 1861. If no supplies were forthcoming, its commander would have to surrender without firing a shot. Lincoln, quite understandably, did not feel that such a weak-kneed course squared with his obligation to protect federal property. But if he sent reinforcements, the South Carolinians would undoubtedly fight back; they could not tolerate a federal fort blocking the mouth of their most important Atlantic seaport.

After agonizing indecision, Lincoln adopted a middle-of-the-road solution. He notified the South Carolinians that an expedition would be sent to *provision* the garrison, though not to re-

---

Secretary of State Seward entertained the dangerous idea that if the North picked a fight with one or more European nations, the South would once more rally around the flag. On April Fool's Day, 1861, he submitted to Lincoln a memorandum recommending "I would demand explanations from Spain and France, categorically, at once. I would seek explanations from Great Britain and Russia. . . . And, if satisfactory explanations are not received from Spain and France . . . would convene Congress and declare war against them." Lincoln quietly but firmly quashed Seward's scheme.

inforce it. But in Southern eyes "provision" spelled "reinforcement."

A Union naval force was next started on its way to Fort Sumter—a move that the South regarded as an act of aggression. On April 12, 1861, the cannons of the Carolinians opened fire on the fort, while crowds in Charleston applauded and waved handkerchiefs. After a thirty-four-hour bombardment, which took no life, the dazed garrison surrendered.

The firing on the fort electrified the North, which at once responded with cries of "Remember Fort Sumter" and "Save the Union." Hitherto countless Northerners had been saying that if the Southern states wanted to go, they should not be pinned to the rest of the nation with bayonets. "Wayward sisters, depart in peace" was a common sentiment, expressed even by the commander of the army, war hero General Winfield Scott, now so feeble at seventy-five that he had to be boosted onto his horse.

But the assault on Fort Sumter provoked the North to a fighting pitch: the fort was lost, but the Union was saved. Lincoln had contrived to win a great strategic victory. Southerners had wantonly fired upon the glorious Stars and Stripes, and honor demanded an armed response. Lincoln promptly (April 15) issued a call to the states for seventy-five thousand mili-

> Lincoln, Kentucky-born like Jefferson Davis, was aware of Kentucky's crucial importance. In September 1861 he remarked: "I think to lose Kentucky is nearly the same as to lose the whole game. Kentucky gone, we cannot hold Missouri, nor, I think, Maryland. These all against us, and the job on our hands is too large for us. We would as well consent to separation at once, including the surrender of this capital [Washington]."

tiamen; and volunteers sprang to the colors in such enthusiastic numbers that many were turned away—a mistake not often repeated. On April 19 and 27 the president proclaimed a leaky blockade of Southern seaports.

The call for troops, in turn, aroused the South much as the attack on Fort Sumter had aroused the North. Lincoln was now waging war—from the Southern view an aggressive war—on the Confederacy. Virginia, Arkansas, and Tennessee, all of which had earlier voted down secession, reluctantly joined their embattled sister states, as did North Carolina. Thus the seven states became eleven as the "submissionists" and "Union shriekers" were overcome. Richmond, Virginia, replaced Mont-

Fort Sumter, South Carolina, April 14, 1861 *The Confederate flag flies over the fortress in Charleston Harbor after its surrender. (National Archives.)*

gomery, Alabama, as the Confederate capital—too near Washington for strategic comfort on either side.

Brothers' Blood and Border Blood

The only slave states left were the crucial Border States. This group consisted of Missouri, Kentucky, Maryland, Delaware, and later West Virginia—the "mountain white" area that somewhat illegally tore itself from the side of Virginia in mid-1861. If the North had fired the first shot, some or all of these doubtful states probably would have seceded, and the South might well have succeeded. The border group actually boasted a white population more than half that of the entire Confederacy. Maryland, Kentucky, and Missouri would almost double the manufacturing capacity of the South and increase by nearly half its supply of horses and mules. The strategic prize of the Ohio River flowed along the northern border of Kentucky and West Virginia. Two of its navigable tributaries, the Cumberland and Tennessee Rivers, penetrated deep into the heart of Dixie, where much of the Confederacy's grain, gunpowder, and iron was produced. Small wonder that Lincoln reportedly said that he hoped to have God on his side, but he *had* to have Kentucky.

In dealing with the Border States, the president did not rely solely on moral suasion but successfully used methods of dubious legality. In Maryland he declared martial law where needed and sent in troops, because this state threatened to cut off Washington from the North. He also deployed Union soldiers in western Virginia and notably in Missouri, where they fought beside Unionists in a local civil war within the larger Civil War.

Any official statement of the North's war aims was profoundly influenced by the teetering Border States. At the very outset, Lincoln was obliged to declare publicly that he was not fighting to free the blacks. An antislavery declaration would no doubt have driven the Border States into the welcoming arms of the South. An antislavery war was also extremely unpopular in the so-called Butternut region of southern Ohio, Indiana, and Illinois. That area had been settled largely by Southerners who had carried their racial prejudices with them when they crossed the Ohio River. It was to be a hotbed of pro-Southern sentiment throughout the war. Sensitive to this delicate political calculus, Lincoln insisted repeatedly—even though weakening his moral cause—that his paramount purpose was to save the Union at all costs. Thus, the war began not as one between slave soil and free soil, but one for the Union—with slaveholders on both sides and many proslavery sympathizers in the North.

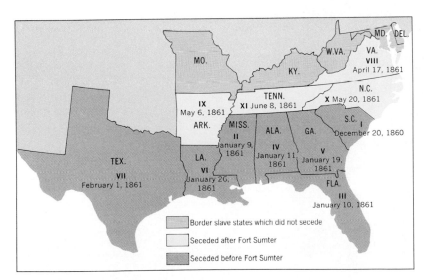

Seceding States (with dates and order of secession) *Note the long period of time between the secession of South Carolina, the first state to go, and that of Tennessee, the last state to leave the Union. These six months were a time of terrible trial for moderate Southerners. When a Georgia statesman pleaded for restraint and negotiations with Washington, he was rebuffed with the cry: "Throw the bloody spear into this den of incendiaries!"*

Unhappily, the conflict between "Billy Yank" and "Johnny Reb" was a brothers' war. There were many Northern volunteers from the Southern states and many Southern volunteers from the Northern states. The "mountain whites" of the South sent north some 50,000 men, and the loyal slave states contributed some 300,000 soldiers to the Union. In many a family of the Border States, one brother rode north to fight with the Blue, another south to fight with the Gray. Senator Crittenden of Kentucky, who fathered the abortive Crittenden Compromise, fathered two sons: one became a general in the Union army, the other a general in the Confederate army. Lincoln's own Kentucky-born wife had four brothers who fought for the Confederacy.

Lincoln wrote to the antislavery editor Horace Greeley in August 1862, even as he was about to announce the Emancipation Proclamation: "If I could save the Union without freeing any slave, I would do it; and if I could save it by freeing all the slaves, I would do it; and if I could do it by freeing some and leaving others alone, I would also do that."

The Balance of Forces

When war broke out, the South seemed to have great advantages. The Confederacy could fight defensively behind interior lines. The North had to invade the vast territory of the Confederacy, conquer it, and drag it bodily back into the Union. In fact, the South did not have to win the war in order to win its independence. If it merely fought the invader to a draw and thereby discouraged him, Confederate independence would be won. Fighting on their own soil for self-determination and preservation of their way of life, Southerners at first enjoyed an advantage in morale as well.

Union Officers The man on the right is George Armstrong Custer. The youngest general in the Union army, this brilliant young officer survived the Civil War only to lose his life and that of every soldier under his command to Sioux warriors at the battle of the Little Big Horn River in 1876—"Custer's Last Stand." (James F. Gibson, Library of Congress.)

Stonewall Jackson *The legendary cavalryman lost his life as a result of accidental injuries he suffered in the Battle of Chancellorsville. (The Bettmann Archive.)*

Militarily, the South had the most talented officers right from the beginning of the war. Most conspicuous among a dozen or so first-rate commanders was gray-haired General Robert E. Lee, whose knightly bearing and sense of honor embodied the Southern ideal. President Lincoln had unofficially offered him the command of the Northern armies, but when Virginia seceded Lee felt honor-bound to go with his native state. Lee's chief lieutenant for much of the war was black-bearded Thomas J. ("Stonewall") Jackson, a gifted tactical theorist and a master of speed and deception.

Besides their brilliant leaders, ordinary Southerners were also bred to fight. Accustomed to managing horses and bearing arms from boyhood, they made excellent cavalrymen and foot soldiers. Their high-pitched "rebel yell" ("yeeeahhh") was designed to strike terror into the hearts of fuzz-chinned Yankee recruits. "There is nothing like it on this side of the infernal region," one Northern soldier declared. "The peculiar corkscrew sensation that it sends down your backbone can never be told. You have to feel it."

As one immense farm, the South seemed to be handicapped by the scarcity of factories. Yet by seizing federal weapons, running Union blockades, and developing their own ironworks, Southerners managed to obtain sufficient weaponry. "Yankee ingenuity" was not confined to Yankees.

Nevertheless, as the war dragged on, grave shortages of shoes, uniforms, and blankets did appear in the South. Even with immense stores of food on Southern farms, civilians and soldiers often went hungry because of supply problems. "Forward, men! They have cheese in their haversacks," cried one Southern officer as he attacked the Yankees. Much of the hunger was caused by a breakdown of the South's rickety transportation system, especially where the railroad tracks were cut or destroyed by the Yankee invaders.

The economy was the greatest Southern weakness; it was the North's greatest strength. The North was not only a huge farm but a sprawling factory as well. Yankees boasted about three-fourths of the nation's wealth, including three-fourths of the thirty thousand miles (forty-eight thousand kilometers) of the railroads.

The North also controlled the sea. With its vastly superior navy, it established a blockade that choked off Southern supplies and eventually shattered Southern morale. Its sea power also enabled the North to exchange huge quantities of grain for munitions and supplies from Europe, thus adding the factories of Europe to its own.

The Union also enjoyed a much larger reserve of manpower. The loyal states had a population of some 22 million; the seceding states had 9 million people, including about 3.5 million slaves. Adding to the North's population strength was the large immigrant population from Europe, which continued to pour into the North even during the war. Over 800,000 newcomers arrived between 1861 and 1865, most of them British, Irish, and German. Large numbers of them were induced to enlist in the

Recruiting Immigrants for the Union Army. *This poster in several languages appeals to immigrants to enlist. Immigrant manpower provided the Union with both industrial and military muscle. (New-York Historical Society.)*

Union armies. Altogether about one-fifth of the Union forces were foreign born, and in some units military commands were given in four different languages.

Whether immigrant or native, ordinary Northern boys were much less prepared than their Southern counterparts for military life. Yet the Northern "clodhoppers" and "shopkeepers" eventually adjusted themselves to soldiering, and became known for their discipline and determination.

The North was much less fortunate in its higher commanders. It was forced to use a costly trial-and-error method to sort out effective leaders from the many incompetent political officers, until it finally uncovered a general, Ulysses Simpson Grant, who would crunch his way to victory.

"The great body of the aristocracy and the commercial classes are anxious to see the United States go to pieces," wrote the American minister to Britain, but "the middle and lower class sympathise with us [because they] see in the convulsion in America an era in the history of the world, out of which must come in the end a general recognition of the right of mankind to the produce of their labor and the pursuit of happiness."

In the long run, as the Northern strengths were brought to bear, they outweighed those of the South. But when the war began, the chances for Southern independence were unusually favorable—certainly better than the prospects for success of the thirteen colonies in 1776. The turn of a few events could easily have produced a different outcome.

The might-have-beens are fascinating. *If* the Border States had seceded, *if* the uncertain states of the upper Mississippi Valley had turned against the Union, *if* a wave of Northern defeatism had demanded an armistice, and *if* England and/or France had broken the blockade, the South probably would have won. All of these possibilities almost became realities, but none of them actually occurred. Successful revolutions, including the American Revolution of 1776, have generally succeeded because of foreign intervention. The South counted on it, did not get it, and lost.

Dethroning King Cotton

Of all the Confederacy's potential assets, none counted more weightily than the prospect of foreign intervention on behalf of the South. Europe's ruling classes were openly sympathetic to the Confederate cause. They had long abhorred the incendiary example of the American democratic experiment, and they cherished a kind of fellow-feeling for the South's semifeudal, aristocratic social order.

In contrast, the masses of workingpeople in England, and to some extent in France, were pulling and praying for the North. Many of

"NOT ANY. WE THANK YOU MR DAVIS."

Europe Spurns the Confederacy *Despite repeated pleas from Confederate diplomats for recognition and aid, both France's Napoleon III and Britain's Queen Victoria remained officially neutral in the American Civil War. (New-York Historical Society.)*

them had read *Uncle Tom's Cabin,* and they sensed that the war—though at the outset officially fought only over the question of union—might extinguish slavery if the North emerged victorious. The common folk of Britain could not yet cast the ballot, but they could cast the brick. Their certain hostility to any official intervention on behalf of the South evidently had a sobering effect on the British government. Thus, the dead hands of Uncle Tom helped Uncle Sam by restraining the British and French ironclads from breaking the Union blockade. Yet the fact remained that British textile mills depended on the American South for 75 percent of their cotton supplies. Humanitarian sympathies aside, Southerners counted on hard economic need to bring Britain to their aid. Why did King Cotton fail them?

He failed in part because he had been so lavishly productive in the immediate prewar years of 1857–1860. Enormous exports of cotton in those years had piled up surpluses in British warehouses. When the shooting started in 1861, English manufacturers had on hand a heavy oversupply of fiber. The real pinch did not come until about a year and a half later, when thousands of hungry operatives were thrown out of work. But by this time Lincoln had announced his slave-emancipation policy, and the "wage slaves" of England were not go-

ing to demand a war to defend the slaveowners of the South.

The direst effects of the "cotton famine" in England were relieved in several ways. Hunger among unemployed workers was partially eased when certain kindhearted Americans sent over several cargoes of foodstuffs. As Union armies penetrated the South, they captured or bought considerable supplies of cotton and shipped them to England; and the Confederates also ran a limited quantity through the blockade. In addition, the cotton growers of Egypt and India, responding to high prices, increased their output. Finally, booming war industries in England, which supplied both North and South, relieved unemployment.

King Wheat and King Corn—of the Northern agricultural royalty—proved to be more potent potentates than King Cotton. During these war years the North, blessed with ideal weather, produced bountiful crops of grain and harvested them with McCormick's mechanical reaper. In the same period the British suffered a series of bad harvests. They were forced to import huge quantities of grain from America, which happened to have the cheapest and most abundant supply. If the British had broken the blockade to get cotton, they would have provoked the North to war and would have cut off this precious granary. Unemployment for some seemed

> *As the Civil war neared the end of its third year, the London* Times *(January 7, 1864) could boast: "We are as busy, as rich, and as fortunate in our trade as if the American war had never broken out, and our trade with the States had never been disturbed. Cotton was no King, notwithstanding the prerogatives which had been loudly claimed for him."*

better than hunger for all. Hence, one Yankee journal could exult:

> Wave the stars and stripes high o'er us,
> Let every freeman sing . . .
> Old King Cotton's dead and buried:
>   brave young Corn is King.

The Decisiveness of Diplomacy

America's diplomatic front has seldom been so critical as during the Civil War. The South never wholly abandoned its dream of foreign intervention, and Europe's rulers schemed to take advantage of America's distress.

The first major crisis with Britain came over the *Trent* affair, late in 1861. A Union warship cruising on the high seas north of Cuba stopped a British mail steamer, the *Trent,* and forcibly removed two Confederate diplomats who were on their way to Europe.

Britons were outraged: upstart Yankees could not do this sort of thing to the Mistress of the Seas. War preparations buzzed, and red-coated troops embarked for Canada, with bands blaring "I Wish I Was in Dixie." The London Foreign Office prepared an ultimatum demanding surrender of the prisoners and an apology. But luckily, slow communications gave passions on both sides a chance to cool. Lincoln came to see the *Trent* prisoners as "white elephants," and reluctantly released them. "One war at a time," he reportedly said.

Another major crisis in Anglo-American relations arose over the unneutral building in England of Confederate commerce-raiders, notably the *Alabama*. These vessels were not warships within the meaning of loopholed British law, because they left their shipyards unarmed and picked up their guns elsewhere. The *Alabama* escaped in 1862 to the Portuguese Azores, and

Tredegar Iron Works, Richmond, Virginia   *This was by far the most important of the Confederate iron works. Using skilled slave labor, this plant equipped the army with nearly twelve hundred scarce cannons. Without these works, the Confederacy probably would have collapsed. Their presence in Richmond helps to explain why the South fought so hard to keep the city. (The Granger Collection.)*

Manufacturing by Sections, 1860

SECTION	NUMBER OF ESTABLISHMENTS	CAPITAL INVESTED	AVERAGE NUMBER OF LABORERS	ANNUAL VALUE OF PRODUCTS	PERCENTAGE OF TOTAL VALUE
New England	20,671	$ 257,477,783	391,836	$ 468,599,287	24%
Middle states	53,387	435,061,964	546,243	802,338,392	42
Western states	36,785	194,212,543	209,909	384,606,530	20
Southern states	20,631	95,975,185	110,721	155,531,281	8
Pacific states	8,777	23,380,334	50,204	71,229,989	3
Territories	282	3,747,906	2,333	3,556,197	1
	140,533	$1,009,855,715	1,311,246	$1,885,861,676	

Immigration to United States, 1860–1866

YEAR	TOTAL	BRITAIN	IRELAND	GERMANY	ALL OTHERS
1860	153,640	29,737	48,637	54,491	20,775
1861	91,918	19,675	23,797	31,661	16,785
1862	91,985	24,639	23,351	27,529	16,466
1863	176,282	66,882	55,916	33,162	20,322
1864	193,418	53,428	63,523	57,276	19,191
1865*	248,120	82,465	29,772	83,424	52,459
1866	318,568	94,924	36,690	115,892	71,062

*Only the first three months of 1865 were war months.

On the Deck of the Alabama *Captain Raphael Semmes leans jauntily against a deck-gun aboard his fearful Confederate raider. The Alabama sank sixty-four Union ships before she was herself sent to the bottom by the U.S.S. Kearsarge off the coast of Cherbourg, France, in June 1864. (U.S. Navy.)*

there took on weapons and a crew from two English ships that followed it. Although flying the Confederate flag and officered by Confederates, it was manned by Britons and never entered a Confederate port. England was thus the chief naval base of the Confederacy.

The *Alabama* lighted the skies from Europe to the Far East with the burning hulks of Yankee merchantmen. All told, this "British pirate"

Charles Francis Adams (1807–1886) *Son of President John Quincy Adams, grandson of President John Adams, and father of author Henry Adams, he was himself widely regarded as of presidential timber, especially in 1872. His chief claim to distinction was his bold and dignified diplomacy in London during the Civil War. (Courtesy of the Fogg Art Museum, Harvard University.)*

captured over sixty vessels. Competing British shippers were delighted, while an angered North had to divert naval strength from its blockade for wild goose chases. The barnacled *Alabama* finally accepted a challenge from a stronger Union cruiser off the coast of France in 1864 and was quickly destroyed.

The *Alabama* was beneath the waves, but the issue of British-built Confederate raiders stayed afloat. Under prodding by the American minister, Charles Francis Adams, the British gradually perceived that allowing such ships to be built was a dangerous precedent that might be used against them. In 1863 London openly violated its own leaky laws and seized another raider being built for the South. But despite greater official efforts by Britain to remain truly neutral, Confederate commerce-destroyers, chiefly British-built, captured more than 250 Yankee ships, severely crippling the American merchant marine, which never fully recovered. Angered Americans talked openly of securing revenge by seizing Canada when the war was over.

Foreign Flare-Ups

A final Anglo-American crisis was touched off in 1863 by the Laird rams—two Confederate warships being constructed in Great Britain. Designed to destroy the wooden ships of the Union navy with their iron rams and large-caliber guns, they were far more dangerous than the swift and lightly armed *Alabama*. If delivered to the South, they probably would have sunk the blockading squadrons and then brought Northern cities under their fire. In angry retaliation, the North doubtless would have invaded Canada, and a full-dress war with Britain would have erupted. But Minister Adams took a hard line, warning that "this is war" if the rams were released. At the last minute the London government relented and bought the two ships for the Royal Navy. Everyone seemed satisfied—except the disappointed Confederates. Britain also eventually repented its sorry role in the *Alabama* business. It agreed in 1871 to submit the *Alabama* dispute to arbitration, and in 1872 paid American claimants $15.5 million for damages caused by wartime commerce raiders.

American anger was also directed at Canada, where despite the vigilance of British authorities, Southern agents plotted to burn Northern cities. One Confederate raid into Vermont left three banks plundered and one American citizen dead. Hatred of England burned especially fiercely among Irish-Americans, and they unleashed their fury on Canada. They raised several tiny "armies" of a few hundred green-shirted men and launched invasions of Canada, notably in 1866 and 1870. The Canadians condemned the Washington government for permitting such violations of neutrality, but the administration was hampered by the presence of so many Irish-American voters.

As fate would have it, two great nations emerged from the fiery furnace of the American Civil War. One was a reunited United States, the other was a united Canada. The British Parliament established the Dominion of Canada in 1867. It was partly designed to bolster the Canadians, both politically and spiritually, against the possible vengeance of the United States.

Emperor Napoleon III of France, taking advantage of America's preoccupation with its own internal problems, dispatched a French army to occupy Mexico City in 1863. The following year he installed on the ruins of the crushed republic his puppet, Austrian Archduke Maximilian, as emperor of Mexico. Both sending the army and enthroning Maximilian were done in flagrant violation of the Monroe Doctrine. Napoleon was gambling that the Union would collapse and thus America would be too weak to enforce its "hands off" policy in the western hemisphere.

The North, as long as it was convulsed by war, pursued a walk-on-eggs policy toward France. But when the shooting stopped in 1865, Secretary of State Seward, speaking with the authority of nearly a million bayonets, prepared to march south. Napoleon realized that his costly gamble was doomed. He reluctantly took "French leave" of his ill-starred puppet in 1867, and Maximilian soon crumpled ingloriously before a Mexican firing squad.

President Davis
versus President Lincoln

The Confederate government, like King Cotton, betrayed fatal weaknesses. Its constitution, borrowing liberally from that of the Union, had one deadly defect. Created by secession, it could not logically deny future secession to its states. Jefferson Davis, while making his bow to states' rights, had in view a well-knit central government. But determined states' rights supporters fought him bitterly to the end. The Richmond regime even encountered difficulty in persuading certain state troops to serve outside their own borders. Governor Brown of Georgia, a belligerent states' righter, at times seemed ready to secede from the secession and fight both sides. States' rights were no less damaging to the Confederacy than Yankee sabers.

Sharp-featured President Davis—tense, humorless, legalistic, stubborn—was repeatedly in hot water. Though an eloquent orator and an

President Davis, the Acrobat, on Rope of Cotton
The "Confederacy" is a fuse bomb; the flag reads, "Let Us Alone," a Davis theme. The cotton rope is unraveling.

able administrator, he at no time enjoyed real personal popularity and was often at loggerheads with his congress. At times there was serious talk of impeachment. Unlike Lincoln, Davis was somewhat imperious and inclined to defy rather than lead public opinion. Suffering acutely from neuralgia and other nervous disorders (including a tic), he overworked himself with the details of both civil government and military operations. No one could doubt his courage, sincerity, integrity, and devotion to the South, but the task proved beyond his powers. It was probably beyond the powers of any mere mortal.

Lincoln also had his troubles, but on the whole they were less prostrating. The North enjoyed the prestige of a long-established government, financially stable and fully recognized both at home and abroad. Lincoln, the inexperienced prairie politician, proved superior to the more experienced but less flexible Jefferson

Davis. Able to relax with droll stories at critical times, "Old Abe" grew as the war dragged on. Tactful, quiet, patient, yet firm, he developed a genius for interpreting and leading a fickle public opinion. Holding aloft the banner of Union with inspiring utterances, he revealed charitableness toward the South and forbearance toward backbiting colleagues. "Did [Secretary] Stanton say I was a damned fool?" he reportedly replied to a talebearer. "Then I dare say I must be one, for Stanton is generally right and he always says what he means."

Limitations on Wartime Liberties

"Honest Abe" Lincoln, when inaugurated, laid his hand on the Bible and swore a solemn oath to uphold the Constitution. Then, driven by sheer necessity, he proceeded to tear a few holes in that hallowed document. He sagely

A Satanic Lincoln Signs the Emancipation Proclamation In this vicious cartoon by Confederate caricaturist Adalbert Volck, a diabolical Lincoln, urged on by the devil, signs the Emancipation Proclamation. Underfoot he tramples the Constitution—a significant point, since the South had long invoked the Constitution in defense of slavery, and the Proclamation's technical legality was debatable. It later took a Constitutional amendment to put a definitive end to the "peculiar instution." (Boston Museum of Fine Arts.)

concluded that if he did not do so, and patch the parchment later, there might not be a Constitution of a *united* United States to mend. The "rail-splitter" was no hairsplitter.

But such infractions were not, in general, sweeping. Congress, as is often true in time of crisis, generally accepted or confirmed the president's questionable acts. Lincoln, though accused of being a "Simple Susan Tyrant," did not believe that his ironhanded authority would continue, once the Union was preserved. As he pointedly remarked in 1863, a man suffering from "temporary illness" would not persist in feeding on bitter medicines for "the remainder of his healthful life."

Congress was not in session when war erupted, so Lincoln gathered the reins into his own hands. Brushing aside legal objections, he boldly proclaimed a blockade. (His action was later upheld by the Supreme Court.) He arbitrarily increased the size of the federal army—something that only Congress can do under the Constitution (see Art. I, Sec. VIII, para. 12). (Congress later approved.) He directed the secretary of the treasury to advance $2 million without appropriation or security to three private citizens for military purposes—a grave irregularity contrary to the Constitution (see Art. I, Sec. IX, par. 7). He suspended the precious privilege of the writ of habeas corpus, so that anti-Unionists might be summarily arrested. In taking this step, he defied a dubious ruling by the chief justice that the safeguards of habeas corpus could be set aside only by authorization of Congress (see Art. I, Sec. IX, para. 2).

Lincoln's regime was guilty of many other high-handed acts. For example, it arranged for "supervised" voting in the Border States. There the intimidated citizen, holding a colored ballot indicating his party preference, had to march between two lines of armed troops. The federal officials also ordered the suspension of certain newspapers and the arrest of their editors on grounds of obstructing the war.

Jefferson Davis was less able than Lincoln to exercise arbitrary power, mainly because of confirmed states' righters who revealed an intense spirit of localism. To the very end of the conflict the owners of horse-drawn vans in Petersburg, Virginia, prevented the joining of the incoming and outgoing tracks of a militarily vital railroad. The South seemed willing to lose the war before it would surrender local rights—and it did.

Volunteers and Draftees: North and South

Ravenous, the gods of war demanded men—lots of men. Northern armies were at first manned solely by volunteers, with each state assigned a quota based on population. But in 1863, after volunteering had slackened off, Congress passed a federal conscription law for the first time on a nationwide scale in the United States. The provisions were grossly unfair to the poor. Rich boys, including young John D. Rockefeller, could hire substitutes to go in their places or purchase exemption outright by paying $300. "Three-hundred-dollar men" was the scornful epithet applied to these slackers. Draftees who did not have the necessary cash complained that their banditlike government demanded "three hundred dollars or your life."

The draft was especially damned in the Democratic strongholds of the North, notably in New York City. A frightful riot broke out in 1863, touched off largely by underprivileged and antiblack Irish-Americans who shouted, "Down with Lincoln!" and "Down with the draft!" For several days the city was at the mercy of a burning, drunken, pillaging mob, and scores of lives were lost, including many lynched blacks. Elsewhere in the North conscription met with resentment and an occasional minor riot.

More than 90 percent of the Union troops were volunteers, since social and patriotic pressures to enlist were strong. As able-bodied men became scarcer, generous bounties for enlistment were offered by federal, state, and local authorities. An enterprising and moneywise volunteer might legitimately pocket more than $1000.

With money flowing so freely, an unsavory crew of "bounty brokers" and "substitute brokers" sprang up, at home and abroad. They combed the poorhouses of the British Isles and Western Europe; and many an Irishman or Ger-

The New York Draft Riot, 1863   *Irish workers resented competition for jobs by "nagurs." The free blacks in turn called the Irish "white niggers." (Museum of the City of New York.)*

man was befuddled with whiskey and induced to enlist. A number of the slippery "bounty boys" deserted, volunteered elsewhere, and netted another handsome haul. The records reveal that one "bounty jumper" repeated his profitable operation thirty-two times. But desertion was by no means confined to "bounty jumpers." The rolls of the Union army recorded about 200,000 deserters of all classes, and the Confederate authorities were plagued with a problem of similar dimensions.

Like the North, the South relied mainly on volunteers. But since the Confederacy was much less populous, it scraped the bottom of its manpower barrel much more quickly. Quipsters observed that any man who could see lightning and hear thunder was judged fit for service. The Richmond regime, robbing both "cradle and grave" (ages 17 to 50), was forced to resort to conscription as early as April 1862, nearly a year earlier than the Union.

Number of Men in Uniform at Date Given

DATE	UNION	CONFEDERATE
July 1861	186,751	112,040
January 1862	575,917	351,418
March 1862	637,126	401,395
January 1863	918,121	446,622
January 1864	860,737	481,180
January 1865	959,460	445,203

Confederate draft regulations also worked serious injustices. As in the North, a rich man could hire a substitute or purchase exemption. Slaveowners or overseers with twenty slaves might also claim exemption. These special privileges, later modified, made for bad feeling among the less prosperous, many of whom complained that this was a "a rich man's war but a poor man's fight." Why sacrifice one's life to save slavery? No large-scale draft riots broke out in the South, as in New York City. But the Confederate conscription agents often found it prudent to avoid those areas inhabited by sharp-shooting mountain whites, who were branded "Tories," "traitors," and "Yankee-lovers."

The Dollar Goes to War

Blessed with a lion's share of the wealth, the North rode through the financial breakers much more smoothly than the South. Excise taxes on tobacco and alcohol were substantially increased by Congress. An income tax was levied for the first time in the nation's experience; and although the rates were painlessly low by later standards, they netted millions of dollars.

Customs receipts likewise proved to be important revenue-raisers. Early in 1861, after enough antiprotection Southern members had seceded, Congress passed the Morrill Tariff Act, superseding the low Tariff of 1857. It increased the existing duties some 5 to 10 percent, boosting them to about the moderate level of the Walker Tariff of 1846. But these modest rates were soon pushed sharply upward by the necessities of war. The increases were designed partly to raise additional revenue and partly to provide more protection for the prosperous manufacturers who were being plucked by the new internal taxes. A protective tariff thus became identified with the Republican party, as American industrialists, predominantly Republicans, waxed fat on these welcome benefits.

The Washington Treasury also issued greenbacked paper money, totaling nearly $450 million at face value. This printing-press currency was inadequately supported by gold, and hence its value was determined by the nation's credit. Greenbacks thus fluctuated with the fortunes of Union arms and at one low point were worth only 39 cents on the gold dollar. The holders of the notes, victims of creeping inflation, were indirectly taxed as the value of the currency slowly withered in their hands.

Yet borrowing far outstripped both greenbacks and taxes as a money-raiser. The Federal Treasury netted $2,621,916,786 through the sale of bonds, which bore interest and which were payable at a later date. The modern technique of selling these issues to the people directly through "drives" and payroll deductions had not yet been devised. Accordingly, the Treasury was forced to market its bonds through the private banking house of Jay Cooke and Company, which received a commission of three-eighths of 1 percent on all sales. With both profits and patriotism at stake, the bankers succeeded in making effective appeals to citizen purchasers.

A financial landmark of the war was the National Banking System, authorized by Congress in 1863. Launched partly as a stimulant to the sale of government bonds, it was also designed to establish a standard bank-note currency. (The country was then flooded with depreciated "rag money" issued by unreliable bankers.) Banks that joined the National Banking System could buy government bonds and issue sound paper money backed by them. The war-born National Banking Act thus turned out to be the first significant step taken toward a unified banking network since 1836, when the "monster" Bank of the United States was killed by Andrew Jackson. Spawned by the war, this new system continued to function for fifty years.

Taxation by Inflation

An impoverished South was beset by different financial problems. Customs duties were choked off as the coils of the Union blockade tightened. Large issues of Confederate bonds were sold at home and abroad, amounting to nearly $400 million. The Richmond regime also increased taxes sharply and imposed a 10 percent levy on farm produce. But in general the states' rights Southerners were vigorously opposed to heavy direct taxation by the central authority: only about 1 percent of the total income was raised in this way.

As revenue began to dry up, the Confederate government was forced to print blue-backed paper money with complete abandon. "Runaway inflation" occurred as Southern presses continued to grind out the poorly backed treasury notes, totaling in all more than $1 billion. One breakfast for three in Richmond in 1864 cost $141. The Confederate paper dollar finally sank to the point where it was worth only 1.6 cents when Lee surrendered. Overall, the war inflicted a 9,000 percent inflation rate on the Confederacy, contrasted with 80 percent for the Union.

A contemporary (October 22, 1863) Richmond diary portrays the ruinous effects of inflation: "A poor woman yesterday applied to a merchant in Carey Street to purchase a barrel of flour. The price he demanded was $70. 'My God!' exclaimed she, 'how can I pay such prices? I have seven children; what shall I do?' 'I don't know, madam,' said he coolly, 'unless you eat your children.'"

"Shoddy" Millionaires in the North

Wartime prosperity in the North was little short of miraculous. The marvel is that a divided nation could fight a costly conflict for four long years and then emerge seemingly more prosperous than ever before.

New factories, sheltered by the friendly umbrella of the new protective tariffs, mushroomed forth. Soaring prices, resulting from inflation, unfortunately pinched the day laborer and the white-collar worker to some extent. But the manufacturers and businesspeople raked in "the fortunes of war."

The Civil War spawned a millionaire class for the first time in American history, though a few individuals of extreme wealth could have been found earlier. Many of these newly rich were noisy, gaudy, brassy, and given to extravagant living. Their emergence merely illustrates the truth that some gluttony and greed always mar the devotion and self-sacrifice called forth by war. The story of speculators and peculators was roughly the same in both camps. But graft was more flagrant in the North than in the South, partly because there was more to steal.

Yankee "sharpness" appeared at its worst. Dishonest agents, putting profits above patriotism, palmed off aged and blind horses on government purchasers. Unscrupulous Northern manufacturers supplied shoes with cardboard soles and fast-disintegrating uniforms of reprocessed or "shoddy" wool, rather than virgin wool. Hence, the reproachful term "shoddy millionaires." One profiteer reluctantly admitted that his profits were "painfully large."

Newly invented laborsaving machinery enabled the North to expand economically, even though the cream of its manpower was being drained off to the fighting front. The sewing machine wrought wonders in fabricating uniforms and military footwear.

The marriage of military need and new machinery largely ended the production of custom-tailored clothing. Graduated standard measurements were introduced, creating "sizes" that were widely used in the civilian garment industry forever after.

Clattering mechanical reapers, which num-

"Nightmare of a War Profiteer" *A dead soldier forces on him the same poisonous food and drink with which he supplied the army. (Vanity Fair, 1861.)*

bered about 250,000 by 1865, proved hardly less potent than thundering guns. They not only released tens of thousands of farm boys for the army but fed them while there. They produced vast surpluses of grain that, when sent abroad, helped dethrone King Cotton. They provided profits with which the North was able to buy munitions and supplies from abroad. They contributed to the feverish prosperity of the North—a prosperity that enabled the Union to weather the war with flying colors.

Other industries were humming. The discovery of petroleum gushers in 1859 had led to a rush of "Fifty-Niners" to Pennsylvania. The result was the birth of a new industry, with its "petroleum plutocracy" and "coal oil Johnnies." Pioneers continued to push westward during the war, altogether an estimated 300,000 souls. Major magnets were free gold nuggets and free land under the Homestead Act of 1862. Strong propellants were the federal draft agents. The only major Northern industry to suffer a crippling setback was the ocean-carrying trade, which fell prey to the *Alabama* and other raiders.

The war also opened new opportunities for women. The booming military demand for shoes and clothing, combined with the availability of new technology like the sewing machine and the unavailability of male workers who had gone to war, drew countless women into industrial employment. Female workers increased their proportion of the manufacturing labor force from one-fourth to one-third during the conflict.

Other women went to the fighting front—or close behind it. America's first female physician, Dr. Elizabeth Blackwell, helped to organize the United States Sanitary Commission to provide medical supplies and assistance to the armies in the field. Here many women acquired the organizational skills and the self-confidence that would propel the women's movement forward after the war. Still others, such as the heroically energetic Clara Barton, helped to transform nursing from a lowly service into a respected profession—and in the process opened up another major category of employment for women in the postwar era.

A Crushed Cotton Kingdom

Dismally different was the plight of the South, which fought to exhaustion. The suffocation caused by the blockade, together with the destruction by invaders, took a terrible toll. Possessing 30 percent of the national wealth in 1860, the South claimed only 12 percent in 1870. Before the war the average per capita income of southerners (including slaves) was about two-thirds that of northerners. The war pushed average southern income to two-fifths of the northern level, where it remained for the rest of the century. The South's bid for independence exacted a cruel and devastating cost.

Transportation collapsed. The South was even driven to the economic cannibalism of pulling up rails from the less-used lines to repair the main ones. Window weights were melted down into bullets; gourds replaced dishes; pins became so scarce that they were loaned with reluctance.

To the brutal end, the South revealed remarkable resourcefulness and spirit. Women

Women of the U.S. Sanitary Commission at a Civil-War Nursing Station. *(The Bettmann Archive.)* **Dr. Elizabeth Blackwell** *Born in England, she migrated to America and was the first woman to receive a medical degree in the United States. In later life she returned to England to found the London School of Medicine for Women, where she served as professor of gynecology. (Schlesinger Library, Radcliffe College.)*

buoyed up their menfolk, many of whom had seen enough of war at first hand to be heartily sick of it. A proposal was made by a number of women that they cut off their long hair and sell it abroad. But the project was not adopted, partly because of the blockade. The self-sacrificing women took pride in denying themselves the silks and satins of their Northern sisters. The chorus of a song, "The Southern Girl," touched a cheerful note:

So hurrah! hurrah! For Southern Rights, hurrah!
Hurrah! for the homespun dress the Southern ladies wear.

At war's end, the Northern Captains of Industry had conquered the Southern Lords of the Manor. A crippled South left the capitalistic North free to work its own way, with high tariffs and other benefits. The industrial giants of the North, ushering in the full-fledged industrial revolution, were destined for increased dominance over American economic and political life. Hitherto the agrarian "slavocracy" of the South, by using sectional alliances, had partially checked the rising plutocracy of the North. Now cotton capitalism had lost out to industrial capitalism. The South of 1865 was to be rich in little but amputees, war heroes, ruins, and memories.

CHRONOLOGY

1861	Lincoln takes office
	Fort Sumter fired upon
	Four Upper South states secede
	Morrill Tariff Act passed
	Trent affair
	Lincoln suspends writ of habeas corpus
1862–1864	*Alabama* raids Northern shipping
1863	Union enacts conscription
	New York City draft riot
	National Banking System established
1863–1864	Napoleon III installs Archduke Maximilian as emperor of Mexico
1864	*Alabama* sunk by Union warship

Varying Viewpoints

When the Civil War ended, slavery was officially defunct, secession was a dead issue, and industrial growth was surging forward. Charles Beard later hailed the war as the "Second American Revolution," because it had transformed the legal and institutional structure of government and placed the levers of power firmly in the hands of a new business class.

But did the bloody conflict neatly bisect the nation's history? In recent years many scholars have questioned the concept that the war constituted a dramatic turning point. Slavery may have formally disappeared, but blacks remained a scandalously subordinated social group. Regional differences persisted, even down to the present day. Thomas Cochran has even argued that the Civil War may have *retarded* overall industrialization. As for the rising commercial class of the postwar "Gilded Age," many historians now point to its antecedents in both the Whig and Jacksonian movements. History, it seems, is a mighty stream, which in time partially submerges even momentous events like the Civil War beneath the surface of its relentless flow.

Select Readings

Primary Source Documents

The Constitution of the Confederacy* (1861) makes an interesting contrast to the United States Constitution. Two diaries that describe life behind the Confederate lines are those of John B. Jones, published as Earl S. Miers, ed., *A Rebel War Clerk's Diary** (1958), and Paul B. Barringer, *The Natural Bent** (1949). Lincoln's Gettysburg Address (1863) (in Henry Steele Commager, *Documents of American History*) poetically proclaims the president's highest war aims, as does his Second Inaugural Address (1865), in Roy P. Basler, ed., *The Collected Works of Abraham Lincoln* (1953), Vol. VIII, pp. 332–333.

Secondary Sources

The best one-volume biography is Stephen B. Oates, *With Malice Toward None: The Life of Abraham Lincoln* (1977). An excellent collection is Don E. Fehrenbacher, *Lincoln in Text and Context: Collected Essays* (1987). Home-front politics are treated in James A. Rawley, *The Politics of Union* (1974), and in Joel Silbey, *A Respectable Minority: The Democratic Party in the Civil War Era* (1977). See also Jean H. Baker, *Affairs of Party: The Political Culture of the Northern Democrats in the Mid–Nineteenth Century* (1983). Lincoln's problems are analyzed in LaWanda Cox, *Lincoln and Black Freedom* (1981); William B. Hesseltine, *Lincoln and the War Governors* (1948); and T. Harry Williams, *Lincoln and the Radicals* (1941). For a different view of the same subject, see Hans L. Trefousse, *The Radical Republicans: Lincoln's Vanguard for Racial Justice* (1969).

Richard N. Current, *The Lincoln Nobody Knows* (1958), and David Donald, *Lincoln Reconsidered* (1956), offer interesting insights. Eugene C. Murdoch analyzes the military draft in the North in *One Million Men* (1971), while Adrian Cook treats an important by-product of the draft, the New York City riots, in *Armies of the Street* (1974). Gerald F. Linderman examines the motivations of soldiers in *Embattled Courage: The Experience of Combat in the Civil War* (1987). Mary E. Massey presents the interesting story of women in the Civil War in *Bonnet Brigades* (1966); that topic also figures in Anne Firor Scott's *The Southern Lady* (1970). On the Confederacy, see Charles P. Roland, *The Confederacy* (1960), and Emory M. Thomas, *The Confederate Nation, 1861–1865* (1979). Economic matters are handled in Ralph L. Andreano, ed., *The Economic Impact of the American Civil War* (1962), and David T. Gilchrist and W. David Lewis, eds., *Economic Change in the Civil War Era* (1965). Two useful anthologies are David Donald, ed., *Why the North Won the Civil War* (1960), and Robert P. Swierenga, ed., *Beyond the Civil War Synthesis: Political Essays on the Civil War Era* (1975). Richard E. Beringer et al. present a different viewpoint in *Why the South Lost the Civil War* (1986). The war's literary legacy is keenly analyzed in Edmund Wilson's classic *Patriotic Gore* (1962) and in Daniel Aaron's *The Unwritten War: American Writers and the Civil War* (1973). For a fascinating discussion of Northern intellectuals and the conflict, consult George M. Frederickson, *The Inner Civil War* (1965).

22

The Furnace of Civil War, 1861–1865

My paramount object in this struggle is to save the Union, and is not either to save or to destroy slavery.

Abraham Lincoln, 1862

Bull Run Ends the "Ninety-Day War"

When President Lincoln, on April 15, 1861, issued his call to the states for seventy-five thousand militiamen, he envisioned them serving for only ninety days. He reaffirmed that he had "no purpose, directly or indirectly, to interfere with slavery in the States where it exists." He hoped, with a swift flourish of federal force, to show the folly of secession and rapidly return the rebellious states to the Union. Northern newspapers, also eager for a quick resolution of the crisis, raised the cry "On to Richmond!"

In this expectant atmosphere, a Union army of some thirty thousand men drilled near Washington in the summer of 1861. It was ill prepared for battle, but the press and the public clamored for action. Lincoln eventually concluded that an attack on a smaller Confederate

force at Bull Run (Manassas Junction), some thirty miles (forty-eight kilometers) southwest of Washington, might be worth a try. If successful, it would demonstrate the superiority of Union arms. It might even lead to the capture of the Confederate capital at Richmond, one hundred miles to the south. If Richmond fell, secession would be thoroughly discredited and the Union could be restored without damage to the economic and social system of the South.

Raw Yankee recruits marched or straggled out of Washington toward Bull Run on July 21, 1861, as if they were headed for a sporting event. Congressmen, ladies, and all manner of spectators trailed along with their lunch baskets to witness the fun. At first the battle went well for the Yankees. But "Stonewall" Jackson's gray-clad warriors stood like a stone wall (here he won his nickname), and Confederate rein-

Union Troops Parading Before the Battle of Bull Run, 1861 *The colorful uniforms are worn by a regiment of Zouaves, who adopted the name and style of military dress from a legendarily dashing French infantry unit. But bright uniforms were not enough to win battles, and these troops were soon to be routed by the Confederates at the Battle of Bull Run. (Collection of Alexander McCook Craighead.)*

forcements arrived unexpectedly. Panic seized the green Union troops, many of whom fled in shameful confusion. The Confederates, themselves too exhausted or disorganized to pursue, feasted on captured lunches.

The "military picnic" at Bull Run, though not decisive militarily, had significant psychological and political consequences. Victory was worse than defeat for the South, because it inflated an already dangerous overconfidence. Many of the Southern soldiers promptly deserted, some boastfully to display their trophies, others feel-

The Union Routed at Bull Run, July 1861 *The chaos and humiliation of the Union retreat are vividly evident in this contemporary drawing. (Library of Congress.)*

An observer behind the Union lines described the Federal troops' pell-mell retreat from the battlefield at Bull Run: "We called to them, tried to tell them there was no danger, called them to stop, implored them to stand. We called them cowards, denounced them in the most offensive terms, put out our heavy revolvers, and threatened to shoot them, but all in vain; a cruel, crazy, mad, hopeless panic possessed them, and communicated to everybody about in front and rear. The heat was awful, although now about six; the men were exhausted—their mouths gaped, their lips cracked and blackened with the powder of the cartridges they had bitten off in battle, their eyes staring in frenzy; no mortal ever saw such a mass of ghastly wretches."

caused the Northerners to buckle down to the staggering task at hand. It also set the stage for a war that would be waged not merely for the cause of Union but also, eventually, for the abolitionist ideal of emancipation.

"Tardy George" McClellan and the Peninsula Campaign

Northern hopes brightened later in 1861, when General George B. McClellan was given command of the Army of the Potomac, as the major Union force near Washington was now called. Red-haired and red-mustached, strong and stocky, McClellan was a brilliant, thirty-four-year-old West Pointer. As a serious student of warfare who was dubbed "Young Napoleon," he had seen plenty of fighting, first in the Mexican War and then as an observer of the Crimean War in Russia.

Cocky George McClellan embodied a curious mixture of virtues and defects. He was a superb organizer and drillmaster, and he injected splendid morale into the Army of the Potomac.

ing that the war was now surely over. Southern enlistments fell off sharply, and preparations for a protracted conflict slackened. Defeat was better than victory for the Union, because it dispelled all illusions of a one-punch war and

Battle of the Merrimack and the Monitor, March 9, 1862. *(Library of Congress.)*

Hating to sacrifice his troops, he was idolized by his men, who affectionately called him "Little Mac." But he was a perfectionist who seems not to have realized that an army is never ready to the last button and that wars cannot be won without running some risks. He consistently but erroneously believed that the enemy outnumbered him, partly because his intelligence reports from the head of Pinkerton's Detective Agency were unreliable. He was overcautious—Lincoln once accused him of having "the slows"—and he addressed the president in an arrogant tone that a less forgiving person would never have tolerated. Privately the general referred to his chief as a "baboon."

As McClellan discreetly continued to drill his army without moving it toward Richmond, the derisive Northern watchword became "All Quiet along the Potomac." The song of the hour was "Tardy George" (McClellan). After threatening to "borrow" the army if it was not going to be used, Lincoln finally issued firm orders to move.

A reluctant McClellan at last decided upon a water-borne approach to Richmond, which lies at the western base of a narrow peninsula formed by the James and York Rivers—hence the name given to this historic encounter: the

Lincoln treated McClellan's demands for reinforcements and his excuses for inaction with infinite patience. One exception came when the general complained that his horses were tired. Lincoln wrote: "I have just read your dispatch about sore-tongued and fatigued horses. Will you pardon me for asking what the horses of your army have done since the battle of Antietam that fatigues anything?" (October 24, 1862.)

Peninsula Campaign. McClellan warily advanced toward the Confederate capital in the spring of 1862 with about one hundred thousand men. After taking a month to capture historic Yorktown, which bristled with imitation wooden cannons, he finally came within sight of the spires of Richmond. At this crucial juncture Lincoln diverted McClellan's anticipated reinforcements to chase "Stonewall" Jackson, whose lightning feints in the Shenandoah Valley seemed to put Washington, D.C., in jeopardy. Stalled in front of Richmond, McClellan was further frustrated when "Jeb" Stuart's Con-

"Masterly Inactivity, or Six Months on the Potomac"
McClellan and his Confederate foe view each other cautiously, while their troops engage in visiting, marrying, and sports. (Frank Leslie's Illustrated Newspaper, 1862.)

Army Camp Life This photograph of the federal camp at Cumberland Landing on Virginia's Pamunkey River during the Peninsula Campaign of 1862 illustrates the abundance of material resources available to the Union forces. Confederate camps were typically much less lavishly outfitted. But even this logistical bounty could not produce a Yankee victory on the Peninsula in 1862. (Library of Congress.)

federate cavalry rode completely around his army on reconnaissance. Then General Robert E. Lee launched a devastating counterattack—the Seven Days' Battles—June 26–July 2, 1862. The Confederates slowly drove McClellan back to the sea. The Union forces abandoned the Peninsula Campaign as a costly failure, and Lincoln temporarily abandoned McClellan as commander of the Army of the Potomac—though Lee's army had suffered some twenty thousand casualties to McClellan's ten thousand.

Lee had achieved a brilliant, if bloody, triumph. Yet the ironies of his accomplishment are striking. If McClellan had succeeded in taking Richmond and ending the war in mid-1862, the Union would probably have been restored with minimal disruption to the "peculiar institution." Slavery would have survived, at least for a time. By his successful defense of Richmond and defeat of McClellan, Lee had in effect ensured that the war would endure until slavery was uprooted and the Old South thoroughly destroyed. Lincoln himself, who had earlier professed his unwillingness to tamper with slavery where it already existed, now declared that the rebels "cannot experiment for ten years trying

to destroy the government and if they fail still come back into the Union unhurt." He began to draft an emancipation proclamation.

Union strategy now turned toward total war. As finally developed, the Northern military plan had six components: first, slowly suffocate the South by blockading its coasts; second, liberate the slaves and hence undermine the very economic foundations of the Old South; third, cut the Confederacy in half by seizing control of the Mississippi River backbone; fourth, chop it to pieces by sending troops through Georgia and the Carolinas; fifth, decapitate it by capturing

A Confederate soldier assigned to burial detail after the Seven Days' Battles wrote: "The sights and smells that assailed us were simply indescribable . . . corpses swollen to twice their original size, some of them actually burst asunder with the pressure of foul gasses. . . . The odors were so nauseating and so deadly that in a short time we all sickened and were lying with our mouths close to the ground, most of us vomiting profusely."

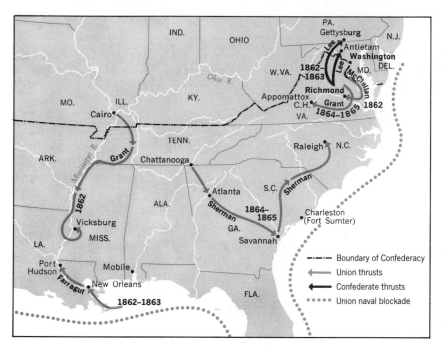

Main Thrusts, 1861–1865
Northern strategists at first believed that the rebellion could be snuffed out quickly by a swift, crushing blow. But the stiffness of Southern resistance to the Union's early probes revealed that the conflict would be a war of attrition, long and bloody.

its capital at Richmond; and sixth (this was Ulysses Grant's idea, especially), try everywhere to engage the enemy's main strength and grind it into submission.

The War at Sea

The blockade started leakily: it was not clamped down all at once but was extended by degrees. An airtight patrol of some 3,500 miles (5,635 kilometers) of coast was impossible for the hastily improvised Northern navy, which consisted partly of converted yachts and ferry boats. But blockading was simplified by concentrating on the principal ports and inlets. Only at such places were dock facilities available for loading bulky bales of cotton.

How was the blockade regarded by the naval powers of the world? Ordinarily, they probably would have defied it, for it was never completely effective and was especially sievelike at the outset. But England, the greatest maritime nation, recognized it as binding and warned its shippers that they ignored it at their peril. An explanation is easy. Blockade happened to be the chief offensive weapon of Britain, which was still Mistress of the Seas. Britain plainly did not

want to tie its hands in a future war by insisting that Lincoln maintain impossibly high blockading standards.

Blockade-running soon became riskily profitable, as the growing scarcity of Southern goods drove prices skyward. The most successful runners were swift, gray-painted steamers, scores of which were specially built in Scotland. A leading rendezvous was the West Indian port of Nassau, in the British Bahamas, where at one time thirty-five of the speedy ships were counted. The low-lying craft would take on cargoes of arms brought in by tramp steamers from England, leave with fraudulent papers for "Halifax" (Canada), and return a few days later with a cargo of cotton. The risks were great, but the profits would mount to 700 percent and more for lucky gamblers. Two successful voyages might well pay for capture on a third. The lush days of blockade-running finally passed as Union squadrons gradually pinched off the leading Southern ports, from New Orleans to Charleston.

The Northern navy enforced the blockade with high-handed practices. Yankee captains, for example, would seize British freighters on the high seas, if laden with war supplies for the tiny port of Nassau and other halfway stations.

When news reached Washington that the Merrimack *had sunk two wooden Yankee warships with ridiculous ease, President Lincoln, much "excited," summoned his advisers. Secretary of the Navy Welles records: "The most frightened man on that gloomy day. . .was the Secretary of War [Stanton]. He was at times almost frantic. . . . The* Merrimack, *he said, would destroy every vessel in the service, could lay every city on the coast under contribution, could take Fortress Monroe. . . . Likely the first movement of the* Merrimack *would be to come up the Potomac and disperse Congress, destroy the Capital and public buildings."*

The justification was that obviously these shipments were "ultimately" destined, by devious routes, for the Confederacy.

London, although not happy, acquiesced in this disagreeable doctrine of "ultimate destination" or "continuous voyage." British blockaders might find such a farfetched interpretation highly useful in a future war—as in fact they did in the World War of 1914–1918.

The most alarming Confederate threat to the blockade came in 1862. Resourceful Southerners raised and reconditioned a former wooden U.S. warship, the *Merrimack,* and plated its sides with old iron railroad rails. Renamed the *Virginia,* this clumsy but powerful monster easily destroyed two wooden ships of the Union navy in the Virginia waters of Chesapeake Bay; it also threatened catastrophe to the entire Yankee blockading fleet. (Actually the homemade ironclad was not a seaworthy craft.)

A tiny Union ironclad, the *Monitor,* built in about 100 days, arrived on the scene in the nick of time. For four hours, on March 9, 1862, the little "Yankee cheesebox on a raft" fought the wheezy *Merrimack* to a standstill. Britain and France had already built several powerful ironclads, but the first battle-testing of these new craft heralded the doom of wooden warships. A few months after the historic battle, the Confederates destroyed the *Merrimack* to keep it from the grasp of advancing Union troops.

The Pivotal Point: Antietam

Robert E. Lee, having broken the back of McClellan's assault on Richmond, next moved northward. At the Second Battle of Bull Run (August 29–30, 1862), he encountered a Federal force under General John Pope. A handsome, dashing, soldierly figure, Pope boasted that in the western theater of war, from which he had recently come, he had seen only the backs of the ·enemy. Lee quickly gave him a front view, furiously attacking Pope's troops and inflicting a crushing defeat.

Emboldened by this success, Lee daringly thrust into Maryland. He hoped to strike a blow that would not only encourage foreign intervention but also seduce the still wavering Border State and its sisters from the Union. The Confederate troops sang lustily:

> Thou wilt not cower in the dust,
>   Maryland! my Maryland!
> Thy gleaming sword shall never rust,
>   Maryland! my Maryland!

But the Marylanders did not respond to the siren song. The presence among the invaders of so many blanketless, hatless, and shoeless soldiers dampened the state's ardor.

Events finally converged toward a critical battle at Antietam Creek, Maryland. Lincoln, responding to popular pressure, hastily restored "Little Mac" to active command of the main Northern army. His soldiers tossed their caps skyward and hugged his horse as they hailed his return. Fortune shone upon McClellan when two Union soldiers found a copy of Lee's battle plans wrapped around a packet of three cigars dropped by a careless Confederate officer. With this crucial piece of intelligence in hand, McClellan succeeded in halting Lee at Antietam on September 17, 1862, in one of the bitterest and bloodiest days of the war.

Antietam was more or less a draw militarily. But Lee, finding his thrust parried, retired across the Potomac. McClellan, from whom much more had been hoped, was removed from his field command for the second and final

Confederate Corpses at Antietam *Unknown to Lee, who had dangerously divided his army, McClellan had obtained a copy of the Confederate battle plan. The Union forces thus had a great tactical advantage, and the result was appalling slaughter. The twelve-hour fight at Antietam Creek ranks as the bloodiest day of the war, with more than ten thousand Confederate casualties and even more on the Union side. "At last the sun went down and the battle ended," one historian wrote, "smoke heavy in the air, the twilight quivering with the anguished cries of thousands of wounded men." (Library of Congress.)*

time. His numerous critics, condemning him for not having boldly pursued the ever-dangerous Lee, finally got his scalp.

The landmark Battle of Antietam was one of the decisive engagements of world history—probably the most decisive of the Civil War. Jefferson Davis was perhaps never again so near victory as on that fateful summer day. The British and French governments were on the verge of diplomatic mediation, a species of interference sure to be angrily resented by the North. An almost certain rebuff by Washington might well have spurred Paris and London into armed intervention. But both capitals cooled off when the Union displayed unexpected power at Antietam, and their chill deepened with the passing months.

Bloody Antietam was also the long-awaited "victory" that Lincoln needed for launching his Emancipation Proclamation. The abolitionists had long been clamoring for action: Wendell Phillips was denouncing the president as a "first-rate second-rate man." By midsummer of 1862, with the Border States safely in the fold,

Lincoln was ready to move. But he believed that to issue such an edict on the heels of a series of military disasters would be folly. It would seem like a confession that the North, unable to conquer the South, was forced to call upon the slaves to murder their masters. Lincoln therefore decided to wait for the outcome of Lee's invasion.

Antietam served as the needed emancipation springboard. The halting of Lee's offensive was just enough of a victory to justify Lincoln's issuing, on September 23, 1862, the preliminary Emancipation Proclamation. This hope-giving document announced that on January 1, 1863, the president would issue a final proclamation.

On the scheduled date he fully redeemed his promise, and the Civil War became more of a moral crusade. It also became more of what Lincoln called a "remorseless revolutionary struggle." After January 1, 1863, Lincoln said, "The character of the war will be changed. It will be one of subjugation. . . The [old] South is to be destroyed and replaced by new propositions and ideas."

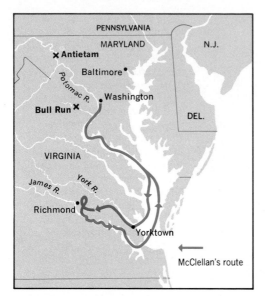

Peninsula Campaign, 1862

> Many of the British aristocrats were unfriendly to the North, and the London Spectator sneered at Lincoln's so-called Emancipation Proclamation: "The Government liberates the enemy's slaves as it would the enemy's cattle, simply to weaken them in the coming conflict. . . . The principle asserted is not that a human being cannot justly own another, but that he cannot own him unless he is loyal to the United States."

A Proclamation without Emancipation

Lincoln's Emancipation Proclamation of 1863 declared "forever free" the slaves in those Confederate states still in rebellion. The blacks in the loyal Border States were not affected, nor were those in specific conquered areas in the South—all told, about 800,000. The tone of the document was dull and legalistic: there was no clarion call for a holy war to achieve freedom. Lincoln in fact is on record as late as February of 1865 as favoring cash compensation to the owners of all slaves.

The presidential pen did not formally strike the shackles from a single slave. Where Lincoln could presumably free the slaves—that is, in the loyal Border States—he refused to do so, lest he spur disunion. Where he could not—that is, in the Confederate states—he tried to. In short, where he *could* he would not, and where he *would* he could not. Thus, the Emancipation Proclamation was stronger on proclamation than emancipation.

Yet much unofficial do-it-yourself liberation did take place. Thousands of jubilant slaves, learning of the proclamation, flocked to the invading Union armies, stripping already run-down plantations of their work force. In this sense the Emancipation Proclamation was heralded by the drumbeat of running feet. But many fugitives would have come anyhow, as they had from the war's outset. Actually, Lincoln did not go so far as legislation already passed by Congress for freeing enemy-owned slaves. His immediate goal was not so much to liberate the slaves as to strengthen the moral cause of the Union at home and abroad. This he succeeded in doing. At the same time, Lincoln's proclamation, though of dubious constitutionality, clearly foreshadowed the ultimate doom of slavery. This was legally achieved by action of the individual states and by their ratification of the Thirteenth Amendment in 1865, eight months after the Civil War had ended. (For text, see the Appendix; see also p. 484.)

Public reactions to the long-awaited proclamation of 1863 were varied. "God bless Abraham Lincoln," exulted the antislavery editor Horace Greeley in his New York *Tribune*. But many ardent abolitionists complained that Lincoln had not gone far enough. On the other hand, formidable numbers of Northerners, especially in the "Butternut" regions of the Old Northwest and the Border States, felt that he had gone too far. A Democratic rhymester sneered:

> Honest old Abe, when the war first began,
> Denied abolition was part of his plan;
> Honest old Abe has since made a decree,
> The war must go on till the slaves are all free.
> As both can't be honest, will some one tell how,
> If honest Abe then, he is honest Abe now?

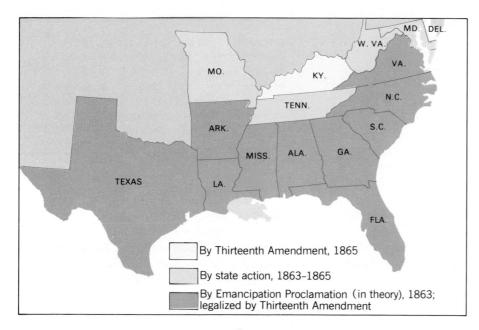

Emancipation in the South   *President Lincoln believed that compensated emancipation of the slaves would be fairest to the South. He formally proposed such an amendment to the Constitution in December 1862. What finally emerged was the Thirteenth Amendment of 1865, which freed all slaves without compensation.*

By Thirteenth Amendment, 1865

By state action, 1863–1865

By Emancipation Proclamation (in theory), 1863; legalized by Thirteenth Amendment

Opposition mounted in the North against supporting an "abolition war"; ex-president Pierce and others felt that emancipation should not be "inflicted" on the slaves. Many Boys in Blue, especially from the Border States, had volunteered to fight for the Union, not against slavery. Desertions increased sharply. The cru-

cial congressional elections in the autumn of 1862 went heavily against the administration, particularly in New York, Pennsylvania, and Ohio. Democrats even carried Lincoln's Illinois, although they did not secure control of Congress.

The Emancipation Proclamation caused an

Lincoln Plays His Last Card
Lincoln's last card was the Emancipation Proclamation, shown as a black spade. (Punch, 1862.)

outcry to rise from the South that "Lincoln the fiend" was trying to stir up the "hellish passions" of a slave insurrection. Aristocrats of Europe, noting that the proclamation applied only to rebel slaveholders, were inclined to sympathize with Southern protests. But the Old World working classes, especially in England, reacted otherwise. They sensed that the proclamation spelled the ultimate doom of slavery, and many laborers were more determined than ever to oppose intervention. Gradually the diplomatic position of the Union improved.

The North now had much the stronger moral cause. In addition to preserving the Union, it had committed itself to freeing the slaves. The moral position of the South was correspondingly weakened.

Blacks Battle Bondage

As Lincoln moved to emancipate the slaves, he also took steps to enlist blacks in the armed forces. Though some African-Americans had served in the Revolution and the War of 1812, the regular army contained no blacks at the war's outset, and the War Department refused to accept those free Northern blacks who tried to volunteer. (The Union navy, however, en-

> *Lincoln defended his policies toward blacks in an open letter to Democrats on August 26, 1863: "You say you will not fight to free negroes. Some of them seem willing to fight for you; but, no matter. Fight you, then, exclusively to save the Union. I issued the proclamation on purpose to aid you in saving the Union."*

rolled many blacks, mainly as cooks, stewards, and firemen.)

But as manpower ran low and emancipation was proclaimed, black enlistees were accepted, sometimes over ferocious protests from Northern as well as Southern whites. By war's end some 180,000 blacks served in the Union armies, most of them from the slave states, but many from the free-soil North. Blacks accounted for about 10 percent of the total enlistments in the Union forces, on land and sea, and included two Massachusetts regiments raised largely through the efforts of the ex-slave Frederick Douglass.

Black fighting men unquestionably had their hearts in the war against slavery that the Civil War had become after Lincoln proclaimed emancipation. Participating in about five hundred engagements, they received twenty-two

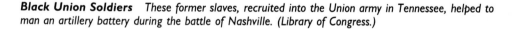

Black Union Soldiers *These former slaves, recruited into the Union army in Tennessee, helped to man an artillery battery during the battle of Nashville. (Library of Congress.)*

An affidavit by a Union sergeant described the fate of one group of black Union troops captured by the Confederates: "All the negroes found in blue uniform or with any outward marks of a Union soldier upon him was killed—I saw some taken into the woods and hung—Others I saw stripped of all their clothing, and they stood upon the bank of the river with their faces riverwards and then they were shot—Still others were killed by having their brains beaten out by the butt end of the muskets in the hands of the Rebels."

In August 1863 Lincoln wrote to Grant that enlisting black soldiers "works doubly, weakening the enemy and strengthening us." In December 1863 he announced that "it is difficult to say they are not as good soldiers as any." In August 1864 he said, "Abandon all the posts now garrisoned by black men, take 150,000 [black] men from our side and put them in the battlefield or cornfield against us, and we would be compelled to abandon the war in three weeks."

Congressional Medals of Honor—the highest military award. Their casualties were extremely heavy; more than thirty-eight thousand died, whether from battle, sickness, or reprisals from vengeful masters. Many were put to death as slaves in revolt, for not until 1864 did the South recognize them as prisoners of war. In one notorious case, several black soldiers were massacred after they had formally surrendered at Fort Pillow, Mississippi. Thereafter vengeful black units cried "Remember Fort Pillow" as they swung into battle, and vowed to take no prisoners.

For reasons of pride, prejudice, and principle, the Confederacy could not bring itself to enlist slaves until a month before the war ended, and then it was too late. Meanwhile tens of thousands were impressed into labor battalions, the building of fortifications, the supplying of armies, and other war-connected activities. Slaves moreover were "the stomach of the Confederacy," for they kept the farms going while the white men fought.

Ironically, the great mass of Southern slaves did little to help their Northern liberators, white or black. A thousand scattered torches in the

Slaves Helping to Build the Fortifications at Savannah, Georgia *The Confederacy employed blacks only as common laborers in the war effort; the Union eventually recruited them to bear arms. (The Granger Collection.)*

hands of a thousand slaves would have brought the Southern soldiers home, and the war would have ended. Through the "grapevine," the blacks learned of Lincoln's Emancipation Proclamation. Yet the bulk of them, whether because of fear, loyalty, lack of leadership, or strict policing, did not cast off their chains. But tens of thousand revolted "with their feet," when they abandoned their plantations upon the approach or arrival of Union armies, with or without emancipation proclamations. About twenty-five thousand joined Sherman's march through Georgia in 1864, and their presence in such numbers created problems of supply and discipline.

Lee's Last Lunge at Gettysburg

After Antietam, Lincoln replaced McClellan as commander of the Army of the Potomac with General A. E. Burnside, whose ornate side-whiskers came to be known as "burnsides" or "sideburns." Protesting his unfitness for this responsibility, Burnside proved it when he launched a rash frontal attack on Lee's strong position at Fredericksburg, Virginia, on December 13, 1862. A chicken could not have lived in the line of fire, remarked one Confederate

Lee's Chief Battles, December 1862–July 1863

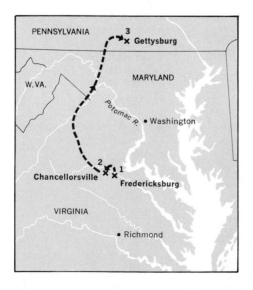

officer. More than ten thousand Northern soldiers were killed or wounded in "Burnside's Slaughter Pen."

A new slaughter pen was prepared when General Burnside yielded his command to "Fighting Joe" Hooker, an aggressive officer but a headstrong subordinate. At Chancellorsville, Virginia, May 2–4, 1863, Lee daringly divided his numerically inferior force and sent "Stonewall" Jackson to attack the Union flank. The strategy worked. Hooker, temporarily dazed by a near hit from a cannonball, was badly beaten but not crushed. This victory was probably Lee's most brilliant, but it was dearly bought. Jackson was mistakenly shot by his own men in the gathering dusk and died a few days later. "I have lost my right arm," lamented Lee. Southern folklore relates how Jackson outflanked the angels while galloping into Heaven.

Lee now prepared to follow up his stunning victory by invading the North again, this time through Pennsylvania. A decisive blow would add strength to the noisy peace movement in the North and would also encourage foreign intervention—still a Southern hope. Three days before the battle was joined, General George G. Meade—scholarly, unspectacular, abrupt—was aroused from his sleep at 2 A.M. with the unwelcome news that he would replace Hooker.

Quite by accident, Meade took his stand atop a low ridge flanking a shallow valley near quiet little Gettysburg, Pennsylvania. There his ninety-two thousand men in blue locked in furious combat with Lee's seventy-six thousand gray-clad warriors. The battle seesawed across the rolling green slopes for three agonizing days, July 1–3, 1863, and the outcome was in doubt until the very end. The failure of General George Pickett's magnificent but futile charge finally broke the back of the Confederate attack—and of the Confederate cause.

Pickett's charge has been called the "high tide of the Confederacy." It defined both the northernmost point reached by any significant Southern force and the last real chance for the Confederates to win the war. As the battle of Gettysburg raged, a Confederate peace delegation was moving under flag of truce toward the

> *In his address at Gettysburg, Lincoln cast the war as a struggle to preserve a nation "conceived in liberty, and dedicated to the proposition that all men are created equal." In his conclusion he declared "that these dead shall not have died in vain—that this nation, under God, shall have a new birth of freedom and that government of the people, by the people, and for the people shall not perish from the earth."*

Union lines near Norfolk, Virginia. Jefferson Davis hoped his negotiators would arrive in Washington from the south just as Lee's triumphant army marched on it from Gettysburg to the north. But the victory at Gettysburg belonged to Lincoln, who refused to allow the Confederate peace mission to pass through Union lines. From now on the Southern cause was doomed. Yet the men of Dixie fought on for nearly two years longer, through sweat, blood, and weariness of spirit.

Later in that dreary autumn of 1863, with the graves still fresh, Lincoln journeyed to Gettysburg to dedicate the cemetery. He read a two-minute address, following a two-hour speech by the orator of the day. Lincoln's noble remarks were branded by the London *Times* as "ludicrous" and by Democratic editors as "dishwatery" and "silly." The address attracted relatively little attention at the time, but the president was speaking for the ages.

The War in the West

Events in the western theater of the war at last provided Lincoln with an able general who did not have to be shelved after every reverse. Ulysses S. Grant had been a mediocre student at West Point, distinguishing himself only in horsemanship, although he did fairly well at mathematics. After fighting creditably in the Mexican War, he was stationed at isolated frontier posts, where boredom and loneliness drove him to drink. Resigning from the army to avoid

a court-martial for drunkenness, he failed at various business ventures, and when war came, he was working in his father's leather store in Illinois for $50 a month.

Grant did not cut much of a figure. The shy and silent shopkeeper was short, stooped, awkward, stubble-bearded, and sloppy in dress. He managed with some difficulty to secure a colonelcy in the volunteers. From then on his military experience—combined with his boldness, resourcefulness, and doggedness—catapulted him on a meteoric rise.

Grant's first signal success came in the northern Tennessee theater. After heavy fighting, he captured Fort Henry and Fort Donelson on the Tennessee and Cumberland Rivers in February 1862. When the Confederate commander at Fort Donelson asked for terms, Grant bluntly demanded "an unconditional and immediate surrender."

Grant's triumph in Tennessee was crucial. It not only riveted Kentucky more securely to the Union but also opened the gateway to the strategically important region of Tennessee, as well as to Georgia and the heart of Dixie. Grant next attempted to exploit his victory by capturing the junction of the main Confederate north-south and east-west railroads in the Mississippi Valley at Corinth, Mississippi. But a Confederate force foiled his plans in a gory battle at Shiloh, just over the Tennessee border from Corinth, on April 6–7, 1862.

Lincoln resisted all demands for the removal of "Unconditional Surrender" Grant, saying "I can't spare this man; he fights." When talebearers later told Lincoln that Grant drank too much, the president allegedly replied, "Find me the brand, and I'll send a barrel to each of my other generals." There is no evidence that Grant's drinking habits seriously impaired his military performance.

Other Union thrusts in the West were in the making. In the spring of 1862, a flotilla commanded by David G. Farragut joined with a Northern army to strike the South a staggering blow by seizing New Orleans. With Union gunboats both ascending and descending the Mississippi, the eastern part of the Confederacy was left with a precarious back door. Through

General Ulysses S. Grant and General Robert E. Lee *Trained at West Point, Grant (left) proved to be a better general than a president. Oddly, he hated the sight of blood and recoiled from rare beef. Lee (right), a gentlemanly general in an ungentlemanly business, remarked when the Union troops were bloodily repulsed at Fredericksburg. "It is well that war is so terrible, or we should get too fond of it." (Left and right, National Archives.)*

this narrowing entrance, between Vicksburg and Port Hudson, flowed herds of vitally needed cattle and quantities of other provisions from Louisiana and Texas. The fortress of Vicksburg, located on a hairpin turn of the Mississippi, was the South's sentinel protecting the lifeline to the western sources of supply.

General Grant was now given command of the Union forces attacking Vicksburg and in the teeth of grave difficulties displayed rare skill and daring. This was his best-fought campaign of the war. Vicksburg at length surrendered, on July 4, 1863, with the garrison reduced to eating mules and rats. Five days later came the fall of Port Hudson, the last Southern bastion on the Mississippi. The spinal cord of the Confederacy was now severed and, in Lincoln's quaint phrase, the Father of Waters at last flowed "unvexed to the sea."

The Union victory at Vicksburg came the day after the Confederate defeat at Gettysburg—July 4 and 3, 1863, respectively. The political significance of these back-to-back military successes was epochal. Reopening the Mississippi helped to quell the Northern peace agitation in the "Butternut" area of the Ohio River Valley. Confederate control of the Mississippi had cut off that region's usual trade routes down the Ohio-Mississippi river system to New Orleans, thus adding economic pain to that border section's already shaky support for the "abolition war." The twin victories also conclusively tipped the diplomatic scales in favor of the North, as England stopped delivery of the Laird rams to the Confederates and as France killed a deal for the sale of six naval vessels to the Richmond government. By the end of 1863 all Confederate hopes for foreign help were irretrievably lost.

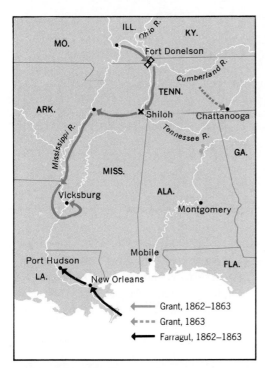

The Mississippi River and Tennessee, 1862–1863

Sherman Scorches Georgia

General Grant, the victor of Vicksburg, was now transferred to the east Tennessee theater, where Confederates had driven Union forces from the battlefield at Chickamauga into the city of Chattanooga, to which they then laid siege. Grant won a series of desperate engagements in November 1863 in the vicinity of besieged Chattanooga; including Missionary Ridge and Lookout Mountain ("the Battle above the Clouds"). Chattanooga was liberated, the state was cleared of Confederates, and the way was thus opened for an invasion of Georgia. Grant was rewarded by being made general-in-chief.

The conquest of Georgia was entrusted to General William Tecumseh Sherman. Red-haired and red-bearded, grim-faced and ruthless, he captured and burned Atlanta in September 1864. He then daringly undertook to cut loose from his base of supplies, live off the country for some 250 miles (402 kilometers), and emerge at Savannah on the sea. As a rous-

ing Northern song ("Marching through Georgia") put it:

> "Sherman's dashing Yankee boys will never reach the coast!"
> So the saucy rebels said—and 't was a handsome boast.

Sherman's March, 1864–1865

But Sherman's hated "Blue Bellies," sixty thousand strong, cut a sixty-mile (ninety-seven-kilometer) swath of destruction through Georgia. They burned buildings, leaving only the blackened chimneys ("Sherman's Sentinels"). They tore up railroad rails, heated them red-hot, and twisted them into "iron doughnuts" and "Sherman's hairpins." They bayoneted family portraits and ran off with valuable "souvenirs." "War . . . is all hell," admitted Sherman later, and he proved it by his efforts to "make Georgia howl." One of his major purposes was to destroy supplies destined for the Confederate army and to weaken the morale of the men at the front by waging war on their homes.

Sherman was a pioneer practitioner of "total war." His success in "Shermanizing" the South was attested by increasing numbers of Confederate desertions. Although his methods were brutal, he probably shortened the struggle and hence saved lives. But there can be no doubt that the discipline of his army at times broke down, as roving riffraff (Sherman's "bummers")

> A letter picked up on a dead Confederate in North Carolina and addressed to his "deer sister" concluded that it was "dam fulishness" trying to "lick shurmin." He had been getting "nuthin but hell & lots uv it" ever since he saw the "dam yanks," and he was "tirde uv it." He would head for home now, but his old horse was "plaid out." If the "dam yankees" had not got there yet, it would be a "dam wunder." They were thicker than "lise on a hen and a dam site ornerier."

engaged in an orgy of pillaging. "Sherman the Brute" was universally damned in the South.

After seizing Savannah as a Christmas present for Lincoln, Sherman's army veered north into South Carolina, where the destruction was even more vicious. Many Union soldiers believed that this state, the "hell-hole of secession," had wantonly provoked the war. The

Sherman's Raiders Rip Up Confederate Railroad Tracks Sherman's mission was to break the will of Southern civilians to carry on the fight. One of his chief means to that end was to disrupt the South's already meager transportation system. In this contemporary drawing, note that the "rails" consist of nothing more than metal strips on a wooden base. Most northern railroads were built to much higher standards, with full metal rails. (Old Print Shop.)

capital city, Columbia, burst into flames, in all probability the handiwork of the Yankee invader. Crunching northward, Sherman's conquering army had rolled deep into North Carolina by the time the war ended.

The Politics of War

Presidential elections come by the calendar and not by the crisis. As fate would have it, the election of 1864 fell most inopportunely in the midst of war.

Political infighting in the North added greatly to Lincoln's cup of woe. Factions within his own party, distrusting his ability or doubting his commitment to abolition, sought to tie his hands or even remove him from office. Conspicuous among his critics was a group led by the overambitious secretary of the treasury, Salmon Chase. Especially burdensome to Lincoln was the creation of the Congressional Committee on the Conduct of the War, formed in late 1861. It was dominated by "radical" Republicans who resented the expansion of presidential power in wartime and who pressed Lincoln zealously on emancipation.

Most dangerous of all to the Union cause were the Northern Democrats. Deprived of the talent that had departed with the Southern wing of the party, those Democrats remaining in the North were left with the taint of association with the seceders. Tragedy befell the Democrats—and the Union—when their gifted leader, Stephen A. Douglas, died of typhoid fever seven weeks after the war began. Unshakably devoted to the Union, he probably could have kept much of his following on the path of loyalty.

Lacking a leader, the Democrats divided. A large group of "War Democrats" patriotically supported the Lincoln administration, but tens of thousands of "Peace Democrats" did not. At the extreme were the so-called Copperheads, named for the poisonous snake, which strikes without a rattle. Copperheads openly obstructed the war through attacks against the draft, against Lincoln, and especially, after 1863, against emancipation. They denounced the president as the "Illinois Ape" and condemned the "Nigger War." They commanded considerable political strength in the southern parts of Ohio, Indiana, and Illinois.

Notorious among the Copperheads was a sometime congressman from Ohio, Clement L. Vallandigham. This tempestuous character possessed brilliant oratorical gifts and unusual talents for stirring up trouble. A Southern partisan, he publicly demanded an end to the "wicked and cruel" war. The civil courts in Ohio

The Copperhead Party *The cartoon shows the party in favor of a vigorous prosecution of peace. (Harper's Weekly, 1863.)*

were open, and he should have been tried in them. But he was convicted by a military tribunal in 1863 for treasonable utterances and was then sentenced to prison. Lincoln decided that if Vallandigham liked the Confederates so much, he ought to be banished to their lines. This was done.

Vallandigham was not so easily silenced. Working his way to Canada, he ran for the governorship of Ohio on foreign soil and polled a substantial but insufficient vote. He returned to his own state before the war ended, and although he defied "King Lincoln" and spat upon a military decree, he was not further prosecuted. The strange case of Vallandigham inspired Edward Everett Hale to write his moving but fictional story of Philip Nolan, "The Man without a Country" (1863), which was immensely popular in the North and which helped stimulate devotion to the Union. Nolan was a young army officer found guilty of participation in the Aaron Burr plot of 1806. He had cried out in court, "Damn the United States! I wish I may never hear of the United States again!" For this outburst he was condemned to a life of complete exile on American warships.

The Election of 1864

As the election of 1864 approached, Lincoln's precarious authority depended on his retaining Republican support while spiking the threat from the Peace Democrats and Copperheads.

Fearing defeat, the Republican party executed a clever maneuver. Joining with the War Democrats, it proclaimed itself to be the Union party. Thus the Republican party passed temporarily out of existence.

Lincoln's renomination at first encountered surprisingly strong opposition. Hostile factions whipped up considerable agitation to shelve homely "Old Abe" in favor of handsome Secretary of the Treasury Chase. Lincoln was accused of lacking force, of being overready to compromise, of not having won the war, and of having shocked many sensitive souls by his ill-timed and earthy jokes. ("Prince of Jesters," one journal called him.) But the "ditch Lincoln" move collapsed, and he was nominated by the Union party without serious dissent.

Lincoln's running mate was ex-tailor Andrew Johnson, a loyal War Democrat from Tennessee who had been a small slaveowner when the conflict began. He was placed on the Union party ticket to "sew up" the election by attracting War Democrats and the voters in the Border States, and not with proper regard for the possibility that Lincoln might die in office. Southerners and Copperheads alike condemned both candidates as birds of a feather: two ignorant, third-rate, boorish, backwoods politicians born in log cabins.

Embattled Democrats—regular and Copperhead—nominated the deposed and overcautious war hero, General McClellan. The Copperheads managed to force into the Democratic platform a plank denouncing the prosecution of the war as a failure. But McClellan, who could not otherwise have faced his old comrades-in-arms, repudiated this defeatist declaration.

The ensuing campaign was noisy and heated. The Democrats cried, "Old Abe removed McClellan. We'll now remove Old Abe." They also sang, "Mac Will Win the Union Back." The Union party supporters shouted for "Uncle Abe and Andy" and urged, "Vote as you shot." Their most effective slogan, growing out of a remark by Lincoln, was: "Don't swap horses in the middle of the river."

Lincoln's reelection was at first gravely in doubt. The war was going badly, and Lincoln himself gave way to despondency, fearing that political defeat was imminent. The anti-Lincoln

Union Party, 1864 *The shaded area represents the Union Party.*

NORTHERN DEMOCRATS

REPUBLICANS

| COPPER-HEADS | PEACE DEMO-CRATS | WAR DEMO-CRATS |

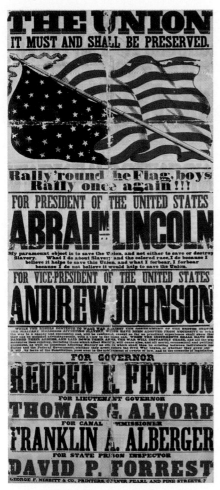

A Lincoln-Johnson Campaign Poster, 1864 *(New-York Historical Society.)*

Republicans, taking heart, started a new movement to "dump" Lincoln in favor of someone else.

But the atmosphere of gloom was changed electrically, as balloting day neared, by a succession of Northern victories. Admiral Farragut captured Mobile, Alabama, after defiantly shouting the now famous, "Damn the torpedoes! Go ahead." General Sherman seized Atlanta. General ("Little Phil") Sheridan laid waste the verdant Shenandoah Valley of Virginia so thoroughly that in his words "a crow could not fly over it without carrying his rations with him."

The president pulled through, but nothing more than necessary was left to chance. At election time many Northern soldiers were furloughed home to support Lincoln. One Pennsylvania veteran voted forty-nine times—once for himself and once for each absent member of his company. Other soldiers were permitted to cast their ballots at the front.

Lincoln, bolstered by the so-called bayonet vote, vanquished General McClellan by 212 electoral votes to 21, with the loss of only Kentucky, Delaware, and New Jersey. But "Little Mac" ran a much closer race than the electoral count indicates. He netted a surprising 45 percent of the popular vote, 1,803,787 to Lincoln's 2,206,938, piling up much support in the Southerner-infiltrated states of the Old Northwest, in New York, and also in his native state of Pennsylvania.

Presidential Election of 1864 (showing popular vote by county) *Lincoln also carried California, Oregon, and Nevada, but there was a considerable McClellan vote in each.*

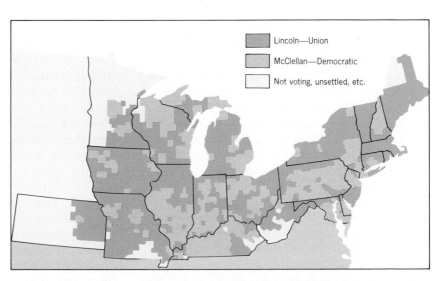

Lincoln—Union

McClellan—Democratic

Not voting, unsettled, etc.

One of the most crushing defeats suffered by the South was the defeat of the Northern Democrats in 1864. The removal of Lincoln was the last ghost of a hope for a Confederate victory, and the Southern soldiers would wishfully shout, "Hurrah for McClellan!" When Lincoln triumphed, desertions from the sinking Southern ship increased sharply.

Grant Outlasts Lee

After Gettysburg, Grant was brought in from the West over Meade, who was blamed for failing to pursue the defeated but always dangerous Lee. Lincoln needed a general who, employing the superior resources of the North, would have the intestinal stamina to drive straight ahead, regardless of casualties. A soldier of bulldog tenacity, Grant was the man for this meat-grinder type of warfare. His overall basic strategy was to assail the enemy's armies simultaneously, so that they could not assist one another and hence could be destroyed piecemeal. His personal motto was "When in doubt, fight." Lincoln urged him to "chew and choke, as much as possible."

A grimly determined Grant, with more than 100,000 men, struck for Richmond. He engaged Lee in a series of furious battles in the Wilderness of Virginia, during May and June of 1864, notably in the leaden hurricane of the "Bloody Angle" and "Hell's Half Acre." In this Wilderness Campaign Grant suffered about 50,000 casualties, or nearly as many men as Lee had at the start. But Lee lost about as heavily in proportion.

In a ghastly gamble, on June 3, 1864, Grant ordered a frontal assault on the impregnable position of Cold Harbor. The Union soldiers advanced to almost certain death with papers pinned on their backs bearing their names and addresses. In a few minutes, about seven thousand men were killed or wounded.

Public opinion in the North was appalled by this "blood and guts" type of fighting. Critics cried that "Grant the Butcher" had gone insane. But his basic strategy of hammering ahead seemed brutally necessary; he could trade two men for one and still beat the enemy to its knees. "I propose to fight it out on this line," he

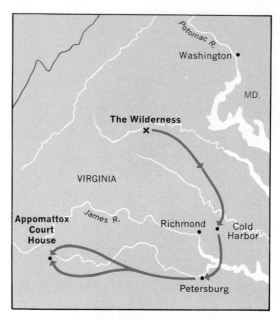

Grant's Virginia Campaign, 1864–1865

wrote, "if it takes all summer." It did—and it also took all autumn, all winter, and a part of the spring.

Early in 1865 the Confederates, tasting the bitter dregs of defeat, tried desperately to negotiate for peace between the "two countries." But Lincoln could accept nothing short of Union, and the Southerners could accept nothing short of independence. So the war had to grind on—amid smoke and agony—to its terrible climax.

The end came with dramatic suddenness. Rapidly advancing Northern troops captured Richmond and cornered Lee at Appomattox Court House in Virginia, in April 1865. Grant—stubble-bearded and informally dressed—met with Lee on Palm Sunday and granted generous terms of surrender. Among other concessions, the hungry Confederates were allowed to keep their own horses for spring plowing.

Tattered Southern veterans—"Lee's Ragamuffins"—wept as they took leave of their beloved commander. The elated Union soldiers cheered, but they were silenced by Grant's stern admonition, "The war is over; the rebels are our countrymen again."

Lincoln himself traveled to conquered Richmond and sat in Jefferson Davis's evacuated office just forty hours after the Confederate president had left it. "Thank God I have lived to see this," he said. With a small escort of sailors, he walked the blasted streets of the city. Freed slaves began to recognize him, and crowds gathered to see and touch "Father Abraham." One black man fell to his knees before the Emancipator, who said to him: "Don't kneel to me. This is not right. You must kneel to God only, and thank Him for the liberty you will enjoy hereafter." Sadly, as many freed slaves were to discover, the hereafter of their full liberty was a long time coming.

The Martyrdom of Lincoln

On the night of April 14, 1865 (Good Friday), only five days after Lee's surrender, Ford's Theater in Washington witnessed its most sensational drama. A half-crazed, fanatically pro-Southern actor, John Wilkes Booth, slipped behind Lincoln as he sat in his box and shot him in the head. After lying unconscious all night, the Great Emancipator died the following morning. "Now he belongs to the ages," remarked the once-critical Secretary Stanton—probably the finest thing he ever said.

Lincoln expired in the arms of victory, at the very pinnacle of his fame. From the standpoint of his reputation, his death could not have been better timed if he had hired the assassin. A large number of his countrymen had not suspected his greatness, and many others had even doubted his ability. But his dramatic death helped to erase the memory of his shortcomings and caused his nobler qualities to stand out in clearer relief.

The full impact of Lincoln's death was not at once apparent to the South. Hundreds of bedraggled ex-Confederate soldiers cheered, as did some Southern civilians and Northern Copperheads, when they learned of the assassination. This reaction was only natural, because Lincoln had kept the war grinding on to the bitter end. If he had only been willing to stop the shooting, the South would have won.

Lincoln's Funeral Parade in New York, 1865 *The flag-draped building on the left was the Roosevelt mansion, from which future president Theodore Roosevelt, then a boy of six, watched Lincoln's funeral procession pass. (International Museum of Photography, George Eastman House.)*

As time wore on, increasing numbers of Southerners perceived that Lincoln's death was a calamity for them. Belatedly they recognized that his kindliness and moderation would have been the most effective shields between them and vindictive treatment by the victors. The assassination unfortunately increased the bitterness in the North, partly because of the fantastic rumor that Jefferson Davis had plotted it.

A few historians have argued that Andrew Johnson, now president-by-bullet, was crucified for Lincoln. The implication is that if the "railsplitter" had lived, he would have run into serious trouble, perhaps impeachment, at the hands of the embittered members of his own party who demanded harsh treatment of the South.

The crucifixion thesis does not stand up under scrutiny. Lincoln no doubt would have clashed with Congress; in fact, he had already found himself in some hot water. The legislative branch normally struggles to win back the power that has been wrested from it by the ex-

> The powerful London Times, voice of the upper classes, had generally criticized Lincoln during the war, especially after the Emancipation Proclamation of 1862. He was then condemned as "a sort of moral American Pope" destined to be "Lincoln the Last." When the president was shot, the Times reversed itself (April 29, 1865): "Abraham Lincoln was as little of a tyrant as any man who ever lived. He could have been a tyrant had he pleased, but he never uttered so much as an ill-natured speech. . . . In all America there was, perhaps, not one man who less deserved to be the victim of this revolution than he who has just fallen."

ecutive in time of crisis. But the surefooted and experienced Lincoln could hardly have blundered into the same quicksands that engulfed Johnson. Lincoln was a victorious president, and there is no arguing with victory. Enjoying battle-tested powers of leadership, Lincoln pos-

The Burning of Richmond, April, 1865 *The proud Confederate capital, after holding out against repeated Union assaults, was evacuated and burned in the final days of the war. (Library of Congress.)*

sessed in full measure tact, sweet reasonableness, and an uncommon amount of common sense. Andrew Johnson, hot-tempered and impetuous, lacked all of these priceless qualities.

Ford's Theater, with its tragic murder of Lincoln, set the stage for the terrible ordeal of Reconstruction.

The Aftermath of the Nightmare

The Civil War took a grisly toll in gore, about as much as all of America's subsequent wars combined. Over 600,000 men died in action or of disease, and in all over a million were killed or seriously wounded. To its lasting hurt, the nation lost the cream of its young manhood and potential leadership. In addition, tens of thousands of babies went unborn because potential fathers were at the front.

Direct monetary costs of the conflict totaled about $15 billion. But this colossal figure does not include continuing expenses, such as pensions and interest on the national debt. The intangible costs—dislocations, disunities, wasted energies, lowered ethics, blasted lives, bitter memories, and burning hates—cannot be calculated.

The greatest constitutional decision of the century, in a sense, was written in blood and handed down at Appomattox Court House, near which Lee surrendered. The extreme states' righters were crushed. The national government, tested in the fiery furnace of war, emerged unbroken. Nullification and secession, those twin nightmares of previous decades, were laid to rest.

Beyond doubt the Civil War—the nightmare of the Republic—was the supreme test of American democracy. It finally answered the question, in the words of Lincoln at Gettysburg, whether a nation dedicated to such principles

Prisoners from the Front   *This celebrated painting of 1866 by Winslow Homer reflected the painter's first-hand observations of the war. He brilliantly captured the enduring depths of sectional animosity. The Union officer somewhat disdainfully asserts his command of the situation; the beaten and disarmed Confederates exhibit an out-at-the-elbows pride and defiance. (The Metropolitan Museum of Art. Gift of Mrs. Frank B. Porter, 1922.)*

"can long endure." The preservation of democratic ideals, though not an officially announced war aim, was subconsciously one of the major objectives of the North.

Victory for Union arms also provided inspiration to the champions of democracy and liberalism the world over. The great English Reform Bill of 1867, under which Britain became a true political democracy, was passed two years after the Civil War ended. American democracy had proved itself, and its success was an additional argument used by the disfranchised British masses in securing similar blessings for themselves.

The "Lost Cause" of the South was lost, but few Americans today would argue that the result was not for the best. The shameful cancer of slavery was sliced away by the sword, and African-Americans were at last in a position to claim their rights to life, liberty, and the pursuit of happiness. The nation was again united politically, though for many generations still divided spiritually by the passions of the war. Grave dangers were averted by a Union victory, including the indefinite prolongation of the "peculiar institution," the unleashing of the slave power on weak Caribbean neighbors, and the transformation of the area from Panama to Hudson's Bay into an armed camp, with several heavily armed and hostile states constantly snarling and sniping at one another. America still had a long way to go to make the promises of freedom a reality for all its citizens, black and white. But emancipation laid the necessary groundwork, and a united and democratic United States was free to fulfill its destiny as the dominant republic of the hemisphere—and eventually of the world.

CHRONOLOGY

1861	First Battle of Bull Run
1862	Grant takes Forts Henry and Donelson
	Battle of Shiloh
	McClellan's Peninsula Campaign
	Seven Days' Battles
	Second Battle of Bull Run
	Battle of Antietam
	Preliminary Emancipation Proclamation
	Battle of Fredericksburg
1863	Final Emancipation Proclamation
	Battle of Chancellorsville
	Battle of Gettysburg
	Fall of Vicksburg
	Fall of Port Hudson
1864	Sherman's march through Georgia
	Grant's Wilderness Campaign
	Battle of Cold Harbor
	Lincoln defeats McClellan for presidency
1865	Lee surrenders to Grant at Appomattox
	Lincoln assassinated
	Thirteenth Amendment ratified

Varying Viewpoints

Why did the North win the Civil War? The usual answer is that superior industry and transportation tipped the scales in the Union's favor. This line of reasoning leads to the conclusion that the Civil War was the first "modern" war, in which victory turned at least as much on home-front economic mobilization as on battlefield prowess.

Another approach focuses on military strategy. Historians of this persuasion argue that Union successes in the western theater more than compensated for the early debacles in Virginia. Victories in the West allowed the emergence of tacticians like Grant and Sherman, who were better equipped to wage a modern total war than the valiant but old-fashioned Confederate generals.

A third answer emphasizes political leadership. In this view, the Lincoln administration was able through political skill to maintain control at home and prevent unfavorable foreign intervention in the conflict. The government of Jefferson Davis had no such domestic or diplomatic success. One historian has even suggested that if the North and South had traded presidents, the Confederacy would have won its independence. Even today, heated debate continues over the relative importance of battlefront and behind-the-lines factors in accounting for the North's crushing victory.

Select Readings

Primary Source Documents

Abraham Lincoln's reply in 1862 to Horace Greeley's "Prayer of Twenty Millions"* (*Collected Works of Abraham Lincoln,* edited by Roy P. Basler, 1953) is an early statement of the president's war aims. See also, in the same collection, the Emancipation Proclamation (1863). Reminiscences of the military struggle include Eliza Andrews, *The War-Time Journal of a Georgia Girl*(1908); *Memoirs of General William T. Sherman*(1887); and C. Vann Woodward, ed., *Mary Chestnut's Civil War* (rev. ed., 1981). See also Stephen Crane's classic war novel *The Red Badge of Courage* (1895).

Secondary Sources

The most compelling single-volume account of the war is James M. McPherson, *Battle Cry of Freedom: The Civil War Era* (1988). An able survey is James G. Randall and David Donald, *The Civil War and Reconstruction* (rev. ed., 1969); greater detail appears in James G. Randall, *Lincoln the President* (4 vols.,

1945–1955). Other capable one-volume studies include Peter J. Parish, *The American Civil War* (1975), and James M. McPherson, *Ordeal by Fire: The Civil War and Reconstruction* (1982). See also the multivolume study by Shelby Foote, *The Civil War* (3 vols., 1958–1974), and Allan Nevins's monumental *Ordeal of the Union* (8 vols., 1947–1971). Bruce Catton has a series of a dozen or so books on aspects of the Civil War, all readable and knowledgeable, including *A Stillness at Appomattox* (1953) and *This Hallowed Ground* (1956). Russell T. Weigley, *The American Way of War* (1973), puts military history in a broader context. Richard N. Current, *Lincoln and the First Shot* (1963), partially exculpates Lincoln. See also T. Harry Williams, *Lincoln and His Generals* (1952). Herman Hattaway and Archer Jones discuss *How the North Won* (1983). An intriguing analysis of Confederate strategy is Grady McWhiney and Perry D. Jamison, *Attack and Die* (1982). Bell I. Wiley's descriptions of common soldiers, *The Life of Johnny Reb* (1943) and *The Life of Billy Yank* (1952), are classics. See also Benjamin Quarles, *The Negro in the Civil War* (1953), and James M. McPherson's collection of documents, *The*

Negro's Civil War (1965). Emancipation is treated in Louis Gerteis, *From Contraband to Freedmen: Federal Policy toward Southern Blacks, 1861–1865* (1973); Herman Belz, *Emancipation and Equal Rights: Politics and Constitutionalism during the Civil War Reconstruction* (1978); and LaWanda Cox, *Lincoln and Black Freedom* (1981). On the abolitionists' role in securing emancipation, see James M. McPherson, *The Struggle for Equality* (1964). The Southern response is discussed in Robert Durden, *The Gray and the Black: The Confederate Debate on Emancipation* (1973). The two leading Civil War generals are masterfully treated in Douglas S. Freeman, *R. E. Lee* (4 vols., 1934–1935), and William S. McFeely, *Grant* (1981).

23

The Ordeal of Reconstruction, 1865–1877

With malice toward none, with charity for all, with firmness in the right as God gives us to see the right, let us strive on to finish the work we are in, to bind up the nation's wounds, to care for him who shall have borne the battle and for his widow and orphan, to do all which may achieve and cherish a just and lasting peace among ourselves and with all nations.

Abraham Lincoln, Second Inaugural, March 4, 1865

The Problems of Peace

The battle was done, the buglers silent. Bone-weary and bloodied, the American people, North and South, now faced the staggering challenges of peace. Four questions loomed large. How would the South, physically devastated by war and socially revolutionized by emancipation, be rebuilt? How would the liberated blacks fare as free men and women? How would the Southern states be reintegrated into the Union? And who would direct the process of Reconstruction—the Southern states themselves, the president, or the Congress?

Other questions also clamored for answers. What should be done with the captured Confederate ringleaders, all of whom were liable to charges of treason? During the war a popular Northern song had been "Hang Jeff Davis to a Sour Apple Tree," and even innocent children had lisped it. Davis was temporarily clapped into irons during the early days of his two-year imprisonment. But he and his fellow "conspirators" were finally released, partly because the odds were that no Virginia jury would convict them. All rebel leaders were finally pardoned by President Johnson as sort of a Christmas present in 1868. But Congress did not remove all

Richmond Devastated *Charleston, Atlanta, and other Southern cities looked much the same, resembling bombed-out Berlin and Dresden in 1945. (Library of Congress.)*

remaining civil disabilities until thirty years later and only posthumously restored Davis's citizenship more than a century later.

Dismal indeed was the picture presented by the war-racked South when the rattle of musketry faded. Not only had an age perished, but a civilization had collapsed, in both its economic and its social structure. The moonlight-and-magnolia Old South, largely imaginary in any case, had forever gone with the wind.

Handsome cities of yesteryear, such as Charleston and Richmond, were rubble-strewn and weed-choked. An Atlantan returned to his once-fair hometown and remarked, "Hell has laid her egg, and right here it hatched."

Economic life had creaked to a halt. Banks and business houses had locked their doors, ruined by runaway inflation. Factories were smokeless, silent, dismantled. The transportation system had broken down completely. Be-fore the war, five different railroad lines had converged on Columbia, South Carolina; now the nearest connected track was 29 miles (47 kilometers) away. Efforts to untwist the rails corkscrewed by Sherman's soldiers proved bumpily unsatisfactory.

Agriculture—the economic lifeblood of the South—was almost hopelessly crippled. Once-white cotton fields now yielded a lush harvest of nothing but green weeds. The slave-labor system had collapsed, seed was scarce, and live-stock had been driven off by plundering Yankees. Pathetic instances were reported of men hitching themselves to plows, while women and children gripped the handles. Not until 1870 did the seceded states produce as large a cotton crop as that of the fateful year 1860, and much of that came from new acreage in the Southwest.

The princely planter aristocrats were hum-

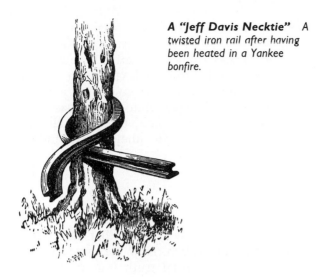

A "Jeff Davis Necktie" *A twisted iron rail after having been heated in a Yankee bonfire.*

...led by the war—at least temporarily. Reduced to proud poverty, they faced charred and gutted mansions, lost investments, and almost worthless land. Their investment of more than $2 billion in slaves, their primary form of wealth, had evaporated with emancipation.

Beaten but unbent, many high-spirited white Southerners remained dangerously defiant. They cursed the "damnyankees" and spoke of "your government" in Washington, instead of "our government." One Southern bishop refused to pray for President Andrew Johnson, though Johnson proved to be in sore need of divine guidance. Conscious of no crime, these former Confederates continued to believe that their view of secession was correct and that the "lost cause" was still a just war. One popular anti-Union song ran:

> I'm glad I fought agin her, I only wish we'd
>   won,
> And I ain't axed any pardon for anything I've
>   done.

Such attitudes boded ill for the prospects of painlessly binding up the Republic's wounds.

Unfettered Freedmen

Confusion abounded in the still-smoldering South about the precise meaning of "freedom" for blacks. Emancipation took effect haltingly and unevenly in different parts of the conquered Confederacy, and in some regions planters stubbornly protested that slavery was legal until state legislatures or the Supreme Court might act. Newspapers in Mississippi earnestly discussed *gradual* emancipation. For many bondsmen, the shackles of slavery were not struck off in a single mighty blow; long-suffering blacks often had to struggle out of their chains link by link.

The variety of responses to emancipation, by whites as well as blacks, illustrated the sometimes startling complexity of the master-slave relationship. Unbending loyalty to "ole Massa" prompted many slaves to help their owners resist the liberating Union armies. Blacks blocked the door of the "big house" with their bodies or stashed the plantation silverware under mattresses in their own humble huts, where it would be safe from the plundering "bluebellies." On other plantations, pent-up bitterness burst violently forth on the day of liberation. A group of Virginia slaves laid twenty lashes on the back of their former master—a painful dose of his own favorite medicine. Newly emancipated slaves sometimes eagerly accepted the invitation of Union troops to join in the pillaging of their master's possessions. One freedman said that he felt entitled to steal a chicken or two, since the whites had robbed him of his labor and his children.

Emancipation followed by re-enslavement, or worse, was the bewildering lot of many blacks, as Union armies marched in and out of various localities. A North Carolina slave estimated that

Carl Schurz described a Fourth of July affair in Savannah, Georgia, in 1865: "The colored firemen of this city desired to parade their engine on the anniversary of our independence. . . . In the principal street of the city the procession was attacked with clubs and stones by a mob . . . and by a crowd of boys swearing at the d———d niggers. The colored firemen were knocked down, some of them severely injured, their engine was taken away from them, and the peaceable procession dispersed."

he had celebrated emancipation about twelve times. As blacks in one Texas county flocked to the free soil of the liberated county next door, their owners bushwacked them with rifle fire as they swam for freedom across the river that marked the county line. The next day, trees along the riverbank were bent with swinging corpses—a grisly warning to others dreaming of liberty.

Prodded by the bayonets of Yankee armies of occupation, all masters were eventually forced to recognize their slaves' permanent freedom. The once-commanding planter would assemble his former human chattels in front of the porch of the "big house" and announce their liberty. This "Day of Jubilo" was the occasion of wild rejoicing. Tens of thousands of blacks naturally took to the roads. They sought long-separated loved ones, as formalizing a "slave marriage" was the first goal of many newly free men and women. Others traveled in search of economic opportunity in the towns or in the still-wild West. Many moved simply to test their new freedom.

Desperately trying to bootstrap themselves up from slavery, blacks assembled in "Conventions of Freedmen" to fight to make their freedom a reality. Led by ministers of God and freeborn blacks from the North, these conventions expressed surprisingly moderate views. But moderation could not guarantee a warm reception by embittered white Southerners. The freed blacks were going to need all the friends—and the power—they could find in Washington.

The Freedmen's Bureau

Abolitionists had long preached that slavery was a degrading institution. Now the emancipators had to face the brutal truth that the former slaves were in many ways indeed degraded. The freedmen were overwhelmingly unskilled, unlettered, without property or money, and with scant knowledge of how to survive as free persons. To cope with this problem throughout the conquered South, Congress created the Freedmen's Bureau in 1865.

On paper at least, the bureau was intended to be a kind of primitive welfare agency. It was to provide food, clothing, and education both to

Free at Last *A black family in South Carolina photographed just after emancipation. Three generations are apparently present here, suggesting the cohesiveness and endurance of the African-American family, despite the harshness of slavery. (Library of Congress.)*

Primary School for Freedmen in Vicksburg, Mississippi, 1866 *Note the wide range of ages. (The Granger Collection.)*

freedmen and to white refugees. It was also authorized to distribute up to forty acres of abandoned or confiscated land to black settlers. Heading the bureau was a warmly sympathetic friend of the blacks, Union General Oliver O. Howard, who later founded and served as president of Howard University in Washington, D.C.

The bureau achieved its greatest successes in education. It taught an estimated 200,000 blacks how to read. Many former slaves had a passion for learning, partly because they wanted to close the gap between themselves and the whites and partly because they longed to read the Word of God. In one elementary class in North Carolina sat four generations of the same family, ranging from a six-year-old tot to a seventy-five-year-old grandmother.

But in other areas the Bureau's accomplishments were meager—or even mischievous. It distributed virtually no land. Its local administrators often collaborated with planters in expelling blacks from towns and cajoling them into signing labor contracts to work for their former masters. Yet the white South resented the bureau as a meddlesome federal interloper that threatened to upset white racial dominance. President Andrew Johnson, who shared the white-supremacist views of most white Southerners, repeatedly tried to kill it, and it expired in 1872.

Johnson: The Tailor President

Few presidents have ever been faced with a more perplexing sea of troubles than that confronting Andrew Johnson. What manner of man was this medium-built, dark-eyed, black-haired Tennessean, now chief executive by virtue of the bullet that killed Lincoln?

No citizen, not even Lincoln, has ever reached the White House from humbler beginnings. Born to impoverished parents in North Carolina and early orphaned, Johnson never attended school but was apprenticed to a tailor at age ten. Ambitious to get ahead, he taught himself to read, and later his wife taught him to write and do simple arithmetic. Like many another self-made man, he was inclined to overpraise his maker.

President Andrew Johnson (1808–1875) *An "accidental president," Andrew Johnson was the only chief executive to be impeached by the House, though narrowly acquitted by the Senate. A former U.S. senator from Tennessee, he was reelected in 1875 to the Senate that had formally tried him seven years earlier. As he said in a public speech in 1866, "I love my country. Every public act of my life testifies that is so. Where is the man who can put his finger upon one act of mine . . . to prove the contrary." (Library of Congress.)*

Johnson early became active in politics in Tennessee, to which he had moved when seventeen years old. He shone as an impassioned champion of the poor whites against the planter aristocrats, although he himself ultimately owned a few slaves. He excelled as a two-fisted stump speaker before angry and heckling crowds, among whom on occasion he could hear a pistol being cocked. Elected to Congress, he attracted much favorable attention in the North (but not the South) when he refused to secede with his own state. After Tennessee was partially "redeemed" by Union armies, he was appointed war governor and served courageously in an atmosphere of danger.

Destiny next thrust Johnson into the vice-presidency. Lincoln's Union party in 1864 needed to attract support from the War

Democrats and other pro-Southern elements, and Johnson, a Democrat, seemed to be the ideal man. Unfortunately, he appeared at the vice-presidential inaugural ceremonies the following March in a scandalous condition. He had recently been afflicted with typhoid fever, and although not known as a heavy drinker, he was urged by his friends to take a stiff bracer of whiskey. This he did—with disgraceful results.

"Old Andy" Johnson was no doubt a man of parts—unpolished parts. He was intelligent, able, forceful, and gifted with homespun honesty. Steadfastly devoted to duty and to the people, he was a dogmatic champion of states' rights and the Constitution. He would often present a copy of the document to visitors, and he was buried with one as a pillow.

Yet the man who had raised himself from the tailor's bench to the president's chair was a misfit. A Southerner who did not understand the North, a Tennessean who had earned the distrust of the South, a Democrat who had

Johnson as a Parrot *He was constantly invoking the Constitution. (Harper's Weekly.)*

never been accepted by the Republicans, a president who had never been elected to the office, he was not at home in a Republican White House. Hotheaded, contentious, and stubborn, he was the wrong man in the wrong place at the wrong time. A Reconstruction policy devised by the angels might well have failed in his tactless hands.

Presidential Reconstruction

Even before the shooting war had ended, the political war over Reconstruction had begun. Abraham Lincoln believed that the Southern states had never legally withdrawn from the Union. Their formal restoration to the Union would therefore be relatively simple. Accordingly, Lincoln in 1863 proclaimed his "10 percent" Reconstruction plan. It decreed that a state could be reintegrated into the Union when 10 percent of its voters in the presidential election of 1860 had taken an oath of allegiance to the United States and pledged to abide by emancipation. The next step would be formal erection of a state government. Lincoln would then recognize the purified regime.

Lincoln's proclamation provoked a sharp reaction in Congress, where Republicans feared the restoration of the planter aristocracy to power and the possible re-enslavement of the blacks. Republicans therefore rammed through Congress in 1864 the Wade-Davis Bill. It required that 50 percent of a state's voters take the oath of allegiance and demanded stronger safeguards for emancipation than Lincoln's as the price of readmission. Lincoln "pocket-vetoed" this bill by refusing to sign it after Congress had adjourned. Republicans were outraged. They refused to seat delegates from Louisiana after that state had reorganized its government in accordance with Lincoln's 10 percent plan in 1864.

The controversy surrounding the Wade-Davis Bill had revealed deep differences between the president and Congress. Unlike Lincoln, many in Congress insisted that the seceders had indeed left the Union—had "committed suicide" as republican states—and

had therefore forfeited all their rights. They could be readmitted only as "conquered provinces" on such conditions as Congress should decree.

This episode further revealed differences among Republicans. Two factions were emerging. The majority moderate group tended to agree with Lincoln that the seceded states should be restored to the Union as simply and swiftly as reasonable—though on Congress's terms, not the president's. The minority radical group believed that the South should suffer more severely for its sins. Before the South should be restored, the radicals wanted its social structure uprooted, the haughty planters punished, and the helpless blacks protected by federal power.

Some of the radicals were secretly pleased when the assassin's bullet felled Lincoln, for the martyred president had shown tenderness toward the South. Spiteful "Andy" Johnson, who shared their hatred for the planter aristocrats, would presumably also share their desire to reconstruct the South with a rod of iron.

Johnson soon disillusioned them. He agreed with Lincoln that the seceded states had never legally been outside the Union. Thus, he quickly recognized several of Lincoln's 10 percent governments, and on May 29, 1865, he issued his own Reconstruction proclamation. It disfranchised certain leading Confederates, in-

Before President Johnson softened his Southern policy, his views were radical. Speaking on April 21, 1865, he declared: "It is not promulgating anything that I have not heretofore said to say that traitors must be made odious, that treason must be made odious, that traitors must be punished and impoverished. They must not only be punished, but their social power must be destroyed. If not, they will still maintain an ascendancy, and may again become numerous and powerful; for, in the words of a former Senator of the United States, 'When traitors become numerous enough, treason becomes respectable.'"

cluding those with taxable property worth more than $20,000, though they might petition him for personal pardons. It called for special state conventions, which were required to repeal the ordinances of secession, repudiate all Confederate debts, and ratify the slave-freeing Thirteenth Amendment. States that complied with these conditions, Johnson declared, would be readmitted.

Johnson, savoring his dominance over the high-toned aristocrats who now begged his favor, granted pardons in abundance. Bolstered by the political resurrection of the planter elite, the recently rebellious states moved rapidly in the second ·half of 1865 to organize governments. But as the pattern of the new governments became clear, Republicans of all stripes grew furious.

The Baleful Black Codes

Among the first acts of the new Southern regimes sanctioned by Johnson was the passage of the iron-toothed Black Codes. These laws were designed to regulate the affairs of the emancipated blacks, much as the slave statutes had done in pre–Civil War days. The Black Codes aimed, first of all, to ensure a stable labor supply. The crushed Cotton Kingdom could not rise from its weeds until the fields were once again put under hoe and plow—and many whites feared that black field hands and plow drivers would not work unless forced to do so.

Severe penalties were therefore imposed by the codes on blacks who "jumped" their labor contracts, which usually committed them to work for the same employer for one year, and generally at pittance wages. Violators could be made to forfeit back wages or could be forcibly dragged back to work by a paid "Negro-catcher." In Mississippi the captured freedmen could be fined and then hired out to pay their fines—an arrangement that closely resembled slavery itself.

The codes also sought to restore as nearly as possible the pre-emancipation system of race relations. Freedom was legally recognized, as were some other privileges, such as the right to

Early in 1866 one congressman quoted a Georgian: "The blacks eat, sleep, move, live, only by the tolerance of the whites, who hate them. The blacks own absolutely nothing but their bodies; their former masters own everything, and will sell them nothing. If a black man draws even a bucket of water from a well, he must first get the permission of a white man, his enemy. . . . If he asks for work to earn his living, he must ask it of a white man; and the whites are determined to give him no work, except on such terms as will make him a serf and impair his liberty."

A Family of Sharecroppers at the End of the Civil War *They were free at last, but most freed slaves would have to wait a century or more to escape slavery's cruel legacy of poverty, ignorance, and discrimination. (Valentine Museum.)*

marry. But all the codes forbade a black to serve on a jury; some even barred blacks from renting or leasing land. A black could be punished for "idleness" by being sentenced to work on a chain gang. Nowhere were blacks allowed to vote.

These oppressive laws mocked the ideal of freedom, so recently purchased by buckets of blood. The Black Codes imposed terrible burdens on the unfettered blacks, struggling against ignorance and poverty to make their way as free persons. The worst features of the Black Codes would eventually be repealed, but their revocation could not by itself lift the liberated blacks into economic independence. Lacking capital, and with little to offer but their labor, thousands of impoverished former slaves slipped into the status of sharecropper farmers, as did many landless whites. Luckless sharecroppers gradually sank into a morass of virtual peonage and remained there for generations. Formerly slaves to masters, countless blacks as well as poorer whites in effect became slaves to the soil and to their creditors. Yet the dethroned planter aristocracy resented even this pitiful concession to freedom. Sharecropping was the "wrong policy," said one planter. "It makes the laborer too independent; he becomes a partner, and has a right to be consulted."

The Black Codes made an ugly impression in the North. If the former slaves were being re-enslaved, people asked one another, had not the Boys in Blue spilled their blood in vain? Had the North really won the war?

Congressional Reconstruction

These questions grew more insistent when the congressional delegations from the newly reconstituted Southern states presented themselves in the Capitol in December 1865. To the shock and disgust of the Republicans, many former Confederate leaders were on hand to claim their seats.

The appearance of these ex-rebels was a natural but costly blunder. Voters of the South, seeking able representatives, had turned instinctively to their experienced statesmen. But most of the Southern leaders were tainted by active association with the "lost cause." Among them were four former Confederate generals, five colonels, and various members of the Richmond cabinet and Congress. Worst of all, there was the shrimpy but brainy Alexander Stephens, ex-vice-president of the Confederacy, still under indictment for treason.

The presence of these "whitewashed rebels" infuriated the Republicans in Congress. The war had been fought to restore the Union, but not on these kinds of terms. The Republicans were in no hurry to embrace their former enemies—virtually all of them Democrats—in the chambers of the Capitol. While the South had been "out" from 1861 to 1865, the Republicans in Congress had enjoyed a relatively free hand. They had passed much legislation that favored the North, such as the Morrill Tariff, the Pacific Railroad Act, and the Homestead Act. Now many Republicans balked at giving up this political advantage. On the first day of the congressional session, December 4, 1865, they banged shut the door in the face of the newly elected Southern delegations.

Looking to the future, the Republicans were alarmed to realize that a restored South would be stronger than ever in national politics. Before the war a black slave had counted as three-fifths of a person in apportioning congressional representation. Now the slave was five-fifths of a person. Eleven Southern states had seceded and been subdued by force of arms. But now, owing to full counting of free blacks, the rebel states were entitled to twelve more votes in Congress, and twelve more presidential electoral votes, than they had previously enjoyed. Again, angry voices in the North raised the cry: Who won the war?

Republicans had good reason to fear that ultimately they might be elbowed aside. Southerners might join hands with Democrats in the North and win control of Congress or maybe even the White House. If this happened, they could perpetuate the Black Codes, perhaps even formally re-enslave the blacks. They could dismantle the economic program of the Republican party by lowering tariffs, rerouting the transcontinental railroad, repealing the free-farm Homestead Act, possibly even repudiating the national debt. President Johnson thus deeply provoked the congressional Republicans when he announced on December 6, 1865, that the recently rebellious states had satisfied his conditions and that in his view the Union was now restored.

Johnson Clashes with Congress

A clash between president and Congress was now inevitable. It exploded into the open in February 1866, when the president vetoed a bill (later repassed) extending the life of the controversial Freedmen's Bureau.

Aroused, the Republicans swiftly struck back. In March 1866 they passed the Civil Rights Bill, which conferred on the blacks the privilege of American citizenship and struck at the Black Codes. President Johnson resolutely vetoed this forward-looking measure on constitutional grounds, but in April congressmen steamrollered it over his veto—something they repeatedly did henceforth. The hapless president, dubbed "Sir Veto" and "Andy Veto," had his presidential wings clipped short, as Congress assumed the dominant role in running the government. One critic called Johnson "the dead dog of the White House."

The Republicans now undertook to rivet the principles of the Civil Rights Bill into the Constitution as the Fourteenth Amendment. They feared that the Southerners might one day win control of Congress and repeal the hated law. The proposed amendment, as approved by Congress and sent to the states in June 1866, was

An Inflexible President *This Republican cartoon shows Johnson knocking blacks out of the Freedmen's Bureau by his veto. (Thomas Nast,* Harper's Weekly, *1866.)*

sweeping. It (1) conferred civil rights, including citizenship but excluding the franchise, on the freedmen; (2) reduced proportionately the representation of a state in Congress and in the Electoral College if it denied blacks the ballot; (3) disqualified from federal and state office for-

Principal Reconstruction Proposals and Plans

YEAR	PROPOSAL OR PLAN
1864–1865	Lincoln's 10 percent proposal
1865–1866	Johnson's version of Lincoln's proposal
1866–1867	Congressional plan: 10 percent plan with Fourteenth Amendment
1867–1877	Congressional plan of military Reconstruction: Fourteenth Amendment plus black suffrage, later established nationwide by Fifteenth Amendment

Andrew Johnson's Reconstruction Policies Criticized *"Dost thou mock me?" an Othello-like black soldier asks Andrew Johnson, rendered as Shakespeare's Iago. Johnson's mild Reconstruction policies were sharply criticized by Republicans who wanted to take stronger measures to protect and help the freed slaves. Black troops who had fought for the Union felt particularly betrayed by Johnson's policies. (Library of Congress.)*

mer Confederates who as federal officeholders had once sworn "to support the Constitution of the United States"; and (4) guaranteed the federal debt, while repudiating all Confederate debts. (See text of Fourteenth Amendment in the Appendix.)

The radical faction was disappointed that the Fourteenth Amendment did not grant the right to vote, but all Republicans were agreed that no state should be welcomed back into the Union fold without first ratifying the Fourteenth Amendment. Yet President Johnson advised the Southern states to reject it, and all of the "sinful eleven," except Tennessee, defiantly spurned the amendment. Their spirit was reflected in a Southern song:

And I don't want no pardon for what I was or
  am,
I won't be reconstructed and I don't give a
  damn.

Swinging 'Round the Circle with Johnson

As 1866 lengthened, the battle grew between the Congress and the president. The root of the controversy was Johnson's "10-percent" governments that had passed the most severe Black Codes. Congress had tried to temper the worst features of the codes by extending the life of the embattled Freedmen's Bureau and passing the Civil Rights Bill. Both measures Johnson had vetoed. Now the issue was whether Reconstruction was to be carried on with or without the drastic Fourteenth Amendment. The Republicans would settle for nothing less.

The crucial congressional elections of 1866—more crucial than some presidential elections—were fast approaching. President Johnson was naturally eager to escape from the clutch of Congress by securing a majority favorable to his soft-on-the-South policy. Invited to dedicate a Chicago monument to Stephen A. Douglas, he undertook to speak at various cities en route in support of his views.

Johnson's famous "swing around the circle," beginning in the late summer of 1866, was a seriocomedy of errors. The president delivered a series of "give 'em hell" speeches, in which he accused the radicals in Congress of having planned large-scale antiblack riots and murder in the South. As he spoke, hecklers hurled insults at him. Reverting to his stump-speaking days in Tennessee, he shouted back angry retorts, amid cries of "You be damned" and "Don't get mad, Andy." The dignity of his high office sank to a new low, as the old charges of drunkenness were revived.

As a vote-getter, Johnson was highly successful—for the opposition. His inept speechmaking heightened the cry "Stand by Congress" against the "Tailor of the Potomac." When the ballots were counted, the Republicans had rolled up more than a two-thirds majority in both Houses of Congress.

Republican Principles and Programs

The Republicans now had a veto-proof Congress and virtually unlimited control of Reconstruction policy. But moderates and radicals still disagreed over the best course to pursue in the South.

The radicals in the Senate were led by the courtly and principled idealist Charles Sumner, now recovered from his prewar caning on the Senate floor, who tirelessly labored not only for black freedom but for racial equality. In the House the most powerful radical was Thaddeus Stevens, crusty and vindictive congressman from Pennsylvania. Seventy-four years old in 1866, he was a curious figure, with a protruding lower lip, a heavy black wig covering his bald head, and a deformed foot. An unswerving friend of blacks, he had defended runaway

Representative Thaddeus Stevens, in a congressional speech on January 3, 1867, urged the ballot for blacks out of concern for them and out of bitterness against the whites: "I am for Negro suffrage in every rebel state. If it be just, it should not be denied; if it be necessary, it should be adopted; if it be a punishment to traitors, they deserve it."

Thaddeus Stevens (1792–1868)   Stevens, who regarded the seceded states as "conquered provinces," promoted much of the major Reconstruction legislation, including the Fourteenth (civil rights) Amendment. Reconstruction, he said, must "revolutionize Southern institutions, habits, and manners. . . . The foundation of their institutions . . . must be broken up and relaid, or all our blood and treasure have been spent in vain." (Library of Congress.)

slaves without fee and, before dying, insisted on burial in a black cemetery. His affectionate devotion to blacks was matched by his vitriolic hatred of rebellious white Southerners. A masterly parliamentarian with a razor-sharp mind and withering wit, Stevens was a leading figure on the Joint (House-Senate) Committee on Reconstruction.

Still opposed to rapid restoration of the Southern states, the radicals wanted to keep them out as long as possibe and apply federal power to bring about a drastic social and economic transformation in the South. But moderate Republicans, more attuned to time-honored Republican principles of states' rights and self-government, recoiled from the full implications of the radical program. They preferred policies that restrained the states from abridging citizens' rights, rather than policies that directly involved the federal government in individual lives. The actual policies adopted by Congress showed the influence of both these schools of thought, though the moderates, as the majority faction, had the upper hand. And one thing both groups had come to agree on by 1867 was the necessity to enfranchise black voters, even if it took federal troops to do it.

Reconstruction by the Sword

Against a backdrop of vicious and bloody race riots that had erupted in several Southern cities, Congress passed the Military Reconstruction Act of March 2, 1867. Supplemented by later measures, this drastic legislation divided the South into five military districts, each commanded by a Union general and policed by blue-clad soldiers, about twenty thousand all

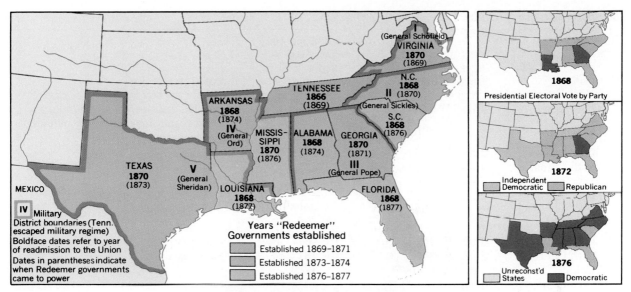

Military Reconstruction, 1867 (five districts and commanding generals)
For many white Southerners, military Reconstruction amounted to turning the knife in the wound of
defeat. An often-repeated story of later years had a Southerner remark, "I was sixteen years old before
I discovered that damnyankee was two words."

told. The act also temporarily disfranchised tens
of thousands of former Confederates.

Congress additionally laid down stringent
conditions for the readmission of the seceded
states. The wayward states were required to ratify the Fourteenth Amendment, giving the former slaves their rights as citizens. The bitterest
pill of all to white Southerners was the stipulation that they guarantee in their state constitutions full suffrage for their former adult male
slaves. Yet the act, reflecting moderate sentiment, stopped short of giving the freedmen land
or education at federal expense. The overriding
purpose of the moderates was to create an electorate in Southern states that would vote those
states back into the Union on acceptable terms
and thus free the federal government from direct responsibility for the protection of black
rights. As later events would demonstrate, this
approach proved woefully inadequate to the
cause of justice for the blacks.

The radical Republicans were still worried.
The danger loomed that once the unrepentant
states were readmitted, they would amend their
constitutions so as to withdraw the ballot from
the blacks. The only ironclad safeguard was to
incorporate black suffrage in the federal Consti-

tution. This goal was finally achieved by the Fifteenth Amendment, passed by Congress in
1869 and ratified by the required number of
states in 1870. (For text, see the Appendix.)

Military Reconstruction of the South not only
usurped certain functions of the president as
commander in chief but set up a martial regime
of dubious legality. The Supreme Court had already ruled, in the case *Ex parte Milligan*
(1866), that military tribunals could not try
civilians, even during wartime, in areas where
the civil courts were open. Peacetime military
rule seemed starkly contrary to the spirit of the
Constitution. But the circumstances were extraordinary in the Republic's history, and for the
time being the Supreme Court avoided giving
offense to the Republican Congress.

Prodded into line by federal bayonets, the
Southern states got on with the task of constitution making. By 1870 all of them had reorganized their governments and had been accorded
full rights. Yet the hated "bluebellies" remained
until the new Republican regimes—usually
called "radical" regimes—appeared to be firmly
entrenched. When the federal troops did leave a
state, its government swiftly passed into the
hands of white "Redeemers," or "Home Rule"

Southern Reconstruction by State

STATE	READMITTED TO REPRESENTATION IN CONGRESS	HOME RULE (DEMOCRATIC OR "REDEEMER" REGIME) REESTABLISHED	COMMENTS
Tennessee	July 24, 1866		Ratified Fourteenth Amendment in 1866 and hence avoided military Reconstruction.*
Arkansas	June 22, 1868	1874	
North Carolina	June 25, 1868	1870	
Alabama	June 25, 1868	1874	
Florida	June 25, 1868	1877	Federal troops restationed in 1877, as result of Hayes-Tilden electoral bargain.
Louisiana	June 25, 1868	1877	Same as above.
South Carolina	June 25, 1868	1877	Same as above.
Virginia	January 26, 1870	1869	
Mississippi	February 23, 1870	1876	
Texas	March 30, 1870	1874	
Georgia	[June 25, 1868] July 15, 1870	1872	Readmitted June 25, 1868, but returned to military control after expulsion of blacks from legislature.

*For many years Tennessee was the only state of the secession to observe Lincoln's birthday as a legal holiday. Many Southern states still observe the birthdays of Jefferson Davis and Robert E. Lee.

regimes, which were invariably Democratic. Finally, in 1877, the last federal muskets were removed from state politics, and the "solid" Democratic South congealed.

The Realities of Radical Reconstruction in the South

The blacks now had freedom, of a sort. Their friends in Congress had only haltingly and somewhat belatedly secured the franchise for them. Both Presidents Lincoln and Johnson had proposed to give the ballot gradually to selected blacks who qualified for it through education, property ownership, or military service. Moderate Republicans and even many radicals at first hesitated to bestow suffrage on the freedmen. The Fourteenth Amendment, in many ways the heart of the Republican program for Reconstruction, had fallen short of guaranteeing the right to vote. (It envisioned for blacks the same status as women—citizenship without voting rights.) But by 1867 hesitation had given way to a hard determination to enfranchise the former

slaves wholesale and immediately, while thousands of white Southerners were being denied the vote. By glaring contrast most of the Northern states, before ratification of the Fifteenth

A white Virginian wrote from his deathbed: "Now with what will be my lastest breath, I here repeat and would willingly proclaim my unmitigated hatred to Yankee rule . . . and all connections with Yankees, and the perfidious, malignant and vile Yankee race." A Virginia woman noted at about the same time: "I have this morning witnessed a procession of nearly a thousand children belonging to colored schools. . . .When I thought that the fetters of ignorance were broken, and that they might not be forced from their parents and sold at auction to the highest bidder, my heart went up in adoring gratitude to the great God; not only on their account, but that we white people were no longer permitted to go on in such wickedness, heaping up more and more wrath of God upon our devoted heads."

Freedmen Voting, Richmond, Virginia, 1871   *The exercise of democratic rights by former slaves constituted a political and social revolution in the South, and was bitterly resented by whites. (The Granger Collection.)*

Amendment in 1870, withheld the ballot from their tiny black minorities. White Southerners naturally concluded that the Republicans were hypocritical in insisting that blacks in the South be allowed to vote.

In five states—Alabama, Florida, Louisiana, Mississippi, and South Carolina—the black voters enfranchised by the new state constitutions made up a majority of the electorate. But only in South Carolina did blacks predominate in the lower house of the legislature. No state senate had a black majority, and there were no black governors during what the whites called "black reconstruction." Many of the newly elected black legislators were literate and able; more than a few came from the ranks of the prewar free blacks who had acquired considerable education. More than a dozen black congressmen and two black United States senators, Hiram Revels and Blanche K. Bruce, both of Mississippi, did creditable work in the national capital.

Yet in many Southern capitals, former slaves held offices ranging from doorkeeper up to Speaker, to the bitter resentment of their one-time masters. Some untutored blacks fell under the control of white "scalawags" and "carpetbaggers," who used the blacks as political henchmen. The "scalawags" were Southerners, sometimes former Unionists and Whigs. By collaborating in creating the new regimes, they earned the undying enmity of the former Confederates, who accused them, often with wild exaggeration, of plundering the treasuries of the Southern states through their political influence in the radical governments. "Carpetbaggers" were mainly Northerners who supposedly had packed all their worldly goods into a single carpetbag suitcase at war's end and had come South to seek their fortune.

How well did the radical regimes rule? In many of them, graft did indeed run rampant. This was especially true in South Carolina and Louisiana, where conscienceless promoters and other pocket-padders used politically inexperienced blacks as cat's-paws. The worst "black-

Black Reconstruction A composite portrait of the first black senators and representatives in the 41st and 42nd congresses. Senator Hiram Revels, on the left, was elected in 1870 to the seat that had been occupied by Jefferson Davis when the South seceded. (The Granger Collection.)

and-white" legislatures purchased, as "legislative supplies," such "stationery" as hams, perfumes, suspenders, bonnets, corsets, champagne, and a coffin. One "thrifty" carpetbag governor in a single year "saved" $100,000 from a salary of $8,000. Yet this sort of corruption was by no means confined to the South in these postwar years. The crimes of the Reconstruction governments were no more outrageous than the scams and felonies being perpetrated in the North at the same time, especially in Boss Tweed's New York.

The radical legislatures also passed much desirable legislation and introduced many badly

needed reforms. For the first time in Southern history, steps were taken toward establishing adequate public schools. Tax systems were streamlined; public works were launched; and property rights were guaranteed to women. Many of these reforms were so welcome that they were retained by the all-white "redeemer" governments that later returned to power.

The Ku Klux Klan

Deeply embittered, some Southern whites resorted to savage measures against "radical" rule. Many whites resented the success and ability of black legislators as much as they resented alleged "corruption." A number of secret organizations mushroomed forth, the most notorious of which was the "Invisible Empire of the South," or Ku Klux Klan, founded in Tennessee in 1866. Besheeted night riders, their horses' hoofs muffled, would approach the cabin of an "upstart" black and hammer on the door. In ghoulish tones one thirsty horseman would demand a bucket of water. Then, under pretense of drinking, he would pour it into a rubber attachment concealed beneath his mask and gown, smack his lips, and declare that this was

In a 1900 speech Senator Tillman of South Carolina brutally boasted: "We preferred to have a United States army officer rather than a government of carpetbaggers and thieves and scallywags and scoundrels who had stolen everything in sight and mortgaged posterity . . . by issuing bonds. When that happened we took the government away. We stuffed the ballot boxes. We shot them. We are not ashamed of it."

the first water he had tasted since he was killed at the Battle of Shiloh. If fright did not produce the desired effect, force was employed.

Such tomfoolery and terror proved partially effective. Many ex-bondsmen and white "carpetbaggers," quick to take a hint, shunned the polls. Those stubborn souls who persisted in their "upstart" ways were flogged, mutilated, or even murdered. In one Louisiana parish in 1868, the whites in two days killed or wounded two hundred victims; a pile of twenty-five bodies was found half-buried in the woods. By such atrocious practices were blacks "kept in their place"—that is, down. The Klan became a refuge for numerous bandits and cutthroats. Any scoundrel could don a sheet.

Congress, outraged by this night-riding lawlessness, passed the harsh Force Acts of 1870 and 1871. Federal troops were able to stamp out much of the "lash law," but by this time the "Invisible Empire" had already done its work of intimidation. Many of the outlawed groups continued their tactics in the guise of "dancing clubs," "missionary societies," and "rifle clubs," though the net effect of all the hooded terrorists has probably been exaggerated. Economic reprisals were often more effective, especially when causing blacks to lose their jobs.

Attempts to empower the blacks politically failed miserably. The white South, for many decades, openly flouted the Fourteenth and Fifteenth Amendments. Wholesale disfranchisement of the blacks, starting conspicuously about 1890, was achieved by intimidation, fraud, and trickery. Among various underhanded schemes were the literacy tests, un-

The Ku Klux Klan   *A contemporary view of the Klan. (Archives of Rutherford B. Hayes Library.)*

The following excerpt is part of a heartrending appeal to Congress in 1871 by a group of Kentucky blacks:

"We believe you are not familiar with the description of the Ku Klux Klans riding nightly over the country, going from county to county, and in the county towns, spreading terror wherever they go by robbing, whipping, ravishing, and killing our people without provocation, compelling colored people to break the ice and bathe in the chilly waters of the Kentucky River.

"The [state] legislature has adjourned. They refused to enact any laws to suppress Ku-Klux disorder. We regard them [the Ku-Kluxers] as now being licensed to continue their dark and bloody deeds under cover of the dark night. They refuse to allow us to testify in the state courts where a white man is concerned. We find their deeds are perpetrated only upon colored men and white Republicans. We also find that for our services to the government and our race we have become the special object of hatred and persecution at the hands of the Democratic Party. Our people are driven from their homes in great numbers, having no redress only [except] the United States court, which is in many cases unable to reach them."

Persons in United States Lynched
[by race], 1882–1970*

YEAR	WHITES	BLACKS	TOTAL
1882	64	49	113
1885	110	74	184
1890	11	85	96
1895	66	113	179
1900	9	106	115
1905	5	57	62
1910	9	67	76
1915	13	56	69
1920	8	53	61
1925	0	17	17
1930	1	20	21
1935	2	18	20
1940	1	4	5
1945	0	1	1
1950	1	1	2
1965	0	0	0

*There were no lynchings in 1965–1970. In every year from 1882 (when records were first kept) to 1964, the number of lynchings corresponded roughly to the figures given here. The worst year was 1892, when 161 blacks and 69 whites were lynched (total 230); the next worst was 1884, when 160 whites and 51 blacks were lynched (total 211).

fairly administered by whites to the advantage of illiterate whites. In the eyes of white Southerners, the goal of white supremacy fully justified dishonorable devices.

Johnson Walks the Impeachment Plank

Radicals meanwhile had been sharpening their hatchets for President Johnson. Annoyed by the obstruction of the "drunken tailor" in the White House, they falsely accused him of maintaining there a harem of "dissolute women." Not content with curbing his authority, they decided to remove him altogether by constitutional processes.* Under existing law the president pro tempore of the Senate, the unscrupulous and

*For impeachment, see Art. I, Sec. II, para. 5; Art. I, Sec. III, paras. 6, 7; Art. II, Sec. IV, in the Appendix.

rabidly radical "Bluff Ben" Wade of Ohio, would then become president.

As an initial step, Congress in 1867 passed the Tenure of Office Act—as usual over Johnson's veto. Contrary to precedent, the new law required the president to secure the consent of the Senate before he could remove his appointees once they had been approved by that body. One purpose was to freeze into the cabinet the secretary of war, Edwin M. Stanton, a holdover from the Lincoln administration. Though outwardly loyal to Johnson, he was secretly serving as a spy and informer for the radicals. Another purpose was to goad Johnson into breaking the law and thus establish grounds for his impeachment.

An aroused Johnson was eager to get a test case before the Supreme Court, for he believed the Tenure of Office Act to be unconstitutional. (That slow-moving tribunal finally ruled indirectly in his favor fifty-eight years later.) Expecting reasonable judicial speed, Johnson abruptly dismissed the two-faced Stanton early in 1868. The president did not believe that the law applied to Lincoln's holdovers, even though the radicals insisted otherwise.

A radical-influenced House of Representatives struck back swiftly. By a count of 126 to 47, it voted to impeach Andrew Johnson for "high crimes and misdemeanors," as called for by the Constitution. Most of the specific accusations grew out of the president's so-called violation of the ("unconstitutional") Tenure of Office Act. Two additional articles related to Johnson's verbal assaults on the Congress, involving "disgrace, ridicule, hatred, contempt, and reproach."

A black leader protested to whites in 1868: "It is extraordinary that a race such as yours, professing gallantry, chivalry, education, and superiority, living in a land where ringing chimes call child and sire to the Gospel of God—that with all these advantages on your side, you can make war upon the poor defenseless black man."

A Not-Guilty Verdict for Johnson

With evident zeal, the radical-led Senate now sat as a court to try Johnson on the dubious impeachment charges. The House conducted the prosecution. The trial aroused intense public interest and, with one thousand tickets printed, proved to be the biggest show of 1868. Johnson kept his dignity and sobriety and maintained a discreet silence. His battery of attorneys was extremely able, while the House prosecutors, including oily-tongued Benjamin F. Butler and embittered Thaddeus Stevens, bungled their flimsy case.

On May 16, 1868, the day for the first voting in the Senate, the tension was electric, and heavy breathing could be heard in the galleries. By a margin of only one vote, the radicals failed to muster the two-thirds majority for Johnson's removal. Seven independent-minded Republican senators, courageously putting country above party, voted "not guilty."

The radicals were infuriated. "The country is going to the Devil!" cried the crippled Stevens as he was carried from the hall. President-to-be Wade had even chosen his cabinet, with the unscrupulous Benjamin F. Butler as secretary of state. But the nation, though violently aroused, accepted the verdict with a good temper that did credit to its political maturity. In a

less stable republic, an armed uprising might have erupted against the president.

The nation thus narrowly avoided a bad precedent that would have gravely weakened one of the three branches of the federal government. Johnson was clearly guilty of bad speeches, bad judgment, and bad temper, but not of "high crimes and misdemeanors." From the standpoint of the radicals, his greatest crime had been to stand inflexibly in their path.

The Purchase of Alaska

Johnson's administration, though largely reduced to a figurehead, achieved its most enduring success in the field of foreign relations.

The Russians by 1867 were in a mood to sell the vast and chilly expanse now known as Alaska. They had already overextended themselves in North America, and they saw that in the likely event of another war with England, they probably would lose their defenseless province to the sea-dominant British. Alaska, moreover, had been ruthlessly "furred out" and was a growing economic liability. The Russians were therefore eager to unload their "frozen asset" on the Americans, and they put out seductive feelers in Washington. They preferred the United States to any other purchaser, primarily because they wanted to strengthen further the

Alaska and the Lower Forty-Eight States (a size comparison)

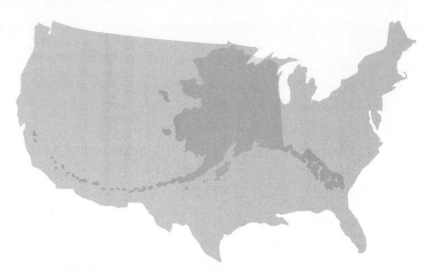

Republic as a barrier against their ancient enemy, Britain.

In 1867 Secretary of State Seward, an ardent expansionist, signed a treaty with Russia that transferred Alaska to the United States for the bargain price of $7.2 million. But Seward's enthusiasm for these frigid wastes was not shared by his ignorant or uninformed countrymen, who jeered at "Seward's Folly," "Seward's Icebox," "Frigidia," and "Walrussia." The American people, still preoccupied with Reconstruction and other internal vexations, were economyminded and antiexpansionist.

Then why did Congress and the American public sanction the purchase? For one thing Russia, alone among the powers, had been conspicuously friendly to the North during the recent Civil War. Americans did not feel that they could offend their great and good friend, the czar, by hurling his walrus-covered icebergs back into his face. Besides, the territory was rumored to be teeming with furs, fish, and gold, and it might yet "pan out" profitably—as it later did with natural resources, including oil and gas. So Congress and the country accepted "Seward's Polar Bear Garden," somewhat wryfacedly and derisively but nevertheless hopefully.

The Heritage of Reconstruction

Many white Southerners regarded Reconstruction as a more grievous wound than the war itself. It left an angry scar that would take generations to heal. They resented the upending of their social and racial system, the humiliation of being ruled by blacks, and the insult of federal intervention in their local affairs. Yet few rebellions have ended with the victors sitting down to a love feast with the vanquished. Given the explosiveness of the issues that had caused the war, and the bitterness of the fighting, the wonder is that Reconstruction was not far harsher

The remarkable ex-slave Frederick Douglass wrote in 1882: "Though slavery was abolished, the wrongs of my people were not ended. Though they were not slaves, they were not yet quite free. No man can be truly free whose liberty is dependent upon the thought, feeling, and action of others, and who has himself no means in his own hands for guarding, protecting, defending, and maintaining that liberty. Yet the Negro after his emancipation was precisely in this state of destitution. . . . He was free from the individual master, but the slave of society. He had neither money, property, nor friends. He was free from the old plantation, but he had nothing but the dusty road under his feet. He was free from the old quarter that once gave him shelter, but a slave to the rains of summer and the frosts of winter. He was, in a word, literally turned loose, naked, hungry, and destitute, to the open sky."

than it was. The fact is that Lincoln, Johnson, and most Republicans had no clear picture at war's end of what federal policy toward the South should be. Policymakers groped their way, influenced as much by Southern responses to defeat and emancipation as by any plans of their own to impose a specific program on the South.

The Republicans acted from a mixture of idealism and political expediency. They wanted both to protect the freed slaves and to promote the fortunes of the Republican party. In the end, their efforts backfired badly. Republican Reconstruction conferred only fleeting benefits on the blacks, envenomed the whites, and virtually extinguished the Republican party in the South for nearly one hundred years.

In the light of hindsight, the Republican Reconstruction program seems too narrowly conceived. Moderate Republicans in particular never appreciated the efforts necessary to make the freed slaves completely independent citizens, nor the lengths to which Southern whites would go to preserve their system of racial dominance. Had Thaddeus Stevens's radical program of drastic economic reforms and heftier protection of political rights been enacted, things might well have been different. But ingrained American resistance to tampering with property rights and violating the principle of local self-government, combined with spreading indifference in the North to the plight of the blacks, formed too formidable an obstacle.

CHRONOLOGY

1863	Lincoln announces "10 percent" Reconstruction plan
1864	Lincoln vetoes Wade-Davis Bill
1865	Johnson proclaims presidential Reconstruction
	Congress refuses to seat Southern congressmen
	Freedmen's Bureau established
	Southern states pass Black Codes
1866	Congress passes Civil Rights Bill over Johnson's veto
	Congress passes Fourteenth Amendment
	Johnson-backed candidates lose congressional election
	Ex parte Milligan case
	Ku Klux Klan founded
1867	Military Reconstruction Act
	Tenure of Office Act
	United States purchases Alaska from Russia
1868	Johnson impeached and acquitted
	Johnson pardons Confederate leaders
1870	Fifteenth Amendment ratified
1870–1871	Force Acts
1872	Freedmen's Bureau ended
1877	Military Reconstruction ends

Varying Viewpoints

Few topics have triggered as much intellectual warfare as the "dark and bloody ground" of Reconstruction. The period provoked questions—sectional, racial, and constitutional—about which people felt deeply and remain deeply divided even today. Scholarly argument goes back conspicuously to a Columbia University historian, William A. Dunning, whose students, in the early years of the twentieth century, published a series of histories of the Reconstruction South. Dunning and his disciples were influenced by the turn-of-the-century spirit of sectional conciliation as well as by current theories about black racial inferiority. Sympathizing with the white South, they wrote about Reconstruction as a kind of national disgrace, foisted upon a prostrate region by vindictive, self-seeking radical Republican politicians. If the South had wronged the North by seceding, the North had wronged the South by reconstructing.

A second cycle of scholarship in the 1920s was impelled by a widespread suspicion that the Civil War itself had been a tragic and unnecessary blunder. Attention now shifted to Northern politicians. Scholars like Howard Beale further questioned the motives of the radical Republicans. To Beale and others, the radicals had masked a ruthless desire to exploit Southern labor and resources behind a false front of "concern" for the freed slaves. Moreover, Northern advocacy of black voting rights was merely a calculated attempt to ensure a Republican political presence in the defeated South. The unfortunate Andrew Johnson, in this view, had valiantly tried to uphold constitutional principles in the face of this cynical Northern onslaught.

Following the Second World War, Kenneth Stampp, among others, turned this view on its head. Influenced by the modern civil rights movement, Stampp argued that Reconstruction had been a noble attempt to extend American principles of equity and justice. The radical Republicans and the carpetbaggers were now heroes, while Andrew Johnson was castigated for his obstinate racism. By the early 1970s, this view had become orthodoxy, and it generally holds sway today. Yet some scholars such as Michael Benedict and Leon Litwack, disillusioned with the inability to achieve full racial justice in the 1960s, began once more to scrutinize the motives of Northern politicians immediately after the Civil War. They claimed to discover that Reconstruction had never been very radical and that the Freedmen's Bureau and other agencies had merely allowed the white planters to maintain their dominance over local politics and the local economy.

More recently, Eric Foner has powerfully reasserted the argument that Reconstruction was a truly radical and noble attempt to establish an interracial democracy. Drawing upon the work of black scholar W. E. B. Du Bois, Foner emphasizes the comparative approach to the American Reconstruction. Clearly, Foner admits, Reconstruction did not create full equality, but it did allow blacks to form political organizations and churches, to vote, and to establish some measure of economic independence. In South Africa, the Caribbean, and other areas once marked by slavery, the freed slaves never received these opportunities. Many of the benefits of Reconstruction were taken away by white southerners during the Gilded Age, but in the twentieth century, the constitutional principles and organizations developed during Reconstruction provided the focus and foundation for the modern civil-rights movement—which some have called the Second Reconstruction.

Select Readings

Primary Source Documents

Booker T. Washington's classic autobiography *Up from Slavery** (1901) records one freedman's experiences. Contemporary comments on the process of Reconstruction include the laments of editor Edwin L. Godkin, *The Nation* (December 7, 1871, p. 364),* and Frederick Douglass, *Life and Times of Frederick Douglass** (1882), as well as the debates in the *Congressional Globe* (1867–1868)* between radicals like Thaddeus Stevens and moderates like Lyman Trumbull.

Secondary Sources

Eric Foner, *Reconstruction: America's Unfinished Revolution, 1863–1877* (1988) is a superb synthesis of current scholarship. Overall accounts may be found in James G. Randall and David Donald, *The Civil War and Reconstruction* (rev. ed., 1969), and James McPherson, *Ordeal By Fire: The Civil War and Reconstruction* (1981), perhaps the best brief introduction. Lincoln's early efforts at Reconstruction are handled in Peyton McCrary, *Abraham Lincoln and Reconstruction* (1978); LaWanda Cox, *Lincoln and Black Freedom* (1981); and Herman Belz, *Emancipation and Equal Rights* (1978). Willie Lee Rose engagingly describes a *Rehearsal for Reconstruction: The Port Royal Experiment* (1964). Otis A. Singletary discusses *The Negro Militia and Reconstruction* (1957). Dan Carter, *When the War Was Over: The Failure of Self-Reconstruction in the South, 1865–1867* (1985), charts the first years of the period. Following up the story of national politics is Eric L. McKitrick, *Andrew Johnson and Reconstruction: Principle and Prejudice, 1865–1866* (1963). Sympathetic to the radical Republicans are James M. McPherson, *The Struggle for Equality* (1964), and Hans L. Trefousse, *The Radical Republicans* (1969). See also David Montgomery, *Beyond Equality: Labor and the Radical Republicans, 1862–1872* (1967). Siding with the radicals in the impeachment fight are Michael L. Benedict, *The Impeachment and Trial of Andrew Johnson* (1973), and Hans L. Trefousse, *Impeachment of a President* (1975). Conditions in the South are analyzed in W. E. B. Du Bois's controversial classic *Black Reconstruction* (1935) and in Leon F. Litwack's brilliantly evocative *Been in the Storm So Long* (1979), a revealing study of the initial responses, by both blacks and whites, to emancipation. An excellent account of the Southern economy after the war is Gavin Wright, *Old South, New South: Revolutions in the Southern Economy Since the Civil War* (1986). It can be usefully supplemented by Roger Ransom and Richard L. Sutch, *One Kind of Freedom: The Economic Consequences of Emancipation* (1977). See also James Roark, *Masters without Slaves: Southern Planters in the Civil War and Reconstruction* (1977), and Lawrence Powell, *New Masters: Northern Planters during the Civil War and Reconstruction* (1980). Roger Shugg, *Origins of Class Struggle in Louisiana* (1968), Dwight Billings, *Planters and the Making of a "New South": Class, Politics and Development in North Carolina, 1865–1900* (1979), and Jonathan Wiener, *Social Origins of the New South: Alabama, 1860–1885* (1978), elucidate the political economy of the postbellum South. Joel Williamson offers a psychological portrait of race relations in *The Crucible of Race: Black-White Relations in the American South Since Emancipation* (1984). Consult also Thomas Holt, *Black over White: Negro Political Leadership in South Carolina during Reconstruction* (1977). C. Vann Woodward's *The Strange Career of Jim Crow* (rev. ed., 1974) is a classic study of the origins of segregation. His views have drawn criticism in Harold O. Rabinowitz, *Race Relations in the Urban South, 1865–1890* (1977). See also Rabinowitz's *Southern Black Leaders of the Reconstruction Era* (1982). Special studies of value are William P. Vaughn, *Schools for All* (1974); William S. McFeely, *Yankee Stepfather: General O. O. Howard and the Freedmen* (1968); William C. Gillette, *The Right to Vote: Politics and the Passage of the 15th Amendment* (1965); Stanley I. Kutler, *Judicial Power and Reconstruction Politics* (1968); Harold M. Hyman, *A More Perfect Union: The Impact of the Civil War and Reconstruction on the Constitution* (1973). Richard N. Current rehabilitates the maligned carpetbaggers in *Those Terrible Carpetbaggers* (1988). Fresh scholarship is presented in Kenneth M. Stampp and Leon Litwack, eds., *Reconstruction: An Anthology of Revisionist*

---

* An asterisk indicates that the document, or an excerpt from it, can be found in Thomas A. Bailey and David M. Kennedy, eds., *The American Spirit: United States History as Seen by Contemporaries, 7th ed.* (Lexington, Mass.: D.C. Heath and Company, 1991).

Writings (1969), and Robert P. Swierenga, ed., *Beyond the Civil War Synthesis* (1975). J. Morgan Kousser and James M. McPherson, eds., *Region, Race, and Reconstruction: Essays in Honor of C. Vann Woodward* (1982), contains some intriguing essays. Eric Foner looks at emancipation in a comparative perspective in *Nothing but Freedom* (1983). A comprehensive study of the climax of this troubled period is William Gillette, *Retreat from Reconstruction, 1869–1879* (1979). Also see Michael Perman, *The Road to Redemption: Southern Politics, 1869–1879* (1984).

Appendix

Declaration of Independence

In Congress, July 4, 1776

The Unanimous Declaration of the Thirteen United States of America

[Bracketed material in color has been inserted by the authors. For adoption background, see pp. 126–127.]

When, in the course of human events, it becomes necessary for one people to dissolve the political bands which have connected them with another, and to assume, among the powers of the earth, the separate and equal station to which the laws of nature and of nature's God entitle them, a decent respect to the opinions of mankind requires that they should declare the causes which impel them to the separation.

We hold these truths to be self-evident: That all men are created equal; that they are endowed by their Creator with certain unalienable rights; that among these are life, liberty, and the pursuit of happiness; that, to secure these rights, governments are instituted among men, deriving their just powers from the consent of the governed; that whenever any form of government becomes destructive of these ends, it is the right of the people to alter or to abolish it, and to institute new government, laying its foundation on such principles, and organizing its powers in such form, as to them shall seem most likely to effect their safety and happiness. Prudence, indeed, will dictate that governments long established should not be changed for light and transient causes; and accordingly all experience hath shown that mankind are more disposed to suffer, while evils are sufferable, than to right themselves by abolishing the forms to which they are accustomed. But when a long train of abuses and usurpations, pursuing invariably the same object, evinces a design to reduce them under absolute despotism, it is their right, it is their duty, to throw off such government, and to provide new guards for their future security. Such has been the patient sufferance of these colonies; and such is now the necessity which constrains them to alter their former systems of government. The history of the present King of Great Britain is a history of repeated injuries and usurpations, all having in direct object the establishment of an absolute tyranny over these states. To prove this, let facts be submitted to a candid world.

He has refused his assent to laws, the most wholesome and necessary for the public good. [See royal veto, p. 105.]

He has forbidden his governors to pass laws of immediate and pressing importance, unless suspended in their operation till his assent should be obtained; and, when so suspended, he has utterly neglected to attend to them.

He has refused to pass other laws for the accommodation of large districts of people [by establishing new counties], unless those people would relinquish the right of representation in the legislature, a right inestimable to them, and formidable to tyrants only.

He has called together legislative bodies at places unusual, uncomfortable, and distant from the depository of their public records, for the sole purpose of fatiguing them into compliance with his measures. [E.g., removal of Massachusetts Assembly to Salem, 1774.]

He has dissolved representative houses repeatedly, for opposing, with manly firmness, his invasions on the rights of the people. [E.g., Virginia Assembly, 1765.]

He has refused for a long time, after such dissolutions, to cause others to be elected; whereby the legislative powers, incapable of annihilation, have returned to the people at large for their exercise; the state remaining, in the mean time, exposed to all the dangers of invasions from without and convulsions within.

He has endeavored to prevent the population [populating] of these states; for that purpose obstructing the laws for naturalization of foreigners; refusing to pass others to encourage their migration hither, and raising the conditions of new appropriations of lands. [E.g., Proclamation of 1763, p. 99.]

He has obstructed the administration of justice, by refusing his assent to laws for establishing judiciary powers.

He has made judges dependent on his will alone, for the tenure of their offices, and the amount and payment of their salaries. [See Townshend Acts, p. 110.]

He has erected a multitude of new offices, and sent hither swarms of officers to harass our people and eat out their substance. [See enforcement of Navigation Laws, p. 112.]

He has kept among us, in times of peace, standing armies, without the consent of our legislatures. [See pp. 107, 111.]

He has affected to render the military independent of, and superior to, the civil power.

He has combined with others to subject us to a jurisdiction foreign to our constitution, and unacknowledged by our laws, giving his assent to their acts of pretended legislation:

For quartering large bodies of armed troops among us [see Boston Massacre, p. 110.];

For protecting them, by a mock trial, from punishment for any murders which they should commit on the inhabitants of these states [See 1774 Acts, pp. 113–114];

For cutting off our trade with all parts of the world [See Boston Port Act, p. 114];

For imposing taxes on us without our consent [see Stamp Act, p. 107];

For depriving us, in many cases, of the benefits of trial by jury;

For transporting us beyond seas, to be tried for pretended offenses;

For abolishing the free system of English laws in a neighboring province [Quebec], establishing therein an arbitrary government, and enlarging its boundaries, so as to render it at once an example and fit instrument for introducing the same absolute rule into these colonies [Quebec Act, p. 114];

For taking away our charters, abolishing our most valuable laws, and altering fundamentally the forms of our governments [E.g., in Massachusetts, p. 114];

For suspending our own legislatures, and declaring themselves invested with power to legislate for us in all cases whatsoever [see Stamp Act repeal, p. 109].

He has abdicated government here, by declaring us out of his protection and waging war against us. [Proclamation, p. 124.]

He has plundered our seas, ravaged our coasts, burned our towns, and destroyed the lives of our people. [E.g., the burning of Falmouth (Portland), p. 124]

He is at this time transporting large armis of foreign mercenaries [Hessians, p. 124] to complete the works of death, desolation, and tyranny already begun with circumstances of cruelty and perfidy scarcely paralleled in the most barbarous ages, and totally unworthy the head of a civilized nation.

He has constrained our fellow-citizens, taken captive on the high seas [by impressment], to bear arms against their country, to become the executioners of their friends and brethren, or to fall themselves by their hands.

He has excited domestic insurrection among us [i.e., among slaves], and has endeavored to bring on the inhabitants of our frontiers the merciless Indian savages, whose known rule of warfare is an undistinguished destruction of all ages, sexes, and conditions.

In every stage of these oppressions we have petitioned for redress in the most humble terms; our repeated petitions have been answered only by repeated injury. [E.g., pp. 122–125.] A prince, whose character is thus marked by every act which may define a tyrant, is unfit to be the ruler of a free people.

Nor have we been wanting in our attentions to our British brethren. We have warned them, from time to time, of attempts by their legislature to extend an unwarrantable jurisdiction over us. We have reminded them of the circumstances of our emigration and settlement here. We have appealed to their native justice and magnanimity; and we have conjured them, by the ties of our common kindred, to disavow these usurpations, which would inevitably interrupt our connections and correspondence. They, too, have been deaf to the voice of justice and of consanguinity [blood relationship]. We must, therefore, acquiesce in the necessity which denounces [announces] our separation, and hold them, as we hold the rest of mankind, enemies in war, in peace friends.

We, therefore, the representatives of the United States of America, in General Congress assembled, appealing to the Supreme Judge of the world for the rectitude of our intentions, do, in the name and by the authority of the good people of these colonies, solemnly publish and declare, That these United Colonies are, and of right ought to be, FREE AND INDEPENDENT STATES; that they are absolved from all allegiance to the British crown, and that all political connection between them and the state of Great Britain is, and ought to be, totally dissolved; and that, as free and independent states, they have full power to levy war, conclude peace, contract alliances, establish commerce, and do all other acts and things which independent states may of right do. And for the support of this declaration, with a firm reliance on the protection of Divine Providence, we mutually pledge to each other our lives, our fortunes, and our sacred honor.

[Signed by]   JOHN HANCOCK [President]
                                                     [and fifty-five others]

Constitution of the United States of America

[Boldface headings and bracketed explanatory matter and marginal comments (both in color) have been inserted for the reader's convenience. Passages that are no longer operative are printed in italic type.]

PREAMBLE

On "We the people," see p. 258n.

We the people of the United States, in order to form a more perfect union, establish justice, insure domestic tranquillity, provide for the common defense, promote the general welfare, and secure the blessings of liberty to ourselves and our postcrity, do ordain and establish this CONSTITUTION for the United States of America.

Article I.   Legislative Department

Section I.   Congress

Legislative power vested in a two-house Congress. All legislative powers herein granted shall be vested in a Congress of the United States, which shall consist of a Senate and a House of Representatives.

Section II.   House of Representatives

1. The people elect representatives biennially. The House of Representatives shall be composed of members chosen every second year by the people of the several States, and the electors [voters] in each State shall have the qualifications requisite for electors of the most numerous branch of the State Legislature.

2. Who may be representatives. No person shall be a Representative who shall not have attained to the age of twenty-five years, and been seven years a citizen of the United States, and who shall not, when elected, be an inhabitant of that State in which he shall be chosen.

See 1787 compromise, p. 155.

See 1787 compromise, p. 155.

3. Representation in the House based on population; census. Representatives and direct taxes[1] shall be apportioned among the several States which may be included within this Union, according to their respective numbers, *which shall be determined by adding to the whole number of free persons, including those bound to service for a term of years* [apprentices and indentured servants], *and excluding Indians not taxed, three-fifths of all other persons* [slaves].[2] The actual enumeration [census] shall be made within three years after the first meeting of the Congress of the United States, and within every subsequent term of ten years, in such manner as they shall by law direct. The number of Representatives shall not exceed one for every thirty thousand, but each State shall have at least one Representative; *and until such enumeration shall be made, the State of New Hampshire shall be entitled to choose three, Massachusetts eight, Rhode Island and Providence Plantations one, Connecticut five, New York six, New Jersey four, Pennsylvania eight, Delaware one, Maryland six, Virginia ten, North Carolina five, South Carolina five, and Georgia three.*

---

[1] Modified in 1913 by the Sixteenth Amendment re income taxes (see p. 695).
[2] The word *slave* appears nowhere in the original, unamended Constitution. The three-fifths rule ceased to be in force when the Thirteenth Amendment was adopted in 1865 (see, p. 48 and amendments below).

4. Vacancies in the House are filled by election. When vacancies happen in the representation from any State, the Executive authority [governor] thereof shall issue writs of election [call a special election] to fill such vacancies.

See Chase and Johnson trials, pp. 194, 494; Nixon trial preliminaries, pp. 958–959.

5. The House selects its Speaker; has sole power to vote impeachment charges (i.e., indictments). The House of Representatives shall choose their Speaker and other officers; and shall have the sole power of impeachment.

Section III.   Senate

1. Senators represent the states. The Senate of the United States shall be composed of two Senators from each State, *chosen by the legislature thereof,*[1] for six years; and each Senator shall have one vote.

2. One-third of senators chosen every two years; vacancies. *Immediately after they shall be assembled in consequence of the first election, they shall be divided as equally as may be into three classes. The seats of the Senators of the first class shall be vacated at the expiration of the second year, of the second class at the expiration of the fourth year, and of the third class at the expiration of the sixth year,* so that one-third may be chosen every second year; *and if vacancies happen by resignation or otherwise, during the recess of the legislature of any State, the Executive* [governor] *thereof may make temporary appointments until the next meeting of the legislature, which shall then fill such vacancies.*[2]

3. Who may be senators. No person shall be a Senator who shall not have attained to the age of thirty years, and been nine years a citizen of the United States, and who shall not, when elected, be an inhabitant of that State for which he shall be chosen.

4. The vice-president presides over the Senate. The Vice-President of the United States shall be President of the Senate, but shall have no vote, unless they be equally divided [tied]

5. The Senate chooses its other officers. The Senate shall choose their other officers, and also a President *pro tempore*, in the absence of the Vice-President, or when he shall exercise the office of President of the United States.

See Chase and Johnson trials, pp. 194, 494.

6. The Senate has sole power to try impeachments. The Senate shall have the sole power to try all impeachments. When sitting for that purpose, they shall be on oath or affirmation. When the President of the United States is tried, the Chief Justice shall preside:[3] and no person shall be convicted without the concurrence of two-thirds of the members present.

7. Penalties for impeachment conviction. Judgment in cases of impeachment shall not extend further than to removal from office, and disqualification to hold and enjoy any office of honor, trust or profit under the United States: but the party convicted shall nevertheless be liable and subject to indictment, trial, judgment and punishment, according to law.

Section IV.   Election and Meetings of Congress

1. Regulation of elections. The times, places and manner of holding elections for Senators and Representatives shall be prescribed in each State by the legislature thereof; but the Congress may at any time by law make or alter such regulations, except as to the places of choosing Senators.

---

[1] Repealed in favor of popular election in 1913 by the Seventeenth Amendment.
[2] Changed in 1913 by the Seventeenth Amendment.
[3] The vice-president, as next in line, would be an interested party.

2. Congress must meet once a year. The Congress shall assemble at least once in every year, and such meeting *shall be on the first Monday in December, unless they shall by law appoint a different day.*[1]

Section V. Organization and Rules of the Houses

1. Each house may reject members; quorums. Each house shall be the judge of the elections, returns and qualifications of its own members, and a majority of each shall constitute a quorum to do business; but a smaller number may adjourn from day to day, and may be authorized to compel the attendance of absent members, in such manner, and under such penalties, as each house may provide.

See "Bully" Brooks case, pp. 410–411.

2. Each house makes its own rules. Each house may determine the rules of its proceedings, punish its members for disorderly behavior, and with the concurrence of two-thirds, expel a member.

3. Each house must keep and publish a record of its proceedings. Each house shall keep a journal of its proceedings, and from time to time publish the same, excepting such parts as may in their judgment require secrecy; and the yeas and nays of the members of either house on any question shall, at the desire of one-fifth of those present, be entered on the journal.

4. Both houses must agree on adjournment. Neither house, during the session of Congress, shall, without the consent of the other, adjourn for more than three days, nor to any other place than that in which the two houses shall be sitting.

Section VI. Privileges of and Prohibitions upon Congressmen

1. Congressional salaries; immunities. The Senators and Representatives shall receive a compensation for their services, to be ascertained by law and paid out of the treasury of the United States. They shall in all cases except treason, felony and breach of the peace, be privileged from arrest during their attendance at the session of their respective houses, and in going to and returning from the same; and for any speech or debate in either house, they shall not be questioned in any other place [i.e., they shall be immune from libel suits]

2. A congressman may not hold any other federal civil office. No Senator or Representative shall, during the time for which he was elected, be appointed to any civil office under the authority of the United States, which shall have been created, or the emoluments whereof shall have been increased, during such time; and no person holding any office under the United States shall be a member of either house during his continuance in office.

Section VII. Method of Making Laws

See 1787 compromise, p. 155.

Nixon, more than any predecessors, "impounded" billions of dollars voted by Congress for specific purposes, because he disapproved of them. The courts generally failed to sustain him, and his impeachment foes regarded wholesale impoundment as a violation of his oath to "faithfully execute" the laws.

1. Money bills must originate in the House. All bills for raising revenue shall originate in the House of Representatives; but the Senate may propose or concur with amendments as on other bills.

2. The president's veto power; Congress may override. Every bill which shall have passed the House of Representatives and the Senate, shall, before it become a law, be presented to the President of the United States; if he approve he shall sign it, but if not he shall return it with his objections to that house in which it shall have originated, who shall enter the objections at large on their journal, and proceed to reconsider it. If after such reconsideration two-thirds of that house shall agree to pass the bill, it shall be sent, together with the objections, to the other house, by which it shall likewise be recon-

---

[1] Changed in 1933 to January 3 by the Twentieth Amendment (see pp. 805–806 and below).

sidered, and, if approved by two-thirds of that house, it shall become a law. But in all such cases the votes of both houses shall be determined by yeas and nays, and the names of the persons voting for and against the bill shall be entered on the journal of each house respectively. If any bill shall not be returned by the President within ten days (Sundays excepted) after it shall have been presented to him, the same shall be a law, in like manner as if he had signed it, unless the Congress by their adjournment prevent its return, in which case it shall not be a law [this is the so-called pocket veto]

3. All measures requiring the agreement of both houses go to president for approval. Every order, resolution, or vote to which the concurrence of the Senate and House of Representatives may be necessary (except on a question of adjournment) shall be presented to the President of the United States; and before the same shall take effect, shall be approved by him, or being disapproved by him, shall be repassed by two-thirds of the Senate and House of Representatives, according to the rules and limitations prescribed in the case of a bill.

Section VIII.   Powers Granted to Congress

Congress has certain enumerated powers:

1. It may lay and collect taxes. The Congress shall have power to lay and collect taxes, duties, imposts, and excises, to pay the debts and provide for the common defense and general welfare of the United States; but all duties, imposts and excises shall be uniform throughout the United States;

2. It may borrow money. To borrow money on the credit of the United States;

3. It may regulate foreign and interstate trade. To regulate commerce with foreign nations, and among the several States, and with the Indian tribes;

4. It may pass naturalization and bankruptcy laws. To establish an uniform rule of naturalization, and uniform laws on the subject of bankruptcies throughout the United States;

For 1798 naturalization, see p. 180.

5. It may coin money. To coin money, regulate the value thereof, and of foreign coin, and fix the standard of weights and measures;

6. It may punish counterfeiters. To provide for the punishment of counterfeiting the securities and current coin of the United States;

7. It may establish a postal service. To establish post offices and post roads;

8. It may issue patents and copyrights. To promote the progress of science and useful arts by securing for limited times to authors and inventors the exclusive right to their respective writings and discoveries;

9. It may establish inferior courts. To constitute tribunals inferior to the Supreme Court;

See Judiciary Act of 1789, p. 168.

10. It may punish crimes committed on the high seas. To define and punish piracies and felonies committed on the high seas [i.e., outside the three-mile limit] and offenses against the law of nations [international law];

11. It may declare war; authorize privateers. To declare war,[1] grant letters of marque and reprisal,[2] and make rules concerning captures on land and water;

---

[1] Note that presidents, though they can provoke war (see the case of Polk, p. 374) or wage it after it is declared, cannot declare it.
[2] Papers issued private citizens in wartime authorizing them to capture enemy ships.

12. It may maintain an army. To raise and support armies, but no appropriation of money to that use shall be for a longer term than two years;[1]

13. It may maintain a navy. To provide and maintain a navy;

14. It may regulate the army and navy. To make rules for the government and regulation of the land and naval forces;

See Whiskey Rebellion, p. 171.

15. It may call out the state militia. To provide for calling forth the militia to execute the laws of the Union, suppress insurrections, and repel invasions;

16. It shares with the states control of militia. To provide for organizing, arming, and disciplining the militia, and for governing such part of them as may be employed in the service of the United States, reserving to the States respectively the appointment of the officers, and the authority of training the militia according to the discipline prescribed by Congress;

17. It makes laws for the District of Columbia and other federal areas. To exercise exclusive legislation in all cases whatsoever, over such district (not exceeding ten miles square) as may, by cession of particular States, and the acceptance of Congress, become the seat of government of the United States,[2] and to exercise like authority over all places purchased by the consent of the legislature of the State, in which the same shall be, for the erection of forts, magazines, arsenals, dock-yards, and other needful buildings; —and

Congress has certain implied powers:

This is the famous "elastic clause"; see p. 170.

18. It may make laws necessary for carrying out the enumerated powers. To make all laws which shall be necessary and proper for carrying into execution the foregoing powers, and all other powers vested by this Constitution in the government of the United States, or in any department or officer thereof.

Section IX.

Powers Denied to the Federal Government

See 1787 slave compromise, p. 156.

1. Congressional control of slave trade postponed until 1808. *The migration or importation of such persons as any of the States now existing shall think proper to admit shall not be prohibited by the Congress prior to the year 1808; but a tax or duty may be imposed on such importation, not exceeding $10 for each person.*

See Lincoln's unlawful suspension, p. 443.

2. The writ of habeas corpus[3] may be suspended only in case of rebellion or invasion. The privilege of the writ of habeas corpus shall not be suspended, unless when in cases of rebellion or invasion the public safety may require it.

3. Attainders[4] and ex post facto laws[5] forbidden. No bill of attainder or ex post facto law shall be passed.

4. Direct taxes must be apportioned according to population. No capitation [head or poll tax] or other direct, tax shall be laid, unless in proportion to the census or enumeration herein before directed to be taken.[6]

5. Export taxes fobidden. No tax or duty shall be laid on articles exported from any State.

---

[1] A reflection of fear of standing armies earlier expressed in the Declaration of Independence.

[2] The District of Columbia, ten miles square, was established in 1791 with a cession from Virginia (see p. 169).

[3] A writ of habeas corpus is a document that enables a person under arrest to obtain an immediate examination in court to ascertain whether he or she is being legally held.

[4] A bill of attainder is a special legislative act condemning and punishing an individual without a judicial trial.

[5] An ex post facto law is one that fixes punishments for acts committed before the law was passed.

[6] Modified in 1913 by the Sixteenth Amendment (see p. 695, and amendments below).

6. Congress must not discriminate among states in regulating commerce. No preference shall be given by any regulation of commerce or revenue to the ports of one State over those of another; nor shall vessels bound to, or from, one State, be obliged to enter, clear, or pay duties in another.

See Lincoln's unlawful infraction, p. 443.

7. Public money may not be spent without congressional appropriation; accounting. No money shall be drawn from the treasury, but in consequence of appropriations made by law; and a regular statement and account of the receipts and expenditures of all public money shall be published from time to time.

8. Titles of nobility prohibited; foreign gifts. No title of nobility shall be granted by the United States: and no person holding any office of profit or trust under them, shall, without the consent of the Congress, accept of any present, emolument, office, or title, of any kind whatever, from any king, prince, or foreign state.

Section X. Powers Denied to the States

Absolute prohibitions on the states:

On contracts, see Fletcher v. Peck, p. 235.

1. The states are forbidden to do certain things. No State shall enter into any treaty, alliance, or confederation; grant letters of marque and reprisal [i.e., authorize privateers]; coin money; emit bills of credit [issue paper money]; make anything but gold and silver coin a [legal] tender in payment of debts; pass any bill of attainder,[1] ex post facto,[1] or law impairing the obligation of contracts, or grant any title of nobility.

Conditional prohibitions on the states:

Cf. Confederation chaos, p. 147.

2. The states may not levy duties without the consent of Congress. No State shall, without the consent of the Congress, lay any imposts or duties on imports or exports, except what may be absolutely necessary for executing its inspection laws: and the net produce of all duties and imposts, laid by any State on imports or exports, shall be for the use of the treasury of the United States; and all such laws shall be subject to the revision and control of the Congress.

3. Certain other federal powers are forbidden the states except with the consent of Congress. No State shall, without the consent of Congress, lay any duty of tonnage [i.e., duty on ship tonnage], keep [nonmilitia] troops or ships of war in time of peace, enter into any agreement or compact with another State, or with a foreign power, or engage in war, unless actually invaded, or in such imminent danger as will not admit of delay.

Article II. Executive Department

Section I. President and Vice-President

1. The president is the chief executive; term of office. The executive power shall be vested in a President of the United States of America. He shall hold his office during the term of four years,[2] and, together with the Vice-President, chosen for the same term, be elected as follows:

See 1787 compromise, p. 155.

See 1876 Oregon case, p. 510.

2. The president is chosen by electors. Each State shall appoint, in such manner as the legislature thereof may direct, a number of electors, equal to the whole number of Senators and Representatives to which the State may be entitled in the Congress; but no Senator or Representative, or person holding an office of trust or profit under the United States, shall be appointed an elector.

---

[1] For definitions, see footnotes 4 and 5 on preceding page.
[2] No reference to reelection; for antithird term Twenty-second Amendment, see below.

A majority of the electoral votes needed to elect a president. *The electors shall meet in their respective States, and vote by ballot for two persons, of whom one at least shall not be an inhabitant of the same State with themselves. And they shall make a list of all the persons voted for, and of the number of votes for each; which list they shall sign and certify, and transmit sealed to the seat of government of the United States, directed to the President of the Senate. The President of the Senate shall, in the presence of the Senate and House of Representatives, open all the certificates, and the votes shall then be counted. The person having the greatest number of votes shall be the President, if such number be a majority of the whole number of electors appointed; and if there be more than one who have such majority, and have an equal number of votes, then the House of Representatives shall immediately choose by ballot one of them for President; and if no person have a majority, then from the five highest on the list the said house shall in like manner choose the President. But in choosing the President the votes shall be taken by States, the representation from each State having one vote; a quorum for this purpose shall consist of a member or members from two-thirds of the States, and a majority of all the States shall be necessary to a choice. In every case, after the choice of the President, the person having the greatest number of votes of the electors shall be the Vice-President. But if there should remain two or more who have equal votes, the Senate shall choose from them by ballot the Vice-President.* [1]

See Burr-Jefferson disputed election of 1800, p. 189.

See Jefferson as vice-president in 1796, p. 177.

3. Congress decides time of meeting of Electoral College. The Congress may determine the time of choosing the electors and the day on which they shall give their votes; which day shall be the same throughout the United States.

4. Who may be president. No person except a natural-born citizen, *or a citizen of the United States at the time of the adoption of this Constitution,* shall be eligible to the office of President; neither shall any person be eligible to that office who shall not have attained to the age of thirty-five years, and been fourteen years a resident within the United States [i.e., a legal resident]

To provide for foreign-born persons, like Alexander Hamilton, born in the British West Indies.

5. Replacements for president. In case of the removal of the President from office or of his death, resignation, or inability to discharge the powers and duties of the said office, the same shall devolve on the Vice-President, and the Congress may by law provide for the case of removal, death, resignation, or inability, both of the President and Vice-President, declaring what officer shall then act as President, and such officer shall act accordingly, until the disability be removed, or a President shall be elected.

Modified by Twentieth and Twenty-fifth Amendments below.

6. The president's salary. The President shall, at stated times, receive for his services a compensation, which shall neither be increased nor diminished during the period for which he shall have been elected, and he shall not receive within that period any other emolument from the United States, or any of them.

7. The president's oath of office. Before he enter on the execution of his office, he shall take the following oath or affirmation:—"I do solemnly swear (or affirm) that I will faithfully execute the office of the President of the United States, and will to the best of my ability preserve, protect and defend the Constitution of the United States."

Section II.   Powers of the President

See cabinet evolution, p. 167.

1. The president has important military and civil powers. The President shall be commander in chief of the army and navy of the United States, and of the militia of the several States, when called into the actual service of the United States; he may require

---

[1] Repealed in 1804 by the Twelfth Amendment (for text, see amendments below).

the opinion, in writing, of the principal officer in each of the executive departments, upon any subject relating to the duties of their respective offices, and he shall have power to grant reprieves and pardons for offenses against the United States, except in cases of impeachment.[1]

For president's removal power, see pp. 494–495.

2. The president may negotiate treaties and nominate federal officials. He shall have power, by and with the advice and consent of the Senate, to make treaties, provided two-thirds of the Senators present concur; and he shall nominate, and by and with the advice and consent of the Senate, shall appoint ambassadors, other public ministers and consuls, judges of the Supreme Court, and all other officers of the United States, whose appointments are not herein otherwise provided for, and which shall be established by law: but the Congress may by law vest the appointment of such inferior officers, as they think proper, in the President alone, in the courts of law, or in the heads of departments.

3. The president may fill vacancies during Senate recess. The President shall have power to fill up all vacancies that may happen during the recess of the Senate, by granting commissions which shall expire at the end of their next session.

Section III. Other Powers and Duties of the President

For president's personal appearances, see p. 695.

Messages; extra sessions; receiving ambassadors: execution of the laws. He shall from time to time give to the Congress information of the state of the Union, and recommend to their consideration such measures as he shall judge necessary and expedient; he may, on extraordinary occasions, convene both houses, or either of them, and in case of disagreement between them, with respect to the time of adjournment, he may adjourn them to such time as he shall think proper; he shall receive ambassadors and other public ministers; he shall take care that the laws be faithfully executed, and shall commission all the officers of the United States.

Section IV. Impeachment

See Johnson's acquittal p. 495; also Nixon's near impeachment, pp. 958–959.

Civil officers may be removed by impeachment. The President, Vice-President and all civil officers[2] of the United States shall be removed from office on impeachment for, and on conviction of, treason, bribery, or other high crimes and misdemeanors.

Article III. Judicial Department

Section I. The Federal Courts

See Judiciary Act of 1789, p. 168.

The judicial power belongs to the federal courts. The judicial power of the United States shall be vested in one Supreme Court, and in such inferior courts as the Congress may from time to time ordain and establish. The judges, both of the Supreme and inferior courts, shall hold their offices during good behavior, and shall, at stated times, receive for their services a compensation which shall not be diminished[3] during their continuance in office.

Section II. Jurisdiction of Federal Courts

1. Kinds of cases that may be heard. The judicial power shall extend to all cases, in law and equity, arising under this Constitution, the laws of the United States, and treaties made, or which shall be made, under their authority; —to all cases affecting ambassa-

---

[1] To prevent the president's pardoning himself or his close associates, as was feared in the case of Richard Nixon. See pp. 958–959.

[2] I.e., all federal executive and judicial officers, but not members of Congress or military personnel.

[3] In 1978, in a case involving federal judges, the Supreme Court ruled that diminution of salaries by inflation was irrelevant.

dors, other public ministers and consuls; —to all cases of admiralty and maritime jurisdiction; —to controversies to which the United States shall be a party; —to controversies between two or more States; —*between a State and citizens of another State;*[1] —between citizens of different States; —between citizens of the same State claiming lands under grants of different States, and between a State, or the citizens thereof, and foreign states, citizens or subjects.

2. Jurisdiction of the Supreme Court. In all cases affecting ambassadors, other public ministers and consuls, and those in which a State shall be party, the Supreme Court shall have original jurisdiction.[2] In all the other cases before mentioned, the Supreme Court shall have appellate jurisdiction,[3] both as to law and fact, with such exceptions, and under such regulations, as the Congress shall make.

3. Trial for federal crime is by jury. The trial of all crimes, except in cases of impeachment, shall be by jury; and such trial shall be held in the State where the said crimes shall have been committed; but when not committed within any State, the trial shall be at such place or places as the Congress may by law have directed.

Section III.   Treason

See Burr trial, p. 200.

1. Treason defined. Treason against the United States shall consist only in levying war against them, or in adhering to their enemies, giving them aid and comfort. No person shall be convicted of treason unless on the testimony of two witnesses to the same overt act, or on confession in open court.

2. Congress fixes punishment for treason. The Congress shall have power to declare the punishment of treason, but no attainder of treason shall work corruption of blood, or forfeiture except during the life of the person attainted.[4]

Article IV.   Relations of the States to One Another

Section I.   Credit to Acts, Records, and Court Proceedings

Each state must respect the public acts of the others. Full faith and credit shall be given in each State to the public acts, records, and judicial proceedings of every other State.[5] And the Congress may by general laws prescribe the manner in which such acts, records, and proceedings shall be proved [attested], and the effect thereof.

Section II.   Duties of States to States

This stipulation is sometimes openly flouted. In 1978 Governor Jerry Brown of California, acting on humanitarian grounds, refused to surrender to South Dakota an American Indian, Dennis Banks, who was charged with murder in an armed uprising.

1. Citizenship in one state is valid in all. The citizens of each State shall be entitled to all privileges and immunities of citizens in the several States.

2. Fugitives from justice must be surrendered by the state to which they have fled. A person charged in any State with treason, felony, or other crime, who shall flee from justice, and be found in another State, shall on demand of the executive authority [governor] of the State from which he fled, be delivered up, to be removed to the State having jurisdiction of the crime.

---

[1] The Eleventh Amendment (see amendments below) restricts this to suits by a state against citizens of another state.
[2] I.e., such cases must originate in the Supreme Court.
[3] I.e., it hears other cases only when they are appealed to it from a lower federal court or a state court.
[4] I.e., punishment only for the offender; none for his or her heirs.
[5] E.g., a marriage valid in one is valid in all.

*Basis of fugitive-
slave laws;
see pp. 389–390.*

3. Slaves and apprentices must be returned. *No person held to service or labor in one State, under the laws thereof, escaping into another, shall, in consequence of any law or regulation therein, be discharged from such service or labor, but shall be delivered up on claim of the party to whom such service or labor may be due.* [1]

Section III.   New States and Territories

*E.g., Maine (1820);
see p. 231.*

1. Congress may admit new states. New States may be admitted by the Congress into this Union; but no new State shall be formed or erected within the jurisdiction of any other State; nor any State be formed by the junction of two or more States, or parts of States, without the consent of the legislatures of the States concerned as well as of the Congress. [2]

2. Congress regulates federal territory and property. The Congress shall have power to dispose of and make all needful rules and regulations respecting the territory or other property belonging to the United States; and nothing in this Constitution shall be so construed as to prejudice any claims of the United States, or of any particular State.

Section IV.   Protection to the States

*See Cleveland and
the Pullman strike,
pp. 616–617.*

United States guarantees to states representative government and protection against invasion and rebellion. The United States shall guarantee to every State in this Union a republican form of government, and shall protect each of them against invasion; and on application of the legislature, or of the executive [governor] (when the legislature cannot be convened), against domestic violence.

Article V.   The Process of Amendment

The Constitution may be amended in four ways. The Congress, whenever two-thirds of both houses shall deem it necessary, shall propose amendments to this Constitution, or, on the application of the legislatures of two-thirds of the several States, shall call a convention for proposing amendments, which, in either case, shall be valid to all intents and purposes, as part of this Constitution, when ratified by the legislatures of three-fourths of the several States, or by conventions in three-fourths thereof, as the one or the other mode of ratification may be proposed by the Congress; provided *that no amendments which may be made prior to the year one thousand eight hundred and eight shall in any manner affect the first and fourth clauses in the ninth section of the first article;* [3] and that no State, without its consent, shall be deprived of its equal suffrage in the Senate.

Article VI.   General Provisions

*This pledge
honored by Hamilton,
p. 168.*

1. The debts of the Confederation are taken over. All debts contracted and engagements entered into, before the adoption of this Constitution, shall be as valid against the United States under this Constitution, as under the Confederation.

2. The Constitution, federal laws, and treaties are the supreme law of the land. This Constitution, and the laws of the United States which shall be made in pursuance thereof; and all treaties made, or which shall be made, under the authority of the United States, shall be the supreme law of the land; and the judges in every State shall be bound

---

[1] Invalidated in 1865 by the Thirteenth Amendment (for text see amendments below).
[2] Loyal West Virginia was formed by Lincoln in 1862 from seceded Virginia. This act was of dubious constitutionality and was justified in part by the wartime powers of the president. See pp. 433–434.
[3] This clause, re slave trade and direct taxes, became inoperative in 1808.

thereby, anything in the Constitution or laws of any State to the contrary notwithstanding.

3. Federal and state officers bound by oath to support the Constitution. The Senators and Representatives before mentioned, and the members of the several State legislatures, and all executive and judicial officers, both of the United States and of the several States, shall be bound by oath or affirmation to support this Constitution; but no religious test shall ever be required as a qualification to any office or public trust under the United States.

Article VII.   Ratification of the Constitution

See 1787 irregularity, p. 157.

The Constitution effective when ratified by conventions in nine states. The ratification of the conventions of nine States shall be sufficient for the establishment of this Constitution between the States so ratifying the same.

Done in Convention by the unanimous consent of the States present, the seventeenth day of September in the year of our Lord one thousand seven hundred and eighty-seven and of the Independence of the United States of America the twelfth. In witness whereof we have hereunto subscribed our names.

[Signed by]

G° WASHINGTON
Presidt and Deputy from Virginia
[and thirty-eight others]

AMENDMENTS TO THE CONSTITUTION

Amendment I.   Religious and Political Freedom

For background of Bill of Rights, see p. 167.

Congress must not interfere with freedom of religion, speech or press, assembly, and petition. Congress shall make no law respecting an establishment of religion,[1] or prohibiting the free exercise thereof; or abridging the freedom of speech, or of the press; or the right of the people peaceably to assemble, and to petition the government for a redress of grievances.

Amendment II.   Right to Bear Arms

The people may bear arms. A well-regulated militia being necessary to the security of a free State, the right of the people to keep and bear arms [i.e., for military purposes] shall not be infringed.[2]

Amendment III.   Quartering of Troops

See Declaration of Independence and British quartering above.

Soldiers may not be arbitrarily quartered on the people. No soldier shall, in time of peace, be quartered in any house without the consent of the owner, nor in time of war, but in a manner to be prescribed by law.

---

[1] In 1787 "an establishment of religion" referred to an "established church," or one supported by all taxpayers, whether members or not. But the courts have often acted under this article to keep religion, including prayers, out of the public schools.

[2] The courts, with "militia" in mind, have consistently held that the "right" to bear arms is a limited one.

Amendment IV. Searches and Seizures

A reflection of colonial grievances against crown.

Unreasonable searches are forbidden. The right of the people to be secure in their persons, houses, papers, and effects, against unreasonable searches and seizures, shall not be violated, and no [search] warrants shall issue but upon probable cause, supported by oath or affirmation, and particularly describing the place to be searched, and the persons or things to be seized.

Amendment V. Right to Life, Liberty, and Property

When witnesses refuse to answer questions in court, they routinely "take the Fifth Amendment."

The individual is guaranteed certain rights when on trial and the right to life, liberty, and property. No person shall be held to answer for a capital, or otherwise infamous crime, unless on a presentment [formal charge] or indictment of a grand jury, except in cases arising in the land or naval forces, or in the militia, when in actual service in time of war or public danger; nor shall any person be subject for the same offense to be twice put in jeopardy of life or limb; nor shall be compelled in any criminal case to be a witness against himself, nor be deprived of life, liberty, or property, without due process of law; nor shall private property be taken for public use [i.e., by eminent domain] without just compensation.

Amendment VI. Protection in Criminal Trials

See Declaration of Independence above.

An accused person has important rights. In all criminal prosecutions, the accused shall enjoy the right to a speedy and public trial, by an impartial jury of the State and district wherein the crime shall have been committed, which district shall have been previously ascertained by law, and to be informed of the nature and cause of the accusation; to be confronted with the witnesses against him; to have compulsory process [subpoena] for obtaining witnesses in his favor, and to have the assistance of counsel for his defense.

Amendment VII. Suits at Common Law

The rules of common law are recognized. In suits at common law, where the value in controversy shall exceed twenty dollars, the right of trial by jury shall be preserved, and no fact tried by a jury shall be otherwise re-examined in any court of the United States, than according to the rules of the common law.

Amendment VIII. Bail and Punishments

Excessive fines and unusual punishments are forbidden. Excessive bail shall not be required, nor excessive fines imposed, nor cruel and unusual punishments inflicted.

Amendment IX. Concerning Rights Not Enumerated

The Ninth and Tenth Amendments were bulwarks of southern states' rights before the Civil War.

The people retain rights not here enumerated. The enumeration in the Constitution, of certain rights, shall not be construed to deny or disparage others retained by the people.

Amendment X. Powers Reserved to the States and to the People

A concession to states' rights, p. 170.

Powers not delegated to the federal government are reserved to the states and the people. The powers not delegated to the United States by the Constitution, nor prohibited by it to the States, are reserved to the States respectively, or to the people.

Amendment XI.	Suits against a State

The federal courts have no authority in suits by citizens against a state. The judicial power of the United States shall not be construed to extend to any suit in law or equity, commenced or prosecuted against one of the United States by citizens of another State, or by citizens or subjects of any foreign state. [Adopted 1798.]

Amendment XII. Election of President and Vice-President

Forestalls repetition of 1800 electoral dispute, p. 190.

See 1876 disputed election, p. 509.

See 1824 election, pp. 246–247.

1. Changes in manner of electing president and vice-president; procedure when no presidential candidate receives electoral majority. The electors shall meet in their respective States, and vote by ballot for President and Vice-President, one of whom, at least, shall not be an inhabitant of the same State with themselves; they shall name in their ballots the person voted for as President, and in distinct ballots the person voted for as Vice-President, and they shall make distinct lists of all persons voted for as President, and of all persons voted for as Vice-President, and of the number of votes for each, which lists they shall sign and certify, and transmit sealed to the seat of government of the United States, directed to the President of the Senate; —the President of the Senate shall, in the presence of the Senate and House of Representatives, open all the certificates and the votes shall then be counted; —the person having the greatest number of votes for President shall be the President, if such number be a majority of the whole number of electors appointed; and if no person have such majority, then from the persons having the highest numbers not exceeding three on the list of those voted for as President, the House of Representatives shall choose immediately, by ballot, the President. But in choosing the President, the votes shall be taken by States, the representation from each State having one vote; a quorum for this purpose shall consist of a member or members from two-thirds of the States, and a majority of all the States shall be necessary to a choice. And if the House of Representatives shall not choose a President whenever the right of choice shall devolve upon them, before *the fourth day of March*[1] next following, then the Vice-President shall act as President, as in the case of the death or other constitutional disability of the President.

2. Procedure when no vice-presidential candidate receives electoral majority. The person having the greatest number of votes as Vice-President shall be the Vice-President, if such number be a majority of the whole number of electors appointed; and if no person have a majority, then from the two highest numbers on the list the Senate shall choose the Vice-President; a quorum for the purpose shall consist of two-thirds of the whole number of Senators, and a majority of the whole number shall be necessary to a choice. But no person constitutionally ineligible to the office of President shall be eligible to that of Vice-President of the United States. [Adopted 1804.]

Amendment XIII. Slavery Prohibited

For background, see p. 458.

Slavery forbidden. 1. Neither slavery[2] nor involuntary servitude, except as a punishment for crime whereof the party shall have been duly convicted, shall exist within the United States, or any place subject to their jurisdiction.

2. Congress shall have power to enforce this article by appropriate legislation. [Adopted 1865.]

---

[1] Changed to January 20 by the Twentieth Amendment (for text, see amendments below).
[2] The only explicit mention of slavery in the Constitution.

Amendment XIV.

Civil Rights for Ex-slaves,[1] etc.

*For background,
see p. 486.*

*For corporations
as "persons,"
see p. 543.*

1. Ex-slaves made citizens; U.S. citizenship primary. All persons born or naturalized in the United States, and subject to the jurisdiction thereof, are citizens of the United States and of the State wherein they reside. No State shall make or enforce any law which shall abridge the privileges or immunities of citizens of the United States; nor shall any State deprive any person of life, liberty, or property, without due process of law; nor deny to any person within its jurisdiction the equal protection of the laws.

*Abolishes
three-fifths rule
for slaves,
Art. I, Sec. II,
para. 3.*

2. When a state denies citizens the vote, its representation shall be reduced. Representatives shall be apportioned among the several States according to their respective numbers, counting the whole number of persons in each State, excluding Indians not taxed. But when the right to vote at any election for the choice of Electors for President and Vice-President of the United States, Representatives in Congress, the executive and judicial officers of a State, or the members of the legislature thereof, is denied to any of the male inhabitants of such State, being twenty-one years of age and citizens of the United States, or in any way abridged, except for participation in rebellion, or other crime, the basis of representation therein shall be reduced in the proportion which the number of such male citizens shall bear to the whole number of male citizens twenty-one years of age in such State.[2]

*Leading
ex-Confederates
denied office.
See p. 483.*

3. Certain persons who have been in rebellion are ineligible for federal and state office. No person shall be a Senator or Representative in Congress, or Elector of President and Vice-President, or hold any office, civil or military, under the United States, or under any State, who, having previously taken an oath, as a member of Congress, or as an officer of the United States, or as a member of any State legislature, or as an executive or judicial officer of any State, to support the Constitution of the United States, shall have engaged in insurrection or rebellion against the same, or given aid or comfort to the enemies thereof. But Congress may, by a vote of two-thirds of each house, remove such disability.

*The ex-Confederates
were thus forced to
repudiate their debts
and pay pensions to
their own veterans,
plus taxes for the
pensions of Union
veterans, their
conquerors.*

4. Debts incurred in aid of rebellion are void. The validity of the public debt of the United States, authorized by law, including debts incurred for payment of pensions and bounties for services in suppressing insurrection or rebellion, shall not be questioned. But neither the United States nor any State shall assume or pay any debt or obligation incurred in aid of insurrection or rebellion against the United States, or any claim for the loss or emancipation of any slave; but all such debts, obligations, and claims shall be held illegal and void.

5. Enforcement. The Congress shall have power to enforce, by appropriate legislation, the provisions of this article. [Adopted 1868.]

Amendment XV.

Suffrage for Blacks

*For background,
see p. 489.*

Black males are made voters. 1. The right of citizens of the United States to vote shall not be denied or abridged by the United States or by any State on account of race, color, or previous condition of servitude.

2. The Congress shall have power to enforce this article by appropriate legislation. [Adopted 1870.]

---

[1] Occasionally an offender is prosecuted under the Thirteenth Amendment for keeping an employee or other person under conditions approximating slavery.
[2] The provisions concerning "male" inhabitants were modified by the Nineteenth Amendment, which enfranchised women. The legal voting age was changed from twenty-one to eighteen by the Twenty-sixth Amendment.

Amendment XVI.	Income Taxes

For background, see pp. 617, 695.

Congress has power to lay and collect income taxes. The Congress shall have power to lay and collect taxes on incomes, from whatever source derived, without apportionment among the several States, and without regard to any census or enumeration. [Adopted 1913.]

Amendment XVII.	Direct Election of Senators

Senators shall be elected by popular vote. 1. The Senate of the United States shall be composed of two Senators from each State, elected by the people thereof, for six years; and each Senator shall have one vote. The electors in each State shall have the qualifications requisite for electors of [voters for] the most numerous branch of the State legislatures.

2. When vacancies happen in the representation of any State in the Senate, the executive authority of such State shall issue writs of election to fill such vacancies: Provided, that the Legislature of any State may empower the executive thereof to make temporary appointments until the people fill the vacancies by election as the Legislature may direct.

3. This amendment shall not be so construed as to affect the election or term of any Senator chosen before it becomes valid as part of the Constitution. [Adopted 1913.]

Amendment XVIII.	National Prohibition

For background, see p. 738.

The sale or manufacture of intoxicating liquors is forbidden. 1. *After one year from the ratification of this article the manufacture, sale, or transportation of intoxicating liquors within, the importation thereof into, or the exportation thereof from the United States and all territory subject to the jurisdiction thereof, for beverage purposes, is hereby prohibited.*

2. *The Congress and the several States shall have concurrent power to enforce this article by appropriate legislation.*

3. *This article shall be inoperative unless it shall have been ratified as an amendment to the Constitution by the legislatures of the several States, as provided by the Constitution, within seven years from the date of the submission thereof to the States by the Congress.* [Adopted 1919; repealed 1933 by Twenty-first Amendment.]

Amendment XIX.	Woman Suffrage

For background, see p. 715.

Women guaranteed the right to vote. 1. The right of citizens of the United States to vote shall not be denied or abridged by the United States or by any State on account of sex.

2. The Congress shall have power to enforce this article by appropriate legislation. [Adopted 1920.]

Amendment XX.	Presidential and Congressional Terms

Shortens lame-duck periods by modifying Art. I, Sec. IV, para. 2.

1. Presidential, vice-presidential, and congressional terms of office begin in January. The terms of the President and Vice-President shall end at noon on the 20th day of January, and the terms of Senators and Representatives at noon on the 3d day of January, of the years in which such terms would have ended if this article had not been ratified; and the terms of their successors shall then begin.

2. New meeting date for Congress. The Congress shall assemble at least once in every year, and such meeting shall begin at noon on the 3d day of January, unless they shall by law appoint a different day.

3. Emergency presidential and vice-presidential succession. If, at the time fixed for the beginning of the term of the President, the President-elect shall have died, the Vice-President-elect shall become President. If a President shall not have been chosen before the time fixed for the beginning of his term, or if the President-elect shall have failed to qualify, then the Vice-President-elect shall act as President until a President shall have qualified; and the Congress may by law provide for the case wherein neither a President-elect nor a Vice-President-elect shall have qualified, declaring who shall then act as President, or the manner in which one who is to act shall be selected, and such persons shall act accordingly until a President or Vice-President shall have qualified.

4. The Congress may by law provide for the case of the death of any of the persons from whom the House of Representatives may choose a President whenever the right of choice shall have devolved upon them, and for the case of the death of any of the persons from whom the Senate may choose a Vice-President whenever the right of choice shall have devolved upon them.

5. Sections 1 and 2 shall take effect on the 15th day of October following the ratification of this article.

6. This article shall be inoperative unless it shall have been ratified as an amendment to the Constitution by the Legislatures of three-fourths of the several States within seven years from the date of its submission. [Adopted 1933.]

Amendment XXI.   Prohibition Repealed

For background, see p. 795.

1. Eighteenth Amendment repealed. The eighteenth article of amendment to the Constitution of the United States is hereby repealed.

2. Local laws honored. The transportation or importation into any State, Territory, or Possession of the United States for delivery or use therein of intoxicating liquors, in violation of the laws thereof, is hereby prohibited.

3. This article shall be inoperative unless it shall have been ratified as an amendment to the Constitution by conventions in the several States, as provided in the Constitution, within seven years from the date of the submission thereof to the States by the Congress. [Adopted 1933.]

Amendment XXII.   Anti–Third Term Amendment

Sometimes referred to as the anti–Franklin Roosevelt amendment.

Presidential term is limited. 1. No person shall be elected to the office of President more than twice, and no person who has held the office of President, or acted as President, for more than two years of a term to which some other person was elected President shall be elected to the office of President more than once. But this article shall not apply to any person holding the office of President when this article was proposed by the Congress [i.e., Truman], and shall not prevent any person who may be holding the office of President, or acting as President, during the term within which this article becomes operative [i.e., Truman] from holding the office of President or acting as President during the remainder of such term.

2. This article shall be inoperative unless it shall have been ratified as an amendment to the Constitution by the legislatures of three-fourths of the several States within seven years from the date of its submission to the States by the Congress. [Adopted 1951.]

Amendment XXIII.

Designed to give the District of Columbia three electoral votes and to quiet the century-old cry of "No taxation without representation." Yet the District of Columbia still has only one nonvoting member of Congress.

District of Columbia Vote

1. Presidential electors for the District of Columbia. The District, constituting the seat of government of the United States, shall appoint in such manner as the Congress may direct:

A number of electors of President and Vice-President equal to the whole number of Senators and Representatives in Congress to which the District would be entitled if it were a State, but in no event more than the least populous State; they shall be in addition to those appointed by the States, but they shall be considered for the purposes of the election of President and Vice-President, to be electors appointed by a State; and they shall meet in the District and perform such duties as provided by the twelfth article of amendment.

2. Enforcement. The Congress shall have the power to enforce this article by appropriate legislation. [Adopted 1961.]

Amendment XXIV.

Designed to end discrimination against blacks and other poor folk. An aspect of the civil rights crusade under President Lyndon Johnson. See p. 930.

Poll Tax

1. Payment of poll tax or other taxes not to be prerequisite for voting in federal elections. The right of citizens of the United States to vote in any primary or other election for President or Vice-President, for electors for President or Vice-President, or for Senator or Representative in Congress, shall not be denied or abridged by the United States or any State by reason of failure to pay any poll tax or other tax.

2. Enforcement. The Congress shall have the power to enforce this article by appropriate legislation. [Adopted 1964.]

Amendment XXV.

Gerald Ford was the first "appointed president." See pp. 956, 960.

Presidential Succession and Disability

1. Vice-president to become president. In case of the removal of the President from office or of his death or resignation, the Vice-President shall become President.[1]

2. Successor to vice-president provided. Whenever there is a vacancy in the office of the Vice-President, the President shall nominate a Vice-President who shall take office upon confirmation by a majority vote of both Houses of Congress.

3. Vice-president to serve for disabled president. Whenever the President transmits to the President pro tempore of the Senate and the Speaker of the House of representatives his written declaration that he is unable to discharge the powers and duties of his office, and until he transmits to them a written declaration to the contrary, such powers and duties shall be discharged by the Vice-President as Acting President.

4. Procedure for disqualifying or requalifying president. Whenever the Vice-President and a majority of either the principal officers of the executive departments or of such other body as Congress may by law provide, transmit to the President pro tempore of the Senate and the Speaker of the House of Representatives their written declaration that the President is unable to discharge the powers and duties of his office, the Vice-President shall immediately assume the powers and duties of the office as Acting President.

Thereafter, when the President transmits to the President pro tempore of the Senate and the Speaker of the House of Representatives his written declaration that no inability

[1] The original Constitution (Art. II, Sec. I, para. 5) was vague on this point, stipulating that "the powers and duties" of the president, but not necessarily the title, should "devolve" on the vice-president. President Tyler, the first "accidental president," assumed not only the powers and duties but the title as well.

exists, he shall resume the powers and duties of his office unless the Vice-President and a majority of either the principal officers of the executive department [s] or of such other body as Congress may by law provide, transmit within four days to the President pro tempore of the Senate and the Speaker of the House of Representatives their written declaration that the President is unable to discharge the powers and duties of his office. Thereupon Congress shall decide the issue, assembling within forty-eight hours for that purpose if not in session. If the Congress, within twenty-one days after receipt of the latter written declaration, or, if Congress is not in session, within twenty-one days after Congress is required to assemble, determines by two-thirds vote of both Houses that the President is unable to discharge the powers and duties of his office, the Vice-President shall continue to discharge the same as Acting President; otherwise, the President shall resume the powers and duties of his office. [Adopted 1967.]

Amendment XXVI. Lowering Voting Age

A response to the current revolt of youth; see p. 950.

1. Ballot for eighteen-year-olds. The right of citizens of the United States, who are eighteen years of age or older, to vote shall not be denied or abridged by the United States or by any State on account of age.

2. Enforcement. The Congress shall have power to enforce this article by appropriate legislation. [Adopted 1971.]

An American Profile: The United States and Its People

Growth of U.S. Population and Area

CENSUS	POPULATION OF UNITED STATES	INCREASE OVER THE PRECEDING CENSUS		LAND AREA (SQ. MI.)	POP. PER SQ. MI.	PERCENT OF POP. IN URBAN AND RURAL TERRITORY	
		NUMBER	PERCENT			URBAN	RURAL
1790	3,929,214			867,980	4.5	5.1	94.9
1800	5,308,483	1,379,269	35.1	867,980	6.1	6.1	93.9
1810	7,239,881	1,931,398	36.4	1,685,865	4.3	7.2	92.8
1820	9,638,453	2,398,572	33.1	1,753,588	5.5	7.2	92.8
1830	12,866,020	3,227,567	33.5	1,753,588	7.3	8.8	91.2
1840	17,069,453	4,203,433	32.7	1,753,588	9.7	10.8	89.2
1850	23,191,876	6,122,423	35.9	2,944,337	7.9	15.3	84.7
1860	31,433,321	8,251,445	35.6	2,973,965	10.6	19.8	80.2
1870	39,818,449	8,375,128	26.6	2,973,965	13.4	24.9	75.1
1880	50,155,783	10,337,334	26.0	2,973,965	16.9	28.2	71.8
1890	62,947,714	12,791,931	25.5	2,973,965	21.2	35.1	64.9
1900	75,994,575	13,046,861	20.7	2,974,159	25.6	39.7	60.3
1910	91,972,266	15,997,691	21.0	2,973,890	30.9	45.7	54.3
1920	105,710,620	13,738,354	14.9	2,973,776	35.5	51.2	48.8
1930	122,775,046	17,064,426	16.1	2,977,128	41.2	56.2	43.8
1940	131,669,275	8,894,229	7.2	2,977,128	44.2	56.5	43.5
1950	150,697,361	19,028,086	14.5	2,974,726*	50.7	64.0	36.0
1960†	179,323,175	28,625,814	19.0	3,540,911	50.6	69.9	30.1
1970	203,235,298	23,912,123	13.3	3,536,855	57.5	73.5	26.5
1980	226,504,825	23,269,527	11.4	3,536,855	64.0	73.7	26.3
1990 (est.)	250,410,000	23,905,175	10.6	3,536,855	70.8	N.A.	N.A.

*As remeasured in 1940; shrinkage offset by increase in water area.
†First year for which figures include Alaska and Hawaii.
Source: Census Bureau, *Historical Statistics of the United States*, updated by relevant *Statistical Abstract of the United States*.

Characteristics of the U.S. Population

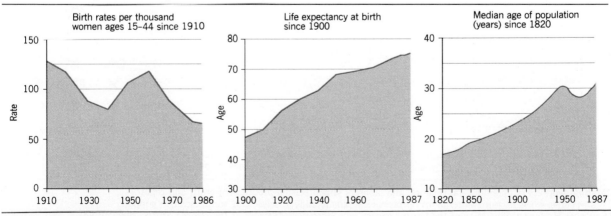

(Sources: *Historical Statistics of the United States* and *Statistical Abstract of the United States*, relevant years. Department of Health and Human Services, *Health, United States, 1988.*)

Changing Lifestyles in the Twentieth Century

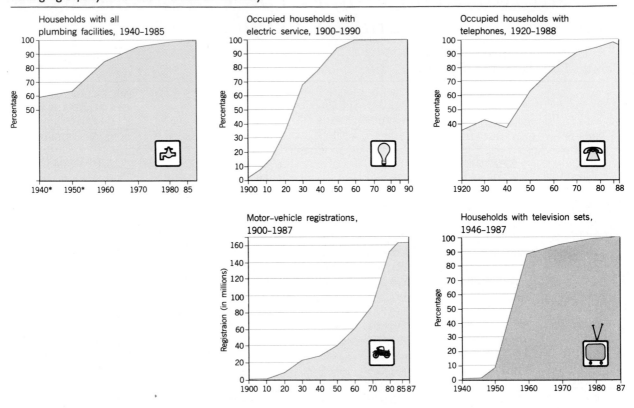

*Except for 1940 and 1950, figures are for "all plumbing facilities" (not defined in source). For 1940, figure is for flush toilet, inside structure, private use (64.7 percent had flush toilet, and private and/or shared inside structure, and 60.9 percent had installed bath or shower). For 1950, figure designates units with private toilet and bath, and hot running water (flush toilet, private or shared inside structure is 74.3 percent; installed bathtub or shower, 72.9 percent).
(Sources: *Historical Statistics of the United States* and *Statistical Abstract of the United States*, relevant years.)

Characteristics of the U.S. Labor Force

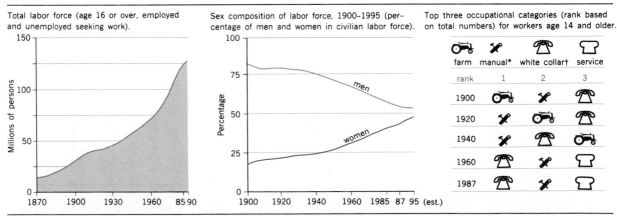

*Manual workers = operators, fabricators, and laborers plus precision production, craft, and repair.
†White collar workers = managerial and professional plus technical, sales, and administrative support.
(Sources: *Historical Statistics of the United States* and *Statistical Abstract of the United States*, relevant years, and Department of Labor Statistics, *Handbook of Labor Statistics*, relevant years.)

Leading Economic Sectors (Various Years)

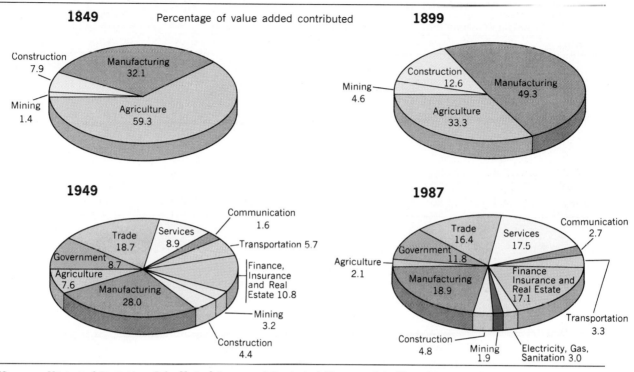

1849   Percentage of value added contributed   **1899**

1849:
- Construction 7.9
- Manufacturing 32.1
- Mining 1.4
- Agriculture 59.3

1899:
- Construction 12.6
- Mining 4.6
- Manufacturing 49.3
- Agriculture 33.3

1949   **1987**

1949:
- Trade 18.7
- Services 8.9
- Communication 1.6
- Transportation 5.7
- Government 8.7
- Agriculture 7.6
- Manufacturing 28.0
- Finance, Insurance and Real Estate 10.8
- Mining 3.2
- Construction 4.4

1987:
- Trade 16.4
- Services 17.5
- Communication 2.7
- Government 11.8
- Agriculture 2.1
- Manufacturing 18.9
- Finance, Insurance and Real Estate 17.1
- Transportation 3.3
- Construction 4.8
- Mining 1.9
- Electricity, Gas, Sanitation 3.0

(Sources: *Historical Statistics of the United States* and *Statistical Abstract of the United States*, relevant years.)

Per Capita Disposable Personal Income in Constant (1982) Dollars, 1929–1988

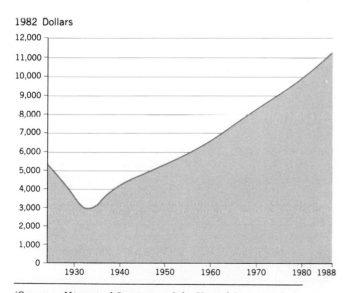

1982 Dollars

(Sources: *Historical Statistics of the United States* and *Statistical Abstract of the United States*.)

Comparative Tax Burdens (Percentage of Gross Domestic Product paid as taxes in major industrial countries, 1986)

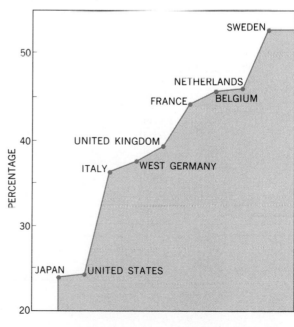

SWEDEN

NETHERLANDS

FRANCE   BELGIUM

UNITED KINGDOM

ITALY   WEST GERMANY

PERCENTAGE

JAPAN   UNITED STATES

Value of Imports by Place of Origin (Millions of Dollars)

| YEAR | WESTERN HEMISPHERE | | EUROPE | | ASIA | | AUSTRALIA AND OCEANIA | AFRICA |
	TOTAL	CANADA	TOTAL	U.K.	TOTAL	JAPAN		
1900	224	39	441	160	146	33	29	11
1910	503	95	806	271	210	66	20	17
1920	2,424	612	1,228	514	1,397	415	80	150
1930	1,195	402	911	210	854	279	33	68
1940	1,089	424	390	155	981	158	35	131
1950	5,063	1,960	1,449	335	1,638	182	208	494
1960	6,864	2,901	4,268	993	2,721	1,149	266	534
1970	16,928	11,092	11,395	2,194	9,621	5,875	871	1,113
1980	78,687	41,459	48,039	9,842	80,299	30,714	3,392	34,410
1987	117,954	71,085	97,419	17,341	174,452	84,575	4,136	11,939

Value of U.S. Exports by Destination

| YEAR | WESTERN HEMISPHERE | | EUROPE | | ASIA | | AUSTRALIA AND OCEANIA | AFRICA |
	TOTAL	CANADA	TOTAL	U.K.	TOTAL	JAPAN		
1900	227	95	1,040	534	68	29	41	19
1910	479	216	1,136	506	78	22	34	19
1920	2,553	972	4,466	1,825	872	378	172	166
1930	1,357	659	1,838	678	448	165	108	92
1940	1,501	713	1,645	1,011	619	227	94	161
1950	4,902	2,039	3,306	548	1,539	418	151	376
1960	7,684	3,810	7,398	1,487	4,186	1,447	514	793
1970	15,612	9,079	14,817	2,536	10,027	4,652	1,189	1,580
1980	74,114	35,395	71,372	12,694	60,168	20,792	4,876	9,060
1987	94,795	59,814	71,917	14,114	73,268	28,249	6,526	6,283

Principal Exports, 1900–1987 (Leading Three Exports by Value in Dollars)

YEAR	FIRST	SECOND	THIRD
1900	cotton	wheat and wheat flour	meat products
1910	cotton	machinery	petroleum and products
1920	cotton	wheat and wheat flour	petroleum and products
1930	machinery	cotton	petroleum and products
1940	machinery	iron and steel mill products	petroleum and products
1950	machinery	cotton	automobiles*
1960	machinery	automobiles*	wheat and wheat flour
1970	machinery	automobiles*	wheat and wheat flour
1980	machinery	road motor vehicles*	metals and manufactures
1987	automobiles, motor vehicles*	office machinery, computers	aircraft*

*includes parts

U.S. Foreign Trade, Ratio of Raw Materials to Manufactured Goods

YEAR	U.S. DOMESTIC EXPORTS		U.S. GENERAL IMPORTS	
	PERCENTAGE OF RAW MATERIALS	PERCENTAGE OF MANUFACTURED GOODS*	PERCENTAGE OF RAW MATERIALS	PERCENTAGE OF MANUFACTURED GOODS
1900	41.3	58.7	44.7	55.3
1910	40.0	60.0	46.4	53.6
1920	34.7	65.3	44.8	55.2
1930	26.7	73.3	45.8	54.2
1940	13.7	86.3	51.0	49.0
1950	26.8	73.2	47.7	52.3
1960	21.8	78.2	31.4	68.6
1970	17.2	82.8	16.8	83.2
1970	27	73	31.0	69.0
1980	29.6	70.4	45.0	55.0
1987*	21.3	78.7	19.8	80.2

*petroleum accounts for 55 percent of raw material imports

Value of Exports and Imports and Status of the Balance of Trade

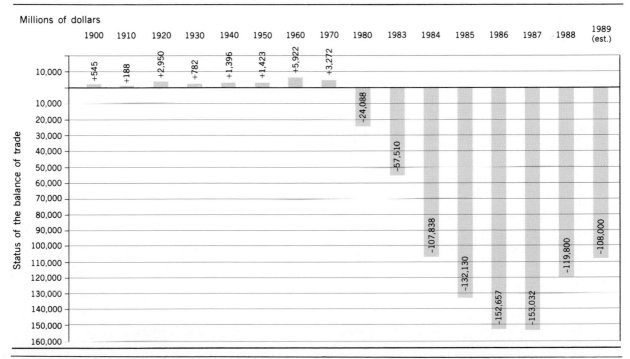

(Sources for tables and graph: *Historical Statistics of the United States* and *Statistical Abstract of the United States*, relevant years.)

Tariff Levies on Dutiable Imports, 1821–1987 (Ratio of Duties to Value of Dutiable Imports)

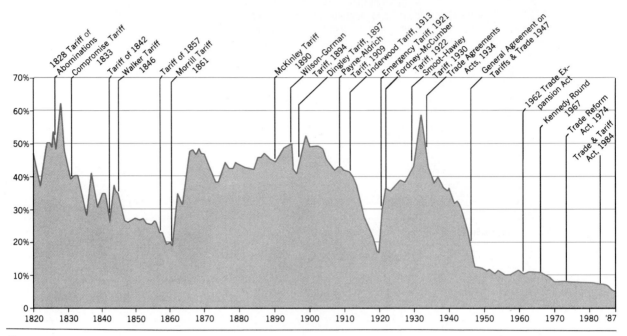

(Sources: *Historical Statistics of the United States* and *Statistical Abstract of the United States,* relevant years.)

Gross National Product in Current and Constant (1982) Dollars, 1900–1988

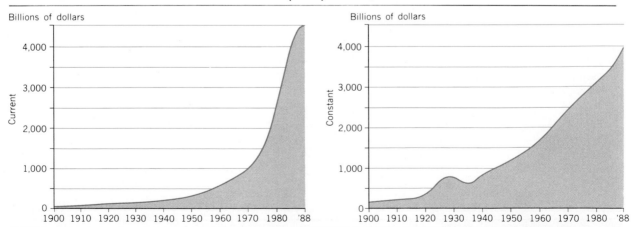

(Source: *1989 Economic Report of the President.*)

Presidential Elections *

ELECTION	CANDIDATES	PARTIES	POPULAR VOTE	ELECTORAL VOTE
1789	GEORGE WASHINGTON	No party designations		69
	JOHN ADAMS			34
	MINOR CANDIDATES			35
1792	GEORGE WASHINGTON	No party designations		132
	JOHN ADAMS			77
	GEORGE CLINTON			50
	MINOR CANDIDATES			5
1796	JOHN ADAMS	Federalist		71
	THOMAS JEFFERSON	Democratic-Republican		68
	THOMAS PINCKNEY	Federalist		59
	AARON BURR	Democratic-Republican		30
	MINOR CANDIDATES			48
1800	THOMAS JEFFERSON	Democratic-Republican		73
	AARON BURR	Democratic-Republican		73
	JOHN ADAMS	Federalist		65
	CHARLES C. PINCKNEY	Federalist		64
	JOHN JAY	Federalist		1
1804	THOMAS JEFFERSON	Democratic-Republican		162
	CHARLES C. PINCKNEY	Federalist		14
1808	JAMES MADISON	Democratic-Republican		122
	CHARLES C. PINCKNEY	Federalist		47
	GEORGE CLINTON	Democratic-Republican		6
1812	JAMES MADISON	Democratic-Republican		128
	DEWITT CLINTON	Federalist		89
1816	JAMES MONROE	Democratic-Republican		183
	RUFUS KING	Federalist		34
1820	JAMES MONROE	Democratic-Republican		231
	JOHN Q. ADAMS	Independent Republican		1
1824	JOHN Q. ADAMS (Min.)[†]	Democratic-Republican	108,740	84
	ANDREW JACKSON	Democratic-Republican	153,544	99
	WILLIAM H. CRAWFORD	Democratic-Republican	46,618	41
	HENRY CLAY	Democratic-Republican	47,136	37
1828	ANDREW JACKSON	Democratic	647,286	178
	JOHN Q. ADAMS	National Republican	508,064	83
1832	ANDREW JACKSON	Democratic	687,502	219
	HENRY CLAY	National Republican	530,189	49
	WILLIAM WIRT	Anti-Masonic ⎫	33,108	7
	JOHN FLOYD	National Republican ⎬		11
1836	MARTIN VAN BUREN	Democratic	765,483	170
	WILLIAM H. HARRISON	Whig ⎫		73
	HUGH L. WHITE	Whig ⎪	739,795	26
	DANIEL WEBSTER	Whig ⎬		14
	W. P. MANGUM	Whig ⎭		11
1840	WILLIAM H. HARRISON	Whig	1,274,624	234
	MARTIN VAN BUREN	Democratic	1,127,781	60
1844	JAMES K. POLK (Min.)[†]	Democratic	1,338,464	170
	HENRY CLAY	Whig	1,300,097	105
	JAMES G. BIRNEY	Liberty	62,300	

*Candidates receiving less than 1 percent of the popular vote are omitted. Before the Twelfth Amendment (1804), the Electoral College voted for two presidential candidates, and the runner-up became vice-president. Basic figures are taken primarily from *Historical Statistics of the United States, Colonial Times to 1970* (1975), pp. 1073–1074, and *Statistical Abstract of the United States,* appropriate years.
[†]"Min." indicates minority president—one receiving less than 50 percent of all popular votes.

ELECTION	CANDIDATES	PARTIES	POPULAR VOTE	ELECTORAL VOTE
1848	ZACHARY TAYLOR	Whig	1,360,967	163
	LEWIS CASS	Democratic	1,222,342	127
	MARTIN VAN BUREN	Free Soil	291,263	
1852	FRANKLIN PIERCE	Democratic	1,601,117	254
	WINFIELD SCOTT	Whig	1,385,453	42
	JOHN P. HALE	Free Soil	155,825	
1856	JAMES BUCHANAN (Min.)*	Democratic	1,832,955	174
	JOHN C. FRÉMONT	Republican	1,339,932	114
	MILLARD FILLMORE	American	871,731	8
1860	ABRAHAM LINCOLN (Min.)*	Republican	1,865,593	180
	STEPHEN A. DOUGLAS	Democratic	1,382,713	12
	JOHN C. BRECKINRIDGE	Democratic	848,356	72
	JOHN BELL	Constitutional Union	592,906	39
1864	ABRAHAM LINCOLN	Union	2,206,938	212
	GEORGE B. MCCLELLAN	Democratic	1,803,787	21
1868	ULYSSES S. GRANT	Republican	3,013,421	214
	HORATIO SEYMOUR	Democratic	2,706,829	80
1872	ULYSSES S. GRANT	Republican	3,596,745	286
	HORACE GREELEY	Democratic Liberal Republican	2,843,446	66
1876	RUTHERFORD B. HAYES (Min.)*	Republican	4,036,572	185
	SAMUEL J. TILDEN	Democratic	4,284,020	184
1880	JAMES A. GARFIELD (Min.)*	Republican	4,453,295	214
	WINFIELD S. HANCOCK	Democratic	4,414,082	155
	JAMES B. WEAVER	Greenback-Labor	308,578	
1884	GROVER CLEVELAND (Min.)*	Democratic	4,879,507	219
	JAMES G. BLAINE	Republican	4,850,293	182
	BENJAMIN F. BUTLER	Greenback-Labor	175,370	
	JOHN P. ST. JOHN	Prohibition	150,369	
1888	BENJAMIN HARRISON (Min.)*	Republican	5,447,129	233
	GROVER CLEVELAND	Democratic	5,537,857	168
	CLINTON B. FISK	Prohibition	249,506	
	ANSON J. STREETER	Union Labor	146,935	
1892	GROVER CLEVELAND (Min.)*	Democratic	5,555,426	277
	BENJAMIN HARRISON	Republican	5,182,690	145
	JAMES B. WEAVER	People's	1,029,846	22
	JOHN BIDWELL	Prohibition	264,133	
1896	WILLIAM MCKINLEY	Republican	7,102,246	271
	WILLIAM J. BRYAN	Democratic	6,492,559	176
1900	WILLIAM MCKINLEY	Republican	7,218,491	292
	WILLIAM J. BRYAN	Democratic; Populist	6,356,734	155
	JOHN C. WOOLLEY	Prohibition	208,914	
1904	THEODORE ROOSEVELT	Republican	7,628,461	336
	ALTON B. PARKER	Democratic	5,084,223	140
	EUGENE V. DEBS	Socialist	402,283	
	SILAS C. SWALLOW	Prohibition	258,536	
1908	WILLIAM H. TAFT	Republican	7,675,320	321
	WILLIAM J. BRYAN	Democratic	6,412,294	162
	EUGENE V. DEBS	Socialist	420,793	
	EUGENE W. CHAFIN	Prohibition	253,840	
1912	WOODROW WILSON (Min.)*	Democratic	6,296,547	435
	THEODORE ROOSEVELT	Progressive	4,118,571	88
	WILLIAM H. TAFT	Republican	3,486,720	8
	EUGENE V. DEBS	Socialist	900,672	
	EUGENE W. CHAFIN	Prohibition	206,275	

*"Min." indicates minority president—one receiving less than 50 percent of all popular votes.

ELECTION	CANDIDATES	PARTIES	POPULAR VOTE	ELECTORAL VOTE
1916	WOODROW WILSON (Min.)*	Democratic	9,127,695	277
	CHARLES E. HUGHES	Republican	8,533,507	254
	A. L. BENSON	Socialist	585,113	
	J. F. HANLY	Prohibition	220,506	
1920	WARREN G. HARDING	Republican	16,143,407	404
	JAMES M. COX	Democratic	9,130,328	127
	EUGENE V. DEBS	Socialist	919,799	
	P. P. CHRISTENSEN	Farmer-Labor	265,411	
1924	CALVIN COOLIDGE	Republican	15,718,211	382
	JOHN W. DAVIS	Democratic	8,385,283	136
	ROBERT M. LA FOLLETTE	Progressive	4,831,289	13
1928	HERBERT C. HOOVER	Republican	21,391,993	444
	ALFRED E. SMITH	Democratic	15,016,169	87
1932	FRANKLIN D. ROOSEVELT	Democratic	22,809,638	472
	HERBERT C. HOOVER	Republican	15,758,901	59
	NORMAN THOMAS	Socialist	881,951	
1936	FRANKLIN D. ROOSEVELT	Democratic	27,752,869	523
	ALFRED M. LANDON	Republican	16,674,665	8
	WILLIAM LEMKE	Union, etc.	882,479	
1940	FRANKLIN D. ROOSEVELT	Democratic	27,307,819	449
	WENDELL L. WILLKIE	Republican	22,321,018	82
1944	FRANKLIN D. ROOSEVELT	Democratic	25,606,585	432
	THOMAS E. DEWEY	Republican	22,014,745	99
1948	HARRY S TRUMAN (Min.)*	Democratic	24,179,345	303
	THOMAS E. DEWEY	Republican	21,991,291	189
	J. STROM THURMOND	States' Rights Democratic	1,176,125	39
	HENRY A. WALLACE	Progressive	1,157,326	
1952	DWIGHT D. EISENHOWER	Republican	33,936,234	442
	ADLAI E. STEVENSON	Democratic	27,314,992	89
1956	DWIGHT D. EISENHOWER	Republican	35,590,472	457
	ADLAI E. STEVENSON	Democratic	26,022,752	73
1960	JOHN F. KENNEDY (Min.)*†	Democratic	34,226,731	303
	RICHARD M. NIXON	Republican	34,108,157	219
1964	LYNDON B. JOHNSON	Democratic	43,129,566	486
	BARRY M. GOLDWATER	Republican	27,178,188	52
1968	RICHARD M. NIXON (Min.)*	Republican	31,785,480	301
	HUBERT H. HUMPHREY, JR.	Democratic	31,275,166	191
	GEORGE C. WALLACE	American Independent	9,906,473	46
1972	RICHARD M. NIXON	Republican	47,169,911	520
	GEORGE S. MC GOVERN	Democratic	29,170,383	17
1976	JIMMY CARTER	Democratic	40,828,657	297
	GERALD R. FORD	Republican	39,145,520	240
1980	RONALD W. REAGAN	Republican	43,899,248	489
	JIMMY CARTER	Democratic	35,481,435	49
	JOHN B. ANDERSON	Independent	5,719,437	0
1984	RONALD W. REAGAN	Republican	52,609,797	525
	WALTER MONDALE	Democratic	36,450,613	13
1988	GEORGE BUSH	Republican	47,946,000	426
	MICHAEL DUKAKIS	Democratic	41,016,000	111

*"Min." indicates minority president—one receiving less than 50 percent of all popular votes.
†Six Democratic electors in Alabama, all eight unpledged Democratic electors in Mississippi, and one Republican elector in Oklahoma voted for Senator Harry F. Byrd.

Presidents and Vice-Presidents

TERM	PRESIDENT	VICE-PRESIDENT
1789–1793	George Washington	John Adams
1793–1797	George Washington	John Adams
1797–1801	John Adams	Thomas Jefferson
1801–1805	Thomas Jefferson	Aaron Burr
1805–1809	Thomas Jefferson	George Clinton
1809–1813	James Madison	George Clinton (d. 1812)
1813–1817	James Madison	Elbridge Gerry (d. 1814)
1817–1821	James Monroe	Daniel D. Tompkins
1821–1825	James Monroe	Daniel D. Tompkins
1825–1829	John Quincy Adams	John C. Calhoun
1829–1833	Andrew Jackson	John C. Calhoun (resigned 1832)
1833–1837	Andrew Jackson	Martin Van Buren
1837–1841	Martin Van Buren	Richard M. Johnson
1841–1845	William H. Harrison (d. 1841) John Tyler	John Tyler
1845–1849	James K. Polk	George M. Dallas
1849–1853	Zachary Taylor (d. 1850) Millard Fillmore	Millard Fillmore
1853–1857	Franklin Pierce	William R. D. King (d. 1853)
1857–1861	James Buchanan	John C. Breckinridge
1861–1865	Abraham Lincoln	Hannibal Hamlin
1865–1869	Abraham Lincoln (d. 1865) Andrew Johnson	Andrew Johnson
1869–1873	Ulysses S. Grant	Schuyler Colfax
1873–1877	Ulysses S. Grant	Henry Wilson (d. 1875)
1877–1881	Rutherford B. Hayes	William A. Wheeler
1881–1885	James A. Garfield (d. 1881) Chester A. Arthur	Chester A. Arthur
1885–1889	Grover Cleveland	Thomas A. Hendricks (d. 1885)
1889–1893	Benjamin Harrison	Levi P. Morton
1893–1897	Grover Cleveland	Adlai E. Stevenson
1897–1901	William McKinley	Garret A. Hobart (d. 1899)
1901–1905	William McKinley (d. 1901) Theodore Roosevelt	Theodore Roosevelt
1905–1909	Theodore Roosevelt	Charles W. Fairbanks
1909–1913	William H. Taft	James S. Sherman (d. 1912)
1913–1917	Woodrow Wilson	Thomas R. Marshall
1917–1921	Woodrow Wilson	Thomas R. Marshall
1921–1925	Warren G. Harding (d. 1923) Calvin Coolidge	Calvin Coolidge
1925–1929	Calvin Coolidge	Charles G. Dawes
1929–1933	Herbert C. Hoover	Charles Curtis
1933–1937	Franklin D. Roosevelt	John N. Garner
1937–1941	Franklin D. Roosevelt	John N. Garner
1941–1945	Franklin D. Roosevelt	Henry A. Wallace
1945–1949	Franklin D. Roosevelt (d. 1945) Harry S Truman	Harry S Truman
1949–1953	Harry S Truman	Alben W. Barkley
1953–1957	Dwight D. Eisenhower	Richard M. Nixon
1957–1961	Dwight D. Eisenhower	Richard M. Nixon
1961–1965	John F. Kennedy (d. 1963) Lyndon B. Johnson	Lyndon B. Johnson
1965–1969	Lyndon B. Johnson	Hubert H. Humphrey, Jr.

Presidents and Vice-Presidents

TERM	PRESIDENT	VICE-PRESIDENT
1969–1974	Richard M. Nixon	Spiro T. Agnew (resigned 1973); Gerald R. Ford
1974–1977	Gerald R. Ford	Nelson A. Rockefeller
1977–1981	Jimmy Carter	Walter F. Mondale
1981–1985	Ronald Reagan	George Bush
1985–1989	Ronald Reagan	George Bush
1989–	George Bush	J. Danforth Quayle III

Admission of States

(See p. 160 for order in which the original thirteen entered the union.)

ORDER OF ADMISSION	STATE	DATE OF ADMISSION	ORDER OF ADMISSION	STATE	DATE OF ADMISSION
14	Vermont	Mar. 4, 1791	33	Oregon	Feb. 14, 1859
15	Kentucky	June 1, 1792	34	Kansas	Jan. 29, 1861
16	Tennessee	June 1, 1796	35	W. Virginia	June 20, 1863
17	Ohio	Mar. 1, 1803	36	Nevada	Oct. 31, 1864
18	Louisiana	April 30, 1812	37	Nebraska	Mar. 1, 1867
19	Indiana	Dec. 11, 1816	38	Colorado	Aug. 1, 1876
20	Mississippi	Dec. 10, 1817	39	N. Dakota	Nov. 2, 1889
21	Illinois	Dec. 3, 1818	40	S. Dakota	Nov. 2, 1889
22	Alabama	Dec. 14, 1819	41	Montana	Nov. 8, 1889
23	Maine	Mar. 15, 1820	42	Washington	Nov. 11, 1889
24	Missouri	Aug. 10, 1821	43	Idaho	July 3, 1890
25	Arkansas	June 15, 1836	44	Wyoming	July 10, 1890
26	Michigan	Jan. 26, 1837	45	Utah	Jan. 4, 1896
27	Florida	Mar. 3, 1845	46	Oklahoma	Nov. 16, 1907
28	Texas	Dec. 29, 1845	47	New Mexico	Jan. 6, 1912
29	Iowa	Dec. 28, 1846	48	Arizona	Feb. 14, 1912
30	Wisconsin	May 29, 1848	49	Alaska	Jan. 3, 1959
31	California	Sept. 9, 1850	50	Hawaii	Aug. 21, 1959
32	Minnesota	May 11, 1858			

Estimates of Total Costs and Number of Battle Deaths of Major U.S. Wars*

	TOTAL COSTS** (MILLIONS OF DOLLARS)	ORIGINAL COSTS	NUMBER OF BATTLE DEATHS
Vietnam Conflict	352,000	140,600	47,318[†]
Korean Conflict	164,000	54,000	33,629
World War II	664,000	288,000	291,557
World War I	112,000	26,000	53,402
Spanish-American War	6,460	400	385
Civil War { Union only	12,952	3,200	140,414
Civil War { Confederacy (est.)	N.A.	1,000	94,000
Mexican War	147	73	1,733
War of 1812	158	93	2,260
American Revolution	190	100	6,824

*Deaths from disease and other causes are not shown. In earlier wars especially, owing to poor medical and sanitary practices, non-battle deaths substantially exceeded combat casualties.
**The difference between total costs and original costs is attributable to continuing postwar payments for such items as veterans' benefits, interest on war debts, etc.
†1959–1983
Sources: *Historical Statistics of the United States, Statistical Abstract of the United States,* relevant years, and *The World Almanac and Book of Facts, 1986.*

Index

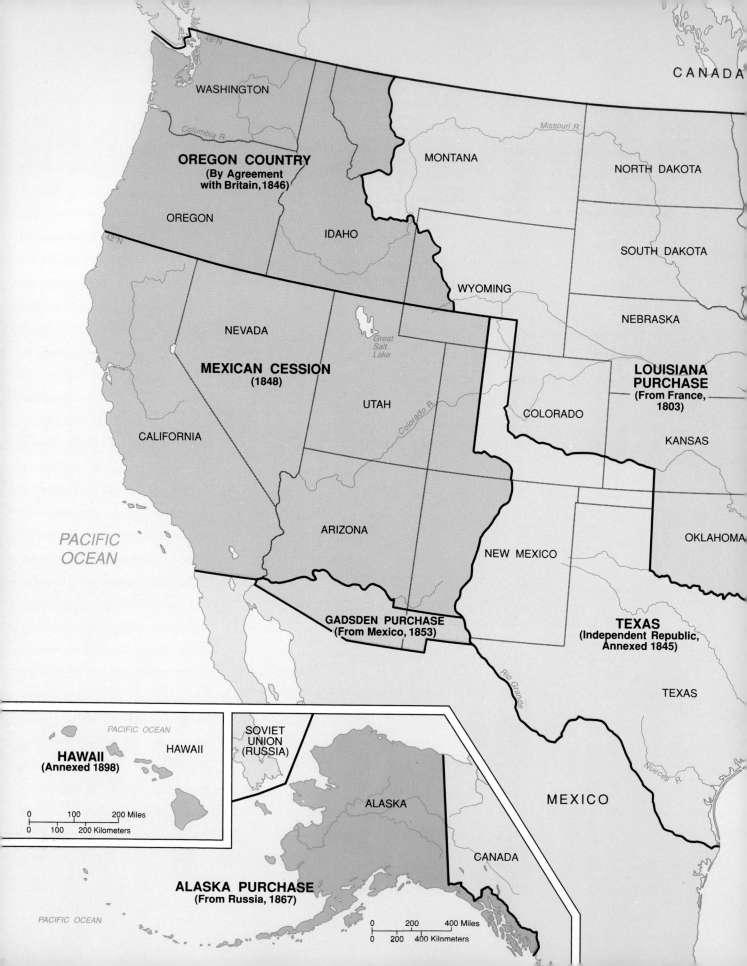

CANADA

WASHINGTON

Columbia R.

OREGON COUNTRY
(By Agreement
with Britain, 1846)

OREGON

IDAHO

MONTANA

Missouri R.

NORTH DAKOTA

SOUTH DAKOTA

WYOMING

42°N

NEVADA

Great
Salt
Lake

NEBRASKA

MEXICAN CESSION
(1848)

UTAH

Colorado R.

COLORADO

LOUISIANA
PURCHASE
(From France,
1803)

KANSAS

CALIFORNIA

PACIFIC
OCEAN

ARIZONA

NEW MEXICO

OKLAHOMA

GADSDEN PURCHASE
(From Mexico, 1853)

TEXAS
(Independent Republic,
Annexed 1845)

TEXAS

Rio Grande

Nueces R.

MEXICO

HAWAII
(Annexed 1898)

PACIFIC OCEAN

HAWAII

SOVIET
UNION
(RUSSIA)

0   100   200 Miles
0   100   200 Kilometers

ALASKA

CANADA

ALASKA PURCHASE
(From Russia, 1867)

0   200   400 Miles
0   200   400 Kilometers

PACIFIC OCEAN

Territorial Growth of the United States

MAINE

V.T.

N.H.

MASS.

CONN.

R.I.

NEW YORK

PENNSYLVANIA

NEW JERSEY

MASON-DIXON LINE

MARYLAND

DELAWARE

WISCONSIN

MICHIGAN

ILLINOIS

INDIANA

OHIO

WEST VIRGINIA

VIRGINIA

KENTUCKY

THE ORIGINAL UNITED STATES
(By Treaty with Britain, 1783)

THE ORIGINAL THIRTEEN COLONIES

NORTH CAROLINA

TENNESSEE

SOUTH CAROLINA

GEORGIA

MISSISSIPPI

ALABAMA

(Seized from Spain, 1810, 1813)

FLORIDA
(By Treaty with Spain, 1819)

FLORIDA

IOWA

MISSOURI

ARKANSAS

LOUISIANA

ESOTA

36°30' N

ATLANTIC OCEAN

GULF OF MEXICO

BAHAMAS

CUBA

DOMINICAN REPUBLIC

HAITI

Lake Superior

Lake Michigan

Lake Huron

Lake Erie

Lake Ontario

St. Lawrence R.

Ohio R.

Mississippi R.

PUERTO RICO
(Acquired from Spain, 1898)

VIRGIN IS.
(Acquired from Denmark, 1916-1917)

PUERTO RICO

VIRGIN ISLANDS

0   50   100 Miles

0   50   100 Kilometers

0   200   400 Miles

0   200   400 Kilometers

Albers Equal-Area Projection

CANAD

Vancouver I.

Seattle
Olympia ★
Spokane

WASHINGTON

Portland
Salem ★

Eugene

OREGON

Great
Falls
Helena ★

MONTANA

NORTH DAKOTA

Bismarck ★

Fargo

IDAHO

Boise ★

Snake R.

WYOMING

SOUTH DAKOTA

BLACK
HILLS

Pierre ★

Sioux
Falls

GREAT

Reno
Carson City

Sacramento ★

San Francisco

San Jose

Fresno

GREAT

BASIN

SIERRA NEVADA

NEVADA

Salt
Lake
City ★

UTAH

Cheyenne ★

ROCKY MOUNTAINS

Boulder
Denver ★

COLORADO

NEBRASKA

PLAINS

Platte R.

KANSAS

Omah

Lincoln ★

Tope

Wichit

Arkansas R.

Las
Vegas

CALIFORNIA

Los Angeles

San Diego

ARIZONA

Phoenix ★

Tucson

NEW MEXICO

Santa Fe ★
Albuquerque

Amarillo

Lubbock

Oklahoma
City ★

OKLAHOM

Tuls

Red R.

Ft. Worth

Dall

PACIFIC
OCEAN

GULF
OF
CALIFORNIA

El Paso

Rio Grande

TEXAS

Austin ★

San Antonio

MEXICO

HAWAII

Niihau Kauai

Oahu

Honolulu ★

Molokai

Lanai Maui

Kaho'olawe

Hawaii

PACIFIC OCEAN

0   100   200 Miles
0   100   200 Kilometers

SOVIET
UNION

ARCTIC
OCEAN

BROOKS RANGE

Yukon R.

ALASKA

Bering Strait

ALASKA RANGE

Anchorage

CANADA

BERING
SEA

Aleutian Islands

GULF OF
ALASKA

Juneau ★

0   200   400 Miles
0   200   400 Kilometers

The United States of America

MAINE
★ Augusta
● Portland

Burlington
Montpelier ★
VT. N.H.
NEW YORK ● Concord
● Manchester
Albany ● ● Boston
Hartford ★ ● Providence
CONN. R.I.
Buffalo
New York

MINNESOTA
● Minneapolis
● St. Paul

WISCONSIN
Madison ★ ● Milwaukee

MICHIGAN
● Lansing
Detroit ●

IOWA
★ Des Moines

ILLINOIS
● Chicago
★ Springfield

INDIANA
Indianapolis ★

OHIO
Cleveland ●
Columbus ●
● Cincinnati

PENNSYLVANIA
● Pittsburgh Harrisburg ★ ● Philadelphia
● Wheeling Baltimore ● Trenton
NEW JERSEY
Dover
Annapolis ★
WEST Washington, D.C. ★ **DELAWARE**
VIRGINIA **MARYLAND**
● Charleston ★

Richmond ★
VIRGINIA
Norfolk ●
Chesapeake Bay

KANSAS CITY
● Kansas City
Jefferson ★ City St. ● Louis

MISSOURI

KENTUCKY
Frankfort ★
● Louisville

TENNESSEE
● Nashville
Knoxville ●
Chattanooga ●
Memphis ●

ARKANSAS
Little ● Rock ★

Winston-Salem ●
NORTH CAROLINA
★ Raleigh
● Charlotte

SOUTH CAROLINA
★ Columbia
● Charleston

MISSISSIPPI
★ Jackson

ALABAMA
● Birmingham
Montgomery ★

GEORGIA
● Atlanta ★

LOUISIANA
Shreveport ●
Baton Rouge ★ ● New Orleans
Houston

Mobile ●
● Tallahassee ★

FLORIDA
Jacksonville ●
Orlando ●
Tampa ●
Lake Okeechobee
● Miami
Key West ●

GULF OF MEXICO

ATLANTIC OCEAN

Lake of the Woods
Lake Superior
Lake Michigan
Lake Huron
Lake Erie
Lake Ontario
Mississippi R.
St. Lawrence R.
Delaware R.
Hudson R.
Connecticut R.
Cumberland R.
Tennessee R.

APPALACHIAN MOUNTAINS

BAHAMAS
CUBA
DOMINICAN REPUBLIC
HAITI

Land Elevation

Feet		Meters
10,000		3,000
5,000		1,500
2,000		600
1,000		300
500		150
0		0
Below Sea Level		Below Sea Level

ATLANTIC OCEAN

VIRGIN ISLANDS
San Juan ●
PUERTO RICO

0   50   100 Miles
0   50   100 Kilometers

0   200   400 Miles
0   200   400 Kilometers

Albers Equal-Area Projection